P9-DDU-958

Teacher's Edition
Level A

Peggy Palo Boyles
Oklahoma City, OK

Myriam Met
Rockville, MD

Richard S. Sayers
Longmont, CO

Carol Eubanks Wargin
Glen Ellyn, IL

Needham, Massachusetts
Upper Saddle River, New Jersey

Front and back covers: Insert photo: Café Zurich, Barcelona, Spain
Background photo: Parque del Buen Retiro, Madrid, Spain

Special thanks to the American Council on the Teaching of Foreign Languages for the use of the logo that accompanies the references to the Standards for Foreign Language Learning.

ISBN 0-13-035956-4

2 3 4 5 6 7 8 9 10 VH 07 06 05 04

REALIDADES A Professional Development

Table of Contents

REALIDADES, Research, and the Standards for Foreign Language Learning T4

- REALIDADES and Research-based Instruction T4
- Achieving the Standards with REALIDADES T6

Program Organization T8

- Articulation T10
- Resources T14

Getting Started T16

Chapter Organization T18

Using the Teacher's Edition T28

Assessment T32

Universal Access T36

Instructional Planning and Support T42

Professional Resources................... T49

- Bibliography T50

Index of Cultural References T52

REALIDADES, Research, and the Standards for Foreign Language Learning

Topics covered:

- ***REALIDADES* and Research-based Instruction**
- **Achieving the Standards with *REALIDADES***

R*EALIDADES* is based on the belief that the purpose of learning Spanish is to communicate with the people who speak it and to understand their cultures. *REALIDADES* presents a fresh, exciting approach to Spanish by making language learning real for today's students.

REALIDADES and Research-based Instruction

REALIDADES reflects the most current research on how students learn languages and what teachers and materials need to do to help them become proficient language users. Let's take a look at some of the basic premises about language and language learning.

Communication

Communication is an authentic exchange of information for a real purpose between two or more people. By this we mean that people tell each other (through speech or writing) something the other person doesn't already know.

Communicating meaning has several aspects. Students need to listen to and read Spanish in order to interpret intended meanings. Students need to express meaning by conveying their own messages for a purpose and to a real audience. They also need to negotiate meaning through the natural give-and-take involved in understanding and making oneself understood. Research tells us that classroom activities must provide students practice in interpreting, expressing, and negotiating meaning through extensive and frequent peer interactions.

Throughout *REALIDADES*, students are engaged in understanding messages, in sending their own messages, and thus in communicating real ideas and real meanings for real purposes.

Comprehensible input

Research states that students learn best when they have ample opportunities to internalize meanings before they have to produce them. In other words, comprehension precedes production. The term "comprehensible input" suggests that learners acquire language by understanding what they hear and read. Students need many opportunities to match what they hear with visual cues (pictures, video, or teacher pantomime) or experiences (physical actions). Reading input should be supported by a close connection between text and visuals. All these strategies for comprehensible input help students associate meaning with forms.

In keeping with this research, *REALIDADES* begins each chapter with a section called *A primera vista.* These six pages of language input give students opportunities to comprehend new language before producing it. The visualized presentation of vocabulary in context, the reading input in the *Videohistoria,* and the listening input in the *A primera vista* video segment provide a wide range of comprehensible input of new language that addresses all students and all learning styles.

Practice activities

Research tells us that students need extensive practice in using their new language to create and convey their own messages. The *Manos a la obra* section provides a wide range of practice activities. New vocabulary and grammar are first practiced in skill-getting activities that provide concrete practice. This basic practice helps to develop accuracy in using the language and prepares students to transition into more communicative tasks. In these transitional activities, students work with a partner or in small groups with information- or opinion-gap activities that are characteristic of real-life communication. Students then continue on to more open-ended, personalized speaking or writing tasks.

> "Communication is an authentic exchange of information for a real purpose between two or more people."

Meaningful context in language learning

All effective learning is rooted in a meaningful context. We know from research that information is most likely to be retained when it is connected to other information in a meaningful way. Thus, language learning is most successful and retention more likely when we present new language organized into topics or by situations.

REALIDADES is organized into themes. All material in a chapter—vocabulary, grammar, culture—is rooted in a context and used meaningfully. Students engage in communicative tasks that are relevant to their lives. Students work with readings, realia, photography, and art that are authentic to the Spanish-speaking world. The video programs and Internet links show native speakers engaged in real-life situations and experiences.

Understanding grammar

Students learn grammar most effectively when it is presented and practiced in a meaningful context and when it connects to real communication needs. Students also benefit when shown how the patterns of grammar work.

In *REALIDADES,* new structures are foreshadowed through lexical presentation (grammar is presented as vocabulary) in the *A primera vista* language input section. In addition, early vocabulary activities in the *Manos a la obra* section have students work with the grammar lexically. This allows students to see the grammar and work with it in a meaningful context before being formally presented with the rules or paradigms.

Grammar is formally presented with clear explanations and examples. Comparisons between English and Spanish grammar are made whenever possible. Students then practice the grammar concepts in a variety of tasks that range from concrete activities that focus primarily on the structures to more open-ended tasks that focus on communication.

REALIDADES, Research, and the Standards

To further facilitate the learning of grammar, *REALIDADES* offers *GramActiva,* a multi-modality approach to grammar that includes grammar videos and hands-on grammar activities. By teaching and practicing grammar through different learning styles, more students will be able to learn grammar.

Building cultural perspectives

The *Standards for Foreign Language Learning* have expanded how culture is taught in today's classroom. We want students to understand the *why* (perspectives) of culture that determines the *what* (products and practices).

The approach to culture in *REALIDADES* not only teaches students the *what* but asks students to explore the *why.* Cultural products, practices, and comparisons are presented throughout *REALIDADES* in features such as *Fondo cultural, La cultura en vivo,* and *Perspectivas del mundo hispano,* and in *REALIDADES 3, Puente a la cultura.* Students read information about cultures that offer different perspectives and they are asked questions that encourage them to think and make observations about cultures.

Strategies for success

Research shows that effective learners know how to help themselves become successful learners. One way they do this is by using specific problem-solving strategies.

REALIDADES teaches students strategies to be effective communicators whether listening, speaking, reading, or writing. Each reading selection is supported by a reading strategy. Each performance-based task includes a useful strategy that connects to a step-by-step approach that helps students plan, rehearse, and present or publish. Each also includes a rubric so students know how they might be evaluated.

We know more than ever about how foreign languages are learned. *REALIDADES* is based on solid research in second-language acquisition, on accepted theories about the teaching of culture, and on sound pedagogical practices that are common to all disciplines. We are sure that you and your students will find this an exciting, motivating, and enormously successful approach to learning Spanish.

Achieving the Standards with *REALIDADES*

The *Standards for Foreign Language Learning* provide an important and useful framework to guide the teaching and learning of foreign languages. This framework should result in a new generation of language learners prepared to meet the demand for competence in other languages that our nation will face as we move into an increasingly interdependent world.

REALIDADES is written based upon the Standards. This means that instruction used in *REALIDADES* will help students develop the competencies delineated in the *Standards for Foreign Language Learning.* Teachers will find a correlation to the Standards at the beginning of each chapter and with the notes that accompany each activity (if appropriate) in the Teacher's Edition.

Goal 1: Communication

1.1 (Interpersonal): Each chapter provides a wide range of paired and group activities. Students speak with a partner, work in small groups, and interview classmates.

1.2 (Interpretive): *REALIDADES* builds the interpretive listening skill through the Audio Program. This CD program supports activities in the Student Edition (input checks, dictations, listening comprehension, and test preparation) and the *Writing, Audio, & Video Workbook.* The Video Program also develops listening through the different language, grammar, and storyline mystery video segments.

REALIDADES provides extensive support for the interpretive reading skill. Students read throughout the chapter: comprehensible input, practice activities, realia, culture notes, and reading selections. Reading is seamlessly integrated with practice and anchored in real-life contexts. Whenever possible, readings are supported by focused strategies.

1.3 (Presentational): Each chapter ends with a performance-based task: in the "A" chapters, a speaking task, in the "B" chapters a presentation writing task. Both presentations are supported by strategies and by the speaking or writing process, step-by-step support to help students successfully complete the task.

Goal 2: Culture
2.1 (Practices and Perspectives); 2.2 (Products and Perspectives): Each chapter in *REALIDADES* explores a cultural theme through a wide range of practices, products, and perspectives. Students see authentic culture through realia, art, photographs, popular sayings, tongue twisters, rhymes and songs, hands-on projects, readings, and authentic literature. In addition, the unique *Fondo cultural* readings generally include a Standards-based critical thinking question.

Goal 3: Connections
3.1 (Cross-curricular Connections): *REALIDADES* integrates cross-curricular activities within the *Manos a la obra* section. Students make connections to a variety of disciplines through activities that integrate the language of the chapter.

3.2 (Connections to Target Culture): *REALIDADES* exposes students to perspectives only available within the target culture through art, realia, pronunciation activities, and readings.

Goal 4: Comparisons
4.1 (Language Comparisons): *REALIDADES* enables students to see comparisons between languages in the grammar explanations in the text, on the *GramActiva* video, and in a unique section called *Exploración del lenguage.* Students learn to look for language connections, to understand how language works, and to integrate these new skills as they continue in their study of Spanish.

4.2 (Cultural Comparisons): *REALIDADES* is rich in cultural comparisons. A unique feature called *Fondo cultural* generally informs students about a cultural product or practice and is followed by a question that challenges students to think critically and make comparisons between cultures.

Goal 5: Communities
5.1 (Outside the Classroom): *REALIDADES* provides informative features called *El español en la comunidad* and *El español en el mundo del trabajo.* These sections help students see how to use Spanish beyond the classroom, in their communities, and in the world of work.

5.2 (Lifelong Learners): For a textbook to help students achieve this goal, it must motivate students to want to communicate and want to learn more about the culture. The core of *REALIDADES*—real language, real culture, real tasks—motivates students. The video programs and other technology support engage learners in ways that may encourage them to continue their exploration of the Spanish language and cultures.

Standards for Foreign Language Learning

Goal 1: Communicate In Languages Other Than English

- Standard 1.1: Students engage in conversation, provide and obtain information, express feelings and emotions, and exchange opinions.
- Standard 1.2: Students understand and interpret written and spoken language on a variety of topics.
- Standard 1.3: Students present information, concepts and ideas to an audience of listeners or readers on a variety of topics.

Goal 2: Gain Knowledge And Understanding Of Other Cultures

- Standard 2.1: Students demonstrate an understanding of the relationship between the practices and perspectives of the culture studied.
- Standard 2.2: Students demonstrate an understanding of the relationship between the products and perspectives of the culture studied.

Goal 3: Connect With Other Disciplines And Acquire Information

- Standard 3.1: Students reinforce and further their knowledge of other disciplines through the foreign language.
- Standard 3.2: Students acquire information and recognize the distinctive viewpoints that are only available through the foreign language and its cultures.

Goal 4: Gain Insight Into The Nature Of Language And Culture

- Standard 4.1: Students demonstrate understanding of the nature of language through comparisons of the language studied and their own.
- Standard 4.2: Students demonstrate understanding of the concept of culture through comparisons of the cultures studied and their own.

Goal 5: Participate In Multilingual Communities At Home And Around The World

- Standard 5.1: Students use the language both within and beyond the school setting.
- Standard 5.2: Students show evidence of becoming lifelong learners by using the language for personal enjoyment and enrichment.

Program Organization

Middle School

REALIDADES A and ***B*** are separate middle school books that meet the needs of younger learners. Taken together, these Student Editions provide the same content as ***REALIDADES 1*** but they have been adapted with new art, photographs, and activities that are age-appropriate for the younger learner. Students completing ***REALIDADES B*** will make a smooth transition into ***REALIDADES 2.***

High School

Each high school Student Edition provides the complete curriculum for one year of instruction. The spiraling of themes and extensive recycling of content allows for smooth articulation between the three levels. Students completing ***REALIDADES 3*** will have a solid foundation for advanced Spanish study.

R*EALIDADES* is a communication-based five-level series with a full range of print and technology components that allow teachers to meet the needs of the different students in today's Spanish classroom.

REALIDADES A
- Introductory section ***Para empezar***
- Themes 1–4

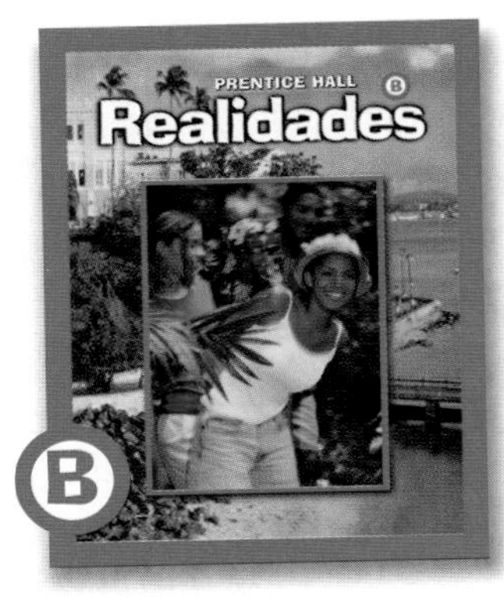

REALIDADES B
- Review section ***Para empezar***
- Themes 5–9

REALIDADES 1
- Introductory section ***Para empezar***
- Themes 1–9

REALIDADES 2
- Review section ***Para empezar***
- Themes 1–9

REALIDADES 3
- Review section ***Para empezar***
- Chapters 1–10

Chapter Organization

Temas

***REALIDADES* A begins with an introductory section followed by four thematic chapters. Each chapter is divided into two sections.**

Tema	Capítulo A	Capítulo B
Para empezar	1. En la escuela 2. En la clase 3. El tiempo	
1: Mis amigos y yo	1A *¿Qué te gusta hacer?*	1B: *Y tú, ¿cómo eres?*
2: La escuela	2A: *Tu día en la escuela*	2B: *Tu sala de clases*
3: La comida	3A: *¿Desayuno o almuerzo?*	3B: *Para mantener la salud*
4: Los pasatiempos	4A: *¿Adónde vas?*	4B: *¿Quieres ir conmigo?*

Chapters

Each chapter in *REALIDADES* is built around a clear sequence of instruction.

Chapter Section	Pedagogical support
A primera vista	Provides comprehensible language input for the chapter's new vocabulary and grammar within an authentic context. Input includes words, dialogues, narration, visuals, audio, and video. Students' language production focuses on comprehension and limited production.
Manos a la obra	Provides productive language practice with a variety of concrete, transitional, and open-ended activities. The activities develop all four language skills and focus on relevant language tasks. Many activities build off of authentic documents, *realia,* and photographs.
¡Adelante!	Provides culminating theme-based activities that have students apply what they have learned. The section features a culturally-based reading, performance-based speaking or writing tasks, cultural activities, and the storyline mystery video *¿Eres tú, María?*
Repaso del capítulo	Provides complete support for the end-of-chapter assessment. One page summarizes what students need to know (vocabulary and grammar). The second page outlines the proficiency and culture sections of the test by describing the task, providing a practice task, and referring students to chapter activities for review.

Program Organization

Articulation

Scope and Sequence

REALIDADES offers a completely articulated Scope and Sequence across all levels. The recursive themes allow for the recycling, review, and reteaching of vocabulary and grammar.

REALIDADES 1

Tema	Capítulo A	Capítulo B
Para empezar	• En la escuela: greetings; introductions; leave-takings; numbers; time; body parts • En la clase: classroom, date, asking for help • El tiempo: weather, seasons	
1: Mis amigos y yo	**1A ¿Qué te gusta hacer?** **Vocabulary:** activities and expressions for saying what you like and don't like to do **Grammar:** infinitives; making negative statements	**1B Y tú, ¿cómo eres?** **Vocabulary:** adjectives and vocabulary to ask about and describe someone's personality **Grammar:** adjectives; definite and indefinite articles; word order
2: La escuela	**2A Tu día en la escuela** **Vocabulary:** classroom items and furniture; parts of the classroom; prepositions of location **Grammar:** subject pronouns; the present tense of *-ar* verbs	**2B Tu sala de clases** **Vocabulary:** classroom items and furniture; parts of the classroom; prepositions of location **Grammar:** the verb *estar;* plurals of nouns and articles
3: La comida	**3A ¿Desayuno o almuerzo?** **Vocabulary:** foods; beverages; adverbs of frequency; expressions to show surprise **Grammar:** present tense of *-er* and *-ir* verbs; *me gusta(n), me encanta(n)*	**3B Para mantener la salud** **Vocabulary:** food; beverages; expressions to discuss health; expressions to discuss preferences, agreement, disagreement, and quantity; adjectives to describe food **Grammar:** the plural of adjectives; the verb *ser*
4: Los pasatiempos	**4A ¿Adónde vas?** **Vocabulary:** leisure activities; places; expressions to tell where and with whom you go; expressions to talk about when things are done **Grammar:** the verb *ir;* interrogative words	**4B ¿Quieres ir conmigo?** **Vocabulary:** leisure activities; feelings; expressions for extending, accepting, and declining invitations; expressions to tell when something happens **Grammar:** *ir* + *a* + infinitive; the verb *jugar*
5: Fiesta en familia	**5A Una fiesta de cumpleaños** **Vocabulary:** family and parties **Grammar:** the verb *tener;* possessive adjectives	**5B ¡Vamos a un restaurante!** **Vocabulary:** describing people and ordering a meal **Grammar:** the verb *venir;* the verbs *ser* and *estar*
6: La casa	**6A En mi dormitorio** **Vocabulary:** bedroom items; electronic equipment; colors; adjectives to describe things **Grammar:** comparisons and superlatives; stem-changing verbs: *poder* and *dormir*	**6B ¿Cómo es tu casa?** **Vocabulary:** rooms in a house and household chores **Grammar:** affirmative *tú* commands; the present progressive tense
7: De compras	**7A ¿Cuánto cuesta?** **Vocabulary:** clothing; shopping; numbers 200-1,000 **Grammar:** stem-changing verbs: *pensar, querer,* and *preferir;* demonstrative adjectives	**7B ¡Qué regalo!** **Vocabulary:** places to shop; gifts; accessories; buying and selling **Grammar:** preterite of *-ar, -car,* and *-gar* verbs; direct object pronouns *lo, la, los, las*
8: Experiencias	**8A De vacaciones** **Vocabulary:** vacation places; activities; modes of transportation **Grammar:** preterite of *-er* and *-ir* verbs; preterite of *ir*; the personal *a*	**8B Ayudando en la comunidad** **Vocabulary:** recycling and volunteer work; places in a community **Grammar:** the verb *decir;* indirect object pronouns; preterite of *hacer* and *dar*
9: Medios de comunicación	**9A El cine y la televisión** **Vocabulary:** television shows; movie genres; giving opinions **Grammar:** *acabar de* + infinitive; *gustar* and similar verbs	**9B La tecnología** **Vocabulary:** computers; communication; computer-related activities **Grammar:** the verbs *pedir* and *servir; saber* and *conocer*

Scope and Sequence

REALIDADES A and *B* provide the same Scope and Sequence as *REALIDADES 1*.

REALIDADES A covers the same content as the *Para empezar* section and *Temas* 1–4.

Tema	Capítulo A	Capítulo B
Para empezar	• En la escuela: greetings; introductions; leave-takings; numbers; time; body parts • En la clase: classroom, date, asking for help • El tiempo: weather, seasons	
1: Mis amigos y yo	**1A ¿Qué te gusta hacer?** **Vocabulary:** activities and expressions for saying what you like and don't like to do **Grammar:** infinitives; making negative statements	**1B Y tú, ¿cómo eres?** **Vocabulary:** adjectives and vocabulary to ask about and describe someone's personality **Grammar:** adjectives; definite and indefinite articles; word order
2: La escuela	**2A Tu día en la escuela** **Vocabulary:** classroom items and furniture; parts of the classroom; prepositions of location **Grammar:** subject pronouns; the present tense of *-ar* verbs	**2B Tu sala de clases** **Vocabulary:** classroom items and furniture; parts of the classroom; prepositions of location **Grammar:** the verb *estar;* plurals of nouns and articles
3: La comida	**3A ¿Desayuno o almuerzo?** **Vocabulary:** foods; beverages; adverbs of frequency; expressions to show surprise **Grammar:** present tense of *-er* and *-ir* verbs; *me gusta(n), me encanta(n)*	**3B Para mantener la salud** **Vocabulary:** food; beverages; expressions to discuss health; expressions to discuss preferences, agreement, disagreement, and quantity; adjectives to describe food **Grammar:** the plural of adjectives; the verb *ser*
4: Los pasatiempos	**4A ¿Adónde vas?** **Vocabulary:** leisure activities; places; expressions to tell where and with whom you go; expressions to talk about when things are done **Grammar:** the verb *ir;* interrogative words	**4B ¿Quieres ir conmigo?** **Vocabulary:** leisure activities; feelings; expressions for extending, accepting, and declining invitations; expressions to tell when something happens **Grammar:** *ir + a +* infinitive; the verb *jugar*

REALIDADES B provides a review section called *Para empezar* and continues with *Temas* 5–9.

Tema	Capítulo A	Capítulo B
5: Fiesta en familia	**5A Una fiesta de cumpleaños** **Vocabulary:** family and parties **Grammar:** the verb *tener;* possessive adjectives	**5B ¡Vamos a un restaurante!** **Vocabulary:** describing people and ordering a meal **Grammar:** the verb *venir;* the verbs *ser* and *estar*
6: La casa	**6A En mi dormitorio** **Vocabulary:** bedroom items; electronic equipment; colors; adjectives to describe things **Grammar:** comparisons and superlatives; stem-changing verbs: *poder* and *dormir*	**6B ¿Cómo es tu casa?** **Vocabulary:** rooms in a house and household chores **Grammar:** affirmative *tú* commands; the present progressive tense
7: De compras	**7A ¿Cuánto cuesta?** **Vocabulary:** clothing; shopping; numbers 200-1,000 **Grammar:** stem-changing verbs: *pensar, querer,* and *preferir;* demonstrative adjectives	**7B ¡Qué regalo!** **Vocabulary:** places to shop; gifts; accessories; buying and selling **Grammar:** preterite of *-ar, -car,* and *-gar* verbs; direct object pronouns *lo, la, los, las*
8: Experiencias	**8A De vacaciones** **Vocabulary:** vacation places; activities; modes of transportation **Grammar:** preterite of *-er* and *-ir* verbs; preterite of *ir;* the personal *a*	**8B Ayudando en la comunidad** **Vocabulary:** recycling and volunteer work; places in a community **Grammar:** the verb *decir;* indirect object pronouns; preterite of *hacer* and *dar*
9: Medios de comunicación	**9A El cine y la televisión** **Vocabulary:** television shows; movie genres; giving opinions **Grammar:** *acabar de* + infinitive; *gustar* and similar verbs	**9B La tecnología** **Vocabulary:** computers; communication; computer-related activities **Grammar:** the verbs *pedir* and *servir; saber* and *conocer*

Program Organization

Scope and Sequence

REALIDADES 2 uses a recursive Scope and Sequence that revisits the themes from *REALIDADES A, B* or *1*. This natural recycling allows for important review and reteaching. In addition, students expand their vocabulary, grammar, and cultural understanding as they revisit each theme in greater depth.

REALIDADES 2

Tema	Capítulo A	Capítulo B
Para empezar	A. ¿Cómo eres tú? *Repaso:* describing people; asking for information; nationalities; adjective agreement; the verb *ser* B. ¿Qué haces? *Repaso*: leisure activities; seasons of the year; regular *-ar, -er*, and *-ir* verbs	
1: Tu día escolar	**1A ¿Qué haces en la escuela?** **Vocabulary:** classroom items, activities, and rules **Grammar:** *(Repaso)* stem-changing verbs; affirmative and negative words	**1B ¿Qué haces después de las clases?** **Vocabulary:** extracurricular activities **Grammar:** making comparisons; *(Repaso)* the verbs *saber* and *conocer; hace* + time expressions
2: Un evento especial	**2A ¿Cómo te preparas?** **Vocabulary:** daily routines, getting ready for an event **Grammar:** reflexive verbs; *(Repaso)* the verbs *ser* and *estar;* possessive adjectives *mío, tuyo, suyo*	**2B ¿Qué ropa compraste?** **Vocabulary:** shopping vocabulary, prices, money **Grammar:** *(Repaso)* the preterite of regular verbs; demonstrative adjectives
3: Tú y tu comunidad	**3A ¿Qué hiciste ayer?** **Vocabulary:** running errands; locations in a downtown; items purchased **Grammar:** *(Repaso)* direct object pronouns; the irregular preterite of the verbs *ir, ser, hacer, tener, estar, poder*	**3B ¿Cómo se va?** **Vocabulary:** places in a city or town; driving terms; modes of transportation **Grammar:** *(Repaso)* direct object pronouns: *me, te, nos;* irregular affirmative *tú* commands; *(Repaso)* present progressive: irregular forms
4: Recuerdos del pasado	**4A Cuando éramos niños** **Vocabulary:** toys; play terms; describing children **Grammar:** the imperfect tense: regular verbs and irregular verbs; *(Repaso)* indirect object pronouns	**4B Celebrando los día festivos** **Vocabulary:** expression describing etiquette; holiday and family celebrations **Grammar:** the imperfect tense: describing a situation; reciprocal actions
5: En las noticias	**5A Un acto heróico** **Vocabulary:** natural disasters; emergencies; rescues; heroes **Grammar:** the imperfect tense: other uses; the preterite of the verbs *oír, leer, creer,* and *destruir*	**5B Un accidente** **Vocabulary:** parts of the body; accidents; events in the emergency room **Grammar:** the irregular preterites: *venir, poner; decir, traer;* the imperfect progressive and preterite
6: La televisión y el cine	**6A ¿Viste el partido en la televisión?** **Vocabulary:** watching television programs; sporting events **Grammar:** the preterite of *-ir* stem-changing verbs; other reflexive verbs	**6B ¿Qué película has visto?** **Vocabulary:** movies; making a movie **Grammar:** verbs that use indirect objects; the present perfect
7: Buen provecho	**7A ¿Cómo se hace la paella?** **Vocabulary:** cooking expressions; food; appliances; following a recipe; giving directions in a kitchen **Grammar:** negative *tú* commands; the impersonal *se*	**7B ¿Te gusta comer al aire libre?** **Vocabulary:** camping and cookouts; food **Grammar:** *Usted* and *Ustedes* commands; uses of *por*
8: Cómo ser un buen turista	**8A Un viaje en avión** **Vocabulary:** visiting an airport; planning a trip; traveling safely **Grammar:** the present subjunctive; irregular verbs in the subjunctive	**8B Quiero que disfrutes de tu viaje** **Vocabulary:** staying in a hotel; appropriate tourist behaviors; traveling in a foreign city **Grammar:** the present subjunctive with impersonal expressions; the present subjunctive of stem-changing verbs
9: ¿Cómo será el futuro?	**9A ¿Qué profesión tendrás?** **Vocabulary:** professions; making plans for the future; earning a living **Grammar:** the future tense; the future tense of irregular verbs	**9B ¿Qué haremos para mejorar el mundo?** **Vocabulary:** environment; environmental issues and solutions **Grammar:** the future tense: other irregular verbs; the present subjunctive with expressions of doubt

Scope and Sequence

REALIDADES 3 offers ten thought-provoking thematic chapters that integrate rich vocabulary groups and a thorough presentation of grammar. Chapter activities combine communication, culture, and cross-curricular content with authentic literature and poetry.

REALIDADES 3

Each thematic chapter is divided into two sections. Each of these sections (1 and 2) presents and practices vocabulary and grammar.

Capítulo	1	2
Para empezar	1. Tu día diaria *Repaso:* daily routines; school life; leisure activities; present tense verbs; reflective verbs 2. Días especiales *Repaso:* weekend activities; celebrations; special events; verbs like *gustar;* possessive adjectives	
1: Un día inolvidable	**Vocabulary:** hiking objects, activities, and perils; weather **Grammar:** *(Repaso)* preterite verbs with the spelling change *i–y; (Repaso)* preterite of irregular verbs; *(Repaso)* preterite of verbs with the spelling change *e–i* and *o–u*	**Vocabulary:** getting ready for an athletic or academic competition; emotional responses to competition; awards and ceremonies **Grammar:** *(Repaso)* the imperfect; uses of the imperfect
2: ¿Cómo te expresas?	**Vocabulary:** describing art and sculpture; tools for painting; describing what influences art **Grammar:** *(Repaso)* the preterite vs. the imperfect; *estar* + participle	**Vocabulary:** musical instruments; describing dance; describing drama **Grammar:** *(Repaso) ser* and *estar;* verbs with special meanings in the preterite vs. the imperfect
3: ¿Qué haces para estar en forma?	**Vocabulary:** nutrition; illnesses and pains; medicine; habits for good health **Grammar:** *(Repaso)* affirmative *tú* commands; *(Repaso)* affirmative and negative commands with *Ud.* and *Uds.*	**Vocabulary:** exercises; getting and staying in shape; health advice **Grammar:** *(Repaso)* the subjunctive: regular verbs; *(Repaso)* the subjunctive: irregular verbs; *(Repaso)* the subjunctive with stem changing *-ar* and *-er* verbs
4: ¿Cómo te llevas con los demás?	**Vocabulary:** personality traits; interpersonal behavior; friendship **Grammar:** *(Repaso)* the subjunctive with verbs of emotion; *(Repaso)* the uses of *por* and *para*	**Vocabulary:** expressing and resolving interpersonal problems; interpersonal relationships **Grammar:** commands with *nosotros;* possessive pronouns
5: Trabajo y comunidad	**Vocabulary:** after-school work; describing a job **Grammar:** *(Repaso)* the present perfect; *(Repaso)* the past perfect	**Vocabulary:** volunteer activities; the benefits and importance of volunteer work **Grammar:** the present perfect subjunctive; demonstrative adjectives and pronouns
6: ¿Qué nos traerá en el futuro?	**Vocabulary:** jobs and professions; qualities of a good employee **Grammar:** *(Repaso)* the future; *(Repaso)* the future of probability	**Vocabulary:** technology; inventions; jobs in the future **Grammar:** the future perfect; *(Repaso)* the use of direct and indirect object pronouns
7: ¿Mito o realidad?	**Vocabulary:** archeological terms and activities; describing archeological sites **Grammar:** the present and past subjunctive in expressions of doubt	**Vocabulary:** myths and legends; ancient beliefs; Precolumbian scientific discoveries **Grammar:** the subjunctive in adverbial clauses
8: Encuentro entre culturas	**Vocabulary:** architecture and history of Spain **Grammar:** the conditional	**Vocabulary:** Spain in the Americas; the encounter between Cortés and the Aztecs; family heritage **Grammar:** the past subjunctive; the past subjunctive with *si* clauses
9: Cuidemos nuestro planeta	**Vocabulary:** caring for the environment **Grammar:** present subjunctive with conjunctions (*mientras, tan pronto como,* etc.); relative pronouns *que, quien, lo que*	**Vocabulary:** environmental issues, endangered animals **Grammar:** present subjunctive with other conjunctions (*a menos que, sin que, para que,* etc.)
10: ¿Cuáles son tus derechos y responsabilidades?	**Vocabulary:** rights and responsibilties **Grammar:** the passive voice: *ser* + past participle; the present vs. the past subjunctive	**Vocabulary:** government; the role of government; individual rights **Grammar:** the past perfect subjunctive; the conditional perfect

Program Organization

Program Resources

REALIDADES offers a wide range of print and technology support for students and teachers.

Student Print Resources

Practice Workbook	• focused practice for new vocabulary and grammar • end-of-chapter crossword puzzle • end-of-chapter Organizer • go online Web Codes for linking to Web site
Writing, Audio & Video Workbook	• additional writing practice • student response pages for the Audio Program • student response pages for the *A primera vista* video segments • lyrics to songs
Heritage Learner Workbook	• builds on students' prior knowledge • focused practice on the basics of language • extensions to chapter content • additional reading and writing tasks
Grammar Study Guide	• quick summary of grammar for Levels 1 and 2 • laminated and 3-hole punched

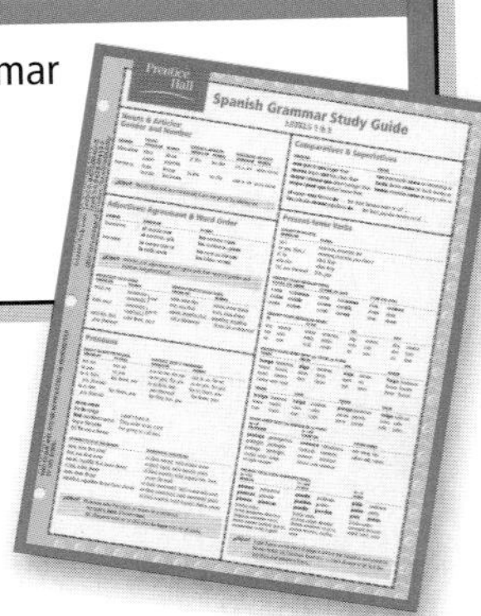

Student Technology

 **REALIDADES Companion Web site**	• instant access using Web Codes • tutorial practice for vocabulary and grammar • Internet links and activities • end-of-chapter vocabulary and grammar lists • end-of-chapter self-test
 **MindPoint Quiz Show CD-ROM**	• interactive game show format for review • competition against computer, a partner, or entire class
 **Interactive text online**	• interactive Student Edition online • access to audio and video • interactive activities
 **Interactive text on CD-ROM**	• interactive Student Edition on CD-ROM • access to audio and video • interactive activities

Teacher Transparencies

Vocabulary and Grammar Transparencies
- Maps
- Graphic Organizers
- *A primera vista*
  - *Vocabulario y gramática en contexto*
  - *Videohistoria*
- *Gramática*
  - verb paradigms and grammar charts
- Realia
- Rapid Review

Answers on Transparencies
- Student Edition answers
- *Practice Workbook* answers

Fine Art Transparencies
- Beautiful transparencies to be used across all five levels
- Accompanying notes and activities

Teacher Print Resources

Teacher's Resource Books

Organized by chapters:
- Input Script
- Video Script
- Audio Script
- *Practice Workbook* Answer Key
- *Writing, Audio & Video Workbook* Answer Key
- Communication Activities on Blackline Masters
- Situation Cards on Blackline Masters
- School to Home Letters
- *GramActiva* and *Juego* Blackline Masters

TPR Storytelling
- Complete support for integrating TPR storytelling with *REALIDADES.*

Teacher Technology

Teacher Express CD-ROM

Complete teacher support including:
- teaching resources to preview and print
- lesson plans at the click of a mouse
- vocabulary clip art

Video Program (VHS or DVD)
- *A primera vista* segments expand each chapter's *Videohistoria*
- *GramActiva* segments teach the new grammar using humor and graphics
- *¿Eres tú, María?* mystery video

Companion Web site
- teaching ideas
- links to other resources

Audio Program (22 CDs)
- *A primera vista*
  - *Vocabulario y gramática en contexto*
  - *Videohistoria*
- Student Edition *Escuchar* Activities
- *Pronunciación*
- *Writing, Audio & Video Workbook* Listening Activities
- Listening section of *Examen del capítulo*
- Songs

Computer Test Bank with CD-ROM
- Variety of questions per chapter
- Create tests and alternate versions

Teacher Assessment

Assessment Program
- Professional Development articles
- Rubrics
- Placement Test
- Chapter Quizzes
- Chapter Tests
- Cumulative Tests

Computer Test Bank with CD-ROM
- Variety of questions per chapter
- Create tests and alternate versions

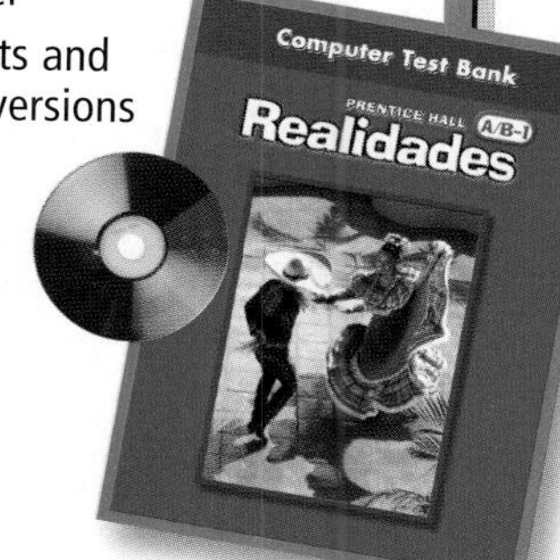

Getting Started

Students get started in ***REALIDADES A*** with these colorful reference and introductory sections:

- **Mapas**
- **Why Study Spanish?**
- **Study Tips**
- **Para empezar**

Mapas

Colorful atlas pages support geography skills. Students can go online to learn more about each country.

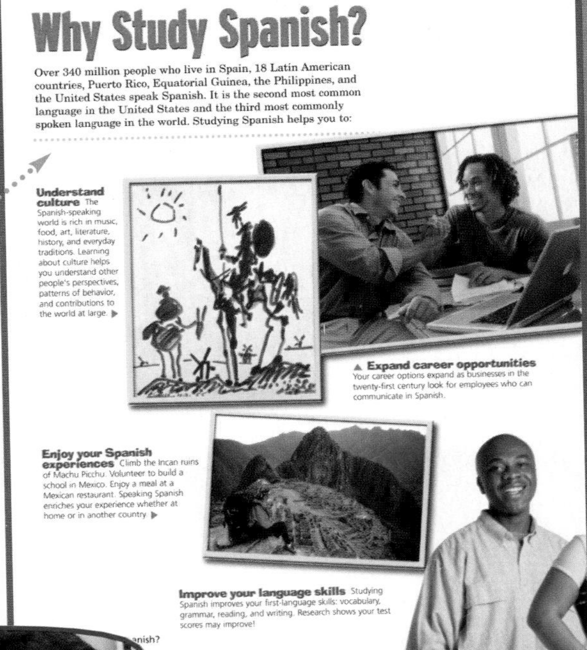

Why Study Spanish?

Over 340 million people who live in Spain, 18 Latin American countries, Puerto Rico, Equatorial Guinea, the Philippines, and the United States speak Spanish. It is the second most common language in the United States and the third most commonly spoken language in the world. Studying Spanish helps you to:

Understand culture The Spanish-speaking world is rich in music, food, art, literature, history, and everyday traditions. Learning about culture helps you understand other people's perspectives, patterns of behavior, and contributions to the world at large.

▲ Expand career opportunities Your career options expand as businesses in the twenty-first century look for employees who can communicate in Spanish.

Enjoy your Spanish experiences Climb the Incan ruins of Machu Picchu. Volunteer to build a school in Mexico. Enjoy a meal at a Mexican restaurant. Speaking Spanish enriches your experience whether at home or in another country.

Improve your language skills Studying Spanish improves your first-language skills: vocabulary, grammar, reading, and writing. Research shows your test scores may improve!

Why Study Spanish?

Students focus on real-life purposes for learning Spanish.

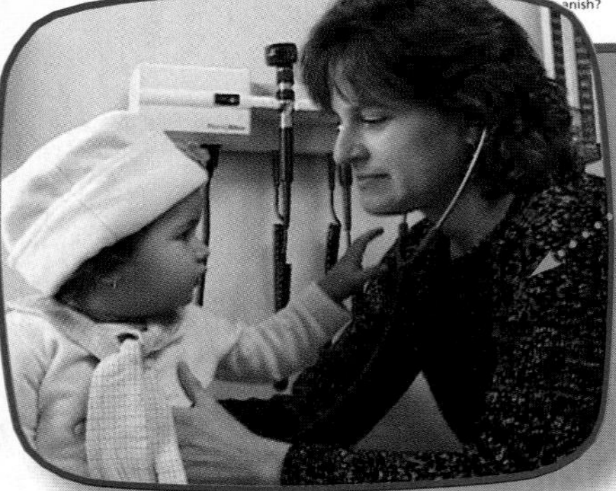

Why Study Spanish? **Video**

Why Study Spanish? Video

This motivating video introduces students to the Spanish-speaking world and to several people who talk about how speaking Spanish has helped them personally and professionally.

Study Tips

Go Online PHSchool.com
For: More tips for studying Spanish
Visit: www.phschool.com
Web Code: jce-0003

Take risks, relax, and be patient. The goal of studying Spanish is to communicate! So don't wait until you get it perfect. Just start talking, and you'll get better and better! You'll make some mistakes, but the longer you practice, the more improvement you'll see.

Here are some easy tips to help you learn Spanish!

Use what you already know. You already know lots of Spanish words such as *rodeo, hasta la vista, tacos, armadillo, sombrero, piñata, mesa,* and *tango*. Use your knowledge of English to help you figure out new words such as *comunicación, delicioso, limón,* and *oficina*. You'll find Spanish is easier if you use what you already know.

You don't need to understand everything. As you hear or read Spanish, you'll come across words or expressions you don't know. Try to figure out what the meaning might be. Above all, don't stop! Keep on listening or reading. You'll be surprised how much you can understand without knowing every word.

Look for Strategy and ¿Recuerdas? boxes. Throughout **Realidades**, you'll see boxes that provide strategies or remind you of something you've already learned. The information in the boxes will help you learn.

Make flashcards. One way to learn a new word is to make a flashcard. Create a picture of the word on an index card. On the back, write the word in Spanish. Then use the card to study: look at the picture and say the word or look at the picture and write the word.

Have fun! You'll find lots of activities that allow you to work with other students, play games, act out skits, explore the Internet, create projects, and use technology. Try out all of the activities and you'll have fun.

Strategy
Using graphic organizers
Drawing diagrams can help you understand how things are related.

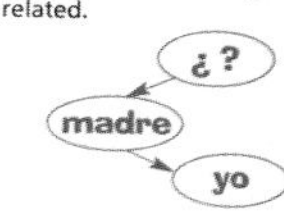

Study tips

Get students started with useful tips for success! Students can find additional strategies online at **PHSchool.com**.

Para empezar

Objectives

1 En la escuela
- Greet people at different times of the day
- Introduce yourself to others
- Respond to classroom directions
- Begin using numbers
- Tell time
- Identify parts of the body

2 En la clase
- Talk about things in the classroom
- Ask questions about new words and phrases
- Use the Spanish alphabet to spell words
- Talk about things related to the calendar

3 El tiempo
- Describe weather conditions
- Identify the seasons

uno 1
Para empezar

Para empezar

This introductory section gets students started in Spanish. Topics include greetings, classroom items and commands, the calendar and dates, and weather expressions.

Chapter Organization

Chapter Sequence

- A primera vista
- Manos a la obra
- ¡Adelante!
- Repaso del capítulo

A primera vista

This six-page section gives students a "first look" at the new vocabulary and grammar through comprehensible input that integrates visuals and text with audio and video.

Visualized vocabulary

New words are presented visually and in context.

Language input

Input continues with visuals accompanied by narrative. All new vocabulary words and grammar are highlighted in blue.

Chapter opener *Capítulo 3A*

Listening comprehension

Short listening activities check comprehension.

More practice

Extra practice is available in the *Practice Workbook* and online.

Reading and language input

The input of new vocabulary and grammar continues through a short, engaging reading written as a *videohistoria*. This story is based upon the accompanying *A primera vista* video segment.

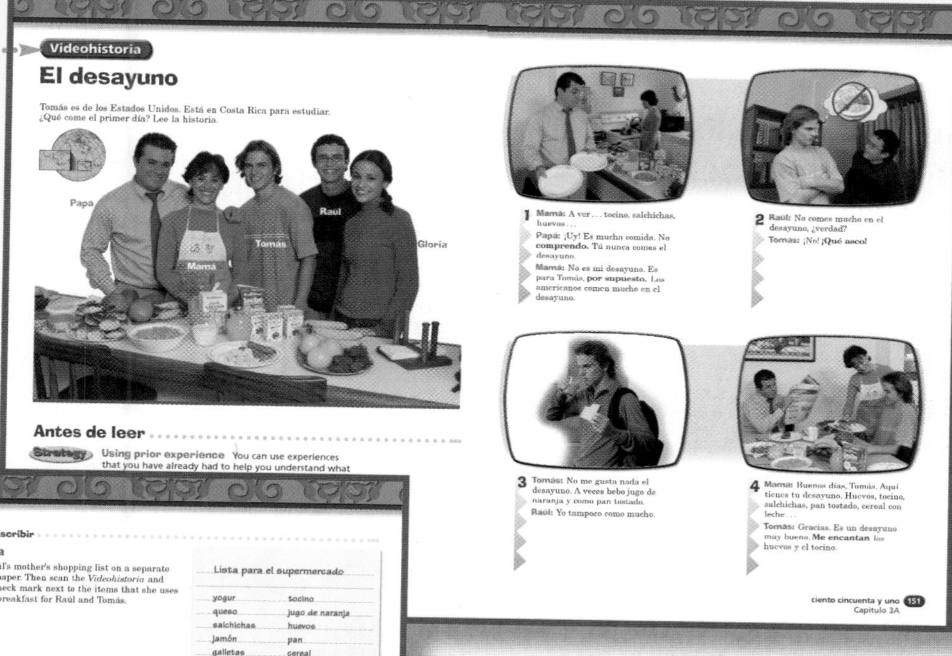

Videohistoria

El desayuno

Tomás es de los Estados Unidos. Está en Costa Rica para estudiar. ¿Qué come el primer día? Lee la historia.

1 **Mamá:** A ver... tocino, salchichas, huevos...
Papá: ¡Uy! Es mucha comida. No **comprendo.** Tú nunca comes el desayuno.
Mamá: No es mi desayuno. Es para Tomás, **por supuesto.** Los americanos comen mucho en el desayuno.

2 **Raúl:** No comes mucho en el desayuno, ¿verdad?
Tomás: ¡No! **¡Qué asco!**

3 **Tomás:** No me gusta nada el desayuno. A veces bebo jugo de naranja y como pan tostado.
Raúl: Yo tampoco como mucho.

4 **Mamá:** Buenos días, Tomás. Aquí tienes tu desayuno. Huevos, tocino, salchichas, pan tostado, cereal con leche...
Tomás: Gracias. Es un desayuno muy bueno. **Me encantan** los huevos y el tocino.

Antes de leer

Strategy **Using prior experience** You can use experiences that you have already had to help you understand what

ciento cincuenta y uno 151
Capítulo 3A

5 **Tomás: Comparto** los huevos, el tocino y las salchichas.
Raúl: ¿Compartes tu desayuno? Muchas gracias, Tomás.

6 **Raúl:** ¿Y qué **bebes?**
Tomás: Jugo de naranja, por favor.
Mamá: Te gusta la leche, ¿no?
Tomás: Más o menos.

7 **Raúl:** Papá, ¿unos huevos?
Papá: No, gracias. ¡La comida es para Uds.!

8 **Mamá: ¿Cuál** es tu almuerzo favorito, Tomás?
Tomás: Me gustan las hamburguesas, la pizza, **la ensalada...**
Mamá: Bueno... ¡pizza, hamburguesas y ensalada en el almuerzo!

Actividad 3 **Escribir**

La lista

Copy Raúl's mother's shopping list on a separate sheet of paper. Then scan the *Videohistoria* and place a check mark next to the items that she uses to make breakfast for Raúl and Tomás.

Lista para el supermercado	
yogur	tocino
queso	jugo de naranja
salchichas	huevos
jamón	pan
galletas	cereal
plátanos	leche

Actividad 4 **Leer/Hablar**

Los gustos de Tomás

Read the following sentences and tell how Tomás would react, according to the *Videohistoria*. If he would like what is mentioned, say "¡*Me encanta!*" If he wouldn't like it, say "¡*Qué asco!*"

1. En el desayuno hay pan tostado.
2. En el desayuno hay jugo de naranja.
3. En el almuerzo hay pizza.
4. Hoy hay un desayuno muy grande.
5. Hoy hay ensalada en el almuerzo.

Actividad 5 **Leer**

¿Comprendes?

Read the following sentences. Write the numbers 1–6 on your paper and write *C* (*cierto*) if a sentence is true, or *F* (*falso*) if it is false.

1. Tomás está en Costa Rica.
2. La mamá de Raúl siempre come mucho en el desayuno.
3. A Tomás le gusta comer mucho en el desayuno.
4. Hoy Tomás no come mucho en el desayuno.
5. Tomás comparte el desayuno con Raúl.
6. A Tomás le gustan las hamburguesas y la pizza.

Más práctica
Practice Workbook 3A-3, 3A-4

Go Online
PHSchool.com
For: Vocabulary practice
Visit: www.phschool.com
Web Code: jad-0302

152 ciento cincuenta y dos
Tema 3 • La comida

ciento cincuenta y tres 153
Capítulo 3A

Reading comprehension

Questions check students' comprehension of the story while practicing the new vocabulary and grammar.

Videos and language input

The language, characters, and culture of the *Videohistoria* come to life in the *A primera vista* video segment. Each video segment is approximately 5 minutes in length. The videos were filmed in San Antonio, Mexico City, Costa Rica, and Spain (Madrid and Toledo). To help students with language input, each video is shown twice. The first time, key vocabulary is labeled on the screen. The second time the words are not shown. Additional video activities can be found in the *Writing, Audio & Video Workbook*.

From the *A primera vista* video segment

Manos a la obra

Students "get to work" using the chapter's new vocabulary and grammar.

Focused practice

Students start with activities that focus on reading, listening, and basic writing.

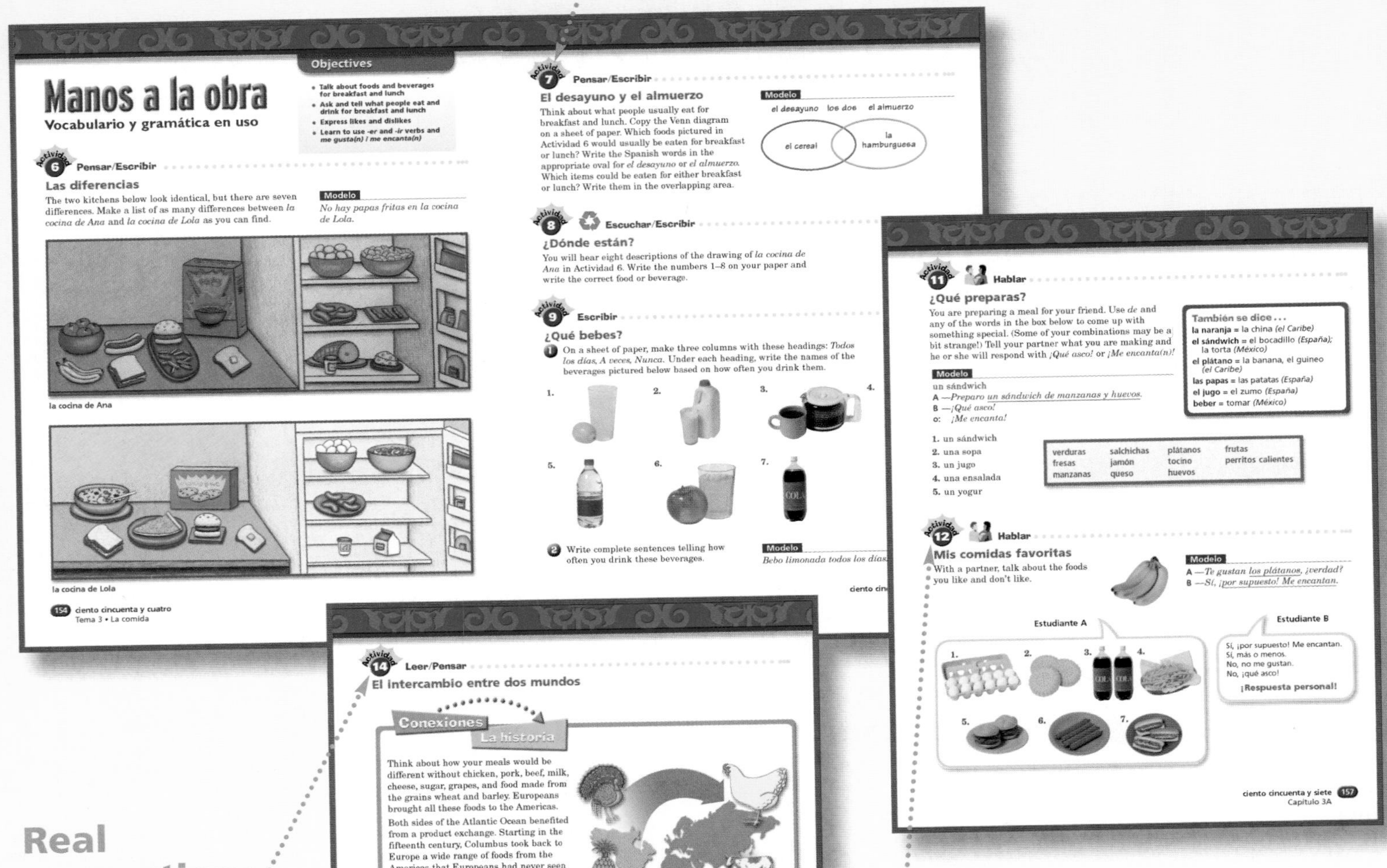

Manos a la obra

Vocabulario y gramática en uso

Objectives

- Talk about foods and beverages for breakfast and lunch
- Ask and tell what people eat and drink for breakfast and lunch
- Express likes and dislikes
- Learn to use *-er* and *-ir* verbs and *me gusta(n)* / *me encanta(n)*

Actividad 6 Pensar/Escribir

Las diferencias

The two kitchens below look identical, but there are seven differences. Make a list of as many differences between *la cocina de Ana* and *la cocina de Lola* as you can find.

Modelo

No hay papas fritas en la cocina de Lola.

la cocina de Ana

la cocina de Lola

154 ciento cincuenta y cuatro
Tema 3 • La comida

Actividad 7 Pensar/Escribir

El desayuno y el almuerzo

Think about what people usually eat for breakfast and lunch. Copy the Venn diagram on a sheet of paper. Which foods pictured in Actividad 6 would usually be eaten for breakfast or lunch? Write the Spanish words in the appropriate oval for *el desayuno* or *el almuerzo.* Which items could be eaten for either breakfast or lunch? Write them in the overlapping area.

Modelo

Actividad 8 Escuchar/Escribir

¿Dónde están?

You will hear eight descriptions of the drawing of *la cocina de Ana* in Actividad 6. Write the numbers 1–8 on your paper and write the correct food or beverage.

Actividad 9 Escribir

¿Qué bebes?

1 On a sheet of paper, make three columns with these headings: *Todos los días, A veces, Nunca.* Under each heading, write the names of the beverages pictured below based on how often you drink them.

1. 2. 3. 4. 5. 6. 7.

2 Write complete sentences telling how often you drink these beverages.

Modelo

Bebo limonada todos los días.

ciento cin

Actividad 11 Hablar

¿Qué preparas?

You are preparing a meal for your friend. Use *de* and any of the words in the box below to come up with something special. (Some of your combinations may be a bit strange!) Tell your partner what you are making and he or she will respond with *¡Qué asco!* or *¡Me encanta(n)!*

Modelo

un sándwich
A —*Preparo un sándwich de manzanas y huevos.*
B —*¡Qué asco!*
o: *¡Me encanta!*

1. un sándwich
2. una sopa
3. un jugo
4. una ensalada
5. un yogur

verduras	salchichas	plátanos	frutas
fresas	jamón	tocino	perritos calientes
manzanas	queso	huevos	

También se dice . . .

la naranja = la china *(el Caribe)*
el sándwich = el bocadillo *(España);* la torta *(México)*
el plátano = la banana, el guineo *(el Caribe)*
las papas = las patatas *(España)*
el jugo = el zumo *(España)*
beber = tomar *(México)*

Actividad 12 Hablar

Mis comidas favoritas

With a partner, talk about the foods you like and don't like.

Modelo

A —*Te gustan los plátanos, ¿verdad?*
B —*Sí, ¡por supuesto! Me encantan.*

Estudiante A

1. 2. 3. 4. 5. 6. 7.

Estudiante B

Sí, ¡por supuesto! Me encantan.
Sí, más o menos.
No, no me gustan.
No, ¡qué asco!
¡Respuesta personal!

ciento cincuenta y siete 157
Capítulo 3A

Actividad 14 Leer/Pensar

El intercambio entre dos mundos

Conexiones La historia

Think about how your meals would be different without chicken, pork, beef, milk, cheese, sugar, grapes, and food made from the grains wheat and barley. Europeans brought all these foods to the Americas.

Both sides of the Atlantic Ocean benefited from a product exchange. Starting in the fifteenth century, Columbus took back to Europe a wide range of foods from the Americas that Europeans had never seen before. These foods included corn, beans, squash, tomatoes, limes, avocados, chiles, peanuts, cashews, turkey, pineapples, yams, potatoes, vanilla, and chocolate. Today these foods are found in dishes in many countries.

- What is your favorite meal? Do the ingredients originally come from the Americas, Europe, or elsewhere?

Actividad 15 Leer/Escribir

Enchiladas de pollo

Read the list of ingredients for a traditional Mexican dish of *enchiladas.* Based upon the information you just read and saw in the map, write which ingredients had their origins in the Americas and which came from Europe.

Enchiladas de pollo con salsa de tomate

Ingredientes

12 tortillas de maíz[1]
1 taza[2] de pollo[3]
1 taza de queso fresco
6 tomates grandes
2 cebollas[4] no muy grandes
crema
aceite[5] de maíz

[1]corn [2]cup [3]chicken [4]onions [5]oil

ciento cincuenta y nueve 159
Capítulo 3A

Real connections

Cross-curricular activities are woven into the practice sequence.

Paired practice

Students transition to paired practice activities that focus on the new vocabulary.

Grammar integrated with communication

The complete grammar presentation features clear explanations and examples.

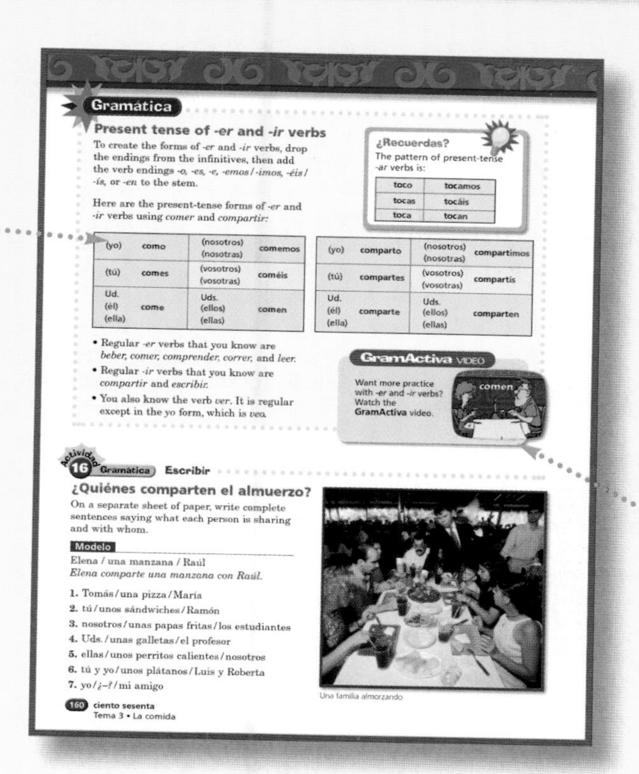

Gramática

Present tense of *-er* and *-ir* verbs

To create the forms of *-er* and *-ir* verbs, drop the endings from the infinitives, then add the verb endings *-o, -es, -e, -emos / -imos, -éis / -ís,* or *-en* to the stem.

Here are the present-tense forms of *-er* and *-ir* verbs using *comer* and *compartir:*

(yo)	como	(nosotros) (nosotras)	comemos
(tú)	comes	(vosotros) (vosotras)	coméis
Ud. (él) (ella)	come	Uds. (ellos) (ellas)	comen

(yo)	comparto	(nosotros) (nosotras)	compartimos
(tú)	compartes	(vosotros) (vosotras)	compartís
Ud. (él) (ella)	comparte	Uds. (ellos) (ellas)	comparten

¿Recuerdas?

The pattern of present-tense *-ar* verbs is:

toco	tocamos
tocas	tocáis
toca	tocan

- Regular *-er* verbs that you know are *beber, comer, comprender, correr,* and *leer.*
- Regular *-ir* verbs that you know are *compartir* and *escribir.*
- You also know the verb *ver*. It is regular except in the *yo* form, which is *veo.*

GramActiva VIDEO

Want more practice with *-er* and *-ir* verbs? Watch the **GramActiva** video.

Actividad 16 Gramática Escribir

¿Quiénes comparten el almuerzo?

On a separate sheet of paper, write complete sentences saying what each person is sharing and with whom.

Modelo

Elena / una manzana / Raúl
Elena comparte una manzana con Raúl.

1. Tomás / una pizza / María
2. tú / unos sándwiches / Ramón
3. nosotros / unas papas fritas / los estudiantes
4. Uds. / unas galletas / el profesor
5. ellas / unos perritos calientes / nosotros
6. tú y yo / unos plátanos / Luis y Roberta
7. yo / ¿–? / mi amigo

Una familia almorzando

160 ciento sesenta
Tema 3 • La comida

Reinforce grammar through videos

Graphics and humor in the *GramActiva* video segments help students "see" how grammar works!

Hands-on learning

Fun, interactive games help students learn new concepts.

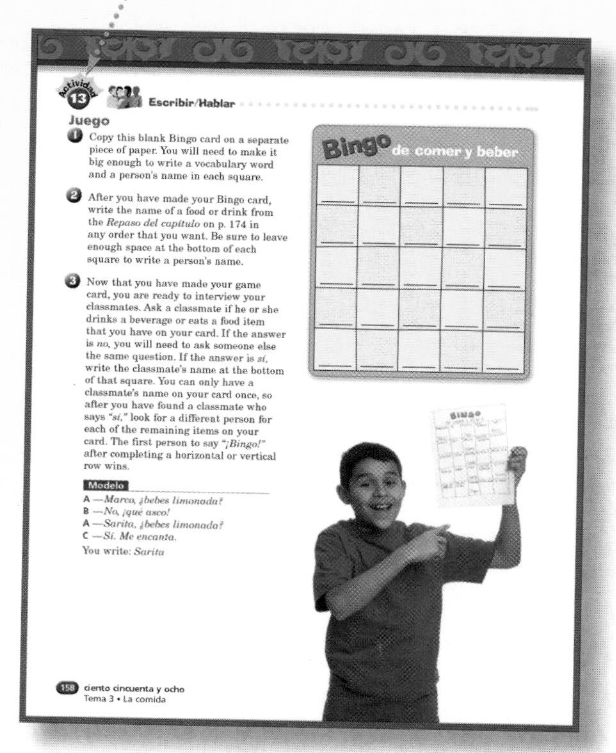

Actividad 13 Escribir/Hablar

Juego

1. Copy this blank Bingo card on a separate piece of paper. You will need to make it big enough to write a vocabulary word and a person's name in each square.
2. After you have made your Bingo card, write the name of a food or drink from the *Repaso del capítulo* on p. 174 in any order that you want. Be sure to leave enough space at the bottom of each square to write a person's name.
3. Now that you have made your game card, you are ready to interview your classmates. Ask a classmate if he or she drinks a beverage or eats a food item that you have on your card. If the answer is *no,* you will need to ask someone else the same question. If the answer is *sí,* write the classmate's name at the bottom of that square. You can only have a classmate's name on your card once, so after you have found a classmate who says "*sí,*" look for a different person for each of the remaining items on your card. The first person to say "*¡Bingo!*" after completing a horizontal or vertical row wins.

Modelo

A —*Marco, ¿bebes limonada?*
B —*No, ¡qué asco!*
A —*Sarita, ¿bebes limonada?*
C —*Sí. Me encanta.*
You write: *Sarita*

158 ciento cincuenta y ocho
Tema 3 • La comida

Language and culture

Culture is woven together with language practice.

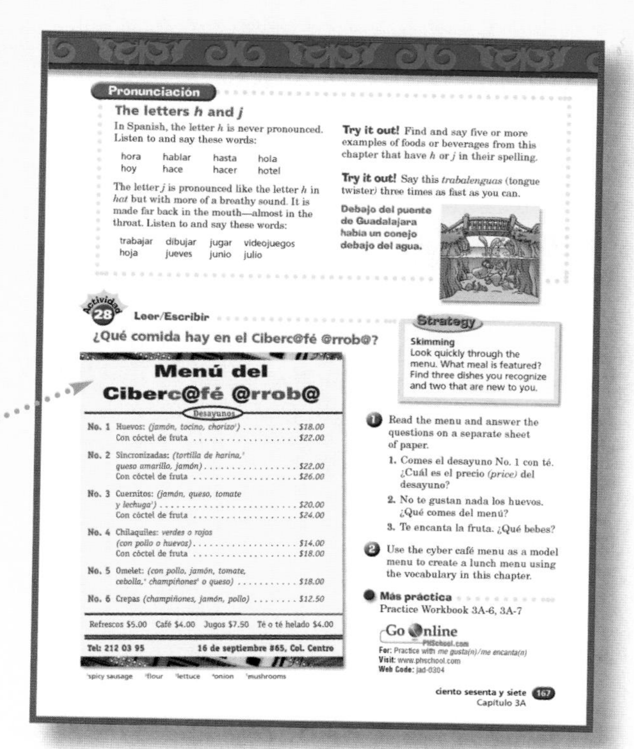

Pronunciación

The letters *h* and *j*

In Spanish, the letter *h* is never pronounced. Listen to and say these words:

hora	hablar	hasta	hola
hoy	hace	hacer	hotel

The letter *j* is pronounced like the letter *h* in *hat* but with more of a breathy sound. It is made far back in the mouth—almost in the throat. Listen to and say these words:

trabajar	dibujar	jugar	videojuegos
hoja	jueves	junio	julio

Try it out! Find and say five or more examples of foods or beverages from this chapter that have *h* or *j* in their spelling.

Try it out! Say this *trabalenguas* (tongue twister) three times as fast as you can.

Debajo del puente de Guadalajara había un conejo debajo del agua.

Actividad 28 Leer/Escribir

¿Qué comida hay en el Ciberc@fé @rrob@?

Menú del Ciberc@fé @rrob@

Desayunos

No. 1	Huevos: *(jamón, tocino, chorizo[1])*	$18.00
	Con cóctel de fruta	$22.00
No. 2	Sincronizadas: *(tortilla de harina,[2] queso amarillo, jamón)*	$22.00
	Con cóctel de fruta	$26.00
No. 3	Cuernitos: *(jamón, queso, tomate y lechuga[3])*	$20.00
	Con cóctel de fruta	$24.00
No. 4	Chilaquiles: *verdes o rojos (con pollo o huevos)*	$14.00
	Con cóctel de fruta	$18.00
No. 5	Omelet: *(con pollo, jamón, tomate, cebolla,[4] champiñones[5] o queso)*	$18.00
No. 6	Crepas *(champiñones, jamón, pollo)*	$12.50

Refrescos $5.00 Café $4.00 Jugos $7.50 Té o té helado $4.00

Tel: 212 03 95 16 de septiembre #65, Col. Centro

[1]spicy sausage [2]flour [3]lettuce [4]onion [5]mushrooms

Strategy

Skimming
Look quickly through the menu. What meal is featured? Find three dishes you recognize and two that are new to you.

1. Read the menu and answer the questions on a separate sheet of paper.
   1. Comes el desayuno No. 1 con té. ¿Cuál es el precio *(price)* del desayuno?
   2. No te gustan nada los huevos. ¿Qué comes del menú?
   3. Te encanta la fruta. ¿Qué bebes?
2. Use the cyber café menu as a model menu to create a lunch menu using the vocabulary in this chapter.

Más práctica
Practice Workbook 3A-6, 3A-7

Go Online PHSchool.com
For: Practice with *me gusta(n)/me encanta(n)*
Visit: www.phschool.com
Web Code: jad-0304

ciento sesenta y siete 167
Capítulo 3A

¡Adelante!

Students apply their language skills with culminating activities that include culturally-authentic readings, performance-based speaking and writing tasks, and a variety of cultural activities.

Strategies

Reading strategies help students become better readers.

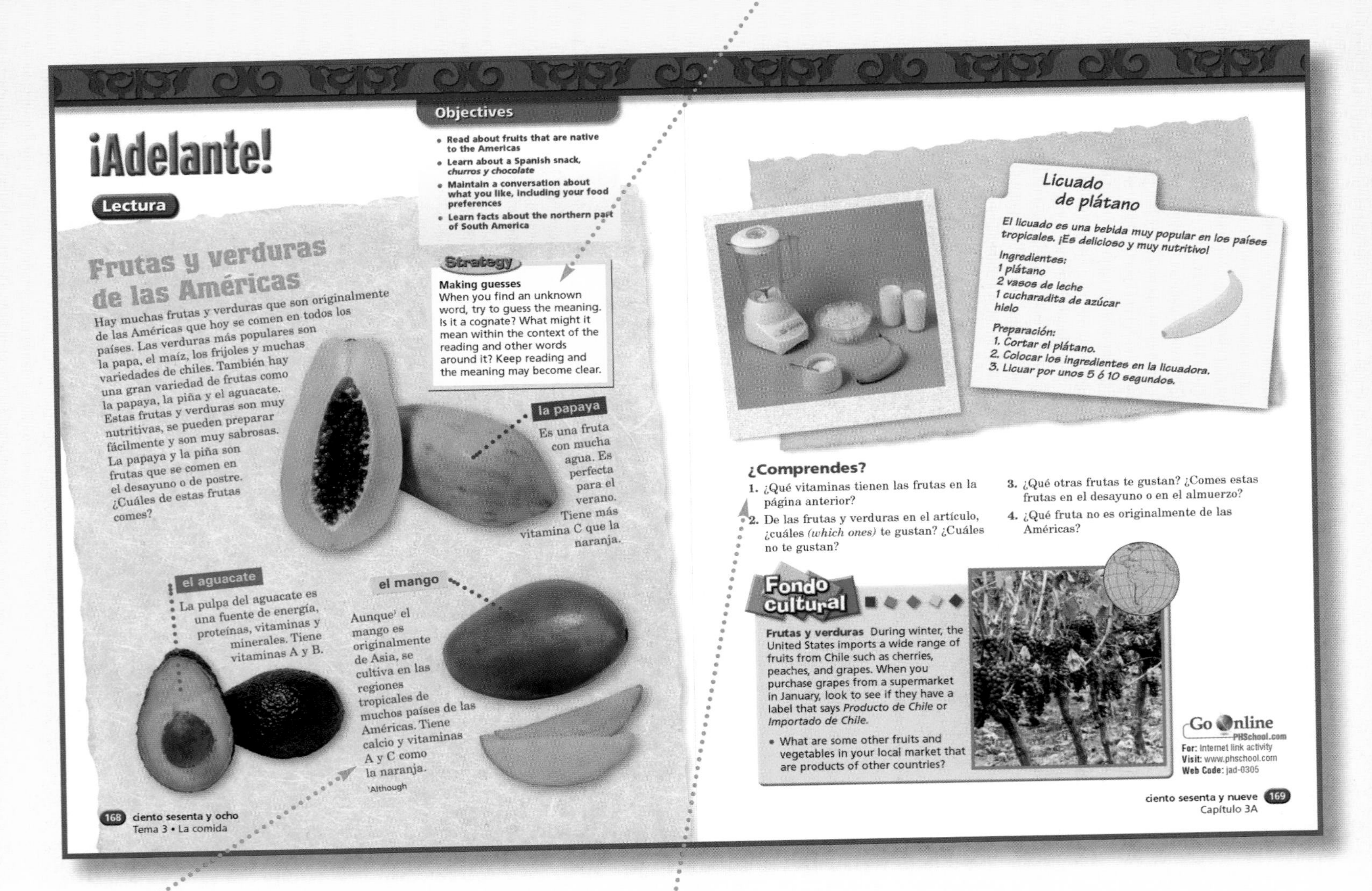

¡Adelante!

Lectura

Objectives
- Read about fruits that are native to the Americas
- Learn about a Spanish snack, *churros y chocolate*
- Maintain a conversation about what you like, including your food preferences
- Learn facts about the northern part of South America

Strategy
Making guesses
When you find an unknown word, try to guess the meaning. Is it a cognate? What might it mean within the context of the reading and other words around it? Keep reading and the meaning may become clear.

Frutas y verduras de las Américas

Hay muchas frutas y verduras que son originalmente de las Américas que hoy se comen en todos los países. Las verduras más populares son la papa, el maíz, los frijoles y muchas variedades de chiles. También hay una gran variedad de frutas como la papaya, la piña y el aguacate. Estas frutas y verduras son muy nutritivas, se pueden preparar fácilmente y son muy sabrosas. La papaya y la piña son frutas que se comen en el desayuno o de postre. ¿Cuáles de estas frutas comes?

la papaya Es una fruta con mucha agua. Es perfecta para el verano. Tiene más vitamina C que la naranja.

el aguacate La pulpa del aguacate es una fuente de energía, proteínas, vitaminas y minerales. Tiene vitaminas A y B.

el mango Aunque[1] el mango es originalmente de Asia, se cultiva en las regiones tropicales de muchos países de las Américas. Tiene calcio y vitaminas A y C como la naranja.

[1]Although

168 ciento sesenta y ocho
Tema 3 • La comida

Licuado de plátano

El licuado es una bebida muy popular en los países tropicales. ¡Es delicioso y muy nutritivo!

Ingredientes:
1 plátano
2 vasos de leche
1 cucharadita de azúcar
hielo

Preparación:
1. Cortar el plátano.
2. Colocar los ingredientes en la licuadora.
3. Licuar por unos 5 ó 10 segundos.

¿Comprendes?
1. ¿Qué vitaminas tienen las frutas en la página anterior?
2. De las frutas y verduras en el artículo, ¿cuáles *(which ones)* te gustan? ¿Cuáles no te gustan?
3. ¿Qué otras frutas te gustan? ¿Comes estas frutas en el desayuno o en el almuerzo?
4. ¿Qué fruta no es originalmente de las Américas?

Fondo cultural

Frutas y verduras During winter, the United States imports a wide range of fruits from Chile such as cherries, peaches, and grapes. When you purchase grapes from a supermarket in January, look to see if they have a label that says *Producto de Chile* or *Importado de Chile*.
- What are some other fruits and vegetables in your local market that are products of other countries?

Go Online PHSchool.com
For: Internet link activity
Visit: www.phschool.com
Web Code: jad-0305

ciento sesenta y nueve 169
Capítulo 3A

Real-world readings

Students are able to connect to the cultural richness and diversity in the Spanish-speaking world.

Reading comprehension

Questions provide a quick check for comprehension.

Hands-on culture

La cultura en vivo offers a fun, hands-on experience with a wide range of cultural products and practices.

La cultura en vivo

Churros y chocolate

In many Spanish-speaking countries, a popular snack is the combination of *churros y chocolate. Churros* are long, slender doughnut-like pastries fried in hot oil. Small restaurants called *churrerías* specialize in *churros* and cups of delicious hot chocolate. You can also find *churros* being sold in stands from the street.

Chocolate y churros

Try it out! Here's the recipe to try. *Churros* are high in fat and calories, so you won't want to sample too many of them!

Churros

1 cup water	$\frac{1}{2}$ cup unsalted butter *(= 1 stick)*
$\frac{1}{4}$ teaspoon salt	1 cup all-purpose flour
4 large eggs	oil for deep-frying
1 cup sugar	

Un molinillo

In a heavy saucepan, bring water, butter, and salt to a full boil. Remove from heat. Add the flour all at once, stirring briskly. Stir until the mixture pulls away from the side of the pan and forms a ball. Put the mixture in a bowl. With an electric mixer on medium speed, add one egg at a time. After adding the last egg, beat the mixture for one more minute.

With adult supervision, heat 2–3 inches of oil to 375° F in a deep, heavy pan. Fit a pastry bag or cookie press with a $\frac{1}{2}$-inch star tip. Pipe out 6 inch-long tubes of dough into the oil. ***Be extremely cautious adding dough to the oil, because the oil may spatter and burn you!*** Fry, turning a few times, for 3–5 minutes or until golden brown. Place the sugar on a plate. Drain the *churros* well on paper towels and then roll them in the sugar.

Chocolate caliente

To make hot chocolate in Mexico, cacao beans are ground to a powder. Cinnamon, powdered almonds, and sugar are then added, and hot milk is poured in. The mixture is whipped with a wooden whisk called *un molinillo* or *un batidor.* You can find Mexican-style chocolate for making *chocolate caliente* in many supermarkets.

Think about it! What kinds of food and drink do you and your friends like? Is chocolate among the popular choices? Can you think of combinations of food and drink that are popular with many people in the United States? Are these combinations popular elsewhere?

170 ciento setenta
Tema 3 • La comida

Perspectivas del mundo hispano

¿Qué haces para mantener la salud?

Have you ever eaten chicken soup when you have a cold? How about putting aloe on a sunburn? In many countries, including those in the Spanish-speaking world, traditional remedies consisting of medicinal herbs have been used for centuries to treat common medical problems. In Mexico, a mint known as *yerbabuena* may be made into tea and given to someone with a stomachache. Remedies such as these may not be prescribed by licensed physicians, but people have confidence in them because they have been passed down through the generations. Many of those herbs are very safe, though some may have harmful side effects.

En la selva de Amazonas, Perú

Researchers are studying traditional herbal remedies to find modern-day medical solutions. In the Amazon rainforest in South America, an amazing abundance of plant life may hold the key to treating a wide variety of common ailments and diseases. Drug companies are looking for cures found in these plants and herbs that could be reproduced in today's modern drugs.

Increasingly, medicinal herbs are accepted not only as the basis for pharmaceutical drugs, but also for their own inherent healing qualities. In many countries, including the United States, herbal remedies are sometimes used in combination with conventional healthcare.

En un mercado en la Ciudad de México

Check it out! What alternatives to conventional medical care are available in your community? Make a list of all the healthcare services you can think of that are not traditional physicians. Are there health stores that sell herbal medicines? What types of herbal medicines are being sold and what remedies are attributed to these medicines?

Think about it! In many Spanish-speaking cultures, herbal remedies have been accepted for centuries. Do you think that medicinal herbs can provide relief and cures? Why or why not?

200 doscientos
Tema 3 • La comida

Cultural perspectives

Perspectivas del mundo hispano provides a thought-provoking overview of a product or practice (and its related perspectives) from the Spanish-speaking world.

Presentación oral

¿Y qué te gusta comer?

Task
An exchange student from the United States is going to Uruguay. You and a partner will role-play a telephone conversation in which you each take one of the roles and gather information about the other person.

1. **Prepare** You will role-play this conversation with a partner. Be sure to prepare for both roles. Here's how to prepare:

   Host Student: Make a list of at least four questions that you might ask the exchange student. Find out what he or she likes to study, his or her favorite activities, and what he or she likes to eat and drink for breakfast and lunch.

   Strategy
   Making lists
   Making lists of questions can help you in conversations where you need to find out specific information.

   Exchange Student: Jot down some possible answers to questions that the host student might ask and be prepared to provide information about yourself.

2. **Practice** Work in groups of four in which there are two exchange students and two host students. Work together to practice different questions and different responses. Here's how you might start your phone conversation:

   Host Student: ¡Hola, Pablo! Soy Rosa.
   Exchange Student: Hola, Rosa. ¿Cómo estás?
   Host Student: Bien, gracias. Pues Pablo, ¿te gusta . . . ?

   Continue the conversation using your notes. You can use your notes in practice, but not during the role-playing.

3. **Present** You will be paired with another student, and your teacher will tell you which role to play. The host student begins the conversation. Listen to your partner's questions and responses and keep the conversation going.

4. **Evaluation** Your teacher may give you a rubric for how the presentation will be graded. You will probably be graded on:
   - completion of task
   - how well you were understood
   - your ability to keep the conversation going

ciento setenta y u
Capítulo

Performance-based speaking tasks

Real-life speaking tasks are supported by strategies and a step-by-step process that helps all students to be successful. The *Assessment Program* contains the rubric for this task.

Presentación escrita

Para mantener la salud

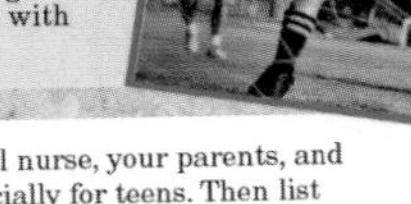

Task
You are doing some research for your health class on good eating and exercise habits. Make a poster in Spanish with five suggestions for better health.

1. **Prewrite** Talk to classmates, teachers, the school nurse, your parents, and so on, about good eating and exercise habits, especially for teens. Then list their ideas under the following headings to help you organize your information:
   - Debes comer . . .
   - Debes beber . . .
   - No debes comer mucho(a) . . .
   - No debes beber mucho(a) . . .
   - Debes ____ para mantener la salud.

   Strategy
   Gathering information
   Gathering information from a variety of sources helps you create a more complete presentation on a topic.

2. **Draft** Write the first draft. Decide how to present the information in a logical manner. Think about using visuals for clarity. Sketch them on your draft. Give the poster a title.

3. **Revise** Share your draft with a partner. Your partner should check the following:
   - Have you communicated the five suggestions well?
   - Do the visuals help convey meaning and make the poster attractive?
   - Are the vocabulary and grammar correct?

   Decide whether to use your partner's suggestions, and then rewrite your poster.

4. **Publish** Make a final copy, adding attractive illustrations or designs and making necessary changes. You might want to:
   - post it in the nurse's office, at a local community center, or in your classroom
   - include it in your portfolio

5. **Evaluation** Your teacher may give you a rubric for how the poster will be graded. You will probably be graded on:
   - completion of task
   - accuracy of vocabulary and grammar
   - effective use of visuals

doscientos uno 201
Capítulo 3B

Performance-based writing tasks

Students become better writers with real-life tasks that are supported with the writing process and focused strategies. As with the speaking tasks, a rubric has been specially written for each *Presentación escrita*.

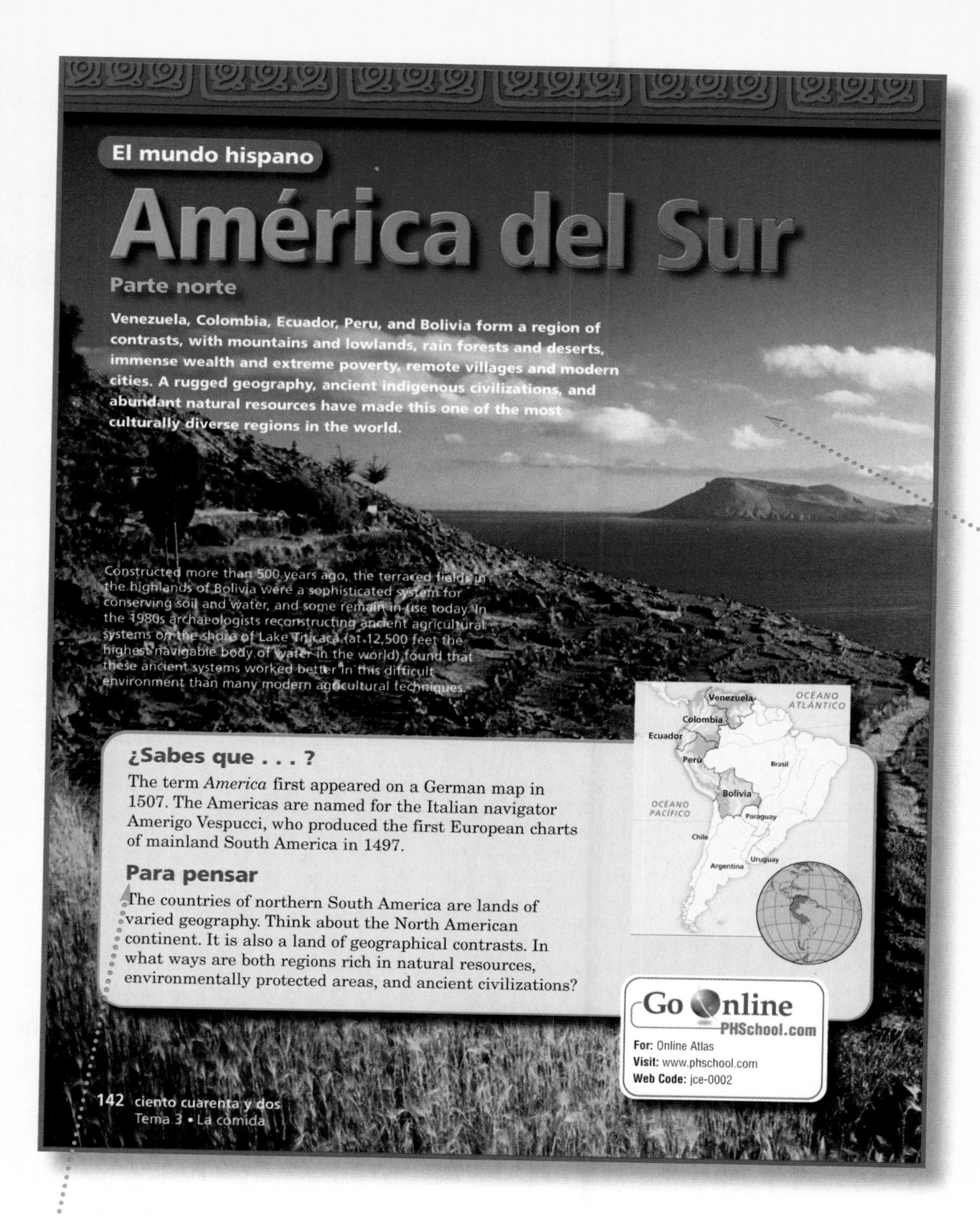

Learn about the Spanish-speaking world

The colorful *El mundo hispano* sections provide information and tasks that focus on people, places, and things in different regions.

Critical thinking

Students are given a question or small task that requires them to think critically as they make comparisons between the United States and the region being studied.

Repaso del capítulo

These two pages provide complete review and preparation for the chapter test.

Online self-test

Students can get extra test practice online.

Chapter Review

Repaso del capítulo

To prepare for the test, check to see if you . . .
- know the new vocabulary and grammar
- can perform the tasks on p. 175

Vocabulario y gramática

to talk about breakfast

en el desayuno	for breakfast
el cereal	cereal
el desayuno	breakfast
los huevos	eggs
el pan	bread
el pan tostado	toast
el plátano	banana
la salchicha	sausage
el tocino	bacon
el yogur	yogurt

to talk about lunch

en el almuerzo	for lunch
la ensalada	salad
la ensalada de frutas	fruit salad
las fresas	strawberries
la galleta	cookie
la hamburguesa	hamburger
el jamón	ham
la manzana	apple
las papas fritas	French fries
el perrito caliente	hot dog
la pizza	pizza
el queso	cheese
el sándwich de jamón y queso	ham and cheese sandwich
la sopa de verduras	vegetable soup

to talk about beverages

el agua *f.*	water
el café	coffee
el jugo de manzana	apple juice
el jugo de naranja	orange juice
la leche	milk
la limonada	lemonade
el refresco	soft drink
el té	tea
el té helado	iced tea

to talk about eating and drinking

beber	to drink
comer	to eat
la comida	food, meal
compartir	to share

to indicate how often

nunca	never
siempre	always
todos los días	every day

to show surprise

por supuesto	of course
¡Qué asco!	How awful!
¿Verdad?	Really? Right?

to say that you like / love something

Me / te encanta(n) ___.	I / you love ___.
Me / te gusta(n) ___.	I / you like ___.

other useful words

comprender	to understand
con	with
¿Cuál?	Which? What?
más o menos	more or less
sin	without

present tense of *-er* verbs

como	comemos
comes	coméis
come	comen

present tense of *-ir* verbs

comparto	compartimos
compartes	compartís
comparte	comparten

Más práctica
Practice Workbook Puzzle 3A-8
Practice Workbook Organizer 3A-9

For *Vocabulario adicional*, see pp. 268–269.

Go Online PHSchool.com
For: Test preparation
Visit: www.phschool.com
Web Code: jad-0306

Preparación para el examen

On the exam you will be asked to . . .	Here are practice tasks similar to those you will find on the exam . . .	If you need review . . .
1 Escuchar Listen and understand as people describe what they eat and drink for lunch	Listen as three students describe what they typically eat and drink for lunch. Which one is most like the kind of lunch you eat? Did they mention anything you could not buy in your school cafeteria?	**pp. 148–149** *A primera vista* **p. 149** Actividades 1–2 **pp. 150–152** *Videohistoria* **p. 155** Actividad 8
2 Hablar Tell someone what you typically eat for breakfast and ask the same of others	Your Spanish club is meeting for breakfast before school next week. Find out what other people in your class typically eat for breakfast. After you tell at least two people what you eat for breakfast, ask what they like to eat. Does everyone eat the same kind of breakfast or do you all like to eat different things?	**p. 156** Actividad 10 **p. 157** Actividad 12 **p. 162** Actividades 19–20 **p. 163** Actividad 21 **p. 171** *Presentación oral*
3 Leer Read and understand words that are typically found on menus	You are trying to help a child order from the lunch menu below, but he is very difficult to please. He doesn't like any white food. And he refuses to eat anything that grows on trees. Which items from the menu do you think he would refuse to eat or drink? ALMUERZO hamburguesa plátanos pizza manzana ensalada leche	**pp. 148–149** *A primera vista* **pp. 150–152** *Videohistoria* **p. 159** Actividad 15 **p. 167** Actividad 28 **pp. 168–169** *Lectura*
4 Escribir Write a list of foods that you like and others that you dislike	Your Spanish club is sponsoring a "Super Spanish Saturday." Your teacher wants to know what foods the class likes and dislikes so that the club can buy what most people like. Write the headings *Me gusta(n)* and *No me gusta(n)* in two columns. List at least four items that you like to eat and drink for breakfast and four items for lunch. Then list what you don't like to eat and drink for these same meals.	**p. 155** Actividades 7, 9 **p. 160** Actividad 16 **p. 163** Actividad 21 **p. 164** Actividad 24
 **5 Pensar** Demonstrate an understanding of cultural differences regarding snacks	Explain to a North American friend the popular snack of *churros y chocolate* in Spanish-speaking countries. How does this compare with popular snacks among students at your school?	**p. 170** *La cultura en vivo*

Vocabulary list

Chapter vocabulary is listed as language functions and with English translations.

Grammar summary

Chapter grammar is conveniently summarized.

Complete test preparation

This page prepares students for the proficiency and culture sections of the chapter test. Students are told how they will be tested, what the task might be like, and how to review.

End-of-Book Student Resources

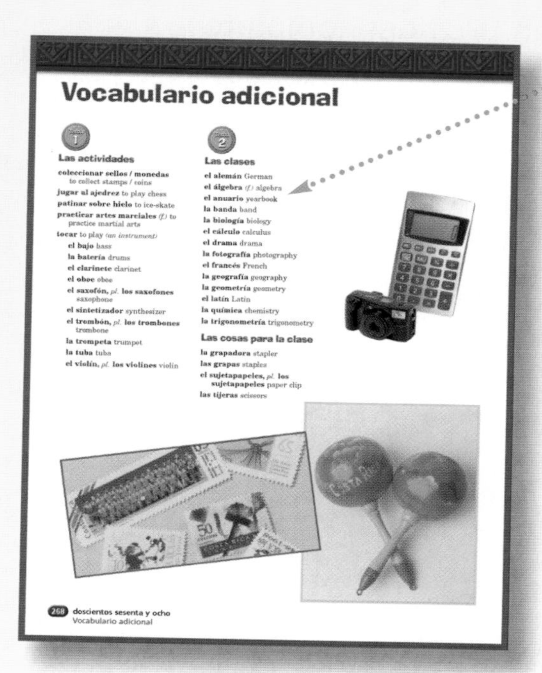
Vocabulario adicional

1

Las actividades

coleccionar sellos / monedas to collect stamps / coins
jugar al ajedrez to play chess
patinar sobre hielo to ice-skate
practicar artes marciales *(f.)* to practice martial arts
tocar to play *(an instrument)*
el bajo bass
la batería drums
el clarinete clarinet
el oboe oboe
el saxofón, *pl.* **los saxofones** saxophone
el sintetizador synthesizer
el trombón, *pl.* **los trombones** trombone
la trompeta trumpet
la tuba tuba
el violín, *pl.* **los violines** violin

2

Las clases

el alemán German
el álgebra *(f.)* algebra
el anuario yearbook
la banda band
la biología biology
el cálculo calculus
el drama drama
la fotografía photography
el francés French
la geografía geography
la geometría geometry
el latín Latin
la química chemistry
la trigonometría trigonometry

Las cosas para la clase

la grapadora stapler
las grapas staples
el sujetapapeles, *pl.* **los sujetapapeles** paper clip
las tijeras scissors

268 doscientos sesenta y ocho
Vocabulario adicional

Additional thematic vocabulary

Useful lists provide additional thematic vocabulary.

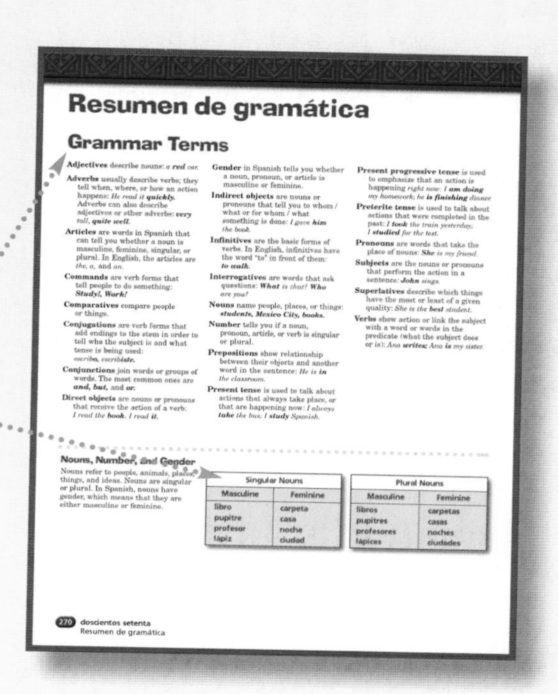
Resumen de gramática

Grammar Terms

Adjectives describe nouns: *a red car.*

Adverbs usually describe verbs; they tell when, where, or how an action happens: *He read it quickly.* Adverbs can also describe adjectives or other adverbs: *very tall, quite well.*

Articles are words in Spanish that can tell you whether a noun is masculine, feminine, singular, or plural. In English, the articles are *the, a,* and *an.*

Commands are verb forms that tell people to do something: *Study!, Work!*

Comparatives compare people or things.

Conjugations are verb forms that add endings to the stem in order to tell who the subject is and what tense is being used: *escribo, escribiste.*

Conjunctions join words or groups of words. The most common ones are *and, but,* and *or.*

Direct objects are nouns or pronouns that receive the action of a verb: *I read the book. I read it.*

Gender in Spanish tells you whether a noun, pronoun, or article is masculine or feminine.

Indirect objects are nouns or pronouns that tell you to whom / what or for whom / what something is done: *I gave him the book.*

Infinitives are the basic forms of verbs. In English, infinitives have the word "to" in front of them: *to walk.*

Interrogatives are words that ask questions: *What is that? Who are you?*

Nouns name people, places, or things: *students, Mexico City, books.*

Number tells you if a noun, pronoun, article, or verb is singular or plural.

Prepositions show relationship between their objects and another word in the sentence: *He is in the classroom.*

Present tense is used to talk about actions that always take place, or that are happening now: *I always take the bus; I study Spanish.*

Present progressive tense is used to emphasize that an action is happening right now: *I am doing my homework; he is finishing dinner.*

Preterite tense is used to talk about actions that were completed in the past: *I took the train yesterday. I studied for the test.*

Pronouns are words that take the place of nouns: *She is my friend.*

Subjects are the nouns or pronouns that perform the action in a sentence: *John sings.*

Superlatives describe which things have the most or least of a given quality: *She is the best student.*

Verbs show action or link the subject with a word or words in the predicate (what the subject does or is): *Ana writes; Ana is my sister.*

Nouns, Number, and Gender

Nouns refer to people, animals, places, things, and ideas. Nouns are singular or plural. In Spanish, nouns have gender, which means that they are either masculine or feminine.

Singular Nouns	
Masculine	Feminine
libro	carpeta
pupitre	casa
profesor	noche
lápiz	ciudad

Plural Nouns	
Masculine	Feminine
libros	carpetas
pupitres	casas
profesores	noches
lápices	ciudades

270 doscientos setenta
Resumen de gramática

Grammar summary and charts

This quick reference guide helps students build a strong grammar foundation.

Vocabulario español-inglés

The *Vocabulario español-inglés* contains all active vocabulary from the text, including vocabulary presented in the grammar sections.

A dash (—) represents the main entry word. For example, **pasar la —** after **la aspiradora** means **pasar la aspiradora.**

The number following each entry indicates the chapter in which the word or expression is presented. The letter *P* following an entry refers to the *Para empezar* section.

The following abbreviations are used in this list: *adj.* (adjective), *dir. obj.* (direct object), *f.* (feminine), *fam.* (familiar), *ind. obj.* (indirect object), *inf.* (infinitive), *m.* (masculine), *pl.* (plural), *prep.* (preposition), *pron.* (pronoun), *sing.* (singular).

A

a to *(prep.)* (4A)
— **casa** (to) home (4A)
— **la una de la tarde** at one (o'clock) in the afternoon (4B)
— **las ocho de la mañana** at eight (o'clock) in the morning (4B)
— **las ocho de la noche** at eight (o'clock) in the evening / at night (4B)
— **mí también** I do (like to) too (1A)
— **mí tampoco** I don't (like to) either (1A)
¿— **qué hora?** (At) what time? (4B)
— **veces** sometimes (1B)
— **ver** Let's see (2A)
al (*a* + *el*), **a la,** to the (4A)
al lado de next to (2B)
abril April (P)
aburrido, -a boring (2A)
acuerdo:
Estoy de —. I agree. (3B)
No estoy de —. I don't agree. (3B)

¡Adiós! Good-bye! (P)
¿Adónde? (To) where? (4A)
agosto August (P)
el **agua** *f.* water (3A)
al (*a* + *el*), **a la,** to the (4A)
al lado de next to (2B)
algo something (3B)
allí there (2B)
el **almuerzo** lunch (2A)
en el — for lunch (3A)
el **año** year (P)
aquí here (2B)
el **arroz** rice (3B)
el **arte: la clase de —** art class (2A)
artístico, -a artistic (1B)
asco: ¡Qué —! How awful! (3A)
atrevido, -a daring (1B)
¡Ay! ¡Qué pena! Oh! What a shame / pity! (4B)

B

bailar to dance (1A)
el **baile** dance (4B)
la **bandera** flag (2B)
el **básquetbol: jugar al —** to play basketball (4B)
beber to drink (3A)
las **bebidas** beverages (3B)
el **béisbol: jugar al —** to play baseball (4B)
la **biblioteca** library (4A)
bien well (P)
el **bistec** beefsteak (3B)
la **boca** mouth (P)
el **bolígrafo** pen (P)
el **brazo** arm (P)
bueno (buen), -a good (1B)
Buenas noches. Good evening (P)
Buenas tardes. Good afternoon. (P)
Buenos días. Good morning (P)

C

la **cabeza** head (P)
cada día every day (3B)
el **café** coffee (3A); café (4A)
la **calculadora** calculator (2A)
calor: Hace —. It's hot. (P)
caminar to walk (3B)
el **campo** countryside (4A)
cansado, -a tired (4B)
cantar to sing (1A)
la **carne** meat (3B)
la **carpeta** folder (P)
la — de argollas three-ring binder (2A)
el **cartel** poster (2B)
la **casa** home, house (4A)
a — (to) home (4A)
en — at home (4A)
catorce fourteen (P)
la **cebolla** onion (3B)
la **cena** dinner (3B)
el **centro: el — comercial** mall (4A)
el **cereal** cereal (3A)
cero zero (P)
la **chica** girl (1B)
el **chico** boy (1B)
cien one hundred (P)
las **ciencias:**
la clase de — naturales science class (2A)
la clase de — sociales social studies class (2A)
cinco five (P)
cincuenta fifty (P)
el **cine** movie theater (4A)
la **clase** class (2A)
la sala de clases classroom (P)
comer to eat (3A)
la **comida** food, meal (3A)

276 doscientos setenta y seis
Vocabulario español-inglés

Expressions for communication

This handy list can help students become better communicators.

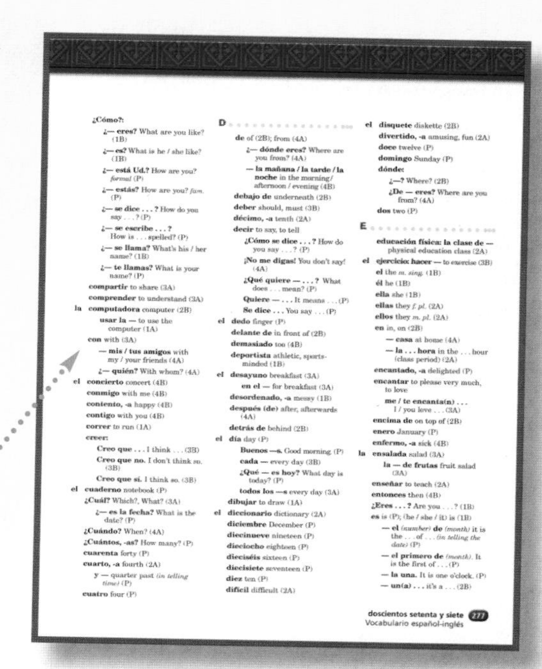
¿Cómo?:
¿— **eres?** What are you like? (1B)
¿— **es?** What is he / she like? (1B)
¿— **está Ud.?** How are you? *formal* (P)
¿— **estás?** How are you? *fam.* (P)
¿— **se dice . . . ?** How do you say . . . ? (P)
¿— **se escribe . . . ?** How is . . . spelled? (P)
¿— **se llama?** What's his / her name? (1B)
¿— **te llamas?** What is your name? (P)
compartir to share (3A)
comprender to understand (3A)
la **computadora** computer (2B)
usar la — to use the computer (1A)
con with (3A)
— **mis / tus amigos** with my / your friends (4A)
¿— **quién?** With whom? (4A)
el **concierto** concert (4B)
conmigo with me (4B)
contento, -a happy (4B)
contigo with you (4B)
correr to run (1A)
creer:
Creo que . . . I think . . . (3B)
Creo que no. I don't think so. (3B)
Creo que sí. I think so. (3B)
el **cuaderno** notebook (P)
¿Cuál? Which?, What? (3A)
¿— **es la fecha?** What is the date? (P)
¿Cuándo? When? (4A)
¿Cuántos, -as? How many? (P)
cuarenta forty (P)
cuarto, -a fourth (2A)
y — quarter past *(in telling time)* (P)
cuatro four (P)

D

de of (2B); from (4A)
¿— **dónde eres?** Where are you from? (4A)
— **la mañana / la tarde / la noche** in the morning / afternoon / evening (4B)
debajo de underneath (2B)
deber should, must (3B)
décimo, -a tenth (2A)
decir to say, to tell
¿Cómo se dice . . . ? How do you say . . . ? (P)
¡No me digas! You don't say! (4A)
¿Qué quiere — . . . ? What does . . . mean? (P)
Quiere — . . . It means . . . (P)
Se dice . . . You say . . . (P)
el **dedo** finger (P)
delante de in front of (2B)
demasiado too (4B)
deportista athletic, sports-minded (1B)
el **desayuno** breakfast (3A)
en el — for breakfast (3A)
desordenado, -a messy (1B)
después (de) after, afterwards (4A)
detrás de behind (2B)
el **día** day (P)
Buenos —s. Good morning (P)
cada — every day (3B)
¿Qué — es hoy? What day is today? (P)
todos los —s every day (3A)
dibujar to draw (1A)
el **diccionario** dictionary (2A)
diciembre December (P)
diecinueve nineteen (P)
dieciocho eighteen (P)
dieciséis sixteen (P)
diecisiete seventeen (P)
diez ten (P)
difícil difficult (2A)

el **disquete** diskette (2B)
divertido, -a amusing, fun (2A)
doce twelve (P)
domingo Sunday (P)
dónde:
¿—? Where? (2B)
¿**De — eres?** Where are you from? (4A)
dos two (P)

E

educación física: la clase de — physical education class (2A)
el **ejercicio: hacer —** to exercise (3B)
el the *m. sing.* (1B)
él he (1B)
ella she (1B)
ellas they *f. pl.* (2A)
ellos they *m. pl.* (2A)
en in, on (2B)
— **casa** at home (4A)
— **la . . . hora** in the . . . hour (class period) (2A)
encantado, -a delighted (P)
encantar to please very much, to love
me / te encanta(n) . . . I / you love . . . (3A)
encima de on top of (2B)
enero January (P)
enfermo, -a sick (4B)
la **ensalada** salad (3A)
la — de frutas fruit salad (3A)
enseñar to teach (2A)
entonces then (4B)
¿**Eres . . . ?** Are you . . . ? (1B)
es is (P); (he / she / it) is (1B)
— **el** *(number)* **de** *(month)* it is the . . . of . . . *(in telling the date)* (P)
— **el primero de** *(month).* It is the first of . . . (P)
— **la una.** It is one o'clock. (P)
— **un(a) . . .** it's a . . . (2B)

doscientos setenta y siete 277
Vocabulario español-inglés

End glossaries

Helpful Spanish-English and English-Spanish glossaries are located at the end of the book.

Using the Teacher's Edition

- Teaching the Theme
- Planning for Instruction
- Alignment with the Standards for Foreign Language Learning
- Complete Teaching Support

Teaching the Theme

The Teacher's Edition provides complete planning support for teaching the themes.

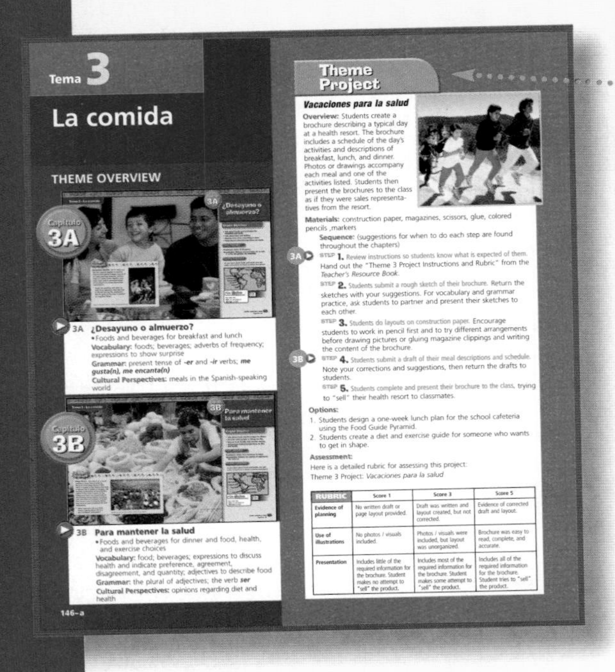

Tema 3

La comida

THEME OVERVIEW

Capítulo 3A

3A ¿Desayuno o almuerzo?
- Foods and beverages for breakfast and lunch

Vocabulary: foods; beverages; adverbs of frequency; expressions to show surprise
Grammar: present tense of *-er* and *-ir* verbs; ***me gusta(n), me encanta(n)***
Cultural Perspectives: meals in the Spanish-speaking world

Capítulo 3B

3B Para mantener la salud
- Foods and beverages for dinner and food, health, and exercise choices

Vocabulary: food; beverages; expressions to discuss health and indicate preference, agreement, disagreement, and quantity; adjectives to describe food
Grammar: the plural of adjectives; the verb ***ser***
Cultural Perspectives: opinions regarding diet and health

146–a

Theme Project

Vacaciones para la salud

Overview: Students create a brochure describing a typical day at a health resort. The brochure includes a schedule of the day's activities and descriptions of breakfast, lunch, and dinner. Photos or drawings accompany each meal and one of the activities listed. Students then present the brochures to the class as if they were sales representatives from the resort.

Materials: construction paper, magazines, scissors, glue, colored pencils ,markers

Sequence: (suggestions for when to do each step are found throughout the chapters)

3A STEP **1.** Review instructions so students know what is expected of them. Hand out the "Theme 3 Project Instructions and Rubric" from the *Teacher's Resource Book*.

STEP **2.** Students submit a rough sketch of their brochure. Return the sketches with your suggestions. For vocabulary and grammar practice, ask students to partner and present their sketches to each other.

STEP **3.** Students do layouts on construction paper. Encourage students to work in pencil first and to try different arrangements before drawing pictures or gluing magazine clippings and writing the content of the brochure.

3B STEP **4.** Students submit a draft of their meal descriptions and schedule. Note your corrections and suggestions, then return the drafts to students.

STEP **5.** Students complete and present their brochure to the class, trying to "sell" their health resort to classmates.

Options:
1. Students design a one-week lunch plan for the school cafeteria using the Food Guide Pyramid.
2. Students create a diet and exercise guide for someone who wants to get in shape.

Assessment:
Here is a detailed rubric for assessing this project:
Theme 3 Project: *Vacaciones para la salud*

RUBRIC	Score 1	Score 3	Score 5
Evidence of planning	No written draft or page layout provided.	Draft was written and layout created, but not corrected.	Evidence of corrected draft and layout.
Use of illustrations	No photos / visuals included.	Photos / visuals were included, but layout was unorganized.	Brochure was easy to read, complete, and accurate.
Presentation	Includes little of the required information for the brochure. Student makes no attempt to "sell" the product.	Includes most of the required information for the brochure. Student makes some attempt to "sell" the product.	Includes all of the required information for the brochure. Student tries to "sell" the product.

Theme project

Each theme begins with an optional project. The project is divided into manageable steps and includes a rubric.

Theme support

Additional support per theme includes bulletin board ideas, games, hands-on culture activities, and teaching resources.

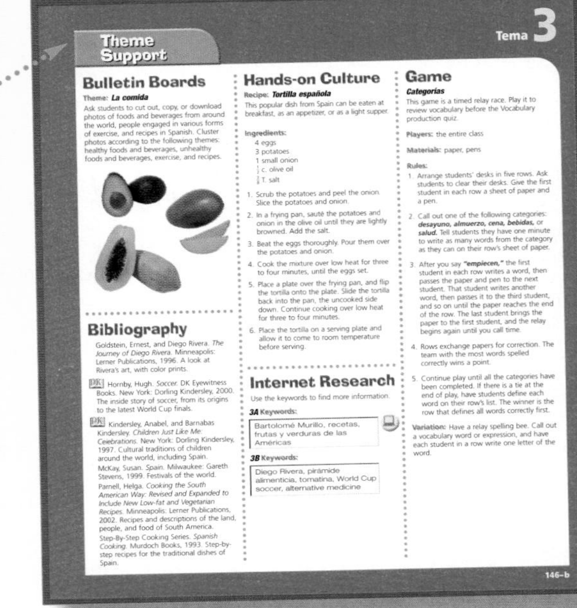

Theme Support

Tema 3

Bulletin Boards

Theme: ***La comida***

Ask students to cut out, copy, or download photos of foods and beverages from around the world, people engaged in various forms of exercise, and recipes in Spanish. Cluster photos according to the following themes: healthy foods and beverages, unhealthy foods and beverages, exercise, and recipes.

Bibliography

Goldstein, Ernest, and Diego Rivera. *The Journey of Diego Rivera*. Minneapolis: Lerner Publications, 1996. A look at Rivera's art, with color prints.

DK Hornby, Hugh. *Soccer*. DK Eyewitness Books. New York: Dorling Kindersley, 2000. The inside story of soccer, from its origins to the latest World Cup finals.

DK Kindersley, Anabel, and Barnabas Kindersley. *Children Just Like Me: Celebrations*. New York: Dorling Kindersley, 1997. Cultural traditions of children around the world, including Spain.

McKay, Susan. *Spain*. Milwaukee: Gareth Stevens, 1999. Festivals of the world.

Parnell, Helga. *Cooking the South American Way: Revised and Expanded to Include New Low-fat and Vegetarian Recipes*. Minneapolis: Lerner Publications, 2002. Recipes and descriptions of the land, people, and food of South America.

Step-By-Step Cooking Series. *Spanish Cooking*. Murdoch Books, 1993. Step-by-step recipes for the traditional dishes of Spain.

Hands-on Culture

Recipe: ***Tortilla española***

This popular dish from Spain can be eaten at breakfast, as an appetizer, or as a light supper.

Ingredients:
4 eggs
3 potatoes
1 small onion
$\frac{1}{2}$ c. olive oil
$\frac{3}{8}$ T. salt

1. Scrub the potatoes and peel the onion. Slice the potatoes and onion.
2. In a frying pan, sauté the potatoes and onion in the olive oil until they are lightly browned. Add the salt.
3. Beat the eggs thoroughly. Pour them over the potatoes and onion.
4. Cook the mixture over low heat for three to four minutes, until the eggs set.
5. Place a plate over the frying pan, and flip the tortilla onto the plate. Slide the tortilla back into the pan, the uncooked side down. Continue cooking over low heat for three to four minutes.
6. Place the tortilla on a serving plate and allow it to come to room temperature before serving.

Internet Research

Use the keywords to find more information.

3A Keywords:
Bartolomé Murillo, recetas, frutas y verduras de las Américas

3B Keywords:
Diego Rivera, pirámide alimenticia, tomatina, World Cup soccer, alternative medicine

Game

Categorías

This game is a timed relay race. Play it to review vocabulary before the Vocabulary production quiz.

Players: the entire class

Materials: paper, pens

Rules:
1. Arrange students' desks in five rows. Ask students to clear their desks. Give the first student in each row a sheet of paper and a pen.
2. Call out one of the following categories: ***desayuno, almuerzo, cena, bebidas,*** or ***salud.*** Tell students they have one minute to write as many words from the category as they can on their row's sheet of paper.
3. After you say ***"empiecen,"*** the first student in each row writes a word, then passes the paper and pen to the next student. That student writes another word, then passes it to the third student, and so on until the paper reaches the end of the row. The last student brings the paper to the first student, and the relay begins again until you call time.
4. Rows exchange papers for correction. The team with the most words spelled correctly wins a point.
5. Continue play until all the categories have been completed. If there is a tie at the end of play, have students define each word on their row's list. The winner is the row that defines all words correctly first.

Variation: Have a relay spelling bee. Call out a vocabulary word or expression, and have each student in a row write one letter of the word.

146–b

Planning for Instruction

The Teacher's Edition provides four pages of planning support interleaved at the beginning of each chapter.

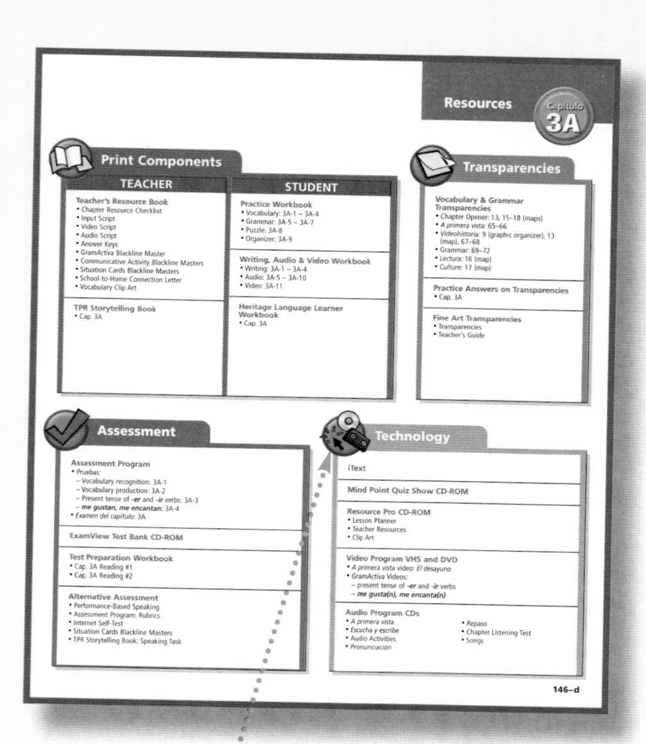

Resources — Capítulo 3A

Print Components

TEACHER	STUDENT
Teacher's Resource Book • Chapter Resource Checklist • Input Script • Video Script • Audio Script • Answer Keys • GramActiva Blackline Master • Communicative Activity Blackline Masters • Situation Cards Blackline Masters • School-to-Home Connection Letter • Vocabulary Clip Art	Practice Workbook • Vocabulary: 3A-1 – 3A-4 • Grammar: 3A-5 – 3A-7 • Puzzle: 3A-8 • Organizer: 3A-9
TPR Storytelling Book • Cap. 3A	Writing, Audio & Video Workbook • Writing: 3A-1 – 3A-4 • Audio: 3A-5 – 3A-10 • Video: 3A-11
	Heritage Language Learner Workbook • Cap. 3A

Transparencies

Vocabulary & Grammar Transparencies
• Chapter Opener: 13, 15–18 (maps)
• *A primera vista*: 65–66
• *Videohistoria*: 9 (graphic organizer), 13 (map), 67–68
• Grammar: 69–72
• *Lectura*: 16 (map)
• Culture: 17 (map)

Practice Answers on Transparencies
• Cap. 3A

Fine Art Transparencies
• Transparencies
• Teacher's Guide

Assessment

Assessment Program
• *Pruebas*:
– Vocabulary recognition: 3A-1
– Vocabulary production: 3A-2
– Present tense of *-er* and *-ir* verbs: 3A-3
– *me gustan, me encantan*: 3A-4
• *Examen del capítulo*: 3A

ExamView Test Bank CD-ROM

Test Preparation Workbook
• Cap. 3A Reading #1
• Cap. 3A Reading #2

Alternative Assessment
• Performance-Based Speaking
• Assessment Program: Rubrics
• Internet Self-Test
• Situation Cards Blackline Masters
• TPR Storytelling Book: Speaking Task

Technology

iText

Mind Point Quiz Show CD-ROM

Resource Pro CD-ROM
• Lesson Planner
• Teacher Resources
• Clip Art

Video Program VHS and DVD
• *A primera vista* video: *El desayuno*
• GramActiva Videos:
– present tense of *-er* and *-ir* verbs
– *me gusta(n), me encanta(n)*

Audio Program CDs
• *A primera vista* • *Escucha y escribe* • Audio Activities • *Pronunciación* • *Repaso* • Chapter Listening Test • Songs

146–d

Program Resources

This section shows all the program resources available for this chapter. All resources are conveniently referenced at point of use in the chapter.

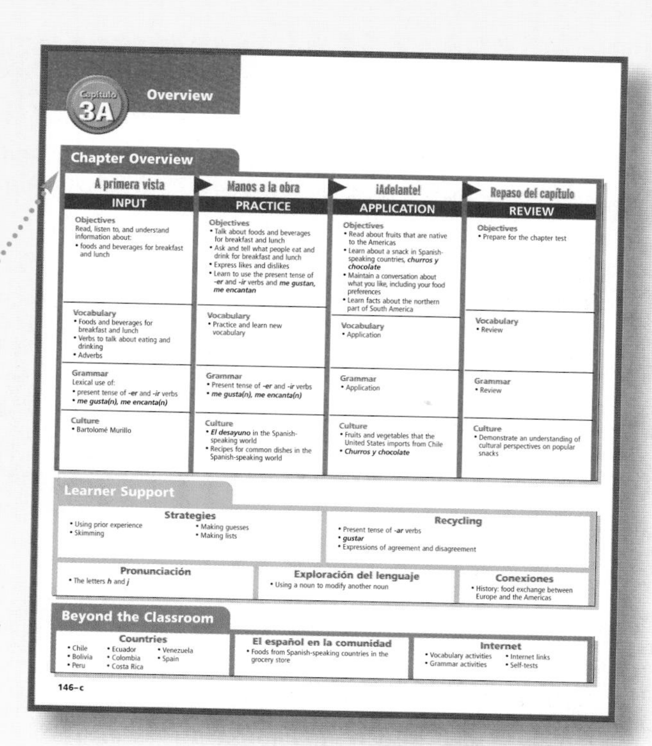

Capítulo 3A Overview

Chapter Overview

A primera vista INPUT	*Manos a la obra* PRACTICE	*¡Adelante!* APPLICATION	*Repaso del capítulo* REVIEW
Objectives: Read, listen to, and understand information about: • foods and beverages for breakfast and lunch	Objectives: • Talk about foods and beverages for breakfast and lunch • Ask and tell what people eat and drink for breakfast and lunch • Express likes and dislikes • Learn to use the present tense of *-er* and *-ir* verbs and *me gustan, me encantan*	Objectives: • Read about fruits that are native to the Americas • Learn about a snack in Spanish-speaking countries, *churros y chocolate* • Maintain a conversation about what you like, including your food preferences • Learn facts about the northern part of South America	Objectives: • Prepare for the chapter test
Vocabulary: • Foods and beverages for breakfast and lunch • Verbs to talk about eating and drinking • Adverbs	Vocabulary: • Practice and learn new vocabulary	Vocabulary: • Application	Vocabulary: • Review
Grammar: Lexical use of: • present tense of *-er* and *-ir* verbs • *me gusta(n), me encanta(n)*	Grammar: • Present tense of *-er* and *-ir* verbs • *me gusta(n), me encanta(n)*	Grammar: • Application	Grammar: • Review
Culture: • Bartolomé Murillo	Culture: • *El desayuno* in the Spanish-speaking world • Recipes for common dishes in the Spanish-speaking world	Culture: • Fruits and vegetables that the United States imports from Chile • *Churros y chocolate*	Culture: • Demonstrate an understanding of cultural perspectives on popular snacks

Learner Support

Strategies: • Using prior experience • Skimming • Making guesses • Making lists

Recycling: • Present tense of *-ar* verbs • *gustar* • Expressions of agreement and disagreement

Pronunciación: • The letters *h* and *j*

Exploración del lenguaje: • Using a noun to modify another noun

Conexiones: • History: food exchange between Europe and the Americas

Beyond the Classroom

Countries: • Chile • Bolivia • Peru • Ecuador • Colombia • Costa Rica • Venezuela • Spain

El español en la comunidad: • Foods from Spanish-speaking countries in the grocery store

Internet: • Vocabulary activities • Grammar activities • Internet links • Self-tests

146–c

Scope and Sequence

This section gives a quick overview of the chapter sections, objectives, and content.

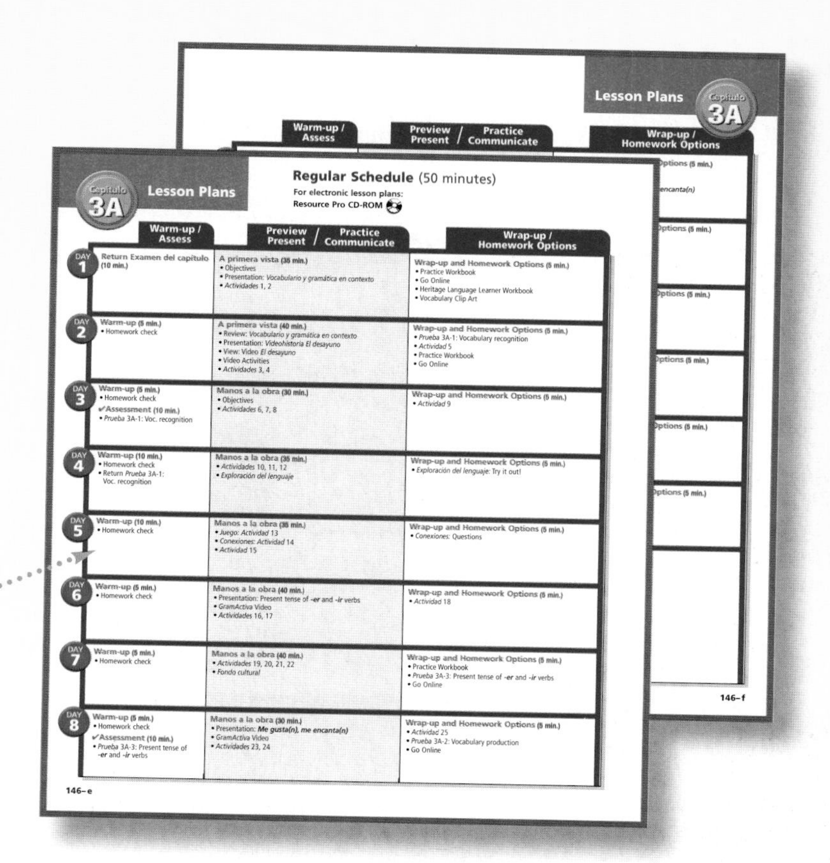

Capítulo 3A Lesson Plans

Regular Schedule (50 minutes)
For electronic lesson plans: Resource Pro CD-ROM

Day	Warm-up / Assess	Preview / Present / Practice / Communicate	Wrap-up / Homework Options
1	Return *Examen del capítulo* (10 min.)	*A primera vista* (35 min.) • Objectives • Presentation: *Vocabulario y gramática en contexto* • *Actividades* 1, 2	Wrap-up and Homework Options (5 min.) • Practice Workbook • Go Online • Heritage Language Learner Workbook • Vocabulary Clip Art
2	Warm-up (5 min.) • Homework check	*A primera vista* (40 min.) • Review: *Vocabulario y gramática en contexto* • Presentation: *Videohistoria El desayuno* • View: Video *El desayuno* • Video Activities • *Actividades* 3, 4	Wrap-up and Homework Options (5 min.) • *Prueba* 3A-1: Vocabulary recognition • *Actividad* 5 • Practice Workbook • Go Online
3	Warm-up (5 min.) • Homework check ✓Assessment (10 min.) • *Prueba* 3A-1: Voc. recognition	*Manos a la obra* (30 min.) • Objectives • *Actividades* 6, 7, 8	Wrap-up and Homework Options (5 min.) • *Actividad* 9
4	Warm-up (10 min.) • Homework check • Return *Prueba* 3A-1: Voc. recognition	*Manos a la obra* (35 min.) • *Actividades* 10, 11, 12 • *Exploración del lenguaje*	Wrap-up and Homework Options (5 min.) • *Exploración del lenguaje*: Try it out!
5	Warm-up (10 min.) • Homework check	*Manos a la obra* (35 min.) • *Juego*: *Actividad* 13 • *Conexiones*: *Actividad* 14 • *Actividad* 15	Wrap-up and Homework Options (5 min.) • *Conexiones*: Questions
6	Warm-up (5 min.) • Homework check	*Manos a la obra* (40 min.) • Presentation: Present tense of *-er* and *-ir* verbs • GramActiva Video • *Actividades* 16, 17	Wrap-up and Homework Options (5 min.) • *Actividad* 18
7	Warm-up (5 min.) • Homework check	*Manos a la obra* (40 min.) • *Actividades* 19, 20, 21, 22 • *Fondo cultural*	Wrap-up and Homework Options (5 min.) • Practice Workbook • *Prueba* 3A-3: Present tense of *-er* and *-ir* verbs • Go Online
8	Warm-up (5 min.) • Homework check ✓Assessment (10 min.) • *Prueba* 3A-3: Present tense of *-er* and *-ir* verbs	*Manos a la obra* (30 min.) • Presentation: *Me gusta(n), me encanta(n)* • GramActiva Video • *Actividades* 23, 24	Wrap-up and Homework Options (5 min.) • *Actividad* 25 • *Prueba* 3A-2: Vocabulary production • Go Online

146–e

146–f

Lesson Plans

Lesson plans are provided for each chapter.

Alignment with the Standards for Foreign Language Learning

REALIDADES is fully aligned with the Standards for Foreign Language Learning. Correlations to the Standards are provided throughout the Teacher's Edition.

Standards correlation

A complete correlation of chapter activities to the Standards is provided at the beginning of each chapter.

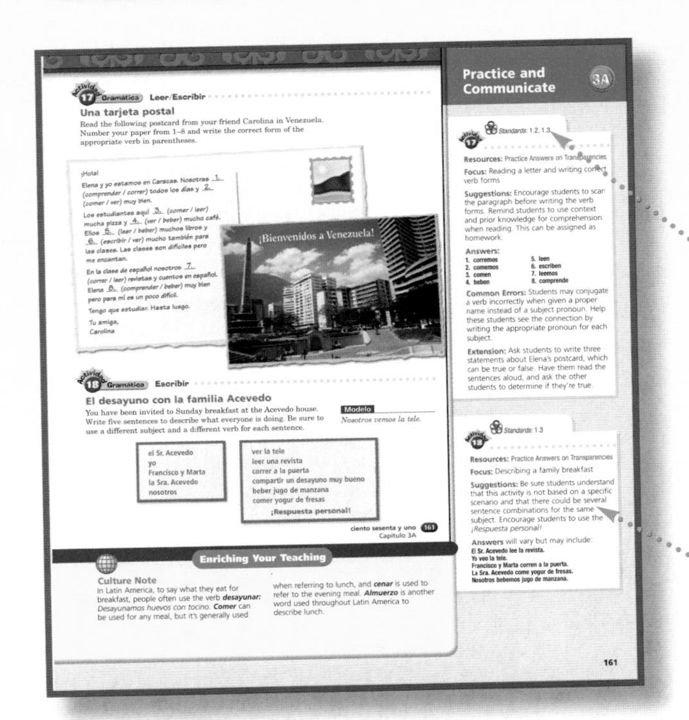

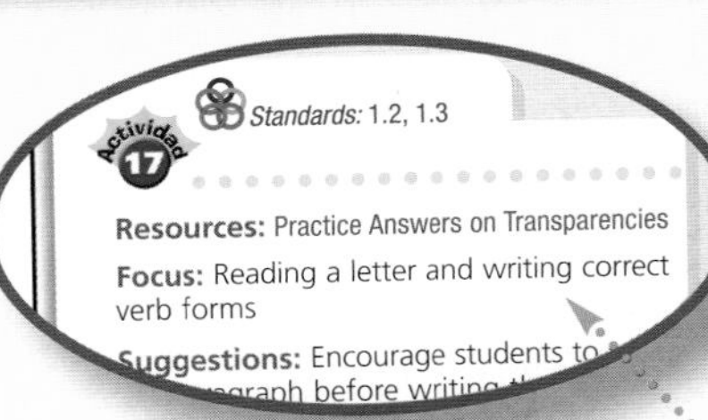

Standards correlation per activity

Teaching support includes references to specific Standards.

Direct instruction

Support for direct instruction is provided for each activity.

Complete Teaching Support

REALIDADES provides teachers with complete instructional support that can be found in the Teacher's Edition and in the various print and technology resources.

Program Organization

Each chapter provides a well-organized structure, clear student outcomes and goals, and a variety of activities that develop all language skills.

Chapter Objectives

- Describe families
- Talk about celebrations and parties
- Ask and tell ages
- Express possession
- Understand cultural perspectives on family and celebrations

Assessment

Teachers are provided with multiple print and technology tools that measure student progress in listening, speaking, reading, and writing.

Assessment

- Prueba 5A-3: The verb ***tener***

Go Online PHSchool.com

For: Test preparation
Visit: www.phschool.com
Web Code: jcd-0508

Presentación oral

Mi familia

Task
You are on an exchange program in Chile and your host family wants to know about your family back home. Show them photographs of three family members and talk about the people shown.

Universal Access

REALIDADES provides teaching suggestions to help all students learn Spanish.

Universal Access

Students with Learning Difficulties
Provide photocopies of the invitation for students to use. Preview the *¿Comprendes?* questions with students, and have them highlight pertinent information on photocopies. When students write their ***nombre completo,*** they might draw a family tree with their parents' and grandparents' names to help them.

Heritage Language Learners
If students have been to a ***fiesta de quince años*** celebration, ask them to describe it. Who was there? What food was served? What did people do during the celebration? If they can, have them describe the gifts and decorations.

Universal Access

Advanced Learners
Have students create and describe a fictional "royal family" and a fictional country for the family to rule. Encourage them to write humorous stories that will be entertaining when reviewed by the class. Some students may want to illustrate their royal families after writing their descriptions.

Special Education
Matching the silhouette to the photograph may be especially difficult for students with visual problems. Pair students who have strong spatial skills with those who don't.

Instructional Planning and Support

REALIDADES provides complete support for implementing the Standards. The Teacher's Edition, program resources, and Companion Web Site provide direct instruction and complete support to implement the program and accompanying resources.

Assessment

Topics covered:

- Assessing Student Progress
- Purposes of Assessment
- Forms of Assessment
- Portfolios and Assessment
- Self-Assessment
- Tools for Self-Assessment
- Assessment Resources
- Making Assessment Real

An assessment program in a second language classroom should be based on the premise that the main purpose of learning a language is to communicate in a meaningful and culturally appropriate way. As you begin to teach a unit of instruction, you might want to start by asking a few key questions: What do I expect my students to learn? What do I want them to be able to do? How can I assess what I am looking for in student performance?

Assessing Student Progress

There are several assessment strategies that will enable students to develop proficiency in a language other than English. This particular list comes from *The Foreign Language Framework for California Public Schools*. These strategies include:

- Have a clear purpose readily communicated to teachers, students, and parents;
- Provide information to guide the teacher in planning instruction;
- Measure how well students perform in reading, writing, listening, and speaking;
- Have clear and concise criteria;
- Include instruments that provide representative samples of what students know and are able to do;
- Integrate the speaking, listening, reading, and writing skills;
- Include a wide range of assessment strategies that allow for a variety of responses;
- Provide students and parents with ongoing information on their progress;
- Allow students to monitor and adjust their individual learning strategies; and
- Employ various forms of assessment.

"What do I expect my students to learn? What do I want them to be able to do? How can I assess what I am looking for in student performance?"

Purposes of Assessment

The following chart outlines the various purposes for assessment:

Purposes of Assessment	
Entry-level assessment	• Analyzes students' ability to communicate as a basis for placing students at an appropriate level in an established foreign language program.
Progress/monitoring assessment	• Gathers evidence about students' progress towards achieving objectives as measured in relation to the stage of the curriculum. • Will occur on an ongoing basis. • May occur at any point in an instructional sequence other than at the end of the course of study.
Summative assessment	• Judges students' achievement at the end of a unit, chapter, or course of study.

Forms of Assessment

Achievement assessment determines what students know by evaluating them on specific, previously learned material, such as the names of items of clothing or the conjugation of *-ar* verbs. Students are tested on discrete bits of information. Achievement tests are used to measure the incremental steps involved in learning a second language—for example, to cover what was taught in a specific chapter. Achievement may be quizzed or tested with some frequency as proof of regular progress for both student and teacher.

Proficiency or **performance-based assessment** measures what students can do with this knowledge and how well they can perform in the language. These tests do not involve testing specific items; rather they are performance-based, checking how well students integrate what they have learned. Their characteristic open-endedness permits students to use what they know to receive or communicate a message, since the emphasis is on communication needs. Proficiency tests address the questions: How well and at what level can the student use the language to receive and express meaningful communication?

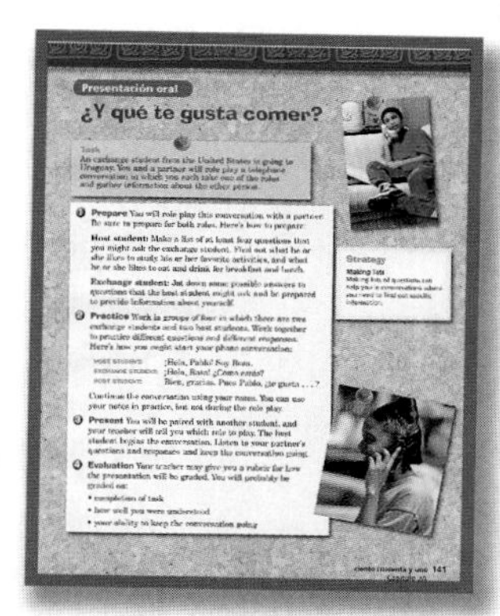
Presentación oral

¿Y qué te gusta comer?

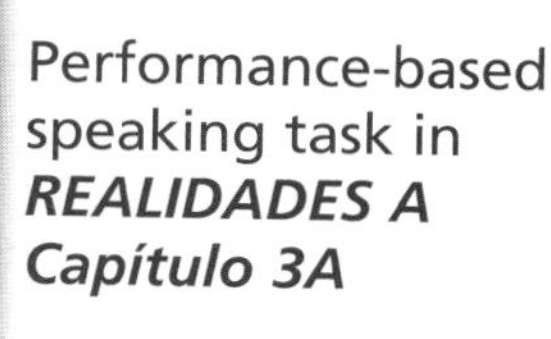
Performance-based speaking task in ***REALIDADES A* Capítulo 3A**

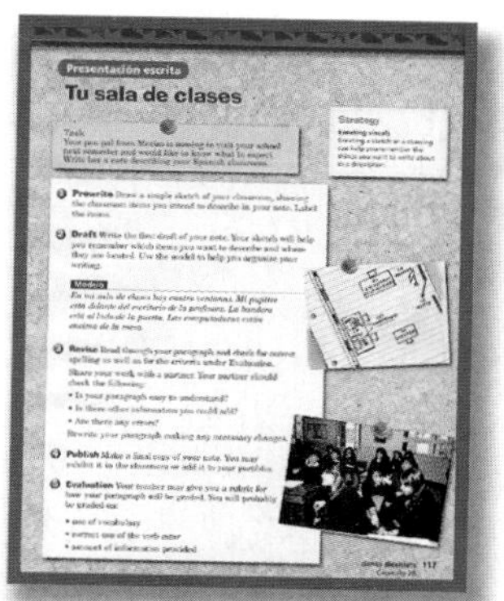
Presentación escrita

Tu sala de clases

Performance-based writing task in ***REALIDADES A* Capítulo 2B**

Assessment

Portfolios and Assessment

Portfolios are another form of assessment that can measure student progress and growth. Portfolios contain samples of a student's work collected over time. This enables both the teacher and the student to observe the progress being made. Portfolios provide students the opportunity to examine and reflect upon what they have produced so that they become more involved in improving their work. The portfolio can be useful to determine grade/level placement.

Self-Assessment

Essential to any assessment program is the inclusion of self-assessment opportunities that allow students to become independent evaluators of their own progress and to take more responsibility for their learning.

Tools for Self-Assessment in *REALIDADES*

- Clear objectives that guide chapter content, activities, and assessment
- Online activities to practice vocabulary and grammar
- Rubrics with clearly written criteria and descriptors
- Test preparation with practice tasks
- Online end-of-chapter Self-test
- End-of-chapter Chapter Checklist and Self-Assessment Worksheet

Contents of the Portfolio

- written work, such as short paragraphs, compositions, short stories, poems, or journals
- audio and/or video cassettes of student performance
- quizzes and tests
- evidence of reading comprehension
- evidence of listening comprehension
- individual student projects
- art work
- cultural projects
- technology projects and web research
- picture dictionaries
- story boards
- evidence that language skills were practiced outside the classroom
- evidence of contact with Hispanic cultures in the community
- evidence of student reflection on his or her own writing or speaking

If the portfolio is to be used in the assessment of progress and proficiency in the language, then students must know that it is more than just a collection of materials. They need to know that it will be integrated with daily, weekly, or monthly activities. The portfolio can be used as the sole means of assessing student progress, as an integral part of the overall grade, or only as a showcase of what students have accomplished. Portfolios reflect a student's progression and are a motivating and rewarding assessment of how well students are developing proficiency in a second language.

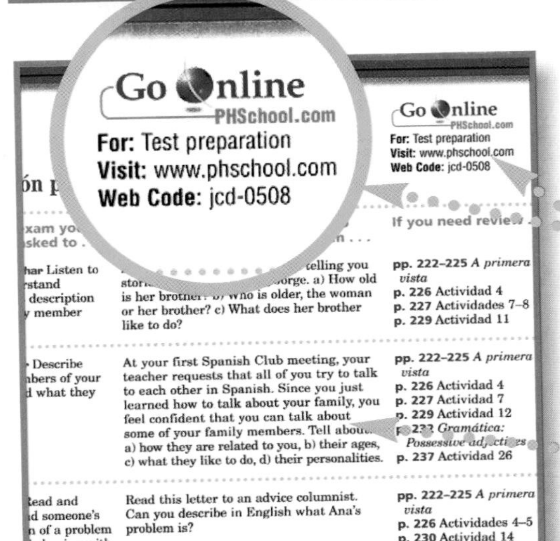

Online Self-tests
Interactive test provides instant feedback.

Test preparation
Students know exactly how to prepare for the chapter test.

Assessment Resources in *REALIDADES*

The Student Edition, print ancillaries, and technology components offer a wide range of assessment options to be used for different purposes and for both achievement and performance assessments. Teachers are encouraged to pick and choose from the many resources.

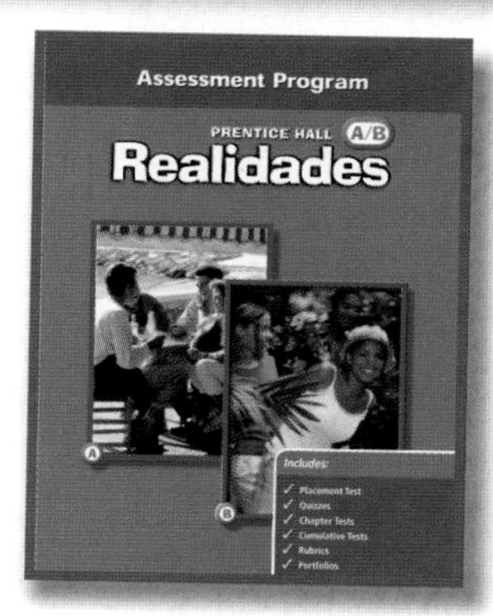

Assessment Program

- Placement Test
- Chapter Quizzes
- Chapter Tests
- Chapter Checklist and Self-Assessment
- Cumulative Tests
- Rubrics
- Portfolios
- Review and Remediation

Assessment Resources

Assessment Resources	Achievement	Proficiency	Self-Assessment
Student Edition			
• *Actividades* (various)	✔	✔	
• *Lectura*		✔	
• *Presentación oral*		✔	
• *Presentación escrita*		✔	
• *Preparación para el examen*	✔	✔	✔
Assessment Program			
• Placement Tests	✔	✔	
• Chapter Quizzes	✔		
• Chapter Tests	✔	✔	
• Cumulative Tests	✔	✔	
• Rubrics		✔	✔
• Portfolio Assessment		✔	✔
• Chapter Checklist and Self-Assessment Worksheet			✔
Teacher Resource Book			
• Communicative Activities		✔	
• Situation Cards		✔	
Technology			
• Computer Test Bank with CD-Rom	✔	✔	
• MindPoint Quiz Show	✔		✔
• Companion Web site	✔		✔

Making Assessment Real

The Latin root of "assess" is to "sit beside." The goal of our assessment program is indeed a sitting beside the student, encouraging performance to the best of his or her ability in the language. Although learning a language is a complicated endeavor, *REALIDADES* provides students with many opportunities to practice these real-life tasks before their performance is evaluated and graded. Conversely, *REALIDADES* offers a wide range of assessment options that reflect each chapter's communication and culture goals.

Universal Access

Instructional Strategies

- Success in Universal Access
- Effective Instructional Strategies
- Planning Instruction for Students with Special Needs
- Teaching Spanish to Students with Learning Disabilities
- Teaching Spanish to Students with Special Physical Needs
- Teaching Spanish to Advanced Learners
- Teaching Heritage Learners

The nation is more diverse than ever and this diversity is a significant asset to the strength of our nation. Yet this diversity also places considerable stress on the educational system to effectively accommodate the range of learning needs found in today's classrooms. The range of student needs, interests, motivation, and skill levels often presents heightened challenges to both curriculum and instruction. It should be clearly acknowledged that the individual needs of some students require additional specialized support. However, the goal of a comprehensive Spanish program remains the provision of "universal access" for all students to a communicative and culturally rich program in addition to whatever specialized intervention may be required.

Success in Universal Access

Universal access occurs when teachers provide curriculum and instruction in ways that allow all learners in the classroom to participate and to achieve the instructional and behavioral goals of general education, as well as of the core curriculum. Success is achieved in classrooms that are heterogeneous, inclusive and that consistently and systematically integrate instructional strategies that are responsive to the needs of all learners with special focus on advanced learners, heritage learners, students with learning difficulties, and students who are eligible for and receiving special education services.

Effective Instructional Strategies

Here are general strategies that deliver effective instruction in a classroom with diverse learners.

- **Clarify the objectives for a chapter.** Students need to understand the outcomes for which they will be assessed.
- **Provide "thinking time" before students have to talk.** You may want to ask a question and then count to 10 before expecting a response. If a student is struggling, state that you want him/her to think about it, and indicate that you'll be back for the response in a minute. Move on to another student, and then return to the student for his/her response.

- **Write all assignments on the board.** Assignments given both verbally and visually are clearer to all students.
- **Use visuals throughout the lesson.** Present vocabulary visually. Use charts to present grammar. Use video that provides visual support such as vocabulary words highlighted on the screen and grammar videos that visualize grammar patterns. Use graphic organizers whenever possible. Connect communicative tasks to photos, art, and *realia*.
- **Assist in time management.** When requiring students to complete projects, or long-term assignments, provide a calendar that breaks down requirements by due dates. Many students experience significant difficulties in self-managing the time needed to complete complex projects.
- **Build in opportunities for reteaching and practice vocabulary words and grammar.** Students need many opportunities to learn new concepts and need to practice in a variety of formats.
- **Build vocabulary skills by teaching the patterns of language.** Teach the meaning of prefixes, suffixes, and the role of cognates. Point out connections between English, Spanish, and Latin.
- **Consider alternative means for demonstrating understanding.** Think beyond the common modes of reading and writing. Students could present information orally, create a poster or visual representation of work, tape-record their ideas, or act out their understanding.

> "The goal of a comprehensive Spanish program remains the provision of "universal access" for all students to a communicative and culturally rich program in addition to whatever specialized intervention may be required."

- **Have students begin all work in class.** Prior to class dismissal, check to ensure that each student has a good start and understands what is expected.
- **Consider setting up a homework hotline using voicemail or e-mail.** Homework assignments could be posted and easily accessed by parents and students outside of school hours.

Planning Instruction for Students with Special Needs

Students needing additional instructional support are a highly diverse student group. Although their learning needs vary greatly, their difficulties in learning Spanish may parallel the learning difficulties experienced in learning their first language. Through instruction that incorporates clear directions and scaffolding, possible adaptations and modifications, and grouping that incorporates collaboration, students with special needs and learning difficulties can gain proficiency in Spanish.

Teaching Spanish to Students with Learning Disabilities

There are many reasons why students may experience difficulties in learning a second language. In general, these difficulties may be characterized by the inability to spell or read well, problems with auditory discrimination and in understanding auditory input, and difficulty with abstract thinking. Research by Ganchow and Sparks (1991) indicates that difficulties with one's first language are a major factor in foreign language learning difficulties.

It is not always evident which students will experience difficulties with learning a second language. Many times these students are bright and outgoing. They may have experienced reading or spelling problems in elementary school, but they have learned to compensate over time. However, when they are confronted with a new language in middle school or high school, the language disabilities return.

Students with learning disabilities can develop a level of proficiency in a second language with some modifications to instruction and testing. These learners benefit from a highly structured approach that teaches new content in context and in incremental amounts. Presentation and practice must include multiple modalities. Many students benefit when instruction combines seeing, hearing, saying, and writing. For example, a teacher would first show a visual of a word and say it aloud. This is followed by using the new word in context. The teacher then writes the word on the board. Students would say the word aloud with the teacher. They then write it down and say it aloud again.

As is evident in this sequence, instruction that combines seeing and hearing with spelling/writing is important for many students with learning disabilities. In subsequent days, many students benefit from frequent reviews of learned auditory materials.

Each student is different and no one suggestion works with all students. Here are general suggestions recommended by Sax Mabbott (1994):

- Ask students what problems they may have experienced with their first language, especially in the areas of reading and dictation.
- Work with students based upon their strengths rather than their weaknesses. Allow students to experience success by using their strengths while still working on areas of weakness.
- Tape reading assignments.
- Give students extra time to look over written work.
- Provide visual representations, such as charts, diagrams, and pictures.
- Include media (video, audio, computers) in addition to print materials.
- Allow students to take a test orally if they have trouble reading.
- Let students take a test a second time if they did not do well the first time.
- Allow students to use grammar charts, study organizers, or dictionaries during a test.
- Try a different testing format if the students are experiencing difficulties.

Teaching Spanish to Students with Special Physical Needs

Here are suggestions for instruction for students with special physical needs:

Auditory impairments

- **Provide students with scripts for the Audio Program.** Teachers will find a complete script in the Audio Scripts section for each chapter in the *Teacher's Resource Book*.
- **Provide students with a copy of the scripts for the Video Program.** Teachers will find a complete script in the Video Scripts section for each chapter in the *Teacher's Resource Book*.
- **Use the closed-captioned version** of the Video Program.
- **Allow students to refer to their textbooks or to other written materials** during oral presentations.
- **Prepare written script of oral activities** to assist students with comprehension difficulties.
- **Ask a student to be a notetaker** during discussions.
- **Provide preferred seating arrangements** in the front of the class, face-to-face talk if students read lips, or interpreters if needed.

Visual impairments

- **Obtain the Braille edition** of *REALIDADES*.
- **Provide students with audio resources** such as copies of the Audio Program or reading services.
- **Allow for oral examinations** to alleviate the need for writing.
- **Allow for preferred seating** in the classroom including providing space for a guide dog if necessary.

Teaching Spanish to Advanced Learners

Advanced learners need opportunities to use all of their abilities and to acquire new knowledge and skills.

- **Provide opportunities for in-depth study and research.** Have students do in-depth research in English or in Spanish as appropriate on certain cultural topics. Throughout the Teacher's Edition, teachers will find "Keywords" listed. These are suggestions for additional cultural research that work perfectly with advanced learners.
- **Provide more challenging extensions for classroom activities.** Advanced learners can take a task "to the next level". This might include a writing extension of a speaking task or adding more requirements to a writing task. Throughout the Teacher's Edition, there are suggestions called "Extensions" which provide ideas for how to extend an activity. There are also notes listed under "Advanced Learners" notes in the "Universal Access" section.
- **Provide opportunities for the creative use of the language.** To expand speaking skills, have students write skits or prepare additional presentations. You might place these students in conversational groups where they are given visuals to talk about or specific questions to discuss. To expand writing skills, encourage journal writing.
- **Provide opportunities to use technology.** Have students explore topics on the Internet as allowed using Spanish browsers. Presentations can be greatly enhanced by Powerpoint and word processing with clip art. Students can film presentations or videos and edit using the latest in video editing tools.

Universal Access

Teaching Heritage Learners

A diverse background

These who have a home language other than English are called "heritage learners" and bring a wider range of language abilities to the classroom. These abilities range from students who are minimally functional in the language to those who are completely fluent and literate. It is important for teachers to assess the language skills of the different heritage learners in the classroom. This diversity includes:

- Students who are able to understand the spoken language, but are unable to respond in the language beyond single-word answers.
- Students who are able to understand the language and communicate at a minimal level. These students may be able to read some items, but because of their limited vocabulary, they may not comprehend much information. They may write what they are able to sound out, but errors are evident.
- Students who can speak the language fluently but who have little to no experience with the language in its written form.
- Students who have come to the United States from non-English-speaking countries. They can understand and speak the language fluently; however, their reading and writing skills may be limited due to lack of a formal education in their country of origin.
- Fluent bilingual students who can understand, speak, read, and write another language very well and have possibly received formal instruction in that language in the United States or in another country.

Program goals

Heritage learners bring rich home language experiences to the classroom that can serve as a foundation for learning. Because of their language background, these students have the potential to be bilingual, biliterate, and bicultural. Heritage learners need to be exposed to a program that can improve and maintain the home language. This is accomplished through the formal study of the language, for example, Spanish. Students need to study the grammar and focus on vocabulary development. Emphasis should be placed on the development of reading and writing skills. It is important that students develop a sensitivity to when in a social situation standard and non-standard language should be employed and comfortably adjust their language accordingly. In addition, students should be exposed to the diverse cultures within the Spanish-speaking community while developing a sense of pride in their own heritage. Heritage learners need to reach a high level of proficiency and accuracy that will ensure success at the advanced level of language study and testing. These students should also be ready to transition into a focused study of Spanish in specific professional areas.

Focus on individual needs

Due to their diverse backgrounds, heritage learners differ greatly in language skills and may need individualized instruction. In many of today's classrooms, teachers encounter classes that contain a mixture of beginning-level students and heritage learners. Each of these groups needs different materials, different instructional approaches, and different objectives. Here are several strategies that may be helpful for heritage learners:

- Build upon their background knowledge. Develop instructional units around themes and topics that relate to their life experiences. Encourage students to use these experiences as the foundation for building language skills through vocabulary development, reading, and writing.

- Help students connect aural with written language. If students don't understand a word in a reading, have them read it aloud or ask a friend or teacher to read it aloud. Often they can recognize the word once hearing it. Allow opportunities for students to follow along as a story is read aloud.

- Use the strategies that are effective in a language arts classroom, such as building schema, teaching language learning strategies, using graphic organizers, and incorporating pre- and post-reading tasks. Use the writing process to develop good writers.

- Encourage students to begin communicating, especially in writing. Have them write down their thoughts in the way it sounds to them. Then have students work with the teacher or another student for corrections. Students can also look through textbooks and dictionaries to assist with error correction.

- Maintain high standards. Require students to focus on accuracy and proficient communication. Many heritage learners experience frustration with reading and writing in the home language when they have good aural/oral skills. Building language skills takes time.

Summary

The diverse needs of today's Spanish students pose a challenge to teachers, curriculum developers and school administrators as they design programs to ensure that all students develop language proficiency. Teachers have at their disposal a variety of materials and strategies to enable them to provide access to Spanish for all learners. Clearly, some students will require additional tutoring and specialized services to reach their full learning potential. However, the activities and materials that accompany *REALIDADES* coupled with instructional strategies described within this article constitute a viable framework for reaching and teaching all learners.

Instructional Planning and Support

Topics covered:

- Creating a Communicative Learning Community
- The Role of Grammar in a Communicative Classroom
- Pair and Group Activities in a Communicative Classroom
- Integrating Technology in the Classroom
- Teaching the Middle School Learner

Today's Spanish classroom is a vibrant and interactive learning community, integrating language with culture. Teachers are planning for instruction that is communicative, motivating, and real for ***all*** students. They are incorporating a wide range of strategies, activities, and technology to achieve clearly defined teaching objectives. This section provides an overview of instructional strategies that will help teachers achieve these goals.

Creating a Communicative Learning Community

A communicative classroom is built upon activities that enable students to use language in meaningful and purposeful ways. One of the challenges is to get students ready, willing, and able to communicate. Here are several strategies that can be built into communicative tasks to help all students be successful.

Teach and use learning strategies

Research states that successful language students use a wide range of learning strategies. In contrast, unsuccessful students employ fewer strategies and tend to give up quickly. Strategies are inherently student-centered and when employed by learners, allow them to become more independent and more successful. Learning strategies enable students to:

- Learn and recall information more efficiently
- Interpret and comprehend language when reading or writing
- Speak more effectively
- Write more effectively
- Take more risks and be more positive
- Work more cooperatively with others

Use activities based upon multiple intelligences

The Multiple Intelligences Theory tells us that students learn in different ways. If new material is presented in a variety of formats, more students will likely learn and be able to demonstrate proficiency with the new material. Howard Gardner in 1983 proposed the theory of Multiple Intelligences in his book, *Frames of Mind.* This theory states that a person has many different ways of acquiring and demonstrating intelligence. Some people remember just about anything if learned to the tune of a jingle or chant, while someone else may be able to grasp an idea, concept, or grammatical point if presented as a graph, chart, or picture.

Gardner presents the notion that there is no "general intelligence," but rather that the mind is organized around distinct functional capacities, which he defines as "intelligences". Though each of the intelligences is developed independently of the others over the course of a lifetime, they usually work together and do not often appear in isolation. Gardner has identified and labeled eight main styles of acquiring and demonstrating knowledge; those eight intelligences are:

- Verbal/Linguistic
- Visual/Spatial
- Bodily/Kinesthetic
- Logical/Mathematical
- Interpersonal/Social
- Intrapersonal/Introspective
- Musical/Rhythmic
- Naturalist

In the Teacher's Edition, you will find frequent specific suggestions for accommodating and teaching to the Multiple Intelligences. This is not meant to be construed as a paradigm for labeling every student in your class. On the contrary, they are presented as tools to help more students access content while recognizing that they are intelligent in many ways and that their overall "intelligence" is based upon the sum of all their intelligences.

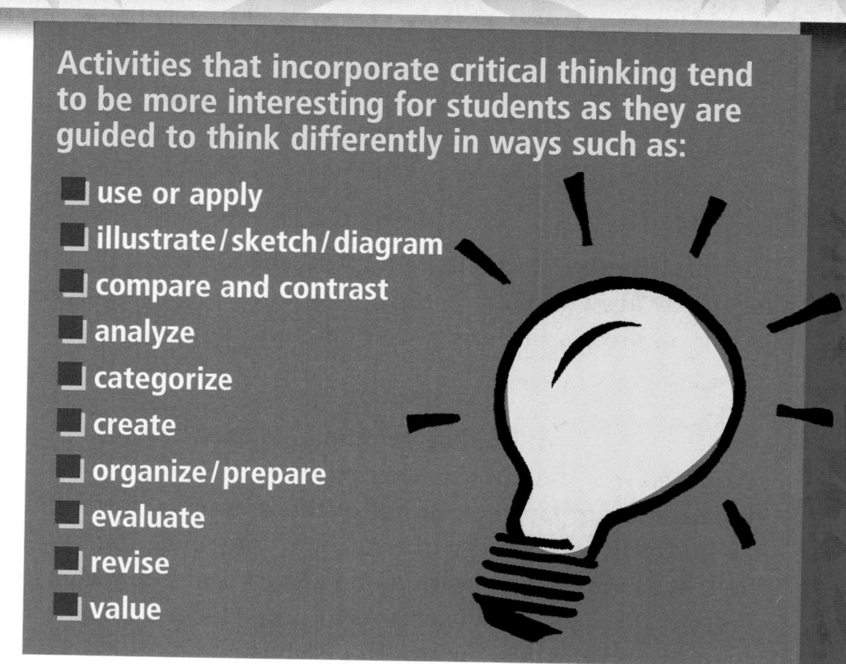

Provide activities that require critical thinking

All students learn more effectively when activities help them make connections and see and use information in new and different ways. Critical thinking skills can be used as tools for learning and are easily integrated in a variety of tasks beginning in the first year of language study in both communication and culture activities.

Scaffolded tasks

Step-by-step support builds success.

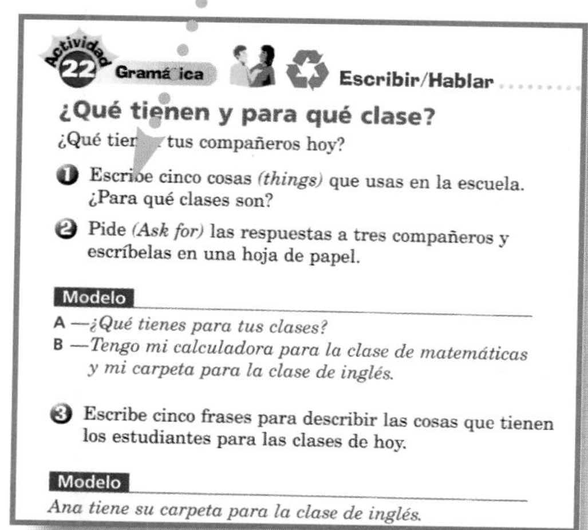

Scaffold communicative tasks

Communicating in a second language is a complicated task. There are mental steps that take place as a student attempts to communicate a message. Activities that help students get through these mental steps allow students to be successful. This "scaffolded" support is provided throughout *REALIDADES*.

For example, in preparing for a speaking task, students think through what they might want to say using a chart. In writing, they might fill out a word web before attempting the first draft. By providing a scaffold that asks students to think, plan, process, and then communicate, more students will become effective communicators.

The Role of Grammar in a Communicative Classroom

In a proficiency-based curriculum, vocabulary and grammar are viewed as tools that students need in order to communicate, rather than as ends in themselves.

Input grammar in context

For students to internalize grammar, it needs to be presented in a meaningful context. For example, students can grasp the concept of the preterite more easily if it is presented within a topic, like shopping. As the teacher presents clothing and store vocabulary, she can tell the class what items of clothing she or another person bought, when they were purchased, and how much was paid. As the teacher points to a picture of a sweater on an overhead transparency or clip art or an actual sweater, she begins with comprehensible input that uses the *yo* form of the preterite: *Ayer, yo fui de compras y compré un suéter nuevo. Y pagué veinte dólares. No es mucho, ¿verdad?* Repetition of the input can continue with other articles of clothing allowing students to easily deduce and internalize the meaning of *compré* and *pagué*. The teacher then begins to ask students questions using *compraste* and *pagaste* and makes summary comments about what is said in the class, drawing other students into the discussion as she introduces other preterite forms. As students begin to internalize these forms and the chapter vocabulary, they begin to make simple statements or ask a partner questions about shopping for clothing.

Input grammar in small, manageable chunks

Present new grammar in manageable chunks that can be immediately practiced. In the example above, students can use a few preterite forms of *comprar* and *pagar* as they talk about shopping. Additional *-ar* verbs and other preterite forms can be added as students become comfortable using *comprar* and *pagar*.

Input grammar in readings

Grammar input can also take place through reading. As students read sentences, short paragraphs, and dialogues with supporting contextual and visual cues, they can understand new grammatical forms. Through carefully planned out questions asked by their teacher, students can be led to explain grammatical concepts.

Teach what is needed for the immediate communication objectives

Teach students the grammar needed to accomplish the communicative objective. This allows students to learn the concept in context and practice. For example, if you teach *pensar* or *querer* in connection with a theme, don't give students an additional list of all *-ie-* stem-changing verbs. Rather, teach additional *-ie-* verbs in later chapters as they connect to the themes.

Practice grammar in a variety of activities

Just as there are several ways to provide input, there are many useful methods for practicing grammar. This practice can involve hands-on activities and games that let students manipulate grammatical structures. Grammar practice is effectively integrated into communicative activities such as surveys, Venn diagrams, and paired and group activities. In addition, practice can involve computerized activities on a Web site that let students practice grammar again and again at their own pace.

Grammar and communication

Grammar can be successfully integrated in a communicative classroom with activities that deal with grammatical accuracy at different levels. When presented in meaningful contexts, in manageable chunks, and with presentation and practice that incorporate a variety of activities, students will develop increasing accuracy with grammar.

Pair and Group Activities in a Communicative Classroom

Benefits of grouping work

Effective group work develops a friendly and cooperative atmosphere by giving students a chance to get to know each other better. This sense of camaraderie leads to a more relaxed classroom in which students are more willing to talk and to participate. Group work also allows more opportunity for "student talk", thereby increasing the quantity of student practice in the target language.

Grouping options and techniques

The communicative activities in a Spanish classroom allow for a variety of grouping options.

The most common option is random grouping that includes pairing up two students or creating small groups of three to five students. Some possible ways to randomly group students include:

- Count off by going left to right or up and down in rows.
- Place on pieces of paper vocabulary words (English/Spanish), countries/capitals, opposites, colors, or categories that can be matched up in a bag. Have students draw a piece of paper and find their partner(s).
- Order students along a continuum by birthday, height, phone numbers, etc.
- Place numbers or a deck of cards in a hat, bag, or box and have students draw.
- Turn to the student to the left or right, front or back.

Another grouping option is to place students by their ability level. Homogeneous grouping allows students of similar ability to work together. In this case, teachers assign tasks based upon the ability level of the group. Advanced students are given a more challenging task. Other students are given tasks that they can successfully complete. Heterogeneous grouping places students of varying abilities together. This allows for stronger students to help weaker students.

Grouping students by interest level is another option to consider. Students could group themselves for an activity or longer project based upon mutual interest.

Planning and facilitating an effective group activity

- Make sure that the task involves a true exchange of information.
- Think through the language functions and content information to make certain students can complete the task.
- Prepare all materials in advance and anticipate questions.
- Explain the task before the students break up into groups. Be sure to model the task if necessary.
- Determine in advance how students will be evaluated and share that criteria with the class.
- Allow adequate time for the task. Make sure at least three quarters of the students at different ability levels can complete it. Tell students how much time they have and stick to the plan.
- Encourage students to stay on-task by walking around the class and monitoring the groups.
- Build into your grading system a way to include group participation and staying on-task.
- Develop some sort of follow-up upon completion of the task.

Error correction

As students work in groups, they will be making mistakes. Here are strategies that can help students to focus on accuracy while doing group work.

- Listen for common errors while monitoring the class. If the error is one of vocabulary usage or grammar, discuss the error with the class and do some focused practice once the task is completed. If the error is one of meaning (very common in beginning writing), have the class work together to determine how best to express the message.
- If you want to correct an individual student error, correct the student only after he or she has spoken. Restate the student's response using the correction in your restatement.

Integrating Technology in the Classroom

REALIDADES Video Program

Technology in today's Spanish classroom

Technology offers teachers and students a wide range of useful, creative, and motivating tools that build language proficiency and cultural understanding. Whether through listening to the vibrating rhythms of *salsa*, clicking on an authentic Internet link from the Spanish-speaking world, practicing basic vocabulary and grammar at a Web site, or by listening to and watching engaging video programs, technology provides new ways to connect with today's learners.

Reaching today's learners

Technology enables teachers to reach more students through resources that include audio, transparencies, video, CD-ROMs, computers, interactive textbooks, or the Internet. Technology enables all students to learn by effectively delivering instruction that:

- Motivates students by making language real
- Helps students learn content through different learning styles: visual, auditory, kinesthetic
- Enables more students to learn on their own and at their own pace through online tutorial and practice opportunities
- Connects students to the Spanish-speaking world beyond the classroom.

Time-saving teacher tools

Technology can save teachers time by offering a wide range of support at the click of a mouse. It also can connect teachers to a network of professional resources and educators who are collaborating and sharing ideas. Technology can support instruction and planning by offering:

- Time-saving electronic lesson plans
- Instant access to previewing teaching resources
- Online links to professional development and teaching resources
- Online communication with networks of educators

> "Technology provides new ways to reach and teach today's learners."

Technology in *REALIDADES A and B*

REALIDADES A and B **provide a complete, state-of-the-art technology package for each chapter at all levels of the program. Technology is integrated into the instruction design of each chapter as follows:**

Chapter Section	Chapter Opener	A primera vista	Manos a la obra	¡Adelante!	Repaso del capítulo
Student Learning Tools	**Web Site** • Atlas **Interactive textbook**	**Web Site** • Vocabulary practice **Interactive textbook**	**Web Site** • Grammar practice **Interactive textbook**	**Web Site** • Internet link and activity • *¿Eres tú, María?* link **Interactive textbook**	**Web Site** • *Vocabulario y gramática* • Self-test **Interactive textbook** **Mindpoint Quiz Show CD-ROM**
Teacher Planning	**Resource Pro CD-ROM** **Web Site**	**Resource Pro CD-ROM** **Web Site**	**Resource Pro CD-ROM** **Web Site**	**Resource Pro CD-ROM** **Web Site**	**Resource Pro CD-ROM** **Web Site**
Instruction	**Fine Art Transparencies** **Vocabulary and Grammar Transparencies** • Maps	**Vocabulary and Grammar Transparencies** • *Vocabulario y gramática en contexto* • *Videohistoria* **Answers on Transparencies** **Audio Program** • *Vocabulario y gramática en contexto* • *Actividades* 1 and 2 • Audio Activities *(Writing, Audio & Video Workbook)* **Video Program** • *A primera vista* segments	**Vocabulary and Grammar Transparencies** • *Gramática* (verbs and charts) • Rapid Review • Graphic Organizers **Answers on Transparencies** **Fine Art Transparencies** **Audio Program** • *Actividades* • *Pronunciación* • Audio Activities *(Writing, Audio & Video Workbook)* **Video Program** • *GramActiva* segments	**Vocabulary and Grammar Transparencies** • Graphic Organizers **Answers on Transparencies** **Video Program** • *¿Eres tú, María?* (starting *Tema* 5)	**Audio Program** • *Repaso del capítulo (Vocabulario y gramática)* • *Escuchar (Preparación para el examen)* • *Canciones*
Assessment					**Computer Test Bank with CD-ROM**

Videohistoria

A primera vista

GramActiva

mi perro

GramActiva

Videomisterio

DETECTIVES PRIVADOS

¿Eres tú, María?

Teaching the Middle School Learner

The middle school learner is not a smaller, shorter version of a high school student and materials for middle school students should not be shorter versions of high school materials. Rather, middle school materials should reflect the unique characteristics of early adolescent learners. There is extraordinary variety among middle school learners as they enter and progress through adolescence at different times and at different rates. As such, middle school materials need to address the variety that characterizes the learners who use them.

Personalized activities

Because middle school learners are egocentric, it is important that students have extensive opportunities for personalized and meaningful self-expression. The materials should have themes and topics that relate to their lives. The photographs and artwork should reflect the age of the learner and be visually appealing, motivating, and colorful.

Social interaction

Middle school students are also social beings: they actively seek out interaction with peers. As a result, pair and group activities should be plentiful. Pair activities should be carefully structured to be manageable with these students.

Physical activity

Because students this age need physical activity, activities should provide for physical involvement of students as they encounter new vocabulary. Early adolescents also seek variety as they explore new identities, experiences, and challenges. Activities should include a variety of formats and challenge levels.

Concrete experiences

The middle school learner is making the transition from a concrete to an abstract learner. At this age, students continue to benefit from concrete learning experiences. For example, early practice that focuses on vocabulary might start out with a contextualized activity for which there is only one answer. A beginning grammar activity might focus on understanding the pattern of grammar before using it communicatively. These students also benefit from the extensive use of visuals (such as pictured vocabulary, video, and clip art). In addition, middle school learners learn better when meaning is contextualized. Materials that are presented within student-centered themes work best. As with all learners, middle school learners benefit from the scaffolding of materials. Instructional scaffolding provides the support that allows learners to stretch beyond where they might succeed on their own.

Cross-curricular connections

In many middle schools, thematic interdisciplinary units characterize instruction across the curriculum. Middle school materials can provide numerous connections with mathematics, science, literature, and social studies concepts. Special emphasis should be made in middle school materials to develop reading and writing skills. Reading should be accompanied by strategies, speaking tasks supported by the speaking process, and writing activities should be structured around the writing process. Students also should see connections to English and how language works. Grammar comparisons to English grammar are helpful and deepen students' understanding of grammar. Language exploration tasks should explain cognates, prefixes, suffixes and the relationship between languages. In general, middle school students benefit from materials that connect to areas in the middle school curriculum.

REALIDADES A and *B* represent a serious, deliberate attempt to address the needs of middle school learners. The two middle school books are not a "younger" version of the high school text. Rather, they meet learners on their own terms, and provide the foundation for successful articulation with second-year high school programs and beyond.

Professional Resources

- National Organizations
- State Organizations
- Regional Conferences
- Listservs
- Web sites

National Organizations

These national organizations provide an annual conference and a wide range of teaching support.

The American Council on the Teaching of Foreign Languages (ACTFL)
http://www.actfl.org

American Association of Teachers of Spanish and Portuguese (AATSP)
http://www.aatsp.org

State Organizations

Each state offers the support of a language association. These organizations provide workshops, conferences, job placement, networking opportunities, and updates on state and second language issues. Teachers are encouraged to contact their state organizations and get involved.

Regional Conferences

These regional conferences provide annual conferences and support teacher advocacy in their regions. They can each be reached via their Web sites.

Central States Conference on the Teaching of Foreign Languages
http://www.centralstates.cc

Northeast Conference on the Teaching of Foreign Languages
http://www.dickinson.edu/nectfl

Southern Conference on Language Teaching
http://www.valdosta.edu/scolt

Southwest Conference on the Teaching of Foreign Languages
http://www.swcolt.org

NOTE: Web site addresses are subject to change.

Listservs

The following electronic resources are helpful to language teachers and curriculum developers. To subscribe to a listserv, send a message with no subject line as follows:

subscribe [name of listserv] your first name your last name

for example: subscribe ***FLTEACH*** Abraham Lincoln

FLTEACH: a forum for discussion among foreign language educators

listserv@ listserv.acsu.buffalo.edu

SLART-L: focuses on second language acquisition research and teaching

listserv@cunyvm.cuny.edu

IECC: an e-mail listserv that helps teachers find partners for intercultural e-mail classroom connections

iecc-request@stolaf.edu

LLTI: a forum to discuss language learning and technology

listserv @dartcms1.dartmouth.edu

http://www.nclrc.org

Web sites

The number of Web sites of interest to foreign language educators is too large to list. Below are some places to begin.

http://www.clta.net/lessons
- excellent source of Web-based activities for the foreign language classroom

http://www.cortland.edu/www/flteach/flteach.html
- allows for keyword searches of the archives of the FLTEACH listserv and provides an extensive number of links with other sites of interest to foreign language teachers

http://www.cal.org/ericcll/
- provides information to foreign language educators in many areas, including publications, study abroad, and links

http://www.elok.com/rendezvous/
- penpal and penfriends service for teachers looking to link with students in other countries

http://www.nclrc.org
- Georgetown University/George Washington University/Center for Applied Linguistics

http://www.educ.iastate.edu/nflrc
- Iowa State University

Bibliography

Assessment

Boyles, Peggy. *"Assessing the Speaking Skill in the Classroom: New Solutions to an Ongoing Problem."* Northeast Conference Reports: Testing Teaching, and Assessment, ed. Charles R. Hancock. Lincolnwood, IL: National Textbook Company, 1994.

Burke, K., R. Fogarty, and S. Belgard. *The Mindful School: The Portfolio Connection.* Palatine, IL: IRI/Skylight Publishing Inc., 1994.

Cohen, Andrew D. *Assessing Language Ability in the Classroom,* 2nd ed. Boston: Heinle and Heinle, 1994.

Liskin-Gasparro, Judith. *"Assessment: From Content Standards to Student Performance."* National Standards. A Catalyst for Reform, ed. Robert Lafayette. Lincolnwood, IL: National Textbook Company, 1996.

Pettigrew, Frances and Ghislaine Tulou. *"Performance Assessment for Language Students."* Language Learners of Tomorrow: Process and Promise, ed. Margaret Ann Kassen. Lincolnwood, IL: National Textbook Company, 1999.

Block Scheduling

Blaz, Deborah. *Teaching Foreign Languages on the Block.* Larchmont, NY: Eye on Education, 1998.

Canady, R. L., and M. D. Rettig. *Block Scheduling: A Catalyst for Change in High Schools.* Larchmont, NY: Eye on Education, 1995.

———. Teaching on the Block: *Strategies for Engaging Active Learners.* Larchmont, NY: Eye on Education, 1996.

Culture

Byram, Michael. *Teaching and Assessing Intercultural Competence.* Clevedon, U.K.: Multilingual Matters, 1997.

Fantini, Alvino. *"Comparisons: towards the Development of Intercultural Competence."* Foreign Language Standards: Linking Theory, Research, and Practice, ed. June Phillips. Lincolnwood, IL: National Textbook Co., 1999.

Galloway, Vicki. *"Bridges and Boundaries: Growing the Cross-Cultural Mind."* Language Learners of Tomorrow: Process and Promise. Lincolnwood, IL: National Textbook Co., 1999.

Seelye, H. Ned. *Teaching Culture, 3rd ed.* Lincolnwood, IL: National Textbook Co., 1993.

Curriculum and Instruction

ACTFL Performance Guidelines for K-12 Learners. Yonkers, NY: ACTFL, 1999.

"Challenge for a New Era." Nebraska K-12 Foreign Language Frameworks. Lincoln: Nebraska Department of Education, 1996.

Chamot, Anna U. ***"Reading and Writing Processes: Learning Strategies in Immersion Classrooms,"*** Language Learners of Tomorrow: Process and Promise, ed. Margaret Ann Kassen. Lincolnwood, IL: National Textbook Company, 1999.

Davis, Robert. *"Group Work is NOT Busy Work: Maximizing Success of Group Work in the L2 Classroom."* Foreign Language Annals, Vol. 30 (1997): 265-279.

Foreign Language Framework for California Public Schools Kindergarten Through Grade Twelve. Sacramento: California State Department of Education, 2002

Guntermann, G., ed. *Teaching Spanish with the Five C's: A Blueprint for Success.* New York: Harcourt College Publishers, 2000.

Hall, Joan Kelly. *"The Communication Standards,"* Foreign Language Standards: Linking Theory, Research, and Practice, ed. June Phillips. Lincolnwood, IL: National Textbook Co., 1999.

Heining-Boyton, Audrey L., and David B. Heining-Boyton. *"Incorporating Higher-Order Thinking Skills in the Foreign Language Curriculum,"* Foreign Languages: Internationalizing the Future, ed. Robert M. Terry. Valdosta, GA: Southern Conference on Language Teaching, 1993.

Jackson, Claire, et al. *Articulation & Achievement: Connecting Standards, Performance, and Assessment in Foreign Language.* New York: College Board of Publications, 1996.

Klee, Carol A. ***"Communication as an Organizing Principle in the National Standards: Sociolinguistic Aspects of Spanish Language Teaching."*** Hispania. Vol. 81 (2) (1998), pp. 339-351.

Knerr, Jennifer and Charles James. *"Partner Work and Small-Group Work for Cooperative and Communicative Learning,"* Focus on the Foreign Language Learner: Priority and Strategies, ed. Lorraine Strasheim. Lincolnwood, IL: National Textbook Company, 1991.

Krashen, Stephen. *Principles and Practice in Second Language Acquisition.* Oxford: Pergamon Press, 1982.

Lafayette, R. C., ed. *National Standards: A Catalyst for Reform.* Lincolnwood, IL: National Textbook Company, 1996.

Met, Myriam, with J. Phillips. *Curriculum Handbook.* Association for Supervision and Curriculum Development, 1999.

———. *"Making Connections."* Foreign Language Standards: Linking Theory, Research, and Practice, ed. June Phillips. Lincolnwood, IL: National Textbook Co., 1999.

National K-12 Foreign Language Resource Center. ***"A Guide to Aligning Curriculum with the Standards."*** Ames: Iowa State University, 1996.

———. ***Bringing the Standards into the Classroom: A Teacher's Guide.*** Ames: Iowa State University, 1997.

Standards for Foreign Language Learning in the 21st Century: *Including Chinese, Classical Languages, French, German, Italian, Japanese, Portuguese, Russian, and Spanish.* Lawrence, KS: Allen Press, 1999.

Trayer, Marie. *"Foreign Language Standards: The Nebraska Story."* ACTFL Newsletter, IX: 3 (Spring 1997): 10.

Van Patton, Bill. *"Grammar Teaching for the Acquisition-Rich Classroom,"* Foreign Language Annals, Vol. 25 (1993): 435-450.

Zaslow, Brandon. *"Teaching Language for Proficiency: From Theory to Practice (An Instructional Framework)."* Unpublished document. School of Education, University of California, Los Angeles, 2001.

Heritage Learners

Colombi, Cecilia M. and Francisco X. Alarcón, eds. *La enseñanza del español a hispanohablantes: Praxis y teoría.* Boston: Houghton Mifflin Co., 1997.

Miller, Barbara L., and John B. Webb, eds. *Teaching Heritage Language Learners: Voices from the Classroom, ACTFL Series.* Princeton: Princeton University, 2000.

Rodriguez-Pino, Cecilia, and Daniel Villa. *"A Student-Centered Spanish for Native Speakers Program: Theory, Curriculum Design and Outcome Assessment."* Faces in a Crowd: The Individual Learner in Multisection Courses, ed. Carol Klee. Boston: Heinle & Heinle, 1994.

Valdés, Guadalupe. *"The Role of Foreign Language Teaching Profession in Maintaining Non-English Languages in the United States."* Northeast Conference Reports: Languages for a Multicultural World in Transition, ed. H. Byrnes. Lincolnwood, IL: National Textbook, 1992.

Methodology

Hadley, Alice Omaggio. *Teaching Language in Context, 2nd ed.* Boston: Heinle & Heinle, 1993.

Hall, Joan Kelly. *Methods for Teaching Foreign Languages: Creating a Community of Learners in the Classroom.* Upper Saddle River, NJ: Merrill Prentice Hall, 2001.

Lee, James, and Bill Van Patten. *Making Communicative Language Teaching Happen.* New York: McGraw-Hill, 1995.

Oxford, Rebecca L. *Language Learning Strategies: What Every Teacher Should Know.* New York: Newbury House, 1990.

Shrum, Judith, and Eileen Glisan. *Teacher's Handbook: Contextualized Language Instruction.* Boston: Heinle & Heinle, 1994.

Multiple Intelligences

Armstrong, Thomas. *Awakening Your Child's Natural Genius.* Los Angeles, CA: Heremy P. Tarcher, Inc., 1991.

———. ***Multiple Intelligences in the Classroom.*** Alexandria, VA: Association for Supervision and Curriculum Development, 1994.

Gardner, Howard. *Frames of Mind: The Theory of Multiple Intelligences.* New York, NY: Basic Books, 1983.

Lazear, David. *Seven Pathways of Learning: Teaching Students and Parents about Multiple Intelligences.* Tuczon, AZ: Zephyr Press, 1994.

Middle School

Raven, Patrick T. and Jo Anne S. Wilson. *"Middle-School Foreign Language: What Is It? What Should It Be?,"* Visions and Reality in Foreign Language Teaching: Where We Are, Where We Are Going, ed. William N. Hatfield. Lincolnwood, IL: National Textbook Company, 1993.

Verkler, Karen W. *"Middle School Philosophy and Second Language Acquisition Theory: Working together for Enhanced Proficiency,"* Foreign Language Annals, Vol. 27 (1994): 19-42.

Students with Learning Disabilities

Ganschow, Leonore, and Richard Sparks. *"A Screening Instrument for the Identification of Foreign Language Learning Problems,"* Foreign Language Annals, Vol. 24 (1991): 383-398.

———, and James Javorsky, John Patton, Jane Pohlman, Richard Sparks. *"Test Comparisons among Students Identified as High-Risk, Low-Risk, and Learning Disabled in High School Foreign Language Courses,"* The Modern Language Journal, Vol. 76 (1992): 142-159.

Sax Mabbott, Ann. *"An Exploration of Reading Comprehension, Oral Reading Errors, and Written Errors by Subjects Labeled Learning Disabled,"* Foreign Language Annals, Vol. 27 (1994): 294-324.

Sheppard, Marie. *"Proficiency as an Inclusive Orientation: Meeting the Challenge of Diversity,"* Reflecting on Proficiency from the Classroom Perspective, ed. June Phillips. Lincolnwood, IL: National Textbook Company, 1993.

Technology

Blyth, C. S. *Untangling the Web*. New York: St. Martin's Press, 1998.

Bush, M.D., and R. M. Terry, eds. *Technology-Enhanced Language Learning.* Lincolnwood, IL: National Textbook Company, 1997.

Muyskens, Judith Ann., ed. *New Ways of Learning and Teaching: Focus on Technology and Foreign Language Education.* Boston: Heinle & Heinle, 1997.

Index of Cultural References

A

Africans in the Caribbean, 81
agriculture, Bolivia, 172
agua de melón, recipe, 155
Alamo, the, 29, 234
Alhambra, the (Granada, Spain), 51
aloe vera, 205
Americans of Spanish or Hispanic descent, xxiii, 35, 45, 222, 261, 264–265
Andes, 202
    music, 231
animals, domestic, introduced to the Americas, 203
architecture: Central America, xiii
    Puerto Rico, 229
Arecibo Observatory, Puerto Rico, 81
Argentina, xviii–xix, 202–203
    Buenos Aires, 203
    country facts, xviii
    estancias, gauchos, and cowboy culture, 203
    maps, xix, 202
    national drink, 185
    Patagonia, xix
    temperatures, 21
    tourist attractions, 202
    writers, 203
art and artists, 24, 25, 40, 54, 84, 146, 176, 177, 206
    Botero, Fernando (Colombia), 84
    cubism, 24, 25
    González Colson, Jaime Antonio (Dominican Republic), 40
    Goya, Francisco de (Spain), 206
    Kahlo, Frida (Mexico), 54
    mural art, 177
    Murillo, Bartolomé (Spain), 146
    Picasso, Pablo (Spain), 24
    Rivera, Diego (Mexico), 176
    textile art, *huipil,* 77, 143
athletes, eating habits, 198
Aztecs, 113
    calendar, 17
    empire, 176, 203
    Spanish words borrowed from Náhuatl, 185

B

Ballet Folklórico de México, 113
Bamba: "La Bamba," 223
baseball in the Caribbean, 257
Basque Country, the (Spain), 51
Belize. *See* Central America.
bibliographical resources, xxvi-b, 24-b, 84-b, 146-b, 206-b
Bilbao Guggenheim Museum (Bilbao, Spain), 51
Bolívar, Simón, 68
Bolivia, xvii. *See also* South America.
    Andean music, 231
    country facts, xvii
    highlands, 172
    maps, xvii, 172
bomba, Puerto Rican music, 228
Botero, Fernando, 84
breakfast in the Spanish-speaking world, 163
Buenos Aires, Argentina, 203
bullfighting, Pamplona (Spain), 16
Buñol, Spain, *Fiesta de la Tomatina,* 195
butterfly reserve, El Rosario, Michoacán, Mexico, 112

C

cafés, outdoor, 33
calendar, Aztec, 17
calle *Ocho,* Miami (Florida), 265
camping, Spain, 259
Canal Zone, Panama, 142
Canary Islands, map, xxi
Caribbean, the, xv, 80–81. *See also* Cuba; Dominican Republic; Puerto Rico.
    geography, xiv
    history, xv
    maps, xv, 80
    musical styles, 80–81, 228
    people of African origin, 81
Castillo de San Marcos, 235
celebrations. *See* festivals.
Central America, 142–143. *See also individual countries;* Aztecs; indigenous cultures; Mayas.
    country facts, xii–xiii
    geography, xii
    history, xiii
    maps, xiii, 142
    pre-Columbian civilizations, 106
Cerro Aconcagua, Argentina, 202
charango guitar, 231
children's rights, 138
Chile, xviii–xix, 202–203, 231
    Andean music, 231
    country facts, xviii
    Incan empire, 173, 203
    indigenous cultures, 203
    maps, xix, 202
    Torres del Paine, 202
churros (Spain), 163
churros y chocolate (recipes), 170
Cinco de Mayo, 15
Colombia, xvi–xvii, 84, 172
    art and artists, 84
    country facts, xvi
    cumbia, 41
    cycling, 105
    maps, xvii, 172
    oil production, 173
Columbus, Christopher, 80, 229
Córdoba, Spain, 51
Costa Rica, xiii, 142
    conservation in, 142
    country facts, xiii

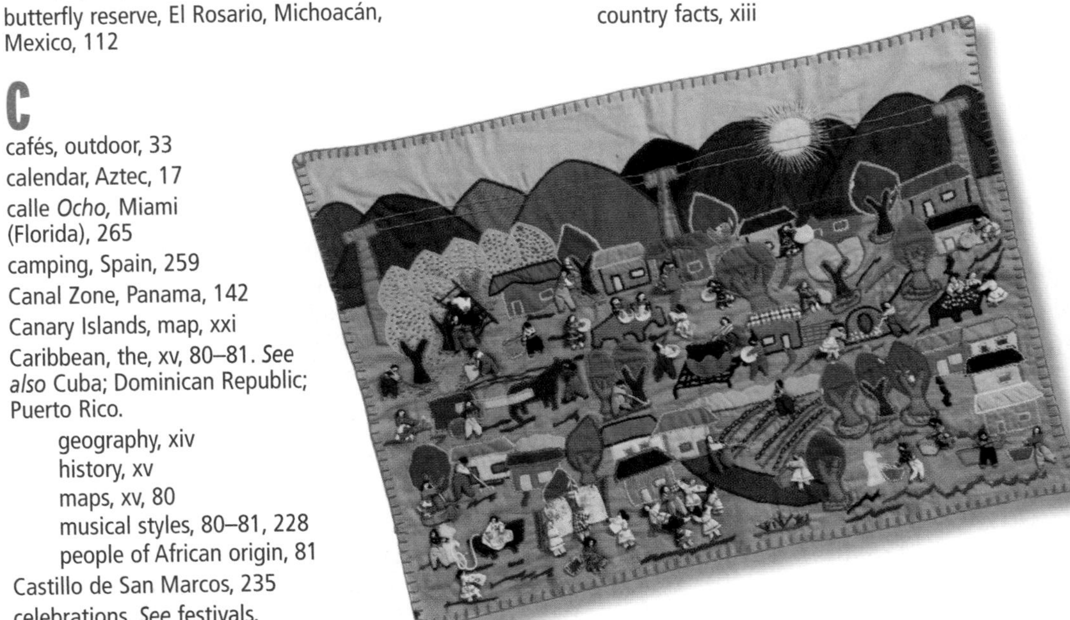

maps, xiii, 142
Spanish-language school, 108–109
country facts
Argentina, xviii
Bolivia, xvii
Chile, xviii
Colombia, xvi
Costa Rica, xiii
Cuba, xv
Dominican Republic, xv
Ecuador, xvi
El Salvador, xii
Equatorial Guinea, xxi
Guatemala, xii
Honduras, xii
Mexico, x
Nicaragua, xiii
Panama, xiii
Paraguay, xviii
Peru, xvi
Puerto Rico, xv
Spain, xx
United States, xxii
Uruguay, xix
Venezuela, xvii
cowboy culture in the Americas, 203
craft resources, *maracas,* 24-b
crafts, modeling with soft bread, 206-b
creole languages, 80
Cruz, Sor Juana Inés de la, 116
Cuba, xv, 80
baseball, 257
country facts, xv
languages, 80
maps, xv, 80
cubism, 24, 25
cuisine, varied across cultures, 197
cumbia, 41
currencies in Spanish-speaking countries, 131
customs. *See* social activities, customs, and recreation.
cybercafés in the Spanish-speaking world, 75
cycling in Colombia, 105

D

dance styles, 41, 48, 113, 203
flamenco, 41
mambo, 48
Mexico, 113
tango, 41, 203
domestic animals introduced to the Americas, 203
Dominican Republic, xv, 40, 80–81
art, 40
baseball, 257
country facts, xv
Guerra, Juan Luis (*merengue* composer), 41
maps, xv, 80
Universidad Autónoma de Santo Domingo, 81

E

earthquakes, Mexico, x
Ecuador, xvi–xvii, 172–173, 199, 231
Andean music, 231
country facts, xvi
Galapagos Islands, 173
Incan Empire, 173
map, xvii, 172
soccer, 199
El Rosario, Michoacán, Mexico (butterfly reserve), 112
El Salvador, xii–xiii
country facts, xii
maps, xiii, 142
enchiladas, recipe, 159
English, studied in other countries, 97
Equatorial Guinea, country facts and map, xxi
geography, xx
history and population, xxi
extracurricular activities. *See* social activities and recreation in the Spanish-speaking world.

F

family life
mealtimes, 147
Sunday activities, 209
festivals and celebrations, 15, 16, 196, 247
Mexico, 15, 247
Spain, *Fiesta de la Tomatina,* Buñol, 196
Spain, "Running of the Bulls," Pamplona, 16
flamenco, 41
folk art, 77, 143, 247
food and drink
agua de melón, recipe, 155
athletes' eating habits, 198
banana juice (smoothie), recipe, 169
breakfast, 163, 167
Caribbean cuisine, xv
churros y chocolate, 170
cuisine across cultures, 197
festivals, *Fiesta de la Tomatina* (Buñol, Spain), 196
festivals, *noche de los rábanos* (Oaxaca, Mexico), 247
from the Americas, 159, 168
fruit and vegetables, 168-169
fruit from Chile, 169
green beans, 179
guacamole, recipe, xxvi-b
horchata, soft drink, 149
imported, 169
mate, 185
meals and mealtimes, 147, 151, 161
Mexican, 159
refrescos in Costa Rica, 183
restaurant, 149
rice and beans, 181
sandwiches in Spain and Mexico, 157
supermarket, 148
Tex-Mex cuisine, 187
tomatoes, 195
tortilla española (omelet), recipe, 146-b
footpaths *(senderos),* in Spain, 55
forms of address, 5, 89, 93
French Quarter, the, in New Orleans, 235
friendship and formality, 5, 89, 93
friendship in Spanish-speaking countries, xxx, 78
Fuerte San Lorenzo, Panama, 143

G

Galapagos Islands, 173
gallo pinto (rice and beans), 181
García, Sergio (Spanish golfer), 260
gauchos, 203
gestures used in Spanish-speaking countries, 127
golf, Spain, 260–261
González Colson, Jaime Antonio, 40
Goya, Francisco de, 206
Gran Vía, Madrid, Spain, 207
Granada, Nicaragua, 143
Granada, Spain, 51
green beans, different names for, 179
greetings in Spanish-speaking countries, xxx, 1, 2–4, 275
Spanish forms of address, 5, 89, 93
guacamole recipe, xxvi–b
Guatemala, xii, 77, 131, 142–143
country facts, xii
currency, 131
maps, xiii, 142
Mayan weaving, 77, 143
Guerra, Juan Luis, *merengue* composer, 41
Guinea Ecuatorial. *See* Equatorial Guinea.
güiro (gourd instrument), 40, 41

Index of Cultural References

H

herbal remedies in the Spanish-speaking world, 200
hieroglyphics, Mayan, 13
Hispanics in the United States. *See* Americans of Spanish or Hispanic descent.
Hispaniola, 80
Honduras, xii–xiii, 142, 215
- country facts, xii
- main square (Plaza Morazán), 215
- maps, xiii, 142

horchata (soft drink), 147
huipil (Mayan blouse), 77, 143

I

Iguazú Falls, Argentina, 202
Incas, 173, 203
indigenous cultures. *See also* Aztecs; Incas; Mayas.
- Bolivia and Peru (Quechua and Aymara), xvii
- Chile, 203
- Guatemala, 77, 143
- Mexico, xi, 234

Internet use, cybercafés, 75
Iztaccíhuatl, Mexico, x

K

Kahlo, Frida, 54

L

Lake Titicaca, 172
languages, 50, 80, 112, 234
- creole, 80
- Cuba, 80
- Mayan, xiii, 112
- Native American, 234
- of Spain, 50
- Quechua, xviii

Laredo, Texas, 265
leisure activities. *See* social activities, customs, and recreation.
licuado (smoothie), 169
Little Havana, Miami (Florida), 265
Lobo, Rebecca (basketball player), 261
Lucumí language, 80

M

Machu Picchu, Peru, 173
Madrid (Spain): map, 217
- Gran Vía, 207
- Parque del Buen Retiro, 51
- Plaza Mayor, 33

mambo (dance) steps, 48
Managua, Nicaragua, xii
maps
- Canary Islands, xxi
- Caribbean, the, xv, 80
- Central America, xiii, 142
- Equatorial Guinea, xxi
- Madrid (Spain), 217
- Mexico, xi, 112
- Puerto Rico, 229
- South America, xvii, xix, 172, 202
- Spain, v, xxi, 50, 259
- United States, xxiii, 234, 264

maracas, how to make, 24-b
mate (herbal tea), 185
Mayas, xiii, 13, 77, 106, 107, 112, 143
- languages, xiii
- mathematics and zero, 107
- numerals, 106
- Tulum, 112
- weaving, 77, 143
- writing, 13

mercados, open-air markets in Latin America, 193
merengue, 40, 41
Mexico, x–xi, 112–113
- art and artists, 54, 176
- Aztec empire, 17, 113, 176, 203
- country facts, x
- currency, 131
- dances, 113
- festivals, 247
- food, *enchiladas* (recipe), 159
- geography, x
- history, xi
- indigenous peoples, 234
- maps, xi, 112
- Mexico City, x
- Oaxaca, x
- school schedules, 92
- writers and intellectuals, 116

Mezquita, the (Córdoba, Spain), 51
Miami, Florida, Little Havana, 265
migajón (soft bread), used in modeling, 206-b
Mission San Xavier del Bac, 235
Moors, 51
Morazán, General Francisco, 215
Morro: El Morro (fortress), San Juan, Puerto Rico, xiv
mural art, 177
Murillo, Bartolomé, 146
musical instruments, 40, 41, 231, 241
musical styles, 41, 80-81, 228, 231

N

Nahua peoples of Central Mexico, 234
Náhuatl, words from, 186
names and naming, 5
New Orleans, 235
Nicaragua, xiii, 142–143. *See also* Central America.
- country facts, xiii
- earthquakes, xii
- history, 143
- maps, xiii,142

noche de los rábanos, Oaxaca (Mexico), 247
nonverbal language, 127
Nuyorican Poets Café, New York City, 265

O

Oaxaca, Mexico, x, 247
Ochoa Reyes, Lorena (Mexican golfer), 261
oil, in Venezuela, 173
Old San Juan (Puerto Rico), 229
oldest university in the Americas, 81
open-air markets in Latin America, 193

P

Pamplona (Spain), "Running of the Bulls," 16
pan dulce, breakfast food, 163
Panama, xiii, 142–143
- country facts, xiii
- history, 143
- maps, xiii, 142
- Pacific coast, 143
- Panama Canal, 142

Paraguay, xviii–xix, 202
- country facts, xviii
- maps, xix, 202
- national drink, 185

Paralympics, International Games, 189, 238
Parque del Buen Retiro (Madrid, Spain), 51
Patagonia, Argentina, xix
Pehuenche, indigenous culture in Chile, 203
Pelé and soccer, 199
Peru, xvi–xvii, 172–173
  Andean music, 231
  country facts, xvi
  currency, 131
  Incan empire, 173, 203
  Machu Picchu, 173
  maps, xvii, 172
Picasso, Pablo, 24
Pilsen neighborhood, Chicago, Illinois, 222
pirates, in Spanish America, 143
Plaza Mayor (Madrid, Spain), 33
Plaza Morazán, Tegucigalpa (Honduras), 215
plena, Puerto Rican music, 228
Ponce de León, Juan, 229
Popocatépetl, Mexico, x
Portillo, Chile, 219
pre-Columbian cultures and civilizations. *See* Aztecs; Incas; indigenous cultures; Mayas.
proverbs, rhymes, songs, and tongue twisters, 35, 84–b, 110, 155, 167, 223, 232, 254
Puerto Rico, xv, 80–81, 228–229
  Arecibo Observatory, 81
  country facts, xv
  currency, 131
  maps, xv, 80, 229
  musical styles, 228
  Old San Juan, 229
  salsa, 41

Q

Quechua language, xvii
quena flute, 231

R

recipes, xxvi-b, 146-b, 155, 159, 169, 170
  agua de melón, 155
  churros y chocolate, 170
  enchiladas, 159
  guacamole, xxvi-b
  licuado, 169
  tortilla española, 146-b
recreation. *See* social activities, customs, and recreation.
recreo: el recreo (break) in Spanish-speaking countries, 103
restaurant menus, 149, 167
rhymes. *See* proverbs, rhymes, songs, and tongue-twisters.
rice and beans *(gallo pinto),* 181
Río Bravo (Río Grande), Mexico, x
Rivera, Diego, 176
Roman empire, 50, 95
Roman numerals, 94
"Running of the Bulls," Pamplona (Spain), 16

S

Salamanca, Spain, 211
salsa, 41
San Juan, Puerto Rico, 229
sandwiches in Spain and Mexico, 157
Sanfermines, Pamplona (Spain), 16
Santa Rosa, Costa Rica, 142
Santo Domingo, Universidad Autónoma de (Dominican Republic), 81
schools, 85, 91, 92, 127, 134, 140
  addressing teachers, 93
  extracurricular activities, 213
  grading, 85
  in Spanish-speaking countries, 134, 140
  schedules, Mexico, 92
  teaching methods, 91
  technology in the classroom, 123
  uniforms, in Spanish-speaking countries, 127
  year, length of, 140
sea turtle, nesting sites in Costa Rica, 142
seasons in the Southern Hemisphere, 20
Segovia, Spain, Roman aqueduct, 95
Seville, Spain, 217
shopping, 193, 231
siku panpipes, 231
soccer, 105, 199, 221, 261
social activities, customs, and recreation, 27, 103, 147, 209, 213, 215, 221, 229, 249, 262. *See also* festivals and celebrations.
  family life on Sundays, 209
  family meals and mealtimes, 147
  invitations, declining, 249
  host / hostess gifts, 249
  outdoor leisure activities, 27, 55
  plazas and public places, 43, 215, 229
  resort vacations (Portillo, Chile), 219
  sports clubs and gyms, 221, 262
  teenagers, 1, 43, 102, 103, 213, 229, 262
Sor Juana Inés de la Cruz, 116
Sosa, Sammy, 257
South America, xvi–xix, 172–173, 202–203. *See also* individual countries.
  geography, xvi, xviii
  history, xvii, xix
  liberation, 68
  maps, xvii, xix, 172, 202
  urban life, 202–203
Spain, 50–51
  art and artists, 24, 146, 206
  athletes (golf), 260–261
  Canary Islands, xxi
  country facts, xx
  currency, 131
  festivals, 196
  flamenco, 41
  food, 163
  footpaths *(senderos),* 55
  geography, xx
  Gran Vía, Madrid, 207
  Granada and the Alhambra, 51
  history, xxi
  in Roman empire, 50, 95
  languages, 50
  Madrid, map, 217
  maps, v, xxi, 50, 259
  "Running of the Bulls," 16
  Salamanca, 211
  Seville, 217
  Spanish empire, 50
  tourism, 259
Spanish Catholic missions in the Americas, 235
Spanish-language school (immersion), Costa Rica, 108–109

Index of Cultural References

Spanish speakers in the United States, 35, 45, 222. *See also* Americans of Spanish or Hispanic descent.
sports
- basketball, 261
- calories burned, 197
- clubs and gyms in Spanish-speaking countries, 221, 262
- cycling, 105
- golf, 260–261
- in the Spanish-speaking world, 221, 262
- Paralympic Games, 189, 238
- soccer, 105, 199

St. Augustine, Florida, 234
supermarket offerings, 148, 166

T

tango, 41, 203
Tegucigalpa, Honduras, 215
telling time in Spanish-speaking countries, 109
temperatures in Spanish-speaking countries, 21
Tenochtitlán, Mexico, 17, 113, 176
Tenorio, Edwin (Ecuadorian soccer player), 199
terraced fields, Bolivia, 172
Tex-Mex cuisine, 187
Texas, independence from Mexico, 29, 187, 234
textile art, *huipil,* 77, 143
Tomatina, Fiesta de la (Buñol, Spain), 196
tomatoes, cultivated in the Andes, 195
Torres del Paine, Chile, 202
tortilla española (omelet), recipe, 146-b
tourism, Spain, 259
trabalenguas (tongue twisters), 35, 167
traditional remedies in the Spanish-speaking world, 200
traditions. *See* social activities, customs, and recreation.
tropical forest in Central America, 142
Tulum, Mayan city, 112
twenty-four-hour clock, 109

U

UNICEF, 138, 139
United States, 234–235, 264–265
- Alamo, the (San Antonio, Texas), 29, 234
- country facts, xxii
- geography, xxii
- history, xxiii
- maps, xxiii, 234, 264

Universidad Autónoma de Santo Domingo, 81
Uruguay, xix, 202–203
- country facts, xix
- *estancias* and cowboy culture, 203
- maps, xix, 202
- national drink, 185

V

Valens, Ritchie, 223
Venezuela, xvii, 172–173
- country facts, xvii
- currency, 131
- maps, xvii, 172
- oil production, 173

W

water in Central America, xii
week, days of the, 31
women
- artists, 54
- astronauts, 264
- athletes, 261
- writers and intellectuals, 116

women's rights, in Mexican history, 116
women's soccer, 261
women's traditional arts, 77
writing, Mayan, 13

X

Xochimilco, Mexico, 113

Y

yerba buena in Mexico, 200
Yunque: El Yunque (mountain peak), Puerto Rico, xiv

PRENTICE HALL

Realidades A

Peggy Palo Boyles
Oklahoma City, OK

Myriam Met
Rockville, MD

Richard S. Sayers
Longmont, CO

Carol Eubanks Wargin
Glen Ellyn, IL

Needham, Massachusetts
Upper Saddle River, New Jersey

Inset image, front cover: Café on the water front, Barcelona, Spain

Front cover (background) and back cover: Parque del Buen Retiro, Madrid, Spain

ISBN 0-13-035966-1

3 4 5 6 7 8 9 10 VH 07 06 05 04

Realidades Authors

Peggy Palo Boyles

During her foreign language career of over 30 years, Peggy Palo Boyles has taught elementary, secondary, and university students in both private and public schools. She currently serves as the Foreign Language/ESL Curriculum Coordinator for the Putnam City Schools in Oklahoma City, OK. She was a member of the ACTFL Performance Guidelines for K–12 Learners task force and served as a Senior Editor for the project. Ms. Boyles is currently President of the National Association of District Supervisors of Foreign Language (NADSFL). She frequently conducts foreign language workshops for state and national organizations, public school districts, and private schools throughout the country.

Myriam Met

For most of her professional life, Myriam (Mimi) Met has worked in the public schools, starting as a high school teacher in New York City. Other positions include supervisor of language programs in the Cincinnati Public Schools, K–12, and Coordinator of Foreign Languages, K–12, for Montgomery County Public Schools, MD. She is currently deputy director of the National Foreign Language Center, where she is responsible for K–12 language education policy analysis. Dr. Met has served on the Advisory Board for the National Standards in Foreign Language Learning, the task force that developed national standards in Spanish, and co-chaired the Pacesetter Spanish task force for the College Board.

Richard S. Sayers

Rich Sayers has been an educator in world languages for 25 years. He taught Spanish at Niwot High School in Longmont, CO, for 18 years, where he also served as department chair, Teacher on Special Assignment coordinating the district foreign language department, and board member of the Colorado Congress of Foreign Language Teachers. In 1991, Mr. Sayers was selected as one of the Disney Company's Foreign Language Teacher Honorees for the American Teacher Awards. He presently serves as a board member of the Southwest Conference on Language Teaching. Mr. Sayers is Senior National Consultant for Pearson Prentice Hall.

Carol Eubanks Wargin

Carol Eubanks Wargin has taught Spanish for 20 years at Glen Crest Middle School, Glen Ellyn, IL, and has also served as Foreign Languages department chair. In 1997, Ms. Wargin's presentation "From Text to Test: How to Land Where You Planned" was honored as the best presentation at the Illinois Conference on the Teaching of Foreign Languages (ICTFL) and at the Central States Conference on the Teaching of Foreign Languages (CSC). She was twice named Outstanding Young Educator by the Jaycees.

Contributing Writers

Eduardo Aparicio
Chicago, IL

Daniel J. Bender
New Trier High School
Winnetka, IL

Marie Deer
Bloomington, IN

Leslie M. Grahn
Howard County Public Schools
Ellicott City, MD

Thomasina Hannum
Albuquerque, NM

Nancy S. Hernández
World Languages Supervisor
Simsbury (CT) Public Schools

Patricia J. Kule
Fountain Valley School
of Colorado
Colorado Springs, CO

Jacqueline Hall Minet
Upper Montclair, NJ

Alex Paredes
Simi Valley, CA

Martha Singer Semmer
Breckenridge, CO

Dee Dee Drisdale Stafford
Putnam City Schools
Oklahoma City, OK

Christine S. Wells
Cheyenne Mountain
Junior High School
Colorado Springs, CO

Michael Werner
University of Chicago
Chicago, IL

National Consultants

Yvonne Cádiz
Tampa, FL

María R. Hubbard
Braintree, MA

Jan Polumbus
Tulsa, OK

Patrick T. Raven
Milwaukee, WI

Joseph Wieczorek
Baltimore, MD

Tabla de materias

Mapas x

México x
América Central xii
El Caribe xiv
América del Sur *(Parte norte)* xvi
América del Sur *(Parte sur)* xviii
España • Guinea Ecuatorial xx
Estados Unidos xxii

Why Study Spanish? xxiv

Study Tips xxv

Para empezar

1 En la escuela 2
- Greet people at different times of the day
- Introduce yourself to others
- Respond to classroom directions
- Begin using numbers
- Tell time
- Identify parts of the body

2 En la clase 10
- Talk about things in the classroom
- Ask questions about new words and phrases
- Use the Spanish alphabet to spell words
- Talk about things related to the calendar
- Learn about the Aztec calendar

3 El tiempo 18
- Describe weather conditions
- Identify the seasons
- Compare weather in the northern and southern hemispheres

Repaso del capítulo 22

Go Online PHSchool.com
For: Online Table of Contents
Visit: www.phschool.com
Web Code: jak-0001

Tema 1 Mis amigos y yo

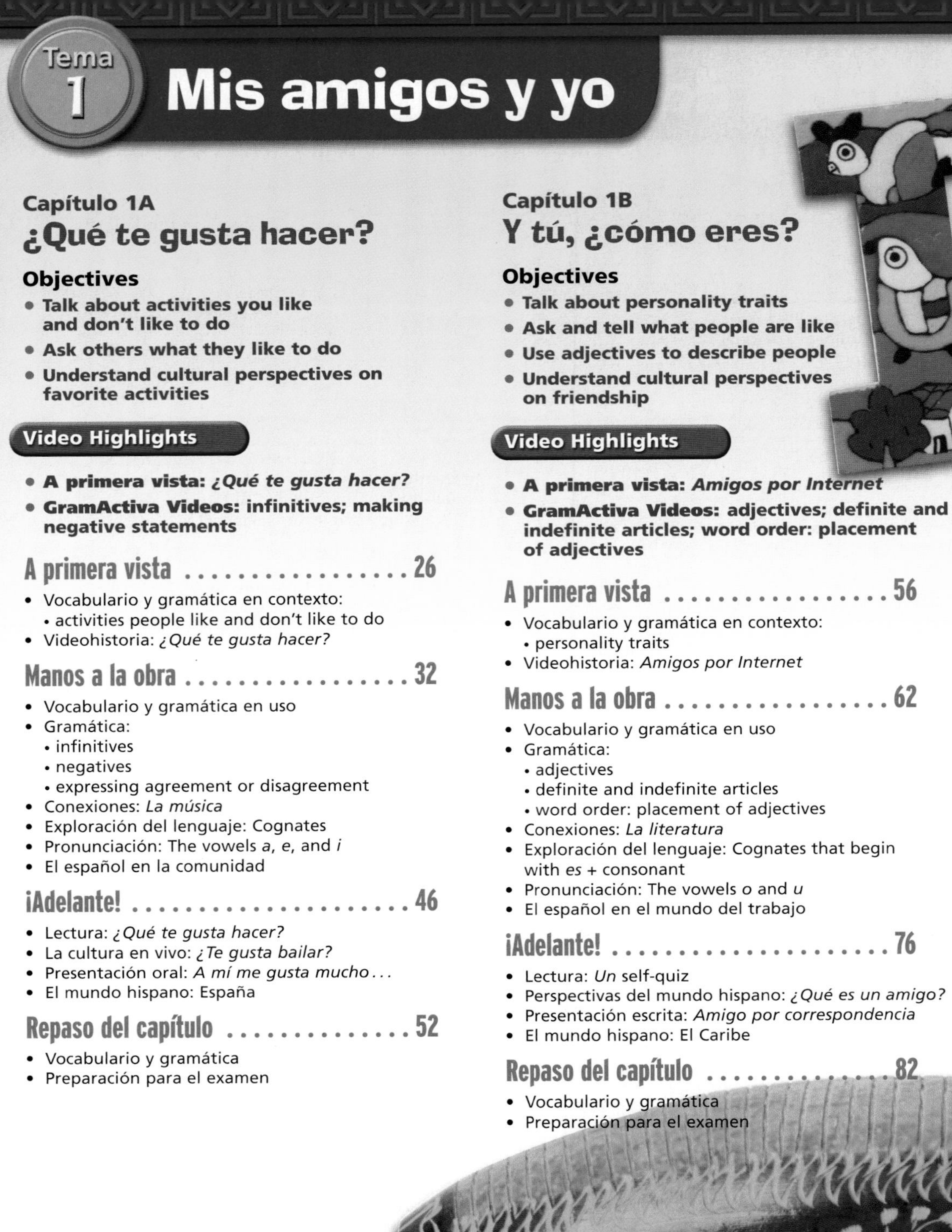

Capítulo 1A
¿Qué te gusta hacer?

Objectives
- **Talk about activities you like and don't like to do**
- **Ask others what they like to do**
- **Understand cultural perspectives on favorite activities**

Video Highlights
- **A primera vista:** ***¿Qué te gusta hacer?***
- **GramActiva Videos: infinitives; making negative statements**

A primera vista 26
- Vocabulario y gramática en contexto:
  - activities people like and don't like to do
- Videohistoria: *¿Qué te gusta hacer?*

Manos a la obra 32
- Vocabulario y gramática en uso
- Gramática:
  - infinitives
  - negatives
  - expressing agreement or disagreement
- Conexiones: *La música*
- Exploración del lenguaje: Cognates
- Pronunciación: The vowels *a*, *e*, and *i*
- El español en la comunidad

¡Adelante! 46
- Lectura: *¿Qué te gusta hacer?*
- La cultura en vivo: *¿Te gusta bailar?*
- Presentación oral: *A mí me gusta mucho...*
- El mundo hispano: España

Repaso del capítulo 52
- Vocabulario y gramática
- Preparación para el examen

Capítulo 1B
Y tú, ¿cómo eres?

Objectives
- **Talk about personality traits**
- **Ask and tell what people are like**
- **Use adjectives to describe people**
- **Understand cultural perspectives on friendship**

Video Highlights
- **A primera vista:** ***Amigos por Internet***
- **GramActiva Videos: adjectives; definite and indefinite articles; word order: placement of adjectives**

A primera vista 56
- Vocabulario y gramática en contexto:
  - personality traits
- Videohistoria: *Amigos por Internet*

Manos a la obra 62
- Vocabulario y gramática en uso
- Gramática:
  - adjectives
  - definite and indefinite articles
  - word order: placement of adjectives
- Conexiones: *La literatura*
- Exploración del lenguaje: Cognates that begin with *es* + consonant
- Pronunciación: The vowels *o* and *u*
- El español en el mundo del trabajo

¡Adelante! 76
- Lectura: *Un* self-quiz
- Perspectivas del mundo hispano: *¿Qué es un amigo?*
- Presentación escrita: *Amigo por correspondencia*
- El mundo hispano: El Caribe

Repaso del capítulo 82
- Vocabulario y gramática
- Preparación para el examen

Tema 2 La escuela

Capítulo 2A
Tu día en la escuela

Objectives

- Talk about school schedules and subjects
- Discuss what students do during the day
- Ask and tell who is doing an action
- Compare your school with that of a student in a Spanish-speaking country

Video Highlights

- **A primera vista:** ***El primer día de clases***
- **GramActiva Videos: subject pronouns; present tense of *-ar* verbs**

A primera vista 86

- Vocabulario y gramática en contexto:
  - the school day
- Videohistoria: *El primer día de clases*

Manos a la obra 92

- Vocabulario y gramática en uso
- Gramática:
  - subject pronouns
  - present tense of *-ar* verbs
- Conexiones: *Las matemáticas*
- Exploración del lenguaje: Connections between Latin, English, and Spanish
- Pronunciación: The letter *c*
- El español en la comunidad

¡Adelante! 108

- Lectura: *La Escuela Español Vivo*
- La cultura en vivo: *Aficionados al fútbol*
- Presentación oral: *Mis clases*
- El mundo hispano: México

Repaso del capítulo 114

- Vocabulario y gramática
- Preparación para el examen

Capítulo 2B
Tu sala de clases

Objectives

- Describe a classroom
- Indicate where things are located
- Talk about more than one object or person
- Understand cultural perspectives on school

Video Highlights

- **A primera vista:** ***Un ratón en la clase***
- **GramActiva Videos: the verb *estar;* the plurals of nouns and articles**

A primera vista 118

- Vocabulario y gramática en contexto:
  - the classroom
  - expressions of location
- Videohistoria: *Un ratón en la clase*

Manos a la obra 124

- Vocabulario y gramática en uso
- Gramática:
  - the verb *estar*
  - the plurals of nouns and articles
- Conexiones: *Las matemáticas*
- Exploración del lenguaje: Language through gestures
- Pronunciación: The letter *g*
- El español en el mundo del trabajo

¡Adelante! 138

- Lectura: *El UNICEF y una convención para los niños*
- Perspectivas del mundo hispano: *¿Cómo es la escuela?*
- Presentación escrita: *Tu sala de clases*
- El mundo hispano: América Central

Repaso del capítulo 144

- Vocabulario y gramática
- Preparación para el examen

Tema 3 La comida

Capítulo 3A
¿Desayuno o almuerzo?

Objectives
- Talk about foods and beverages for breakfast and lunch
- Talk about likes and dislikes
- Express how often something is done
- Understand cultural perspectives on meals

Video Highlights
- **A primera vista:** ***El desayuno***
- **GramActiva Videos:** present tense of *-er* and *-ir* verbs; *me gustan, me encantan*

A primera vista 148
- Vocabulario y gramática en contexto:
  - foods and beverages for breakfast and lunch
- Videohistoria: *El desayuno*

Manos a la obra 154
- Vocabulario y gramática en uso
- Gramática:
  - present tense of *-er* and *-ir* verbs
  - *me gustan, me encantan*
- Conexiones: *La historia*
- Exploración del lenguaje: Using a noun to modify another noun
- Pronunciación: The letters *h* and *j*
- El español en la comunidad

¡Adelante! 168
- Lectura: *Frutas y verduras de las Américas*
- La cultura en vivo: *Churros y chocolate*
- Presentación oral: *¿Y qué te gusta comer?*
- El mundo hispano: América del Sur *(Parte norte)*

Repaso del capítulo 174
- Vocabulario y gramática
- Preparación para el examen

Capítulo 3B
Para mantener la salud

Objectives
- Talk about foods and beverages for dinner
- Describe what people or things are like
- Discuss food, health, and exercise choices
- Understand cultural perspectives on diet and health

Video Highlights
- **A primera vista:** ***Para mantener la salud***
- **GramActiva Videos:** the plurals of adjectives; the verb *ser*

A primera vista 178
- Vocabulario y gramática en contexto:
  - food groups and foods on the Food Guide Pyramid
  - activities to maintain good health
  - ways to describe food
- Videohistoria: *Para mantener la salud*

Manos a la obra 184
- Vocabulario y gramática en uso
- Gramática:
  - the plurals of adjectives
  - the verb *ser*
- Conexiones: *La salud*
- Exploración del lenguaje: Where did it come from?
- Pronunciación: The letters *l* and *ll*
- El español en el mundo del trabajo

¡Adelante! 198
- Lectura: *La comida de los atletas*
- Perspectivas del mundo hispano: *¿Qué haces para mantener la salud?*
- Presentación escrita: *Para mantener la salud*
- El mundo hispano: América del Sur *(Parte sur)*

Repaso del capítulo 204
- Vocabulario y gramática
- Preparación para el examen

Tema 4

Los pasatiempos

Capítulo 4A

¿Adónde vas?

Objectives

- **Talk about locations in your community**
- **Discuss leisure activities**
- **Talk about where you go and with whom**
- **Learn how to ask questions**
- **Understand cultural perspectives on leisure activities**

Video Highlights

- **A primera vista:** ***Un chico reservado***
- **GramActiva Videos: the verb *ir;* asking questions**

A primera vista 208

- Vocabulario y gramática en contexto:
  - places to go to when you're not in school
- Videohistoria: *Un chico reservado*

Manos a la obra 214

- Vocabulario y gramática en uso
- Gramática:
  - the verb *ir*
  - asking questions
- Conexiones: *La geografía; La historia*
- Exploración del lenguaje: Origins of the Spanish days of the week
- Pronunciación: Stress and accents
- El español en la comunidad

¡Adelante! 230

- Lectura: *Al centro comercial*
- La cultura en vivo: *Rimas infantiles*
- Presentación oral: *Un estudiante nuevo*
- El mundo hispano: Los Estados Unidos (Histórico)

Repaso del capítulo 236

- Vocabulario y gramática
- Preparación para el examen

Capítulo 4B

¿Quieres ir conmigo?

Objectives

- **Talk about activities outside of school**
- **Extend, accept, and decline invitations**
- **Tell when an event happens**
- **Understand cultural perspectives on after-school activities**

Video Highlights

- **A primera vista:** ***¡A jugar!***
- **GramActiva Videos: *ir + a* + infinitive; the verb *jugar***

A primera vista 240

- Vocabulario y gramática en contexto:
  - activities outside of school
- Videohistoria: *¡A jugar!*

Manos a la obra 246

- Vocabulario y gramática en uso
- Gramática:
  - *ir + a* + infinitive
  - the verb *jugar*
- Conexiones: *Las matemáticas*
- Exploración del lenguaje: Spanish words borrowed from English
- Pronunciación: The letter *d*
- El español en el mundo del trabajo

¡Adelante! 260

- Lectura: *Sergio y Lorena: El futuro del golf*
- Perspectivas del mundo hispano: *¿Qué haces en tu tiempo libre?*
- Presentación escrita: *Una invitación*
- El mundo hispano: Los Estados Unidos (Contemporáneo)

Repaso del capítulo 266

- Vocabulario y gramática
- Preparación para el examen

Apéndices

- Vocabulario adicional 268
- Resumen de gramática 270
- Verbos 273
- Expresiones útiles para conversar 275
- Vocabulario español-inglés . . 276
- English-Spanish Vocabulary . . . 283
- Grammar Index 290
- Acknowledgments 292

Culture

Standards: 2.1, 2.2, 3.1, 4.2

Geography

Mexico is the fifth largest country in the Western Hemisphere. Its geography ranges from the rugged mountains of the Sierra Madre Occidental and Sierra Madre Oriental to tropical rainforests, volcanic peaks, and world-renowned beaches.

The central area of the country, a high plateau between the ranges of the Sierra Madre, is dry, with limited rainfall. Most of the population lives in this area. Its hub is México D.F. *(Distrito Federal),* the nation's capital. The city is located in a basin known historically as the Valley of Mexico. Earthquakes are not uncommon. In 1985 one of the worst earthquakes in Mexican history shook Mexico City and its environs, causing many deaths and extensive damage.

The central plateau is also home to Mexico's highest peaks and volcanoes, including Popocatépetl and Iztaccíhuatl. Pico de Orizaba is the highest mountain in Mexico at 5,610 meters (18,406 feet).

To the north of the central plateau is the Sierra Tarahumara, or Copper Canyon, the largest canyon system in North America. The climate varies dramatically here. At the rim of the canyons the weather is temperate, with cold winters and mild summers, punctuated by heavy rainfall. Deep below the canyon rims, the climate is tropical, wet and hot for most of the year.

North of the Sierra Tarahumara is the border with the United States, most of which is formed by the Rio Grande, known in Mexico as the Rio Bravo.

To the southwest of Mexico City is Acapulco. Mexican vacationers and tourists from around the world visit the heavily populated city and its tropical ocean beaches. Southeast of the capital, on the Yucatan peninsula, is Cancún. Tourists flock to this area's white sandy beaches and the turquoise waters of the Caribbean.

One of the highlights of southern Mexico is Oaxaca, where the climate is spring-like throughout the year. Here archeological sites dot the landscape, revealing the ancient remains of pre-Columbian settlements.

México

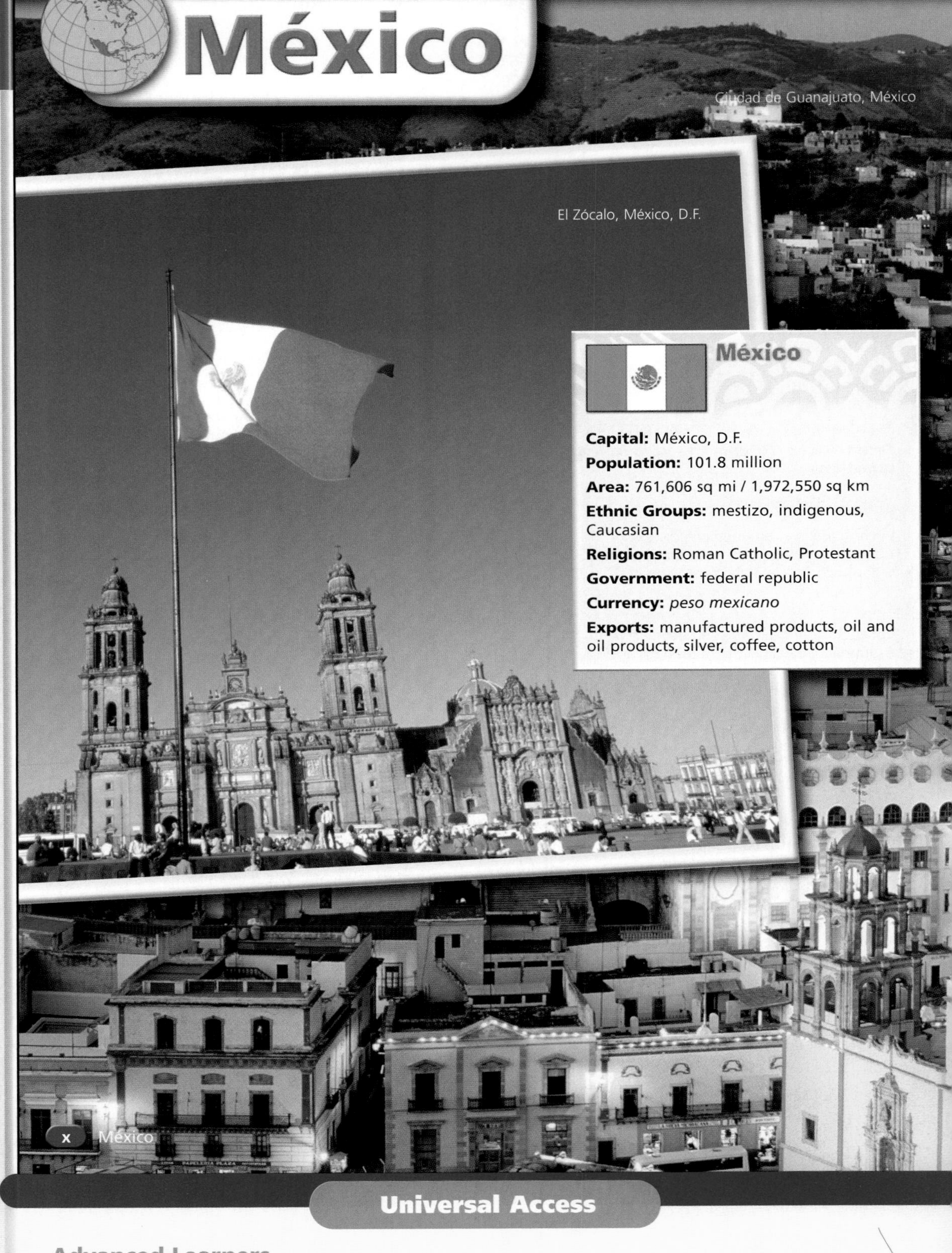

Ciudad de Guanajuato, México

El Zócalo, México, D.F.

México

Capital: México, D.F.

Population: 101.8 million

Area: 761,606 sq mi / 1,972,550 sq km

Ethnic Groups: mestizo, indigenous, Caucasian

Religions: Roman Catholic, Protestant

Government: federal republic

Currency: *peso mexicano*

Exports: manufactured products, oil and oil products, silver, coffee, cotton

Universal Access

Advanced Learners

El Zócalo is Mexico City's central plaza and home of the government, which is housed in the Palacio Nacional, as well as museums, shops, restaurants, and the cathedral (shown in the photo). Ask students to think of a place in the United States that might be similar to Mexico's Zócalo (e.g., the Mall in Washington, D.C., or a central area in their community). Encourage them to speculate about how the two areas might be similar or dissimilar.

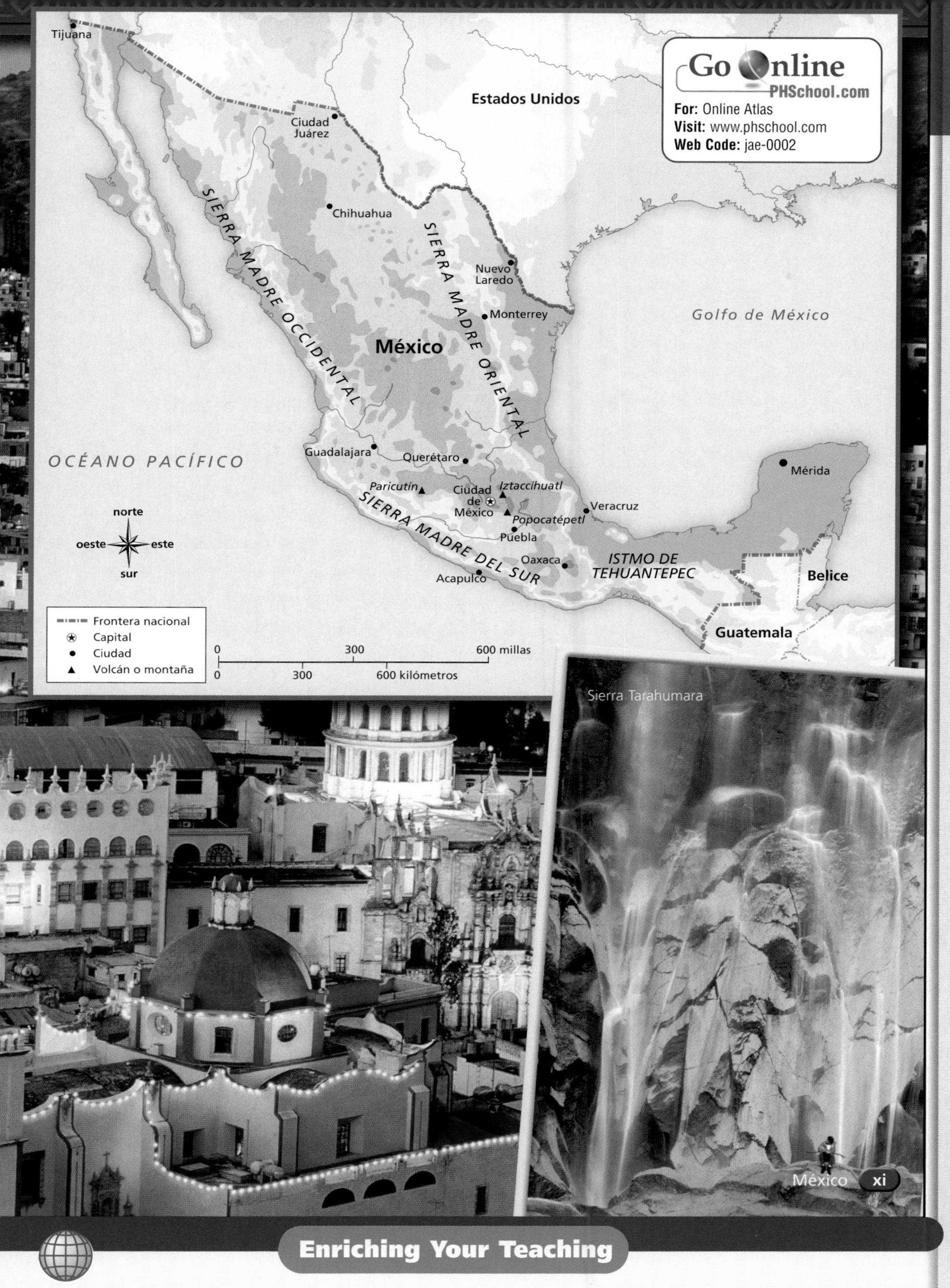

Culture

History

1519 Hernán Cortés conquers the Aztec emperor Moctezuma II and establishes the first Spanish settlement in Mexico.

1810 Mexico declares its independence from Spain.

1845 Mexican-American War begins as U.S. troops capture Mexico City in an effort to annex Texas.

1862–1864 French troops led by Napoleon III march into Mexico City. Maximilian of Austria is declared Emperor of Mexico.

1867 Mexican forces regain control of the country. Maximilian is assassinated.

1876 Porfirio Díaz becomes president of the Republic and eventual dictator (1876–80, 1884–1911).

1910–1911 The Mexican Revolution begins. Francisco I. Madero becomes president.

1913 Madero is assassinated and civil war breaks out.

1934 The Party of Institutionalized Revolution (PRI) is formed and is in power for the next 60 years.

1968 Over 300 students protesting against the government are killed during the Mexico City Olympic games.

1993 The North American Free Trade Agreement (NAFTA) between Canada, the United States, and Mexico is signed.

1994 The Zapatista National Liberation Army (a group of Native American rebels) declares war on the government.

1995 The PRI grip begins to loosen in Mexico with a variety of parties winning provincial elections.

Social Background

Mexico has a diverse population made up of many cultures and customs. The majority of the people (60%) are ***mestizo,*** or a mix of indigenous and European (mostly Spanish) ancestry. Most of the population speaks Spanish as its first language. Indigenous people make up the second largest ethnic group at 30% of the population.

Enriching Your Teaching

Culture Note

The Tarahumara is one of North America's oldest groups of indigenous people. They live communally on small farms in the Sierra Madre Occidental mountains of northwestern Mexico. They have expert knowledge of many different varieties of herbal and edible plants. They are also known for their longevity and for their stamina as long-distance runners.

Culture

Standards: 2.1, 2.2, 3.1

Geography

A series of islands were once scattered between what is now the Caribbean Sea and the Pacific Ocean. Three million years ago (relatively recently in geological terms) they merged to form Central America, a land bridge that links North and South America.

The region is geographically unstable. It is home to at least 14 active volcanoes and experiences frequent earthquakes. Managua, capital of Nicaragua, has been nearly destroyed by earthquakes twice in the last 100 years.

The land is marked by volcanic mountains and ***calderas,*** lakes that have formed in the volcanic craters. Central America's western coastal plain is fairly narrow, sloping dramatically up to the central mountain region. A less dramatic plateau slopes eastward to the Caribbean.

The climate is diverse, mostly due to a variety of altitudes rather than topography. There are three major areas. The hottest (***tierra caliente***) is the lowest area, ranging from sea level to an altitude of roughly 915 meters (3,000 feet). The ***tierra templada*** ranges from 1,830 meters to 3,050 meters (6,000–10,000 feet) and averages temperatures of 65°–75° F. The coldest area (***tierra fría***) is the highest and encompasses the mountain peaks.

Water is key to Central American geography. Bordered on east and west by enormous bodies of water, the region also has several rivers and two very large lakes—Lake Nicaragua and Lake Managua. The Panama Canal is a commercial waterway that links the Caribbean and the Pacific. It was constructed at the narrowest point of Central America so that ships carrying goods between distant ports would not have to sail all the way around the southern tip of South America.

The countries of Central America offer a variety of products and resources that are traded worldwide. Honduras and Nicaragua are rich in minerals, including gold and silver. Honduras also has significant deposits of lead, zinc, copper, and iron ore, while Nicaragua offers offshore oil. Bananas and coffee are key to the economies of Costa Rica and Panama, which are the chief exporters of these products to the United States.

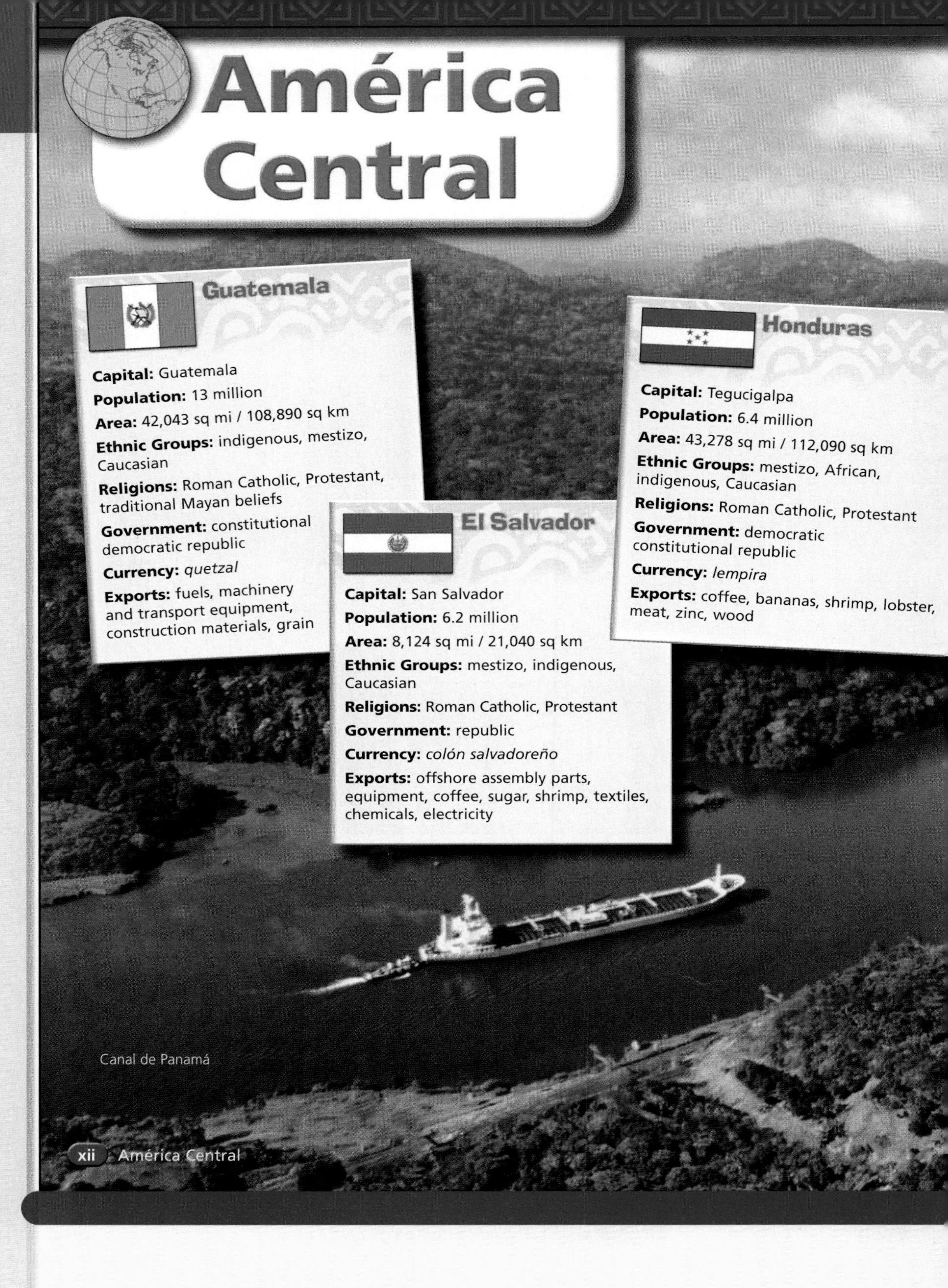

Canal de Panamá

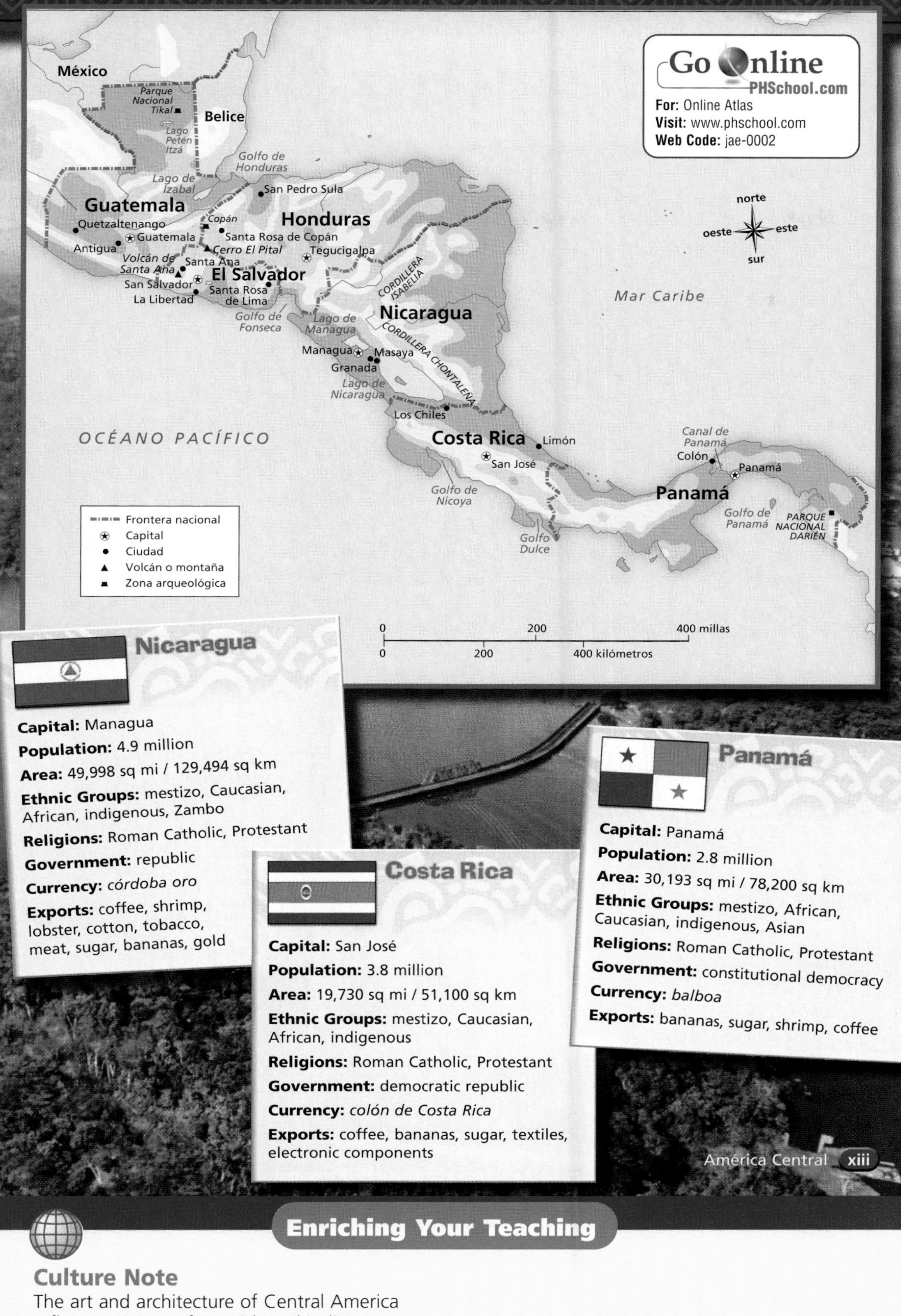

Nicaragua

Capital: Managua
Population: 4.9 million
Area: 49,998 sq mi / 129,494 sq km
Ethnic Groups: mestizo, Caucasian, African, indigenous, Zambo
Religions: Roman Catholic, Protestant
Government: republic
Currency: *córdoba oro*
Exports: coffee, shrimp, lobster, cotton, tobacco, meat, sugar, bananas, gold

Costa Rica

Capital: San José
Population: 3.8 million
Area: 19,730 sq mi / 51,100 sq km
Ethnic Groups: mestizo, Caucasian, African, indigenous
Religions: Roman Catholic, Protestant
Government: democratic republic
Currency: *colón de Costa Rica*
Exports: coffee, bananas, sugar, textiles, electronic components

Panamá

Capital: Panamá
Population: 2.8 million
Area: 30,193 sq mi / 78,200 sq km
Ethnic Groups: mestizo, African, Caucasian, indigenous, Asian
Religions: Roman Catholic, Protestant
Government: constitutional democracy
Currency: *balboa*
Exports: bananas, sugar, shrimp, coffee

Enriching Your Teaching

Culture Note

The art and architecture of Central America reflect a mixture of Spanish and indigenous cultures. Each country has its unique heritage, but similar influences are found throughout the region. A visitor to the region would be struck by the colorful murals, mosaics, and crafts that link the cultures found there.

Culture

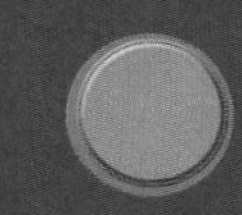

History

1502 On his fourth voyage, Columbus establishes Spain's claim to Central America.

1510–1519 Explorers create and settle colonies. The region is divided into two jurisdictions.

1821–1822 Guatemala, El Salvador, Honduras, Nicaragua, and Costa Rica declare their independence from Spain and create The United Provinces of Central America.

1823 U.S. President James Monroe and Secretary of State John Quincy Adams develop the Monroe Doctrine, warning Europe against intervening in the government or trade of countries in the Western Hemisphere.

1840 Guatemala, Honduras, El Salvador, Nicaragua, and Costa Rica become independent republics.

1855 The Panama Railroad is completed, improving commerce to the Pacific coast ports.

1903 Panama becomes independent from Colombia.

1960 Guatemala, Honduras, El Salvador, and Nicaragua create the Central American Common Market (CACM).

1979 The Sandinistas in Nicaragua overthrow the government of Anastasio Somoza.

1987 Costa Rican president Oscar Arias Sánchez wins the Nobel Peace Prize for creating a peace plan for Central America.

1992 Guatemalan activist Rigoberta Menchú Tum wins the Nobel Peace Prize for her work in justice and ethno-cultural reconciliation. She is the first Native American and the youngest person (33 years old) ever to receive this honor.

1990–present The nations of Central America continue to strive for political stability and economic modernization.

Social Background

The majority of people in America Central are ***mestizo,*** a mix of Native American and European heritage—mostly Spanish. Though the first language of most of the population is Spanish, in Guatemala 23 dialects of Mayan are also spoken.

Culture

Standards: 2.1, 2.2, 3.1

Geography

The Spanish-speaking islands of the Caribbean share common and dramatic geographical features, including a similar topography of mountain ranges and extensive shorelines.

Cuba consists of one main island and several small ones, including la Isla de la Juventud (The Isle of Youth) and four small archipelagos.

Cuba is the largest island in the Caribbean. It is unusual in that three quarters of the country are fertile farmland, where crops such as sugar, tobacco, citrus fruits, and coffee grow in abundance. Cuba's shoreline is home to spectacular beaches, coral reefs, and deep harbors.

The República Dominicana shares the island of Hispaniola with Creole-speaking Haiti. It, too, has fertile farmland, but the majority of the island consists of mountain ranges. Its most valuable natural resources are sugar, cocoa, and tobacco.

Puerto Rico's landscape is marked by steep mountains. The Cordillera Central extends from east to west and divides the country into northern and southern regions. The island's mountain peak of El Yunque (The Anvil) attracts tourists throughout the year. The warm, sunny beaches of the coastline are also a major tourist destination. Puerto Rico's economy relies on industry and tourism rather than agriculture. An estimated five million tourists visit the island each year.

The three countries share a similar climate. Generally, the temperatures are moderate to tropical all year round. The mountainous areas receive the most rainfall, while the beaches remain fairly warm and sunny throughout the year.

Teaching with Photos

Ask students to look at the photo of El Morro and speculate as to what kind of building it is and why it might have been built. Let them know that it is a fortress built by the Spanish to guard San Juan's harbor. Today over two million visitors a year explore the fort's ramparts and passageways.

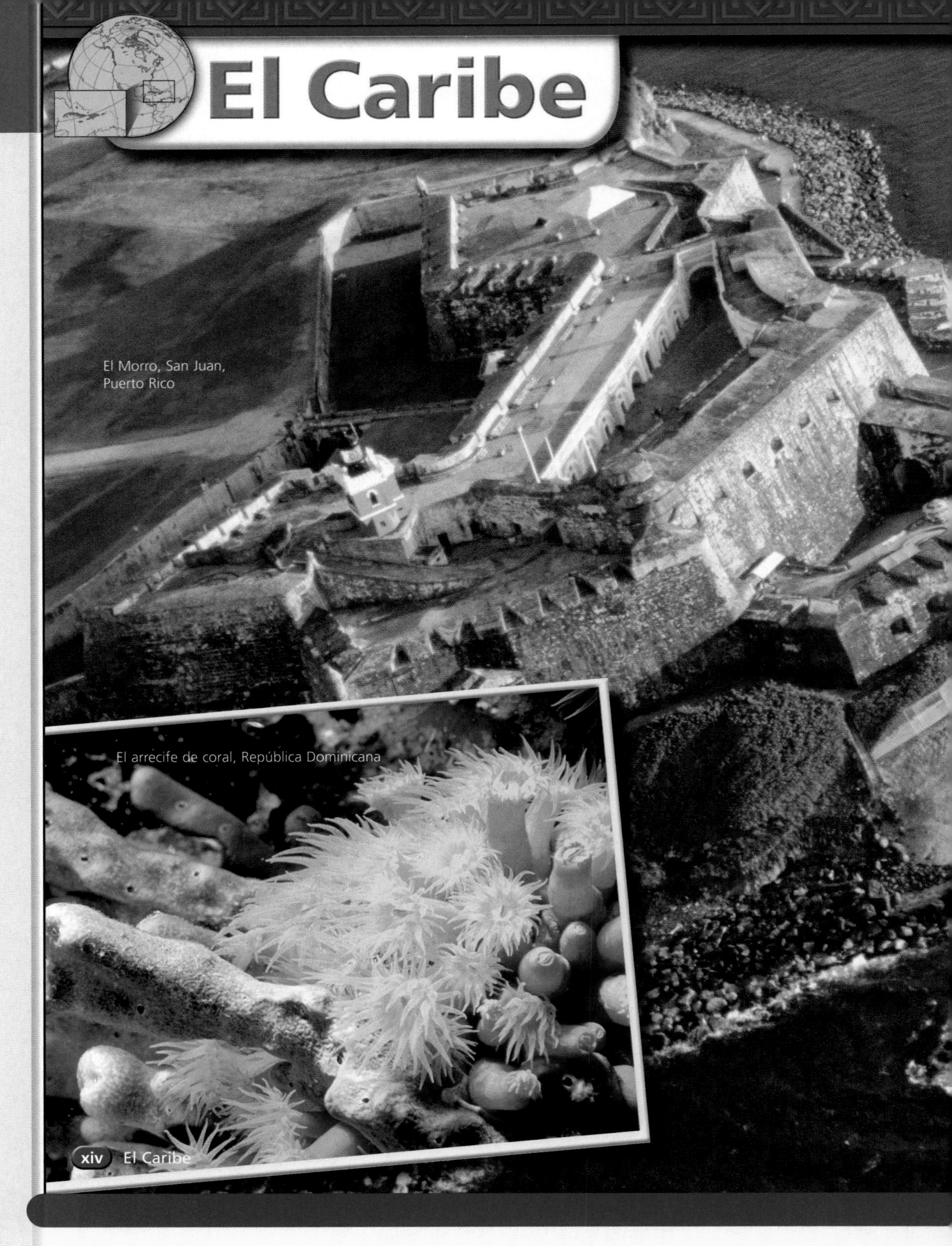

El Morro, San Juan, Puerto Rico

El arrecife de coral, República Dominicana

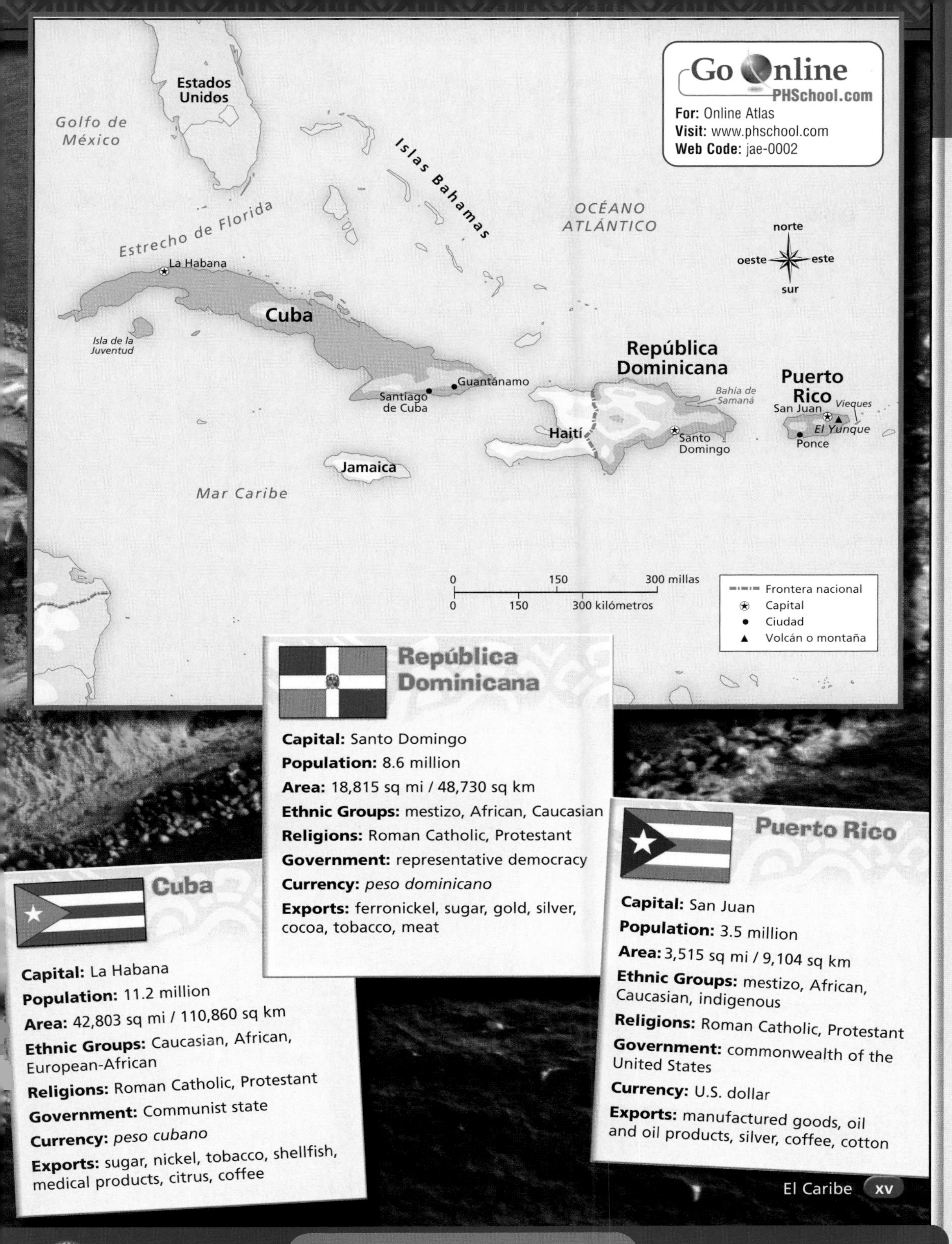

Culture

History

1492 Christopher Columbus explores Hispaniola and Cuba on his first voyage to the Americas.

1493 Puerto Rico is claimed by Spain during Columbus's second voyage.

1496 Santo Domingo, the oldest Spanish settlement in the Western Hemisphere and the capital of the Dominican Republic, is founded.

1898 Puerto Rico is ceded to the U.S. after the Spanish-American War.

1899 Cuba becomes an independent republic under U.S. protection.

1917 Residents of Puerto Rico are granted U.S. citizenship.

1934 Cuba terminates its alliance with the U.S.

1952 Puerto Rico enacts its first consti tution for internal self-government.

1956–1959 Fidel Castro launches the Cuban Revolution. Many Cubans flee to Florida.

1961 The U.S. suspends diplomatic relations with Cuba due to Castro's ties with Communist U.S.S.R.

1996 The Dominican Republic holds its first free elections.

1997 Puerto Rican voters decide to maintain their Commonwealth status.

2002 Castro claims he has 99% of the Cuban electorate's backing to retain its socialist system.

Social Background

Cuba and the Dominican Republic have similar populations, which are largely ***mestizo*** and African. Puerto Rico is different in that most of its inhabitants are Caucasian descendants of Spanish settlers.

Enriching Your Teaching

Culture Note

Each Caribbean country has its own unique cuisine. In Cuba, a visitor might enjoy rice and beans, fried plantains, and pork stew. In the Dominican Republic, one might indulge in fresh seafood, including crayfish and crab. In Puerto Rico, traditional dishes are spiced with three local staples: ***achiote,*** a mixture of seeds and oils; ***sofrito,*** herbs and spices ground together; and ***adobo,*** salt and garlic spiced with lime juice.

Culture

Standards: 2.1, 3.1, 4.1

Geography

The countries of northern South America share dramatic landscapes of high mountains, lush tropical rainforests, and striking coastlines, yet each country has a unique geography that distinguishes it from its neighbors.

Venezuela is the continent's northernmost nation. Most of its population lives in the northern highlands or the coastal regions, where the capital, Caracas, is located. The rest of the country is divided between the Llanos, tropical grasslands, and the Guiana Highlands, a mountainous area comprising over half of the country. The highlands have recently become more populated due to large deposits of iron, manganese, and bauxite that have been discovered there.

Colombia's landscape is divided between east and west by the spectacular Andes Mountains, which extend southward, dividing Ecuador, Peru, and Bolivia as well. Most of the population of Colombia lives in the basins around the Cordillera Oriental. One of the highest ranges of the Andes, the Cordillera's peaks reach to 5,500 meters (18,000 feet). To the east lies a jungle lowland, thinly populated and one of the last minimally explored areas on earth.

Ecuador, named for its location on the Equator, has four distinct geographic regions, including the coastal plain and the Sierra, home to the Andes and one of the world's highest volcanoes, Cotopaxi. The Oriente jungle covers almost half the country, while the Galapagos Islands are a series of 15 islands dotted with volcanic peaks.

Peru lies just south of Ecuador and Colombia. Peru's Andean peaks are some of the highest in the world. Huascarán, at 6,768 meters (22,205 feet), is the highest mountain in the country. Earthquakes occur in this part of Peru, and these mountains are virtually impassable. Peru's long coast is dry and wide and is the economic and population center of the country.

Bolivia is nicknamed "Rooftop of the World," because most of the country sits at a high elevation atop the Andes. Most of the people live in the mountains and in the capital cities of La Paz and Sucre.

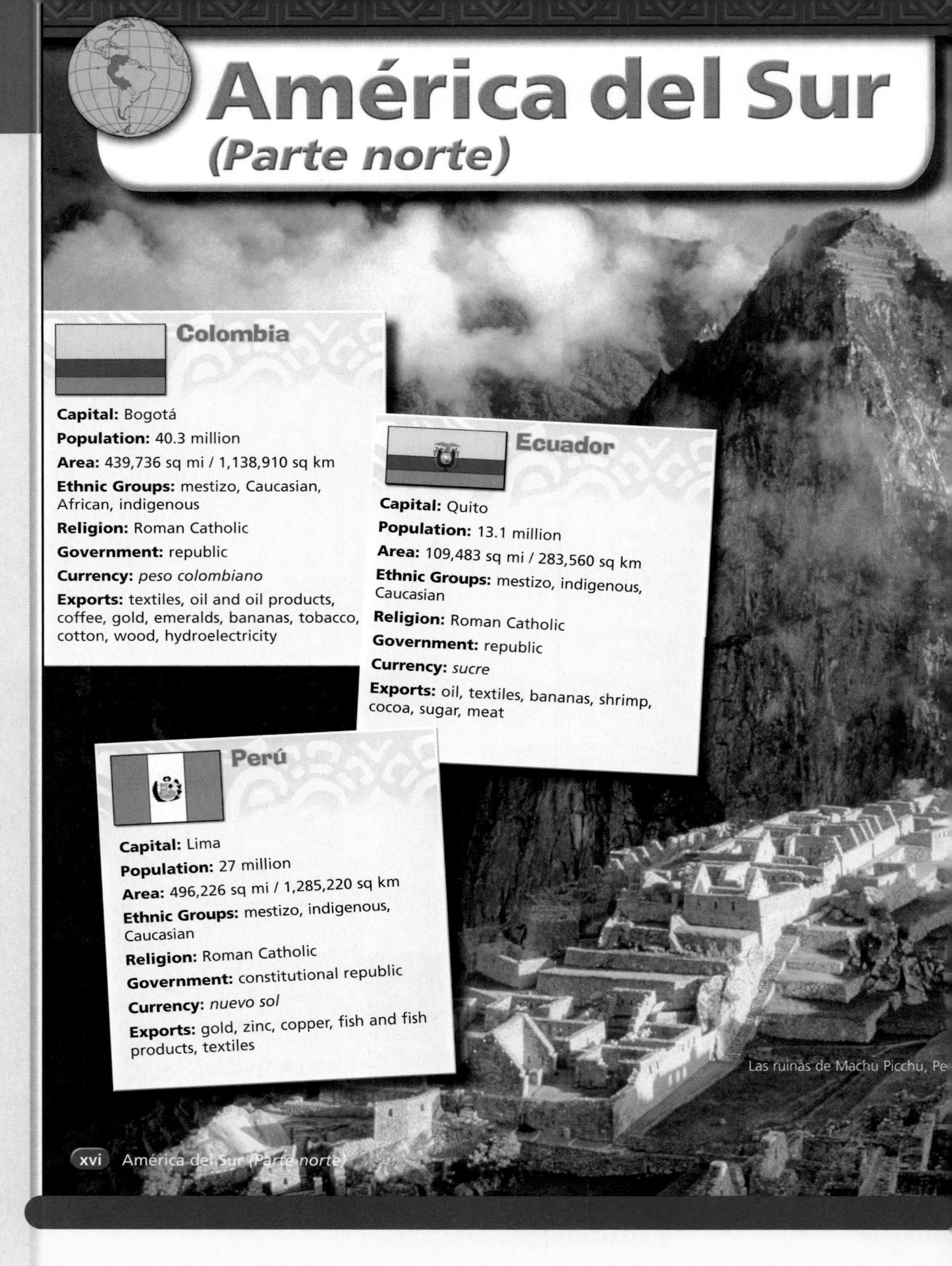

Las ruinas de Machu Picchu, Pe

Enriching Your Teaching

Culture Note

Several words that have become a part of our vocabulary have come from the Quechua languages. These languages were spoken in the Inca empire and are still used in some parts of South America. Some words may be familiar. Have students ever tried beef jerky? The word *jerky* comes from Quechua. And have they seen a llama? That is also a Quechua word, as is *condor*. Why do students think that words for unique natural features and wildlife often come from indigenous languages?

Culture

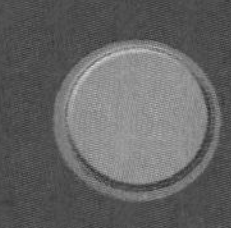

History

1498	Christopher Columbus sights Venezuela on his third voyage.
1502	On his fourth voyage, Columbus explores the Colombian coast.
1532	Francisco Pizarro lands in Peru.
1533	Sebastián de Benalcázar enters Ecuador under the auspices of Pizarro.
1538	Hernando Pizarro, son of Francisco, conquers Bolivian territory.
1811	Venezuela declares its independence from Spain.
1819	Simón Bolívar leads the revolution that unites present-day Colombia and Venezuela as la República de Gran Colombia.
1820	Peru declares its independence from Spain.
1821	Ecuador is liberated from Spain and joins Gran Colombia.
1825	Bolivia declares its independence from Spain.
1830	Ecuador becomes an independent country.
1879	War begins over land disputes between Chile, Peru, and landlocked Bolivia over access to the Pacific.
1970s	Ecuador becomes South America's second largest producer of oil.
1980	Peru begins an economic decline that leads to depression.
1994	Under President Alberto Fujimori, Peru's economy begins to recover.
2000	Fujimori loses popularity and is forced to flee the country.
2002	Venezuela's controversial president, Hugo Chávez, is ousted from power. Three days later he is reinstated.

Social Background

Bolivia and Peru have very large indigenous populations. The two largest groups are the Quechua, descended from the ancient Incas, and the Aymará. Virtually the entire Aymará population of the world—roughly 1.2 million people—lives in the area around Lake Titicaca on the border between Peru and Bolivia.

Culture

Standards: 2.1, 3.1, 4.2

Geography

The southern part of South America contrasts dramatically between the west coast of Chile and the eastern plains of Uruguay. This part of the world, south of the massive country of Brazil, is fascinating in its culture, geography, and history.

Chile's footprint is easy to remember. The country is long and extremely narrow, with a rugged desert coastline punctuated by dozens of undersea volcanic peaks that form islands along its southernmost coast. Like its neighbors to the north—Peru, Ecuador, and Colombia—Chile's principal geographic landmark is the Andes Mountains, which extend the entire length of the country. Chile's population is centered in the Central Valley. This area is only 40 to 80 kilometers wide.

Argentina is almost as long as Chile, but it is much wider. It is geographically and topographically quite diverse. Along its western border, it shares the Andes with Chile. Eastward from the Andes is a flat, rolling plain divided into two territories: Gran Chaco, which it shares with neighboring Paraguay, and the Pampas, which are treeless plains that are the center of the country's prosperous agricultural region. The southernmost plains are part of Patagonia, a dry, desolate, sparsely inhabited region.

Uruguay is one of the smallest countries of South America. Its landscape offers a sharp contrast to the Andean countries. Due to its relatively uniform elevation, Uruguay has a moderate temperature. Along its Atlantic coast, there are beaches, deep lagoons, and wide sand dunes, which extend almost as much as eight kilometers inland. The economy is based largely on agriculture.

Paraguay, to the northeast of Argentina, is characterized mainly by the Paraná plateau, which is 300–600 meters (1,000–2,000 feet) high. The area slopes gently to the Paraná River and boasts spectacular waterfalls. Paraguay's weather averages 60°–80° F. year round.

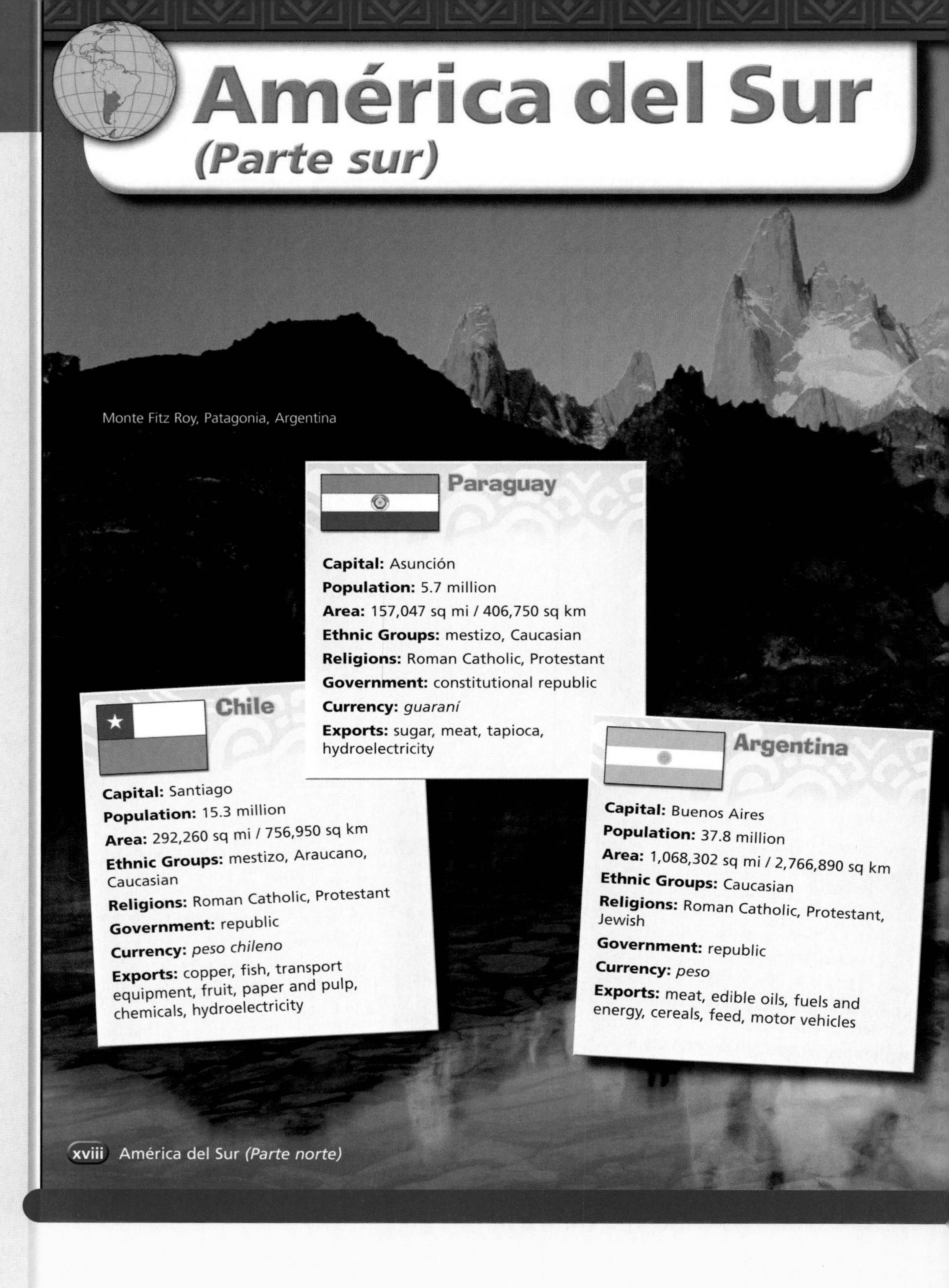

América del Sur
(Parte sur)

Monte Fitz Roy, Patagonia, Argentina

Paraguay

Capital: Asunción
Population: 5.7 million
Area: 157,047 sq mi / 406,750 sq km
Ethnic Groups: mestizo, Caucasian
Religions: Roman Catholic, Protestant
Government: constitutional republic
Currency: *guaraní*
Exports: sugar, meat, tapioca, hydroelectricity

Chile

Capital: Santiago
Population: 15.3 million
Area: 292,260 sq mi / 756,950 sq km
Ethnic Groups: mestizo, Araucano, Caucasian
Religions: Roman Catholic, Protestant
Government: republic
Currency: *peso chileno*
Exports: copper, fish, transport equipment, fruit, paper and pulp, chemicals, hydroelectricity

Argentina

Capital: Buenos Aires
Population: 37.8 million
Area: 1,068,302 sq mi / 2,766,890 sq km
Ethnic Groups: Caucasian
Religions: Roman Catholic, Protestant, Jewish
Government: republic
Currency: *peso*
Exports: meat, edible oils, fuels and energy, cereals, feed, motor vehicles

xviii América del Sur *(Parte norte)*

Uruguay

Capital: Montevideo
Population: 3.3 million
Area: 68,039 sq mi / 176,220 sq km
Ethnic Groups: Caucasian
Religions: Roman Catholic, Protestant
Government: constitutional republic
Currency: *peso uruguayo*
Exports: foods, vehicles, meat, rice, timber

Enriching Your Teaching

Culture Note

The photograph shows one of the world's most breathtaking views. It is in the region of Patagonia, in southern Argentina. Standing at the base of the Monte Fitz Roy, you would see sharp, vertical peaks, hanging glaciers, and trees of twisted and gnarled pine. Even more unnerving would be the continuous moans and creaks underfoot, the sounds of the glaciers constantly shifting.

Culture

History

1520 Portuguese explorer Ferdinand Magellan lands in Chile.

1536 Buenos Aires is founded.

1540 Chile becomes colonial vice-regency of Spain.

1624 First permanent Spanish settlement in Uruguay is founded.

1810 Chile breaks ties with Spain.

1811 Paraguay declares independence.

1814 The Spanish governor is driven from Uruguay.

1815 Representatives from various provinces in Argentina declare independence from Spain.

1816 Bernardo O'Higgins is named supreme dictator of Chile.

1828 Uruguay officially becomes an independent nation.

1839 Chile invades Peru for territorial reasons.

1864–1870 After years of growth under President Carlos Antonio López, Paraguay is devastated in a war with the Triple Alliance (Argentina, Brazil, and Uruguay) over borders.

1906 An earthquake devastates the city of Santiago, Chile.

1946 Juan Perón becomes head of state of Argentina.

1955 Peron's government is ousted.

1970 Salvador Allende Gossens elected president of Chile.

1973 Perón is reinstated as Argentina's president. Allende of Chile dies during Agusto Pinochet's military coup.

1974 Isabel Perón, third wife of Juan Perón, is elected first woman head of state in the Western Hemisphere.

1990 Pinochet is ousted as president of Chile.

Culture

 *Standards:* 2.1, 3.2

Geography

Spain, in the southwest of Europe, occupies most of the Iberian peninsula, which it shares with Portugal. It is surrounded on three sides by the Mediterranean and the Atlantic. The Pyrenees Mountains extend across the northeastern border with France.

The most pronounced topographical feature in Spain is the Meseta Central, or Central Plateau, which slopes downward from north to south and east to west. The eastern coastal plain is narrow, broken by rocky mountains that slope directly to the sea. Barcelona is the only good harbor on Spain's Mediterranean coast.

Spain is separated from Africa by only 13 kilometers at the Strait of Gibraltar. On the southern coast, the people enjoy a subtropical climate; the coldest it gets is around 57° F. It does not rain often, except in the northern mountains. In fact, along the central plateau, the summers are so dry that droughts are not uncommon.

Spain has many environmental concerns, and has embraced international agreements on air quality, marine dumping, and endangered species protection.

Equatorial Guinea is located in Western Africa between Gabon and Cameroon. It includes a mainland territory known as Mbini, and several islands, the largest of which is Bioko Island. The entire country is smaller than the state of Maryland.

The mainland is covered with gently rolling forests and woodland. In contrast, Bioko Island was formed by volcanic eruptions and is quite mountainous, with a steep and rocky coast. Inland, the island is made up of fertile volcanic soils.

Equatorial Guinea has a climate similar to that of the Canary Islands (see inset), its Spanish island neighbor off the coast of Morocco. The weather at Bioko is hot and humid, with a rainy season from December through February.

The primary occupation of the country's nearly half million residents is agriculture. In 1995, however, offshore oil deposits were discovered, which could transform the country's economy.

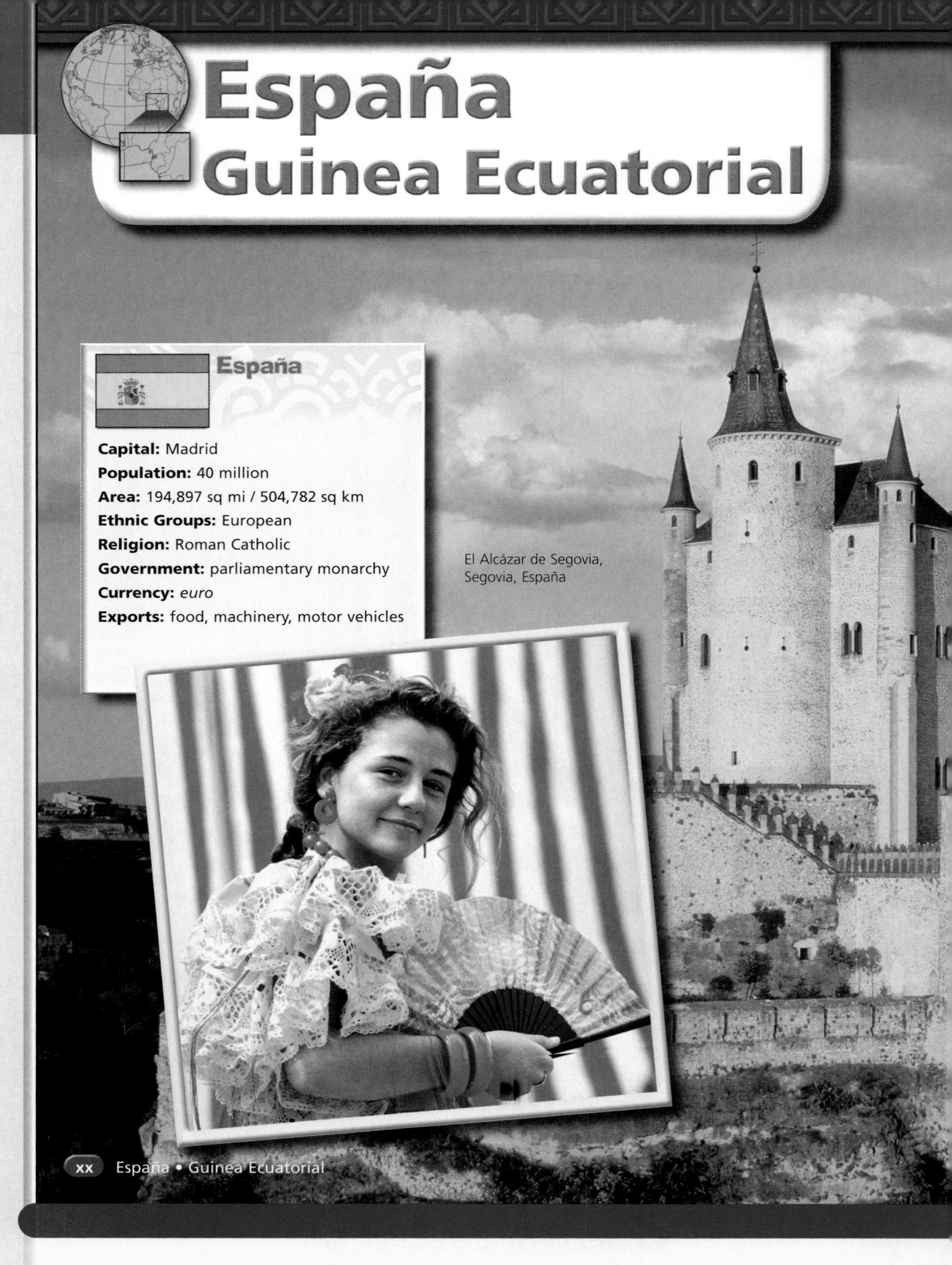

El Alcázar de Segovia, Segovia, España

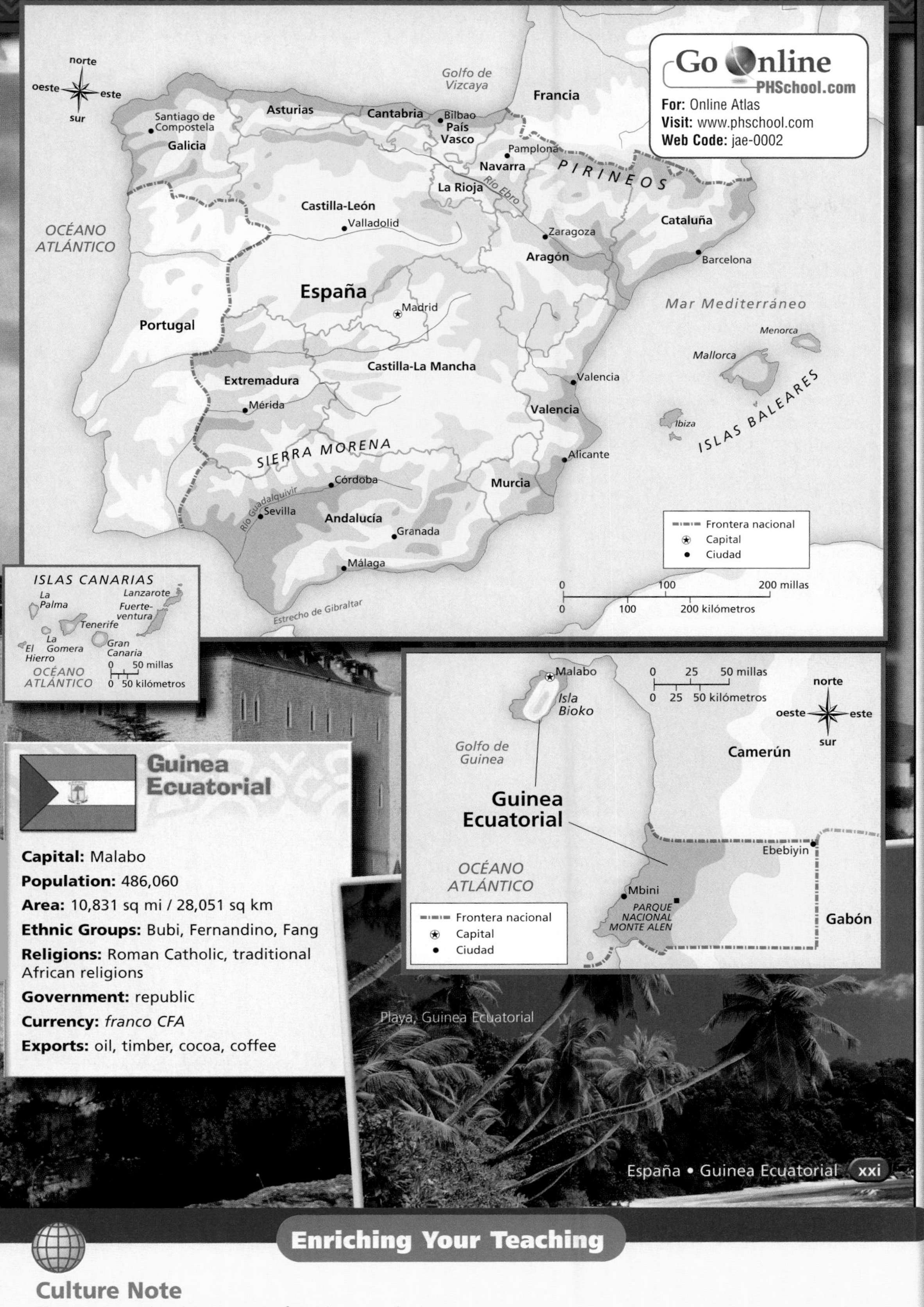

Guinea Ecuatorial

Capital: Malabo
Population: 486,060
Area: 10,831 sq mi / 28,051 sq km
Ethnic Groups: Bubi, Fernandino, Fang
Religions: Roman Catholic, traditional African religions
Government: republic
Currency: *franco CFA*
Exports: oil, timber, cocoa, coffee

Playa, Guinea Ecuatorial

Culture

History

España

1469 The marriage of Ferdinand and Isabella unites the kingdoms of Aragon and Castille.

1492 Spain is created after Grenada falls to Ferdinand and Isabella.

1492 Columbus's first voyage to the Americas.

1519–1580 Spain explores and colonizes throughout the Americas.

1588 The British defeat the Armada, beginning the decline of Spain's hold on large parts of the world.

1826 By 1826, all of the Spanish colonies in the Americas have won their independence.

1898 The Spanish-American War marks the end of the Spanish Empire.

1936–1939 Civil War breaks out. Franco becomes dictator of Spain.

1947 Franco declares Spain a monarchy, but continues to rule.

1955 The United Nations admits Spain as a member.

1975 Franco dies; Juan Carlos I de Borbón becomes king.

1978 A constitution is drafted.

Guinea Ecuatorial

1473 Explorer Fernando Poo claims Equatorial Guinea for Portugal.

1778 Portugal relinquishes the area to Spain.

1904 Bioki Island (known as Fernando Poo) and the mainland (known as Río Muni) become known as Spanish Guinea.

1959 Spanish Guinea becomes an official province of Spain.

1963 Spanish Guinea is granted autonomy.

1972 Spanish Guinea becomes an independent country and is renamed Equatorial Guinea.

Social Background

The Bubi were the original inhabitants of Guinea Ecuatorial. The Fang were indigenous to the mainland and, with the Bubi, migrated to Bioki. The Fernandinos are a mix of Spanish and African people. In Equatorial Guinea, most of the peoples have Spanish first names and African middle and last names, giving them a total of four names. The mother's and father's first names are incorporated into the full name of the child.

Enriching Your Teaching

Culture Note

The Canary Islands are part of Spain—not just a Spanish possession. There are seven main islands and six islets. The Canaries enjoy a comfortable, warm climate most of the year, and their history is steeped in rich folklore.

Culture

Standards: 2.1, 2.2, 3.1

Geography

The geography of the United States is as diverse as its people.

The United States is made up of fifty states and a number of territories, including Puerto Rico, the U.S. Virgin Islands, American Samoa, and Guam. The states vary in size from the largest (Alaska) at 1,593,438 square km (615,230 square miles) to Rhode Island, which is just 3,188 square km (1,231 square miles).

The United States is mountainous, with the Appalachians in the east and the Rocky Mountains, which run north to south in the west-central part of the country. In the center of the country lie flat, fertile plains.

Like the geography, the climate varies greatly from region to region. In general, the northern half of the country experiences cold winters and mild summers. The southern coastal areas are semi-tropical, with mild winters and hot, humid summers, while inland areas in the southwest have a desert climate. The southeastern and east central parts of the country also see more violent weather patterns, such as tornados and hurricanes.

The country is rich in natural resources and has a diverse economy that includes industry, agriculture, technology, and financial services. The eastern part of the country includes uninterrupted urban centers extending from Massachusetts to the Carolinas and is home to one third of the nation's largest corporations. Many of the area's cities are also major tourist attractions.

The central U.S. is home to both industry and agriculture. Rich soils, abundant rainfall, and a long growing season nurture soybean, wheat, corn, and alfalfa crops. Livestock and dairy farms dot the landscape. Manufacturing includes the auto industry, with Ohio and Michigan as its chief centers.

Agriculture, industry, and tourism also dominate the western part of the United States. Wine, cotton, citrus, fruits, and vegetables are the region's principal crops. Aircraft manufacturing, computer technology, aerospace technology, and entertainment are all key factors in the region's economy.

Las grandes llanura

Caras de los Estados Unidos

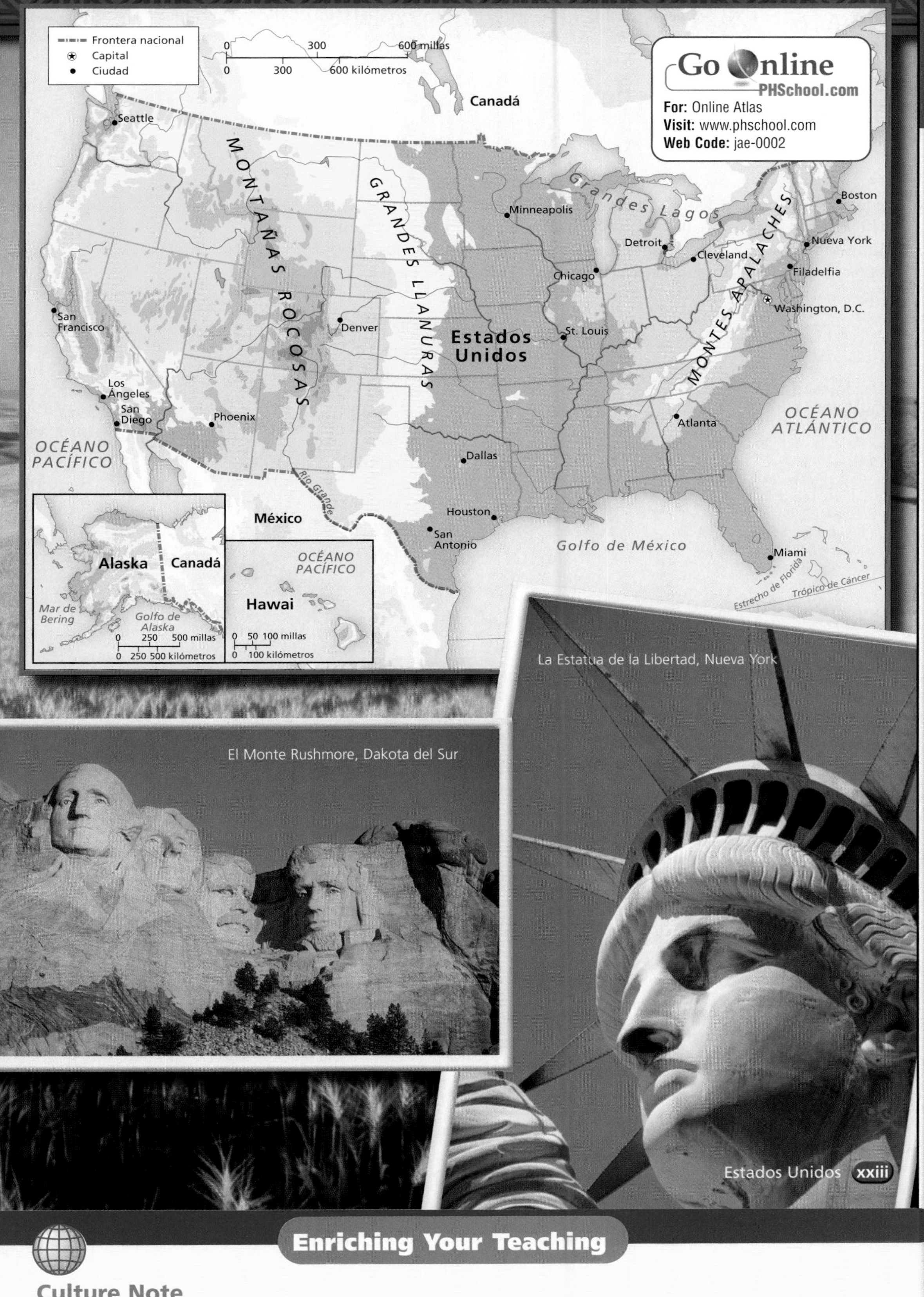

Enriching Your Teaching

Culture Note

The United States is home to many historic monuments. The Statue of Liberty, a gift from the people of France, stands in the harbor in New York City.

South Dakota's Mount Rushmore shows the sculpted faces of four U.S. presidents. Can students identify the presidents depicted? Ask them to name any national or state monuments that may be in or near their community.

Culture

History

1492 Christopher Columbus is the first European to encounter America.

1497–1620 Explorers from Spain, France, Portugal, and England explore and establish colonies.

1763 Britain defeats France in the French and Indian War and gains control of eastern North America.

1775–1781 The Revolutionary War ends with U.S. independence.

1787 U.S. Constitution is ratified.

1803 Louisiana Purchase doubles the size of the U.S.

1821 U.S. purchases Florida from Spain.

1823 The Monroe Doctrine warns European nations not to interfere in the western hemisphere.

1848 U.S. wins the Mexican War and obtains huge areas of land from Texas to California.

1861–1865 U.S. Civil War.

1898 U.S. defeats Spain in the Spanish-American War.

1917 The U.S. joins European allies in fighting World War I.

1941 Japanese attack the U.S. at Pearl Harbor, Hawaii, and U.S. enters World War II.

1945 President Truman orders the use of the atomic bomb against Japan.

1962 U.S.S.R. removes missiles from Cuba, averting war with the U.S.

1969 U.S. astronauts walk on the moon.

2001 Terrorists attack New York (World Trade Center) and Washington (Pentagon).

Social Background

Spanish speakers are rapidly becoming the largest minority group in the United States. Thirty-five million, or 13% of the U.S. population, is considered to be Hispanic. Mexicans make up the majority. Spanish speakers are active in the workforce, and many of their customs and celebrations are becoming part of mainstream U.S. culture. Most U.S. citizens of Hispanic origin live in five states—California, Texas, New York, Florida, and Illinois.

Why Study Spanish?
Presentation

Resources: Video Program: Why Study Spanish?

Suggestions: Ask students why they have chosen to study Spanish and write their ideas on the board. They may have relatives or friends who speak Spanish, or parents who think it's important, or maybe they just think it would be fun to speak another language. Share with students why you chose to study Spanish and how it has enriched your life.

Have students find out how many native Spanish speakers are in your home state or your community. They can present their findings in chart form.

Understand culture:

Have students work in groups and write the following headings on a sheet of paper: Literature, Art, Music, History, and Food. Have them list any examples from Spanish-speaking cultures for these categories that they may know. Have them do interviews or research to add to their lists. Students may be surprised at how much their lives have already been influenced by Spanish-speaking cultures.

Expand career opportunities:

Bring in a list of careers from your guidance center and have students discuss how a professional in each field could use Spanish. Have students look through the newspaper and see how many jobs require Spanish.

Enjoy your Spanish experience:

Some students may have traveled to a Spanish speaking country or may have lived in one. Have students discuss what they did and encourage them to bring in photographs.

Improve your language skills:

Point out to students that some studies suggest a link between language study and higher scores on the verbal portions of standardized exams.

Why Study Spanish?

Over 340 million people who live in Spain, 18 Latin American countries, Puerto Rico, Equatorial Guinea, the Philippines, and the United States speak Spanish. It is the second most common language in the United States and the third most commonly spoken language in the world. Studying Spanish helps you to:

Understand culture The Spanish-speaking world is rich in music, food, art, literature, history, and everyday traditions. Learning about culture helps you understand other people's perspectives, patterns of behavior, and contributions to the world at large. ▶

▲ **Expand career opportunities** Your career options expand as businesses in the twenty-first century look for employees who can communicate in Spanish.

Enjoy your Spanish experiences Climb the Incan ruins of Machu Picchu. Volunteer to build a school in Mexico. Enjoy a meal at a Mexican restaurant. Speaking Spanish enriches your experience whether at home or in another country. ▶

Improve your language skills Studying Spanish improves your first-language skills: vocabulary, grammar, reading, and writing. Research shows your test scores may improve!

Study Tips

Go Online
PHSchool.com
For: More tips for studying Spanish
Visit: www.phschool.com
Web Code: jae-0003

Take risks, relax, and be patient. The goal of studying Spanish is to communicate! So don't wait until you get it perfect. Just start talking, and you'll get better and better! You'll make some mistakes, but the longer you practice, the more improvement you'll see.

Here are some easy tips to help you learn Spanish!

Use what you already know. You already know lots of Spanish words such as *rodeo, hasta la vista, tacos, armadillo, sombrero, piñata, mesa,* and *tango*. Use your knowledge of English to help you figure out new words such as *comunicación, delicioso, limón,* and *oficina*. You'll find Spanish is easier if you use what you already know.

You don't need to understand everything. As you hear or read Spanish, you'll come across words or expressions you don't know. Try to figure out what the meaning might be. Above all, don't stop! Keep on listening or reading. You'll be surprised how much you can understand without knowing every word.

Look for Strategy and ¿Recuerdas? boxes. Throughout **Realidades,** you'll see boxes that provide strategies or remind you of something you've already learned. The information in the boxes will help you learn.

Make flashcards. One way to learn a new word is to make a flashcard. Create a picture of the word on an index card. On the back, write the word in Spanish. Then use the card to study: look at the picture and say the word or look at the picture and write the word.

Have fun! You'll find lots of activities that allow you to work with other students, play games, act out skits, explore the Internet, create projects, and use technology. Try out all of the activities and you'll have fun.

Strategy

Using graphic organizers
Drawing diagrams can help you understand how things are related.

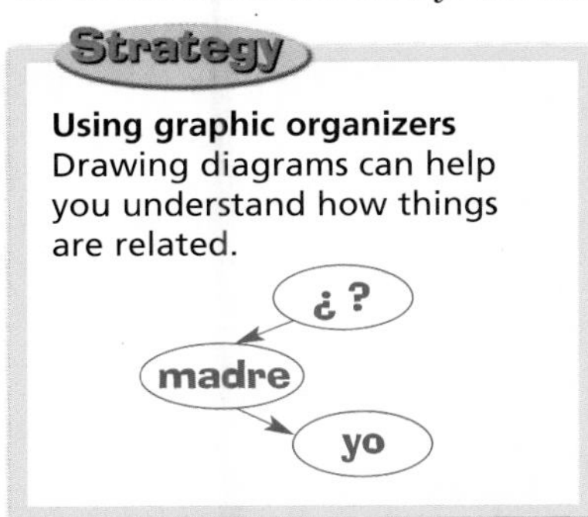

¿Recuerdas?
Adjectives agree in gender with the masculine or feminine nouns they modify:
- **El** bistec es sabros**o**.
- **La** ensalada es sabros**a**.

Study Tips
Presentation
Suggestions:

Using what you already know: Have students brainstorm a list of words or phrases they already know in Spanish. Encourage students to listen to Spanish TV or radio programs, when they can. Although they will not understand everything, they will be training their ears to listen for familiar words (cognates) and accents.

You don't need to understand everything:
Point out that the best language learners are those who don't try to understand every single word. Play a short clip from a Spanish-language advertisement or news broadcast. Demonstrate how visual cues and cognates allow you to understand even when you don't know how to speak.

Look for...boxes:
Have students flip through the book to find examples of *Strategy* and *¿Recuerdas?* boxes. Show them how these can help them learn.

Make flashcards:
The Vocabulary Clip Art in the *Teacher's Resource Book* and on the *Teacher Express CD-ROM* provides a wealth of images you can reproduce for students to use in vocabulary review. Remind them to review their cards daily.

Have fun!:
Some students feel embarrassed or anxious speaking a new language. Remind them they are all in the same position. Tell them that you want them to enjoy their experience, and that they will be doing things in Spanish class that they may not get to do in other classes...such as talking with friends during class!

THEME OVERVIEW

1 **En la escuela**
- Social interactions
- Classroom directions
- Numbers and telling time
- Parts of the body

Vocabulary: greetings; introductions; leave-takings; numbers; time; body parts
Grammar: lexical use of ***estar, ser,*** and plural commands
Cultural Focus: appropriate behavior when greeting someone

2 **En la clase**
- Classroom interactions
- Spanish alphabet
- The calendar

Vocabulary: classroom; date; asking for help
Grammar: nouns; singular definite articles; ***hay; ¿cuántos, -as?***
Cultural Focus: the Aztecs and the Aztec calendar; the Maya and glyphs; holidays

3 **El tiempo**
- The weather
- Seasons

Vocabulary: weather and seasons
Grammar: lexical use of ***hacer***
Cultural Focus: reversed seasons in the Northern and Southern Hemispheres

Theme Project

Pronóstico del tiempo

Overview: Students write a television script and create maps for a weather forecast for four locations in the Western Hemisphere. They then videotape their forecast for the class to view.

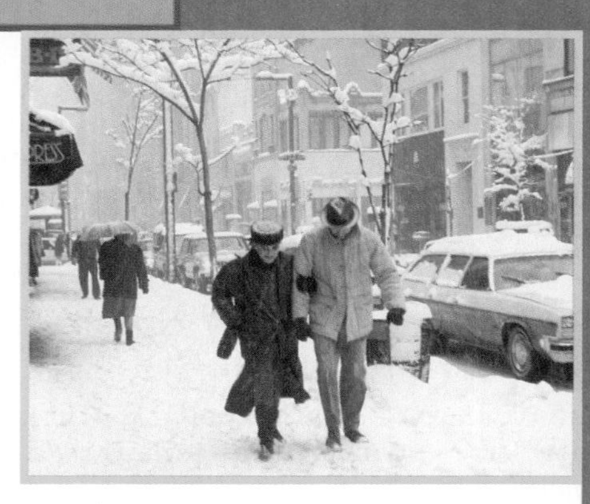

Materials: poster board, markers, video camera, videocassette

Sequence: (suggestions for when to do each step appear throughout the chapter)

STEP **1.** Review instructions so students know what's expected of them. Hand out the "Preliminary Unit Project Instructions and Rubric" from the *Teacher's Resource Book.*

STEP **2.** Students write a rough draft of their weather forecast. They then exchange scripts with a partner for peer editing. Students make corrections based on their partner's comments.

STEP **3.** Students create one or more maps for their forecast on poster board. After completing their map(s), students add drawings or symbols that indicate the weather in each city they plan to talk about and the temperature there.

STEP **4.** Students rehearse their forecast with a partner. Partners give students feedback about the content, accuracy, and presentation of the forecast.

STEP **5.** Students videotape their weather forecast. Show videotapes to the class.

Options:
1. Students present their forecasts to the class "live" instead of videotaping them.
2. Students give a presentation on the weather of one location for each season.

Assessment:
Here is a detailed rubric for assessing this project:
Preliminary Unit Project: *Pronóstico del tiempo*

RUBRIC	Score 1	Score 3	Score 5
Evidence of planning	You submitted no written draft.	Your draft was written but not corrected.	You submitted a corrected draft.
Your use of illustrations	You included no map.	Your map was difficult to read, incomplete, and / or inaccurate.	Your map was easy to read, complete, and accurate.
Your presentation	You did not include the majority of the required elements.	You included some of the following: greeting, name, day, date, weather, and temperature for four locations.	You included all of the following: greeting, name, day, date, weather, and temperature for four locations.

Bulletin Boards

Theme: ***En la escuela***

Ask students to cut out, copy, or download pictures of people greeting each other and saying good-bye, teachers interacting with students, and students interacting with each other. Cluster photos according to what the people are doing in each scene: saying hello, saying goodbye, socializing, asking questions, offering assistance, etc.

Bibliography

Anderson, Robert. *Artists in Their Time: Salvador Dalí.* New York: Franklin Watts, 2002. Dalí's life and work.

Coulter, Laurie, and Sarah Jane English. *Secrets in Stone: All about Maya Hieroglyphs.* Boston: Little, Brown, 2001. Story of the Maya and their language.

MacDonald, Fiona. *Step into Series: Step into the Aztec and Maya Worlds.* New York: Lorenz Books, 1998. History and culture of the Aztecs and Mayans.

Menard, Valerie. *The Latino Holiday Book: From Cinco de Mayo to Día de los Muertos: The Celebrations and Traditions of Hispanic Americans.* New York: Marlowe, 2000. History and description of customs, foods, crafts, and activities associated with holidays celebrated by Spanish speakers.

Hands-on Culture

Recipe: ***Guacamole***

Guacamole is a popular appetizer in Texas and Mexico.

Ingredients:

2 ripe avocados
1 small tomato
1 clove garlic, chopped
1 T. of chopped onion
juice from 1 lemon
2 T. chopped cilantro
salt

1. Cut the avocados in half, remove the pits, and scoop out the pulp with a spoon.
2. Mash the avocados with a fork.
3. Mix in the garlic, onion, lemon juice, and cilantro.
4. Dice the tomato and fold it into the avocado mixture.
5. Add salt to taste.
6. Serve the guacamole with tortilla chips.

Internet Search

Use the keywords to find more information.

1 **Keywords:**

azulejos cerámicos, Salvador Dalí

2 **Keywords:**

Mayan glyphs, Cinco de mayo, Mexican Independence Day

3 **Keywords:**

Andes Mountains, Bariloche, Puerto Montt, Viña del Mar

Game

0 1 2 3 4
5 6 7 8 9

Número

This game practices numbers and is played like Bingo. Use it toward the end of *En la escuela*, after students have learned numbers 1–100.

Players: entire class

Materials: paper and pens with ink of different colors

Rules:

1. Students each prepare their own ***Número*** card by folding a sheet of paper to create 36 squares. To do this, students fold the paper in half vertically, then fold it in thirds. They unfold the paper and repeat the process horizontally. When students unfold the paper again, they should have 36 squares.
2. Students write ***n-ú-m-e-r-o*** in the top six squares. They then fill in the remaining 30 squares with any number from 1–100. The result should look like a Bingo card.
3. Call out a number from 1–100. Note the number you called on a sheet of paper that students can't see. If students have the number on their card, they cross it out. When a player has marked off an entire row of numbers, either vertically, horizontally, or diagonally, he or she calls out ***Número,*** then reads the numbers aloud in Spanish. If the numbers match the ones you have recorded, that student is the winner. If a number is incorrect, play continues until another student calls out ***Número.***
4. Play again, having students use a pen of a different color to cross out numbers.

Variation: Instead of marking off a row, students mark off the four corners, the borders of the square, or the borders of a smaller square within the card.

Overview

Chapter Overview

En la escuela	En la clase	El tiempo	Repaso
INPUT	INPUT	INPUT	REVIEW
Objectives • Greet people at different times of day • Introduce yourself to others • Respond to classroom directions • Begin using numbers • Tell time • Identify parts of the body	**Objectives** • Talk about things in the classroom • Ask questions about new words and phrases • Use the Spanish alphabet to spell words • Talk about things related to the calendar	**Objectives** • Describe weather conditions • Identify the seasons	**Objectives** • Prepare for the test
Vocabulary • Greetings and leave-takings • Introductions • Forms of address • Ask / tell how you and others are • Classroom commands • Numbers 1–100 • Body parts	**Vocabulary** • People and objects in the classroom • Months • Days of the week	**Vocabulary** • Weather expressions • Seasons	**Vocabulary** • Review
Grammar Lexical use of: • ***estar*** • ***ser*** • plural commands	**Grammar** • Nouns • Singular definite articles • ***¿cuántos, -as?*** Lexical use of: • ***hay***	**Grammar** Lexical use of: • ***hacer***	**Grammar** • Review
Culture • Greetings • Social relations • First names in the Spanish-speaking world	**Culture** • Mayan glyphs • The Aztecs • Mexican holidays • The Spanish calendar • ***Los sanfermines*** • Celsius vs. Fahrenheit	**Culture** • Reversed seasons in Northern and Southern Hemispheres	

Learner Support

Strategies
- Sustaining a conversation

Pronunciación
- *el alfabeto*

Exploración del lenguaje
- ***señor, señora,*** and ***señorita***
- ***tú*** vs. ***usted***
- Punctuation and accent marks

Conexiones
- History: Aztec calendar
- Geography: seasons in the Northern and Southern Hemispheres

Beyond the Classroom

Countries
- United States (New Mexico, Texas)
- Argentina
- Mexico
- Chile

Internet
- Vocabulary activities
- Grammar activities
- Internet links
- Self-tests

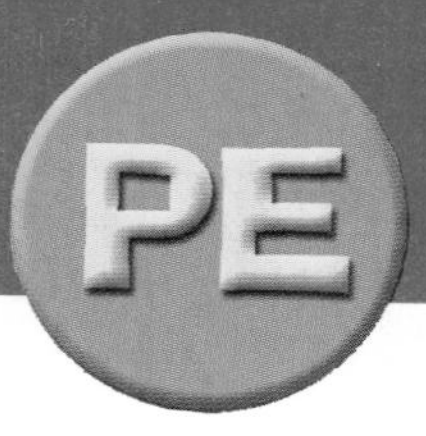

Print Components

TEACHER

Teacher's Resource Book
- Chapter Resource Checklist
- Input Script
- Audio Script
- Answer Keys
- Communicative Activity Blackline Masters
- Situation Cards Blackline Masters
- School-to-Home Connection Letter
- Vocabulary Clip Art

TPR Storytelling Book
- *Para empezar*

STUDENT

Practice Workbook
- Vocabulary: 1–4, 6–9
- Grammar: 5

Writing, Audio & Video Workbook
- *Para empezar*

***Realidades para hispanohablantes* Workbook**
- *En la escuela*
- *En la clase*
- *El tiempo*

Transparencies

Vocabulary & Grammar Transparencies
- *En la escuela:* 21–27
- *En la clase:* 28–30
- *El tiempo:* 31

Practice Answers on Transparencies
- *Para empezar*

Fine Art Transparencies
- Transparencies
- Teacher's Guide

Assessment

Assessment Program
- *Pruebas:*
  - *En la escuela:* PE-1
  - *En la clase:* PE-2
  - *El tiempo:* PE-3
- *Examen del capítulo: Para empezar*

ExamView Test Bank CD-ROM

Test Preparation Workbook

Alternative Assessment
- Performance-Based Speaking
- Assessment Program: Rubrics
- Internet Self-Test
- Situation Cards Blackline Masters
- TPR Storytelling Book: Speaking Task

Technology

iText

Resource Pro CD-ROM
- Lesson Planner
- Teacher Resources
- Clip Art

Video Program VHS and DVD
- *Why Study Spanish?*

Audio Program CDs
- Audio CD 1

Regular Schedule (50 minutes)

For electronic lesson plans: Resource Pro CD-ROM

	Warm-up / Assess	Preview / Present / Practice / Communicate	Wrap-up / Homework Options
DAY 1	**Introduction** (10 min.)	**En la escuela** (35 min.) • Objectives • Presentation: *¡Hola! ¿Cómo te llamas?* • *Actividades* 1, 2, 3 • *Exploración del lenguaje*	**Wrap-up and Homework Options** (5 min.) • Practice Workbook P-1 • Go Online • Heritage Language Learner Workbook • Vocabulary Clip Art
DAY 2	**Warm-up** (10 min.) • Homework check	**En la escuela** (35 min.) • Review: *¡Hola! ¿Cómo te llamas?* • Presentation: *¡Hola! ¿Cómo estás?* • *Exploración del lenguaje* • *Actividades* 4, 5, 6	**Wrap-up and Homework Options** (5 min.) • Practice Workbook P-2 • Go Online
DAY 3	**Warm-up** (10 min.) • Homework check	**En la escuela** (35 min.) • Review: *¡Hola! ¿Cómo estás?* • Presentation: *¡Atención, por favor!* • *Actividad* 7	**Wrap-up and Homework Options** (5 min.) • Practice Workbook P-3
DAY 4	**Warm-up** (10 min.) • Homework check	**En la escuela** (35 min.) • Review: *¡Atención, por favor!* • Presentation: *Los números* • *Actividades* 8, 9, 10	**Wrap-up and Homework Options** (5 min.) • Go Online
DAY 5	**Warm-up** (10 min.) • Homework check	**En la escuela** (35 min.) • Review: *Los números* • Presentation: *¿Qué hora es?* • *Actividades* 11, 12	**Wrap-up and Homework Options** (5 min.) • Practice Workbook P-4 • Go Online
DAY 6	**Warm-up** (10 min.) • Homework check	**En la escuela** (35 min.) • Review: *¿Qué hora es?* • Presentation: *El cuerpo* • *Actividades* 13, 14	**Wrap-up and Homework Options** (5 min.) • Practice Workbook P-5 • *Prueba*: *En la escuela* • Go Online
DAY 7	**Warm-up** (5 min.) • Homework check ✔**Assessment** (10 min.) • *Prueba*: *En la escuela*	**En la clase** (30 min.) • Review: *El cuerpo* • Objectives • Presentation: *La sala de clases* • *Actividades* 1, 2	**Wrap-up and Homework Options** (5 min.) • Practice Workbook P-6 • Go Online
DAY 8	**Warm-up** (10 min.) • Homework check • Return *Prueba*: *En la escuela*	**En la clase** (35 min.) • Review: *La sala de clases* • Presentation: Nouns • *Actividad* 3 • *Exploración del lenguaje* • *Fondo cultural*	**Wrap-up and Homework Options** (5 min.) • Go Online

	Warm-up / Assess	Preview / Present / Practice / Communicate	Wrap-up / Homework Options
DAY 9	**Warm-up** (10 min.) • Homework check	**En la clase** (35 min.) • Review: Nouns • Presentation: *El alfabeto* • *Actividades* 4, 5, 6 • *Juego: Actividad* 7	**Wrap-up and Homework Options** (5 min.) • Go Online: Clip Art
DAY 10	**Warm-up** (10 min.) • Homework check	**En la clase** (35 min.) • Review: *El alfabeto* • Presentation: *El calendario y la fecha* • Presentation: *Los meses del año* • *Actividades* 8, 9	**Wrap-up and Homework Options** (5 min.) • Go Online • Practice Workbook, P-7, P-8
DAY 11	**Warm-up** (5 min.) • Homework check	**En la clase** (40 min.) • Review: *El calendario y la fecha, Los meses del año* • *Actividad* 10, 11, 12 • *Conexiones: La historia* • *Fondo cultural*	**Wrap-up and Homework Options** (5 min.) • Go Online • *Prueba*: *En la clase*
DAY 12	**Warm-up** (5 min.) • Homework check ✔**Assessment** (10 min.) • *Prueba*: *En la clase*	**El tiempo** (30 min.) • Presentation: *¿Qué tiempo hace?* • Presentation: *Las estaciones* • *Actividades* 1, 2, 3	**Wrap-up and Homework Options** (5 min.) • Practice Workbook P-9
DAY 13	**Warm-up** (10 min.) • Homework check	**El tiempo** (35 min.) • Review: *¿Qué tiempo hace?, Las estaciones* • *Actividad* 4, 5, 6 • *Conexiones: La geografía*	**Wrap-up and Homework Options** (5 min.) • Go Online • *Prueba*: *El tiempo*
DAY 14	**Warm-up** (5 min.) • Homework check ✔**Assessment** (10 min.) • *Prueba*: *El tiempo*	**Repaso** (30 min.) • *Vocabulario y gramática* • *Preparación para el examen*	**Wrap-up and Homework Options** (5 min.) • Go Online: Self-test • Practice Workbook P-10, P-11 • *Examen del capítulo*
DAY 15	**Warm-up** (5 min.) • Answer questions ✔**Assessment** (45 min.) • *Examen del capítulo*		

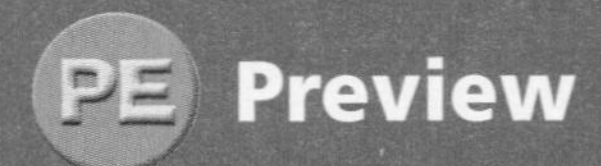

Standards for Para empezar

- To achieve the goals of the Standards, students will:

Communication

1.1 Interpersonal
- Greet and introduce themselves to others
- Use correct leave-taking phrases
- Ask how others are
- Provide others with the correct numbers of or for things
- Ask and provide others the correct time
- Talk about classroom people and objects
- Ask for and provide others the date or day of the week
- Talk about the weather

1.2 Interpretive
- Read and listen to information about appropriate greetings, introductions, and leave-takings
- Read and listen to information about how to ask about how someone is
- Read and listen to information about classroom directions and commands
- Read and listen to information about numbers
- Read and listen to information about telling time
- Read and listen to information about parts of the body
- Read and listen to information about classroom people and objects
- Read and listen to information about the alphabet
- Read and listen to information about the calendar
- Read and listen to information about weather and seasons

1.3 Presentational
- Present information about appropriate greetings, introductions, and leave-takings
- Write the correct numbers of or for things
- Present information about people and things
- Present information about the Spanish alphabet
- Present information about dates and days of the week
- Present information about seasons and the weather

Culture

2.1 Practices and Perspectives
- Talk about ***los sanfermines***

Connections

3.1 Cross-curricular
- Discuss the hieroglyphics of the Maya
- Discuss the Aztec calendar
- Discuss geography and climatology in the southern hemisphere
- Reinforce math and metric conversion skills

Comparisons

4.1 Language
- Explain the difference between ***tú*** and ***usted***
- Discuss that nouns in Spanish are either masculine or feminine
- Discuss some rules of punctuation and accent marks

4.2 Culture
- Compare customs of greetings and introductions
- Compare festivals in which animals play a role

Estudiantes en México

Social relations are somewhat more formal in Spanish-speaking countries than in the United States, since new acquaintances usually greet one another with a handshake. Friends, however, greet each other with a hug or with a kiss on the cheek.

- How does this compare with the way you greet people in the United States?

Estudiantes en Cuzco, Perú

Universal Access

Personalizing the Theme

Ask students how they greet others (both those they know and those they don't) and how they introduce themselves to new people. What body language or gestures are involved? Are there differences according to the age or status of the person, or according to the setting? Are there different greetings for different times of day?

Heritage Language Learners

Have students consider the same questions as in *Personalizing the Theme,* but ask them to extend their answers to the cultural and linguistic differences they may notice between Spanish-speaking cultures that they are familiar with and English-speaking cultures in the United States.

Una escuela en México

Objectives

1 En la escuela

- **Greet people at different times of the day**
- **Introduce yourself to others**
- **Respond to classroom directions**
- **Begin using numbers**
- **Tell time**
- **Identify parts of the body**

2 En la clase

- **Talk about things in the classroom**
- **Ask questions about new words and phrases**
- **Use the Spanish alphabet to spell words**
- **Talk about things related to the calendar**
- **Learn about the Aztec calendar**

3 El tiempo

- **Describe weather conditions**
- **Identify the seasons**
- **Compare weather in the Northern and Southern hemispheres**

Preview

Chapter Opener

Presentation

Suggestions: As you go through the objectives, ask volunteers to identify in English the ways people might introduce themselves, name common classroom objects, or describe the day's weather. Scan the section with students to help familiarize them with the structure of this unit (which follows a different pattern from the other chapters). Explain that the *Para empezar* is an introduction to their language learning that will help them communicate right away, and that the vocabulary and expressions they learn here will then be recycled throughout the book. The emphasis should be on recognition and limited use, not on mastery.

Standards: 4.1

Suggestions: Ask students about the different ways strangers, adults, young people, men, women, and family members greet each other in the United States.

Answers will vary.

Teaching with Photos

Have students look at the three photos. What do they notice about how these students are dressed? How does it compare with the way they dress for school? Explain that there is a great deal of variety in the Spanish-speaking world, and that people in different places do not always dress the same.

Enriching Your Teaching

Planning for Instruction

Resources:

- Teacher Express CD-ROM or Resource Book
  - Teaching resources
  - Lesson Planner
  - Chapter Resource Checklist
  - School-to-Home Connection Letter

Culture Note

Young people in the United States have many colloquialisms for greeting each other. "How's it going," "What's up," and "Hey!" are just a few of them. Teens in Latin America also have informal ways of greeting each other, such as *"¿Cómo te va?"*, *"¿Qué onda?"*, and *"¿Quehúbole?"*

PE Language Input

¡Hola! ¿Cómo te llamas?

Presentation

 *Standards:* 1.2

Resources: Voc. & Gram. Transparencies: 21; Resource Book: Para empezar, Input Script; TPR Storytelling Book: Para empezar; Resource Book: Para empezar, Clip Art; Resource Book: Para empezar, Audio Program: CD Para empezar, Track 1

Focus: Presenting different ways to greet friends and adults in the morning, afternoon, and evening

Suggestions: Use the Input Script from the *Teacher's Resource Book* or the stories from the *TPR Storytelling Book* any time you have new vocabulary to introduce, or use other ideas that work for you. Show the transparencies to introduce the words. Be sure students notice the age differences of the speakers and the different times of day the conversations take place. When students have become familiar with the conversations, ask them to greet you and one another. Point out the *Nota*, and explain that these provide additional explanations and useful information.

Exploración del lenguaje

Presentation

 *Standards:* 4.1

Focus: Explaining different ways to address others

Suggestions: Write examples on the board such as ***Señor Trujillo*** and then write the abbreviation ***Sr. Trujillo.*** Point out the comparison in English to students. They may be surprised at the relative formality with which adults are addressed in Spanish. Have students identify school personnel with the new Spanish titles.

1 En la escuela

¡Hola! ¿Cómo te llamas?

Objectives

- Greet people at different times of the day
- Introduce yourself to others
- Respond to classroom directions
- Begin using numbers
- Tell time
- Identify parts of the body

—**¡Buenos días, señor!**
—¡Buenos días! **¿Cómo te llamas?**
—**Me llamo** Felipe.

—**¡Buenas tardes, señora!**
—¡Buenas tardes! ¿Cómo te llamas?
—Me llamo Beatriz.
—**Mucho gusto.**
—**Encantada.**

Nota

A woman or girl says *encantada*.
A man or boy says *encantado*.

—**¡Buenas noches!** ¿Cómo te llamas?
—**¡Hola!** Me llamo Graciela. **¿Y tú?**
—Me llamo Lorenzo.
—Mucho gusto.
—**Igualmente.**

Exploración del lenguaje

Señor, señora, señorita

The words *señor, señora,* and *señorita* mean "sir," "madam," and "miss" when used alone. When they are used with people's last names they mean "Mr.," "Mrs.," and "Miss," and are abbreviated *Sr., Sra.,* and *Srta.* Note that the abbreviations are capitalized.

In Spanish you should address adults as *señor, señora,* or *señorita* or use the titles *Sr., Sra.,* and *Srta.* with their last names.

Universal Access

Students with Learning Difficulties

If students have problems identifying individual phrases in context, provide them with a list of specific words and phrases that you want them to know. Model different ways in which they can combine the words and phrases for communication.

Advanced Learners

Explain that *¿Cómo te llamas?* and *Me llamo...* do not literally mean "What's your name?" and "My name is...." Use this as an opportunity to demonstrate that languages cannot be translated on a word-to-word basis. Some students may also benefit from further explanation of the *Nota* and of agreement of adjectives.

Escuchar

Buenos días

Listen as people greet each other. Then point to the clock that indicates the time of day when the greetings are probably taking place.

a. 

b. 

c. 

Hablar

¿Cómo te llamas?

Follow the model to ask the name of the classmate on your right. After you have introduced yourself, do the same with the person on your left.

Modelo

A —*¡Hola! ¿Cómo te llamas?*
B —*Me llamo David. ¿Y tú?*
A —*Me llamo Antonio. Mucho gusto.*
B —*Igualmente.*
o: *Encantado.*

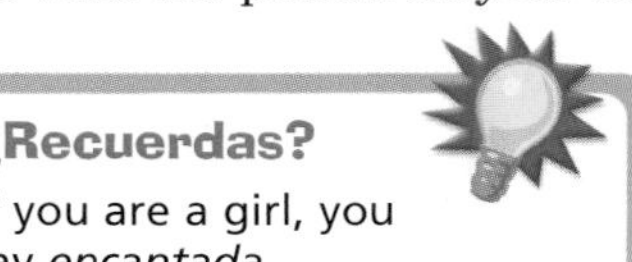
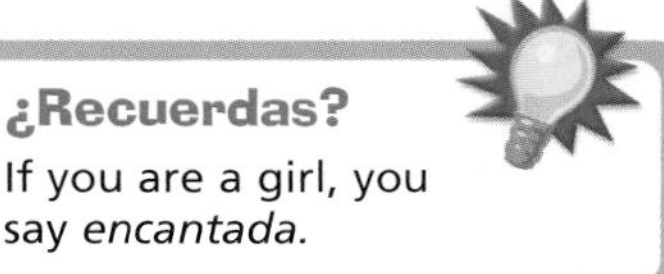

¿Recuerdas?

If you are a girl, you say *encantada*.

Hablar

¡Hola!

Work with a partner. Choose a clock from Actividad 1 and greet each other appropriately for the time of day. Then find out your partner's name. Follow the model. Change partners and repeat.

Modelo

A —*Buenas tardes.*
B —*Buenas tardes. ¿Cómo te llamas?*
A —*Me llamo Paco. ¿Y tú?*
B —*Me llamo Lourdes. Mucho gusto.*
A —*Igualmente.*

For: List of Spanish names
Visit: www.phschool.com
Web Code: jad-0001

Los nombres

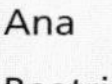

Chicas

Alicia
Ana
Beatriz
Carmen
Cristina
Dolores (Lola)
Elena
Gloria
Inés
Isabel (Isa)
Juana
Luisa
Luz María (Luzma)
Margarita
María
María Eugenia (Maru)
Marta
Teresa (Tere)

Chicos

Alejandro
Antonio (Toño)
Carlos (Chacho, Cacho)
Diego
Eduardo (Edu)
Federico (Kiko)
Francisco (Paco)
Guillermo (Guille)
Jorge
José (Pepe)
Juan
Manuel (Manolo)
Miguel
Pablo
Pedro
Ricardo
Roberto
Tomás

Enriching Your Teaching

Culture Note

In Spain and many other Spanish-speaking countries, ***buenos días*** is used until noon. ***Buenas tardes*** is used from noon until the evening meal. ***Buenas noches*** is considered both a greeting and a farewell.

Teacher-to-Teacher

Bring in a kitchen timer and set it for the time you want to allot for each paired activity. When the bell rings, stop the activity, review the task with students if necessary, and move on. The timer will help you keep track of the time and will help students focus.

Practice and Communicate

Actividad 1  *Standards:* 1.2

Resources: Audio Program: CD Para empezar, Track 2; Resource Book: Para empezar, Audio Script Practice Answers on Transparencies

Focus: Listening to understand greetings

Suggestions: In all *Escuchar* activities, you may either play the *Audio CD* or read the script. Walk around the room to monitor comprehension and check that students are pointing to the correct clocks.

Script and Answers:

1. **—Buenas noches, señor Rodríguez.**
   —Hola, Roberto. ***(c)***
2. **—Buenas tardes, Alicia.**
   —Buenas tardes, señora. ***(b)***
3. **—Buenos días, señora Gómez.**
   —Hola, Ana. ***(a)***
4. **—Buenos días, Pablo.**
   —Buenos días, señor. ***(a)***
5. **—Buenas noches, Jorge.**
   —Hola, María. ***(c)***
6. **—Hola, Juana.**
   —Buenas tardes, Catalina. ***(b)***

Actividad 2  *Standards:* 1.1

Focus: Practicing introductions

Suggestions: Model a personalized version of the conversation with a volunteer and go over roles. Students will need to learn how to do paired practice. Point out that the *¿Recuerdas?* will remind students of things they've already learned.

Actividad 3  *Standards:* 1.1

Focus: Practicing greetings appropriate to time of day; asking and telling names

Suggestions: If you wish, have students choose Spanish names to use in class. Allow students to repeat the activity with several partners.

PE Language Input

¡Hola! ¿Cómo estás?

Presentation

 *Standards:* 1.2

Resources: Voc. & Gram. Transparencies: 22; Audio Program: CD Para empezar, Track 3

Focus: Introducing expressions used to ask and answer how someone is

Suggestions: Use the transparencies and the dialogue to help students guess the meanings of the unfamiliar words in blue. Direct attention to the *¿Recuerdas?* Play the *Audio CD* or read the conversations beneath the pictures. Then role-play the conversations with students. Draw a rising sun at one end of the blackboard, a noontime sun a little to the right with a dividing line under it, a setting sun a little further to the right, and a moon at the far end. Position pairs of students at various points along the board, and have the class identify whether they would say ***buenos días, buenas tardes,*** or ***buenas noches,*** depending on where they are. Point out that ***hasta*** + an expression of time means that you're saying good-bye until that time.

Additional Resources

- Writing, Audio & Video Workbook: Audio Activity 1, Track 5

¡Hola! ¿Cómo estás?

—Buenos días, Adela.
¿Cómo estás?
—**Bien, gracias,** Sr. Ruiz.
¿Y usted?
—Bien, gracias.

—Buenas tardes, Sr. Ruiz.
¿Cómo está Ud.?
—**Muy** bien, gracias. ¿Y tú?
—Bien, gracias.

—Buenas noches, Miguel.
¿Qué tal?
—**Regular.** ¿Y tú, Carlos?
¿Qué pasa?
—**Nada.**

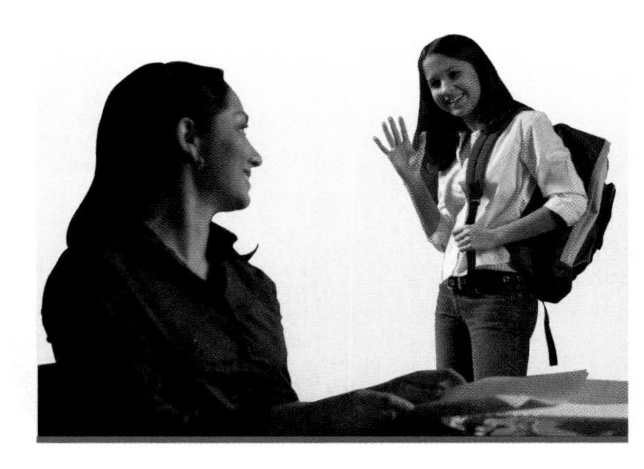

—**¡Adiós, Srta.** Moreno!
¡Hasta luego!
—**¡Hasta mañana!**

—¡Hasta luego, Juan!
—**¡Nos vemos!**

¿Recuerdas?

Señor, señora, and *señorita* are abbreviated to ***Sr., Sra.,*** and ***Srta.*** before a person's last name.

Universal Access

Students with Learning Difficulties

Have students create a section in their notebook for vocabulary and a separate section for grammar. For each chapter, students can enter new vocabulary and grammar concepts into their respective sections. Allow students to accompany vocabulary words with pictures and English translations, as needed.

Heritage Language Learners

Many students who already speak Spanish may have little or no formal experience with the written language. Ask these students to write new versions of the dialogues above, personalizing them in some way. Have them pay special attention to spelling. You can use this exercise to informally assess their written Spanish.

Exploración del lenguaje

Tú vs. *usted*

For most Spanish speakers there are two ways to say "you": *tú* and *usted.* Use *tú* when speaking to friends, family, people your own age, children, and pets. *Usted* is formal. Use it to show respect and when talking to people you don't know well, older people, and people in positions of authority. In writing, *usted* is almost always abbreviated *Ud.,* with a capital *U.*

Would you say *tú* or *Ud.* when talking to the following people?

- your brother
- your teacher
- your best friend
- your friend's mother
- your cat
- your principal
- a new acquaintance who is your age

Escuchar

¿Hola o adiós?

Make a chart on your paper with two columns. Label one *Greeting,* the other *Leaving.* Number your paper from 1–8. As you hear each greeting or leave-taking, place a check mark in the appropriate column next to the number.

	Greeting	Leaving
1.		
2.		
3.		

Hablar

¡Hola! ¿Qué tal?

Work with a partner. Greet each other and ask how your partner is. Say good-bye. Then change partners and repeat.

Modelo

A —*Hola, Luisa. ¿Qué tal?*
B —*Bien, Lupe. ¿Y tú?*
A —*Regular. ¡Hasta luego!*
B —*¡Adiós!*

Leer

Mucho gusto

Read the conversation on the right, then reply *sí* or *no* to these statements.

1. The people in the dialogue knew each other already.
2. The teacher is a man.
3. We know the last names of both people.
4. The student talks to the teacher in a formal tone.
5. Neither person is feeling well today.

Profesor: Buenos días. Me llamo Señor Guzmán. ¿Y tú?
Estudiante: Me llamo María Rosa Hernández. Mucho gusto.
Profesor: Igualmente. ¿Cómo estás, María Rosa?
Estudiante: Bien, gracias. ¿Y Ud.?
Profesor: Muy bien, gracias. Hasta luego.
Estudiante: Adiós, señor.

Más práctica
Practice Workbook P-2

Enriching Your Teaching

Culture Note

In Spain, a newborn child is generally given a first name, no middle name, and two surnames—one from each parent. Usually, the father's surname is first and the mother's surname is second. This is different in the United States, where a child is given a first name, perhaps a middle name, and one last name, usually the father's surname.

Teacher-to-Teacher

To keep students on task and speaking Spanish during a paired activity, circulate and place star stickers on the desks of students who are participating. Give the stars a value—three stars equals a bonus point, for example. When using this system, remind students that stars can be taken away for not participating or for speaking English.

Practice and Communicate

Exploración del lenguaje

Presentation

Standards: 4.1

Resources: Practice Answers on Transparencies

Suggestions: Tell students to use ***Ud.*** for anybody that they call by their last name.

Answers:

1. tú 2. usted 3. tú 4. usted
5. tú 6. usted 7. tú

Standards: 1.2

Resources: Audio Program: CD Para empezar, Track 4; Resource Book: Para empezar, Audio Script; Practice Answers on Transparencies

Focus: Listening to understand greetings

Suggestions: Draw the chart on the board as a model.

Script and Answers:

1. **Hola, Juan. ¿Qué pasa? *(greeting)***
2. **Adiós, Miguel. *(leaving)***
3. **Buenos días, señor García. *(greeting)***
4. **Hola, Elena. *(greeting)***
5. **Nos vemos. *(leaving)***
6. **Hasta mañana, señor Pérez. *(leaving)***
7. **Buenas noches, señora. *(greeting)***
8. **Hasta luego, Ana. *(leaving)***

Standards: 1.1

Focus: Using greetings

Suggestions: Have students switch roles so that each one can both ask and answer questions.

Standards: 1.2, 1.3

Resources: Practice Answers on Transparencies

Focus: Reading comprehension

Suggestions: If the answer is "No," have students provide correct information.

Answers:

1. no 2. sí 3. sí 4. sí 5. no

Language Input

¡Atención, por favor!

Presentation

 *Standards:* 1.2

Resources: Voc. & Gram. Transparencies: 23; Audio Program: CD Para empezar, Track 6; Resource Book: Para empezar, Audio Script

Focus: Presenting common classroom commands

Suggestions: Play the *Audio CD* or refer to the text under the pictures. Dramatize the classroom commands while saying them aloud or playing the CD. Have students guess the commands. Then say them again and have the class respond as asked. Try to do as much classroom management in Spanish as possible.

 *Standards:* 1.2

Resources: Audio Program: CD Para empezar, Track 7; Resource Book: Para empezar, Audio Script; Practice Answers on Transparencies

Focus: Listening and responding to classroom commands

Suggestions: Play the *Audio CD* or read the script. Have students simply listen the first time. Then play or read the script again, having students act out the commands.

Script and Answers:

1. **Abran el libro.** ***(open the book)***
2. **Levántense.** ***(stand up)***
3. **Repitan: Buenas tardes.** ***(repeat: Buenas tardes.)***
4. **Siéntense.** ***(sit down)***
5. **Cierren el libro.** ***(close the book)***
6. **Saquen una hoja de papel.** ***(take out a sheet of paper)***

Los números

Presentation

 *Standards:* 1.2

Resources: Voc. & Gram. Transparencies: 24; Audio Program: CD Para empezar, Track 8

Suggestions: Have students practice by playing bingo or rolling number cubes.

¡Atención, por favor!

—¡Silencio, **por favor!** Abran el libro en la página diez.

—¡Atención! Cierren el libro.

—Repitan, por favor: Buenos días.

—Buenos días.

—Levántense, por favor.

—Siéntense, por favor.

—Saquen una hoja de papel. Escriban los números.

—Entreguen sus hojas de papel.

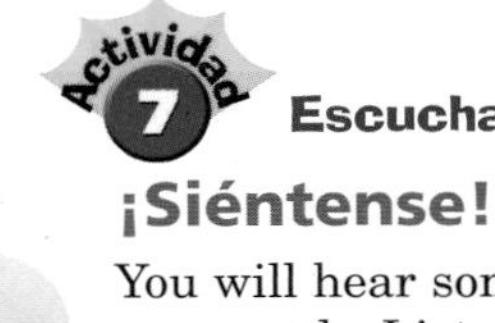

Escuchar

¡Siéntense!

You will hear some classroom commands. Listen carefully and act them out.

Más práctica

Practice Workbook P-3

Universal Access

Students with Special Needs

For students who find the commands difficult to act out, have them discuss with you other ways they might indicate comprehension of the commands. Depending on the students, these might include simple hand or arm movements.

Advanced Learners

Have students turn to p. 100 in their textbook and then flip through the pages, randomly stopping ten times. They should say or write the page number each time they stop. Point out that the numbers are written out on each page.

Los números

cero uno dos tres cuatro

      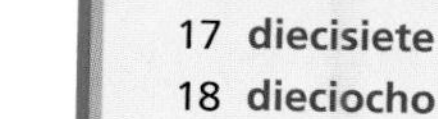

cinco seis siete ocho nueve

10	diez	21	veintiuno, . . .
11	once	30	treinta
12	doce	31	treinta y uno, . . .
13	trece	40	cuarenta
14	catorce	50	cincuenta
15	quince	60	sesenta
16	dieciséis	70	setenta
17	diecisiete	80	ochenta
18	dieciocho	90	noventa
19	diecinueve	100	cien
20	veinte		

Actividad 8 Hablar

Las combinaciones

It is the first day of school, and you are helping some Spanish-speaking exchange students learn their locker combinations. Read the combinations that you see below.

1. 09-26-17
2. 16-07-30
3. 13-20-11
4. 22-19-29
5. 04-12-27
6. 15-01-28
7. 10-06-14
8. 18-21-25

Actividad 9 Pensar/Hablar

Los números

With a partner, provide the missing numbers in each sequence. Then say the number sequence aloud.

1. 1, 2, 3, . . . 10
2. 2, 4, 6, . . . 20
3. 1, 3, 5, . . . 19
4. 5, 10, 15, . . . 60
5. 3, 6, 9, . . . 39
6. 10, 20, 30, . . . 100

Go Online PHSchool.com
For: More practice: *los números*
Visit: www.phschool.com
Web Code: jad-0002

Actividad 10 Hablar/Escuchar/Escribir

Números y más números

Tell your partner these numbers. He or she will write them using numerals, not words. Then check your partner's work.

1. the phone numbers used to dial for information and emergencies
2. the bar code number on the back of your Spanish book
3. the number of months until your next birthday
4. the number of students in your math class
5. the number of minutes it takes you to get from your home to school

Azulejos *(tiles)* cerámicos

Enriching Your Teaching

Teacher-to-Teacher

Give each student a number written large on a piece of paper. Have them tape the numbers to their shirts. Then have the class stand in a circle and clap their hands rhythmically. The student who is ***uno*** says his or her number and then calls out another number. The student who has that number says it, then calls out another number (e.g., *"¡uno, diez!"*; *diez* then responds, saying *"¡diez, cuatro!"*). All the while, students clap the rhythm. If someone makes a mistake, the person and number are out.

Practice and Communicate

Actividad 8 *Standards:* 1.1

Resources: Practice Answers on Transparencies

Focus: Reading numbers

Suggestions: Remind students not to say the zero for single digits in a locker combination.

Answers:
1. nueve, veintiséis, diecisiete
2. dieciséis, siete, treinta
3. trece, veinte, once
4. veintidós, diecinueve, veintinueve
5. cuatro, doce, veintisiete
6. quince, uno, veintiocho
7. diez, seis, catorce
8. dieciocho, veintiuno, veinticinco

Actividad 9 *Standards:* 1.1

Resources: Practice Answers on Transparencies

Focus: Practicing with numbers

Suggestions: Remind students that each item is a different sequence.

Answers:
1. cuatro, cinco, seis, siete, ocho, nueve
2. ocho, diez, doce, catorce, dieciséis, dieciocho
3. siete, nueve, once, trece, quince, diecisiete
4. veinte, veinticinco, treinta, treinta y cinco, cuarenta, cuarenta y cinco, cincuenta, cincuenta y cinco
5. doce, quince, dieciocho, veintiuno, veinticuatro, veintisiete, treinta, treinta y tres, treinta y seis
6. cuarenta, cincuenta, sesenta, setenta, ochenta, noventa

Actividad 10 *Standards:* 1.1, 1.3

Focus: Using numbers

Suggestions: Verify answers using a transparency.

Answers will vary.

Additional Resources

- Resource Book: Para empezar, Communicative Activity BLM

PE Language Input

¿Qué hora es?

Presentation

Standards: 1.2

Resources: Voc. & Gram. Transparencies: 25–26; Audio Program: CD Para empezar, Track 9

Focus: Telling time

Suggestions: Show the transparencies to present the expressions for telling time. Pretend that your watch is broken and ask: *"¿Qué hora es?"* Point to a clock, and have students tell you the time. Mark different times on the clock transparency. Have students say the times aloud.

Standards: 1.1

Resources: Practice Answers on Transparencies

Focus: Asking and telling the time

Suggestions: Point to the classroom clock and prompt students to say what time it is.

Answers:

1. Son las siete.
2. Son las tres y media / treinta.
3. Es la una y cuarto / quince.
4. Son las dos y veinte.
5. Son las nueve y cuarenta. / Son las diez menos veinte.
6. Son las doce y cincuenta. / Es la una menos diez.

Standards: 1.2

Resources: Audio Program: CD Cap. Para empezar, Track 10; Resource Book: Cap. Para empezar, Audio Script; Practice Answers on Transparencies

Focus: Listening to understand time of day

Suggestions: When the activity is complete, repeat each time of day again and ask volunteers for the answers.

Script and Answers:

1. Es la una y media. *(1:30)*
2. Son las diez. *(10:00)*
3. Son las once y cinco. *(11:05)*
4. Son las doce. *(12:00)*
5. Son las seis y media. *(6:30)*
6. Son las siete y cuarenta y cinco. *(7:45)*
7. Son las nueve y veinte. *(9:20)*
8. Son las tres y treinta y cinco. *(3:35)*

¿Qué hora es?

In Spanish, to ask what time it is, you say *¿Qué hora es?* Here are some answers:

Es la una.

Son las dos.

Son las tres y cinco.

Son las cuatro y diez.

Son las cinco y cuarto.

Son las seis y media.

Son las siete menos veinte.

Son las ocho y cincuenta y dos.

Hablar

¿Qué hora es?

Work with a partner to ask and answer questions about the time. Use these clocks.

Modelo

A —*¿Qué hora es?*
B —*Son las diez.*

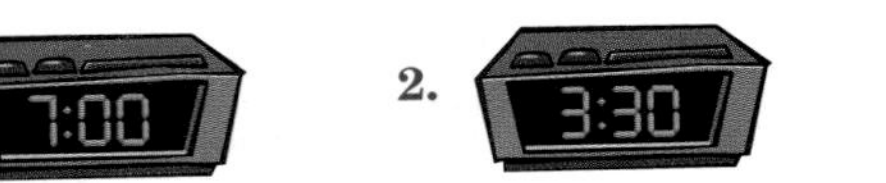

1. 2. 3. 4. 5. 6. (12:50)

Escuchar

La hora

Write the numbers 1–8 on a sheet of paper. Write the times you hear with numerals—1:00, 2:15, and so on.

Más práctica

Practice Workbook P-4

La persistencia de la memoria (1931), Salvador Dalí

Universal Access

Students with Learning Difficulties

Some students may be unable to read clocks with faces and hands. If so, provide times on digital clocks.

Advanced Learners

Have students write a television program guide with the names and times of their favorite programs. Suggest that they use the newspaper listings as a model. Have students exchange program guides. One student will say a time, and the other student will say the name of the program.

El cuerpo

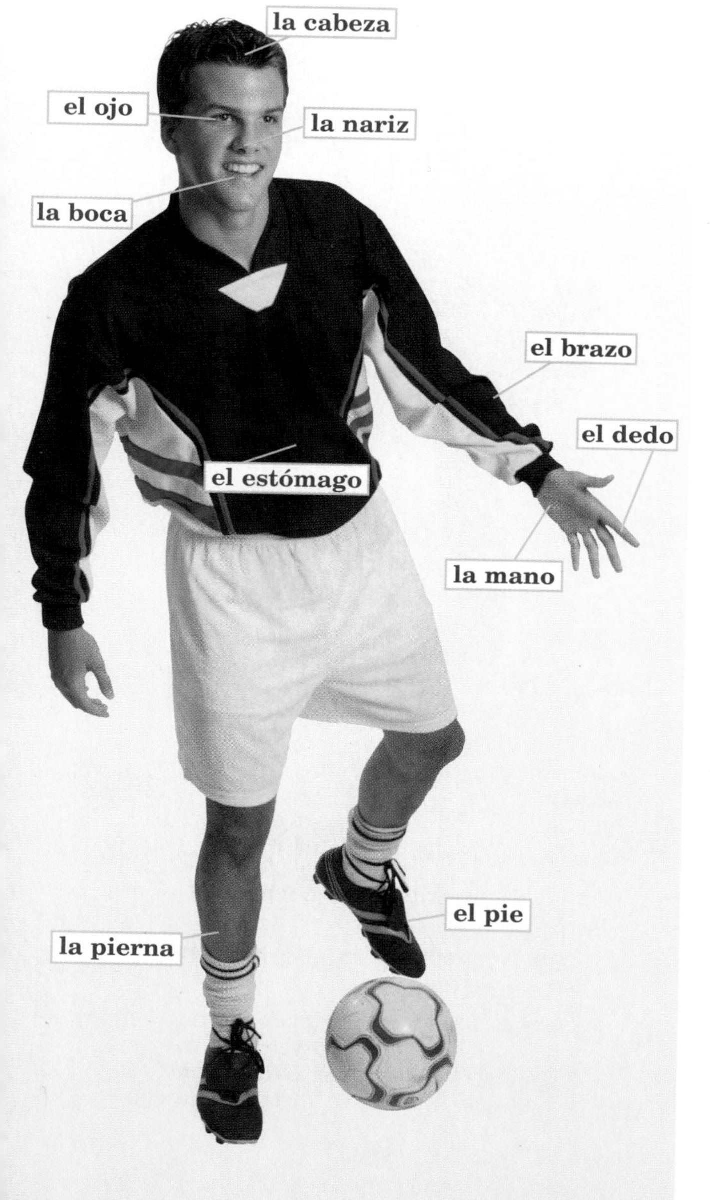

"¡Ay! Me duele el pie."

Actividad 13 — Escuchar

Señalen

You will hear some commands. Listen carefully and act out the commands. When you hear the word *señalen,* you should point to that body part.

Actividad 14 — Escuchar

Juego

Play the game *Simón dice . . .* (Simon Says). Listen and follow the leader's directions. Remember that if the leader does not say *"Simón dice,"* you should not do the action.

Más práctica

Practice Workbook P-5

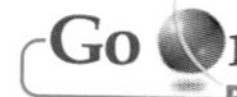

Go Online PHSchool.com

For: More practice: *el cuerpo*
Visit: www.phschool.com
Web Code: jad-0003

Enriching Your Teaching

Teacher-to-Teacher

Have students create a poster of a "creature" using images cut from magazines or newspapers. Their creature can have six arms, four legs, etc. Have them label each of the body parts. Provide plurals as necessary. Display the art in the classroom and ask students true or false questions about each one, or have them list the body parts that they see.

Language Input

El cuerpo

Presentation

Standards: 1.2

Resources: Voc. & Gram. Transparencies: 27; Audio Program: CD Para empezar, Track 12

Focus: Vocabulary for body parts

Suggestions: Play the *Audio CD* and show the transparency. Pretend to be in pain and say: *¡Ay! Me duele el pie.* Continue with the rest of the vocabulary. Note that only singular body parts are used. Point out the use of the article.

Actividad 13

Standards: 1.2

Resources: Audio Program: CD Para empezar, Track 13; Resource Guide: Para empezar, Audio Script; Practice Answers on Transparencies

Focus: Comprehending commands

Suggestions: Play the *Audio CD* or read the script twice. Suggest that students listen first, then perform the action.

Script and Answers:

1. **Señalen la nariz.** ***(nose)***
2. **Señalen el estómago.** ***(stomach)***
3. **Señalen la mano.** ***(hand)***
4. **Señalen la cabeza.** ***(head)***
5. **Señalen el pie.** ***(foot)***
6. **Señalen el brazo.** ***(arm)***

Actividad 14

Standards: 1.2

Focus: Following directions

Suggestions: Have students take turns playing leader in small groups.

Answers will vary.

Additional Resources

- Writing, Audio & Video Workbook: Audio Activity 2, Track 11
- Writing, Audio & Video Workbook: Para empezar, Writing Activity 6

Assessment

- Prueba PE-1: En la escuela

Language Input

La sala de clases

Presentation

Standards: 1.2

Resources: Voc. & Gram. Transparencies: 28; Audio Program: CD Para empezar, Track 14

Focus: Presenting classroom vocabulary

Suggestions: Use the commands from p. 6 to introduce and practice these vocabulary items, using actual items in your classroom. Combine these with other commands for students to carry out. Tell students that for the rest of the year, if they want to know either the Spanish or English word for something, you will only respond if they use the question format presented here.

Standards: 1.2

Resources: Audio Program: CD Para empezar, Track 15; Resource Book: Para empezar, Audio Script; Practice Answers on Transparencies

Focus: Listening comprehension of vocabulary for classroom objects

Suggestions: Tell students that if an object is not visible in the classroom, they may point to the picture in the book. Explain the *También se dice...* but tell students that they will not have to remember these words.

Script and Answers:

1. **la hoja de papel *(sheet of paper)***
2. **el libro *(book)***
3. **la profesora *(el profesor) (teacher)***
4. **el pupitre *(student desk)***
5. **el bolígrafo *(pen)***
6. **el cuaderno *(notebook)***
7. **el lápiz *(pencil)***
8. **la carpeta *(folder)***

Additional Resources

- Writing, Audio & Video Workbook: Para empezar, Writing Activity 10–11
- Heritage Language Learner Workbook: PE-1, PE-2
- Resource Book: Para empezar, Communicative Activity BLM

2 En la clase

La sala de clases

Objectives

- Talk about things in the classroom
- Ask questions about new words and phrases
- Use the Spanish alphabet to spell words
- Talk about things related to the calendar

el cuaderno

la hoja de papel

el lápiz

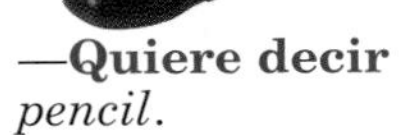
el libro

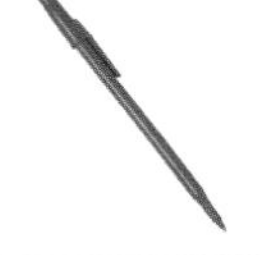
el bolígrafo

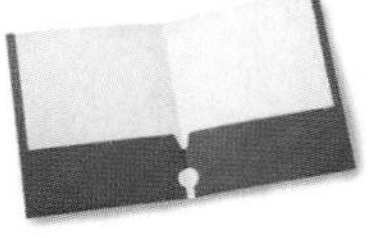
la carpeta

el pupitre

Actividad 1 **Escuchar**

El libro, el lápiz, . . .

You will hear the names of objects in your classroom. After you hear each word, hold up the object if you have it on your desk or point to it if it is somewhere in the classroom.

También se dice . . .

In many Spanish-speaking countries or regions, you will hear different words for the same thing. Words like these are highlighted in the *También se dice . . .* sections throughout your textbook.

For example, in Spain *pencil* is ***el lapicero.*** In Mexico and other countries, *pen* is ***la pluma.***

Universal Access

Students with Learning Difficulties

The concept of gender is sometimes difficult for English speakers. Encourage students to always learn a noun with its article as a means of reinforcing the sound and rhythm. If they are copying new vocabulary into their notebooks, have them use a blue and a pink highlighter to colorcode the words.

Heritage Language Learners

Ask students if they use any words that are different from the vocabulary in the book, but that mean the same thing. For instance, in Spain, a pencil is ***el lapicero,*** but in Mexico, people say ***el lápiz.*** Be sure students understand that their words are valid, but that you may make other vocabulary choices for class.

Actividad 2 Hablar

¿Cómo se dice . . . ?

Discuss with a partner how you would say the following classroom objects in Spanish.

Modelo

A —*¿Cómo se dice* book *en español?*
B —*Se dice* libro.

1. 
2. 
3. 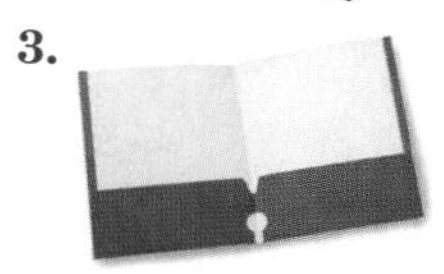
4. 
5. 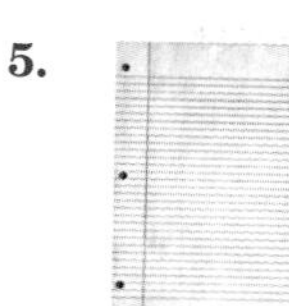

Now ask each other what these Spanish words mean in English.

6. estudiante
7. pie
8. cabeza
9. ojo
10. brazo

Modelo

mano
A —*¿Qué quiere decir* mano?
B —*Quiere decir* hand.

Gramática

Nouns

Nouns refer to people, animals, places, things, and ideas. In Spanish, nouns have gender. They are either masculine or feminine.

Most nouns that end in *-o* are masculine. Most nouns that end in *-a* are feminine.

Masculine	Feminine
el libro	la carpeta
el bolígrafo	la hoja de papel

The definite articles, *el* and *la,* also point out if a word is masculine or feminine. They both mean "the."

Spanish nouns that end in *-e* or a consonant must be learned as masculine or feminine. You should practice them with their definite articles, *el* or *la*.

Masculine	Feminine
el profesor	la noche
el lápiz	la conversación

Actividad 3 Pensar/Escribir

¿Masculino o femenino?

Look at these words and decide whether each one is masculine or feminine. Rewrite each word and add the appropriate definite article (*el* or *la*).

1. pierna
2. nariz
3. cuaderno
4. carpeta
5. pupitre
6. pie
7. profesora
8. lápiz

Más práctica

Practice Workbook P-6

For: More practice: *en la clase*
Visit: www.phschool.com
Web Code: jad-0004

Enriching Your Teaching

Teacher-to-Teacher

Since Spanish nouns have gender, a concept foreign to most native English speakers, students often make overgeneralizations when learning vocabulary. Point out exceptions to the gender rule: ***la mano*** (feminine even though it ends in ***o***) and ***el día*** (masculine even though it ends in ***a***), but stress that in most cases the ***o / a*** rule is accurate. Tell students that they should always learn nouns with the correct article.

Actividad 2 *Standards:* 1.1

Resources: Practice Answers on Transparencies

Focus: Speaking with a partner about items and people in the classroom

Suggestions: Be sure students understand that they are to use the English word in items 1–5 because they are asking for the Spanish word. In items 6–10, they must use the Spanish word because they are asking for an English word.

Answers:

1. pen / bolígrafo
2. notebook / cuaderno
3. folder / carpeta
4. desk / pupitre
5. sheet of paper / hoja de papel
6. estudiante / student
7. pie / foot
8. cabeza / head
9. ojo / eye
10. brazo / arm

Gramática

Presentation

Standards: 4.1

Suggestions: Use the various vocabulary transparencies and have students identify the gender of the nouns. Show the grammar transparencies for reinforcement.

Actividad 3 *Standards:* 1.3

Resources: Practice Answers on Transparencies

Focus: Identifying gender and using appropriate definite articles

Suggestions: Have students identify the gender of nouns ending in ***-o*** or ***-a.*** Point out that ***estudiante*** is tricky, and that ***nariz*** must simply be learned as feminine.

Answers:

1. la
2. la
3. el
4. la
5. el
6. el
7. la
8. el

Language Input

El alfabeto

Presentation

Standards: 1.2

Resources: Voc. & Gram. Transparencies: 29; Audio Program: CD Para empezar, Track 16

Focus: Introducing the Spanish alphabet and spelling in Spanish

Suggestions: Explain that different countries call some of the letters different things. Develop a rap rhythm for the letters. Ask volunteers to say a letter, quickly moving from one student to the next.

Actividad 4 — *Standards:* 1.2, 1.3

Resources: Audio Program: CD Para empezar, Track 17; Resource Book: Para empezar, Audio Script; Practice Answers on Transparencies

Focus: Listening to letters in a word and writing the word

Suggestions: Allow students to listen more than once.

Script and Answers:

1. ge-u-ese-te-o *(gusto)*
2. be-i-e-ene *(bien)*
3. ere-e-ge-u-ele-a-ere *(regular)*
4. o-ene-ce-e *(once)*
5. be-ere-a-zeta-o *(brazo)*
6. pe-i-e-ere-ene-a *(pierna)*
7. pe-u-pe-i-te-ere-e *(pupitre)*
8. ce-a-be-e-zeta-a *(cabeza)*

Actividad 5 — *Standards:* 1.1, 1.3

Resources: Practice Answers on Transparencies

Focus: Speaking and writing letters and words

Suggestions: As students work, walk around the room to monitor their pronunciation.

Answers:

1. carpeta: *ce-a-ere-pe-e-te-a*
2. cuaderno: *ce-u-a-de-e-ere-ene-o*
3. libro: *ele-i-be-ere-o*
4. pupitre: *pe-u-pe-i-te-ere-e*
5. bolígrafo: *be-o-ele-i acento-ge-ere-a-efe-o*

El alfabeto

a	be	ce	de	e	efe
ge	hache	i	jota	ka	ele
eme	ene	eñe	o	pe	cu
ere	erre	ese	te	u	ve *or* uve
doble ve *or* doble u	equis	i griega *or* ye	zeta		

—**¿Cómo se escribe** *libro?*

—**Se escribe** ele-i-be-ere-o.

Actividad 4 **Escuchar/Escribir**

Escucha y escribe

On a sheet of paper, write the numbers 1–8. You will hear several words you know spelled aloud. Listen carefully and write the letters as you hear them.

Actividad 5 **Hablar/Escribir**

Pregunta y contesta

Work with a partner. Use the pictures to ask and answer according to the model. As Student B spells the words, Student A should write them out. When you are finished, check your spelling by looking at p. 10.

1. 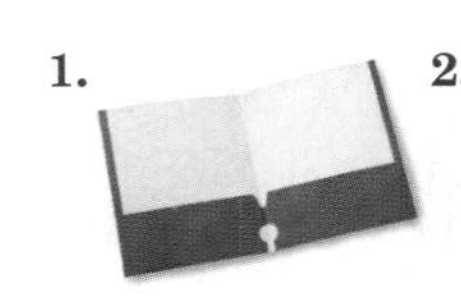
2. 
3. 
4. 
5. 

Modelo

A —*¿Cómo se escribe lápiz?*

B —*Se escribe ele-a acento-pe-i-zeta.*

Universal Access

Heritage Language Learners

Have students look at Spanish newspapers or magazines and write a list of ten words that have accent marks. Then have students spell the words aloud. Remind them to include the accent marks in their spelling.

Advanced Learners

Have students turn to p. 9, make a list of the labeled parts of ***El cuerpo,*** and then write or say the letters for each word.

Hablar

¿Cómo te llamas?

Work with a partner. Follow the model to find out each other's names and how they are spelled. Then change partners and repeat.

Modelo

A —*¿Cómo te llamas?*
B —*Me llamo María.*
A —*¿Cómo se escribe María?*
B —*Se escribe eme-a-ere-i acento-a.*

Fondo cultural

The Maya were among the early civilizations in the Western Hemisphere to develop a form of writing with symbols, known as hieroglyphics *(los jeroglíficos)*. Each symbol, or glyph, represents a word or an idea.

- With what other hieroglyphic writing are you familiar?

Jeroglíficos mayas

Exploración del lenguaje

Punctuation and accent marks

You have probably noticed that questions begin with an upside-down question mark (¿) and exclamations with an upside-down exclamation point (¡). This lets you know at the beginning of a sentence what kind of sentence you are reading.

You probably also noticed the accent marks *(el acento)* on *días* and *estás*. When you write in Spanish, you must include these accent and punctuation marks.

Try it out! Rewrite these phrases and insert the correct punctuation and accent marks.

Como estas   Que tal   Hasta luego   Y tu

Actividad 7

Escuchar/Escribir/Hablar

Juego

1. Play this game in pairs. Each player makes a list of five Spanish words that you have learned. Don't let your partner see your words.
2. Spell your first word aloud in Spanish. Don't forget any accent marks. Your partner will write the word as you spell it. Then your partner will spell a word for you to write. Take turns until you have spelled all the words on your lists.
3. Check each other's papers. The winner is the player with the most words spelled correctly.

Sustaining a conversation
If you need your partner to spell a word again, say: *Repite, por favor.*

Enriching Your Teaching

Teacher-to-Teacher

Have students write two sentences about themselves and then create their own hieroglyphs. Tell them to draw pictures that represent the sentences they wrote. Then have students exchange their glyphs with another student and try to read their hieroglyphic system.

Teacher-to-Teacher

In 1994, the Association of Spanish Language Academies *(**La Real Academia**)* voted to eliminate ***ch*** and ***ll*** as separate letters in the Spanish alphabet. The change was made to simplify dictionaires and computer use. Spelling, pronunciation, and usage are not affected. Some sources treat ***rr*** as a sound and not a letter. In *Realidades,* ***rr*** is listed as a letter.

Practice and Communicate

Standards: 1.1

Focus: Asking partners their names and how to spell them

Suggestions: Direct students' attention to the *Strategy*. Explain that these are tips that will help in language learning. Have students change partners three or four times. When reviewing, call on pairs of students who did not work together to do the dialogue.

Answers will vary.

Exploración del lenguaje

Presentation

Standards: 4.1

Focus: Using punctuation and accent marks

Suggestions: If students need help, have them look at p. 4 to review the words. Stress that accent marks are required for meaning.

Standards: 3.1

Suggestions: Explain that glyphs can be difficult to translate because they are not individual letters that form words, but pictures that represent something—an idea, a person, an action. Glyphs are closer in function to words than letters.

Standards: 1.2

Focus: Listening to and spelling words

Suggestions: Suggest that students choose vocabulary words from different categories, rather than from a single group. This way, their partner will not be able to guess as easily.

Answers will vary.

Language Input

Rapid Review
Use flashcards or transparencies to quickly drill students on numbers 1–31.

El calendario y la fecha

Presentation

Standards: 1.2

Resources: Voc. & Gram. Transparencies: 30; Audio Program: CD Para empezar, Tracks 18–19

Focus: Reading and speaking the months of the year; asking questions about days, months, and dates

Suggestions: You may want to present this vocabulary in three sets: days of the week, months of the year, and asking and telling the date. Show students a calendar or use the transparency, and explain that in most Spanish-speaking countries, calendars start with Monday. Prompt students to ask you: *¿Qué día es hoy?* Respond and point to the day at the top of the calendar, then ask students: *Y mañana, ¿qué día es mañana?* Repeat this exercise for each of the days of the week.

Use the question *¿Cuántos días hay en el mes de...?* to introduce the months in order. Students answer with a number. As they listen, ask students to raise their hand when they hear their birth month.

Direct attention to the *Nota*.

Use the dialogues to introduce how to ask the date. Practice other dates by flipping through a calendar and pointing to random dates. Direct attention to the second *Nota*, then include ***el primero*** in the practice. Each day at the beginning of class, ask students what the date is.

El calendario y la fecha

AGOSTO

lunes	martes	miércoles	jueves	viernes	sábado	domingo
				1	2	3
4	5	6	7	8	9	10
11	12	13	14	15	16	17
18	19	20	21	22	23	24
25	26	27	28	29	30	31

el mes

el día

la semana

—**¿Qué día es hoy?**
—**Hoy** es lunes. **Mañana** es martes.
—**¿Cuántos** días **hay en** el mes de agosto?
—Hay treinta y un días.

Nota

Notice that the days of the week and the months of the year are not capitalized in Spanish, except at the beginning of sentences.

The first day of the week in a Spanish-language calendar is *lunes*.

Los meses del año

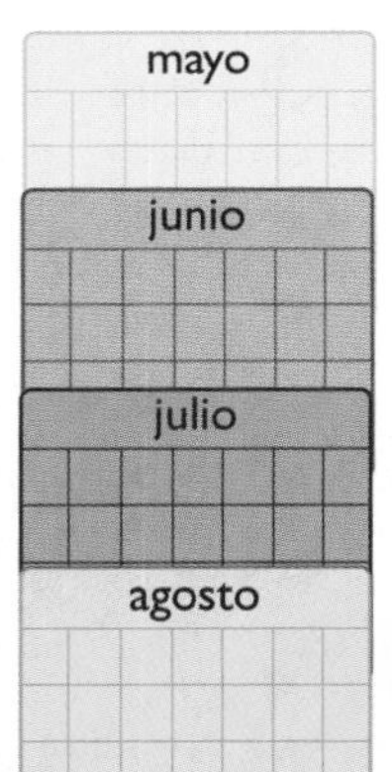

Universal Access

Heritage Language Learners

Have students research and write down the names and dates of three important celebrations in their heritage countries. Give them opportunity to describe the occasion and the festivities that occur during these celebrations. Check their written work for correct spelling, including use of accents.

Advanced Learners

Have students make a twelve-month calendar using the Spanish names for months and days of the week. Students should note important days, such as school holidays and classmates' birthdays. You may want students to research and include important holidays in Spanish-speaking cultures. Post the calendars in the room.

Nota

To say the first day of the month, use *el primero*. For the other days, use the numbers *dos, tres*, and so on.

—**¿Cuál es la fecha?**
—**Es el** 22 **de** agosto.

—¿Cuál es la fecha?
—Es **el primero** de agosto.

Actividad 8 Hablar

Hoy y mañana

Ask and answer according to the model.

Modelo

lunes
A —*¿Qué día es hoy?*
B —*Hoy es lunes. Mañana es martes.*

1. martes
2. sábado
3. jueves
4. miércoles
5. viernes
6. domingo

El Cinco de Mayo es un día festivo en México.

Actividad 9 Leer/Escribir

Días de fiesta

Your friend never gets dates right. Correct the following sentences making the necessary changes.

1. El Día de San Patricio es el 14 de enero.
2. El Día de San Valentín es en junio.
3. Januká es en febrero.
4. La Navidad *(Christmas)* es el 25 de noviembre.
5. El Día de la Independencia de los Estados Unidos *(United States)* es el 4 de junio.
6. El Año Nuevo *(New Year's Day)* es en diciembre.
7. Hoy es el 3 de agosto.

Enriching Your Teaching

Culture Note

Cinco de mayo commemorates the victory of the Mexican army over the invading French army at the Battle of Puebla in 1862. It is not, as is commonly misunderstood, Mexican Independence Day, which is celebrated September 15 and 16. *Cinco de mayo* has become an occasion for parties and celebration in the United States, even among people of other heritages.

Practice and Communicate

Actividad 8

Standards: 1.1

Resources: Practice Answers on Transparencies

Focus: Asking and answering questions about days of the week

Suggestions: Be sure students understand their roles. Have them switch roles and repeat the activity.

Answers:

Student B:
1. **Hoy es martes. Mañana es miércoles.**
2. **... domingo.**
3. **... viernes.**
4. **... jueves.**
5. **... sábado.**
6. **... lunes.**

Extension: Create a spinner with the seven days of the week randomly placed. Have students spin and tell you the day that follows the day shown.

Actividad 9

Standards: 1.3

Resources: Practice Answers on Transparencies

Focus: Writing dates of holiday celebrations

Suggestions: Tell students to first read to identify the errors, then to read again, substituting the correct information before they write their sentences. When students are done, show the answers and have them correct their sentences if necessary.

Answers:

1. **El día de San Patricio es el 17 de marzo.**
2. **El día de San Valentín es en febrero.**
3. **Januká es en diciembre.**
4. **La Navidad es el 25 de diciembre.**
5. **El Día de la Independencia de los Estados Unidos es el 4 de julio.**
6. **El Año Nuevo es en enero.**
7. **Hoy es el ... *(the current date).***

Teaching with Photos

Direct attention to the photo. Ask: *¿Qué día es?* Have students read the caption and answer. Encourage them to look for and read captions throughout *Realidades*, because they will give important information and will also use new words and structures. Explain how photos can support understanding of unfamiliar words.

Practice and Communicate

Standards: 1.3

Resources: Practice Answers on Transparencies

Focus: Writing answers to questions about days of the week

Suggestions: Be sure students understand they are to answer based on the calendar in the book.

Answers:

1. Hoy es el 7 de julio.
2. Hoy es lunes.
3. Mañana es martes.
4. Mañana es el 8 de julio.
5. Hay 31 días en el mes de julio.
6. Hay 7 días en una semana.

Extension: Make transparencies of other months and repeat the activity.

Standards: 2.1, 4.2

Suggestions: Explain that ***Los sanfermines*** dates back to the Middle Ages. There are many other parts of this celebration, including music, dancing, and the Masquerade of the Giants, papier-mâché figures of kings and queens that are paraded through the streets. Stress that the running of the bulls is a very dangerous activity that frequently results in injury or death.

Answers will vary but may include events such as annual rodeos or the Kentucky Derby.

Additional Resources

- Writing, Audio & Video Workbook: Audio Activity 3, Track 20

Escribir

El calendario

Answer the questions based on the calendar page at the right.

julio

lunes	martes	miércoles	jueves	viernes	sábado	domingo
	1	2	3	4	5	6
hoy — 7	8	9	10	11	12	13
14	15	16	17	18	19	20
21	22	23	24	25	26	27
28	29	30	31			

1. ¿Cuál es la fecha de hoy?
2. ¿Qué día de la semana es?
3. ¿Qué día es mañana?
4. ¿Cuál es la fecha de mañana?
5. ¿Cuántos días hay en este *(this)* mes?
6. ¿Cuántos días hay en una semana?

Fondo cultural

Los sanfermines, or the "Running of the Bulls," is a popular two-week festival in Pamplona, Spain, named for the town's patron saint, San Fermín, who is commemorated on July 7 each year. The celebration includes daily bullfights, but before they begin the real fun happens! As the bulls are released from their pens and run through the streets, many people run ahead or alongside them to the bullring.

- What festivals are you familiar with in which animals play a role?

Un día de fiesta en Pamplona, España

Más práctica

Practice Workbook P-7, P-8

Go Online PHSchool.com

For: More practice: *el calendario*

Visit: www.phschool.com

Web Code: jad-0005

Universal Access

Advanced Learners

Ask students to research Pamplona and ***Los sanfermines.*** Remind them to include information on the other aspects of the two-week-long festival, not just on the running of the bulls. Suggest that they create a poster presentation to share with the class.

Students with Special Needs

Some students may have difficulty grasping the abstraction of pretending that it is a different date in *Actividad* 10. If so, make a calendar that shows today's date and have them answer the questions on that basis.

Actividad 11 Leer

El calendario azteca

The Aztecs were a nomadic tribe that finally settled in the valley of central Mexico in 1325. They established their capital, Tenochtitlán, on a swampy lake and built a mighty empire that dominated most of Mexico. The Aztec empire flourished until 1521, when it was defeated by the Spaniards, led by Hernán Cortés.

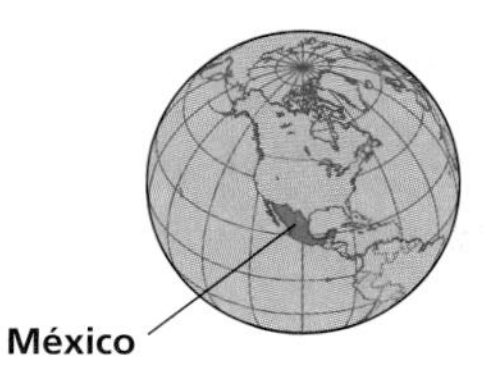

Conexiones — La historia

One of the most famous symbols of Mexico is the monolith, or huge stone, carved by the Aztecs in 1479. Known today as the Aztec calendar or the Sun Stone, the carving weighs almost 24 tons and is approximately 12 feet in diameter. The Aztecs dedicated it to the sun, represented by the face in the center. The calendar represents a 260-day year.

Actividad 12 Pensar

Los símbolos aztecas

Here are several glyphs representing days found on the Sun Stone. Match the glyph with the Spanish word. What do you think each of the glyphs represents? Why do you think the Aztecs included these symbols on their calendar?

1. 
2. 
3. 
4. 
5.  
6. 

a. Jaguar
b. Perro
c. Movimiento
d. Serpiente
e. Cráneo
f. Agua

Enriching Your Teaching

Culture Note

After the Spaniards conquered the Aztec city of Tenochtitlán (now Mexico City) in 1521, the Sun Stone was buried. It was rediscovered December 17, 1790, in what is now the ***Zócalo,*** or main plaza, of Mexico City. It now sits in Mexico's National Museum of Anthropology.

Internet Search

Keywords:

Tenochtitlán, Aztecs, Sun Stone

Practice and Communicate

Actividad 11 *Standards:* 3.1

Focus: Reading about the Aztec calendar, cross-curricular connection to history

Suggestions: Throughout the program, you will find *Conexiones* activities that link language study with other disciplines. Students are moved into working directly in Spanish as quickly as possible. The *Conexiones* will either include activities and questions or will be followed by a related activity. Ask: Why might a tribe like the Aztecs abandon a nomadic lifestyle, settle, and develop agriculture? How long did the Aztecs dominate Mexico? What does the Sun Stone suggest about the Aztec culture?

Actividad 12 *Standards:* 3.1

Resources: Practice Answers on Transparencies

Focus: Speculating about the Aztec glyphs and calendar

Suggestions: Help students define the Spanish words before beginning the activity.

Answers:
1. d 2. e 3. f 4. b 5. a 6. c

Theme Project

Give students copies of the Theme Project outline and rubric from the *Teacher's Resource Book*. Explain the task to them, and have them perform step 1. (For more information, see p. xxxii-a.)

Additional Resources

- Writing, Audio & Video Workbook: Writing Activities 12–13
- Resource Book: Para empezar, Communicative Activity BLM
- Heritage Language Learner Workbook: PE-4, PE-5

Assessment

- Prueba PE-2: En la clase

Language Input

¿Qué tiempo hace?

Presentation

Standards: 1.2

Resources: Voc. & Gram. Transparencies: 31; Audio Program: CD Para empezar, Track 21

Focus: Describing weather conditions and identifying seasons

Suggestions: Show the vocabulary transparencies. Use gestures to convey meaning. Bring in clothing or other items associated with each weather condition and use them in presenting and cueing the vocabulary. Have volunteers choose one of the items to hold up and ask their classmates *¿Qué tiempo hace?* Make this a regular question that you ask at the beginning of each class period. After modeling each expression, ask questions like *¿Hace calor en diciembre?* Say the name of a month and a region of the United States, and ask students for possible logical weather conditions.

To introduce the seasons, model pronunciation. Then say the months of a particular season ***(septiembre, octubre, noviembre)*** and ask students to choose which one it is.

Actividad 1

Standards: 1.2

Resources: Audio Program: CD Para empezar, Track 22; Resource Book: Para empezar, Audio Script; Practice Answers on Transparencies

Focus: Listening to and identifying weather vocabulary

Suggestions: Ask students to briefly describe in English the weather they see in each picture. Explain that there are six items, so some of the pictures will be used more than once.

Script and Answers:

1. **Hace calor. (b)**
2. **Llueve. (d)**
3. **Nieva. (c)**
4. **Hace frío. (c)**
5. **Hace viento. (d)**
6. **Hace sol. No hace calor. (a)**

3 El tiempo

Objectives

- Describe weather conditions
- Identify the seasons
- Compare weather in the northern and southern hemispheres

¿Qué tiempo hace?

Hace sol.

Hace calor.

Hace frío.

Hace viento.

Llueve.

Nieva.

Las estaciones

la primavera

el verano

el otoño

el invierno

Universal Access

Advanced Learners

Assign students a city in the Spanish-speaking world, and have them follow the weather there for one week. They can find weather conditions on the Internet and summarize their findings for the class. Make a bulletin board to track the weather in the cities. Have students provide additional facts about the cities and tell how weather may affect the lifestyle there.

Multiple Intelligences

Bodily / Kinesthetic: Nonverbal cues can often help students retain new vocabulary and expressions. Ask students to work in pairs to pantomime each of the weather conditions and seasons. Have students guess what kind of weather or which season is being represented and say the vocabulary word.

Escuchar

El tiempo

You will hear descriptions of different weather conditions. Write the numbers 1–6 on a sheet of paper. Then, next to each number, write the letter of the photo for which the weather is being described.

a.  b.  c.  d. 

Hablar

¿Qué tiempo hace?

Work with a partner. Ask and answer the questions based on the city and weather information for each item.

Miami / julio / 

Modelo

A —*¿Qué tiempo hace en Miami en julio?*
B —*Hace sol.*

1. Denver / enero / 
2. Chicago / octubre / 
3. San Francisco / noviembre / 
4. Washington, D.C. / junio / 
5. Minneapolis / diciembre / 
6. Dallas / agosto / 

Hablar/Escribir

Las estaciones

Answer the questions based on where you live.

1. ¿Qué tiempo hace en la primavera?
2. ¿Qué tiempo hace en el otoño?
3. ¿En qué estación hace calor?
4. ¿En qué estación hace frío?
5. ¿En qué estación llueve mucho?
6. ¿En qué estación nieva?

Más práctica
Practice Workbook P-9

Enriching Your Teaching

Teacher-to-Teacher

Make photocopies of a newspaper weather map. Have students use the symbols on the map or read the weather for various cities and then write a sentence indicating the weather for those cities.

Internet Search

Keywords:

weather Latin America, weather Spain 

Practice and Communicate

 *Standards:* 1.1

Resources: Practice Answers on Transparencies

Focus: Asking and answering questions about the weather

Suggestions: Ask students to think about what the weather is like in each city. Be sure they understand which words they need to replace in each item.

Answers:

1. Nieva. / Hace frío.
2. Hace viento.
3. Llueve.
4. Hace calor. / Hace sol.
5. Hace frío.
6. Hace calor. / Hace sol.

Extension: Ask: *¿Qué tiempo hace en* (your town) *en* (month)*?* Have volunteers ask questions of their classmates.

 *Standards:* 1.2, 1.3

Focus: Asking and answering questions about weather and seasons

Suggestions: Have students write this activity in paragraph form, giving it a title such as *El tiempo en* (name of town).

Answers will vary.

Theme Project

Students can perform step 2 at this point. (For more information, see p. xxxii-a.)

Practice and Communicate

Actividad 4 — Standards: 1.1, 1.2, 1.3, 3.1

Resources: Voc. & Gram. Transparencies: 15–17, 20 (maps); Practice Answers on Transparencies

Focus: Speaking and writing about weather in the two hemispheres; cross-curricular connection

Suggestions: Ask students to describe the location of Colorado and Chile. Show the map transparencies or a globe. Refer students to the pictures. Be sure they understand the difference between the Northern and Southern Hemispheres. Have students share their answers with the class.

Answers:

1. En febrero hace calor en Chile.
2. En junio hace calor en Colorado.
3. Answers will vary.

Extension: Write on the board the names of ten places in the Northern and Southern Hemispheres and refer students to a world map or globe. Have students identify which hemisphere each place is in and ask them what the weather might be like during ***enero, abril, junio, julio, septiembre,*** and ***noviembre.***

Theme Project

Students can perform step 3 at this point. (For more information, see p. xxxii-a.)

Additional Resources

- Writing, Audio & Video Workbook: Audio Activity 4, Track 23
- Writing, Audio & Video Workbook: Para empezar, Writing Activity 8

Actividad 4 — **Leer/Pensar/Escribir/Hablar**

Dos hemisferios

Read about the seasons in the Northern and Southern Hemispheres and then answer the questions.

Conexiones — La geografía

Did you know that the seasons for the Northern and Southern Hemispheres are reversed? When it's winter in the Northern Hemisphere, it's summer in the Southern Hemisphere and vice versa. So if you want to ski all year round, go from the slopes of the Rockies in Colorado in December to those of the Andes in Bariloche, Argentina, or Puerto Montt, Chile, in July. Or for a December getaway to a warmer climate, go to one of the coastal resorts at Viña del Mar, Chile.

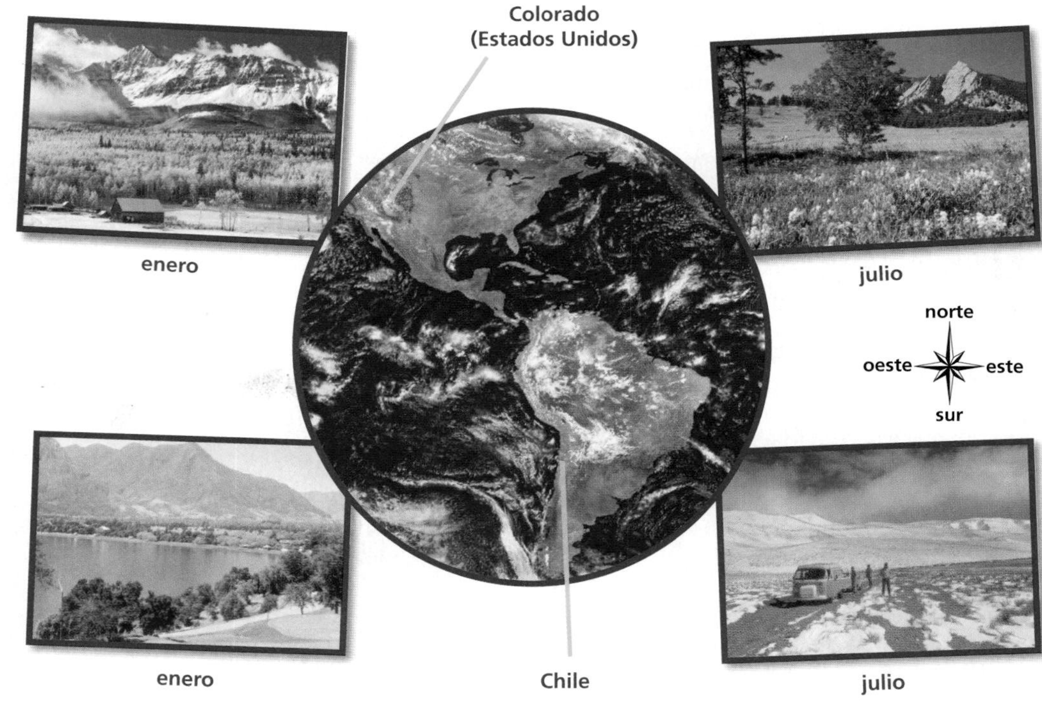

1. En febrero, ¿qué tiempo hace en Chile?
2. En junio, ¿qué tiempo hace en Colorado?
3. En tu comunidad, ¿qué tiempo hace en diciembre? ¿Y en agosto?

Universal Access

Students with Learning Difficulties

You might need to read this passage with students who struggle with reading. Encourage them to read through the questions at the bottom prior to reading. Converting temperatures might prove a challenge for students; the *Nota* section could be an added task not required of all students.

Heritage Language Learners

Have students research the climate and seasons of their heritage countries and write a short paragraph. They should note the country's hemisphere, compare the weather with that of your community, and distinguish the seasons and their temperatures in the two places.

ciudad	diciembre	julio
Chicago	36°F / 2°C	75°F / 24°C
Los Ángeles	67°F / 19°C	88°F / 31°C
Miami	76°F / 24°C	97°F / 36°C
Nueva York	41°F / 5°C	74°F / 23°C
Seattle	41°F / 5°C	66°F / 19°C
St. Louis	36°F / 2°C	81°F / 27°C
Asunción, Paraguay	85°F / 29°C	75°F / 24°C
Bogotá, Colombia	66°F / 19°C	64°F / 17°C
Buenos Aires, Argentina	78°F / 26°C	50°F / 10°C
Caracas, Venezuela	80°F / 27°C	80°F / 27°C
Ciudad de México, México	70°F / 21°C	74°F / 23°C
Guatemala, Guatemala	72°F / 22°C	74°F / 23°C
La Habana, Cuba	76°F / 24°C	82°F / 28°C
La Paz, Bolivia	58°F / 15°C	55°F / 13°C
Lima, Perú	76°F / 24°C	67°F / 19°C
Quito, Ecuador	65°F / 18°C	67°F / 19°C
San José, Costa Rica	78°F / 26°C	78°F / 26°C
San Juan, Puerto Rico	74°F / 23°C	80°F / 27°C
Santiago, Chile	82°F / 28°C	50°F / 10°C
Tegucigalpa, Honduras	70°F / 21°C	81°F / 27°C

Hablar

¿Hace calor o hace frío?

Work with a partner. Discuss the weather in six cities listed in the chart above.

Modelo

A —*¿Qué tiempo hace en Chicago en diciembre?*
B —*Hace frío.*

Hablar

La temperatura es . . .

Working with a partner, ask about the temperature in six different places on the chart.

Modelo

A —*¿Cuál es la temperatura en Quito en diciembre?*
B —*Sesenta y seis grados.*
o: *Dieciocho grados.*

Nota

In most parts of the world, people express temperatures in Celsius. A simple way to convert from Celsius to Fahrenheit is to multiply the temperature by $\frac{9}{5}$, then add 32.

30°C = ? F

$30 \times \frac{9}{5} = 54 + 32$

30°C = 86°F

Para decir más . . .

la temperatura temperature
grados degrees

For: More practice: *el tiempo*
Visit: www.phschool.com
Web Code: jad-0006

Practice and Communicate

Rapid Review

Have students turn to p. 7 and review *Los números.*

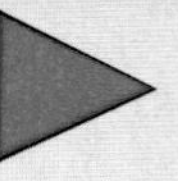

Standards: 1.1, 3.1

Focus: Reading a chart and writing about the weather for cities in the Northern and Southern Hemispheres

Suggestions: Show the map transparencies and help students locate the countries and cities in the chart. Direct their attention to the *Nota*. To internalize the concept, have them practice one or two conversions using a calculator. Have students take turns asking and answering the questions. Both students should write the questions and the answers, indicating the cities they selected and their weather.

Answers will vary.

Extension: Have students take turns asking the class their questions from this activity and eliciting spontaneous answers. Students should also point to the map and show the class the cities they chose.

Standards: 1.1

Focus: Talking about temperatures in the Northern and Southern Hemispheres

Suggestions: Direct students' attention to the *Para decir más. . . .* Point out that these words are helpful for completing the activity but do not have to be memorized.

Answers will vary.

Enriching Your Teaching

Culture Note

The highest temperature in the continental United States,134°F (57°C), was recorded on July 10, 1913, in Death Valley, California. The lowest recorded temperature, –70°F (–57°C), was at Roger's Pass, Montana, on January 20, 1954. In South America, the highest and lowest recorded temperatures were in Argentina: 120°F (49°C) at Rivadavia on December 11, 1905, and –27°F (–33°C) at Sarmiento on June 1, 1907. Remind students that the highest and lowest temperatures happen at opposite times of the year in North and South America. Write these dates and have students read them.

Theme Project

Students can perform step 4 at this point. Be sure they understand their partner's feedback. (For more information, see p. xxxii-a.)

Assessment

- Prueba PE-3: El tiempo

PE Review

Review Activities

Suggestions:

To greet someone and to say goodbye: Have students practice greetings and leave-takings in pairs.

To ask and tell how someone is: Have students circulate from partner to partner asking and telling how they are doing.

To tell time: Have students make a list of five times. Have them take turns asking, *¿Qué hora es?* and answering with different times of day.

To count up to 100: Have students write the numerals 1–9 on index cards. Shuffle the cards and place them face down. Each player draws two cards and says the number that is formed.

To talk about the body: Have students draw the outline of a person and identify the body parts, referring to p. 9 for help.

To talk about the classroom: Have students use the Clip Art in the *Teacher's Resource Book* or on the *Teacher Express CD-ROM* to make flashcards to identify classroom items.

To say the date: Partners can take turns asking and answering *¿Qué día es hoy?* and *¿Cuál es la fecha?* while pointing to a calendar.

To ask for help: Have students quiz one another on word meanings using the questions shown.

To talk about the weather: Have students work in pairs and take turns asking each other, *¿Qué tiempo hace?*

To talk about the seasons: Show students the transparencies and have them identify the seasons.

Portfolio

Invite students to review the activities they completed in this chapter, including written reports, posters and other visuals, and tapes of oral presentations or other projects. Have them select one or two items that they feel best demonstrate their achievements in Spanish to include in their portfolios. Have them include this with the Chapter Checklist and Self-Assessment Worksheet.

Additional Resources

- Audio Program: CD Para empezar, Track 25
- Resource Book: Para empezar, Clip Art
- Resource Book: Para empezar, Situation Cards
- Assessment Program: Para empezar, Chapter Checklist and Self-Assessment Worksheet

Repaso del capítulo

Chapter Review

To prepare for the test, check to see if you . . .
- **recognize the vocabulary**
- **can perform the tasks on p. 23**

Vocabulario y gramática

En la escuela

to greet someone

Buenos días.	Good morning.
Buenas noches.	Good evening.
Buenas tardes.	Good afternoon.
¡Hola!	Hello!
¿Cómo te llamas?	What is your name?
Me llamo . . .	My name is . . .
Encantado, -a.	Delighted.
Igualmente.	Likewise.
Mucho gusto.	Pleased to meet you.
señor (Sr.)	sir, Mr.
señora (Sra.)	madam, Mrs.
señorita (Srta.)	miss, Miss

to ask and tell how someone is

¿Cómo está Ud.? *(formal)*	How are you?
¿Cómo estás? *(familiar)*	How are you?
¿Qué pasa?	What's happening?
¿Qué tal?	How are you?
¿Y tú? / ¿Y usted (Ud.)?	And you?
(muy) bien	(very) well
nada	nothing
regular	okay, so-so
gracias	thank you

to say good-bye

¡Adiós!	Good-bye!
Hasta luego.	See you later.
Hasta mañana.	See you tomorrow.
¡Nos vemos!	See you!

to tell time

¿Qué hora es?	What time is it?
Es la una.	It is one o'clock.
Son las . . . y/ menos . . .	It is . . . *(time)*.
y cuarto/menos cuarto	quarter past / quarter to
y media	thirty, half-past

to count up to 100 (Turn to p. 7.)

to talk about the body (Turn to p. 9.)

En la clase

to talk about the classroom

el bolígrafo	pen
la carpeta	folder
el cuaderno	notebook
el estudiante, la estudiante	student
la hoja de papel	sheet of paper
el lápiz	pencil
el libro	book
el profesor, la profesora	teacher
el pupitre	(student) desk
la sala de clases	classroom

to say the date

el año	year
el día	day
el mes	month
la semana	week
¿Qué día es hoy?	What day is today?
¿Cuál es la fecha?	What is the date?
Es el *(number)* **de** *(month)*.	It is the . . . of . . .
Es el primero de *(month)*.	It is the first of . . .
hoy	today
mañana	tomorrow

to say the days of the week and the months of the year (Turn to p. 14.)

to ask for help

¿Cómo se dice . . . ?	How do you say . . . ?
Se dice . . .	You say . . .
¿Cómo se escribe . . . ?	How is . . . spelled?
Se escribe . . .	It's spelled . . .
¿Qué quiere decir . . . ?	What does . . . mean?
Quiere decir . . .	It means . . .

other useful words

¿cuántos, -as?	how many?
en	in
hay	there is, there are
por favor	please

Universal Access

Students with Learning Difficulties

The *Repaso* page contains a lot of information, and may be too much for some students to absorb and understand at once. Help students take the review section by section. Show them how to focus on things they've not mastered.

Advanced Learners

You may wish to ask students to facilitate review sessions within small groups. Suggest that they write five review questions to share with their group.

Más práctica
Practice Workbook Puzzle P-10
Practice Workbook Organizer P-11

For: Test preparation
Visit: www.phschool.com
Web Code: jad-0007

El tiempo

to talk about the weather

¿Qué tiempo hace?	What's the weather like?
Hace calor.	It's hot.
Hace frío.	It's cold.
Hace sol.	It's sunny.
Hace viento.	It's windy.
Llueve.	It's raining.
Nieva.	It's snowing.

to talk about the seasons

la estación, *pl.* **las estaciones**	season
el invierno	winter
el otoño	fall, autumn
la primavera	spring
el verano	summer

Preparación para el examen

1 Escuchar On the exam you will be asked to listen to and understand people as they greet each other and introduce themselves. To practice, listen to some students greet people in the school halls. Answer these questions about each greeting: What is the time of day? Was the greeting directed to an adult? How did that person respond?

To review, see pp. 2–5 and Actividades 1, 4.

2 Escuchar You will be asked to listen to and understand someone announcing the current date and time. To practice, listen to the message and answer the questions: What is the time of day? What is the date?

To review, see pp. 7–8 and Actividad 11; pp. 14–16 and Actividad 10.

3 Leer You will be asked to read and understand a description of the weather for a given day. To practice, read the weather forecast to the right. Answer the questions: What is the date? What are the high and low temperatures? What is the weather like?

To review, see pp. 18–21 and Actividades 2–6.

El dos de septiembre
Hoy en San Antonio hace sol. La temperatura máxima es 75 grados y la mínima es 54. No llueve.

4 Leer You will be asked to read a list of school supplies and identify them. To practice, copy the school supply list below onto a sheet of paper. Please note: *un, una* mean "a" or "an." Then look to see whether you have any of the items on your desk right now. Make a check mark next to each item you have.

un cuaderno	un lápiz	una hoja de papel
un bolígrafo	una carpeta	un libro

To review, see p. 10.

Enriching Your Teaching

Teacher-to-Teacher

When grouping students for review or other activities, it is important that everyone be on task. Assign groups instead of letting students choose them. Change your method of assignment often so students have the opportunity to work with a variety of classmates. Achieve variety by assigning groups based on the students' favorite class, birth month, or homeroom number.

Review

Performance Tasks

Standards: 1.2, 1.3

Resources:
Audio Program: CD Para empezar, Tracks 26–27; Resource Book: Para empezar, Audio Script; Practice Answers on Transparencies

The test for the *Para empezar* does not ask for active communicative production.

1. Escuchar

Suggestions: Remind students of the greetings for different times of day and for greeting adults versus friends.

Script and Answers:

1. —Buenas tardes, Sr. Ruiz. ¿Cómo está Ud.?
   —Bien, señor. *(afternoon; to an adult; he is well)*
2. —¡Hola, Elena!
   —Buenos días. Nos vemos en la escuela. *(morning; to a teen; she said good morning)*
3. —Julio, ¿qué tal?
   —Regular, ¿y tú? *(either; to a teen; he's so-so)*

2. Escuchar

Suggestions: Play the *Audio CD* or read the script.

Script and Answers:

1. Muy buenos días. Es el veintidós de septiembre. Son las ocho y media de la mañana. *(8:30 in the morning; September 22)*
2. Muy buenas tardes. Es el ocho de enero. Son las dos y veinte de la tarde. *(2:20 in the afternoon; January 8)*
3. Muy buenas noches. Es el cuatro de noviembre. Son las nueve y diez de la noche. *(9:10 in the evening / night; November 4)*

3. Leer

Suggestions: Have volunteers share their answers with the class.

Answers: September 2; high temperature 75°; the low is 54°; it's sunny and not raining

4. Leer

Suggestions: Have students try this activity without consulting the vocabulary list.

Answers will vary.

Theme Project

Students can perform step 5 at this point. Record their presentations on cassette or videotape for inclusion in their portfoliio. (For more information, see p. xxxii-a.)

Assessment

- Examen del capítulo: Para empezar
- Audio Program: CD 20, Track 2

Alternative Assessment

- ExamView Test Bank CD-ROM
- Resource Book: Para empezar, Situation Cards
- Resource Book: Para empezar, Communicative Activities

Tema 1

Mis amigos y yo

THEME OVERVIEW

1A ¿Qué te gusta hacer?

- Activities you and others like and don't like to do

Vocabulary: activities and expressions for saying what you like and don't like to do

Grammar: infinitives; making negative statements

Cultural Perspectives: favorite activities of teens

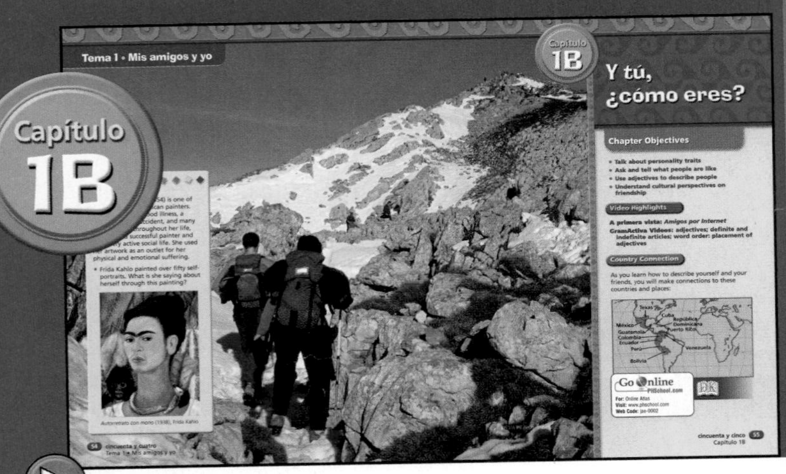

1B Y tú, ¿cómo eres?

- Personality traits

Vocabulary: adjectives and vocabulary to ask about and describe someone's personality

Grammar: adjectives; definite and indefinite articles; word order

Cultural Perspectives: opinions about what makes a good friend

Theme Project

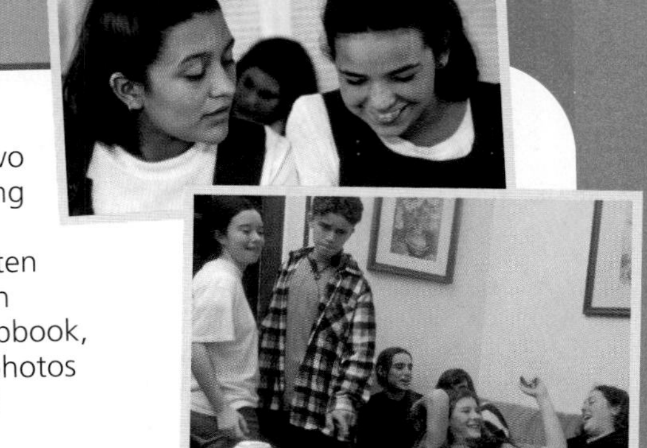

Álbum de recuerdos

Overview: Students create two pages for a scrapbook featuring photos of their friends and themselves with captions written underneath. They then give an oral presentation of their scrapbook, describing the people in the photos and telling what they like and don't like to do.

Materials: construction paper, photographs, magazines, colored pencils, markers, glue, scissors

Sequence: (suggestions for when to do each step appear throughout the chapters)

1A STEP **1.** Review instructions so students know what is expected of them. Hand out the "Theme 1 Project Instructions and Rubric" from the *Teacher's Resource Book.*

STEP **2.** Students submit a rough sketch of their scrapbook pages. Return the sketches with your suggestions. For vocabulary and grammar practice, ask students to work with a partner and present their drafts to each other.

STEP **3.** Students lay out their photos on construction paper. Encourage students to work in pencil first and to try different arrangements before gluing photographs and writing captions.

1B STEP **4.** Students submit a draft of their captions. Note your corrections and suggestions, then return the drafts to students.

STEP **5.** Students complete and present their scrapbook to the class. They should describe the people in the photos and say what they like and don't like to do.

Options:

1. Students feature fictitious friends in their scrapbook.
2. Students create scrapbook pages only about themselves.

Assessment:

Here is a detailed rubric for assessing this project:

Theme 1 Project: *Álbum de recuerdos*

RUBRIC	Score 1	Score 3	Score 5
Evidence of planning	You provided no written draft or page layouts.	Your draft was written and layout created, but not corrected.	You corrected your draft and layout.
Your use of illustrations	You included no photos / visuals.	Your photos / visuals were included, but your layout was unorganized.	Your scrapbook was easy to read, complete, and accurate.
Your presentation	You included little of the required information for each photo.	You included most of the required information for each photo.	You included all the required information for each photo.

Bulletin Boards

Theme: *Mis amigos y yo*

Ask students to cut out, copy, or download photos of people from many different cultures engaged in a variety of academic, social, and leisure activities, sports, crafts, and artistic pursuits. Cluster photos according to the types of activities featured.

Bibliography

Collier, Simon, ed., et al. *Tango! The Dance, the Song, the Story.* New York: Thames & Hudson, 1995. The history of the tango.

Goodnough, David. *Simón Bolívar: South American Liberator.* Springfield, N.J.: Enslow Publishers, 1998. The Life and times of Simón Bolívar.

Klickman, F. Henri, ed. *How to Play Laẗin American Rhythm Instruments.* Warner Brothers Publications, 1995. Explains the rhythmic contributions of Latin American instruments.

Stewart, Sue, and Willie Colón. *Música: The Rhythm of Latin America: Salsa, Rumba, Merengue, and More.* Chronicle Books, 1999. Comprehensive guide to the music of Latin America, its history, and the legendary individuals who perform it.

Venezia, Mike. *Getting to Know the World's Greatest Artists: Picasso.* Chicago: Children's Press, 1994. The life and art of Pablo Picasso.

Hands-on Culture

Craft: *Maracas*

Maracas are very popular percussion instruments in Spanish-speaking countries. They can be made of many materials. Maracas can be used to make noise for a soccer team, to beat rhythm in music, or simply as a toy.

Materials: newspaper, 2 round balloons, 2 jars, white glue, scissors, foil pan, measuring cup, pin, masking tape, 24 dried beans or small pebbles, 2 paper towel tubes, paint, paintbrush, crepe paper

Directions:

1. Cover work area with newspapers.
2. Blow up balloons to grapefruit size.
3. Place each balloon in the mouth of a jar, with the tied end inside the jar.
4. Cut strips of newspaper 6" × $\frac{1}{2}$ ".
5. In the foil pan, mix equal amounts of white glue and water (about $\frac{1}{2}$ cup each). Dip newspaper strips in glue mixture and apply wet strips to balloons, criss-crossing them. Use five layers to make the maraca strong. Be sure only the bottom parts of the balloons show through.
6. Let dry overnight. Hold each balloon by the tied end and burst it with a pin.
7. Remove the balloon. Insert 12 beans or pebbles through the hole in each maraca and tape the hole closed.
8. To make handles, cut four parallel slits (about 3" long) into the end of each paper towel tube, running lengthwise. Circle the tubes with tape just below the slits to keep them from splitting further. Spread the slit pieces apart and fit the maraca onto them. Tape the slit pieces firmly to the maraca, taping all the way around and $\frac{1}{2}$ to $\frac{3}{4}$ of the way up the maraca. Paint and let dry overnight.
9. Cut two strips of crepe paper about 3" wide and 14" long. To make a fringe, cut $1\frac{1}{2}$ " slits all along the edge of each strip, about $\frac{1}{4}$ " apart. Glue the uncut edge of one strip to the handle of one of the maracas, starting just below the maraca. Wind and glue the strip around the handle.

Game

¿Quién es?

This game is played like Twenty Questions. Use it in *Capítulo* 1B after students have learned the vocabulary for describing personality traits.

Players: entire class

Materials: scraps of paper, pen, a paper bag

Rules:

1. Students write their names on scraps of paper and place them in a paper bag.
2. Shake the paper bag to mix up the names. Then call on a volunteer to come to the front of the class. The volunteer draws the name of a student from the paper bag, then gives the paper to you.
3. Students take turns asking the volunteer yes / no questions in an attempt to determine the identity of the person listed on the scrap of paper.
   Student 1: ¿Es una chica?
   Leader: Sí.
   Student 2: ¿Es deportista?
   Leader: Sí.
   Student 3: ¿Le gusta montar en bicicleta?
   Leader: No.
   Student 4: ¿Le gusta patinar?
   Leader: Sí.
   Student 5: ¿Es Mati?
   Leader: Sí.
4. When a student correctly guesses the identity of the person on the paper, he or she becomes the new volunteer. Play continues in this manner until every student has had a chance to ask one or two questions.

Variation: Instead of writing their own names on the scraps of paper, students write the names of celebrities.

Internet Search

Use the keywords to find more information.

Keywords:

Pablo Picasso, Plaza Mayor de Madrid, güiro, flamenco, Frida Kahlo, Simón Bolívar, Mayan civilization

Chapter Overview

A primera vista	Manos a la obra	¡Adelante!	Repaso del capítulo
INPUT	**PRACTICE**	**APPLICATION**	**REVIEW**
Objectives Read, listen to, and explain information about: • activities people like and don't like to do	**Objectives** • Talk about activities • Say what you like and don't like to do • Ask others what they like to do • Talk about infinitives and negative statements	**Objectives** • Read about favorite activities of some teenagers • Explain cultural perspectives regarding dancing • Give an oral presentation about your activities • Talk about Spain	**Objectives** • Prepare for the chapter test
Vocabulary • Activities • Likes and dislikes	**Vocabulary** • Practice and learn new vocabulary	**Vocabulary** • Application	**Vocabulary** • Review
Grammar Lexical use of: • ***gustar*** • infinitives • negatives • structures to express agreement and disagreement	**Grammar** • Infinitives • Negatives • Expressing agreement or disagreement	**Grammar** • Application	**Grammar** • Review
Culture • Pablo Picasso	**Culture** • Outdoor cafés • ***La Plaza Mayor*** in Madrid • Jaime Antonio González Colson • The music and dances of different Spanish-speaking countries • The ***güiro*** and rhythm instruments	**Culture** • Instructions for dancing the ***mambo***	**Culture** • Demonstrate an understanding of cultural differences regarding dancing

Learner Support

Strategies
- Using visuals
- Using a dictionary or glossary
- Recognizing cognates
- Using cognates

Recycling
- Accent marks
- ***nada***

Pronunciación
- Vowels ***a, e, i***

Exploración del lenguaje
- Cognates

Conexiones
- Music and dances

Beyond the Classroom

Countries
- United States (Texas)
- Mexico
- Costa Rica
- Dominican Republic
- Equatorial Guinea
- Colombia
- Puerto Rico
- Argentina
- Spain

El español en la comunidad
- Spanish-language media resources

Internet
- Vocabulary activities
- Grammar activities
- Internet links
- Self-tests

Print Components

TEACHER

Teacher's Resource Book
- Chapter Resource Checklist
- Input Script
- Video Script
- Audio Script
- Answer Keys
- *GramActiva* Blackline Masters
- Communicative Activity Blackline Masters
- Situation Cards Blackline Masters
- School-to-Home Connection Letter
- Vocabulary Clip Art

TPR Storytelling Book
- Cap. 1A

STUDENT

Practice Workbook
- Vocabulary: 1A-1 – 1A-4
- Grammar: 1A-5 – 1A-7
- Puzzle: 1A-8
- Organizer: 1A-9

Writing, Audio & Video Workbook
- Writing: 1A-1 – 1A-4
- Audio: 1A-5 – 1A-10
- Video: 1A-11

Realidades para hispanohablantes
- Cap. 1A

Transparencies

Vocabulary & Grammar Transparencies
- Chapter Opener: 12–20 (maps)
- *A primera vista*: 32–33
- *Videohistoria*: 12–13, 15, 20 (maps), 34–35
- Grammar: 14–18 (maps), 36
- *Lectura*: 14,15,18–19 (maps), 37–38
- *Presentación*: 39

Practice Answers on Transparencies
- Cap. 1A

Fine Art Transparencies
- Transparencies
- Teacher's Guide

Assessment

Assessment Program
- *Pruebas:*
  - Vocabulary recognition: 1A-1
  - Vocabulary production: 1A-2
  - Infinitives: 1A-3
  - Negatives: 1A-4
  - Expressing agreement or disagreement: 1A-5
- *Examen del capítulo:* 1A

ExamView Test Bank CD-ROM

Test Preparation Workbook
- Cap. 1A Reading #1
- Cap. 1A Reading #2

Alternative Assessment
- Performance-Based Speaking
- Assessment Program: Rubrics
- Internet Self-Test
- Situation Cards Blackline Masters
- TPR Storytelling Book: Speaking Task

Technology

iText

Mind Point Quiz Show CD-ROM

Resource Pro CD-ROM
- Lesson Planner
- Teacher Resources
- Clip Art

Video Program VHS and DVD
- *A primera vista* video: *¿Qué te gusta hacer?*
- *GramActiva* Videos:
  - infinitives
  - negatives

Audio Program CDs
- *A primera vista*
- *Escucha y escribe* activities
- Audio activities
- *Pronunciación*
- *Repaso*
- Chapter Listening Test
- Songs

Regular Schedule (50 minutes)

For electronic lesson plans:
Resource Pro CD-ROM

Day	Warm-up / Assess	Preview / Present / Practice / Communicate	Wrap-up / Homework Options
DAY 1	**Return Examen del capítulo (10 min.)**	**A primera vista (35 min.)** • Objectives • Presentation: *Vocabulario y gramática en contexto* • *Actividades* 1, 2 • *Fondo cultural*	**Wrap-up and Homework Options (5 min.)** • Practice Workbook, 1A-1, 1A-2 • Go Online • Heritage Language Learner Workbook • Vocabulary Clip Art
DAY 2	**Warm-up (5 min.)** • Homework check	**A primera vista (40 min.)** • Review: *Vocabulario y gramática en contexto* • Presentation: *Videohistoria ¿Qué te gusta hacer?* • View: Video *¿Qué te gusta hacer?* • *Actividades* 3, 4	**Wrap-up and Homework Options (5 min.)** • *Prueba* 1A-1: Vocabulary recognition • *Actividad* 5 • Practice Workbook 1A-3, 1A-4 • Go Online
DAY 3	**Warm-up (5 min.)** • Homework check **✔Assessment (10 min.)** • *Prueba* 1A-1: Voc. recognition	**Manos a la obra (30 min.)** • Objectives • *Actividades* 6, 7, 9	**Wrap-up and Homework Options (5 min.)** • *Fondo cultural* • Go Online
DAY 4	**Warm-up (10 min.)** • Homework check • Return *Prueba* 1A-1: Voc. recognition	**Manos a la obra (35 min.)** • *Actividades* 10, 11 • *Pronunciación*	**Wrap-up and Homework Options (5 min.)** • *Actividad* 8 • *Prueba* 1A-2: Vocabulary production • Go Online
DAY 5	**Warm-up (5 min.)** • Homework check **✔Assessment (10 min.)** • *Prueba* 1A-2: Voc. production	**Manos a la obra (30 min.)** • Presentation: Infinitives • *GramActiva* Video • *Actividades* 13, 14 • *Fondo cultural*	**Wrap-up and Homework Options (5 min.)** • Practice Workbook 1A-5 • *Actividades* 12, 15 • Go Online
DAY 6	**Warm-up (5 min.)** • Homework check • Return *Prueba* 1A-2: Voc. production	**Manos a la obra (40 min.)** • *Actividades* 16, 17, 18 • *Conexiones: Actividad* 20 • *Juego: Actividad* 19 • *Exploración del lenguaje*	**Wrap-up and Homework Options (5 min.)** • *Prueba* 1A-3: Infinitives
DAY 7	**Warm-up (5 min.)** • Homework check **✔Assessment (10 min.)** • *Prueba* 1A-3: Infinitives	**Manos a la obra (30 min.)** • Presentation: Negatives • *GramActiva* Video • *Actividades* 22, 23	**Wrap-up and Homework Options (5 min.)** • Practice Workbook 1A-6 • *Actividad* 21 • Go Online
DAY 8	**Warm-up (5 min.)** • Homework check • Return *Prueba* 1A-3: Infinitives	**Manos a la obra (40 min.)** • Presentation: Expressing agreement or disagreement • *Actividades* 24, 25, 26 • *El español en la comunidad*	**Wrap-up and Homework Options (5 min.)** • *Prueba* 1A-4: Negatives • Practice Workbook 1A-7 • Go Online

	Warm-up / Assess	Preview / Present / Practice / Communicate	Wrap-up / Homework Options
DAY 9	**Warm-up** (5 min.) • Homework check ✓**Assessment** (10 min.) • *Prueba* 1A-4: Negatives	**¡Adelante!** (30 min.) • Objectives • Presentation: *Presentación oral* • *Presentación oral*: Prepare	**Wrap-up and Homework Options** (5 min.) • *Presentación oral:* Prepare
DAY 10	**Warm-up** (10 min.) • Return *Prueba* 1A-4: Negatives • Homework check	**¡Adelante!** (35 min.) • *Lectura* • *¿Comprendes?*	**Wrap-up and Homework Options** (5 min.) • Go Online
DAY 11	**Warm-up** (5 min.) • Homework check	**¡Adelante!** (40 min.) • *Presentación oral:* Practice • *La cultura en vivo*	**Wrap-up and Homework Options** (5 min.) • Go Online
DAY 12	**Warm-up** (5 min.) • Homework check	**¡Adelante!** (40 min.) • *Presentación oral:* Present	**Wrap-up and Homework Options** (5 min.) • Go Online • Practice Workbook 1A-8, 1A-9
DAY 13	**Warm-up** (5 min.) • Homework check	**¡Adelante!** (20 min.) • *El mundo hispano* **Repaso** (20 min.) • *Vocabulario y gramática* • *Preparación para el examen* 1, 2	**Wrap-up and Homework Options** (5 min.)
DAY 14	**Warm-up** (5 min.) • Homework check	**Repaso** (40 min.) • *Vocabulario y gramática* • *Preparación para el examen* 3, 4, 5	**Wrap-up and Homework Options** (5 min.) • Go Online: Self-test • *Examen del capítulo*
DAY 15	**Warm-up** (5 min.) • Answer questions ✓**Assessment** (45 min.) • *Examen del capítulo*		

1A Preview

Standards for *Capítulo* 1A

- To achieve the goals of the Standards, students will:

Communication

1.1 Interpersonal

- Talk about preferences in leisure activities

1.2 Interpretive

- Read and listen to information about leisure activities and likes; listen to and watch a video about leisure activities; read about leisure and recreational activities
- Listen to and understand information about infinitives; read about traditional dances of Spanish-speaking countries; read about snowboarding; read information of general interest in Spanish language media

1.3 Presentational

- Present information about preferences in leisure activities

Culture

2.1 Practices and Perspectives

- Learn that outdoor ***cafés*** are popular places to relax with friends

2.2 Products and Perspectives

- Learn about Pablo Picasso and his painting; learn about Jaime Antonio González Colson and his painting
- Learn about a dance of the Domincan Republic, the merengue; learn about musical instruments used in the Domincan Republic; learn about traditional dances of Spanish-speaking countries; learn about the mambo; learn about periods in Spain's history that affected its architecture

Connections

3.1 Cross-curricular

- Learn about important artists and their work: Picasso, Colson
- Learn about musical instruments used in the Domincan Republic; learn about traditional dances of Spanish-speaking countries; learn about current events from Spanish language media; understand historical foundations of Spanish language and architecture

3.2 Target Culture

- Acquire information about current events through Spanish language media sources

Comparisons

4.1 Language

- Learn new vocabulary through the recognition of cognates; compare Spanish and English infinitives
- Compare construction of negatives between English and Spanish; compare expressing agreement or disagreement in English and Spanish
- Compare the Spanish vowels ***a, e,*** and ***i*** to their English counterparts

4.2 Culture

- Compare places where teens gather to spend free time; compare the selection of news stories in Spanish language media sources to those in media sources in English
- Compare Latin dances to those in the United States

5.2 Lifelong Learner

- Utilize the language to experience news and entertainment available through print and electronic Spanish language media.

Tema 1 • Mis amigos y yo

Fondo cultural

Pablo Picasso (1881–1973), one of the best-known Spanish artists of the twentieth century, had a long, productive career creating art in a wide range of styles and forms. He showed remarkable artistic talent as a child and had his first exhibition when he was 13 years old. *Three Musicians* is an example of Picasso's cubist painting style.

- Study the painting and list some characteristics that show why this style is known as "cubism."

Musiciens aux masques / Three Musicians (1921), Pablo Picasso

Universal Access

Personalizing the Theme

Ask students to talk about activities they do with their friends. What outdoor activities do they like to do? What do they like to do when they have to stay indoors? Tell students that in this chapter they will talk about activities they like and dislike, as well as learn about favorite activities of young people in Spanish-speaking countries.

Heritage Language Learners

Ask students to name contemporary Spanish-speaking musicians who are popular with young people either in the United States or their heritage country. Have them write names on the board. Encourage students to bring in their CDs or tapes and plan time to listen to them.

Capítulo 1A

¿Qué te gusta hacer?

Chapter Objectives

- Talk about activities you like and don't like to do
- Ask others what they like to do
- Understand cultural perspectives on favorite activities

Video Highlights

A primera vista: ***¿Qué te gusta hacer?***
GramActiva Videos: infinitives; making negative statements

Country Connection

As you learn to talk about what you and your friends like to do, you will make connections to these countries and places:

Texas
España
México
República Dominicana
Costa Rica
Puerto Rico
Colombia
Argentina
Guinea Ecuatorial

Go Online PHSchool.com
For: Online Atlas
Visit: www.phschool.com
Web Code: jae-0002

Un concierto de música latina

Preview 1A

Chapter Opener

Presentation

Resources: Voc. & Gram. Transparencies: 12–20 (maps)

Suggestions: Explain to students that *Capítulo* 1A is the first of two chapters in *Tema 1, Mis amigos y yo.* In this chapter, students will learn language for talking about things they like and do not like to do and ways to express the negative.

The chapter has four parts. *A primera vista* introduces vocabulary and lexical uses of grammar structures through illustrations, conversations, narratives, reading, and video. *Manos a la obra* allows students to practice vocabulary and grammar through reading, writing, speaking, and listening and introduces formal explanations of the grammar. *¡Adelante!* presents opportunities for reading and presentation tasks, while also giving cultural information. *Repaso del capítulo* reviews chapter vocabulary and helps students prepare for tasks on the test.

Introduce students to the theme of the chapter and go over the objectives. Tell them that they will watch videos about what people like to do. The *GramActiva* Videos will help them understand the grammar taught in the chapter.

Standards: 2.2, 3.1

Fondo cultural

Resources: Fine Art Transparencies; Fine Art Transparencies Teacher's Guide

Suggestions: Point out that "cubism" comes from the word "cube." Ask students to describe the properties of a cube before answering the question.

Answers might include the following: The objects in the painting are mostly squares and other geometric figures.

Enriching Your Teaching

Planning for Instruction

Resources:
- Teacher Express CD-ROM or Resource Book
  - Teaching resources
  - Lesson Planner
  - Chapter Resource Checklist
  - School-to-Home Connection Letter

Culture Note

In cubism, the goal is not to make an object look realistic but to explore the shapes in it. The object is broken down into geometrical shapes, and several sides are seen at the same time. Perspective and shading are not used because cubists work with only two dimensions.

Teaching with Art

Resources: Fine Art Transparencies; Fine Art Transparencies Teacher's Guide

Show the transparency. Explain that Picasso developed his cubist style after years of study and work in more traditional styles of painting. He felt he could express ordinary things best by using simple geometric shapes.

1A Language Input

Vocabulario y gramática

Presentation

Standards: 1.2

Resources: Voc. & Gram. Transparencies: 32–33; Resource Book: Cap. 1A, Input Script; TPR Storytelling Book: Cap. 1A; Audio Program: CD Cap. 1A, Tracks 1–2; Resource Book: Cap. 1A, Clip Art;

Focus: Presenting new vocabulary about leisure activities and likes and dislikes

Suggestions: Use the *TPR Storytelling Book* or the Input Script from the *Teacher's Resource Book* as a source of ideas for presentation of new vocabulary and comprehensible input. Keep in mind that the *A primera vista* is designed for input of new words and lexical presentation of grammatical structures explained in the *Manos a la obra*.

Tell students that *A primera vista* means "At first sight." Point out that pictures often help us understand the meanings of unfamiliar words. Show Transparency 32 to guide the presentation. Tell the students that the words in heavy blue type are the words they will be responsible for knowing.

Read each conversation and dramatize each sentence as you say it. Use gestures, facial expressions, and tone to convey meaning. Ask students to guess the meanings. When they understand the statements, begin substituting words from the visuals, using the transparencies to highlight the substitutions.

Ask students to raise their hands when they hear an activity they like. Ask a volunteer to track the responses and tally them on the board to see which are the most- and least-favored leisure activities.

Additional Resources

- Audio Program: Song CD

A primera vista

Vocabulario y gramática en contexto

Objectives

Read, listen to, and understand information about

- **activities people like and don't like to do**

bailar

escuchar música

practicar deportes

nadar

correr

esquiar

—**¡Me gusta mucho** bailar!

—**A mí también. Y también** me gusta escuchar música.

—¡Hola, Beatriz! **¿Qué te gusta hacer? ¿Te gusta** practicar deportes?

—**¡Sí!** Me gusta mucho practicar deportes. Me gusta correr, nadar y esquiar. **¿Y a ti?** ¿Qué te gusta hacer?

Universal Access

Heritage Language Learners

Have students identify the leisure activities that are most popular with young people in their heritage countries. Are there any leisure activities preferred by people in Spanish-speaking countries that are not common in the United States? Are there differences in what the activities are called in various countries?

Students with Learning Difficulties

Use the Organizer from the *Practice Workbook* to create a written vocabulary list for easy reference for oral, listening, and writing activities throughout the chapter. The list will help students to succeed with the activities. Encourage them to use their lists whenever they need them.

escribir cuentos

montar en monopatín

ver la tele

usar la computadora

dibujar

cantar

montar en bicicleta

jugar videojuegos

Actividad 1 Escuchar

¿Te gusta o no te gusta?

You will hear Rosa say what she likes to do and doesn't like to do. Give a "thumbs-up" sign when you hear her say what she likes to do, and a "thumbs-down" sign when she says what she doesn't like to do.

Más práctica

Practice Workbook 1A-1, 1A-2

Actividad 2 Escuchar

Me gusta . . .

Listen to what some people like to do. Point to the picture of the activity each describes.

Go Online PHSchool.com

For: Vocabulary practice
Visit: www.phschool.com
Web Code: jad-0101

Actividad 1 *Standards:* 1.2

Resources: Audio Program: CD Cap. 1A, Track 3; Resource Book: Cap. 1A, Audio Script; Practice Answers on Transparencies

Focus: Listening to someone talk about likes and dislikes; indicating comprehension

Suggestions: Demonstrate the "thumbs-up" and "thumbs-down" signs. Play the *Audio CD* or read the script to the class. Allow students to listen and display the gestures several times.

Script and Answers:

¡Hola! Me llamo Rosa y me gusta mucho bailar. *(up)* También me gusta escuchar música y cantar. *(up)* No me gusta ver la tele ni jugar videojuegos. *(down)* Y tampoco me gusta nadar. *(down)* ¡Uy! ¡Me gusta más bailar! *(up)*

Extension: Choose other new vocabulary to vary and extend the activity.

Actividad 2 *Standards:* 1.2

Resources: Audio Program: CD Cap. 1A, Track 4; Resource Book: Cap. 1A, Audio Script; Practice Answers on Transparencies

Focus: Listening comprehension of leisure activity words

Suggestions: Play the *Audio CD* or read the script as students point to the pictures. Walk around the classroom and check that they select the correct pictures.

Script and Answers:

1. **¡Hola! Me llamo Sebastián y me gusta mucho montar en monopatín. También me gusta escribir cuentos y ver la tele. *(montar en monopatín, escribir cuentos, ver la tele)***
2. **Yo soy Valentina y a mí me gusta bailar, dibujar y montar en bicicleta. *(bailar, dibujar, montar en bicicleta)***
3. **Mi nombre es Carmen. Me gusta usar la computadora, escuchar música y esquiar. *(usar la computadora, escuchar música, esquiar)***
4. **Yo soy Daniel. A mí me gusta correr, practicar deportes y nadar. *(correr, practicar deportes, nadar)***

Enriching Your Teaching

Culture Note

Because the climates and cultures of Spanish-speaking countries are so diverse, a variety of leisure activities is available. People in eastern Chile can engage in mountain climbing. In Caracas, Venezuela, free time is spent surfing and swimming. Throughout Mexico, soccer is played on any open field.

Teacher-to-Teacher

Have students make flashcards using the clip art from the *Resource Pro CD-ROM* or *Teacher's Resource Book.* Students can write a Spanish word on one side of each card and paste the picture on the other. For non-visualized words, have students write the Spanish word.

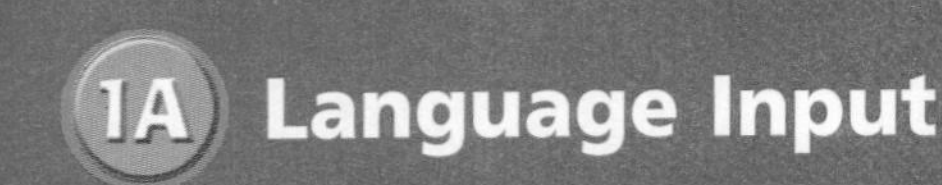

Rapid Review

Have a few students introduce themselves in Spanish to review introductions.

Videohistoria

Presentation

 *Standards:* 1.2, 4.1

Resources: Voc. & Gram. Transparencies: 34–35; Audio Program: CD Cap. 1A, Track 5

Focus: Presenting additional vocabulary and grammar in visual and story context; previewing the language video

Suggestions:

Pre-reading: Direct attention to the *Strategy.* Have students close their books. Present the transparencies, panel by panel, and ask students to predict who likes to do what.

Reading: Explain that the *Videohistoria* is a reading that introduces more vocabulary and will prepare students for watching a video story in each chapter. The characters will appear throughout *Realidades.* Read the captions with students or use the *Audio CD.* Using the transparencies and pantomime, help students understand the new words in blue type. Ask students the comprehension questions found on the transparencies.

Post-reading: Complete *Actividades* 3, 4, and 5 to check comprehension.

Additional Resources

- Writing, Audio & Video Workbook: Cap. 1A, Video Activity 1

Videohistoria

¿Qué te gusta hacer?

You're going to meet eight students from around the Spanish-speaking world and find out what they like and don't like to do. You'll be able to figure out where they live by looking at the globes on the page.

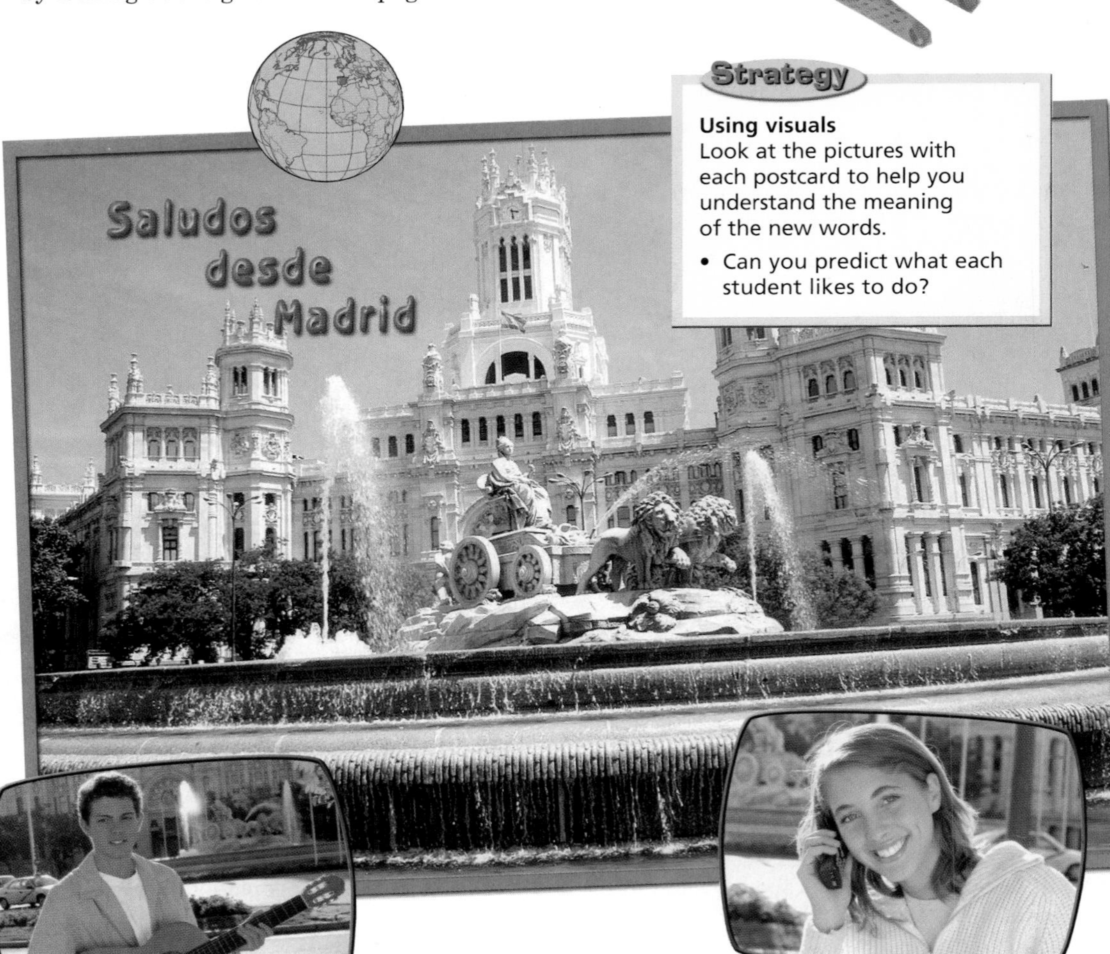

Strategy

Using visuals
Look at the pictures with each postcard to help you understand the meaning of the new words.

- Can you predict what each student likes to do?

"Soy Ignacio.
Me gusta mucho
tocar la guitarra."

"Y yo me llamo Ana.
A mí me gusta **hablar por teléfono.**"

Universal Access

Advanced Learners

Have students choose one of the places named on the postcards and do Internet or other research on the locale's popular places, events, or holidays. Pictures or other graphics showing the city can add visual interest to the written or oral presentation to the class.

Heritage Language Learners

Ask students how people in their heritage country answer the telephone, and explain to the class that people in different countries answer differently. For example, in Mexico, it is often *"¿Bueno?"* In Spain, some say *"¿Diga?"* or *"¿Dígame?"* Colombians favor *"¿A ver?"*, *"¿Con quién?"* or *"¿Aló?"*

“¡Hola! Me llamo Claudia y me gusta usar la computadora y **pasar tiempo con mis amigos.**”

“Yo soy Teresa. También me gusta usar la computadora, pero **me gusta más** jugar videojuegos.”

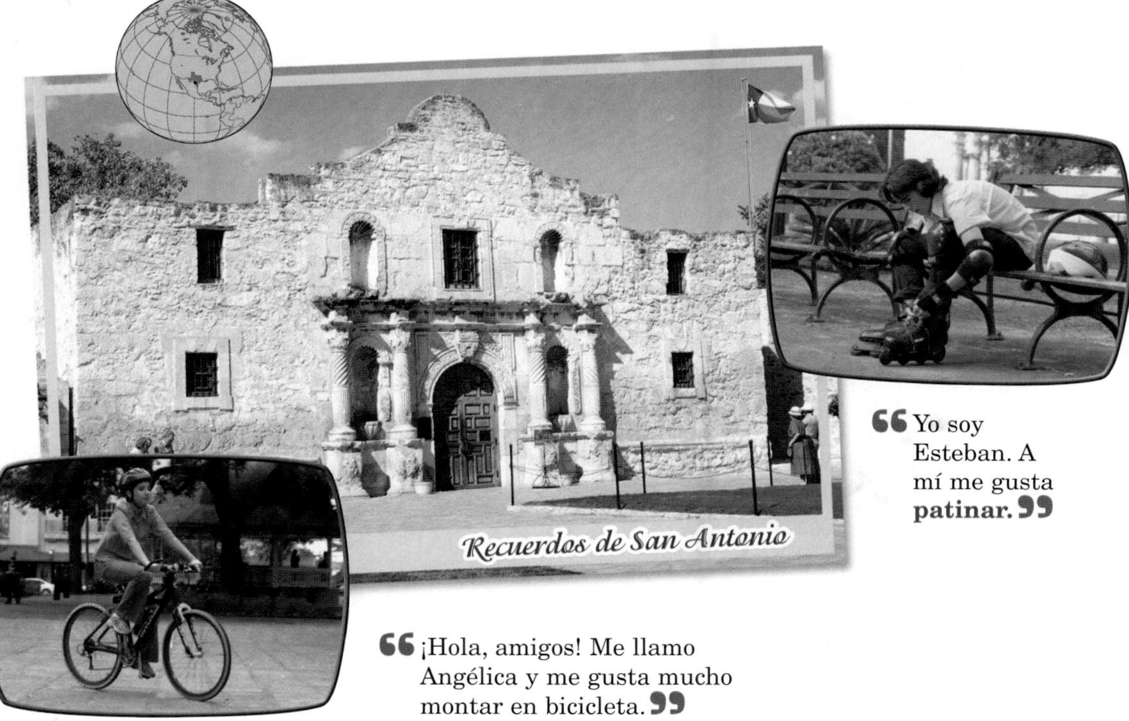

“Yo soy Esteban. A mí me gusta **patinar.**”

“¡Hola, amigos! Me llamo Angélica y me gusta mucho montar en bicicleta.”

Enriching Your Teaching

Culture Note

The Alamo, located in what is now downtown San Antonio, Texas, was originally part of a Franciscan mission, called Misión San Antonio Valero. It was fortified in the early 1800's. In 1836, a relatively small group of separatist Texans led by Colonel William Travis, David (Davy) Crockett, and Jim Bowie defended the Alamo against thousands of Mexican troops for 13 days before they were defeated. The defeat mobilized the movement for independence from Mexico. Today the Alamo remains an important historical symbol to Texans.

Video

Presentation

Standards: 1.2, 4.1

Resources: Video Program: Cap. 1A; Resource Book: Cap. 1A, Video Script

Focus: Comprehending new vocabulary and grammar in authentic context

Suggestions:

Pre-viewing: Remind students that they do not need to understand every word in the video. Encourage them to focus on understanding key concepts.

Viewing: Show the video once without pausing; then show it again, stopping to check comprehension. Show it a final time without pausing.

Post-viewing: Have students complete the Video Activities in the *Writing, Audio & Video Workbook*.

Additional Resources

- Writing, Audio & Video Workbook: Cap. 1A, Video Activities 2–4

Teacher-to-Teacher

Ask students to bring in a postcard or photo of where they live, as well as a photo of themselves. Ask them to use the *Videohistoria* as a model to write a brief caption that tells who they are and what they like to do. Post the photos and captions in the classroom.

Standards: 1.2, 1.3

Resources: Practice Answers on Transparencies

Focus: Recognizing vocabulary

Suggestions: When students have completed the activity, ask volunteers to read their answers to the class.

Answers:
1. b
2. c
3. f
4. a
5. d
6. e

Extension: As homework, ask students to collect several magazine pictures of people doing fun activities that students know how to say. They can create a collage with these images, providing names for the people and quoting each person saying what he or she likes to do.

Standards: 1.2, 1.3

Resources: Practice Answers on Transparencies

Focus: Reading comprehension

Suggestions: When students have completed the activity, ask volunteers to read the statements and give their answers. If the answer is false, have students change it to make it true.

Answers:
1. F
2. C
3. C
4. C
5. F
6. C

Extension: Ask students to find and read at least one statement in *Actividad* 4 with which they personally agree.

"Yo me llamo Raúl. Me gusta ir a la escuela . . . más o menos . . . , pero me gusta más **leer revistas.**"

"¿Qué tal, amigos? Soy Gloria. A mí me gusta **ir a la escuela,** y también me gusta **trabajar.**"

Universal Access

Heritage Language Learners

Ask students to write a paragraph in which they compare their favorite activities with those of the young teens in the video and with those of Spanish speakers they know (family, friends, neighbors, etc.). Help them to focus on spelling. For example: ***hacer*** has an ***h*** but ***Angélica*** and ***jugar videojuegos*** don't.

Multiple Intelligences

Bodily / Kinesthetic: Ask students to make their own video about their favorite activities. Help them focus on using vocabulary and grammar creatively. Have them show the video to the class.

Actividad 3 **Leer**

Actividades favoritas

The students you saw in the video are doing their favorite activities. Number your paper from 1–6 and match the picture to the activity each student likes to do.

1. 

2. 

3. 

4. 

5. 

6. 

a. patinar
b. montar en bicicleta
c. hablar por teléfono
d. tocar la guitarra
e. ir a la escuela
f. leer revistas

Leer

¿Comprendes?

On a sheet of paper, write the numbers 1–6. Read the following statements by the characters in the *Videohistoria* and write *C (cierto)* if the statement is true, or *F (falso)* if it is false.

1. **Angélica:** No me gusta montar en bicicleta.
2. **Raúl:** Me gusta mucho leer revistas.
3. **Esteban:** Me gusta patinar.
4. **Claudia:** Me gusta pasar tiempo con mis amigos.
5. **Teresa:** No me gusta usar la computadora.
6. **Gloria:** Me gusta trabajar.

Escribir/Hablar

Y tú, ¿qué dices?

Choose the activity that you prefer to do on the following days of the week and write it on a separate sheet of paper. Share your answers with a classmate.

1. Hoy es sábado. Me gusta más ___.
   a. trabajar
   b. leer revistas
   c. ver la tele
2. Hoy es lunes. Me gusta más ___.
   a. usar la computadora
   b. patinar
   c. ir a la escuela
3. Hoy es miércoles. Me gusta más ___.
   a. jugar videojuegos
   b. tocar la guitarra
   c. bailar
4. Hoy es domingo. Me gusta más ___.
   a. pasar tiempos con amigos
   b. jugar al fútbol
   c. hablar por teléfono

Más práctica
Practice Workbook 1A-3, 1A-4

Go Online PHSchool.com
For: Vocabulary practice
Visit: www.phschool.com
Web Code: jad-0102

Rapid Review

Review the days of the week before doing *Actividad* 5.

Standards: 1.1, 1.3

Focus: Writing and speaking about what you like to do

Suggestions: After students have done the activity as directed, have them say two sentences for each day.

Answers will vary.

Additional Resources

- Heritage Learner Workbook: 1A-1, 1A-2

Assessment

- Prueba 1A-1: Vocabulary recognition

Enriching Your Teaching

Culture Note

Monteverde, Costa Rica offers tremendous ecological richness. In addition to an active volcano, it contains a cloud forest, a tropical rain forest at such great altitude (4,662 feet), that it passes through the clouds. The forest receives almost 12 feet of rain annually and is home to thousands of different species

Teacher-to-Teacher

Play "Round Robin" with *¿Qué te gusta hacer?* Have a volunteer name an activity and call on a classmate to say "*Me gusta* ______." or "*No me gusta* ______." Then have the student who responded name another activity and call on a different student to answer. Continue the game until all students have participated.

Standards: 1.2, 1.3

Resources: Practice Answers on Transparencies

Focus: Practicing new vocabulary for likes and dislikes; infinitives

Suggestions: Have students do this activity in writing and then say the sentences aloud with a partner.

When students finish the activity, ask volunteers to each write one sentence on the board and then read it to the class.

Answers:
1. usar la computadora
2. montar en bicicleta
3. dibujar
4. cantar
5. correr
6. ver la tele

Extension: Have students draw a picture to represent the three words from the word bank not used in the activity. Then have them write a sentence with ***Me gusta*** to go with each word.

Standards: 1.3

Focus: Practicing vocabulary for likes and dislikes; infinitives

Suggestions: Be sure students understand that the words shown on the chart are models. They do not have to include them in their own charts. Remind them to save their charts for *Actividad* 9.

Answers will vary.

Manos a la obra

Vocabulario y gramática en uso

Objectives

- Talk about activities
- Say what you like and don't like to do
- Ask others what they like to do
- Learn about infinitives and negative statements

Escribir

Actividades populares

Use the word bank to match the vocabulary word with the appropriate picture.

dibujar	usar la computadora
correr	cantar
practicar deportes	ver la tele
bailar	montar en bicicleta
nadar	

Modelo

Me gusta practicar deportes.

1. Me gusta ___.

2. Me gusta ___.

3. Me gusta ___.

4. Me gusta ___.

5. Me gusta ___.

6. Me gusta ___.

Escribir

Mi lista personal

Copy this chart on a separate sheet of paper. Using the activities from pp. 26–30, write four things that you like to do and four things that you don't like to do under the correct columns.

Modelo

Me gusta	No me gusta
correr	cantar

Universal Access

Students with Learning Difficulties

Review *¡A mí tambien!* and *¡A mí no me gusta!* as the two responses for *Actividad* 9. Students might need an immediate reminder in order to succeed.

Heritage Language Learners

You may want to allow heritage language learners to include additional activities on their lists for *Actividad* 7. Use this as an informal opportunity to assess spelling skills. If you choose this option, pair heritage language learners for *Actividad* 9.

Actividad 8 **Escribir**

¿Te gusta o no te gusta?

Using the chart you made in Actividad 7, complete each of the following sentences with a different activity.

Modelo

Me gusta pasar tiempo con mis amigos.

1. Me gusta ___.
2. Me gusta mucho ___.
3. Y también me gusta ___.
4. No me gusta ___.
5. No me gusta nada ___.
6. No me gusta ni ___ ni ___.

Actividad 9 **Hablar**

¡A mí también!

Using the information from Actividad 7, tell your partner three activities you like to do. Your partner will agree or disagree with you. Follow the model. Then switch roles and repeat the activity.

Modelo

A —*Me gusta correr.*
B —*¡A mí también!*
o: *¡A mí no me gusta!*

Fondo cultural

Outdoor cafés are popular throughout the Spanish-speaking world. Friends go there to enjoy a snack, something to drink, or a light meal. A café is a place where young people can sit and talk with one another and watch people go by.

- Are there outdoor cafés in your area that are similar to this one in Madrid's *Plaza Mayor?* What kinds of places do you go to for a snack with your friends? Compare the places where you like to meet with the Spanish café in the photo.

En el verano, me gusta pasar tiempo con mis amigos en la Plaza Mayor.

Enriching Your Teaching

Culture Note

The Plaza Mayor is one of Madrid's most famous meeting places. Built in the seventeenth century by Felipe III, it was designed to display his wealth and power. Ceremonies, festivities, and even bullfights have taken place there. Some days it is used as a marketplace. The Plaza Mayor hosts musical performances and visitors from all over the world.

Actividad 8 *Standards:* 1.3

Resources: Voc. & Gram Transparencies: 32–33

Focus: Practicing new vocabulary for likes and dislikes; infinitives

Suggestions: Show the transparencies to review visualized vocabulary. Leave the transparencies on the projector as a visual reference while students work.

Answers will vary.

Actividad 9 *Standards:* 1.1

Focus: Communicating likes and dislikes to a partner

Suggestions: Help students understand that this is a real conversation, so they will need to listen to their partners carefully. Be sure Student B understands that he or she should answer truthfully.

Answers will vary.

Common Errors: Students often confuse the use and pronunciation of the pronouns ***me*** and ***mí.*** Emphasize the pronunciation of "***A mí***" and "***Me gusta.***"

 *Standards:* 2.1, 4.2

Fondo cultural

Suggestions: Have students study the photo and read the paragraph. Share information from the Culture Note at left or provide other information that you know about plazas and ***cafés.*** Then have students answer the questions.

Answers will vary but might include malls, fast-food restaurants, school activities, etc.

1A Practice and Communicate

Rapid Review

Have students review the "activities" vocabulary in pairs by acting out and identifying each infinitive.

Actividad 10 *Standards:* 1.1

Resources: Practice Answers on Transpaencies

Focus: Asking about likes and dislikes; practicing new vocabulary

Suggestions: Review the visualized vocabulary with the class, and then role-play the model with a student. When students are paired, remind them that *¡Respuesta personal!* in the Student B bubble means that their answer should express their opinion. When students have finished, ask for several volunteers to practice the conversation for the class.

Answers:

Student A:

1. —¿Te gusta hablar por teléfono?
2. —¿Te gusta dibujar?
3. —¿Te gusta bailar?
4. —¿Te gusta pasar tiempo con amigos?
5. — ¿Te gusta tocar la guitarra?
6. —¿Te gusta cantar?
7. —¿Te gusta correr?
8. —¿Te gusta escribir?

Student B: Answers will vary.

Common Errors: Students intent on pronunciation and vocabulary often forget to use proper intonation when asking a question. Model appropriate intonation patterns for questions and answers.

Actividad 10 **Hablar**

¿Qué te gusta hacer?

Ask your partner whether he or she likes doing the activities below. Your partner will answer using one of the two responses shown. Then switch roles and answer your partner's questions.

Modelo

A —*¿Te gusta montar en monopatín?*
B —*Sí, me gusta mucho.*
o: *No, no me gusta nada.*

Estudiante A
¿Te gusta . . . ?

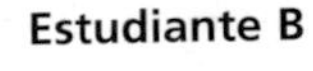

Estudiante B

¡Respuesta personal!

Universal Access

Students with Special Needs

Students with limited or no vision can do *Actividad* 10 by being paired with a student with sight. The student who can see describes the picture in English. The visually impaired student gives the Spanish infinitive. The first student asks "*Te gusta...?*" and the second responds as in the model.

Heritage Language Learners

Point out that the "*kw*" sound (***cuentos, escuela***) is always spelled with ***cu-***, not ***qu-***, in Spanish. Interference from English spelling can often pose difficulties.

Leer/Hablar

¿Calor o frío?

With a partner, look at the following vacation brochures. Ask your partner if he or she likes to do the different activities offered at the two hotels. Then, using that information, decide which vacation destination would be best for him or her.

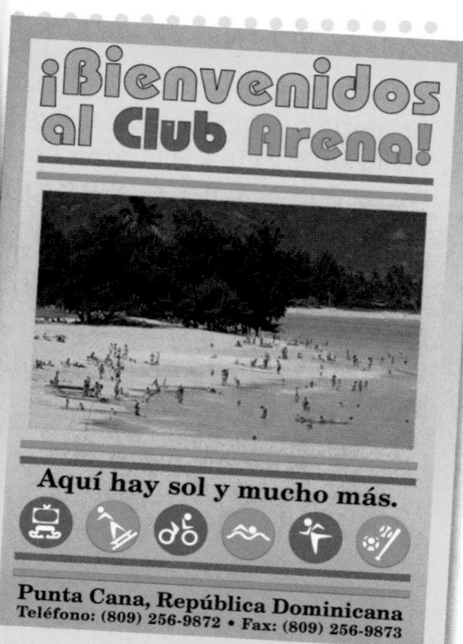

Pronunciación

The vowels *a, e,* and *i*

The vowel sounds in Spanish are different from those in English. In Spanish, each vowel has just one sound. Spanish vowels are also quicker and shorter than those in English.

The letter *a* is similar to the sound in the English word *pop.* Listen to and say these words:

andar	cantar	trabajar
hablar	nadar	pasar

The letter *e* is similar to the sound in the English word *met.* Listen to and say these words:

tele me es Elena deportes

The letter *i* is similar to the sound in the English word *see.* As you have already seen, the letter *y* sometimes has the same sound as *i.* Listen to and say these words:

sí	escribir	patinar
lápiz	ti	mí

Try it out! Listen to and say this rhyme:

A E I El perro canta para ti.
A E I El tigre baila para mí.

Try it again, substituting *el gato* for *el perro* and *la cebra* for *el tigre.*

Enriching Your Teaching

Culture Note

The 2000 Census determined that Spanish-speaking people are the largest minority in 23 of the 50 states. A 2002 Census Survey estimated that 328 million people living in the United States claim Latino heritage, representing one out of nine residents and making Spanish the second most-spoken language in the country.

Teacher-to-Teacher

Use this tongue twister to practice the vowels **a, e,** and ***i:*** *Mi mamá me mima, y mimo a mi mamá."* ("My mom pampers me, and I pamper my mom")

Actividad 11  *Standards:* 1.1, 1.2

Focus: Conversing with a partner about likes and dislikes

Suggestions: Some students may need help interpreting the symbols on the poster. Go over a few of them with the class so you can see who needs help. Model a few questions and answers with different students.

Have the students take notes so they can report to the class. Ask a few pairs of students to perform their conversation for the class.

Answers will vary.

Common Errors: Encourage students to use full sentences in asking each other questions: *"¿Te gusta esquiar?,"* not just *"¿Esquiar?"*

Extension: As homework, students can prepare their own "brochure" with pictures and icons, and present it to the class naming the available activities and asking classmates *"¿Te gusta...?"*

Pronunciación

Presentation

 *Standards:* 4.1

Resources: Audio Program: CD Cap. 1A, Track 6

Suggestions: Go through the *Pronunciación* with students. Have them pronounce the vowels ***a, e,*** and ***i*** and the example words. Let students work individually to memorize the rhymes. Ask volunteers to say the rhyme. Use the drawing to identify the animals. Point out that spelling in Spanish is much simpler than in English because each vowel has just one sound.

Additional Resources

- Writing, Audio & Video Workbook: Cap. 1A, Audio Activities 5–6, Tracks 7–8
- Writing, Audio & Video Workbook: Cap. 1A, Writing Activity 10
- Resource Book: Cap. 1A Communicative Activity BLM

Assessment

- Prueba 1A-2: Vocabulary input

Presentation

 *Standards:* 4.1

Resources: Video Program: Cap. 1A; Resource Book: Cap. 1A, Video Script

Suggestions: Ask students to brainstorm infinitives in English. Write the suggestions on the board or transparency, underlining the word *to* in each infinitive. Give examples of some English sentences containing infinitives, such as "I like to run." Have students call out Spanish infinitives they've learned. Underline the endings in different colors. Play the *GramActiva* Video for reinforcement.

Rapid Review

Use *Vocabulary* and *Grammar Transparencies* to review vocabulary for activities before students complete *Actividad* 12.

Actividad 12

Standards: 1.3

Resources: Practice Answers on Transparencies

Focus: Recognizing infinitive endings

Suggestions: You may want to do this activity with the whole class. Draw the chart on the board and have volunteers write the infinitives in the correct columns. Students should save this chart to use with *Actividad* 14.

Answers:

-ar: nadar, tocar, jugar, bailar
-er: leer, ver, correr
-ir: escribir

Extension: Have students write three *"Me gusta ___."* and *"No me gusta ___."* sentences using infinitives from the chart.

Gramática

Infinitives

Verbs are words that are most often used to name actions. Verbs in English have different forms depending on who is doing the action or when the action is occurring:

I **walk,** she **walks,** we **walked,** etc.

The most basic form of a verb is called the infinitive. In English, you can spot infinitives because they usually have the word "to" in front of them:

to swim, **to** read, **to** write

Infinitives in Spanish, though, don't have a separate word like "to" in front of them. Spanish infinitives are only one word, and they always end in *-ar,* *-er,* or *-ir:*

nad**ar,** le**er,** escrib**ir**

GramActiva VIDEO

Want more help with infinitives? Watch the **GramActiva** video.

Actividad 12 Gramática Escribir

¿Cuál es?

On a sheet of paper, make a chart with three columns for the headings *-ar,* *-er,* and *-ir.* Then look at these pictures of activities. Write the infinitive for each activity under the corresponding head. Save your chart to use in Actividad 14.

Modelo

-ar	-er	-ir
nadar		

Universal Access

Multiple Intgelligences

Interpersonal / Social: Ask students to work together to fill in the chart with more, or all, of the new infinitives in the chapter. Have them work on a conversation, asking each other whether they like or dislike each activity on the chart.

Students with Learning Difficulties

Give several examples of infinitives in English. Have students give examples themselves. Clarify the relationship between "to..." in English and ***-ar, -er, -ir*** in Spanish. You might have them add that to their "activity list" for ready reference until the fact is internalized.

Actividad 13 Gramática **Escuchar/GramActiva**

Tres papeles

Tear a sheet of paper into three equal parts. Write *-ar* on one piece, *-er* on another piece, and *-ir* on the third piece. You will hear several infinitives. Listen carefully to the endings. Hold up the paper with the ending that you hear.

Actividad 14 Gramática **Escribir**

El verbo es . . .

Here are some verbs in English. Look them up in the English-Spanish glossary at the back of the book and write down the infinitive form on the chart you made in Actividad 12.

1. to walk	**2.** to see	**3.** to eat	**4.** to study
5. to talk	**6.** to write	**7.** to share	**8.** to play

Strategy

Using a dictionary or glossary
When you need to look up a verb, always look for the infinitive form.

Actividad 15 Gramática **Escribir**

El diccionario en uso

It's easy to talk about the things you like to do once you know the infinitive, because you just add the infinitive to *Me gusta*. Using the glossary at the back of the book, try writing six sentences about what you like to do.

Modelo

I like to play soccer.
Me gusta jugar al fútbol.

Enriching Your Teaching

Teacher-to-Teacher

Take time to explain the Glossaries to students. For most, this will be the first time they have used a dictionary with two languages. Point out that there are two sections, one that presents words from Spanish to English, and one that presents words from English to Spanish. Warn of the limitations of using dictionaries and glossaries, especially as this relates to words that have multiple meanings in one language, but not the other.

Actividad 13 *Standards:* 1.2

Resources: Audio Program: CD Cap. 1A, Track 9; Resource Book: Cap. 1A, Audio Script; Practice Answers on Transparencies

Focus: Listening for endings

Suggestions: Have students use three colors of index cards so you can immediately see if answers are correct. Play the *Audio CD* or read the script.

Script and Answers:

1. patinar *(-ar)*
2. correr *(-er)*
3. trabajar *(-ar)*
4. escribir *(-ir)*
5. leer *(-er)*
6. nadar *(-ar)*
7. compartir *(-ir)*
8. hacer *(-er)*

Rapid Review

Before doing *Actividad* 14, go over the meanings of several of the infinitives students already know, using the question *"¿Qué es ...?"* Students may respond in English or by pantomiming.

Actividad 14 *Standards:* 1.3, 4.1

Resources: Practice Answers on Transparencies

Focus: Using the glossary or dictionary to look up unfamiliar words

Suggestions: Help students locate the glossary that starts on p. 276. Show them how to find the first item.

Answers:

1. caminar
2. ver
3. comer
4. estudiar
5. hablar
6. escribir
7. compartir
8. jugar

Extension: Call out infinitives in English or Spanish (*to play, to work*, ***lavar, beber***). The first person who finds each word in the glossary is the winner.

Actividad 15 *Standards:* 1.3

Focus: Using the dictionary or glossary; writing about personal likes and dislikes

Suggestions: Encourage students to write about what they don't like as well as what they do like.

Answers will vary.

Standards: 1.1, 1.3

Resources: Voc. & Gram. Transparencies: 36

Focus: Surveying likes and dislikes.

Suggestions: Using the transparencies, have students review infinitives to describe leisure-time activities. Students should save this chart for *Actividad* 17.

Answers will vary.

Standards: 1.1, 1.3

Focus: Compiling results of the class survey on likes and dislikes

Suggestions: Have one group member name the activity, while others respond with their results: ***Dos, "me gusta"; "uno," "no me gusta."*** Ask students whether they are surprised by the results of the survey.

Answers will vary.

Extension: Have students poll their friends or family members about their likes and dislikes using the same kind of chart.

Standards: 1.2, 1.3

Resources: Audio Program: CD Cap. 1A, Track 10; Resource Book: Cap. 1A, Audio Script; Practice Answers on Transparencies

Focus: Listening comprehension and writing accuracy

Suggestions: Read the *¿Recuerdas?* and ask for three examples of words that have accent marks. Play the *Audio CD* or read the script.

Script and Answers:

1. **Me gusta tocar la guitarra.**
2. **Me gusta ver la tele.**
3. **También me gusta jugar videojuegos.**
4. **Me gusta ir a la escuela.**
5. **Me gusta patinar.**
6. **Me gusta usar la computadora.**
7. **¡Y me gusta mucho escuchar música!**

Extension: Continue Raúl's presentation with several questions such as *¿Te gusta practicar deportes? ¿Te gusta hablar por teléfono?* and *¿Qué te gusta hacer los sábados?*

Escribir/Hablar

Encuesta: ¿Qué te gusta hacer?

Ask four classmates to tell you two things they like to do *(¿Qué te gusta hacer?)* and two things they don't like to do *(¿Qué no te gusta hacer?)*. Record their names and responses on a chart like this one.

Modelo

Nombre	Me gusta	No me gusta
Beto	nadar ir a la escuela	patinar cantar

Escribir/Hablar

Encuesta: Los resultados

Working in a group, create a chart like the one to the right using the results of the interviews you did in Actividad 16. Use your chart to find the most popular and least popular activities among your group. Finally, share your findings with the class, using the two sentences below.

1. Las actividades más *(most)* populares:
2. Las actividades menos *(least)* populares:

Actividad	Me gusta	No me gusta
tocar la guitarra	III	I
cantar	I	IIII
trabajar	II	~~IIII~~

Escuchar/Escribir

Escucha y escribe

Write the numbers 1–7 on a sheet of paper. You will hear Raúl say seven things that he likes to do. Write them down as he says them. Spelling counts!

¿Recuerdas?
Remember to include any accent marks when you spell a word.

¿Te gusta hablar por teléfono?

1.
2.
3.
4.
5.
6.
7.

Universal Access

Heritage Language Learners

Students who have not been exposed to written Spanish may tend to omit diacritical marks. Encourage them to keep a list of words with accent marks and add to it throughout the year.

Advanced Learners

Students can work in pairs to write a short paragraph about what they like and don't like to do. Each pair takes turns reading their paragraph to another pair who write down what they hear.

  **Hablar/GramActiva**

Juego

Get together in groups and make a list of at least four things that you like to do. When everyone in the group knows how to say what they like to do in Spanish, you're ready to play.

1. The first person will start the game by saying one thing that he or she likes to do.

First Person:

Me gusta escuchar música.

2. The second person will repeat that information and add another activity.

Second Person:

Me gusta escuchar música y también esquiar.

3. The next person will repeat both activities and add a new one, and so on. See how long your group's sentence gets before someone leaves out an activity.

Next Person:

Me gusta escuchar música, esquiar y también escribir cuentos.

Más práctica
Practice Workbook 1A-5

For: Practice with infinitives
Visit: www.phschool.com
Web Code: jad-0103

Practice and Communicate

Rapid Review

Before doing *Actividad* 19, have students review the chart they made for *Actividad* 17.

Standards: 1.3

Resources: Voc. & Gram. Transparencies: 36

Focus: Talking about likes and dislikes with a group in a game context

Suggestions: Have students try this first in groups of three or four, then in teams, and finally as a whole class. In each case, start out slowly so everybody can do it, and then try to go faster to make the game more challenging and fun.

Answers will vary.

Common Errors: Students will tend to focus on remembering the activities, so they may forget to use complete sentences. Remind them to be careful with their pronunciation.

Extension: Have students prepare a collage or drawing to visually represent the activities they mention.

Additional Resources

- Writing, Audio & Video Workbook: Cap. 1A, Audio Activity 7, Track 17
- Writing, Audio & Video Workbook: Cap. 1A, Writing Activity 11
- Resource Book: Cap. 1A, Communicative Activity BLM

Assessment

- Prueba 1A-3: Infinitives

Enriching Your Teaching

Teacher-to-Teacher

Actividad 19 will work very well for those students who are good at repeating what they hear, but others may struggle. Some students will be able to play better if they are allowed to take notes. One or two students could be involved in the game, without actually playing it, by creating lists or charts to keep track of what is said. As an alternative, students who aren't able to play the game easily in spoken form might enjoy it and be successful playing it in written form. A group of such students can pass around a sheet of paper.

Practice and Communicate

Exploración del lenguaje

Presentation

 *Standards:* 4.1

Resources: Practice Answers on Transparencies

Suggestions: Refer students to the *Strategy.* When they finish *Try it out!,* ask volunteers to identify the cognates. Have them find four additional cognates on these pages.

Answers:
música, practicar, esquiar, usar, computadora, bicicleta, tele, guitarra

Standards: 2.2, 3.1

Resources: Voc. & Gram. Transparencies: 14 (map); Fine Arts Transparencies; Fine Arts Transparencies Teacher's Guide

Suggestions: Have students read the *Fondo cultural.* Then have students find the Dominican Republic on the map on p. 25, or show on the transparency. Ask them to identify the musical instruments they see in the painting. Have students answer the question and discuss their responses.

Teaching with Art

Resources: Fine Art Transparencies; Fine Arts Transparencies Teacher's Guide

Have students examine the painting *Merengue* by Jaime Antonio González Colson. The artist was born in the Dominican Republic in 1901. The indigenous peoples of the Dominican Republic were influenced by both Spanish and African cultures, and its music, dance, and other art reflect these influences. Ask students: What words in Spanish do you know that describe the actions in the painting? ***(hablar, tocar, cantar, bailar)***

Exploración del lenguaje

Cognates

Words that look alike and have similar meanings in English and Spanish are called **cognates** *(cognados).* Here are examples from this chapter:

Spanish	English
popular	popular
usar	to use
guitarra	guitar
computadora	computer

Strategy

Recognizing cognates
Identifying cognates will help you understand what you read and will increase your vocabulary.

Try it out! Look at pp. 26–30 and make a list of seven cognates from the vocabulary on those pages.

Fondo cultural

Jaime Antonio González Colson (1901–1975) was an artist from the Dominican Republic. His works usually focused on the people and culture of his homeland.

The *merengue,* the dance shown in this painting, originated in the Dominican Republic in the nineteenth century. One of the instruments used to accompany it is the *güiro* (shown at the top right of the painting), made from a gourd and played by scraping it with a forked stick.

- What instruments set the rhythms in the music that you listen to?

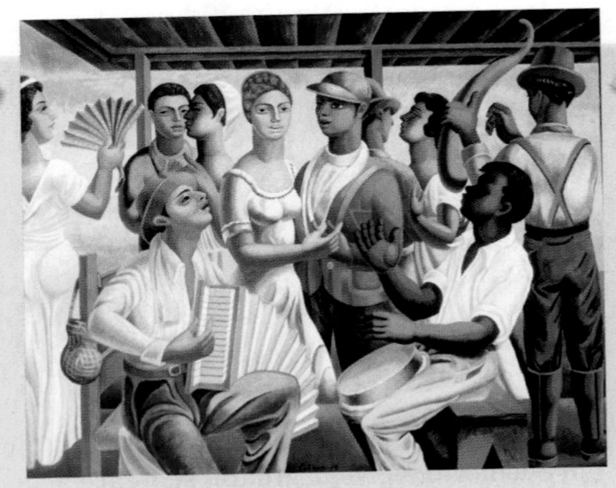

Merengue (1937), Jaime Antonio González Colson
Courtesy of Museo Bellapart, Dominican Republic.

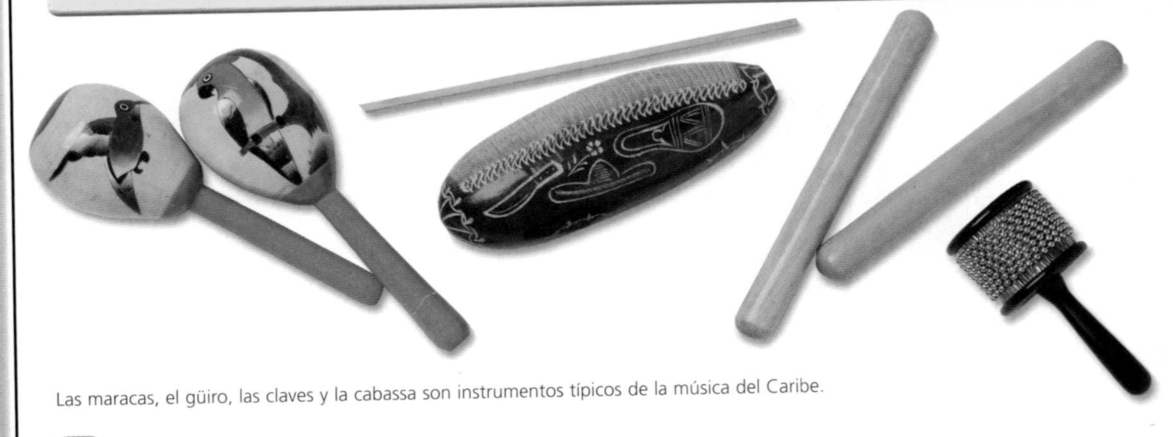

Las maracas, el güiro, las claves y la cabassa son instrumentos típicos de la música del Caribe.

Universal Access

Heritage Language Learners

Students may have items from Spanish-speaking countries in their homes that they can share with their classmates. Ask if anyone has ***maracas, un güiro, un rascador, una clave,*** or ***una cabassa*** to bring to class. Emphasize, however, that students should not bring valuables or rare items.

Advanced Learners

Have students research artist Jaime Antonio González Colson. Ask them to use the Internet or other resources to find information about his life, other artists who influenced his work, and additional examples of his work. Students can share their research with the class.

Actividad 20 Leer/Escuchar/Escribir

El baile y la música del mundo hispano

Each country in the Spanish-speaking world has distinct musical styles and traditions. Many of the unique rhythms and dances of Spanish-speaking countries are now popular in the United States. This music features instruments such as guitars, violins, accordions, and various types of percussion such as *güiros,* sticks, cymbals, cowbells, and drums. As you read the captions, see how many words you can understand due to their similarity with English words. After you read, your teacher will play examples of each type of music. Listen for the different instruments used.

En Argentina, el tango es muy popular. Es un baile romántico.

El flamenco es un baile típico de España. El instrumento más importante en el flamenco es la guitarra.

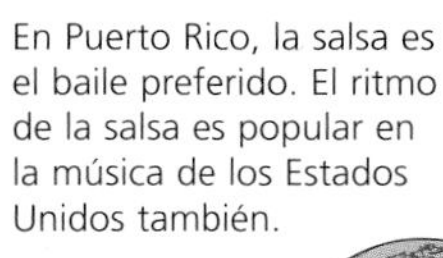

En Puerto Rico, la salsa es el baile preferido. El ritmo de la salsa es popular en la música de los Estados Unidos también.

En la República Dominicana, el baile tradicional es el merengue. El merengue tiene muchos ritmos africanos.

La cumbia es el baile más famoso de Colombia.

- Reread each of the captions and make a list of seven cognates.
- Make a list of instruments you heard in the different pieces of music. You might need to listen to the music again.

Enriching Your Teaching

Culture Note

Play a merengue CD by Juan Luis Guerra, the Dominican Republic's foremost contemporary composer of songs with this rhythm. Tango rhythms by Carlos Gardel and Astor Piazzola, and salsa music by Celia Cruz or Tito Puente are good selections. Cumbia musicians Juan Madera, Walter Choperana Mugno, José Barros, and Mario Gareña are also good choices. The library may have a selection of music, or may find short clips on the Internet.

Internet Search

Keywords:

merengue, tango, salsa, cumbia

Practice and Communicate

Actividad 20 *Standards:* 1.2, 2.2, 3.1

Resources: Audio Program: CD Cap. 1A, Tracks 11–16; Resource Book: Cap. 1A, Audio Script; Practice Answers on Transparencies; Voc. & Gram. Transparencies: 13, 15–18 (maps)

Focus: Reading comprehension using cognates and context; cross-curricular connections to music

Suggestions: Read through *El baile y la música del mundo hispano* with students. Have them read each of the captions silently, using cognates, the photos, and the globe locators to help with comprehension. Ask volunteers to share their understanding of the captions. Then have students complete the activity.

Answers:

Cognates: popular, romántico, preferido, ritmo(s), música, típico, República, tradicional, africanos, famoso
Instruments: Answers will vary.

Common Errors: Some students may be confused by the general placement of adjectives and adjective phrases after the noun they modify. Explain to students that in Spanish the noun usually comes first.

Teacher-to-Teacher

Bring to class a recording of merengue music. Although merengue originated in the 19th century, it is still very popular. If you have time, show students pictures of merengue performers, play a few songs, and have them listen for the rhythm, instruments, and any words they understand.

Theme Project

Give students copies of the Theme Project outline and rubric from the *Teacher's Resource Book.* Explain the task to them, and have them perform step 1. (For more informaion, see p. 24-a.)

Gramática

Presentation

Standards: 4.1

Resources: Video Program: Cap. 1A; Resource Book: Cap. 1A, Video Script

Suggestions: Write on the board the affirmative sentence *Me gusta cantar.* Show students how to make the negative by adding ***No*** in front of ***Me,*** and changing capital *M* to lowercase. Do this with additional examples. Direct attention to the *¿Recuerdas?* Show the *GramActiva* Video to reinforce use of the negative. Note that the video also includes a discussion of ***también*** and ***tampoco,*** so you may want to stop it and use the second part with the grammar presentaiton on p. 44.

Standards: 1.2, 1.3

Resources: Practice Answers on Transparencies

Focus: Reading and writing negatives

Suggestions: Have students silently read the conversation between Ana and Tomás and then write the words that belong in blanks 1–5. When they have finished the activity, have two students role-play the conversation for the class. If any of the answers are incorrect, ask the class to provide a correct negative.

Answers:

1. no **2. ni** **3. ni** **4. nada** **5. tampoco**

Common Errors: Many students will find ***"No, no…"*** difficult to remember. You may have to emphasize that they will use one ***no*** to make a statement and two ***no's*** to answer a question. Point out that by using intonation and a pause (as indicated by the comma), it is easier to say the two ***no's.***

Gramática

Negatives

To make a sentence negative in Spanish, you usually put *no* in front of the verb or expression. In English you usually use the word "not."

No me gusta cantar.	*I do **not** like to sing.*

To answer a question negatively in Spanish you often use *no* twice. The first *no* answers the question. The second *no* says, "I do *not… (don't).*" This is similar to the way you answer a question in English.

¿Te gusta escribir cuentos?	*Do you like to write stories?*
No, no me gusta.	***No, I don't.***

In Spanish, you might use one or more negatives after answering *"no."*

¿Te gusta cantar?	*Do you like to sing?*
No, no me gusta **nada.**	***No,** I **don't** like it **at all.***

If you want to say that you do not like either of two choices, use *ni… ni:*

No me gusta **ni** nadar **ni** dibujar.	*I **don't** like **either** swimming **or** drawing.*
	or: *I like **neither** swimming **nor** drawing.*

¿Recuerdas?

Did you remember that *nada* has another meaning?

- ¿Qué pasa? **Nada.**

In this case, *nada* means "nothing."

GramActiva VIDEO

Want more help with negatives? Watch the **GramActiva** video.

Actividad 21 Gramática **Leer/Escribir**

Una persona muy negativa

Tomás is a new student in the class who is very negative. Number your paper from 1–5. Complete his conversation with Ana by writing one of these negative expressions: *no, nada, ni… ni.*

nada

no

ni

Ana: Hola, Tomás. ¿Te gusta escuchar música?

Tomás: No, __1.__ me gusta.

Ana: Pues, ¿qué te gusta más, jugar videojuegos o usar la computadora?

Tomás: No me gusta __2.__ jugar videojuegos __3.__ usar la computadora.

Ana: ¿Te gusta practicar deportes?

Tomás: No, no me gusta __4.__ practicar deportes.

Ana: Pues, Tomás, __5.__ me gusta pasar tiempo con personas negativas.

Tomás: ¡A mí tampoco! *(Me neither!)*

Universal Access

Advanced Learners

Have students write a paragraph describing what they like to do, what they do not like to do, and what they do not like to do at all. When you hand back their corrected papers, have them rewrite the paragraphs and display them for the class to read.

Students with Learning Difficulties

To help visual learners grasp the pattern for negation, write *No, I don't like to sing* and *No, no me gusta cantar.* Circle *No* and write the number 1, then circle *don't* and write the number 2. In the Spanish version, circle the first ***No*** and write the number 1, then circle the second ***no*** and write the number 2.

Hablar

¡No, no me gusta!

Today you feel as negative as Tomás. With a partner, respond to each question saying that you don't like to do any of these activities.

Modelo

A —*¿Te gusta ver la tele?*
B —*No, no me gusta ver la tele.*

Estudiante A
¿Te gusta . . . ?

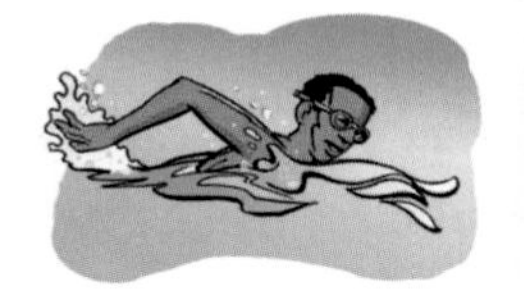

Estudiante B
No, no me gusta . . .

Hablar

¿Qué te gusta más?

Find out what your partner likes more. Then switch roles.

Modelo

A —*¿Qué te gusta más, nadar o esquiar?*
B —*Pues, me gusta más nadar.*
o: *Pues, no me gusta ni nadar ni esquiar.*

1.

2.

3.

4.

Más práctica
Practice Workbook 1A-6

Go Online PHSchool.com
For: Practice with negatives
Visit: www.phschool.com
Web Code: jad-0104

Rapid Review

Ask students to name the activities in the Student *A* bubble.

Standards: 1.1

Resources: Practice Answers on Transparencies

Focus: Asking and answering questions

Suggestions: Remind pairs that Student B will respond in the negative. When students have finished, have them reverse roles and repeat the activity.

Answers:

1. patinar
2. montar en bicicleta
3. nadar
4. usar la computadora
5. dibujar
6. ir a la escuela

Standards: 1.1

Resources: Practice Answers on Transparencies

Focus: Asking and answering questions about likes and dislikes

Suggestions: Review the visualized vocabulary with the class. Role-play the *Modelo* with a student. Stress the ***ni...ni*** to emphasize the negatives. When students have completed the activity, ask several pairs to present the conversation to the class.

Answers:

1. ¿Qué te gusta más, leer o cantar? Pues, me gusta más leer. o: Pues, no me gusta ni leer ni cantar.
2. ¿ . . . ver la tele o tocar la guitarra?
3. ¿ . . . jugar videojuegos o montar en monopatín?
4. ¿ . . . hablar por teléfono o pasar tiempo con amigos?

Enriching Your Teaching

Culture Note

Young people in Spanish-speaking cities generally go out to cafés, movies, and dances in groups. Many leisure activities are planned for public squares or parks. Extracurricular school activities play a much smaller role in Spain than in the United States. For Spanish young people, activities such as after school music and sports usually take place at clubs outside of school.

Additional Resources

- Writing, Audio &Video Workbook: Audio Activity 8, Track 18
- Writing, Audio & Video Workbook: Writing Activity 12
- Resource Book: Cap. 1A, Communicative Activity BLM

Assessment

- Prueba 1A-4: Negatives

Gramática

Presentation

Standards: 4.1

Resources: Video Program: Cap. 1A; Voc. & Gram. Transparencies 34–35

Suggestions: Be sure students understand that you say ***a mí tambien*** to agree with a positive statement and ***a mí tampoco*** to agree with a negative statement. Students may confuse agreeing in the negative, ***a mí tampoco,*** with disagreeing in the affirmative, ***a mí no me gusta.*** Use the second portion of the *GramActiva* Video on negatives.

Standards: 1.3

Resources: Practice Answers on Transparencies

Focus: Expressing agreement

Suggestions: Be sure students understand that they are agreeing with someone when they say, ***A mí tampoco.***

Answers:

1. A mí también. Me gusta...
2. A mí tampoco. No me gusta nada...
3. A mí tampoco. No me gusta nada...
4. A mí también. Me gusta...
5. A mí tampoco. No me gusta nada...
6. A mí también. Me gusta...
7. A mí tampoco. No me gusta nada...
8. A mí tampoco. No me gusta nada...

Common Errors: Perhaps because of similarity to the English *me too* and *me neither* students often leave off the ***a*** from ***a mí también*** and ***a mí tampoco.*** Remind them that the ***a*** is necessary.

Standards: 1.1, 1.3

Resources: Voc. & Gram. Transparencies: 32–33

Focus: Expressing agreement or disagreement in personalized context

Suggestions: Ask students to brainstorm leisure activities they like and do not like to do as you write them on the board. Show the transparencies. Then have students write their own lists.

Answers will vary.

Gramática

Expressing agreement or disagreement

también

tampoco

To agree with what a person likes, you use *a mí también.* It's like saying "me too" in English.

Me gusta pasar tiempo con amigos.	*I like to spend time with friends.*
A mí también.	***Me too.***

If someone tells you that he or she dislikes something, you can agree by saying *a mí tampoco.* It's like saying "me neither" or "neither do I" in English.

No me gusta nada cantar.	*I don't like to sing at all.*
A mí tampoco.	***Me neither.***

Actividad 24 Gramática **Escribir**

Un buen amigo

You have the same likes and dislikes as Miguel, the new Spanish exchange student. Read his statements below and using either *a mí también* or *a mí tampoco,* write a sentence saying that you agree.

Modelo

Me gusta montar en monopatín.
A mí también. Me gusta mucho montar en monopatín.
No me gusta correr.
A mí tampoco. No me gusta nada correr.

1. Me gusta jugar videojuegos.
2. No me gusta ir a la escuela.
3. No me gusta escribir cuentos.
4. Me gusta pasar tiempo con mis amigos.
5. No me gusta usar la computadora.
6. Me gusta mucho patinar.
7. No me gusta tocar la guitarra.
8. No me gusta trabajar.

Actividad 25 **Escribir/Hablar**

¿También o tampoco?

Write a list of three things that you like to do and three things that you don't like to do. Tell your partner the activities on your list. Your partner will agree or disagree based upon his or her personal preferences. Follow the model.

Modelo

A —*Me gusta mucho bailar.*
B —*A mí también.*
o: *Pues, a mí no me gusta nada bailar.*
A —*No me gusta nada cantar.*
B —*A mí tampoco.*
o: *Pues, a mí me gusta cantar.*

Universal Access

Students with Learning Difficulties

Student B may have difficulty understanding the choices in the model for *Actividad* 25. Explain that the first means that they agree with their partner, and the second means that they disagree. Write the model on the board and label the choices as "agree" and "disagree."

Heritage Langugage Leanres

Have students choose two leisure activities studied in this chapter and use the text in *Actividad* 26 as a model to express written opinions appropriate for their selections. Provide feedback on errors in standard Spanish.

Leer/Escribir

¿Comprendes?

Read two students' opinions on snowboarding. On a sheet of paper, answer the questions that follow.

1. Who thinks that snowboarding is "neither a fad nor a sport"? What does he or she consider it to be?
2. What does the other person consider snowboarding to be? What else does this person say about snowboarding?
3. ¿A ti te gusta el *snowboard?* En tu opinión, ¿es un deporte o una moda?

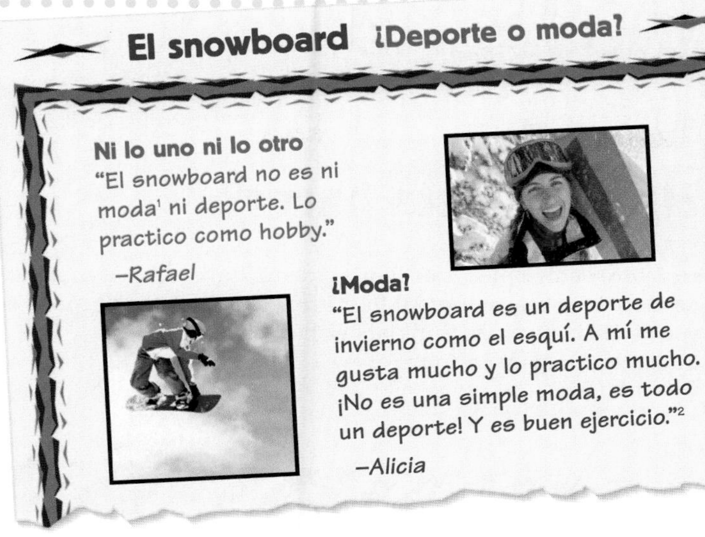

El snowboard ¿Deporte o moda?

Ni lo uno ni lo otro
"El snowboard no es ni moda[1] ni deporte. Lo practico como hobby."
–Rafael

¡Moda!
"El snowboard es un deporte de invierno como el esquí. A mí me gusta mucho y lo practico mucho. ¡No es una simple moda, es todo un deporte! Y es buen ejercicio."[2]
–Alicia

[1] fad [2] good exercise

Más práctica
Practice Workbook 1A-7

For: Practice with agreement or disagreement
Visit: www.phschool.com
Web Code: jad-0105

El español en la comunidad

People of Spanish-speaking heritage in the U.S. make up approximately 13 percent of the total population and are the fastest-growing minority group. By the year 2050, the Hispanic population is expected to be almost 25 percent of the total U.S. population. Because of this, many Spanish-language media sources—magazines, newspapers, television, radio, and Internet—are available throughout the country.

- Make a list of Spanish-language media sources in your community. Try to find local, regional, national, or even international sources. If possible, bring in examples. How much can you understand?

These sources will help you improve your Spanish, and you'll learn about Spanish-speaking cultures as well.

Enriching Your Teaching

Culture Note

Of the more than 30,000,000 Americans who identify themselves as being of Spanish-speaking heritage, 91% speak Spanish at home. Many prefer media in Spanish. Univisión, the number one Spanish-language TV network in the United States, is the fifth largest network overall. *National Geographic, Vogue,* and *Newsweek* are available in Spanish.

Teacher-to-Teacher

One place that students might not think to look for Spanish-language materials is in the grocery store—larger stores that serve a sizeable Spanish-speaking population are likely to carry Spanish-language magazines and newspapers.

Standards: 1.2, 1.3, 4.1

Resources: Practice Answers on Transparencies

Focus: Read for comprehension

Suggestions: Explain to students that they may not know all the words and should use cognates and context for overall comprehension. Direct students to the glosses that define two unfamiliar words. When finished, have volunteers read their answers to the class.

Answers:

1. **Rafael; a hobby**
2. **a sport; it's not just a fad, it's a real sport; it's good exercise**
3. **Answers will vary.**

El español en la comunidad

Presentation

Standards: 1.2, 3.1, 3.2, 4.2, 5.2

Suggestions: Have the class suggest ideas for Spanish-language media sources and write them on the board. Possible answers include local newspapers, radio and television stations, magazines they've seen on newsstands, etc.

Theme Project

Students can perform step 2 at this point. Be sure they understand your corrections and suggestions. (For more information, see p. 24-a.)

Assessment

- Prueba 1A-5: Expressing agreement or disagreement

Additional Resources

- Writing, Audio & Video Workbook: Audio Activity 9, Track 19
- Writing, Audio & Video Workbook: Writing Activity 13
- Heritage Learner Workbook: 1A-3, 1A-4, 1A-5

1A Communicate: Reading

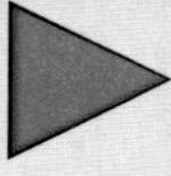

Rapid Review
Ask students to explain what cognates are and give examples.

Lectura

Presentation

*Standards:* 1.2, 1.3, 4.1

Resources: Voc. & Gram. Transparencies: 37–38

Focus: Reading about other teens' likes and dislikes

Suggestions:

Pre-reading: Direct attention to the *Strategy* box. Have students quickly scan the selection to see if they can identify any cognates. Remind them that cognates can help them to understand the notes as they read them.

Reading: Have students read the notes without interruption. They can predict the meaning of the notes from the context and the cognates. Stop arfter each note and ask volunteers to tell what activities were mentioned.

Post-reading: After students finish reading the four notes, review each one with them. Ask a volunteer to read the first note aloud. Ask, "What things does Marisol like to do?" Let students suggest activities until all volunteers have spoken. Make sure the class agrees on all of the activities and that they are correct. Ask students to explain how they arrived at their understanding. Repeat the exercise with all four notes.

Additional Resources

- Heritage Learner Workbook: 1A-6

¡Adelante!

Lectura

¿Qué te gusta hacer?

Here are some notes that four students have written to a popular teen magazine. All four are looking for e-pals. As you read their notes, think about how their likes and interests compare to yours.

Objectives

- Read about favorite activities of some teenagers
- Understand cultural perspectives regarding dancing
- Give an oral presentation about your activities
- Learn facts about Spain

Strategy

Using cognates
Use what you already know about cognates to figure out what new words mean.

Puerto Rico
Marisol, 14 años

"¿Te gusta practicar deportes y escuchar música? ¡A mí me gusta mucho! También me gusta jugar al básquetbol. ¡Hasta luego!"

Colombia
Daniel, 16 años

"Me gusta mucho ver la tele y escuchar música clásica. También me gusta tocar el piano y pasar tiempo con amigos en un café o en una fiesta. ¿Y a ti?"

Universal Access

Students with Learning Difficulties

Have students divide a sheet of paper into four equal sections. In each section, have them list what each student likes and doesn't like to do. They may wish to use this list as an aid in answering the questions in the *¿Comprendes?* section.

Multiple Intelligences

Interpersonal / Introspective: Have students respond to the four young people from Puerto Rico, Colombia, Spain, and Equatorial Guinea by writing an e-pal note to each one. In their e-mails, students should tell Marisol, Daniel, Silvia, and Pablo about themselves, indicating their own likes and dislikes.

España
Silvia, 17 años

"Me gusta leer revistas, bailar y cantar. Soy fanática de la música alternativa. También me gusta hablar por teléfono con amigos. ¿Y a ti? ¿Qué te gusta hacer?"

Guinea Ecuatorial
Pablo, 15 años

"Me gusta mucho jugar al vóleibol y al tenis. Me gusta escribir cuentos y también me gusta organizar fiestas con amigos. No me gusta ni jugar videojuegos ni ver la tele. ¡Hasta pronto!"

¿Comprendes?

1. On a sheet of paper, draw a bar graph like the one below. Indicate on the graph how many of the four young people like each of these types of activities.

ver la tele				
escuchar música				
practicar deportes				
pasar tiempo con amigos				
	1	**2**	**3**	**4**

2. Of the four types of activities, which are the most popular with these four students?
3. Of the four students, with whom do you have the most in common?
4. Write a personal message similar to those in the magazine. Use one of them as a model.

For: Internet link activity
Visit: www.phschool.com
Web Code: jad-0106

Enriching Your Teaching

Teacher-to-Teacher

Using a large wall map, map transparencies, or the maps in the front of the book, help students find the places named on pp. 46–47: *Puerto Rico, Colombia,* and *Ecuatorial Guinea España.* Make sure students understand that Puerto Rico is not a country, but ***un Estado libre asociado,*** a territory—not a state—of the United States.

Communicate: Reading

Standards: 1.1, 1.3

¿Comprendes?

Resources: Practice Answers on Transparencies

Focus: Demonstrate reading comprehension of the e-pal notes by creating a bar graph and writing a similar note

Suggestions: Make sure students understand how to make a bar graph. Have students complete the activity. Draw the bar graph on the board or use the blank bar graph transparency and ask a volunteer to fill it in. Students can compare their charts with the one on the board, suggest corrections, and check their own. After students write their own messages, have several students share their personal messages with the class by reading them or writing them on the board.

Answers:

1. **Students' bar graphs should indicate: 1 televisión; 3 música; 2 deportes; 3 pasar tiempo con amigos.**
2. **Answers will vary.**
3. **Answers will vary.**

Teacher-to-Teacher

If you have the resources, students may enjoy having an e-pal with whom they can practice Spanish. This could take the form of a class-only chat if you have access to a lab or an arrangement with another Spanish class, or with students in a Spanish-speaking country. If Internet access is not available, students may enjoy having a secret pen pal in class. They can draw names and write notes that you collect and distribute.

La cultura en vivo

Presentation

Standards: 2.2, 3.1

Resources: Audio Program: CD Cap. 1A, Track 20

Focus: Reading about ***el mambo*** and learning the dance

Suggestions: Locate in advance some mambo music to play in class. Tell the class that dancing is popular in Spanish-speaking countries and some of the dances have been around for many years. People often learn popular national or regional dances as young children. Direct attention to the diagram. Explain that the dotted line shows the moving foot, and then demonstrate the steps with your back to the students. Have students follow along with you. After a little practice, play the music. Have them listen to the rhythm and the beat. Explain that this music is for dancing the ***mambo,*** a popular dance from Cuba.

Be sensitive to students who do not dance for religious reasons or because of physical limitations. Other students may be hesitant to dance, so create an inviting environment by not putting individuals on the spot. Show that this is fun. Clear a space in the classroom, or move to an open area where students have room to move. Demonstrate the steps slowly. Then, as a class, practice the steps slowly a few times. Try to move more quickly and smoothly each time.

Once students have acquired some proficiency, allow them to practice. Arrange students in pairs with partners facing each other. One partner will begin the dance with the left foot moving forward and the other with the right foot going back at the same time. After a few minutes have each pair change partners.

Play a mambo tune and allow students to dance. If students have fun and become even mildly proficient, they may enjoy holding a dance contest.

Direct attention to the *Think About It!* and have students answer the questions.

Answers will vary.

Additional Resources

- Heritage Learner Workbook: 1A-7

La cultura en vivo

¿Te gusta bailar?

Thanks to the worldwide popularity of Latin music, Latin dances have captured the attention of people of all ages. As a result, people all around the United States are learning dances such as the merengue, tango, and salsa. Here is a dance you can learn. It is called the mambo, and it originated in Cuba in the 1940s.

Bailando el mambo

El mambo

Directions

Beat 1 (of the music): Step forward with the left foot and slightly raise the right foot in a rocking motion.

Beat 2: Step back down on the right foot.

Beat 3: Place the left foot next to the right foot.

Beat 4: Hold both feet in place with the left and right feet next to each other.

Repeat the same motion, now moving backwards.

Beat 5: Step backward with the right foot and slightly raise the left foot in a rocking motion.

Beat 6: Step back down on the left foot.

Beat 7: Place the right foot next to the left foot.

Beat 8: Hold both feet in place with the left and right feet next to each other.

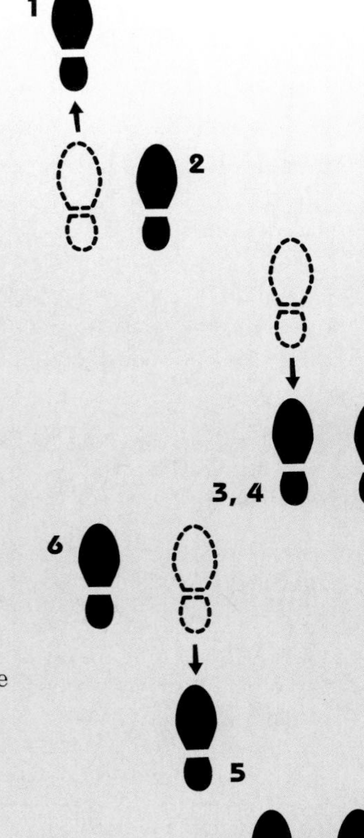

These steps are repeated throughout the music. If partners dance together, then the male should start with his left foot going forward and the female should start with her right foot going backward.

Think about it! How is doing the mambo with a partner different from dances you might do? What dances do you know from the United States that are danced with a partner?

Universal Access

Heritage Language Learners

Some students may be familiar with the ***mambo*** and the music associated with it. If so, allow them to help teach the steps and to share personal experiences if they wish. Others may be familiar with other dances from Spanish-speaking countries and may have interesting stories to share with the class.

Multiple Intelligences

Musical / Rhythmic: If students master the dance quickly, they may find other dances interesting too. Encourage them to research ***salsa, merengue,*** or ***tango*** and present their findings to the class, prefeerably by demonstrating the dance.

Presentación oral

A mí me gusta mucho . . .

Task
You are a new student at school and have been asked to tell the class a little bit about your likes and dislikes.

1 Prepare Copy this diagram on a sheet of paper. Write a list of at least five activities that you can include in the three different ovals.

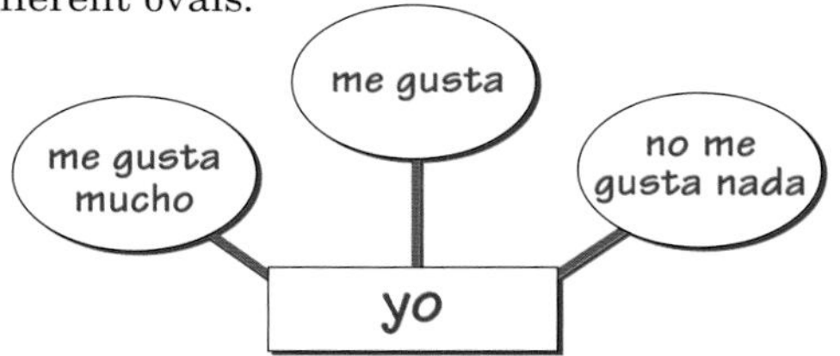

Strategy
Creating visuals
Making a diagram can help you organize a presentation.

Using your list, create a poster or other visual aid to illustrate the three categories and at least five activities. To illustrate the activities, you can make drawings, cut pictures out of magazines, or show photos of yourself doing the activity. Make sure that each activity is easy to identify. You will use this visual as part of your presentation.

2 Practice Go through your presentation with a few class members. You can use your notes the first time or two, but then practice using only the visuals.

Modelo
Me gusta mucho . . .
Me gusta . . .
No me gusta nada . . .

3 Present Talk about yourself using the visual you have created. Remember to look at the Evaluation list below so you know what you need to emphasize in your presentation. Be sure to begin the presentation with your name. During the presentation, try to:
- use complete sentences
- speak clearly
- use the visuals to keep yourself focused

4 Evaluation Your teacher may give you a rubric explaining how the presentation will be graded. You probably will be graded on:
- how much information you communicate
- how easy it is to understand you
- how clearly and neatly your visuals match what you are saying

Enriching Your Teaching

RUBRIC	Score 1	Score 3	Score 5
How much information you communicate	You mention only one detailed example in each category.	You mention only four activities and mention all three categories.	You mention five activities and mention all three categories.
How easily you are understood	You are difficult to understand with many patterns of grammatical errors.	You are fairly easy to understand with occasional patterns of grammatical errors.	You are easy to understand with very few patterns of grammatical errors.
How clearly and neatly your visuals match what you are saying	You include only three visuals that clearly connect to activities.	You include only four visuals that clearly connect to activities.	You include five visuals that clearly connect to activities.

Presentación oral

Presentation

Standards: 1.3

Resources: Voc. & Gram. Transparencies: 39; Resource Book: Cap. 1A, GramActiva BLM

Focus: Communicating about likes and dislikes in a personalized context

Suggestions: Explain the task and 4-step approach to students. Review the rubric with the class to explain how you will grade the performance task (see Assessment below). Do a presentation of your own (an anchor) to model a top-scoring presentation. Have students work through each step of the speaking process.

Teacher-to-Teacher

Display the students' visual presentations for the class. Make time for students to walk around, view each diagram, and take notes or write questions to ask their classmates. Provide time for a class discussion of the diagrams, comments, and questions.

Portfolio

Record students' oral presentations on cassette or videotape for inclusion in their portfolios.

Additional Resources

- Heritage Learner Workbook: 1A-8

Assessment

- Assessment Program: Cap. 1A, Rubrics

Give students copies of the rubric before they begin the activity. Review the different levels of performance. After assessing students, help individuals understand how their performance could be improved.

El mundo hispano

Presentation

*Standards:* 2.2, 3.1

Resources: Voc. & Gram. Transparencies: 18 (map)

Focus: Reading about Spain's heritage

Presentation: After students read the opening page, use a world map to point out Spain and the areas that belonged to the Spanish empire. Discuss how over time Spain's territories gained their independence.

Locate Rome on the map. Point out the proximity of Spain and Rome. Since Spain was once a province of the Roman empire, it is easy to understand why Spanish is called a Romance language.

Have students look at the top two photos and read the paragraphs on p. 50. Discuss how Spain still shows traces of other cultures that influenced it. Ask students to point out evidence of this. Locate North Africa on the map and note where the Moors originated. Indicate a path linking North Africa and Spain, so students can visualize how they came to Spain. Entertain ideas about their method of travel. Point out that the Moors, who ruled Spain for nearly 800 years, spoke Arabic and that Spanish today still reflects its influence. On a map of Spain, have students locate Granada and Córdoba, once important Moorish cities. Help students see that they are in southern Spain, the area closest to North Africa. Point out that the Alhambra and other sites dating back to the time of the Moors still exist. Have students focus on the photo of the Retiro. Talk about its original purpose and how it is used now. Locate Bilbao on the map. Point it out as the location of the museum.

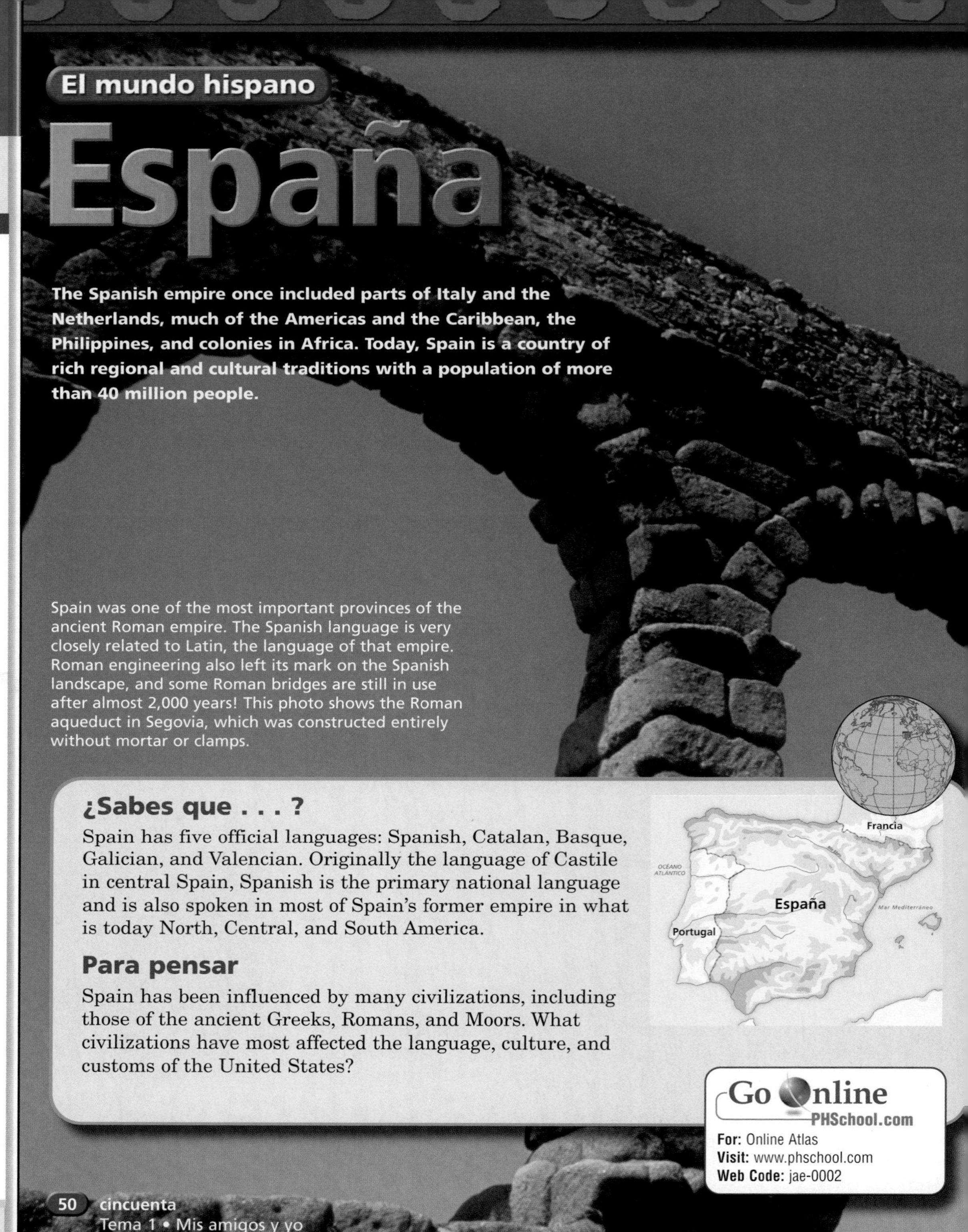

The Spanish empire once included parts of Italy and the Netherlands, much of the Americas and the Caribbean, the Philippines, and colonies in Africa. Today, Spain is a country of rich regional and cultural traditions with a population of more than 40 million people.

Spain was one of the most important provinces of the ancient Roman empire. The Spanish language is very closely related to Latin, the language of that empire. Roman engineering also left its mark on the Spanish landscape, and some Roman bridges are still in use after almost 2,000 years! This photo shows the Roman aqueduct in Segovia, which was constructed entirely without mortar or clamps.

¿Sabes que . . . ?

Spain has five official languages: Spanish, Catalan, Basque, Galician, and Valencian. Originally the language of Castile in central Spain, Spanish is the primary national language and is also spoken in most of Spain's former empire in what is today North, Central, and South America.

Para pensar

Spain has been influenced by many civilizations, including those of the ancient Greeks, Romans, and Moors. What civilizations have most affected the language, culture, and customs of the United States?

Go Online PHSchool.com
For: Online Atlas
Visit: www.phschool.com
Web Code: jae-0002

Universal Access

Advanced Learners

Have students research Spain's monarchy that defeated the Moors in 1492. Have them answer questions such as: Who were the monarchs at that time? What regions were occupied by the Moors? Does the monarchy still exist?

Heritage Language Learners

Have students research the languages that influenced their heritage country. Have them answer the question: Why is Spanish spoken there? Also, have them find some words used in their heritage country that, due to non-Spanish influences, may not be used in Spain.

Culture

Originally a royal retreat, the Parque del Buen Retiro is now a favorite place for the traditional Sunday-afternoon *paseo* (stroll). Throngs of people come to enjoy the Retiro's lakes, gardens, and museums, or simply to spend time with friends or family. What are your favorite places to go walking with friends? Why?

Arabic-speaking Moors from North Africa ruled much of Spain for nearly 800 years. Córdoba in southern Spain became one of the most important cities in Islam, and its mosque, the Mezquita, was one of the largest in the world. The Alhambra in Granada (shown above) is a strongly fortified and beautiful complex of palaces and gardens. It was also the last stronghold of the Moors in Spain, falling to Spain's Catholic monarchs in 1492.

The Bilbao Guggenheim Museum opened in October 1997 and houses a collection of modern and contemporary art. The building's titanium-paneled curves and concrete blocks imitate the harbor of Bilbao, a principal seaport and former shipbuilding center in the heart of the Basque country in the north.

Suggestions: Some students may have difficulty understanding the timeline. Spain was part of the Roman empire before the Moors occupied it and later acquired its own possessions in other regions and continents after defeating the Moors in 1492.

Point out how Spain has maintained its history (the buildings from the time of the Moors) while incorporating the very up-to-date (the Guggenheim Museum).

Direct attention to the *Para pensar* and have students discuss the question.

Answers will vary.

Extension: Have students research the official languages of Spain. Direct them to the *¿Sabes qué ...?* and have them find out where in Spain each language is spoken. Note that Spanish *(Castillian)* was originally the language of Castile.

Go Online

The Online Atlas provides additional maps of the locations mentioned here.

Theme Project

Students can perform step 3 at this point. (For more information, see p. 24-a.)

Enriching Your Teaching

Teacher-to-Teacher

Allow those who did the research describe in the Universal Access sections to present their findings to the class. You may wish to have a bulletin board where students can display photos or reports. This will allow others to review them.

Teacher-to-Teacher

Let students work together to create a map showing Spain as a Roman colony and Spain as a colonial power. Have them display it on a wall or bulletin board in the classroom.

Review Activities

To talk about activities: Have students work in pairs to quiz each other on the vocabulary. Have them create flashcards. Creating and collecting these cards may prove helpful to students throughout the *Realidades* course.

To say what you like and don't like to do: Have students work in pairs and tell each other what they like to do and don't like to do. Students can respond with: ***A mí también*** *or* ***A mí tampoco.***

To ask others what they like to do: Have students interview each other about activities they like to do. Ask students to brainstorm a list of activities and write five questions using ***¿Te gusta...?*** Tell them to interview a different classmate for each question. Encourage students to use the phrases in *Other useful words and expressions* in their responses. After they have completed the interview, ask volunteers: *¿Qué te gusta hacer?*

Portfolio

Invite students to review the chapter activities, including written reports, posters or other visuals, and tapes of oral presentations, or other projects. Have them select one or two items that they feel best demonstrate their achievements in Spanish. Include these products in students' portfolios. Have them include this with the Chapter Checklist and Self-Assessment Worksheet.

Additional Resources

- Audio Program: CD Cap. 1A, Track 21
- Resource Book: Cap. 1A, Clip Art
- Resource Book: Cap. 1A, Situation Cards
- Asssessment Program: Cap. 1A, Chapter Checklist and Self-Assessment Worksheeet

Chapter Review

Repaso del capítulo

Vocabulario y gramática

To prepare for the test, check to see if you...
- know the new vocabulary and grammar
- can perform the tasks on p. 53

to talk about activities

bailar	to dance
cantar	to sing
correr	to run
dibujar	to draw
escribir cuentos	to write stories
escuchar música	to listen to music
esquiar	to ski
hablar por teléfono	to talk on the phone
ir a la escuela	to go to school
jugar videojuegos	to play video games
leer revistas	to read magazines
montar en bicicleta	to ride a bicycle
montar en monopatín	to skateboard
nadar	to swim
pasar tiempo con amigos	to spend time with friends
patinar	to skate
practicar deportes	to play sports
tocar la guitarra	to play the guitar
trabajar	to work
usar la computadora	to use the computer
ver la tele	to watch television

to say what you like to do

(A mí) me gusta ___.	I like to ___.
(A mí) me gusta más ___.	I like to ___ better. (I prefer to ___.)
(A mí) me gusta mucho ___.	I like to ___ a lot.
A mí también.	Me too.

to say what you don't like to do

(A mí) no me gusta ___.	I don't like to ___.
(A mí) no me gusta nada ___.	I don't like to ___ at all.
A mí tampoco.	Me neither.

to ask others what they like to do

¿Qué te gusta hacer?	What do you like to do?
¿Qué te gusta más?	What do you like better (prefer)?
¿Te gusta ___?	Do you like to ___?
¿Y a ti?	And you?

other useful words and expressions

más	more
ni . . . ni	neither . . . nor, not . . . or
o	or
pues	well . . .
sí	yes
también	also, too
y	and

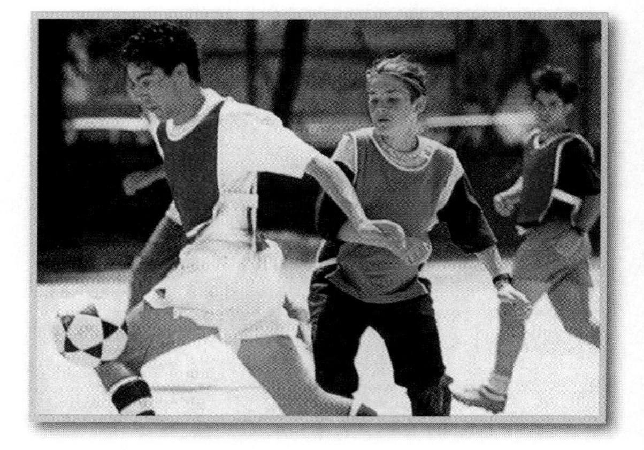

For *Vocabulario adicional,* see pp. 268–269.

Más práctica
Practice Workbook Puzzle 1A-8
Practice Workbook Organizer 1A-9

Universal Access

Students with Learning Difficulties

The *Vocabulario y gramática* page contains a good deal of information, perhaps too much for some students to absorb and understand at once. Break the review into smaller sections and give several examples for each explanation. The Organizer in the *Practice Workbook* is a useful tool for this purpose.

Advanced Learners

Give students copies of the Clip Art *(Teacher's Resource Book)* and copies of the Communicative Activities *(Teacher's Resource Book).* Tell them to use the art to test their vocabulary knowledge, and the Communicative Activities to practice the sentences.

Go Online PHSchool.com
For: Test preparation
Visit: www.phschool.com
Web Code: jad-0107

Preparación para el examen

On the exam you will be asked to . . .	Here are practice tasks similar to those you will find on the exam . . .	If you need review . . .
1 Escuchar Listen to and understand a description of what someone likes to do	Listen to a voice mail from a student looking for a "match-up" to the homecoming dance. a) What are two things this person likes doing? b) What is one thing this person dislikes doing?	**pp. 26–31** *A primera vista* **p. 27** Actividades 1–2 **p. 38** Actividad 18
 **2 Hablar** Talk about yourself and what you like and don't like to do and ask the same of others	You agreed to host a student from the Dominican Republic for a week. What can you tell him or her about yourself in a taped message? Include a brief description of what you like to do. How would you ask the student to tell you something about himself or herself?	**p. 32** Actividad 7 **p. 33** Actividades 8–9 **p. 34** Actividad 10 **p. 38** Actividades 16–17 **p. 43** Actividades 22–23 **p. 49** *Presentación oral*
 **3 Leer** Read and understand someone's description of himself or herself	Read this pen pal e-mail from a Spanish-language magazine. What does the person like to do? Does this person have anything in common with you? What is it? ¡Hola! A mí me gusta mucho usar la computadora y tocar la guitarra. No me gusta ni ir a la escuela ni leer. En el verano me gusta nadar y en el invierno me gusta esquiar. ¿Y a ti? ¿Qué te gusta hacer?	**pp. 26–31** *A primera vista* **p. 31** Actividades 3–4 **p. 35** Actividad 11 **p. 42** Actividad 21 **p. 45** Actividad 26 **pp. 46–47** *Lectura*
 **4 Escribir** Write about yourself with a description of things you like and don't like to do	A school in the Dominican Republic wants to exchange e-mails with your school. Tell your e-pal your name and what you like to do and don't like to do.	**p. 31** Actividad 5 **p. 32** Actividades 6–7 **p. 38** Actividades 16–17 **p. 44** Actividades 24–25 **p. 47** *¿Comprendes?*, no. 3
 **5 Pensar** Demonstrate an understanding of cultural differences regarding dancing	How would you describe the Latin dances that have become popular in the United States? With what countries do you associate each dance? With what type of music or rhythms do you associate each dance?	**p. 41** Actividad 20 **p. 40** *Fondo cultural* **p. 48** *La cultura en vivo*

Enriching Your Teaching

Teacher-to-Teacher

After students review the vocabulary and work together in pairs, organize a "vocabulary bee." Have all students stand in a circle around the room. Give students an English word and ask them to name its Spanish equivalent or give a Spanish word and ask for the English version. One by one, ask them to identify the correct word when you prompt them. When students do not know a word, they have to sit down. The last student standing is the winner.

Performance Tasks

 *Standards:* 1.1, 1.2, 1.3, 4.2

Resources: Audio Program: CD Cap. 1A, Track 22; Resource Book: Cap. 1A, Audio Script; Practice Answers on Transparencies

Suggestions: Explain the format of the chapter test to students. The first portion will assess their knowledge of vocabulary and grammar. The second portion is performance-based and will have tasks very similar to those shown here.

1. Escuchar

Suggestions: Play the *Audio CD* or read the script until all students can say the answers. Ask students to suggest answers to the questions.

Script and Answers:

Pues, ... a mí me gusta practicar deportes y pasar tiempo con mis amigos. *(This person likes to practice sports and spend time with friends.)* ¿Y bailar? No me gusta nada bailar. ¿Y a ti? *(This person doesn't like to dance).*

2. Hablar

Suggestions: Allow time for students to work in class. If they have difficulty speaking spontaneously, have them write their messages and practice them until they can say them without consulting their notes.

Answers will vary.

3. Leer

Suggestions: Remind students that cognates can help them understand unfamiliar words.

Answers: usar la computadora, tocar la guitarra, nadar, esquiar; answers will vary.

4. Escribir

Suggestions: Have students try this activity without consulting the vocabulary list, notes, or completed activities.

5. Pensar

Suggestions: Ask students to call out the names of various dances. Elicit comments about rhythms, instruments, dance steps, etc.

Assessment

- Examen del capítulo: 1A
- Audio Program: CD 20, Track 3

Alternative Assessment

- ExamView Test Bank CD-ROM
- Resource Book: Cap. 1A, Situation Cards
- Resource Book: Cap. 1A, Communicative Activities

Capítulo 1B

Overview

Chapter Overview

A primera vista — INPUT	Manos a la obra — PRACTICE	¡Adelante! — APPLICATION	Repaso del capítulo — REVIEW
Objectives Read, listen to, and explain information about: • personality traits	**Objectives** • Talk about what people are like • Ask people to talk about themselves and others • Describe your own personality traits	**Objectives** • Read and understand an article about personality traits • Compare different views on what makes a good friend • Talk about the Caribbean • Write a letter to a pen pal • Explain cultural perspectives on friendship	**Objectives** • Prepare for the chapter test
Vocabulary • Adjectives to describe people • Words to ask about or answer what someone is like	**Vocabulary** • Practice and learn new vocabulary	**Vocabulary** • Application	**Vocabulary** • Review
Grammar Lexical use of: • adjectives • definite and indefinite articles • word order: placement of adjectives	**Grammar** • Adjectives • Definite and indefinite articles • Word order: placement of adjectives	**Grammar** • Application	**Grammar** • Review
Culture • Frida Kahlo	**Culture** • Simón Bolívar	**Culture** • ***huipil*** • What makes a good friend • Facts about the Caribbean	**Culture** • Demonstrate an understanding of cultural differences regarding dancing

Learner Support

Strategies

- Using cognates
- Learning by repetition
- Using visual clues to get meaning
- Using the writing process

Recycling

- Gender
- Negatives
- Lexical use of ***gustar***

Pronunciación

- Vowels ***o*** and ***u***

Exploración del lenguaje

- Cognates that begin with ***es*** + consonant

Conexiones

- Literature: ***poema diamante***

Beyond the Classroom

Countries

- Bolivia
- Mexico
- Colombia
- Venezuela
- Peru
- Guatemala
- Ecuador
- Cuba
- Puerto Rico
- Dominican Republic
- United States (Texas)

El español en el mundo del trabajo

- Usefulness of Spanish as a work skill

Internet

- Vocabulary activities
- Grammar activities
- Internet links
- Self-tests

Print Components

TEACHER

Teacher's Resource Book
- Chapter Resource Checklist
- Input Script
- Video Script
- Audio Script
- Answer Keys
- *GramActiva* Blackline Master
- Communicative Activity Blackline Masters
- Situation Cards Blackline Masters
- School-to-Home Connection Letter
- Vocabulary Clip Art

TPR Storytelling Book
- Cap. 1B

STUDENT

Practice Workbook
- Vocabulary: 1B-1 – 1B-4
- Grammar: 1B-5 – 1B-7
- Puzzle: 1B-8
- Organizer: 1B-9

Writing, Audio & Video Workbook
- Writing: 1B-1 – 1B-4
- Audio: 1B-5 – 1B-10
- Video: 1B-11

Realidades para hispanohablantes
- Cap. 1B

Transparencies

Vocabulary & Grammar Transparencies
- Chapter Opener: 12–17, 20 (maps)
- *A primera vista:* 40–41
- *Videohistoria:* 12 (map), 42–43
- Grammar: 2 (graphic organizer), 44–46
- *Lectura:* 47

Practice Answers on Transparencies
- Cap. 1B

Fine Art Transparencies
- Transparencies
- Teacher's Guide

Assessment

Assessment Program
- *Pruebas:*
  - Vocabulary recognition: 1B-1
  - Vocabulary production: 1B-2
  - Adjectives: 1B-3
  - Definite and indefinite articles: 1B-4
  - Placement of adjectives: 1B-5
- *Examen del capítulo:* 1B

ExamView Test Bank CD-ROM

Test Preparation Workbook
- Cap. 1B Reading #1
- Cap. 1B Reading #2

Alternative Assessment
- Performance-Based Speaking
- Assessment Program: Rubrics
- Internet Self-Test
- Situation Cards Blackline Masters
- TPR Storytelling Book: Speaking Task

Technology

iText

Mind Point Quiz Show CD-ROM

Resource Pro CD-ROM
- Lesson Planner
- Teacher Resources
- Clip Art

Video Program
- *A primera vista* video: *Amigos por Internet*
- *GramActiva* Videos:
  - adjectives
  - definite and indefinite articles

Audio Program CDs
- *A primera vista*
- *Escucha y escribe* activities
- Audio Activities
- *Pronunciación*
- *Repaso*
- Chapter Listening Test
- Songs

Regular Schedule (50 minutes)

For electronic lesson plans: Resource Pro CD-ROM

	Warm-up / Assess	Preview / Present / Practice / Communicate	Wrap-up / Homework Options
DAY 1	**Return Examen del capítulo (10 min.)**	**A primera vista (35 min.)** • Objectives • Presentation: *Vocabulario y gramática en contexto* • *Actividades* 1, 2 • *Fondo cultural*	**Wrap-up and Homework Options (5 min.)** • Practice Workbook 1B-1, 1B-2 • Go Online • Heritage Language Learner Workbook • Vocabulary Clip Art
DAY 2	**Warm-up (5 min.)** • Homework check	**A primera vista (40 min.)** • Review: *Vocabulario y gramática en contexto* • Presentation: *Videohistoria Amigos por Internet* • View: Video *Amigos por Internet* • Video Activities • *Actividades* 3, 4	**Wrap-up and Homework Options (5 min.)** • *Prueba* 1B-1: Vocabulary recognition • Practice Workbook 1B-3, 1B-4 • Go Online
DAY 3	**Warm-up (5 min.)** • Homework check **✓Assessment (10 min.)** • *Prueba* 1B-1: Voc. recognition	**Manos a la obra (30 min.)** • Objectives • *Actividades* 5, 6	**Wrap-up and Homework Options (5 min.)** • *Actividad* 7
DAY 4	**Warm-up (10 min.)** • Homework check • Return *Prueba* 1B-1: Voc. recognition	**Manos a la obra (35 min.)** • Presentation: Adjectives • *GramActiva* Video • *Actividad* 9 • *Juego: Actividad* 10	**Wrap-up and Homework Options (5 min.)** • *Actividad* 8 • Practice Workbook 1B-5
DAY 5	**Warm-up (10 min.)** • Homework check	**Manos a la obra (35 min.)** • Review: Adjectives • *Actividades* 11, 12	**Wrap-up and Homework Options (5 min.)** • *Actividad* 13
DAY 6	**Warm-up (5 min.)** • Homework check	**Manos a la obra (40 min.)** • Review: Adjectives • *Actividades* 14, 15	**Wrap-up and Homework Options (5 min.)** • *Actividad* 16
DAY 7	**Warm-up (5 min.)** • Homework check	**Manos a la obra (40 min.)** • *Actividad* 18 • *Fondo cultural* • *Exploración del lenguaje* • Audio Activities • *Conexiones: Actividad* 17	**Wrap-up and Homework Options (5 min.)** • *Prueba* 1B-3: Adjectives • Go Online
DAY 8	**Warm-up (5 min.)** • Homework check **✓Assessment (10 min.)** • *Prueba* 1B-3: Adjectives	**Manos a la obra (30 min.)** • Presentation: Definite and indefinite articles • *GramActiva* Video • *Actividades* 19, 20, 21, 22 • *Pronunciación*	**Wrap-up and Homework Options (5 min.)** • Practice Workbook 1B-6 • *Prueba* 1B-2: Vocabulary production • Go Online

	Warm-up / Assess	Preview / Present / Practice / Communicate	Wrap-up / Homework Options
DAY 9	**Warm-up (5 min.)** • Homework check **✔Assessment (10 min.)** • *Prueba* 1B-2: Voc. production	**Manos a la obra (30 min.)** • Review: Direct and indirect articles • Presentation: Word order: Placement of adjectives • *Actividad* 23, 24, 25 • *El español en el mundo del trabajo*	**Wrap-up and Homework Options (5 min.)** • *Actividad* 26, 27 • Go Online • *Prueba* 1B-4: Definite and indefinite articles • Practice Workbook 1B-7
DAY 10	**Warm-up (5 min.)** • Homework check **✔Assessment (10 min.)** • *Prueba* 1B-4: Definite and indefinite articles	**Manos a la obra (10 min.)** • *Actividad* 28 • *Fondo cultural* **¡Adelante! (20 min.)** • *Lectura* • *Fondo cultural*	**Wrap-up and Homework Options (5 min.)** • Go Online • *¿Comprendes?*
DAY 11	**Warm-up (5 min.)** • Homework check • Return *Prueba* 1B-4: Definite and indefinite articles	**¡Adelante! (40 min.)** • Presentation: *Presentación escrita:* Prewrite • *Perspectivas del mundo hispano*	**Wrap-up and Homework Options (5 min.)** • Go Online
DAY 12	**Warm-up (5 min.)** • Homework check	**¡Adelante! (40 min.)** • *Presentación escrita:* Draft, revise	**Wrap-up and Homework Options (5 min.)** • Go Online • *Presentación escrita:* Publish
DAY 13	**Warm-up (5 min.)** • Homework check	**¡Adelante! (40 min.)** • *Presentación escrita:* Present	**Wrap-up and Homework Options (5 min.)** • Writing Activities • Practice Workbook 1B-8, 1B-9
DAY 14	**Warm-up (5 min.)** • Homework check	**¡Adelante! (20 min.)** • *El mundo hispano* **Repaso (20 min.)** • *Vocabulario y gramática* • *Preparación para el examen*	**Wrap-up and Homework Options (5 min.)** • Go Online: Self-test • *Examen del capítulo*
DAY 15	**Warm-up (5 min.)** • Answer questions **✔Assessment (45 min.)** • *Examen del capítulo*		

Standards for *Capítulo* 1B

- To achieve the goals of the Standards, students will:

Communication

1.1 Interpersonal

- Talk about: personality traits; themselves and each other; activities and personality traits; familiar objects

1.2 Interpretive

- Listen to information about personality traits
- Read information about likes and dislikes
- Read a picture-based story; listen to and watch a video about personality traits; listen to and identify the gender of nouns
- Read a personality quiz based on color association

1.3 Presentational

- Present descriptions of traits of themselves and others
- Use poetry to express and describe themselves
- Present information about likes and dislikes
- Present information about parts of the body

Culture

2.1 Practices and Perspectives

- Understand how friendships are formed and maintained in some Spanish-speaking countries
- Learn about the rise in use of cybercafés.
- Understand how Spanish in the Caribbean is influenced by European and African

2.2 Products and Perspectives

- Learn about Frida Kahlo and her painting
- Learn how the ***huipil*** reveals facts about its wearer
- Understand how music in the Caribbean is influenced by the musical styles from around the world

Connections

3.1 Cross-curricular

- Learn about: important artists and their work: Kahlo; the influence of Simón Bolívar
- Learn about and write a type of poem known as the ***diamante***

Comparisons

4.1 Language

- Learn vocabulary through the recognition of cognates
- Learn to build vocabulary through the use of root words; compare cognates that begin with the letters ***es*** plus consonant
- Understand the use of definite and indefinite articles; gender-agreement rules with use of adjectives
- Learn the pronunciation of the letters ***o*** and ***u***; learn the placement of adjectives

4.2 Culture

- Compare: Internet-based chat habits of teenagers clothing choices that reflect personality; public access to computers and the Internet; words used to identify friends and acquaintances; how friendships are formed and maintained; the African influence on music in the Americas
- Learn about and compare the influence of Simón Bolívar to other leaders

Communities

5.1 Beyond the School

- Reflect and discuss careers promoting bilingualism

5.2 Lifelong Learner

- Communicate by e-mail in Spanish

Tema 1 • Mis amigos y yo

Fondo cultural

Frida Kahlo (1907–1954) is one of the best-known Mexican painters. In spite of a childhood illness, a crippling traffic accident, and many hospital stays throughout her life, Kahlo was a successful painter and led a very active social life. She used her artwork as an outlet for her physical and emotional suffering.

- Frida Kahlo painted over fifty self-portraits. What is she saying about herself through this painting?

Autorretrato con mono (1938), Frida Kahlo

Universal Access

Personalizing the Theme

Have students write down the names of two or three of their friends. Ask them to list three adjectives that describe the personalities or characteristics of these friends. Explain that in this chapter they will learn how to describe the traits of people they know.

Heritage Language Learners

Point out that in the United States people use words other than "friend" when referring to their associates. Can students give other words in English that mean "friend"? What words do they use in Spanish other than ***amigo*** that mean the same thing? Can they place them in order of formality?

Capítulo 1B

Y tú, ¿cómo eres?

Chapter Objectives

- Talk about personality traits
- Ask and tell what people are like
- Use adjectives to describe people
- Understand cultural perspectives on friendship

Video Highlights

A primera vista: ***Amigos por Internet***

GramActiva Videos: adjectives; definite and indefinite articles; word order: placement of adjectives

Country Connection

As you learn how to describe yourself and your friends, you will make connections to these countries and places:

Go Online PHSchool.com
For: Online Atlas
Visit: www.phschool.com
Web Code: jae-0002

En los Pirineos, España

Chapter Opener

Presentation

Resources: Voc. & Gram. Transparencies: 12–17, 20 (maps)

Suggestions: Explain that students will learn language for identifying personality traits and describing what people are like. (Physical descriptions will be taught in Level B *Cap.* 5B in the context of family.) The video story focuses on e-mails being exchanged by strangers in two different cities. The *GramActiva* Videos will help students learn to describe things using adjectives.

Standards: 2.2, 3.1

Fondo cultural

Resources: Fine Arts Transparencies; Fine Arts Transparencies Teacher's Guide

Suggestions: After students have studied the paragraph and the painting, explain that Frida Kahlo chose to wear traditional Mexican clothing and jewelry, and this is reflected in her self-portraits. Have students comment on what the painter is wearing and her facial expression. Ask them what they would include in a self-portrait.

Answers will vary but may include personality traits, or that she displays some pain in the serious tone of the self-portrait.

Enriching Your Teaching

Planning for Instruction

Resources:

- Resource Pro CD-ROM or Resource Book
  - Teaching resources
  - Lesson Planner
  - Chapter Resource Checklist
  - School-to-Home Connection Letter

Culture Note

Footpaths (***senderos***) exist in many of the mountainous areas in Spain. The *Federación Española de Montañismo* publishes booklets with maps of ***senderos*** throughout the Pyrenees, Catalonia, Basque country, and the Sierra Nevada mountains in southern Spain.

Vocabulario y gramática

Presentation

 *Standards:* 1.2, 4.1

Resources: Resource Book: Cap. 1B, Input Script; Voc. & Gram. Transparencies: 40–41; Resource Book: Cap. 1B, Clip Art; TPR Storytelling Book: Cap. 1B; Audio Program: CD Cap. 1B, Tracks 1–2

Focus: Presenting vocabulary about personality traits

Suggestions: Use the Input Script from the *Teacher's Resource Book* to present the new vocabulary, or use some of the suggestions here. Show the transparencies and ask students to tell you in English what trait is represented in each image. Then go back and provide input as you describe each one using the language in the book. Present the *Más vocabulario* using pantomime or exaggerated acting. Explain to students that they will be held responsible for knowing the words in the *Más vocabulario*.

Ask a male student to read the description of ***el chico*** and a female student to read the description of ***el chica.*** Explain that many adjectives have different endings depending on whether they're being used to describe a female or a male. Can students begin to deduce the rules? Encourage them to guess meanings of cognates. Can they guess the opposite of ***impaciente?***

You could also use characters from popular culture to demonstrate the vocabulary.

Additional Resources

- Audio Program: Song CD

A primera vista

Objectives

Read, listen to, and understand information about
- personality traits

Vocabulario y gramática en contexto

“¿El chico? **Es mi amigo. ¿Cómo se llama?** Se llama Marcos. **¿Cómo es?** Pues . . .

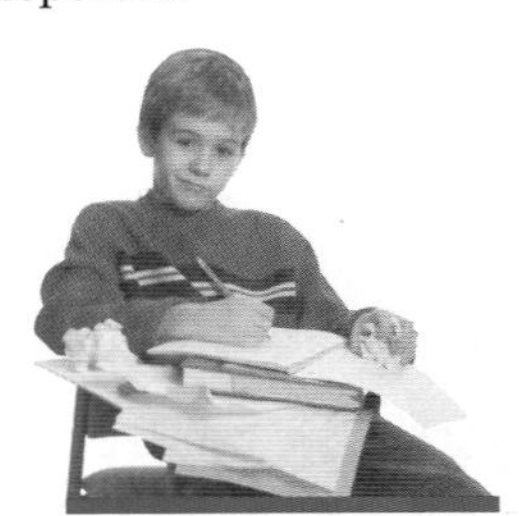

el chico

. . . él es **deportista. Le gusta** mucho practicar deportes.

Pero a veces es **impaciente . . .**

. . . también es **un** chico **desordenado.**”

“Mi amiga Sarita es **una buena** amiga. No es **muy** deportista . . .

la chica

. . . pero es una chica **artística . . .**

. . . y muy **ordenada.**

Es una chica muy **inteligente.**”

Universal Access

Heritage Language Learners

Students may know of other words used to refer to a boy or a girl. Discuss the differences between various terms. Ask them which words they would use with a good friend. Would they use the same ones when talking with an acquaintance or someone they don't know?

Advanced Learners

Have students bring in magazine or newspaper pictures of people in various professions, such as firefighters, judges, athletes, comedians, artists, etc. and write a list of peersonality traits for each profession. Students can use these as flashcards to review or expand their vocabulary.

“Hola, me llamo Luz. **¿Yo?**
¿Cómo **soy**? Pues . . .

. . . soy **estudiosa** . . .

. . . y también **graciosa** . . .

. . . y **trabajadora** . . .

. . . pero **según mi familia** ¡a veces soy **perezosa**! Y tú, **¿cómo eres?**”

Más vocabulario

atrevido, -a daring
paciente patient
reservado, -a shy
simpático, -a nice, friendly
talentoso, -a talented

Actividad 1 **Escuchar**

¿Marcos o Sarita?

Look at the pictures of Marcos and Sarita, and listen to the descriptions. If a word describes Marcos, point to his picture. If a word describes Sarita, point to her picture.

Actividad 2 **Escuchar**

¿Cierto o falso?

You will hear some statements about Luz. Give a “thumbs-up” sign if a statement is true, or a “thumbs-down” sign if it is false.

Más práctica

Practice Workbook 1B-1, 1B-2

For: Vocabulary practice
Visit: www.phschool.com
Web Code: jad-0111

Actividad 1 *Standards:* 1.2

Resources: Audio Program: CD Cap. 1B, Track 3; Resource Book: Cap. 1B, Audio Script; Practice Answers on Transparencies

Focus: Listening comprehension of vocabulary for personality traits

Suggestions: Have students scan the photos and read the captions on p. 56 before beginning the activity. Play the *Audio CD* or read the script. Pause often to monitor that students are identifying the correct person. Have volunteers say the answers aloud.

Script and Answers:

1. deportista *(Marcos)*
2. artística *(Sarita)*
3. inteligente *(Sarita)*
4. impaciente *(Marcos)*
5. ordenada *(Sarita)*
6. desordenado *(Marcos)*
7. el chico *(Marcos)*
8. buena amiga *(Sarita)*

Actividad 2 *Standards:* 1.2

Resources: Audio Program: CD Cap. 1B, Track 4; Resource Book: Cap. 1B, Audio Script; Practice Answers on Transparencies

Focus: Listening comprehension of vocabulary for personality traits

Suggestions: Play the *Audio CD* or read the script. Be sure students understand that the references are to the girl pictured at the top of p. 57. Tell them that words not included in the picture should receive a thumbs down.

Script and Answers:

¿Cómo es Luz?
Es estudiosa. *(up)*
Es impaciente. *(down)*
Es muy graciosa. *(up)*
Es ordenada. *(down)*
Es trabajadora. *(up)*
Es talentosa. *(down)*
Pero, según la familia, ¡a veces es perezosa! *(up)*

Enriching Your Teaching

Teacher-to-Teacher

The more students get to know each other, the more comfortable they will feel using Spanish in the classroom. Pair students up with a partner they may not know very well and ask them to find out what that person is like. Have students give their partner at least three adjectives to describe themselves. When students have completed their interviews, have them introduce their partners and tell the class what they are like.

Videohistoria

Presentation

 *Standards:* 1.2, 4.1

Resources: Voc. & Gram. Transparencies: 42–43; Audio Program: CD Cap. 1B, Track 5

Focus: Presenting additional personality traits vocabulary; extending presentation of contextualized vocabulary and grammar; previewing the language video

Suggestions: Introduce the four new characters by name. Explain that Pedro, who is chatting on the Internet, receives a mystery e-mail from a girl named ***Chica sociable***. Be sure students understand that the boys are in San Antonio and the girls are in Mexico City, and that they don't know one another.

Pre-reading: Direct students' attention to the *Strategy*. Have them scan the story and write a list of possible cognates. Using the transparencies, ask students to predict the story line: Whom would Claudia like, Pedro or Esteban? Tell them to use the photos to answer the pre-reading questions.

Answers will vary but may include:

1. **They are using a computer in a library.**
2. **Yes. The students are in computer labs. They might be writing e-mails to each other.**

Videohistoria

Amigos por Internet

See what happens when *Chica sociable* sends an e-mail message to Esteban.

Antes de leer

Strategy **Using cognates** You will see some unfamiliar words in this story. Many of these are cognates. Use their similarity to English words to determine their meaning.

- What does *sociable* mean? What does *ideal* mean?

1. Look at photo 1. What are the boys doing?
2. Look at photos 3 and 4. Are the students at different locations? Where are they? How do you think the students in the two photos might be connected?

Universal Access

Multiple Intelligences

Bodily / Kinesthetic: As a pre-reading activity, have students play Charades to practice adjectives. Ask them to write one adjective on a strip of paper and drop the paper into a container. Students take turns drawing a word and acting it out while the class guesses the word. The person acting out the word use body language or movement, but may not use any words or make noises.

1 **Pedro:** Esteban, escucha: "Hola, ¿cómo eres? ¿Qué te gusta hacer? Me gusta mucho hablar con mis amigos. Me llamo *Chica sociable.* Escríbeme."

Esteban: ¡Ja! *Chica sociable.* A responder. Escribe, Pedro . . .

2 **Pedro:** "Hola. Me llamo *Chico sociable.* ¡Qué coincidencia!"

3 **Pedro:** "Me gusta pasar tiempo con mis amigos. **No soy** muy **serio**. Según mis amigos, soy gracioso."

4 **Claudia:** *¡Chica sociable!* ¡Ja!

Teresa: Yo soy *Chica sociable.*

Claudia: ¡No! ¿Tú **eres** *Chica sociable?* Mi buena amiga . . .

Suggestions:

Reading: Go through the captions with students. Using the transparencies help students figure out the details of the story.

Post-reading: Have students review their list of cognates and discuss their findings. Did the list of cognates help them with comprehension? Complete *Actividades* 3 and 4 to check comprehension.

Additional Resources

- Writing, Audio & Video Workbook: Cap. 1B, Video Activity 1
- Heritage Learner Workbook: 1B-1, 1B-2

Enriching Your Teaching

Culture Note

Suggest that students research the cities of San Antonio and Mexico City for pictures and information about their common history and culture. The American Southwest was influenced by Spain and Mexico, beginning in the 1500s when the Spaniards explored the region and encountered the indigenous cultures. Many influences of Spanish and Mexican cultures can be seen in the American Southwest today.

Internet Search

Keywords:

Mexico City;
San Antonio, Texas

Video

Presentation

Standards: 1.2, 4.1

Resources: Video Program: Cap. 1B; Resource Book: Cap. 1B, Video Script

Focus: Comprehension of a story about people describing themselves

Suggestions:

Pre-viewing: Remind students that they will not understand every word in the video, but that they should listen and watch for overall understanding.

Viewing: Show the video once without pausing, and then go back and show it again, stopping along the way to check comprehension. Use the graphics-supported version to help reinforce the new words. Show the unsupported segment a final time without pausing.

Post-viewing: Complete the Video Activities in the *Writing, Audio & Video Workbook.*

Additional Resources

- Writing, Audio & Video Workbook: Cap. 1B, Video Activities 2–4

5 **Teresa:** "Soy muy desordenada. Me gusta hablar por teléfono. Y no me gusta ir a la escuela. Escríbeme. *Chica sociable.*"

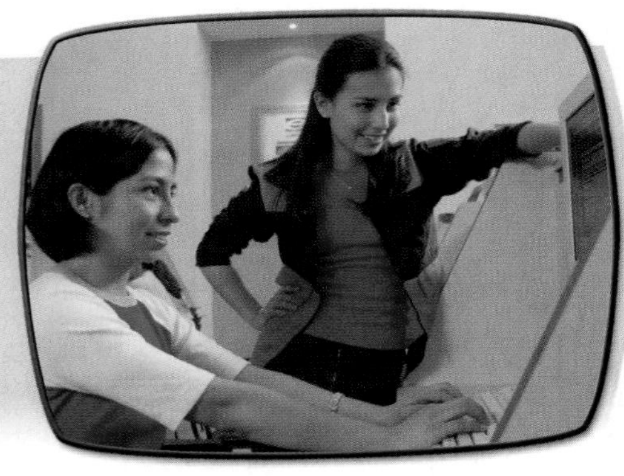

6 **Claudia:** Un momento . . . uno más de mí. Escribe . . . "Yo soy *Chica misteriosa.* Soy amiga de *Chica sociable.* Soy muy simpática."

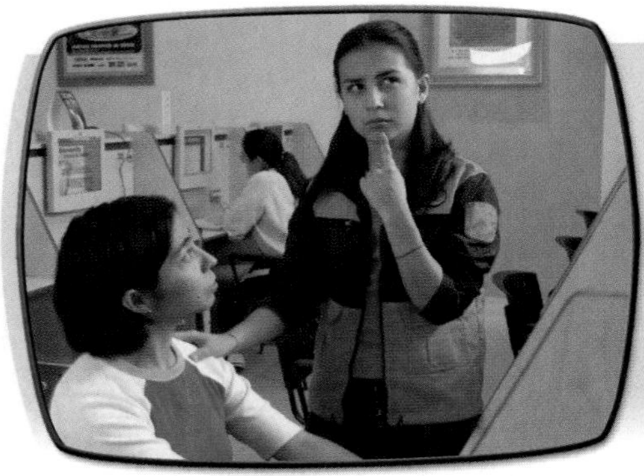

7 **Claudia:** "Y me gusta ir a la escuela. Soy estudiosa y trabajadora. Yo no soy tu chica ideal. *Chica misteriosa.*"

8 **Esteban:** Pues, Pedro. *¿Chica sociable* o *Chica misteriosa?*

Pedro: *Chica misteriosa.* Me gusta la escuela y a ella le gusta la escuela también.

Esteban: Perfecto. A mí me gusta más *Chica sociable.*

Universal Access

Heritage Language Learners

Have students write a paragraph describing the ideal person for ***Chica misteriosa*** or ***Chico sociable.*** Check to be sure they are making appropriate adjective agreements.

Multiple Intelligences

Bodily / Kinesthetic: Ask students to come to the front of the class and role-play the parts of the four students in the video. Encourage them to be dramatic and to act out any adjectives they can. Give them a few minutes to practice beforehand.

Escribir/Hablar

¿Comprendes?

Read each of the sentences below and indicate which character is being described: *Chica sociable* or *Chica misteriosa.*

1. Me gusta hablar por teléfono.
2. Me gusta ir a la escuela.
3. Soy simpática.
4. No soy muy ordenada.
5. Soy trabajadora.

Claudia

Teresa

Leer/Pensar

¿Qué les gusta hacer?

Number your paper 1–8. Based on the *Videohistoria,* decide which characters you think would like to do the activities below. Write the names of all of the characters you have chosen beside each number.

1. trabajar	5. hablar
2. estudiar	7. pasar tiempo con amigos
3. bailar	6. ir a la escuela
4. leer	8. usar la computadora

Esteban

Pedro

Más práctica

Practice Workbook 1B-3, 1B-4

For: Vocabulary practice
Visit: www.phschool.com
Web Code: jad-0112

Enriching Your Teaching

Teacher-to-Teacher

Have students draw a series of three pictures of themselves and label the pictures using the vocabulary introduced on pp. 56–60. Ask volunteers to share their drawings with the class.

Standards: 1.2, 1.3

Resources: Practice Answers on Transparencies

Focus: Reading comprehension

Suggestions: When students tell you the name of the character being described, have them identify the number of the panel that contains this information.

Answers:

1. Chica sociable, panel 5
2. Chica misteriosa, panel 7
3. Chica misteriosa, panel 6
4. Chica sociable, panel 5
5. Chica misteriosa, panel 7

Extension: Have students make a T-chart listing the characteristics of ***Chica sociable*** on one side and the characteristics of ***Chica misteriosa*** on the other. Ask students whom they would prefer to have as a friend and explain why.

Standards: 1.2

Resources: Practice Answers on Transparencies

Focus: Reading comprehension

Suggestions: Before beginning this activity, have students scan the reading and take notes on the adjectives used to describe the characters, as well as each character's likes and dislikes. Remind students that Esteban is ***Chico sociable,*** Teresa is ***Chica sociable,*** Claudia is ***Chica misteriosa,*** and Pedro has the same interests as Claudia.

Answers:

1. Claudia
2. Claudia, Pedro
3. Teresa, Esteban
4. Teresa, Esteban
5. Claudia, Pedro
6. Teresa, Esteban
7. todos
8. todos

 *Standards:* 1.2, 1.3

Resources: Practice Answers on Transparencies

Focus: Using new vocabulary to complete sentences with adjectives

Suggestions: Point out that students should look at the two adjective choices with each picture as well as the pictures.

Answers:

1. artística
2. desordenado
3. perezosa
4. atrevida
5. reservado
6. estudioso

Common Errors: Even when the correct adjective endings are given, beginning students may forget to use the correct gender ending when they focus on vocabulary meanings. Remind students to be careful with spelling.

Extension: To reinforce the meanings of the adjectives, have students name a friend or classmate who could be described by each of the statements. Remind them to keep gender in mind as they substitute their friend's names for ***la chica*** and ***el chico*** in each sentence.

Manos a la obra

Vocabulario y gramática en uso

Objectives

- Talk about what people are like
- Ask people to talk about themselves and others
- Describe your own personality traits

Actividad 5 **Escribir**

¿Cómo es el chico o la chica?

Number your paper 1–6. Choose the correct word to describe each of the people in the pictures and write the complete sentence on your paper.

Modelo

El chico es *(impaciente / estudioso).*
El chico es impaciente.

1. La chica es *(reservada / artística).*

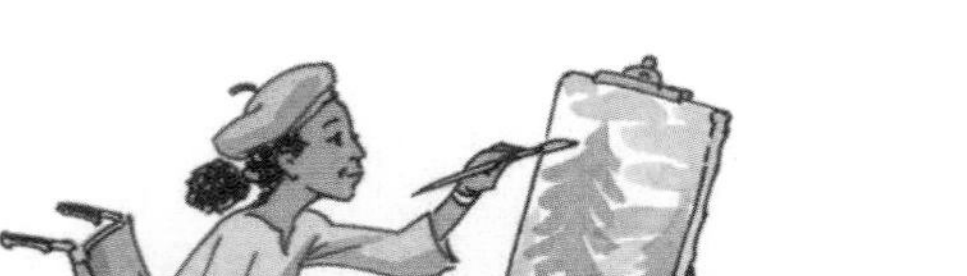

2. El chico es *(desordenado / atrevido).*

3. La chica es *(graciosa / perezosa).*

4. La chica es *(artística / atrevida).*

5. El chico es *(reservado / deportista).*

6. El chico es *(estudioso / desordenado).*

Universal Access

Multiple Intelligences

Visual / Spatial: Have students use digital cameras and word-processing software to make a class directory, using *Actividad* 6 as a model. Alternatively, they could take pictures, enlarge them, and create a bulletin board with the same information.

Students with Learning Difficulties

Before starting *Actividad* 7, have students study the word bank o be sure they understand all the words. Some students will benefit from writing the words on their own paper, then crossing them out as they are used.

Actividad 6 **Leer/Pensar**

Nuevos amigos

Look at the profiles of the following students who are chatting online with you. Put them in pairs according to who you think would make good friends. Base your decision on personality traits and favorite activities.

1. 

Catalina: Me gusta mucho correr. En general, soy deportista.

2. 

Christian: Me gusta escribir cuentos. Soy estudioso.

3. 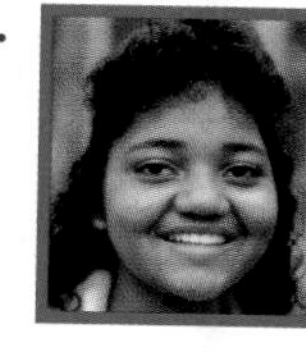

Flor: Soy reservada. No me gusta mucho hablar por teléfono.

4. 

Alejandro: No me gusta nada nadar. Me gusta más jugar videojuegos.

5. 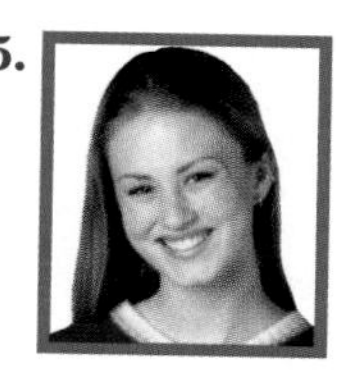

Liliana: Soy inteligente. Me gusta ir a la escuela y leer.

6. **Mayra:** No soy muy sociable, pero a veces me gusta pasar tiempo con amigos.

7. 

Alfonso: No soy deportista. Me gusta mucho usar la computadora.

8. 

Guillermo: Me gusta practicar deportes. No soy muy artístico.

Actividad 7 **Escribir**

Mi amigo José

Maritza is talking about her friend José. Read the sentences, then choose the appropriate word to fill in each blank.

Modelo

No es un chico impaciente. Es muy paciente.

1. Le gusta mucho practicar deportes. Es ___.
2. A veces no es serio. Es un chico ___.
3. Le gusta pasar tiempo con amigos. Es muy ___.
4. No es un chico ordenado. Es ___.
5. Le gusta ir a la escuela. Es ___.
6. No es perezoso. Es un chico muy ___.

trabajador	deportista
paciente	estudioso
gracioso	desordenado
sociable	

Enriching Your Teaching

Teacher-to-Teacher

Have students make a concentration game using antonyms. For example, on one index card have them write ***es trabajador*** and on another ***es perezoso.*** For vocabulary words that do not have opposites, have students write ***no es*** + that vocabulary word. When students are finished making their cards, tell them to turn the cards facedown and mix them up. Have students work in pairs taking turns trying to match adjectives with their opposite meanings. The student with the most matches wins.

Actividad 6

Standards: 1.2

Resources: Practice Answers on Transparencies

Focus: Reading descriptive vocabulary in context

Suggestions: Have students write the numbers 1–8 on their paper and write the names of the students being described and at least one adjective to describe each one. Tell students to review their notes before making their final decisions about who would make good friends.

Answers:

Catalina y Guillermo
Christian y Liliana
Flor y Mayra
Alejandro y Alfonso

Actividad 7

Standards: 1.2, 1.3, 4.1

Resources: Practice Answers on Transparencies

Focus: Writing new vocabulary in a story context

Suggestions: This is a good homework assignment. Make sure students understand the directions and the adjectives.

Answers:

1. **deportista**
2. **gracioso**
3. **sociable**
4. **desordenado**
5. **estudioso**
6. **trabajador**

Additional Resources

- Writing, Audio & Video Workbook: Cap. 1B, Audio Activities 5–6, Tracks 6–7
- Writing, Audio & Video Workbook: Cap. 1B, Writing Activity 10
- Resource Book: Cap. 1B, Communicative Activity BLM

Assessment

- Prueba 1B-2: Vocabulary production

Presentation

Standards: 4.1

Resources: Voc. & Gram. Transparencies: 44; Video Program: Cap. 1B; Resource Book: Cap. 1B, Video Script

Suggestions: Use the *GramActiva* Video either as an initial introduction to adjectives or as a follow-up to your own explanation. Write the adjectives ***gracioso, estudiosa,*** and ***inteligente*** on the board. Ask which one applies to a male, which one to a female, and which one can be applied to either. Use the text on p. 56 and the transparency to demonstrate agreement. Change the genders of the characters and tell the story again. Once students begin to grasp the concept of agreement, introduce invariable adjectives, stressing that there are relatively few of these to learn.

Standards: 1.3

Resources: Voc. & Gram. Transparencies: 2 Practice Answers on Transparencies

Focus: Recognizing feminine, masculine, and neutral endings

Suggestions: To reinforce the idea of gender, draw a large version of the Venn diagram on the board or use the transparency. Lightly shade Roberto's oval with blue, Yolanda's with pink, and the overlapping portion with yellow. Have volunteers write the answers in the appropriate spots.

Answers:
Roberto: **artístico, serio, simpático, reservado, trabajador**
Yolanda: **graciosa, ordenada, atrevida, perezosa, talentosa, estudiosa**
Either: **impaciente, paciente, sociable, deportista, inteligente**

Common Errors: Adjectives ending in ***-ista*** are commonly mistaken as feminine instead of neutral. Remind students that they apply to both.

Gramática

Adjectives

Words that describe people and things are called adjectives *(adjetivos)*.

- In Spanish, most adjectives have both masculine and feminine forms. The masculine form usually ends in the letter *-o* and the feminine form usually ends in the letter *-a*.
- Masculine adjectives are used to describe masculine nouns.

Marcos es ordenado y simpático.	*Marcos is organized and nice.*

- Feminine adjectives are used to describe feminine nouns.

Marta es ordenada y simpática.	*Marta is organized and nice.*

- Adjectives that end in *-e* describe both masculine and feminine nouns.

Anita es inteligente.	*Anita is smart.*
Pedro es inteligente también.	*Pedro is also smart.*

Masculine	Feminine
ordenado	ordenada
trabajador	trabajadora
paciente	paciente
deportista	deportista

- Adjectives whose masculine form ends in *-dor* have a feminine form that ends in *-dora*.

Juan es trabajador.	*Juan is hardworking.*
Luz es trabajadora.	*Luz is hardworking.*

- Some adjectives that end in *-a*, such as *deportista*, describe both masculine and feminine nouns. You will need to learn which adjectives follow this pattern.

Tomás es deportista.	*Tomás is athletic.*
Marta es deportista también.	*Marta is also athletic.*

GramActiva VIDEO

Want more help with masculine and feminine adjectives? Watch the **GramActiva** video.

Escribir

Roberto y Yolanda

Copy the Venn diagram on a sheet of paper. Which words from the list could only describe Roberto? Write them in the oval below his name. Which words could only describe Yolanda? Write them in the oval below her name. Which words could describe either Roberto or Yolanda? Write them in the overlapping area.

Modelo

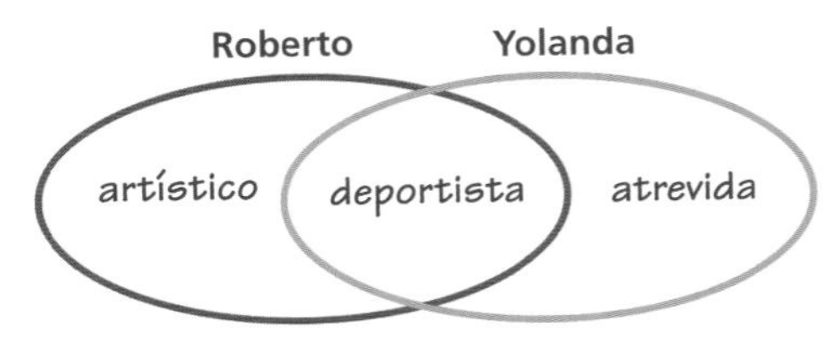

artístico	graciosa	ordenada	serio
atrevida	impaciente	paciente	sociable
deportista	simpático	perezosa	talentosa
estudiosa	inteligente	reservado	trabajador

Universal Access

Students with Special Needs

Students with motor difficulties may find it easier to do *Actividad* 8 if you use colored string or yarn to make ovals on a tabletop. Write the words on index cards for them and have them sort the words into the ovals.

Heritage Language Learners

Have students brainstorm lists of other adjectives they know that end in ***-a*** or ***-e*** but that apply to both males and females. Have them write sentences to put the words in context.

  Hablar

¿Cómo es Paloma?

Work with a partner to ask and answer questions about the people shown below.

Paloma

Modelo

A —*¿Cómo es Paloma?*
B —*Paloma es trabajadora.*

1. Elena

2. Marisol

3. Felipe

4. Juan

5. Lola

6. Gloria

  Hablar/GramActiva

Juego

Choose an adjective to act out for a small group. The other students in the group will take turns asking you questions to guess which word you are demonstrating. The first student to guess the correct adjective, in the correct form, gets to perform the next charade.

Modelo

A —*¿Eres ordenada?*
B —*¡Claro que sí! Soy ordenada.*
o: *¡Claro que no! No soy ordenada.*

Para decir más . . .

¡Claro que sí! Of course!
¡Claro que no! Of course not!
¿De veras? Really?

Enriching Your Teaching

Teacher-to-Teacher

Give each student a blue, a yellow, and a pink index card. As you call out various adjectives, have students hold up the card whose color matches the gender of the word you've said. This allows for a quick check of comprehension.

Teacher-to-Teacher

Have students practice questions and answers with the classmates in their row of desks. Ask the first student in each row: *¿Cómo eres?* That student answers using an appropriate adjective, then asks the second student the same question. Continue until all students have participated.

 Actividad 9 *Standards:* 1.2

Resources: Practice Answers on Transparencies

Focus: Asking and answering questions about what people are like

Suggestions: Pair the class for the activity. Remind Student B to pay attention to the adjective endings. When they have completed the activity, have students reverse roles.

Answers:

1. Elena es perezosa.
2. Marisol es artística/talentosa.
3. Felipe es gracioso.
4. Juan es desordenado.
5. Lola es sociable.
6. Gloria es atrevida.

Extension: Have students bring in pictures of famous people and mount them on poster board. Label the pictures with an attribute of each person: ***Pete Sampras es deportista.***

 Actividad 10 *Standards:* 1.2

Resources: Voc. & Gram. Transparencies: 40–41

Focus: Asking and answering questions about what people are like; using vocabulary in a personalized context

Suggestions: To provide a word bank, use the transparencies. Tell students not to repeat an adjective. Remind them to use the correct endings.

Answers will vary.

Standards: 1.3

Focus: Writing adjectives in a personalized context

Suggestions: Model a chart on the board or overhead that describes you. Be sure students use correct gender endings when they make their charts. Encourage them to use ***muy*** and ***a veces*** when applicable.

Answers will vary.

Extension: Have students create another chart with names of friends and family members at the top. For example, *Mi madre es / no es ..., Mi amigo Brent es / no es ...*, etc. Have students share their charts with the class. Tell students to save their charts to use in *Actividades* 12 and 13.

Standards: 1.1, 1.3

Focus: Asking and answering questions about personality traits; listening comprehension

Suggestions: Show students how to set up the new chart. Use your personal chart and role play the *Modelo* with a volunteer. Tell students to save their answers for *Actividad* 13.

Answers will vary.

Standards: 1.3

Focus: Writing descriptions of yourself and others

Suggestions: Point out that students should refer to both their ***Soy / No soy*** chart from *Actividad* 11 and their notes from *Actividad* 12.

Answers will vary.

Actividad 11 **Escribir**

Yo soy . . .

Make a chart like the one on the right. Write at least three adjectives in each column to say what you are like and are not like. Include *muy* and *a veces* when they are appropriate. Save your chart to use in later activities.

Modelo

Soy	No soy
estudiosa	perezosa
muy trabajadora	impaciente
deportista	

Actividad 12 **Hablar/Escribir**

¿Cómo eres?

Working with a partner, use the chart that you made in Actividad 11 to talk about your personality traits. Take notes on what your partner tells you. You will be asked to use this information in the next Actividad.

Modelo

A —*¿Cómo eres?*
B —*Soy estudiosa y muy trabajadora. También soy deportista. ¿Y tú?*
A —*Soy artístico. Según mis amigos, soy talentoso. No soy perezoso.*

Actividad 13 **Escribir/Hablar**

Mi amigo(a)

Use the information from Actividades 11 and 12 to write a short description of yourself and your partner. Follow the model, and be prepared to report back to the class.

Modelo

Me llamo Luisa. Soy estudiosa y trabajadora. Y soy artística. Mi amiga se llama Susana. Ella es simpática. También es artística y trabajadora.

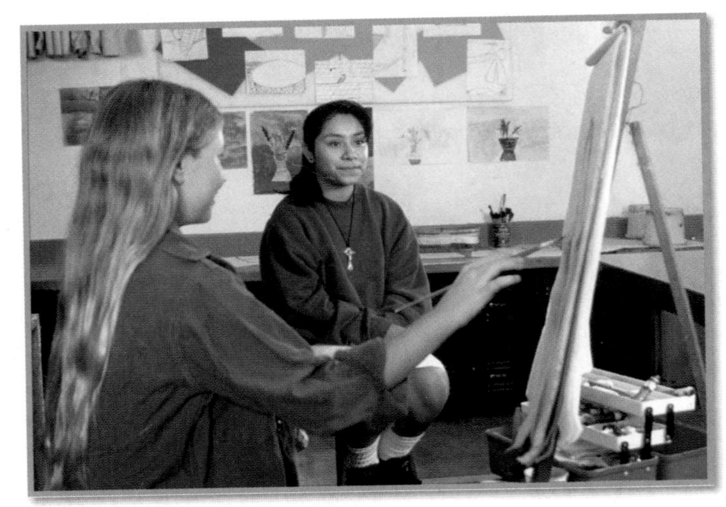

Universal Access

Multiple Intelligences

Intrapersonal / Introspective: Have students choose three or four words to describe themselves. For each of the words, have them write a sentence telling what they like or dislike doing. Example: ***artístico***—*Me gusta tocar la guitarra.*

Students with Special Needs

Allow students to refer to their Organizer and / or their flashcards as they complete the activities. Some students may need to have someone transcribe for them. Having a fellow student do this can benefit both students.

   Hablar

¿Qué te gusta hacer?

Working with a partner, ask each other if you like to do the following activities and answer according to the model.

Modelo

A —*¿Te gusta correr?*
B —*Sí, soy deportista.*
o: *No, no soy deportista.*
o: *Sí, pero no soy muy deportista.*

Estudiante A

Estudiante B

trabajador, -a
sociable
artístico, -a
deportista
estudioso, -a
talentoso, -a

¡Respuesta personal!

Escribir

Una persona famosa

Who is your favorite celebrity? Copy the paragraph on a separate piece of paper, filling in the blanks with words that describe your favorite celebrity and what he or she likes to do.

La persona famosa que me gusta más se llama __1.__. Es __2.__ y __3.__. Le gusta __4.__ pero no le gusta __5.__. No es ni __6.__ ni __7.__.

Enriching Your Teaching

Teacher-to-Teacher

Have students write five names of real or fictional people on a piece of paper, such as Frida Kahlo, Abraham Lincoln, Sally Ride, Donald Duck, Superman, or Goldilocks. Then have them write a sentence using an adjective to describe each person or character.

Rapid Review

Hold up pictures of famous people or people students are familiar with and ask: *¿Cómo es?*

  *Standards:* 1.1

Resources: Practice Answers on Transparencies

Focus: Asking and answering personalized questions about what you and others like to do

Recycle: ***Me / te gusta,*** activities

Suggestions: Be sure students understand their options. Students should answer according to what is true for them. Encourage them to use the *¡Respuesta personal!*

Answers:

Student A: Answers:
1. —¿Te gusta trabajar?
2. —¿...practicar deportes?
3. —¿...dibujar?
4. —¿...esquiar?
5. —¿...pasar tiempo con los amigos?
6. —¿...cantar?
7. —¿...ir a la escuela?

Student B answers will vary.

 *Standards:* 1.3

Focus: Writing descriptions about others

Suggestions: Before beginning this activity, discuss different categories of famous people that students might choose from, such as athletes, musicians, actors, politicians, or authors.

Answers will vary.

Extension: Allow student volunteers to read their descriptions aloud without saying the name of the person. See if anyone in the class can guess who it is.

1B Practice and Communicate

Standards: 3.1, 4.2

Fondo cultural

Resources: Voc. & Gram. Transparencies: 15–17

Suggestions: Ask students what can be inferred from the picture about the time period and the person depicted. What is he grasping in his left hand? *(a sword)* Use the map transparencies to show where Venezuela, Colombia, Ecuador, Peru, and Bolivia are located.

Answers will vary.

Actividad 16

Standards: 1.3

Suggestions: Ask students to name a leader whom they admire. Have them brainstorm a list of adjectives that describe that person and provide as many antonyms as possible for those adjectives.

Answers will vary.

Exploración del lenguaje

Presentation

Standards: 4.1

Suggestions: Remind students of the concept of cognates. Have them work individually with the list in *Try it out!* and then have them share their answers with the class.

Fondo cultural

Simón Bolívar (1783–1830) liberated the territory that is now Venezuela, Colombia, Ecuador, Peru, and Bolivia. Bolívar helped these areas gain their independence from Spain. Simón Bolívar is remembered as a brave and daring leader and is known throughout South America as *El Libertador* (The Liberator).

- Name three leaders who had a similar influence on events of their time.

Simón Bolívar (siglo XIX), Anónimo

Chromolitho. Artist Unknown (pre 20th century). Private Collection / Archives Charmet / Bridgeman Art Library.

Actividad 16 **Pensar/Escribir**

¿Qué es un buen líder?

A good leader has to have certain qualities. Copy this chart onto your paper, and fill in the adjectives that, in your opinion, describe what a good leader is and is not.

Es ...	No es ...

Exploración del lenguaje

Cognates that begin with *es* + consonant

Many words in Spanish that begin with *es* + consonant are easy to understand because they have the same meaning as English words. Knowing this pattern helps you recognize the meaning of new Spanish words and learn them quickly.

Try it out! Look at these words, then cover up the *e* at the beginning. Name English words that come from the same root word.

estudiante **es**tudioso **es**cuela **es**tómago
esquiar **es**pecial **es**tricto **es**cena

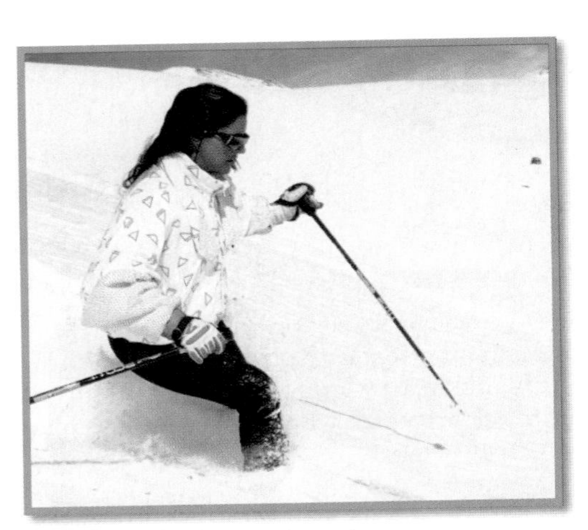

Es muy deportista. Le encanta esquiar.

Universal Access

Heritage Language Learners

Ask students to name a famous person from their heritage country or someone they consider a role model and describe that person using the vocabulary they have learned. Check that they are using appropriate gender endings.

Students with Learning Difficulties

Make a cognate poster and hang it in the classroom. As students move through the chapters, have them add new words to the poster.

Actividad 17 **Leer/Escribir**

El poema "Soy Elena"

The following poem is called a *diamante*. Can you guess why? After you've read the poem, answer the questions.

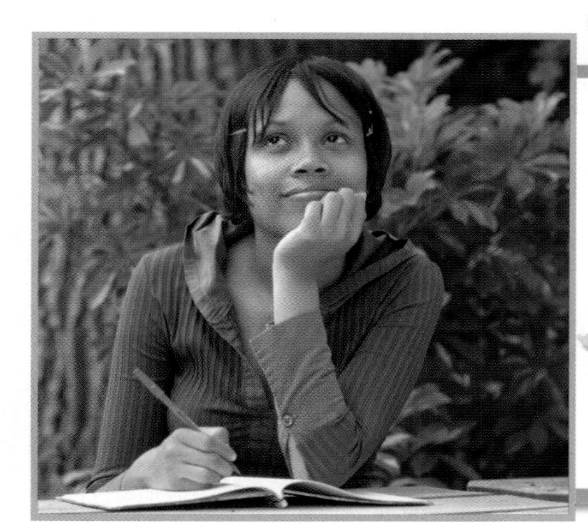

Conexiones — La literatura

Soy Elena
En general, soy
reservada y ordenada.
A veces, soy atrevida,
graciosa o impaciente.
No soy ni deportista
ni artística.
¡Yo soy yo!

1. Which activity would you invite Elena to do based on what she has told you about herself?
   dibujar   montar en monopatín   escuchar música
2. Rewrite the poem replacing *Soy Elena* with *Soy Tomás.*

Actividad 18 **Escribir**

Un poema personal

Write *un poema diamante* about yourself. Choose adjectives that best describe you. Look back at your chart from Actividad 11 for some ideas. Substitute your adjectives in the poem above. Be sure to write the poem in the form of a diamond. You might want to use calligraphy or an appropriate font on the computer and add pictures to illustrate your work.

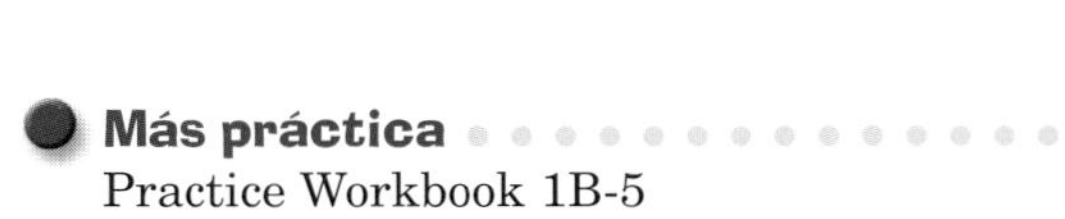

Más práctica
Practice Workbook 1B-5

Go Online PHSchool.com
For: Practice with adjective agreement
Visit: www.phschool.com
Web Code: jad-0114

Enriching Your Teaching

Teacher-to-Teacher

To help students with original writing projects like the one above, prepare a handout with the poem, leaving blank the words that students are expected to fill in. After they fill it in, they can copy over the entire poem and decorate it.

Teacher-to-Teacher

If students enjoy writing poems, you can have them bring photos of friends, family members, or celebrities or pictures from magazine advertisements and use them to write similar poems. These should be in the third-person form. ___: *Es* ___.

Actividad 17 *Standards: 1.2, 1.3, 3.1*

Resources: Resource Book: Cap. 1B, GramActiva BLM; Practice Answers on Transparencies

Focus: Reading and writing using adjectives

Suggestions: Have students answer item 1 aloud and complete item 2 on a sheet of paper, writing in the ***diamante*** form. Ask volunteers to share their poems with the class.

Answers:

1. ***dibujar:*** **No. Elena no es artística.**
   montar en monopatín: **Sí. Elena es atrevida.**
   escuchar música: **No. Elena no es artística.**
   o: Sí, es reservada.
2. **Soy Tomás. En general soy reservado y ordenado. A veces, soy atrevido, gracioso o impaciente. No soy ni deportista ni artístico. ¡Yo soy yo!**

Actividad 18 *Standards: 1.3, 3.1*

Focus: Writing poetry with learned vocabulary

Suggestions: Point out that the title will still be ***Soy*** ___, and the last line will be *¡Yo soy yo!* Students can review the lesson, make a list of adjectives, and refer to the list as they write their poems. Encourage students to decorate their poems and display them in the classroom.

Answers will vary.

Theme Project

Students can perform step 4 at this point. Be sure they understand your corrections and suggestions. (For more information, see p. 24-a.)

Additional Resources

- Writing, Audio & Video Workbook: Cap. 1B, Audio Activity 7, Track 8
- Writing, Audio & Video Workbook: Cap. 1B, Writing Activity 11
- Resource Book: Cap. 1B, Communicative Activity BLM

Assessment

- Prueba 1B-3: Adjectives

Practice and Communicate

Gramática

Presentation

Standards: 4.1

Resources: Voc. & Gram. Transparencies: 45; Video Program: Cap. 1B; Resource Book: Cap. 1B, Video Script

Suggestions: Present the new grammar using the transparencies and show the *GramActiva* Video as reinforcement. Direct attention to the *Strategy.* Use flashcards with familiar nouns and have students say ***el (un)*** or ***la (una)*** as they say each one.

Standards: 1.2

Resources: Audio Program: Cap. 1B, Track 9; Resource Book: Cap. 1B, Audio Script; Practice Answers on Transparencies

Focus: Listening for definite articles; gender agreements

Suggestions: Bring thick markers to class and have students write the articles in large, visible letters. Use blue and pink paper or index cards to reinforce the gender relationship. Play the *Audio CD* or read the script to students.

Script and Answers:

1. libro *(el)*
2. carpeta *(la)*
3. chica *(la)*
4. profesor *(el)*
5. escuela *(la)*
6. chico *(el)*
7. sábado *(el)*
8. amiga *(la)*

Standards: 1.3

Resources: Practice Answers on Transparencies

Focus: Completing a list with definite articles

Suggestions: Have students write the definite article and the noun together to reinforce vocabulary and gender correspondence.

Answers:

1. el 2. la 3. la 4. la 5. el 6. la

Gramática

Definite and indefinite articles

El and *la* are called definite articles and are the equivalent of "the" in English. *El* is used with masculine nouns; *la* is used with feminine nouns. You've already seen words with definite articles:

el libro *the book* la carpeta *the folder*

Un and *una* are called indefinite articles and are the equivalent of "a" and "an" in English. *Un* is used with masculine nouns; *una* is used with feminine nouns.

un libro *a book* una carpeta *a folder*

el	*the*
la	*the*

un	*a, an*
una	*a, an*

Strategy

Learning by repetition
When you learn a new noun, say it aloud, along with its definite article. Eventually you will find that words just "sound right" with the correct definite article and you will know whether the nouns are masculine or feminine.

GramActiva VIDEO

Want more help with definite and indefinite articles? Watch the **GramActiva** video.

Actividad 19 Gramática **Escuchar/GramActiva**

¿El o la?

Write the word *el* in large letters on a sheet of paper or an index card. Write *la* in large letters on another sheet. You will hear eight words you already know. When you hear a masculine word, hold up the paper with *el*. When you hear a feminine word, hold up the paper with the word *la* on it.

Actividad 20 Gramática **Escribir**

Buenos días, Doctor

Julian is at the doctor's office for a check-up. As he examines Julian, the doctor follows a list to be thorough. Copy the list on your paper and help the doctor by adding the appropriate definite article for each body part.

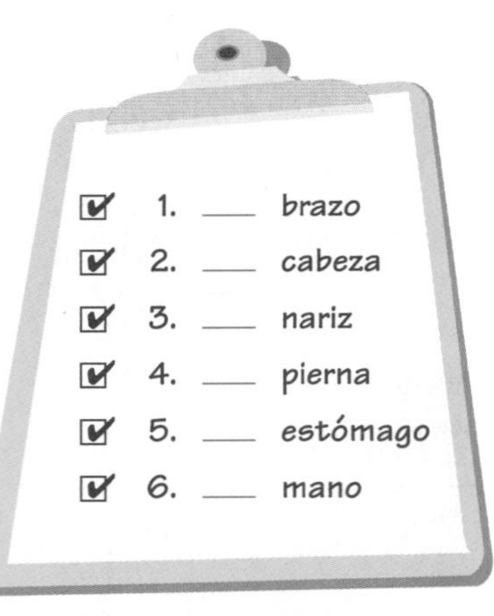

Universal Access

Students with Learning Difficulties

When teaching articles, provide very concrete examples that students can easily write in their Organizer or on flashcards. Students who struggle with writing might need the information provided on a handout that can be put directly into their notebooks. Continue to remind students that ***un*** is masculine and ***una*** is feminine, until you are sure they have mastered this concept.

Actividad 21 Gramática | Escribir

La escuela de Diego

Diego is talking about people at his school. Copy the sentences on your paper and complete each one with *un* or *una*.

1. La Sra. Secada es ___ profesora simpática.
2. Alicia es ___ estudiante trabajadora.
3. Juan Carlos es ___ chico perezoso.
4. Víctor es ___ chico sociable.
5. El Sr. Guzmán es ___ profesor gracioso.
6. Adriana es ___ chica muy seria.
7. La Srta. Cifuentes es ___ profesora paciente.
8. Arturo es ___ estudiante talentoso.

Actividad 22 Gramática 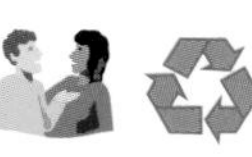  Hablar

¿Qué es?

Tell your partner the name of each object or body part pictured below.

Modelo

A —*¿Qué es?*
B —*Es un brazo.*

1. 

2. 

3. 

4. 

5. 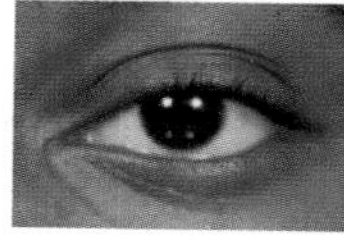 

6. 

7. 

8. 

Pronunciación

The vowels *o* and *u*

In Spanish, the pronunciation of the letter *o* is similar to the vowel sound in the English word *boat*, except that it is short. Listen then say these words, concentrating on making a short *o* sound:

bolígrafo	gracioso	cómo
teléfono	tampoco	otoño

In Spanish, the pronunciation of the letter *u* is similar to the vowel sound in the English word *zoo*. Listen to and say these words:

mucho	lunes	usted
octubre	estudioso	según

¡Ojo! Careful! Sometimes the words we mispronounce most are the ones that remind us of English words.

Try it out! Pronounce these words, concentrating on the Spanish vowel sounds:

agosto	regular	tropical	música
gusto	universidad	Uruguay	Cuba

El mundo

Más práctica

Practice Workbook 1B-6

For: Practice with articles
Visit: www.phschool.com
Web Code: jad-0113

Enriching Your Teaching

Teacher-to-Teacher

For homework, have students write on a piece of paper two columns with the headings *Masculine Nouns:* ***el / un*** and *Feminine Nouns:* ***la / una.*** Instruct them to list ten objects or people, such as ***un profesor,*** in the appropriate columns. After the homework has been checked, have students add other nouns to the list as they learn them. Encourage them to use their lists as an ongoing reference.

Actividad 21 *Standards:* 1.2, 1.3

Resources: Practice Answers on Transparencies

Focus: Writing and using indefinite articles

Suggestions: Remind students to look at the subjects, the nouns after the blanks, and the adjective endings for clues.

Answers:

1. una
2. una
3. un
4. un
5. un
6. una
7. una
8. un

Actividad 22 *Standards:* 1.1

Resources: Practice Answers on Transparencies

Focus: Speaking using indefinite articles

Recycle: School vocabulary, body parts

Suggestions: Review school vocabulary and words for body parts. Have students reverse roles when they have completed the activity.

Answers:

1. Es un bolígrafo.
2. Es una carpeta.
3. Es un lápiz.
4. Es una hoja de papel.
5. Es un ojo.
6. Es un cuaderno.
7. Es un pupitre.
8. Es una pierna.

Pronunciación

Presentation

 *Standards:* 4.1

Resources: Audio Program: Cap. 1B, Track 12

Suggestions: Have students say each word in the *Pronunciación* and in the *Try it out!* To demonstrate the point of the *¡Ojo!,* have students say these Spanish words: ***normal, horror, pronunciación.***

Additional Resources

- Writing, Audio & Video Workbook: Audio Activity 8, Track 10
- Writing, Audio & Video Workbook: Writing Activity 12

Assessment

- Prueba 1B-4: Definite and indefinite articles

1B Practice and Communicate

Presentation

Standards: 4.1

Resources: Voc. & Gram. Transparencies: 46; Audio Program: Cap. 1B, Track 11; Resource Book: Cap. 1B, Audio Script

Suggestions: Contrast English and Spanish word order by having students give English equivalents of the sentences in the chart. Direct students' attention to the *¿Recuerdas?* Use the transparency to reinforce placement of adjectives. Have students practice making negative sentences by placing the word ***no*** in the sample sentences.

Standards: 1.3

Resources: Practice Answers on Transparencies

Focus: Using correct word order with adjectives

Suggestions: Help students identify the various parts of speech before they unscramble the sentences.

Answers:

1. Marina es una chica artística.
2. Marcos es un chico reservado.
3. Tito es un chico perezoso.
4. Teresa es una chica inteligente.
5. Enrique es un chico trabajador.

Extension: Have students make the sentences they wrote negative. Write several additional sentences on strips of paper and cut them apart. Have students work together to unscramble them.

Gramática

Word order: Placement of adjectives

In Spanish, adjectives usually come after the noun they describe. Notice how *artística* follows *chica* in this Spanish sentence:

Margarita es una **chica artística.** *Margarita is an* ***artistic girl.***

Did you notice in the English sentence that the adjective comes before the noun?

Here's a simple pattern you can follow when writing a sentence in Spanish:

Subject	Verb	Indefinite Article + Noun	Adjective
Margarita	es	una chica	muy artística
Pablo	es	un estudiante	inteligente
La señora Ortiz	es	una profesora	muy buena

¿Recuerdas?

To make a sentence negative, you place the word *no* before the verb.

- **Eduardo no es un chico serio.**
- **No me gusta jugar videojuegos.**

Actividad 23 Gramática **Escribir**

Frases desordenadas

Create five sentences using the words in the following bubbles. Follow the "building blocks" pattern above and be sure to add a period at the end of each sentence.

Modelo

Patricia es una chica deportista.

1. 

2. Marcos / chico / es / reservado / un

3. es / un / Tito / perezoso / chico

4. chica / Teresa / es / inteligente / una

5. Enrique / es / trabajador / un / chico

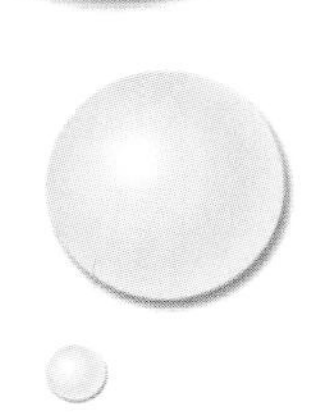

Universal Access

Students with Learning Difficulties

Have students write female and male names, the verb ***es,*** the indefinite articles ***un*** and ***una*** along with appropriate nouns (***chico, chica, estudiante***), and adjectives each on individual index cards. They can use these cards to practice forming sentences using correct word order. Color-coding can help to reinforce the pattern.

Heritage Language Learners

For homework, have students ask family members to describe the personality of their best friend. Tell them to write down what they've heard and use different highlighters to mark the various parts of speech.

Actividad 24 Gramática Escuchar/Escribir

Escucha y escribe

You will hear a description of Arturo, Marta, and Belinda. Write what you hear.

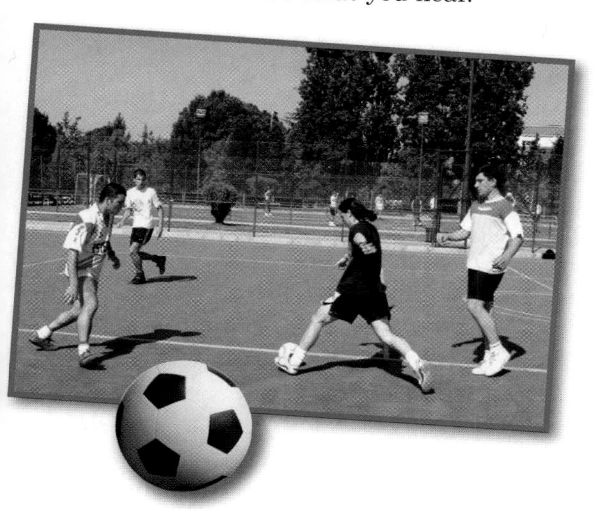

Actividad 25 Leer/Escribir

¿Cómo son los estudiantes?

Each of the following students is going to tell you what they like to do. Based on their statements, write a description of them. Be sure to use the correct word order.

Modelo

José: Me gusta nadar.
José es un chico deportista.

1. **Mariana:** Me gusta estudiar.
2. **Gustavo:** Me gusta mucho pasar tiempo con amigos.
3. **Luz:** Me gusta hablar por teléfono.
4. **Jorge:** Me gusta trabajar.
5. **Silvia:** Me gusta mucho bailar y cantar.
6. **Natalia:** Me gusta mucho el arte.
7. **Julian:** Me gusta usar la computadora.

El español en el mundo del trabajo

Paciente, inteligente, trabajador, ordenado . . .

These four qualities will make you a good candidate for any job. And if you add *bilingüe* to the list, your job qualifications will be enhanced.

- Make a list of careers where your knowledge of Spanish would be an asset. Which of these careers are of interest to you?

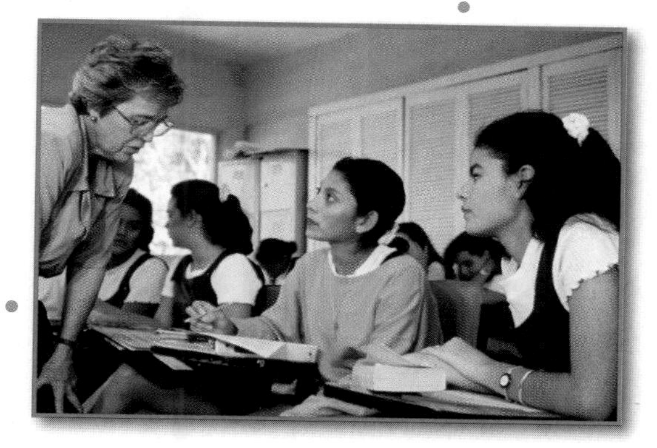

Enriching Your Teaching

Teacher-to-Teacher

Make "human sentences" to reinforce word order. Give each student a color-coded sheet of paper with a word or phrase on it. Use one color for subjects, one color for verbs, one color for indefinite articles + objects, and one color for adjectives. At your signal, students must scramble to place themselves in the correct order so the class can read the sentences that are formed. Have one student be the negative who inserts himself or herself in the various sentences.

Actividad 24

 *Standards:* 1.2, 1.3

Resources: Audio Program: CD Cap. 1B, Track 13; Practice Answer on Transparencies

Focus: Listening comprehension

Suggestions: Play the *Audio CD* or read the script as many times as necessary. Point out that two of the people described are female and one is male. Remind students to listen carefully and write the correct adjective endings. Have students check their work with a partner.

Script and Answers:

Arturo es un chico atrevido y serio. Le gusta mucho esquiar.
Marta es una chica inteligente, paciente y trabajadora.
Belinda es muy sociable. Le gusta hablar con los amigos.

Actividad 25

 *Standards:* 1.2, 1.3

Resources: Practice Answers on Transparencies

Focus: Reading comprehension and writing about personal descriptions

Suggestions: Remind students to be sure that for each sentence, the indefinite article agrees in gender with the noun and the adjective agrees with the word it describes.

Answers will vary but may include:

1. **Mariana es una chica estudiosa.**
2. **Gustavo es un chico sociable.**
3. **Luz es una chica sociable.**
4. **Jorge es un chico trabajador.**
5. **Silvia es una chica talentosa.**
6. **Natalia es una chica artística.**
7. **Julián es un chico inteligente.**

El español en el mundo del trabajo

Presentation

 *Standards:* 5.1

Suggestions: After students have read *El español en el mundo del trabajo* and discussed the question, ask: In addition to being an asset professionally, how else might bilingualism be valuable?

Standards: 1.3

Resources: Practice Answers on Transparencies

Focus: Writing sentences about people

Suggestions: Point out to students that they should write as many adjectives as apply to each person. Tell them to refer to pp. 56–60 if they need help remembering adjectives.

Answers will vary but may include:

Emilia es una chica artística (talentosa).
Carmen es una chica talentosa (graciosa, sociable).
Felipe es un chico estudioso (trabajador, inteligente, serio).
Lilia es una chica impaciente.
María Elena es una chica sociable (graciosa).
Kiko es un chico gracioso (sociable).
***Also accept negative statements, e.g.,* Felipe no es un chico perezoso.**

Standards: 1.1, 1.3

Focus: Writing and speaking about oneself

Suggestions: Be sure students understand the questions, and that they answer in complete sentences. In items 1 and 2, point out that ***tu*** means "your."

Answers will vary.

Actividad 26 Gramática **Escribir**

¿Cómo es . . .?

You are sitting in your school cafeteria with Marcos, a new exchange student from Costa Rica. Describe the other students based on their activities.

Modelo

Emilia es una chica talentosa.

Actividad 27 **Escribir/Hablar**

Y tú, ¿qué dices?

1. Según tu familia, ¿cómo eres?
2. Según tu mejor *(best)* amigo(a), ¿cómo eres?
3. Según tus profesores, ¿cómo eres?

Universal Access

Advanced Learners

Encourage students to bring a notebook with them to lunch and write sentences describing their friends and others in the school cafeteria. Have them read their sentences to the class.

Multiple Intelligences

Verbal / Linguistic: If possible, have students do *Actividad* 28 on a computer. Ask them to type in Andreina's message exactly as it is in their book, and then use the cut and paste function to put it in the correct order. Have them correspond with a classmate using Andreina's message as a model.

Actividad 28 Leer/Escribir

Un mensaje electrónico

You just received an e-mail message from another student in Panama City, but when you opened it up, some of the sentences were scrambled. Unscramble her message and then answer her questions by writing your own message.

Hola,

Me llamo Andreina:

una seria soy estudiante muy Yo. chica Yo artística soy una. ¿Eres inteligente? ¿Eres paciente? Mi mejor amiga es Claudia. **Claudia deportista chica una es. muy estudiante Claudia es trabajadora una.** ¿Cómo se llama tu mejor amigo? ¿Es deportista y talentoso?

Hola Andreina,
Me llamo ___.
Soy ___.
También, yo soy ___.
Mi mejor amigo(a) se llama ___.
Es ___.
También es ___.
Y a ti, ¿qué te gusta hacer?
¡Escríbeme pronto!

Fondo cultural

Cibercafés Many households in Spanish-speaking countries have computers and are online. However, *cibercafés,* places where people can access the Internet, are very popular. Some of the *cibercafés* are regular coffeehouses that serve snacks and drinks and have a few computers for customers to use, while others are equipped with dozens of computers. When people want to surf the Internet, play computer games, or e-mail friends, they can go to a *cibercafé* and get connected for a small fee.

- How much time do you spend on the computer? Would you spend money to go to a *cibercafé* if you didn't have a computer at home or at school? Why or why not?

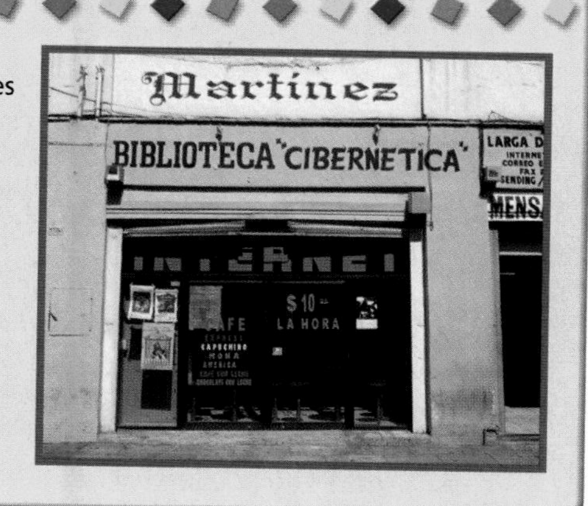

Más práctica
Practice Workbook 1B-7

Go Online PHSchool.com
For: Practice with placement of adjectives
Visit: www.phschool.com
Web Code: jad-0115

Enriching Your Teaching

Teacher-to-Teacher

Have students write e-mails and get real responses. Locate a partner school in a Spanish-speaking country or work with another Spanish class at the same level in another school. Schedule a day each month, or more often, for students to communicate via e-mail. The e-mail correspondence could be posted on a Web site or a bulletin board to share with the class.

Standards: 1.2, 1.3

Actividad 28

Focus: Reading and writing using agreement and correct word order

Suggestions: Have students number their papers 1–4. Point out that the scrambled sentences are in boldface type. Assign the response message for homework.

Standards: 2.1, 4.2

Fondo cultural

Suggestions: Ask students if they have ever been to a cyber café. Have students explain why they think that cyber cafés in the United States are more popular or less popular than those in Spain.

Answers will vary.

Theme Project

Students can perform step 5 at this point. Record their presentatons on cassette or videotape for inclusion in their portfolio. (For more information, see p. 24-a.)

Additional Resources

- Writing, Audio & Video Workbook: Audio Activity 9, Track 11
- Writing, Audio & Video Workbook: Writing Activity 13
- Heritage Language Learner Workbook: 1B-3, 1B-4, 1B-5

Assessment

- Prueba 1B-5: Placement of adjectives

Communicate: Reading

Lectura

Presentation

Standards: 1.2, 1.3, 4.1

Resources: Voc. & Gram. Transparencies: 47

Focus: Reading comprehension of a magazine personality quiz

Suggestions:

Pre-reading: Direct students' attention to the *Strategy* and discuss how visual clues often help in understanding a text. Help them identify the color names. Colors are formally taught in Level B, *Cap.* 6A. You may want to use this as an opportunity to introduce them and demonstrate that color words are adjectives and must agree with the nouns they modify.

Reading: Pair students and have them take turns reading the text to each other. Encourage them to choose their favorite color and see what it reveals about them.

Post-reading: Have students tell what the quiz says about them. Do they agree with the quiz? Have them complete the *¿Comprendes?* to check comprehension.

Additional Resources

- Heritage Learner Workbook: 1B-6

¡Adelante!

Objectives

- Read an article about personality traits
- Understand cultural perspectives on friendship
- Write a letter to a pen pal
- Learn facts about the Caribbean

Lectura

Un *self-quiz*

Is there a relationship between colors and personality? According to a self-quiz in the magazine *Amigos*, your favorite colors reveal perfectly what your personality is like.

Strategy

Using visual clues to get meaning
You have not yet learned the Spanish words for colors, but see if you can figure out what they are from the visual clues in the article.

¿Cómo eres tú? ¡Los colores revelan tu personalidad!

¿Eres una chica? ¿Te gusta el rojo? ¿Eres un chico? ¿Te gusta el rojo?	Eres muy apasionada. Eres atrevido.
¿Eres una chica? ¿Te gusta el verde? ¿Eres un chico? ¿Te gusta el verde?	Eres una chica natural. Eres muy generoso.
¿Eres una chica? ¿Te gusta el azul? ¿Eres un chico? ¿Te gusta el azul?	Eres muy talentosa. Eres un chico sociable.
¿Eres una chica? ¿Te gusta el anaranjado? ¿Eres un chico? ¿Te gusta el anaranjado?	Eres una chica artística. Eres gracioso.
¿Eres una chica? ¿Te gusta el violeta? ¿Eres un chico? ¿Te gusta el violeta?	Eres una chica muy independiente. Eres un chico romántico.
¿Eres una chica? ¿Te gusta el amarillo? ¿Eres un chico? ¿Te gusta el amarillo?	Eres una chica muy trabajadora. Eres muy serio.

Universal Access

Advanced Learners

Have students write a brief poem about themselves using the names of colors and other adjectives. Be sure they understand that the words in the poem do not have to rhyme. Students can decorate their papers using corresponding colors and pictures.

Heritage Language Learners

Have students search through magazines to find additional personality quizzes. They can print these out, then write summaries of what the tests say about them, changing from the second person to the first person.

¿Comprendes?

1. You probably were able to understand most of the words in the quiz. Write the English meaning for these Spanish cognates from the reading:
   - a. revelan
   - b. natural
   - c. independiente
   - d. generoso
   - e. apasionada
   - f. romántico
2. According to the self-quiz, what should be the favorite colors of these teenagers?
   - a. A Beto le gusta estar con amigos.
   - b. A Margarita le gusta dibujar.
   - c. A Lorenzo le gusta el trabajo voluntario *(volunteer work)*.
   - d. A Lupe le gusta estudiar. Es muy seria.
   - e. A Isabel le gusta estar con amigos, pero también le gusta estar sola *(alone)*.
3. Which of the colors in this reading is your favorite? Do you agree with the description? Why or why not?

Modelo

amarillo
¡Sí! Soy una chica trabajadora. Me gusta la escuela.
o: *¡No! Soy una chica perezosa. Me gusta ver la tele.*

Fondo cultural

Huipil is the word for the colorful, hand-woven blouse worn by female descendents of the Maya. The color, design, and style of weaving are unique to each *huipil* and identify the background and specific village of the weaver. Hundreds of designs and styles of weaving have been identified in the Mayan regions, principally Guatemala and parts of Mexico.

- What do you wear that might help someone identify your background?

Una niña con huipil

Go Online PHSchool.com
For: Internet link activity
Visit: www.phschool.com
Web Code: jad-0116

Enriching Your Teaching

Culture Note

Crafting the ***huipil*** is a tradition kept by Mayan women. Other indigenous peoples have similar traditions. For example, the Kuna, who live on small coral islands in the San Blas Archipelago along the Atlantic coast of Panama, are famous for their ***molas. Mola*** is the Kuna word for the elaborate embroidered panels that make up the front and back of a Kuna woman's blouse. Students will learn about ***molas*** in Level B, *Cap.* 7A.

Internet Search

Keywords: huipil, Kuna, mola

Standards: 1.2, 1.3, 4.1

¿Comprendes?

Resources: Practice Answers on Transparencies

Suggestions: Have students share their answers for items 1 and 2. Ask for volunteers to explain their answers for item 3.

Answers:

1. **reveal, natural, independent, generous, passionate, romantic**
2. **a) azul, b) anaranjado, c) verde, d) amarillo, e) violeta**
3. **Answers will vary.**

Standards: 2.2, 4.2

Fondo cultural

Suggestions: Bring in photos or actual examples of clothing from various Spanish-speaking cultures. Help students recognize that even if they purchase clothing rather than making it, it nonetheless is a reflection of their values and personalities.

Answers will vary but might include T-shirts, team uniforms, particular colors or styles of clothing, etc.

Perspectivas del mundo hispano

Presentation

Standards: 2.1, 4.2

Focus: Reading about friendship

Suggestions: Get students thinking about friendship and what it means to them by asking them to think about how many friends they have and the qualities they look for in a friend. Have students read the page. Talk about the experiences of Marcos and Brianna. Do students feel these experiences are realistic? Have any of them had similar experiences? Ask if they differentiate between a friend and an acquaintance. If so, what terms do they use for this distinction? Direct students to the *Check it out!* section. After they have completed it, go over the Spanish terms and have students answer the question.

Some students may have personal experiences similar to those described because of having moved to a foreign country or to another city or community. Have students look at the photos and discuss what they see as compared to their own world.

Direct attention to the *Think about it!* section and have students discuss it.

Answers will vary.

Additional Resources

- Heritage Learner Workbook: 1B-7

Perspectivas del mundo hispano

¿Qué es un amigo?

Marcos, a Costa Rican student on an exchange program in the United States, writes:

“When I arrived in the United States, I was amazed at all the friends my host brother and sister had. They knew a lot of people. These friends came to the house frequently, and we went out in groups. People were very open when meeting me. We'd spend some time together and get to know each other in a short amount of time. And once you got to know them, you ended up talking about everything!”

Brianna, a U.S. student on an exchange program in Colombia, writes:

“After I spent my year in Colombia, I learned that the concept of friendship is a little different than in the United States. My host brother and sisters spent a lot of time with their family. They knew people at school and from after-school activities, but they had just a few close friends and we'd do things with them. It was definitely a smaller group than I was used to. It seems that it took longer to become close friends with people too.”

Dos amigas estudiando en Cozumel, México

In Spanish, two expressions are used frequently to describe friendly relationships: *un amigo,* which means “friend,” and *un conocido,* which means “acquaintance.” You already know the word *amigo. Conocido* comes from the verb *conocer,* which means “to meet.” Each expression implies a different type of relationship.

Check it out! In many Spanish-speaking countries you'll find lots of expressions for someone who is your friend: *hermano, cuate (México), amigote (España),* and *compinche (Uruguay, Argentina, España).* Make a list of the expressions for “a friend” that are popular in your community. How would you explain them to someone from a Spanish-speaking country?

Amigos en una fiesta en España

Think about it! Compare how the United States perspective on friendship is different from that of a Spanish-speaking country. Use the terms *amigo* and *conocido* as you make the comparison.

Universal Access

Heritage Language Learners

Students may have firsthand knowledge of the differences in friendships if they have moved from another country. If so, encourage them to share their experiences with the class.

Presentación escrita

Amigo por correspondencia

Task
Write an e-mail in which you introduce yourself to a prospective pen pal.

1 Prewrite Think about what information you want to give. Answer these questions to help you organize your e-mail message.

- ¿Cómo te llamas?
- ¿Cómo eres?
- ¿Qué te gusta hacer?
- ¿Qué no te gusta hacer?

2 Draft Write a first draft of your e-mail message using the answers to the questions above. Begin by introducing yourself: *¡Hola! Me llamo . . .* When you are finished, end with *Escríbeme pronto.* ("Write to me soon.")

Using the writing process
To create your best work, follow each step in the writing process.

Modelo

¡Hola! Me llamo Patti. Soy atrevida y muy deportista. Me gusta mucho nadar y correr, pero me gusta más esquiar. ¡No me gusta nada jugar videojuegos! Escríbeme pronto.

3 Revise Review the first draft of your e-mail and share it with a partner. Your partner should check the following:

- Is it well organized?
- Does it include all the information from the Prewrite questions?
- Is the spelling accurate? Did you use the correct form of the adjectives to describe yourself?
- Did you include the opening and the closing?

Decide whether or not you want to use your partner's suggestions. Rewrite your draft.

4 Publish Type up the e-mail. You might want to send it to a pen pal in another class or school, send it to your teacher, or print it and give it to someone else in the class to answer.

5 Evaluation Your teacher may give you a rubric for grading the e-mail. You probably will be graded on:

- completion of task
- following the writing process by turning in the Prewrite and first draft
- using adjectives correctly

Enriching Your Teaching

RUBRIC	Score 1	Score 3	Score 5
Completion of task	You only include some of the required information.	You include most of the required information.	You include all of the required information.
Following the writing process	You turn in only the prewrite questions.	You turn in prewrite questions and rough draft.	You turn in prewrite, rough draft, and final product.
Using adjectives correctly	You use only one adjective with grammar errors.	You use two adjectives with some grammar errors.	You use more than two adjectives with very few grammar errors.

Presentación escrita

Presentation

Standards: 1.3

Focus: Writing an e-mail as an introduction to a prospective pen pal

Suggestions: Introduce the *Presentación escrita* to the class and give students copies of the rubic. Then have them work through each step of the process.

Prewrite: Suggest to students that they make an outline or write a list of facts they want to include in their e-mail. Students should use the questions in step 1 to guide their thinking about their message.

Draft: Encourage students to be creative when they write their e-mail, but explain that they can use the example in step 2 to format their own message.

Revise: Tell students to check their e-mail and try to identify errors or better ways to communicate before they share it with a partner. Be sure students know to incorporate mistakes or suggestions to revise their message.

Publish: Remind students to reread their final copy of the e-mail for typing errors before they send it or give it to someone.

Evaluation: See Assessment below.

Portfolio

Have students print out their e-mails for inclusion in their portfolios.

Additional Resources

- Heritage Learner Workbook: 1B-8

Assessment

- Assessment Program: Cap. 1B, Rubrics

Give student copies of the rubric before they begin the activity. Review the different levels of performance. After assessing students, help individuals understand how their e-mails could be improved.

El mundo hispano

Presentation

Standards: 2.1, 2.2, 4.2

Resources: Voc. & Gram. Transparencies: 14 (map)

Focus: Reading about the heritage of the Caribbean

Suggestions: After students read the text, display a map of the Caribbean. Point out the islands mentioned, indicating the Spanish-speaking islands. Explain that Hispaniola is shared by two countries and that only the eastern portion of it, the Dominican Republic, is Spanish-speaking. (The languages of Haiti are Creole and French.)

Discuss the voyage of Columbus, using a map to show how he traveled from Spain to Hispaniola. Have students hypothesize about the origins of the colonists who returned with Columbus to the island on his second voyage.

Direct attention to the top photo on p. 81. Ask students if it looks like other universities they have seen. Have them note that it is the oldest university in the Americas.

Focus on the *¿Sabes que…?* section. Using a map that shows Africa and the Caribbean, indicate how Africans traveled across the ocean to the islands. Discuss the languages spoken, their roots, and how they may have evolved.

Direct attention to the photo at the bottom of p. 81. Guide students to understand that the music of the Caribbean reflects a fusion of many different cultures. Have them discuss which cultures contributed to this fusion and how it came to be.

Have students locate Puerto Rico on the map. Mention that it is not a state, but a territory of the United States. As a territory, its citizens have rights that are similar to those of a citizen, but not as far-reaching. Focus on the photo in the middle of p. 81. This observatory remains very important as we continue to explore space and our universe.

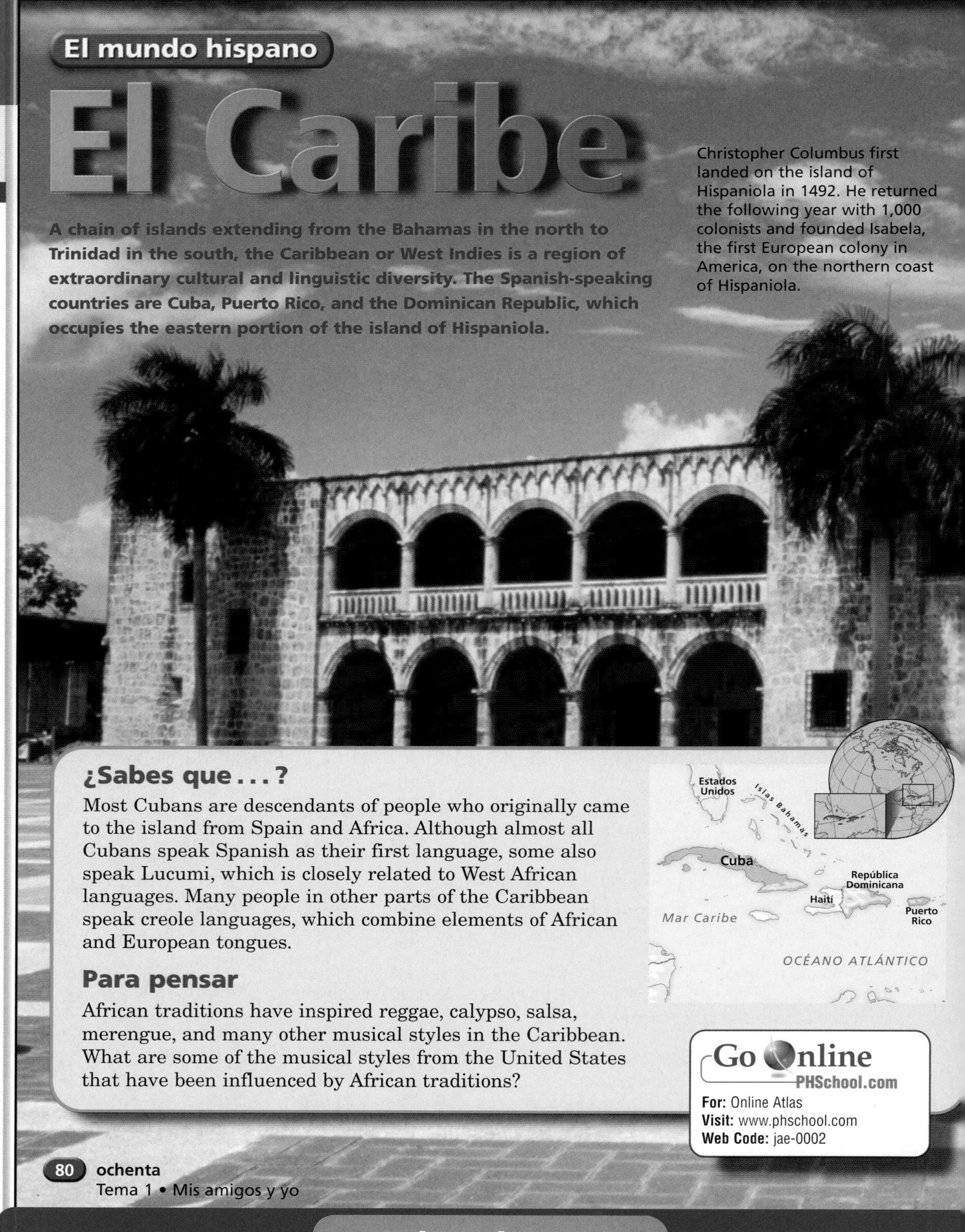

El mundo hispano

El Caribe

A chain of islands extending from the Bahamas in the north to Trinidad in the south, the Caribbean or West Indies is a region of extraordinary cultural and linguistic diversity. The Spanish-speaking countries are Cuba, Puerto Rico, and the Dominican Republic, which occupies the eastern portion of the island of Hispaniola.

Christopher Columbus first landed on the island of Hispaniola in 1492. He returned the following year with 1,000 colonists and founded Isabela, the first European colony in America, on the northern coast of Hispaniola.

¿Sabes que . . . ?

Most Cubans are descendants of people who originally came to the island from Spain and Africa. Although almost all Cubans speak Spanish as their first language, some also speak Lucumi, which is closely related to West African languages. Many people in other parts of the Caribbean speak creole languages, which combine elements of African and European tongues.

Para pensar

African traditions have inspired reggae, calypso, salsa, merengue, and many other musical styles in the Caribbean. What are some of the musical styles from the United States that have been influenced by African traditions?

Go Online
PHSchool.com
For: Online Atlas
Visit: www.phschool.com
Web Code: jae-0002

Universal Access

Advanced Learners

Have students research the history of Puerto Rico and its present relationship to the United States. What rights do United States citizens have that Puerto Ricans do not have? Have students include their opinion on whether or not Puerto Rico should become a state.

Heritage Language Learners

Have students choose a Spanish-speaking country in the Caribbean and research the languages spoken there. In what ways have languages other than Spanish influenced the country?

◀ The Universidad Autónoma de Santo Domingo, located in the capital of the Dominican Republic, Santo Domingo, is the oldest university in the Americas. It was founded in 1538—almost 100 years before Harvard—and continues to be one of the most important in the Caribbean.

Opened in 1963, the Arecibo Observatory in Puerto Rico has the largest single-dish radio telescope in the world. Some 200 scientists from around the world conduct research at Arecibo every year. In the early 1990s astronomers at Arecibo discovered the first planets outside our solar system. ▶

◀ The Caribbean is famous for its diverse musical styles that fuse African and European influences. Some groups even combine salsa, rumba, cha-cha-cha, and other Caribbean musical styles with jazz, hip-hop, and rock and roll.

Culture

Suggestions: Bring in, or have students bring in, recordings of the types of music mentioned. Compare their rhythms and the types of musical instruments used.

Direct attention to the *Para pensar* and have students discuss the question.

Answers will vary.

Go Online

The Online Atlas will provide additional maps of the locations mentioned here.

Enriching Your Teaching

Culture Note

Africans were taken to the Caribbean and enslaved, just as they were to the United States. Families were split up and cultural roots broken. People from different groups spoke different languages, and many transplanted Africans found themselves unable to communicate. Eventually, however, languages and cultures blended.

Teacher-to-Teacher

Have students research musical instruments of the Caribbean. Have them find out how certain instruments came to be and how they are made, and explore making one in class using available materials.

Review Activities

To talk about what you and others are like: Have students work in pairs to quiz each other on the vocabulary. They can pantomime the adjectives and have classmates guess which words they are acting out.

To ask people about themselves or others: Have students walk around the room and ask three people about themselves or another person. Each student should ask and answer three questions.

To talk about what someone likes or dislikes: Have students talk in pairs about what their friends like and dislike, using infinitives from the learned vocabulary in the structure *(No) le gusta* ___.

To describe someone: Have students work in small groups to describe themselves or another person using *(No) Soy* ___. and *Es* ___. Tell them to use as many adjectives as they can.

To tell whom are you talking about: Have the class write short sentences *(Es un chico...)* using correct verb forms and gender endings to describe themselves or someone else.

Other useful words: Refer students to this section and remind them to practice these expressions as they create sentences throughout this review.

Portfolio

Invite students to review the activities they completed in this chapter, including written reports, posters or other visuals, and tapes of oral presentations or other projects. Have them select one or two items that they feel best demonstrate their achievements in Spanish. Include these products in students' portfolios. Have them include this with the Chapter Checklist and Self-Assessment Worksheet.

Additional Resources

- Audio Program: CD, Cap. 1B, Track 14
- Resource Book: Cap. 1B, Clip Art
- Resource Book: Cap. 1B, Situation Cards
- Assessment Program: Cap. 1B, Chaper Checklist and Self-Assessment Worksheet

Chapter Review

Repaso del capítulo

Vocabulario y gramática

To prepare for the test, check to see if you...
- **know the new vocabulary and grammar**
- **can perform the tasks on p. 83**

to talk about what you and others are like

artístico, -a	artistic
atrevido, -a	daring
bueno, -a	good
deportista	athletic
desordenado, -a	messy
estudioso, -a	studious
gracioso, -a	funny
impaciente	impatient
inteligente	intelligent
ordenado, -a	neat
paciente	patient
perezoso, -a	lazy
reservado, -a	reserved, shy
serio, -a	serious
simpático, -a	nice, friendly
sociable	sociable
talentoso, -a	talented
trabajador, -ora	hardworking

to ask people about themselves or others

¿Cómo eres?	What are you like?
¿Cómo es?	What is he/she like?
¿Cómo se llama?	What's his/her name?
¿Eres...?	Are you...?

to talk about what someone likes or doesn't like

le gusta...	he/she likes...
no le gusta...	he/she doesn't like...

to describe someone

es	he/she is
soy	I am
no soy	I am not

For *Vocabulario adicional,* see pp. 268–269.

to tell whom you are talking about

el amigo	male friend
la amiga	female friend
el chico	boy
la chica	girl
él	he
ella	she
yo	I

other useful words

a veces	sometimes
muy	very
pero	but
según	according to
según mi familia	according to my family

adjectives

Masculine	Feminine
ordenado	**ordenada**
trabajador	**trabajadora**
paciente	**paciente**
deportista	**deportista**

definite articles

el	the
la	the

indefinite articles

un	a, an
una	a, an

Más práctica
Practice Workbook Puzzle 1B-8
Practice Workbook Organizer 1B-9

Universal Access

Students with Learning Difficulties

Cut out magazine pictures of people who could be described using the vocabulary in this chapter. Hold up two of the pictures and give a short description of one of them. Have students tell you which one you are describing.

Multiple Intelligences

Logical / Mathematical: Have students make a word-search puzzle with all the new adjectives mixed in among other letters. Instead of listing the words to search for, have students write sentences that are clues. For example: *Me gustan los deportes. Soy (deportista). No soy paciente, soy (impaciente).*

For: Test preparation
Visit: www.phschool.com
Web Code: jad-0117

Preparación para el examen

On the exam you will be asked to . . .	Here are practice tasks similar to those you will find on the exam . . .	If you need review . . .
 **1 Escuchar** Listen to and understand a description of a friend	Listen as a character in a Spanish soap opera describes his ex-girlfriend. What does he think her good qualities are? What does he think her shortcomings are? Can you understand why he broke up with her?	**pp. 56–61** *A primera vista* **p. 62** Actividad 5 **p. 63** Actividades 6–7 **p. 64** Actividad 8 **p. 65** Actividad 10
 **2 Hablar** Talk about yourself in terms of how you see yourself	While you're talking to your Spanish teacher, you realize that she doesn't know the "real you." Tell her some things about yourself that would help her understand you.	**p. 66** Actividades 11–13 **p. 69** Actividad 18 **p. 74** Actividad 27
3 Leer Read and understand a description of someone	In a popular Spanish magazine, you see an interview with the actor who plays the part of a teenager, Carlos, in a TV show you have been watching. See if you can understand what he is saying about the character he plays: ¡No me gusta nada el chico! Él es muy inteligente, pero le gusta hablar y hablar de NADA. Es ridículo. Es muy impaciente y perezoso. Él no es ni simpático ni gracioso. Yo soy un actor . . . ¡no soy como Carlos!	**pp. 56–61** *A primera vista* **p. 69** Actividad 17 **pp. 76–77** *Lectura*
 **4 Escribir** Write a short paragraph describing yourself	The first issue of your school's online newspaper is called "Getting to Know You." Submit a brief profile of yourself. Mention what your family thinks of you and list some things you like to do. For example: Yo soy una chica deportista y muy sociable. Según mi familia, soy graciosa. Me gusta patinar y hablar por teléfono.	**p. 66** Actividades 11–13 **p. 69** Actividad 18 **p. 74** Actividad 27 **p. 75** Actividad 28 **p. 79** *Presentación escrita*
 **5 Pensar** Demonstrate an understanding of cultural perspectives on friendship	Explain the differences between the terms *amigo* and *conocido* in Spanish-speaking cultures. How does this compare to words that we use in the United States?	**p. 78** *Perspectivas del mundo hispano*

Enriching Your Teaching

Teacher-to-Teacher
Have students work in groups, pretending to be the teacher and students. The "teacher" will ask the students questions, focusing on vocabulary from this chapter.

Performance Tasks

Standards: 1.1, 1.2, 1.3, 2.1

1. Escuchar

Resources: Audio Program: CD Cap. 1B, Track 15; Resource Book: Cap. 1B, Audio Script; Practice Answers on Transparencies

Suggestions: Play the *Audio CD* or read the script. Have students suggest answers to the questions. Have students say adjectives that would describe the ideal girlfriend for this boy.

Script:

¿Cómo es María Elena? Pues… es una chica inteligente y talentosa, pero es muuuy seria. Y no es sociable. Yo soy un chico gracioso y muy sociable. A mí me gustan más las chicas atrevidas.

Answers:

Elena is talented and intelligent, but very serious. One of her shortcomings is that she is not sociable. He likes more outgoing or daring girls.

2. Hablar

Suggestions: Tell students to use as many adjectives as they can. For more practice, have students describe themselves as the opposite of what they are like.

Answers will vary.

3. Leer

Suggestions: Remind students to look for cognates. Ask them to point out the phrases that describe personality traits.

Answers may vary but should include:

1. **Es ridículo. Es muy impaciente y perezoso. Él no es ni simpático ni gracioso.**
2. **Él es muy inteligente, pero le gusta hablar y hablar de nada.**

4. Escribir

Suggestions: Tell students they can either describe themselves as they are or write about an imaginary version of themselves.

Answers will vary.

5. Pensar

Suggestion: Allow students to speak spontaneously about the issue or speak from a short outline of their thoughts.

Answers will vary.

Assessment

- Examen del capítulo: 1B
- Audio Program: CD 20, Track 4

Alternative Assessment

- ExamView Test Bank CD-ROM
- Resource Book: Cap. 1B, Situation Cards
- Resource Book: Cap. 1B, Communicative Activities

Tema 2

La escuela

THEME OVERVIEW

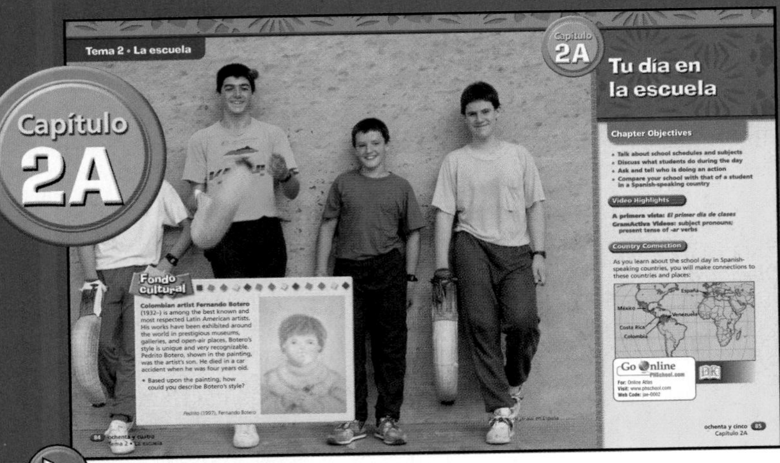

2A Tu día en la escuela
- School subjects and schedules

Vocabulary: class subjects; school activities; school supplies; ordinal numbers
Grammar: subject pronouns; the present tense of *-ar* verbs
Cultural Perspectives: comparing schools

2B Tu sala de clases
- Describing a classroom

Vocabulary: classroom items and furniture; parts of the classroom; prepositions of location
Grammar: the verb ***estar;*** plurals of nouns and articles
Cultural Perspectives: opinions about school

Theme Project

Página Web

Overview: Students create a Web page for their school featuring the school's name, address, and phone number and at least four symbols or photos that represent different classes. Under each symbol or photo, students write a description of the class represented. Students then present their Web page to the class, describing all the information featured on the page.

Materials: poster board, magazines, colored pencils, markers, glue, scissors, bilingual dictionary

Sequence: (suggestions for when to do each step appear throughout the chapters)

2A STEP **1.** Review instructions so students know what is expected of them. Hand out the "Theme 2 Project Instructions and Rubric" from the *Teacher's Resource Book.*

STEP **2.** Students submit a rough sketch of their Web page. Return the sketches with your suggestions. For vocabulary and grammar practice, ask students to work with a partner and present their drafts to each other.

STEP **3.** Students create layouts on poster board. Encourage students to work in pencil first, and to try different arrangements before drawing or gluing photos or symbols and writing descriptions. Encourage students to use as much of the vocabulary from *Capítulos* 2A and 2B as possible in the descriptions. Also, encourage them to use a bilingual dictionary for any words they would like to use but do not yet know.

2B STEP **4.** Students submit a draft of their descriptions. Note your corrections and suggestions, then return the drafts to students.

STEP **5.** Students complete and present their Web page to the class, reading and/or describing all the information featured on the page.

Options:
1. Students create a brochure for their school instead of a Web page.
2. Students create a virtual tour of a classroom, describing its contents.

Assessment:
Here is a detailed rubric for assessing this project:
Theme 2 Project: *Página Web*

RUBRIC	Score 1	Score 3	Score 5
Evidence of planning	You provided no written draft or page layout.	Your draft was written and layout created but not corrected.	Your corrected your draft and layout.
Your use of illustrations	You included no photos or visuals.	You included photos or visuals, but your layout was unorganized.	Your Web page was easy to read, complete, and accurate.
Your poster presentation	You included little of the required information.	You included most of the required information.	You included all the required information.

Bulletin Boards

Theme: ***La escuela***

Ask students to cut out, copy, or download photos of school supplies, items found in a classroom, schools from around the world, and scenes from different school settings. Cluster photos according to these four categories.

Bibliography

Arnold, Karen, and Richard Hewitt. *City of the Gods: Mexico's Ancient City of Teotihuacán.* New York: Clarion Books, 1994. Text and color photographs explore the ruins and history of Teotihuacán.

Morrison, Marion. *Costa Rica. Enchantment of the World.* Second Series. New York: Children's Press, 1998. The history and culture of Costa Rica, with clear color photographs.

Prior, Katherine. *UNICEF.* (World Organizations). New York: Franklin Watts, 2001.

Tingay, Graham I., and Anthony Marks. *The Romans. Illustrated World History Series.* Tulsa, Okla.: EDC Publications, 1991. Describes the world of the Romans.

Wilkes, Angela, John Schakell, and Roger Priddy. *Latin for Beginners.* Lincolnwood, Ill.: NTC Publishing Group, 1995.

Hands-on Culture

Chant for choosing teams

When choosing teams to play a game, students in ***América Latina*** often sing a chant like the one that follows.

Directions:

1. Type out the words to the chant and distribute copies to students.
2. Have students repeat each line of the chant after you to practice pronunciation.
3. Choose a leader to begin the chant, or be the leader yourself. The entire class responds to the leader.

   Leader: Ambos a dos … Matarile, rile, rile. Ambos a dos … Matarile, rile, rile, ron.
   Class: ¿Qué quiere usted? Matarile, rile, rile. ¿Qué quiere usted? Matarile, rile, rile, ron.
   Leader: Yo quiero un paje. Matarile, rile, rile. Yo quiero un paje. Matarile, rile, rile, ron.
   Group: ¿Qué paje quiere usted? Matarile, rile, rile. ¿Qué paje quiere usted? Matarile, rile, rile, ron.
   Leader: Yo quiero a (name of a student). Matarile, rile, rile. Yo quiero a (name of a student). Matarile, rile, rile, ron.
   Group: Aquí tiene usted su paje. Matarile, rile, rile. Aquí tiene usted su paje. Matarile, rile, rile, ron.

4. The student who is named joins the leader, and the chant begins again to choose the next team member.

Internet Search

Use the keywords to find more information.

2A **Keywords:**

Romans in Spain, Costa Rica, Fernando Botero, Mayan Indians

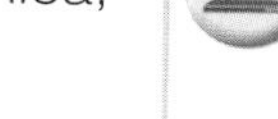

2B **Keywords:**

UNICEF, Convención para los niños

Game

¿Tienes . . . ?

This game is similar to Go Fish. Have students play it after you present the vocabulary from *Capítulo* 2B.

Players: 2 to 4

Materials: index cards, colored pencils or markers

Rules:

1. The cards for this game should be prepared ahead of time. Have students draw on the index cards the classroom items listed on p. 120. There should be four index cards for each item, making a deck of 48 cards for each pair or group.
2. One student deals each player five cards, then places the remaining cards face down on the desk or table.
3. Players examine their cards to see whether they have any matching pairs. If they do, they remove the pairs and set them aside.
4. The dealer begins play by asking whether anyone has a card.
   Dealer: Linda, ¿tienes un reloj?
5. If the player has the card that the dealer is asking for, he or she responds affirmatively and gives the card to the dealer. The dealer then sets the pair aside and takes another turn. If the player doesn't have the card, the dealer must draw one from the pile and the next player takes a turn.
   Player: Sí, tengo un reloj.
   No, no tengo un reloj. Toma un naipe *(card).*
6. The game ends when one player puts down or gives away the last card. All players count their cards. The player with the most pairs wins.

Variation: Have students write the vocabulary words on index cards, then turn them face down on a large table or the floor to play Memory. Students turn over two cards at a time to find matching pairs.

Overview

Chapter Overview

A primera vista INPUT	Manos a la obra PRACTICE	¡Adelante! APPLICATION	Repaso del capítulo REVIEW
Objectives Read, listen to, and explain information about: • the school day	**Objectives** • Discuss the school day • Ask and tell about likes and dislikes • Use subject pronouns • Use verbs that end in ***-ar***	**Objectives** • Read a brochure about a school in Costa Rica • Talk about soccer fan chants • Talk about some of your classes • Discuss facts about Mexico	**Objectives** • Prepare for the chapter test
Vocabulary • Class subjects • Ordinal numbers • School activities • Things you need for school • Adjectives to describe classes	**Vocabulary** • Practice and learn new vocabulary	**Vocabulary** • Application	**Vocabulary** • Review
Grammar Lexical use of: • subject pronouns • present tense of ***-ar*** verbs	**Grammar** • Subject pronouns • Present tense of ***-ar*** verbs	**Grammar** • Application	**Grammar** • Review
Culture • Fernando Botero	**Culture** • Courses students take in Spanish-speaking countries • Romans in Spain • Latin influence on Spanish • ***el recreo*** • The Maya	**Culture** • The 24-hour clock • Facts about Costa Rica • Soccer fan chants	**Culture** • Demonstrate an understanding of cultural practices concerning sports

Learner Support

Strategies
- Using context clues
- Listening for information
- Using photos
- Using graphic organizers

Recycling
- Titles used with adults
- Infinitives
- Negatives
- Lexical use of ***gustar***

Pronunciación
- The letter ***c***

Exploración del lenguaje
- Connections between Latin, English, and Spanish

Conexiones
- Mathematics: Mayan numbers

Beyond the Classroom

Countries
- Spain
- Mexico
- Costa Rica
- Colombia
- Venezuela

El español en la comunidad
- Opportunities to learn Spanish in your community

Internet
- Vocabulary activities
- Grammar activities
- Internet links
- Self-tests

Print Components

TEACHER

Teacher's Resource Book
- Chapter Resource Checklist
- Input Script
- Video Script
- Audio Script
- Answer Keys
- *GramActiva* Blackline Masters
- Communicative Activity Blackline Masters
- Situation Cards Blackline Masters
- School-to-Home Connection Letter
- Vocabulary Clip Art

TPR Storytelling Book
- Cap. 2A

STUDENT

Practice Workbook
- Vocabulary: 2A-1 – 2A-4
- Grammar: 2A-5 – 2A-7
- Puzzle: 2A-8
- Organizer: 2A-9

Writing, Audio & Video Workbook
- Writing: 2A-1 – 2A-4
- Audio: 2A-5 – 2A-10
- Video: 2A-11

Realidades para hispanohablantes
- Cap. 2A

Transparencies

Vocabulary & Grammar Transparencies
- Chapter Opener 12–12,15,18 (maps)
- *A primera vista:* 48–49
- *Videohistoria:* 12 (map), 50–51
- Grammar: 2 (graphic organizer), 12 (map), 52–55
- *Lectura*: 13 (map)
- *Cultura*: 9 (graphic organizer), 12 (map)

Practice Answers on Transparencies
- Cap. 2A

Fine Art Transparencies
- Transparencies
- Teacher's Guide

Assessment

Assessment Program
- *Pruebas:*
  - Vocabulary recognition: 2A-1
  - Vocabulary production: 2A-2
  - Subject pronouns: 2A-3
  - Present tense of ***-ar*** verbs: 2A-4
- *Examen del capítulo:* 2A

ExamView Test Bank CD-ROM

Test Preparation Workbook
- Cap. 2A Reading #1
- Cap. 2A Reading #2

Alternative Assessment
- Performance-Based Speaking
- Assessment Program: Rubrics
- Internet Self-Test
- Situation Cards Blackline Masters
- TPR Storytelling Book: Speaking Task

Technology

iText

Mind Point Quiz Show CD-ROM

Resource Pro CD-ROM
- Lesson Planner
- Teacher Resources
- Clip Art

Video Program VHS and DVD
- *A primera vista* video: *El primer día de clases*
- *GramActiva* Videos:
  - subject pronouns
  - present tense of ***-ar*** verbs

Audio Program CDs
- *A primera vista*
- *Escucha y escribe* activities
- Audio Activities
- *Pronunciación*
- *Repaso*
- Chapter Listening Test
- Songs

Regular Schedule (50 minutes)

For electronic lesson plans:
Resource Pro CD-ROM

Day	Warm-up / Assess	Preview / Present / Practice / Communicate	Wrap-up / Homework Options
DAY 1	**Return Examen del capítulo (10 min.)**	**A primera vista (35 min.)** • Objectives • Presentation: *Vocabulario y gramática en contexto* • *Actividades* 1, 2 • *Fondo cultural*	**Wrap-up and Homework Options (5 min.)** • Practice Workbook 2A-1, 2A-2 • Go Online • Heritage Language Learner Workbook • Vocabulary Clip Art
DAY 2	**Warm-up (5 min.)** • Homework check	**A primera vista (40 min.)** • Review: *Vocabulario y gramática en contexto* • Presentation: *Videohistoria El primer día de clases* • View: Video *El primer día de clases* • Video Activities • *Actividades* 3, 4	**Wrap-up and Homework Options (5 min.)** • *Prueba* 2A-1: Vocabulary recognition • Practice Workbook 2A-3, 2A-4 • Go Online
DAY 3	**Warm-up (5 min.)** • Homework check **✔Assessment (10 min.)** • *Prueba* 2A-1: Voc. recognition	**Manos a la obra (30 min.)** • Objectives • *Actividades* 5, 6, 7	**Wrap-up and Homework Options (5 min.)** • *Actividades* 8, 10
DAY 4	**Warm-up (10 min.)** • Homework check • Return *Prueba* 2A-1: Voc. recognition	**Manos a la obra (35 min.)** • *Actividades* 9, 11 • *Exploración del lenguaje* • *Fondo cultural*	**Wrap-up and Homework Options (5 min.)** • *Exploración del lenguaje:* Try it out!
DAY 5	**Warm-up (10 min.)** • Homework check	**Manos a la obra (35 min.)** • *Actividad* 12 • *El español en la comunidad* • *Fondo cultural*	**Wrap-up and Homework Options (5 min.)** • Go Online
DAY 6	**Warm-up (5 min.)** • Homework check	**Manos a la obra (40 min.)** • Presentation: Subject pronouns • *GramActiva* Video • *Actividades* 13, 14, 15	**Wrap-up and Homework Options (5 min.)** • Practice Workbook 2A-5 • *Prueba* 2A-3: Subject pronouns • Go Online
DAY 7	**Warm-up (5 min.)** • Homework check • *Prueba* 2A-3: Subject pronouns	**Manos a la obra (40 min.)** • Presentation: Present tense of *-ar* verbs • *GramActiva* Video • *Actividades* 16, 18	**Wrap-up and Homework Options (5 min.)** • *Actividad* 17 • Practice Workbook 2A-6, 2A-7
DAY 8	**Warm-up (5 min.)** • Homework check • Return *Prueba* 2A-3: Subject pronouns	**Manos a la obra (40 min.)** • *Juego: Actividad* 20 • *Actividades* 19, 21	**Wrap-up and Homework Options (5 min.)** • *Prueba* 2A-3: Vocabulary production • Go Online

Day	Warm-up / Assess	Preview / Present / Practice / Communicate	Wrap-up / Homework Options
DAY 9	**Warm-up** (5 min.) • Homework check ✔**Assessment** (10 min.) • *Prueba* 2A-3: Voc. production	**Manos a la obra** (30 min.) • *Actividades* 22, 23	**Wrap-up and Homework Options** (5 min.) • Go Online • *Prueba* 2A-4: Present tense of *-ar* verbs
DAY 10	**Warm-up** (5 min.) • Homework check • Return *Prueba* 2A-3: Voc. production ✔**Assessment** (10 min.) • *Prueba* 2A-4: Present tense of *-ar* verbs	**Manos a la obra** (30 min.) • *Actividad* 26 • *Conexiones: Actividad* 25 • *Pronunciación*	**Wrap-up and Homework Options** (5 min.) • *Actividad* 24
DAY 11	**Warm-up** (5 min.) • Homework check • Return *Prueba* 2A-4: Present tense of *-ar* verbs	**¡Adelante!** (40 min.) • *Lectura* • *Fondo cultural* • *Presentación oral:* Prepare	**Wrap-up and Homework Options** (5 min.) • Go Online
DAY 12	**Warm-up** (5 min.) • Homework check	**¡Adelante!** (40 min.) • *Presentación oral:* Practice • *La cultura en vivo*	**Wrap-up and Homework Options** (5 min.) • *Presentación oral:* Practice
DAY 13	**Warm-up** (5 min.) • Homework check	**¡Adelante!** (40 min.) • *Presentación oral:* Present	**Wrap-up and Homework Options** (5 min.) • Writing Activities • Practice Workbook 2A-8, 2A-9
DAY 14	**Warm-up** (5 min.) • Homework check	**¡Adelante!** (20 min.) • *El mundo hispano* **Repaso** (20 min.) • *Vocabulario y gramática* • *Preparación para el examen*	**Wrap-up and Homework Options** (5 min.) • Go Online: Self-test • *Examen del capítulo*
DAY 15	**Warm-up** (5 min.) • Answer questions ✔**Assessment** (45 min.) • *Examen del capítulo*		

2A Preview

Standards for *Capítulo* 2A

- To achieve the goals of the Standards, students will:

Communication

1.1 Interpersonal
- Talk about homework, classes, people, and schedules at school
- Talk about preferences in school subjects and activities

1.2 Interpretive
- Listen to and read information on school subjects, schedules, supplies
- Read a picture-based story
- Listen to and watch a video about school schedules
- Listen to information about present tense of ***-ar*** verbs
- Listen to information about activities during ***recreo***
- Read information about a language school in Costa Rica

1.3 Presentational
- Present information about work, home, school activities, school subjects, schedules, and supplies
- Present school cheers like those in Spanish-speaking countries

Culture

2.1 Practices and Perspectives
- Understand the focus on English language acquisition in Spanish-speaking countries
- Learn about school sporting event celebrations and traditions
- Learn about leisure time during school hours
- Understand Sunday "family time" in Mexico

2.2 Products and Perspectives
- Learn about Fernando Botero and his painting
- Read and learn about school cheers
- Learn about traditional dances of Mexico

Connections

3.1 Cross-curricular
- Learn about important artists and their work: Botero
- Building vocabulary through an understanding of mathematics
- Understand influences of Roman Empire on Spain
- Understand similarities between Mayan numbering system and Roman numerals
- Understand the impact Spanish exploration had on the Maya
- Learn about migration patterns of monarch butterflies

3.2 Target Culture
- Read and recite school cheers

Comparisons

4.1 Language
- Learn new vocabulary through cognate recognition
- Compare personalized school-related vocabulary
- Understand the use of subject pronouns
- Learn the present tense of ***-ar*** verbs
- Understand the pronunciation of the letter ***c***

4.2 Culture
- Compare motivations for foreign language learning
- Compare leisure periods during the school day
- Compare use of the 24-hour and 12-hour clock
- Compare school cheers and sporting event celebrations

Communities

5.1 Beyond the School
- Learn why English-speakers in the community wish to learn Spanish

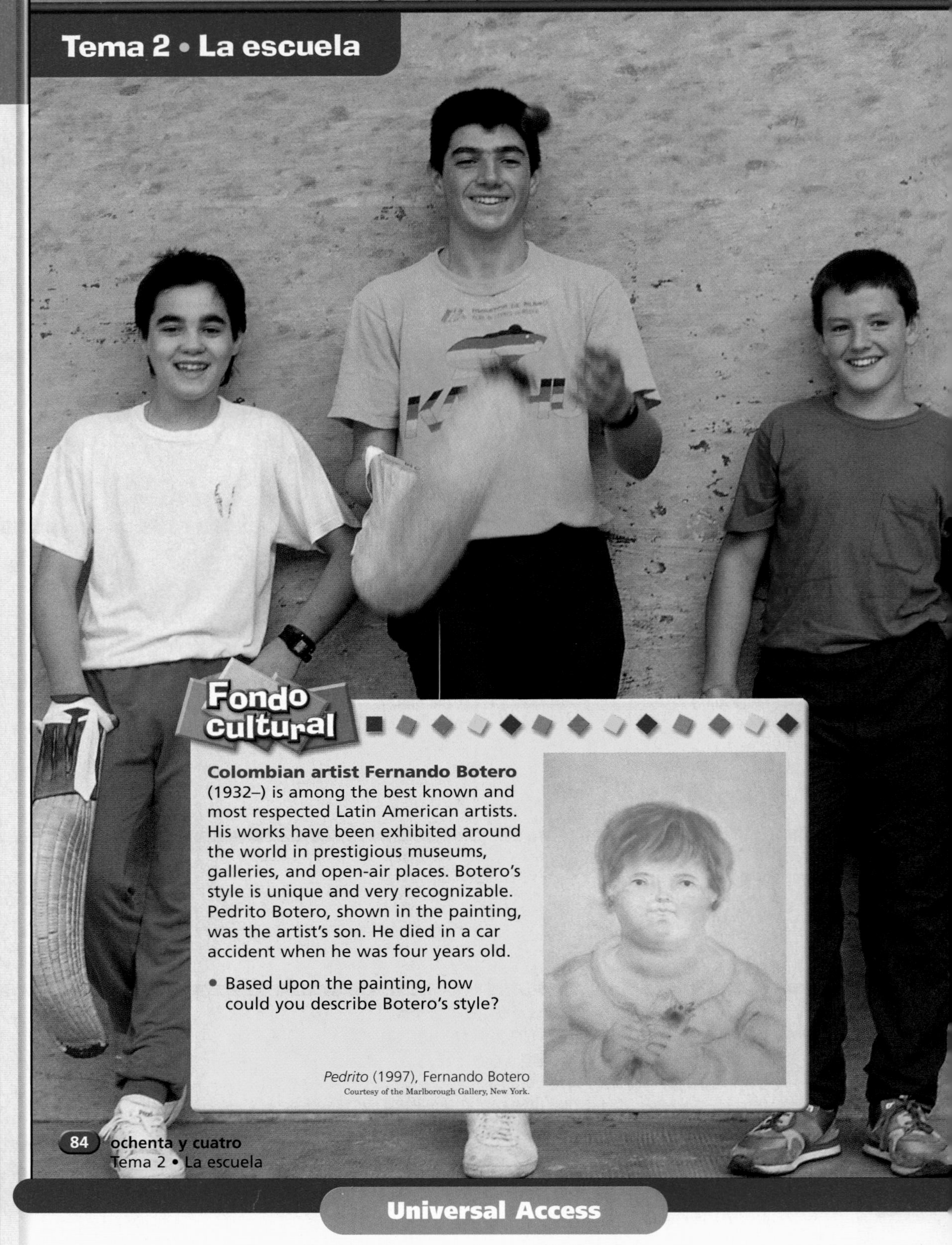

Tema 2 • La escuela

Fondo cultural

Colombian artist Fernando Botero (1932–) is among the best known and most respected Latin American artists. His works have been exhibited around the world in prestigious museums, galleries, and open-air places. Botero's style is unique and very recognizable. Pedrito Botero, shown in the painting, was the artist's son. He died in a car accident when he was four years old.

- Based upon the painting, how could you describe Botero's style?

Pedrito (1997), Fernando Botero
Courtesy of the Marlborough Gallery, New York.

84 ochenta y cuatro
Tema 2 • La escuela

Universal Access

Personalizing the Theme

Have students talk about their school schedules. What classes do they like or dislike? How long are their class periods? How many periods do they have a day? Do all of their classes meet every day? Explain that schools in Spanish-speaking countries often follow different schedules and may have different required courses.

Heritage Language Learners

Ask students who have attended school in a Spanish-speaking country to describe the differences between school there and school in the United States. Ask them to discuss topics such as start and end times, scheduling lunch, and other breaks, and what classes students typically take.

Capítulo 2A

Tu día en la escuela

Chapter Objectives

- Talk about school schedules and subjects
- Discuss what students do during the day
- Ask and tell who is doing an action
- Compare your school with that of a student in a Spanish-speaking country

Video Highlights

A primera vista: ***El primer día de clases***
GramActiva Videos: **subject pronouns; present tense of *-ar* verbs**

Country Connection

As you learn about the school day in Spanish-speaking countries, you will make connections to these countries and places:

For: Online Atlas
Visit: www.phschool.com
Web Code: jae-0002

Jugadores de jai-alai en España

Preview

Chapter Opener

Presentation

Resources: Voc. & Gram. Transparencies: 12–13, 15, 18 (maps)

Suggestions: Introduce students to the theme of the chapter, school schedules, and subjects by discussing what their school day is like now. Ask students to predict what some of the vocabulary words may be, based on the context. Help students locate the countries featured in the chapter using the map transparencies.

Standards: 2.2, 3.1

Resources: Fine Art Transparencies; Fine Art Transparencies Teacher's Guide

Suggestions: Discuss the style in which the artist depicted the child in the painting. You may want to comment on the title of the work, *Pedrito,* and ask students if they notice anything interesting or strange about the proportions of the child: the face, the neck, and the hands.

Answers will vary but may include adjectives such as *strange* or *unrealistic.*

Teaching with Art

Resources: Fine Art Transparencies; Fine Art Transparencies Teacher's Guide

Remind students that not all artists want to recreate an image exactly. You may wish to give examples of other artists who distort reality, such as Salvador Dalí, Pablo Picasso, or Joan Miró. You can find images by these artists on the Internet and in the *Fine Arts Transparencies.*

Enriching Your Teaching

Planning for Instruction

Resources:

- Teacher Express CD-ROM or Resource Book
  - Teaching resources
  - Lesson Planner
  - Chapter Resource Checklist
  - School-to-Home Connection Letter

Culture Note

In the United States it is common to use a letter grading system, where generally A = 90–100%, B = 80–90%, and so on. In the majority of Spanish-speaking countries, however, the grading system is generally based on the numbers 1–10 rather than on letter grades.

Vocabulario y gramática

Presentation

Standards: 1.2

Resources: Resource Book: 2A, Input Script; Voc. & Gram. Transparencies: 48–49; Resource Book: Cap. 2A, Clip Art; TPR Storytelling Book: Cap. 2A; Audio Program: CD Cap. 2A, Tracks 1–2

Focus: Presenting new vocabulary for school subjects, school schedule, school supplies, adjectives

Suggestions: Use the story in *TPR Storytelling* or the Input Script from the *Teacher's Resource Book* to present the new vocabulary and grammar. Using the transparencies, ask students to describe the schedule they see by answering short questions. (Example: *¿Alicia tiene ciencias sociales o matemáticas en la tercera hora?*) You may wish to present the vocabulary in two sections: classes and school supplies.

Additional Resources

- Audio Program: Song CD

Standards: 1.2, 4.1

Resources: Audio Program: CD Cap. 2A, Track 3; Resource Book: Cap. 2A, Audio Script; Practice Answers on Transparencies

Focus: Listening to statements about the school day and the schedule

Suggestions: Play the *Audio CD* or read the script to the class. Give students a chance to listen more than once. Remind students that they should respond based on Alicia's statements about her classes on pp. 86–87.

Script and Answers:

1. Estudio mucho en la clase de español. *(up)*
2. Mi clase favorita es la clase de tecnología. *(up)*
3. La clase de tecnología es fácil. *(down)*
4. Tengo mucha tarea en la clase de inglés. *(up)*
5. Para la clase de español necesito una calculadora. *(down)*
6. ¡No me gusta nada mi horario! *(down)*

Extension: Re-read the statements and have students give you their personal response by signaling "thumbs-up" if they agree or "thumbs-down" if they disagree. Add additional sentences to personalize the activity for your school environment.

A primera vista

Objectives

Read, listen to, and understand information about
- the school day

Vocabulario y gramática en contexto

El horario de Alicia

"Me gusta mucho mi **horario. En la primera hora, tengo la clase de** tecnología . . . ¡es mi clase **favorita!** Es **interesante** y **práctica.** Pero a veces es **difícil.**"

primera hora	tecnología
segunda hora	arte
tercera hora	ciencias sociales
cuarta hora	ciencias naturales
quinta hora	el almuerzo
sexta hora	español
séptima hora	matemáticas
octava hora	inglés
novena hora	educación física

Más vocabulario
décimo, -a tenth

Universal Access

Students with Learning Difficulties

Have students write new words into the vocabulary section of their notebooks and encourage them to accompany each with a picture if possible. Have students look at *El horario de Alicia* on p. 87 while they listen in *Actividades* 1 and 2.

Advanced Learners

Have students prepare a schedule of their classes, like the one above. Have them put their teachers' names under each subject, using ***Profesor*** + (name) and ***Profesora*** + (name). Ask students to write three sentences under their chart: *Mi clase favorita es* (subject); (subject) *es difícil;* (subject) *es fácil.*

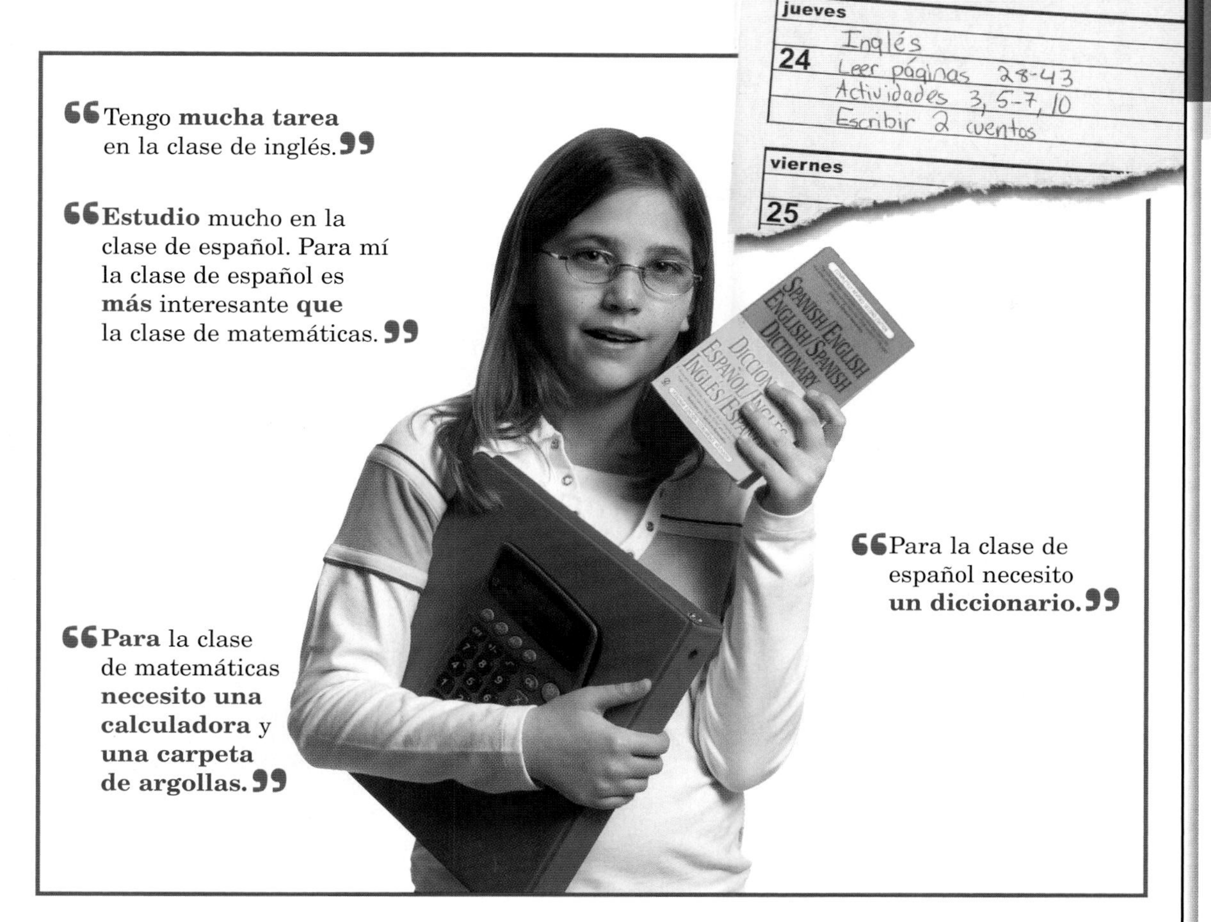

"Tengo **mucha tarea** en la clase de inglés."

"**Estudio** mucho en la clase de español. Para mí la clase de español es **más** interesante **que** la clase de matemáticas."

"**Para** la clase de matemáticas **necesito una calculadora** y **una carpeta de argollas.**"

"Para la clase de español necesito **un diccionario.**"

1 Escuchar

¿Sí o no?

You will hear Alicia make several statements about her school day and schedule. Give a "thumbs-up" sign if what she says is true or a "thumbs-down" sign if what she says is false.

2 Escuchar

El horario de Alicia

Listen to Alicia as she describes her class schedule. Touch the picture of each class as you hear it.

Más práctica

Practice Workbook 2A-1, 2A-2

For: Vocabulary practice
Visit: www.phschool.com
Web Code: jad-0201

Actividad 2 *Standards:* 1.2, 4.1

Resources: Audio Program: CD Cap. 2A, Track 4; Resource Book: Cap. 2A, Audio Script; Practice Answers on Transparencies

Focus: Listening comprehension of statements about the school schedule

Suggestions: Use the *Audio CD* or read the script aloud. Pause in between descriptions so you can verify that students are indicating the correct picture.

Script and Answers:

Tengo ocho clases.

1. **Mi clase favorita, la clase de tecnología, está en la primera hora.** ***(computer)***
2. **La clase de español está en la sexta hora.** ***(Spanish textbook)***
3. **La clase de educación física está en la novena hora.** ***(athletic shoes)***
4. **La clase de matemáticas está en la séptima hora.** ***(math book)***
5. **La clase de arte está en la segunda hora.** ***(palette and brushes)***
6. **La clase de ciencias sociales está en la tercera hora.** ***("El Mundo" book)***
7. **La clase de inglés está en la octava hora.** ***(English literature book)***
8. **La clase de ciencias naturales está en la cuarta hora.** ***(microscope)***
9. **En la quinta hora tengo el almuerzo.** ***(tray of food)***

Extension: Ask volunteers to finish this statement about their favorite class: *Mi clase favorita es* ____. As each student states her favorite, the others continue to point to the chart.

Enriching Your Teaching

Teacher-to-Teacher

A great way to get students on task at the beginning of the class is to put a short, written exercise on an overhead transparency. In this theme, you may ask students to provide vocabulary words or answer short questions about their school day. Stand at the door and pass out small pieces of paper for students to answer the questions on so they can begin immediately. Set a two- or three-minute time limit, and take attendance or collect homework while students work.

Videohistoria

Presentation

 *Standards:* 1.2

Resources: Voc. & Gram. Transparencies: 50–51; Audio Program: CD Cap. 2A, Track 5

Focus: Presenting additional conceptualized vocabulary and grammar; previewing the video

Suggestions:

Pre-reading: Point out the *Strategy* to the class. Have a student answer the question, guessing what ***enseña*** means with the help of the context. Then have students close their books and look at the transparencies. Go panel by panel and ask students to predict what is going to happen.

Videohistoria

El primer día de clases

Es el primer día de clases en la Escuela Bilingüe de la Ciudad de México.

Antes de leer

Using context clues You can often guess the meaning of new words by reading the words around them. Understanding what the rest of the sentence or paragraph is about is helpful in figuring out the meaning of individual words.

- Based on the words around it, what does *enseña* mean in panel 2?

1. What classes do you have every day? What classes do you expect the students in the *Videohistoria* to have?
2. Scan the text to find three classes that the students at the Escuela Bilingüe have. Do you have these classes?
3. Use the photos to see if you can guess what the problem is with Claudia's schedule. Then read the *Videohistoria* to find out whether your prediction was correct or not.

Universal Access

Heritage Language Learners

Have students write a letter to an imaginary friend in their country of origin telling the friend about the first day of school. Then have students exchange letters and answer each other's letters. When reading and reviewing students' letters, make sure to discuss any necessary strategies for improving their writing skills.

Multiple Intelligences

Interpersonal / Social: Have students prepare a short survey to interview their classmates about their opinions on each class. Suggest that they use the words ***interesante, divertida, aburrida, práctica, fácil,*** and ***difícil*** as categories. Have them present the results in a chart, with the adjectives going down the left-hand side, and the names of classes going across the top.

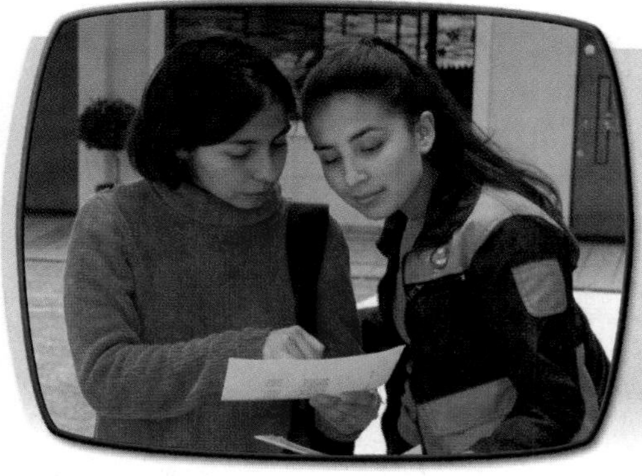

1 **Claudia:** Teresa, ¿qué clase **tienes** en la primera hora?

Teresa: Tengo la clase de inglés.

2 **Claudia:** **¿Quién enseña** la clase de inglés?

Teresa: El señor Marín. Es un profesor muy **divertido.** ¿Y tú? ¿Qué clase tienes en la primera hora?

3 **Claudia:** Tengo la clase de matemáticas. Me gusta mucho. Para mí es muy **fácil.** Y, ¿qué tienes en la segunda hora?

Teresa: La clase de educación física.

4 **Teresa:** Y en la segunda hora, ¿qué clase tienes, Claudia?

Claudia: **A ver . . .** En la segunda hora, tengo la clase de matemáticas. ¡Y también tengo la clase de matemáticas en la tercera, en la cuarta, en la quinta y en la sexta hora!

Suggestions:

Reading: Read the conversations, dramatizing the new words in blue to encourage student comprehension. Model the use of context to figure out some of the new words.

Post-reading: Complete *Actividades* 3 and 4 to check comprehension.

Additional Resources

- Writing, Audio & Video Workbook: Cap. 2A, Video Activity 1
- Heritage Learner Workbook: 2A-1, 2A-2

Enriching Your Teaching

Culture Note

The word ***usted*** came from abbreviating the phrase ***vuestra merced,*** or "your mercy," which was used to address royalty. Students may be interested to know that English also had an informal second person pronoun, "thou." "You" was originally both the plural and formal second person pronoun, but eventually took over all meanings.

Teacher-to-Teacher

As students watch the video, they may get overwhelmed with the language input. It is important to keep them on task. Have different students look for specific details within a segment of the video to discuss as a class. This will help to prepare students for a second or third viewing, when they will be expected to comprehend more.

Video

Presentation

Standards: 1.2

Resources: Video Program: Cap. 2A; Resource Book: Cap. 2A, Video Script

Focus: Hearing new vocabulary in context

Suggestions:

Pre-viewing: Remind students that they will not understand every word in the video, but that they should listen and watch for overall understanding. You may wish to play a short excerpt with the volume down, and then ask students to describe the characters' actions and feelings, based on what they see.

Viewing: Show the video once without pausing, and then go back and show it again, stopping along the way to check comprehension. Make a list of difficult words on the board for review. Depending on student comprehension, you may wish to show the segment a final time without pausing.

Post-viewing: Complete the Video Activities in the *Writing, Audio & Video Workbook*. Have students make predictions about what might happen with Claudia in the second half of the story.

Ask students to identify Claudia's problem as shown in panel 8. How does the teacher react? Have students come up with suggestions that would help her to solve her problem.

Additional Resources

- Writing, Audio & Video Workbook: Cap. 2A, Video Activities 2–4

5 **Teresa: Necesitas hablar** con el señor Treviño, en la oficina.
Claudia: Buena idea.

6 **Claudia:** Buenos días, señor Treviño. Necesito hablar con Ud. Tengo la clase de matemáticas . . .
Sr. Treviño: Sí, sí, Claudia, pero ahora no es posible. Mañana.

7 **Srta. Santoro:** Buenos días, estudiantes. Las matemáticas son muy interesantes y prácticas, ¿verdad?
Estudiantes: Sí, profesora.
Srta. Santoro: Y es muy importante **estudiar** y trabajar mucho . . .

8 **Srta. Santoro:** ¿Claudia?
Claudia: ¡Tengo seis clases de matemáticas hoy!
Srta. Santoro: ¡Seis! Es **aburrido,** ¿no? . . .

Universal Access

Special Education

Provide hearing-impaired students with a copy of the script so that they may follow along when you are showing the video. You may wish to have them read it before viewing, so that they can watch the episode with the class and have some background knowledge about what is happening.

Multiple Intelligences

Bodily / Kinesthetic: Have students prepare a skit about a scheduling conflict, using the *Videohistoria* as a model. Allow students time to prepare in groups. Have volunteers present their skit after reading the *Videohistoria* or viewing the video.

Actividad 3 **Leer/Escribir**

¿Comprendes?

Read each sentence. On your paper, write *sí* if the sentence is correct or *no* if it is incorrect.

1. Es el primer día de clases.
2. A Teresa le gusta la clase de inglés.
3. Para Claudia, la clase de matemáticas es difícil.
4. Claudia tiene la clase de educación física en la segunda hora.
5. Según la Srta. Santoro, la clase de matemáticas es muy práctica.
6. Tener seis clases de matemáticas es interesante.

Pensar/Escribir

¿Dónde están?

Where are the students and faculty of the Escuela Bilingüe? Write the numbers 1–5 on your paper, and then beside each number write the name of the character who belongs in the room. Base your answers on the *Videohistoria*.

Claudia
Teresa
el Sr. Marín
la Srta. Santoro
el Sr. Treviño

1.

2.

3.

4.

5.

Más práctica
Practice Workbook 2A-3, 2A-4

For: Vocabulary practice
Visit: www.phschool.com
Web Code: jad-0202

Actividad 3 *Standards:* 1.2, 1.3

Resources: Practice Answers on Transparencies

Focus: Reading and writing to verify comprehension of the *Videohistoria*

Suggestions: Have different students read each statement to the class. When you call on students, ask them to give you the number of the panel in which the information for their answer is presented.

Answers:
1. sí
2. sí
3. no
4. no
5. sí
6. no

Extension: Have students write or say the correct answer for the sentences that were incorrect.

Standards: 1.3

Resources: Practice Answers on Transparencies

Focus: Writing to verify comprehension of the *Videohistoria*

Suggestions: Work with students to recall the titles of each character, such as ***estudiante, profesor,*** and ***director.***

Answers:
1. el Sr. Treviño
2. el Sr. Marín
3. Claudia, la Srta. Santoro
4. Teresa
5. la Srta. Santoro

Assessment
- Prueba 2A-1: Vocabulary recognition

Enriching Your Teaching

Teacher-to-Teacher

Have each student write one school-related question such as *¿Qué tienes en la tercera hora?* on a small piece of paper. Collect all the papers and put them in a grab bag. Go around the room and have students pull out a question, read it, and call on a classmate to answer. After answering, he or she picks the next question, and so on.

Practice and Communicate

Rapid Review

Have students create two sentences using ***gustar*** to share with the class.

Standards: 1.2, 1.3, 4.1

Actividad 5

Resources: Voc. & Gram. Transparencies: 55; Practice Answers on Transparencies

Focus: Reading and writing about a school schedule in Mexico

Suggestions: Have students review class names, and ask about those they cannot identify. Point out to students that "the arts" may refer to more than art class: the term includes music, dance, and theater, as well as the visual arts. Ask students specific questions about meanings of words, such as ***artes plásticas*** and ***semanales.*** Remind them to use strategies such as background knowledge and cognate identification for comprehension.

Answers:

1. once
2. tres horas
3. dos—historia del mundo y educación cívica y ética
4. dos—biología e introducción a la física
5. danza, teatro, artes plásticas, música

Extension: Have students design their own list of classes based on Ignacio's. Suggest that they total up the number of hours they spend on each subject. You will need to supply names for some classes. Discuss with students which classes are important, practical, fun, and interesting.

Standards: 1.2, 1.3

Actividad 6

Resources: Practice Answers on Transparencies

Focus: Reading about classes, likes, and dislikes

Suggestions: Before beginning the activity, have students look at the words in the box and identify one or two adjectives or nouns that they might be looking for to correspond to each word.

Answers:

1. tecnología
2. educación física
3. inglés
4. matemáticas
5. arte
6. español

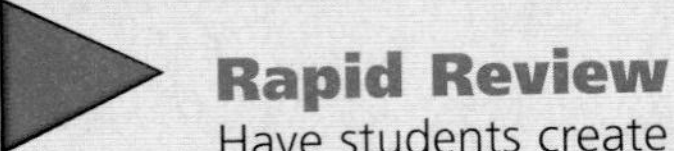

Manos a la obra

Vocabulario y gramática en uso

Objectives

- Discuss the school day
- Ask and tell about likes and dislikes
- Learn to use subject pronouns
- Learn to use verbs that end in *-ar*

Actividad 5 — Leer/Escribir

Un horario

Read the list of classes offered at a school in Querétaro, Mexico, that specializes in the arts. On your paper, answer the questions about the schedule.

1. ¿Cuántas clases hay cada *(each)* semana?
2. ¿Cuántas horas de inglés hay?
3. ¿Cuántas clases de ciencias sociales hay?
4. ¿Cuántas clases de ciencias naturales hay?
5. Escribe los nombres de las diferentes clases de arte.

CENTRO DE EDUCACIÓN ARTÍSTICA
"IGNACIO MARIANO DE LAS CASAS"

PRIMER SEMESTRE	
Español	5 h semanales
Matemáticas	5 h semanales
Historia del mundo	3 h semanales
Educación cívica y ética	3 h semanales
Biología	3 h semanales
Introducción a la física	3 h semanales
Inglés	3 h semanales
Danza	3 h semanales
Teatro	3 h semanales
Artes plásticas	3 h semanales
Música	3 h semanales

Total 37 h semanales

Actividad 6 — Leer/Pensar

¿Qué les gusta?

Read the descriptions of the students below. Then, number your paper 1–6 and write the name of the class that you think each student would like.

1. A Juan le gusta mucho usar la computadora.
2. Sarita es muy deportista.
3. A Roberto le gusta leer.
4. A Miguel le gustan los números.
5. Gabriela es artística y le gusta pintar.
6. A Carolina le gusta hablar con amigos en México.

inglés
educación física
matemáticas
español
arte
tecnología

Universal Access

Heritage Language Learners

Ask students who have attended school in their heritage country to write a short paragraph explaining how scheduling and grading procedures there differ from those in the United States. Ask them to talk about rotating schedules with different classes each day and grading with numbers instead of letters. You may wish to discuss their responses with the class.

Students with Learning Difficulties

When practicing reading comprehension, as in *Actividad* 5, allow students with learning difficulties extra time to use the variety of reading strategies that are accessible. Comprehension may require two or three attempts at the task.

Leer/Hablar

¿Estás de acuerdo?

Yolanda has interviewed her classmates for her school newspaper, *El Diario San Miguel,* to find out what they think about their classes.

1 Number your paper 1–6. Read the article and based on your own classes, write *sí* if you agree with each statement or *no* if you disagree.

2 Now tell your partner how you would change each statement that you disagree with in order to express your own opinion.

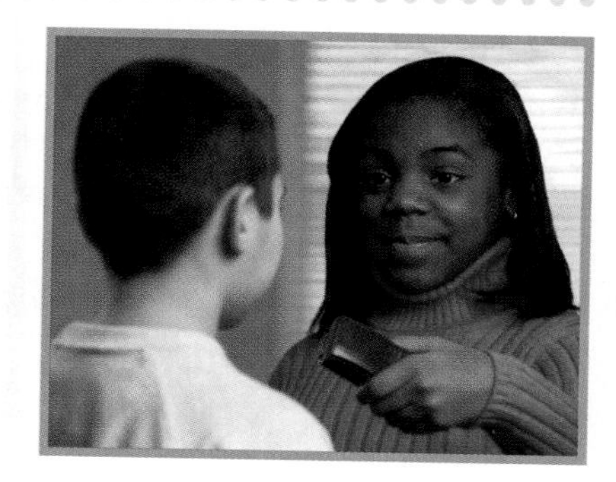

PUEBLA, MÉXICO **22 DE SEPTIEMBRE**

El Diario San Miguel

Periódico de la Escuela San Miguel **TERCERA EDICIÓN**

Las clases en la Escuela San Miguel

¿Te gustan tus clases? Las opiniones de los estudiantes de la Escuela San Miguel son muy diferentes.

Alejandro Zarzalejos, octavo año

"La clase de inglés no es muy difícil. Me gusta leer y escribir." 1.

Ángel Suzuki, séptimo año

"La clase de matemáticas es divertida. La profesora es buena." 2.

Laura Rodríguez, séptimo año

"Mi clase favorita es la educación física. Me gusta mucho el fútbol." 3.

Pilar Soriano, octavo año

"La tecnología es muy aburrida. No me gusta nada jugar videojuegos." 4.

Sara Martínez, octavo año

"El arte es interesante y la profesora es muy talentosa. Me gusta mucho dibujar." 5.

Luis Soto, séptimo año

"La clase de español es fácil. Me gusta la tarea." 6.

Enriching Your Teaching

Culture Note

Point out to your students that in Spanish-speaking countries, students often address their teachers by their titles, to show respect. For example, they would say ***Maestro Smith*** or ***Profesora Johnson.*** Occasionally, students may also address their teacher as ***profe,*** short for ***profesor(a).*** Students in Spain, however, may actually call teachers by their first name.

Teacher-to-Teacher

Have students work in groups to produce their own newspaper article like the one on p. 93. They can create a name for the newspaper and write comments about their favorite or least favorite classes.

Standards: 1.1, 1.2

Focus: Reading and talking about classes and likes and dislikes

Suggestions: Point out to students that ordinal numbers appear in several places in the article. After students complete step 1, ask volunteers to read the comments while students raise their hands to show whether they agree or disagree. Then have them talk in pairs to complete step 2. Invite them to share some of these answers with the class.

Answers will vary.

Extension: Have students choose three of the students' comments and rewrite them, changing a few words to create a new meaning.

Standards: 1.3

Focus: Writing about a class schedule; personalizing vocabulary

Suggestions: If students are in travel groups, and all share the same schedule, have them scramble the classes and teachers in their charts and give them to other students to unscramble.

Answers will vary.

Common Errors: Students may forget to use definite articles. As students are working, circulate around the room and remind students to use articles where appropriate.

Extension: Have students add another column and write one thing they need for each class.

Exploración del lenguaje

Presentation

Standards: 3.1

Suggestions: When possible, pair heritage speakers with non-heritage speakers to complete both *Try it out!* activities. To extend the second *Try it out!* activity, ask students to come up with other words in English or Spanish that have the roots *sept-, oct-, nov-, dic-, or dec-*. Have students share their answers with the class.

Answers will vary.

Possible answers: unisex, primary, dual, bicycle, secondary, tricycle, quadrant, quarter, quintuplets, sexto, September, *séptimo*, octagon, *octavo*, octave, November decade, decimal.

These months were named using ordinals, so September, October, November, and December were the seventh, eighth, ninth, and tenth months, respectively.

  **Escribir**

Mi horario

Write out your class schedule. Copy the chart on a separate sheet of paper and provide the information for each of your classes.

Modelo

Hora	Clase	Profesor(a)
la primera hora	la clase de inglés	la Sra. Sánchez

¿Recuerdas?

Use *señor, señora*, and *señorita* when talking **to** adults. Use *el* in front of *señor* and *la* in front of *señora* or *señorita* when talking **about** adults.

Exploración del lenguaje

Connections between Latin, English, and Spanish

Many words in English and Spanish are based on Latin. Seeing the relationship between these words will help expand your English or Spanish vocabulary. Look at the list of Latin root forms for the numbers one through ten.

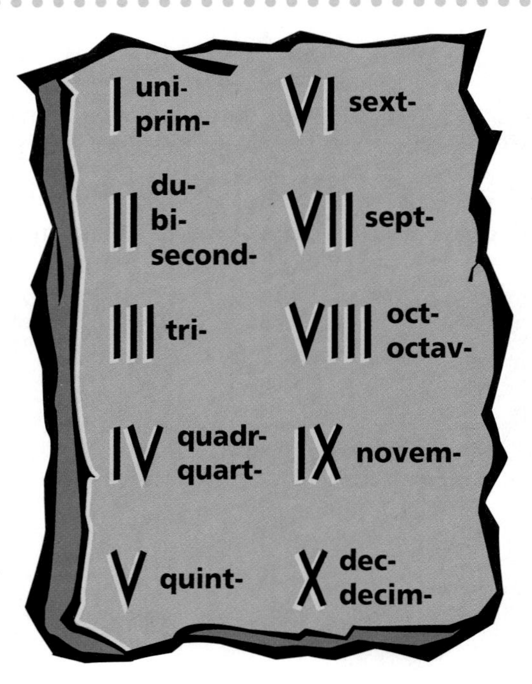

Try it out! For each Roman numeral listed, choose one of the root forms (if more than one is listed) and write down a Spanish and an English word you know that are based on that root.

Try it out! The Roman year used to begin with the month of March. Knowing that, can you explain why *septiembre, octubre, noviembre,* and *diciembre* use the Latin root forms for seven, eight, nine, and ten?

Universal Access

Students with Learning Difficulties

The *Exploración del lenguaje* activity may be easier for some students if you provide a list of words and ask them to identify the Latin roots. Have students discuss the meaning of each word to show how the Latin prefix affects it.

Multiple Intelligences

Visual / Spatial: Have students make a poster with the numbers 1–10 and the Latin root forms. Below each number, have them list all the words they can think of with that root. You may want to let them use a dictionary. Display these on the wall and tell students to add to them as they encounter new vocabulary in either language.

Fondo cultural

Many Spanish words are derived from Latin because Spain was once part of the Roman Empire. Rome occupied most of Spain from about 209 B.C. to 586 A.D. During that time, massive public structures, including aqueducts and theaters, were built. Some of these, such as the aqueduct that towers over the modern city of Segovia, are still standing. The Latin name for Spain was *Hispania*.

- Can you see the similarity between *Hispania* and the country's name in Spanish, *España?*

El acueducto de Segovia

Actividad 9 **Hablar**

Mucha tarea

With a partner, ask and tell if you have homework in each class.

Modelo

A —*¿Tienes mucha tarea en la clase de matemáticas?*
B —*Sí, tengo mucha tarea.*
o: *No, no tengo mucha tarea.*
o: *No estudio matemáticas.*

Estudiante A

Estudiante B

¡Respuesta personal!

Enriching Your Teaching

Culture Note

Spanish is one of the Romance languages, along with French, Italian, Portuguese, Rumanian, and Romansch (one of the official languages of Switzerland). These languages are called "Romance" because they come from the language of Rome, Latin. Spanish is considered the most similar to Latin. More than half of English words are derived from Latin or Greek, though most of these are relative latecomers to the English language.

Internet Search

Keyword: Segovia, Spainl

Standards: 3.1

Fondo cultural

Suggestions: Point out that the historical connection between Rome and Spain goes beyond language. Some of Rome's most successful leaders came from Spain, for example, Trajan (A.D. 98–117) and Hadrian (A.D. 117–138). Students may wish to do further research on these leaders or other Roman influences on Spain.

Teaching with Photos

Point out to students that this structure, like many of the remains of the Roman Empire, is significant because of its size and complexity. Remind students that the Romans did not have modern tools to build such structures. Usually such tasks were extremely arduous and time-consuming for the workers.

Actividad 9 *Standards:* 1.1

Resources: Practice Answers on Transparencies

Focus: Speaking about homework in a personalized context

Suggestions: Briefly review which class each item represents. Have student volunteers read the model. Remind students to take turns being Student A and Student B, so that each one has a chance to ask and answer questions.

Answers:

Student A:

1. ¿Tienes mucha tarea en la clase de tecnología?
2. ¿Tienes mucha tarea en la clase de español?
3. ¿Tienes mucha tarea en la clase de arte?
4. ¿Tienes mucha tarea en la clase de ciencias sociales?
5. ¿Tienes mucha tarea en la clase de educación física?
6. ¿Tienes mucha tarea en la clase de ciencias naturales?
7. ¿Tienes mucha tarea en la clase de inglés?

Student B: Answers will vary.

Common Errors: Remind students that ***tarea*** is feminine, and they should say ***mucha,*** not ***mucho, tarea.***

Practice and Communicate

Rapid Review

Write the sentence *No me gusta ni ... ni ...* on the board. Have students fill in the blanks with the names of two school subjects that they do not like.

Standards: 1.3

Focus: Writing to compare class preferences in a personalized context

Suggestions: If students do not take all of the classes shown, suggest possible alternatives. Remind students to save their answers for *Actividad* 11.

Answers will vary.

Standards: 1.1

Resources: Practice Answers on Transparencies

Focus: Speaking about personal preferences regarding classes

Recycle: ***Te gusta***

Suggestions: Remind students to use the information that they wrote in *Actividad* 10. Point out to students that instead of using ***me gusta*** in the response, they will use ***es más*** (adjective) ***que*** to explain why they prefer one class to another. Ask volunteers to read the model, and then have another pair of students personalize the model before dividing the class into pairs.

Answers will vary for Student B, but Student A will ask:

1. **¿Te gusta más la clase de música o la clase de español?**
2. **¿Te gusta más la clase de arte o la clase de educación física?**
3. **¿Te gusta más la clase de inglés o la clase de matemáticas?**
4. **¿Te gusta más la clase de ciencias sociales o la clase de ciencias naturales?**
5. **¿Te gusta más la clase de tecnología o la clase de música?**
6. **¿Te gusta más la clase de ciencias sociales o la clase de matemáticas?**

Actividad 10 **Escribir**

Me gusta más . . .

On your paper, write sentences stating which of the two classes you like better and why. Use the list of adjectives to help with your responses. Save your paper for Actividad 11.

aburrida	difícil
divertida	fácil
interesante	práctica

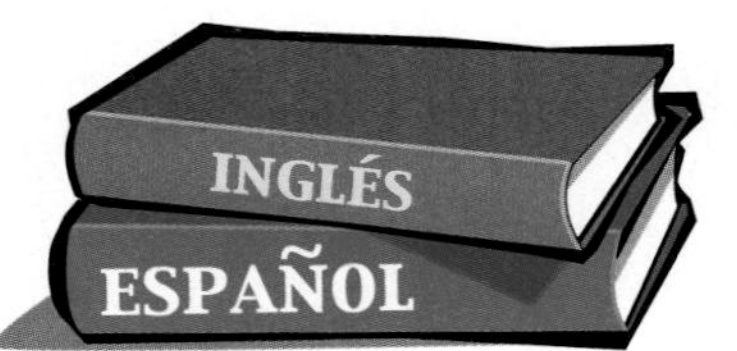

Modelo

Me gusta más la clase de español. Es divertida.
o: *Me gusta más la clase de inglés. No es aburrida.*
o: *No me gusta ni la clase de español ni la clase de inglés.*

1.

2.

3.

4.

5.

6.

Actividad 11 **Hablar**

¿Qué te gusta más?

With a partner, ask and tell which classes from Actividad 10 you like best and why.

Modelo

A —*¿Te gusta más la clase de inglés o la clase de español?*
B —*A ver . . . Para mí, la clase de español es más divertida que la clase de inglés.*

Universal Access

Advanced Learners

Have students write a short summary of their schedule, including how many classes there are, which time slot they fall into, who the teacher is, what they need for the class, and how they feel about it. You may wish to have students peer-edit each other's papers and keep them in a portfolio.

Heritage Language Learners

Have students compare English and Spanish. Do the languages seem closely related? What specific structures in English are different in Spanish? What expressions are difficult to remember? Follow up their comments with a whole-class discussion on some of the challenges and rewards of learning a second language.

Estudiantes mexicanos en una clase de inglés

Fondo cultural

Studying English While you're in Spanish class at your school, large numbers of Spanish-speaking students are studying to learn the most popular foreign language worldwide: English. Many children begin to study English in grade school and continue through high school. They often attend special language school for additional English classes. When visiting a Spanish-speaking country, you might easily find someone who is eager to practice his or her English skills with you in exchange for helping you improve your Spanish.

- Why do you think English is so popular in other countries? Are you studying Spanish for similar reasons?

El español en la comunidad

Do you know if there are any opportunities to learn Spanish outside of your school in your community? Use the Internet, look through college brochures, or look in the phone book to see if there are any Spanish classes or private lessons offered close to where you live.

- Why do you think people in your community would want to study Spanish?

Escribir/Hablar

Y tú, ¿qué dices?

1. ¿Qué clase te gusta más?
2. ¿Cómo es la clase?
3. ¿En qué hora tienes la clase?
4. ¿Quién enseña la clase?
5. ¿Tienes mucha tarea en la clase?

Practice and Communicate

Standards: 2.1, 4.2

Suggestions: Point out that throughout the Spanish-speaking world, learning English is important for success in school and in the working world. Students start studying English at an early age and by middle school are often quite competent.

Answers will vary.

El español en la comunidad

Presentation

Standards: 3.1

Suggestions: Brainstorm names of places in the community where adults and children can learn Spanish. Ask students if they know of anyone who is taking such classes. If so, have them inquire about the courses. Have students compare the community class with their own class.

Answers will vary.

Standards: 1.1, 1.3

Focus: Writing and speaking in a personalized context

Suggestions: Have students work individually or with a partner to prepare their answers. You may want to have students answer the questions in paragraph format, with the title *Mi clase favorita.*

Answers will vary.

Enriching Your Teaching

Teacher-to-Teacher

You may wish to present *Y tú, ¿qué dices?* activities as an opportunity for students to create a project that reflects themselves. Having students answer questions in a paragraph format, and possibly include an illustration, can result in a nice piece for a student's portfolio.

Internet Search

Keywords:

Spanish language schools or classes + (your community)

Additional Resources

- Resource Book: Cap. 2A, Communicative Activity BLM
- Writing, Audio & Video Workbook: Cap. 2A, Audio Activities 5–6, Tracks 6–7
- Writing, Audio & Video Workbook: Cap. 2A, Writing Activity 10

Assessment

- Prueba 2A-2: Vocabulary production

Practice and Communicate

Rapid Review

Before beginning, define subject pronouns and have students list the ones they have seen in Spanish.

Gramática

Presentation

Standards: 4.1

Resources: Voc. & Gram. Transparencies: 52–53; Video Program: Cap. 2A; Resource Book: Cap. 2A, Video Script

Suggestions: Present subject pronouns in context, telling a story about what different people do. Emphasize who the subject pronoun is referring to by pointing to the person or people. Use the transparencies to reinforce the subject pronouns. Use the *GramActiva* Video to reinforce your grammar explanation. Remind students of the distinction between ***tú*** and ***usted.*** Point out that ***nosotros*** and ***vosotros*** have feminine forms, but that the masculine is used if there is at least one male in the group.

Standards: 1.2

Focus: Listening and speaking using subject pronouns

Suggestions: Model this activity for your students, pointing to pre-designated people in the class. You will need to say the subject pronouns aloud. For example, point to yourself for ***yo,*** have students face each other and point for ***tú,*** point to a male or female student when saying ***él*** and ***ella,*** indicate an imaginary circle including yourself when saying ***nosotros,*** point directly to two or more students for ***vosotros,*** and point to a group of male or female students for ***ellos / ellas.*** You might want to draw several adult-like stick figures on the board so students can point to ***ustedes.***

Gramática

Subject pronouns

The subject of a sentence tells who is doing the action. You often use people's names as the subject:

Gregorio escucha música. — ***Gregory*** *listens to music.*
Ana canta y baila. — ***Ana*** *sings and dances.*

yo tú

You also use subject pronouns *(I, you, he, she, we, they)* to tell who is doing an action. The subject pronouns replace people's names:

Él escucha música. — ***He*** *listens to music.*
Ella canta y baila. — ***She*** *sings and dances.*

Here are all the subject pronouns in Spanish:

yo	I	**nosotros** **nosotras**	we we
tú	you *(familiar)*	**vosotros** **vosotras**	you you
usted (Ud.)	you *(formal)*	**ustedes (Uds.)**	you *(formal)*
él **ella**	he she	**ellos** **ellas**	they they

Tú, usted, ustedes, and *vosotros(as)* all mean "you."

- Use *tú* with family, friends, people your age or younger, and anyone you call by his or her first name.
- Use *usted* with adults you address with a title, such as *señor, señora, profesor(a),* etc. *Usted* is usually written as *Ud.*
- In Latin America, use *ustedes* when speaking to two or more people, regardless of age. *Ustedes* is usually written as *Uds.*
- In Spain, use *vosotros(as)* when speaking to two or more people you call *tú* individually: *tú* + *tú* = *vosotros(as).* Use *ustedes* when talking to two or more people you call *usted* individually.

If a group is made up of males only, or of both males and females together, use the masculine forms: *nosotr**os**, vosotr**os**, ell**os**.*

If a group is all females, use the feminine forms: *nosotr**as**, vosotr**as**, ell**as**.*

You can combine a subject pronoun and a name to form a subject.

Alejandro y yo = **nosotros** — Pepe y tú = **ustedes**
Carlos y ella = **ellos** — Lola y ella = **ellas**

GramActiva VIDEO

Want more help with subject pronouns? Watch the **GramActiva** video.

Universal Access

Heritage Language Learners

Give students a paragraph or list of sentences. Ask them to underline the subjects in one color and the subject pronouns in another.

Students with Learning Difficulties

Often, students have difficulty substituting subject pronouns for proper nouns. It is helpful to have students recall their English-language skills. Give students two or three examples in English of how they substitute subject pronouns, and then have them transfer this skill to Spanish.

Escuchar/GramActiva

¡Señala!

Your teacher will name several subject pronouns. Point to people in the classroom who represent the pronoun you hear. After you have practiced with your teacher, practice with a partner.

Actividad 14 Gramática Escribir

¿Es ella?

On your paper, write the subject pronouns you would use to talk about these people.

Modelo
Gloria
Ella.

1. Carlos
2. Felipe y yo
3. Pablo, Tomás y Anita
4. María y Sarita
5. el señor Treviño
6. tú y Esteban

Gramática Hablar

¿Tú, Ud. o Uds.?

Tell whether you would use *tú, Ud.,* or *Uds.* with these people.

1. 
2. 
3. 
4. 
5. 
6. 
7. 
8. 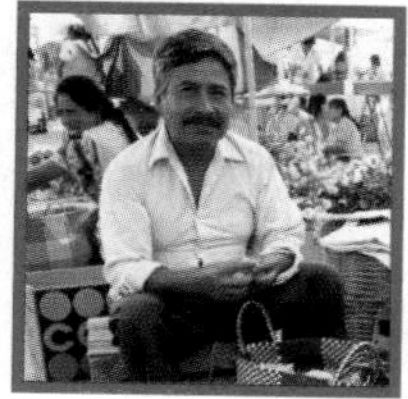

Más práctica
Practice Workbook 2A-5

For: Practice with subject pronouns
Visit: www.phschool.com
Web Code: jad-0203

Enriching Your Teaching

Teacher-to-Teacher

Often, confusion arises when the subject pronouns ***yo*** and ***tú*** are seem in an activity. When given such prompts, students generally should assume that they will stay the same in their answers. When an activity is "talking to" the students (for example, *Y tú ¿qué dices?),* they need to change the ***tú*** in the question to ***yo*** in the answer in order to talk about themselves.

Standards: 1.3

Resources: Practice Answers on Transparencies

Focus: Writing using subject pronouns

Suggestions: Refer students to the notes on p. 98 to decide which subject pronoun is appropriate. For item 6, point out that there are two possible correct responses, depending on the dialect that is being used. Remind students that in *Realidades*, ***ustedes*** is generally used to refer to the second person plural.

Answers:

1. él
2. nosotros
3. ellos
4. ellas
5. él
6. vosotros / ustedes

Standards: 1.1, 1.2

Resources: Practice Answers on Transparencies

Focus: Choosing socially appropriate subject pronouns

Suggestions: Remind students that ***tú*** is used informally, and ***usted*** is generally used for people who would be addressed by their last name. Point out that students will not use ***vosotros / vosotras*** in this activity.

Answers:

1. Ud.
2. tú
3. Ud.
4. Uds.
5. Ud.
6. Uds.
7. tú
8. Ud.

Extension: As a homework assignment, have students prepare three pieces of paper, one labeled ***tú,*** one labeled ***usted,*** and one labeled ***ustedes.*** Ask them to cut out magazine pictures or downloaded images showing individuals and groups of people whom they would address as ***tú, usted,*** or ***ustedes,*** and mount them on the correct sheet. These can be hung on the bulletin board.

Additional Resources

- Writing, Audio & Video Workbook: Cap. 2A, Audio Activity 7
- Writing, Audio & Video Workbook: Cap. 2A, Writing Activity 11
- Heritage Language Learner Workbook: 2A-3

Assessment

- Prueba 2A-3: Subject pronouns

Practice and Communicate

Rapid Review

Have students list all the **-ar** verbs they remember. Ask, *¿Te gusta ...?* followed by one of the verbs. Have students respond with "thumbs-up" or "thumbs-down."

Presentation

Standards: 4.1

Resources: Voc. & Gram. Transparencies: 54; Video Program: Cap. 2A; Resource Book: Cap. 2A, Video Script

Suggestions: Direct students' attention to the *¿Recuerdas?* to remind them that they have seen **-ar** verbs before.

To present the ***-ar*** verbs, you may wish to choose one and break it down to the stem and the ending. Tell students that the stem carries the meaning, so it is the ***habl-*** of ***hablar*** that means "talk." Have students identify stems of the other infinitives that they see.

Use the transparency to point out verbs with ***-ar*** endings, then use the *GramActiva* Video.

Standards: 1.2

Resources: Audio Program: CD Cap. 2A, Track 8; Research Book: Cap. 2A, Audio Script; Practice Answers on Transparencies

Focus: Listening comprehension

Suggestions: Before beginning, direct students' attention to the *Strategy*.

Have students refer to the chart on p. 100 while doing this exercise. Point out that the forms on the left side of the chart are singular (one person doing the action), and those on the right are plural.

Script and Answers:

1. hablo *(one hand)*
2. enseñan *(two hands)*
3. dibujamos *(two hands)*
4. trabaja *(one hand)*
5. cantas *(one hand)*
6. estudian *(two hands)*
7. necesitan *(two hands)*
8. practico *(one hand)*

Gramática

Present tense of *-ar* verbs

You already know that the infinitive forms of Spanish verbs always end in *-ar, -er,* or *-ir.*

The largest group of verbs end in *-ar. Hablar* is one of these *-ar* verbs.

In order to express who is doing an action, you have to use verbs in ways other than in the infinitive form. To do this, you have to drop the *-ar* ending and make changes.

To create the forms of most *-ar* verbs, first drop the *-ar* from the infinitive, saving the stem:

hablar → habl-

Then add the verb endings *-o, -as, -a, -amos, -áis,* or *-an* to the stem.

Here are the forms of *hablar:*

(yo)	**hablo**	(nosotros) (nosotras)	**hablamos**
(tú)	**hablas**	(vosotros) (vosotras)	**habláis**
Ud. (él) (ella)	**habla**	Uds. (ellos) (ellas)	**hablan**

¿Recuerdas?
You already know many *-ar* verbs, such as *cantar* and *bailar.*

In Spanish, the present tense form of a verb can be translated into English in two ways:

Hablo español. *I speak Spanish. / I am speaking Spanish.*

The verb endings always indicate who is doing the action. Because of this, you can often use the verb without a subject:

Hablo inglés.
¿**Hablas** español?

Subject pronouns are often used for emphasis or clarification.

Ella habla inglés pero **él** habla español.

GramActiva VIDEO

Want more help with verbs that end in *-ar*? Watch the **GramActiva** video.

Gramática Escuchar/Pensar/GramActiva

¿Una mano o dos?

You will hear eight *-ar* verbs. If the ending tells you one person is performing the action, raise one hand. If the ending tells you more than one person is doing something, raise both hands.

Strategy

Listening for information
Always listen carefully for the endings on verbs to know who is doing the action.

Universal Access

Multiple Intelligences

Bodily / Kinesthetic: Have students cut out magazine pictures that depict ***-ar*** verbs and paste them on construction paper to make posters. At the bottom of the poster, have students write a sentence describing each action.

Heritage Language Learners

Pay special attention to students' verb formation. Depending on their heritage, students' pronunciation may vary from the "standard" ways of saying these endings. These differences may result in incorrect spelling or adding the wrong verb ending. Some students may also use such forms as the ***voseo,*** which should be recognized.

Actividad 17 **Pensar/Escribir**

El detective

Number your paper 1–10. Play the detective and figure out what everyone is doing by matching the sentences with the correct names under the magnifying glass.

1. ___ estudia mucho en la clase.
2. ___ hablan con amigos.
3. ___ pasas mucho tiempo en la clase.
4. ___ usamos la computadora.
5. ___ dibujan muy bien.
6. ___ no montas en monopatín.
7. ___ hablamos español.
8. ___ escuchas música.
9. ___ baila con Carolina.
10. ___ patinan en el parque.

Tú
María y Graciela
Federico y yo
Carlos

Escribir/Hablar

¿Qué estudian?

Number your paper 1–6. Look at the pictures and tell what these people are studying.

Modelo

Tomás
Tomás estudia música.

1. Laura

2A+B=6

4. Catalina y José

2. Josefina, Elena y yo

5. Joaquín y tú

3. tú

6. yo

Actividad 17 *Standards:* 1.3

Resources: Practice Answers on Transparencies

Focus: Writing to practice subject-verb agreement

Suggestions: Recall the subject pronouns that go with the proper nouns shown. Remind students that they can identify the subject by looking at the verb ending.

Answers:

1. Carlos
2. María y Graciela
3. Tú
4. Federico y yo
5. María y Graciela
6. Tú
7. Federico y yo
8. Tú
9. Carlos
10. María y Graciela

Extension: Have students rewrite the five sentences, personalizing them by inserting the names of their friends and family members who do the same activities.

Actividad 18 *Standards:* 1.1, 1.3

Resources: Practice Answers on Transparencies

Focus: Writing and speaking about classes

Suggestions: While reviewing this activity, you may wish to ask students *¿Quién estudia el arte?* and have students identify the person. This will allow the class to avoid the routine of reviewing questions and answers in the order they appear and will also require them to stay on task.

Answers:

1. **Laura estudia las matemáticas.**
2. **Josefina, Elena y yo estudiamos el arte.**
3. **Tú estudias el inglés.**
4. **Catalina y José estudian el español.**
5. **Joaquín y tú estudian la tecnología.**
6. **Yo estudio las ciencias sociales.**

Enriching Your Teaching

Teacher-to-Teacher

On the board or on a transparency, write the numbers 1–6 and write a different subject next to each number. Make another column, again writing the numbers 1–6, and listing an infinitive for each number. Bring in two different colored dice, and have students take turns rolling them. Assign one color to column one and the other to column two. Students must provide subject-verb formations according to the numbers they have rolled.

Theme Project

Give students copies of the Theme Project outline and rubric from the *Teacher's Resource Book.* Explain the task to them, and have them perform step 1. (For more information, see p. 84-a.)

Practice and Communicate

Standards: 1.2, 1.3

Resources: Practice Answers on Transparencies

Focus: Writing using *-ar* verb conjugations

Recycle: Meanings of *-ar* verbs

Suggestions: Before beginning, review with students which subject pronoun endings they will use for proper noun subjects. Refer students to the *-ar* verb chart on p. 100. Point out that they need both the correct form and the meaning to get the right answer. They will not use all of the verbs in the word bank.

Answers:

1. dibujan
2. necesitas/usas
3. uso
4. practicamos
5. enseña
6. habla

Standards: 1.1, 1.2

Resources: Resource Book: Cap. 2A, GramActiva BLM

Focus: Listening comprehension of contextualized use of verb forms

Suggestions: Have the subject pronoun cards prepared and laminated, as they can be quite useful as students continue learning different verb forms and tenses. Have students keep score on a sheet of notebook paper.

Script:

1. estudiar
2. enseñar
3. trabajar
4. cantar
5. bailar
6. patinar
7. necesitar
8. usar

Answers will vary.

Additional Resources

- Writing, Audio & Video Workbook: Cap. 2A, Audio Activities 8–9
- Writing, Audio & Video Workbook: Cap. 2A, Writing Activities 12–13
- Heritage Language Learner Workbook: 2A-4, 2A-5
- Resource Book: Cap. 2A, Communicative Activity BLM

Assessment

- Prueba 2A-4: Present tense of *-ar* verbs

Actividad 19 Gramática  Escribir

En la escuela

On your paper, use verbs from the box to complete the sentences about what different activities take place during school.

Modelo

Yo estudio mucho en la clase de español.

necesitar	hablar	practicar	enseñar
dibujar	usar	patinar	bailar

1. Lupe y Guillermo ___ mucho en la clase de arte.
2. Tú ___ la computadora en la clase de tecnología.
3. Yo ___ una calculadora y una carpeta para la clase de matemáticas.
4. Tomás y yo ___ deportes en la clase de educación física.
5. ¿Quién ___ la clase de ciencias naturales?
6. Marta ___ mucho en la clase de español.

 Escuchar/Hablar/GramActiva

Juego

1. Work with a partner and tear a sheet of paper into eight pieces of equal size. Write a different subject pronoun on each piece (*yo, tú, él, ella, Ud., nosotros, ellas, Uds.*). Place the subject pronouns face down in a pile.
2. Your teacher will say an infinitive. One partner will select the top piece of paper from the pile, read the subject pronoun, and say the correct verb form. A correct answer earns one point. Place the "used" subject pronouns in a separate pile. Take turns selecting from the pile and answering.
3. When your teacher calls time, shuffle the pieces of paper with subject pronouns and place them in a new pile face down. When the next verb is read aloud, continue play. The partner with the most correct answers is the winner.

En una escuela en México

Más práctica

Practice Workbook 2A-6, 2A-7

For: Practice with *-ar* verbs
Visit: www.phschool.com
Web Code: jad-0204

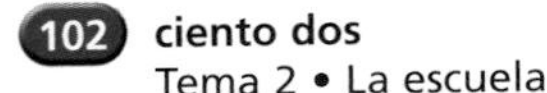

Universal Access

Advanced Learners

Assign students a Spanish-speaking country, and ask them to use the Internet to find information about the education system in that country. Suggest that they include details such as the format and size of schools, subjects offered, and languages of instruction. Have them share their findings with the class.

Students with Learning Difficulties

To help students on task during *Actividad* 20, write each infinitive on a large piece of paper or on the board and display it for students to see while they work. Often, this visual cue helps students to process the conjugation of verbs in their heads.

Actividad 21 Escuchar/Escribir

Escucha y escribe

Listen to a student describe this photo of himself and other students during their *recreo*. Write what you hear.

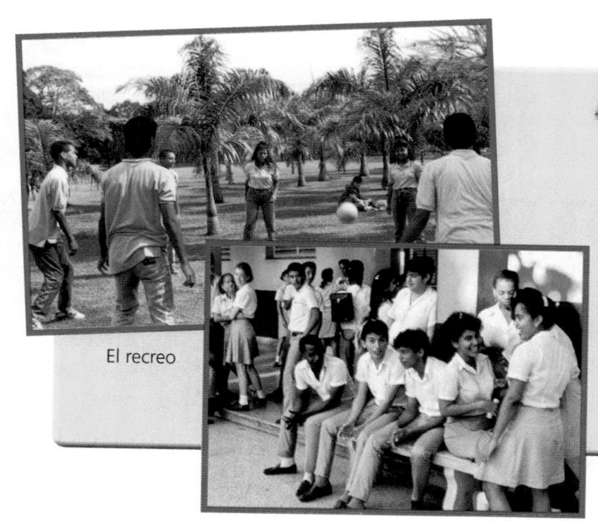

El recreo

Fondo cultural

El recreo In Spanish-speaking countries, students usually have *el recreo* (recess or break) in the school patio. Students take time to relax and spend time with friends, eat a snack, or participate in activities such as a quick game of basketball, soccer, or volleyball.

- How is this similar to your school? How is it different?

Actividad 22 Gramática Leer/Escribir

Durante el recreo

During recess, Lola and the others at the Escuela Rubén Darío are always busy doing something. Based on their personality traits, match the students to the activity they would most likely be doing. After you have matched the person with the activity, write complete sentences on your paper describing what everyone does during *el recreo*.

1. yo *(deportista)*
2. Isabel y Carmen *(artísticas)*
3. Geraldo y yo *(estudiosos)*
4. tú *(sociable)*
5. el Sr. Campo *(trabajador)*

a. enseñar una clase de español
b. usar una calculadora para la tarea
c. dibujar en la cafetería
d. practicar deportes
e. hablar con amigos

Enriching Your Teaching

Culture Note

Because music is such an important part of many Spanish-speaking cultures, students often spend time singing and dancing in groups, even at school during their breaks. While many students from the United States are likely to sing and dance at shows, students in Spanish-speaking countries often do so casually with groups of friends.

Teacher-to-Teacher

Collect pictures that represent ***-ar*** verbs the students know. Tape them on the walls around the room. Ask pairs of students to stand in front of each picture. Give them a few minutes to write a sentence about it. Signal when it's time for them to move to the next picture. Students can give the people in the pictures names and add details if they want to be creative.

Actividad 21 *Standards:* 1.2, 1.3

Resources: Audio Program: CD Cap. 2A, Track 9; Resource Book: Cap. 2A, Audio Script; Practice Answers on Transparencies

Focus: Listening comprehension; writing about school breaktime

Suggestions: Use the *Audio CD* or read the script. Let students hear the script once without writing. Play or read it a second time, pausing after each sentence for students to write. Play or read the script a final time so students can check their work.

Script and Answers:

1. **Dos amigos y yo hablamos de las clases.**
2. **Tomás estudia español.**
3. **Ana canta.**
4. **Y María escucha música.**

Standards: 2.1, 4.2

Fondo cultural

Suggestions: Have students look at the pictures of activities outside the classroom during the break. If students no longer have recess during school, ask them to recall what activities they did in elementary school or encourage them to talk about what they do in the short breaks between classes.

Answers will vary.

Actividad 22 *Standards:* 1.2, 1.3

Resources: Practice Answers on Transparencies

Focus: Writing about school breaktime

Suggestions: Remind students that the word in italics will indicate which activity they should choose.

You may want to review these adjectives by asking students to identify classmates who can be described using these adjectives.

Answers:

1. **Yo practico deportes.**
2. **Isabel y Carmen dibujan en la cafetería.**
3. **Gerardo y yo usamos una calculadora para la tarea.**
4. **Tú hablas con amigos.**
5. **El Sr. Campo enseña una clase de español.**

Standards: 1.1, 1.3

Resources: Voc. & Gram. Transparencies: 2 (graphic organizer); Resource Book: Cap. 2A, Communicative Activity BLM

Focus: Writing and speaking using ***-ar*** verbs and contextualized vocabulary

Recycle: ***-ar*** verb meanings

Suggestions: Pair students with people they usually do not work with. If they pair up with their friends, many of their activities may be the same.

Use the board or an overhead transparency to demonstrate the steps of the activities. Point out that students must write the words in the ***yo*** form for step 2, and in the ***él / ella*** form for step 3. Have volunteers read the *Modelo* for step 3 and then reread it, this time personalizing it with their information. Encourage students to use other words besides ***mucho,*** such as ***bien*** or ***con mis amigos.*** Point out that they will not use the ***nosotros*** section of the Venn diagram until step 4.

Actividad 23   **Escribir/Hablar**

Actividades y más actividades

1. Work with a partner. Look at the model for Step One below. Copy the Venn diagram on a sheet of paper. Label the oval on the left *Yo.* Label the oval on the right with the name of your partner. Label the overlapping area *Nosotros* or *Nosotras.*

2. From the word box, choose five activities you do a lot. Write your activities in the oval labeled *Yo.* Be sure to use the appropriate verb in the *Yo* form. Look at the model for Step Two below.

hablar por teléfono	dibujar
estudiar	cantar
hablar español	nadar
montar en bicicleta	bailar
pasar tiempo con amigos	trabajar
practicar deportes	escuchar música
usar la computadora	

Modelo
Step One

Yo *Nosotros(as)* *Amigo(a)*

Modelo
Step Two

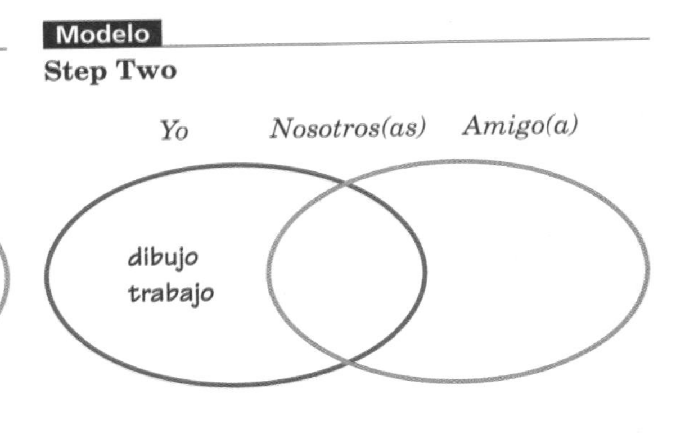

Universal Access

Heritage Language Learners

Often, students will use vocabulary and expressions that are not in the book, but are in their daily speech. Encourage them to limit this when working with a partner who is not a native Spanish speaker. Explain that it is important that other students practice the vocabulary being presented.

Students with Special Needs

For students with hearing difficulties, it is often a good idea to provide a clearly presented copy of the audio script so that they may be included in listening activities.

3 Interview your partner. Ask questions to find out the five activities your partner wrote in the diagram. When you find an activity that your partner does, write it in the oval labeled with his or her name. Be sure to use the appropriate verb form. Look at the model for Step Three below.

4 Compare the two sides of your diagram. Write the activities that you and your partner both do in the center. Be sure to use the appropriate verb form. Look at the model for Step Four below. Then, use the completed diagram to write at least five complete sentences telling what you and/or your partner usually do.

Modelo

A —*¿Dibujas mucho?*
B —*A ver... No, no dibujo mucho.*
A —*Pues, ¿trabajas mucho?*
B —*Sí, trabajo mucho.*

¿Recuerdas?

When you answer in the negative, you often use *no* twice. The first *no* answers the question. The second no goes before the verb and means "not."

Modelo
Step Three

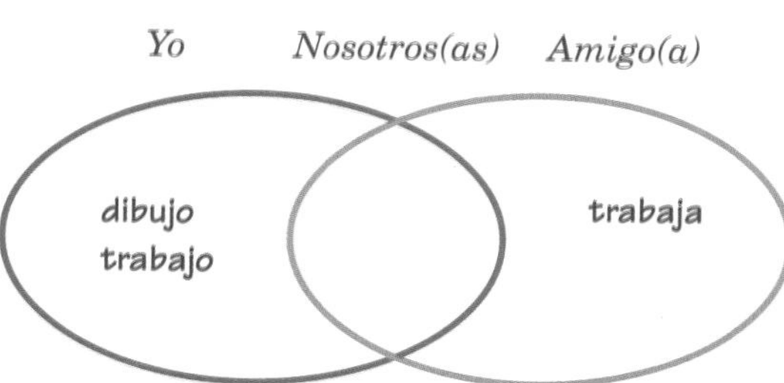

Modelo
Step Four

Yo — *Nosotros(as)* — *Amigo(a)*

dibujo, trabajo | trabajamos | trabaja

Suggestions: After providing a model for step 4, have students write as many sentences as they can in the ***nosotros*** section, according to the actions they both do. Then have them write one negative sentence about an action both of them do not do: *Nosotros no dibujamos.* Ask them to then state who does the action and who doesn't. For example: *Diego dibuja pero yo no dibujo.*

Answers will vary.

Common Errors: While focusing on completing the steps of the activity, students can easily forget to conjugate the verbs to agree with the subjects in each section of the diagram. Circulate among pairs and remind them to think about subject verb agreement.

Extension: After student pairs have written sentences in the ***nosotros / nosotras*** form, have one of them read a sentence aloud. Then have a third student repeat the information, stating in the ***ellos / ellas*** form the action those classmates both do.

Portfolio

You may wish to have students add their Venn diagrams to their portfolios. An alternative is a paragraph that summarizes what they have written in the diagram.

Enriching Your Teaching

Teacher-to-Teacher

Have students bring in action pictures of themselves, their family, or friends, or pictures from magazines. They should prepare 3–5 sentences about the actions shown, using more than one picture if needed. The next day, they can present these orally to a partner, or volunteers can present them to the class. You might want to model this for the class using sample photos; refer students to the word bank in *Actividad* 23 for ***-ar*** verbs.

Practice and Communicate

Standards: 1.3

Focus: Writing about weekend activities

Suggestions: Have students read the letter through before starting and identify the subject of each verb that must be added. Remind students that they must choose a verb to fill in the blank. You may wish to provide them with a word bank, or refer them to the one on p. 104 for ideas.

Answers will vary.

Common Errors: Some students may use the plural verb form with ***familia.*** Point out that, although the word represents a group, it is a singular noun and requires a singular verb form.

Standards: 3.1

Focus: Reading about the Mayan civilization's development of mathematics

Suggestions: Have students read the text silently and then ask a volunteer to summarize the information. Make up two or three additional numbers to review with students before having them decipher the ones in the book.

Answers will vary but may include the Roman numeral system.

Extension: Write simple addition or subtraction problems on the board using the Mayan number system. Have students write their answers in both Mayan symbols and arabic numerals.

Additional Resources

- Heritage Learner Workbook: 2A-3, 2A-4, 2A-5

Escribir

Los fines de semana

You are writing a letter to your friend Pablo who lives in Chile. Use the words that you have already learned to tell him what you and the people you know do on weekends *(los fines de semana).* Be sure to add words like *a veces* and *mucho.*

29 de Septiembre

Hola Pablo:

¿Cómo estás? Aquí los fines de semana son muy divertidos y muy ocupados. El viernes yo __1.__ . El sábado mi amigo(a) y yo __2.__ . El domingo mis amigos __3.__ . El sábado el/la profesor(a) de español __4.__ . El viernes mi familia __5.__ . ¿Y tú? ¿Cómo pasas los fines de semana?

¡Escríbeme pronto!

Leer/Pensar

Los números maya

Long before the Spaniards set foot in the Americas, many different civilizations already existed here. One of these, the Maya, lived in southern Mexico and Central America, where their descendants still make their home. One of the accomplishments of the ancient Maya was the development of a system of mathematics.

Conexiones
Las matemáticas

The Maya used three symbols to write numbers: a dot •, a bar ——, and a drawing of a shell. The dot equals 1, the bar equals 5, and the shell equals 0. Mayan numbers were written from bottom to top, not from left to right. Look at the Mayan numbers below.

0 1 2 3 4

5 6 7 8 9

What would these Mayan numbers be in our numbering system?

1. 2. 3.

Now write these numbers in the Mayan system.

4. 13 5. 16 6. 19

Are you familiar with any other numbering systems that remind you of the Mayan system?

ciento seis
Tema 2 • La escuela

Universal Access

Advanced Learners

Have students use the Internet to do further research on the Mayan number system. They could also explore numbering systems used by other civilizations in the Americas.

Pronunciación

The letter *c*

In Spanish the pronunciation of the letter *c* depends on the letter that follows it.

When the letter *c* comes before *a, o, u,* or another consonant, it is pronounced like the *c* in *cat.* Listen to and say these words:

computadora	**ca**ntar	es**cu**ela
tampo**co**	**có**mo	to**ca**r
correr	practi**ca**r	**Ca**rlos

When the letter *c* comes before *e* or *i,* most Spanish speakers pronounce it like the *s* in *Sally*. Listen to and say these words:

ve**ce**s	so**ci**able	gra**ci**oso	gra**ci**as
ha**ce**r	on**ce**	do**ce**	tre**ce**

Try it out! Listen to this rhyme. Listen particularly for the sound of the letter *c*. Then repeat the rhyme.

Cero más cuatro,
o cuatro más cero,
siempre[1] son cuatro.
¿No es verdadero[2]?

[1]always [2]true

Say the rhyme again, first replacing *cuatro* with *doce,* then replacing *cuatro* with *trece.* Then say the rhyme quickly several times.

Escribir/Hablar

Y tú, ¿qué dices?

1. En tu escuela, ¿quién enseña la clase de arte? ¿Quién enseña la clase de educación física?
2. En tu escuela, ¿quién canta muy bien *(well)*? ¿Quién dibuja muy bien?
3. ¿Escuchan tus amigos(as) mucha música? ¿Bailan bien tú y tus amigos(as)?
4. ¿Qué estudias en la primera hora?
5. ¿Qué clase tienes en la tercera hora?

Una estudiante en la clase de matemáticas

Enriching Your Teaching

Culture Note

The Maya were an agricultural society that began around 3000 B.C. and peaked about A.D. 900. Their territory extended through the Yucatán to the north and through Honduras to the south. Their mathematical accomplishments included early use of the zero. They conducted extensive studies of astronomy and developed their own calendar.

Internet Search

Keywords:

Maya; Mayan mathematics

Pronunciación

Presentation

Standards: 4.1

Resources: Audio Program: CD Cap. 2A, Track 10

Suggestions: Model the pronunciation of the words for the students, then ask them to repeat the words individually. Depending on class size, you may wish to have each student say the word. For larger classes, ask four or five students at a time to repeat the word. For *Try it out!* read the rhyme first, then have student volunteers read it aloud. You may suggest that volunteers say the variations with ***doce*** and ***trece.***

Standards: 1.1, 1.3

Focus: Writing and speaking about school in personalized contexts

Recycle: School subjects; ***-ar*** verb meanings

Suggestions: Before they answer the questions, students should be aware of the change that needs to be made from the forms in the question to those in the answers. Suggest that students ask and answer the questions with a partner before reviewing their answers as a whole class.

Answers will vary.

Common Errors: Students often get confused about which subject to use when answering questions in Spanish. Write this chart on the board for students to copy into their notebooks as a reference, and remind them that this pattern is the same as in English:

Question		Answer
tú / Ud.	→	yo
Uds.	→	nosotros
él / ella	→	él / ella
ellos / ellas	→	ellos / ellas

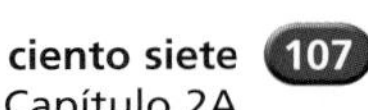

Theme Project

Students can perform step 2 at this point. Be sure they understand your corrections and suggestions. (For more information, see p. 84-a.)

Lectura

Presentation

 *Standards:* 1.2, 1.3

Focus: Reading about a Spanish-language school in Costa Rica

Suggestions:

Pre-reading: Have students look at the title and subtitle, and ask them to predict what the reading is about. Review the *Strategy* and point out that the photos will help them identify the context of the reading.

Reading: Pair students and have them take turns reading the text to one another. Encourage students to deduce the meaning of the passage from context and cognates. Have students share words they could not figure out and write them on the board. Ask volunteers to guess the meanings and explain how they deduced them.

Post-reading: Answer the *¿Comprendes?* questions in class or have students write their answers as homework.

Teaching with Photos

Before reading, have students guess some of the activities offered through the school, based on the climate and atmosphere depicted in the photos. Brainstorm a list of activities that would be done in such an environment, and then check the list as you review the reading.

Additional Resources

- Heritage Learner Workbook: 2A-6

¡Adelante!

Objectives

- Read a brochure about a school in Costa Rica
- Learn soccer fan chants
- Talk about some of your classes
- Learn facts about Mexico

Lectura

¡Estudiar español es divertido!

Consider what an immersion experience in Spanish would be like for you as you read this brochure from a Spanish language school in Costa Rica.

Strategy

Using photos
Look at the photos to help you understand the contents of a brochure or advertisement.

Costa Rica

La Escuela Español Vivo

¡Una experiencia fabulosa en Costa Rica!
¡Estudia español con nosotros en la Escuela Español Vivo!

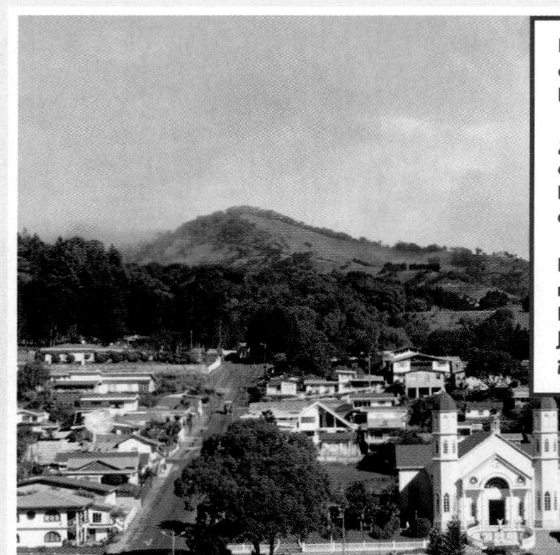

Es verano, el mes de junio. Eres estudiante en Santa Ana, un pueblo en las montañas de Costa Rica.

¿Y cómo es una clase? Hay cinco estudiantes en tu clase. Uds. escuchan, hablan y practican el español todo el día. También usan la computadora.

En la escuela hay estudiantes de muchos países: Estados Unidos, Inglaterra, Francia, Brasil, Canadá, Japón, India, Sudáfrica y otros. ¡Todos estudian español!

Universal Access

Heritage Language Learners

If applicable, ask students to comment on immersion. If they came from another country, did they know English at all before coming to the United States? If not, or if their English skills were limited, ask them to list the advantages and disadvantages of being immersed in an English-speaking culture.

Multiple Intelligences

Logical / Mathematical: Have students rewrite their own schedules in Spanish, including after-school activities, using the 24-hour clock. Have them use a chart format.

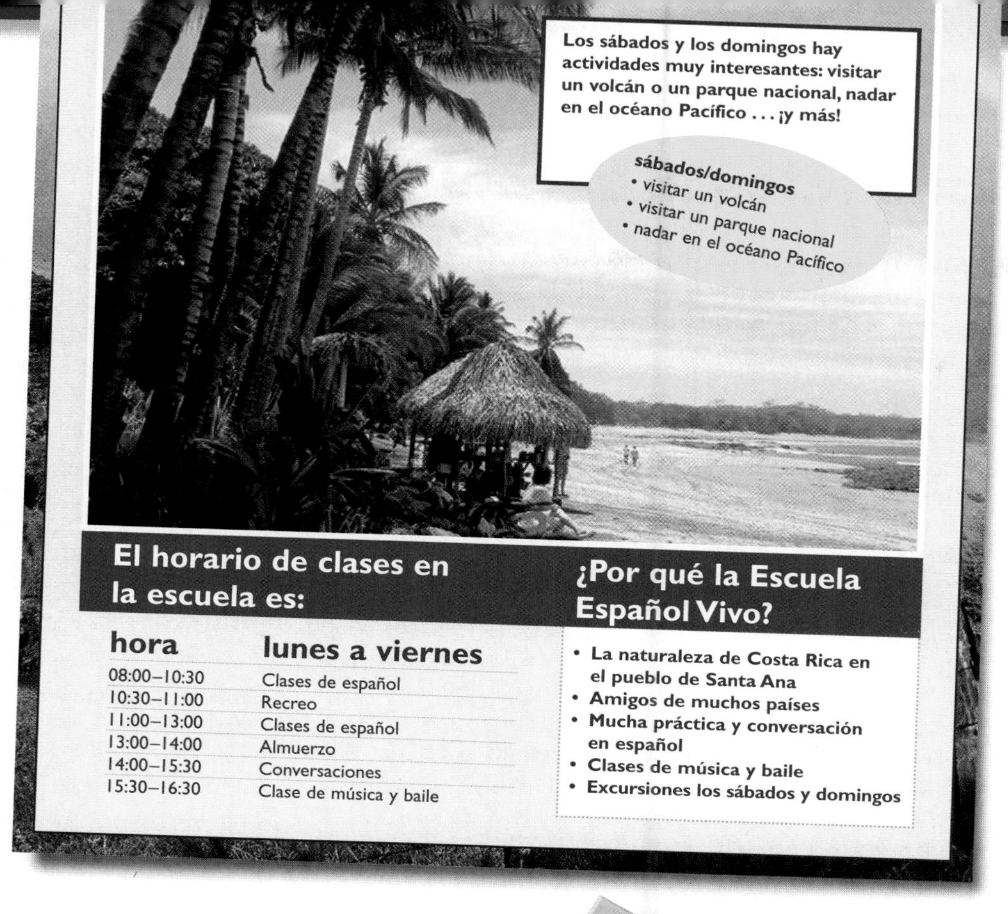

El horario de clases en la escuela es:

hora	lunes a viernes
08:00–10:30	Clases de español
10:30–11:00	Recreo
11:00–13:00	Clases de español
13:00–14:00	Almuerzo
14:00–15:30	Conversaciones
15:30–16:30	Clase de música y baile

¿Por qué la Escuela Español Vivo?

- La naturaleza de Costa Rica en el pueblo de Santa Ana
- Amigos de muchos países
- Mucha práctica y conversación en español
- Clases de música y baile
- Excursiones los sábados y domingos

¿Comprendes?

1. When does the program take place?
2. Describe what a class is like.
3. What activities are offered on the weekends?
4. How many hours are spent on learning and using Spanish each week?
5. Would you like to study Spanish in Costa Rica? Why or why not?

For: Internet link activity
Visit: www.phschool.com
Web Code: jad-0205

Fondo cultural

La hora in Spanish-speaking countries is usually shown using the 24-hour clock on official schedules and timetables. Times in the morning are shown as 00:00 (midnight) through 11:59 (11:59 A.M.), 1:00 P.M. is shown as 13:00, 2:00 P.M. is 14:00, and so on.

- Look at the times in the *horario* from the brochure. What times are the conversation class and the music and dance classes?

En una estación de trenes de Madrid

Standards: 4.2

¿Comprendes?

Resources: Practice Answers on Transparencies

Focus: Writing answers to questions using the information in the reading

Suggestions: Have students read the question, and then reread the *Lectura* before answering.

Answers:

1. In the summer, in June.
2. There are five students in a class. They listen, speak, and practice Spanish all day, and also use the computer.
3. You can visit a volcano or a park, or you can swim in the ocean.
4. Six hours a day.
5. Answers will vary.

Standards: 4.2

Suggestions: Read the text to the class and give students some extra examples of schedules in the 24-hour format. Point out that the 24-hour clock is used in the United States Armed Forces, and therefore is often referred to as military time. Ask students what the benefits are of using this system.

Answers:

The conversation class is from 2:00 P.M.–3:30 P.M.
The dance and music class is from 3:30 P.M.–4:30 P.M.

Enriching Your Teaching

Culture Note

In Spanish-speaking countries, the 24-hour clock is also used for public events such as concerts, bullfights, sports events, radio and television schedules, and for invitations to private events like graduations and weddings. It may also be used in ordinary conversation to specify that an event people are talking about is occurring in the evening.

Teacher-to-Teacher

Have students choose a destination in the United States and create a brochure for an English-language institute similar to *La escuela español vivo.* Suggest that they include a schedule of classes and other activities that students can participate in.

La cultura en vivo

Presentation

Standards: 1.3, 2.1, 2.2, 3.2, 4.2

Focus: Reading cheers for sports teams and creating one

Suggestions: Before reading, poll students to determine their favorite sports. List them on the board and have them arrive at a class favorite. After noting the favorite sport of the class, ask what they think the favorite sport is in the entire world.

Direct attention to the opening paragraph. After students have finished reading, find out if any correctly predicted the world's most popular sport. If your school has a soccer team, talk about it.

Many teams have cheerleaders who cheer the team on enthusiastically, boost spirits, and help create a winning attitude. Have students think about cheers they know and their meaning, if any. Point out those in the book. Read one aloud with enthusiasm. Emphasize the rhythm. Have students repeat after you. Move on to the second and do the same. Direct students to the *Try it out!* Allow them to work on their cheers and present them another day.

Some students will have no interest in soccer (or perhaps in any sport at all). You may find it helpful to allow them to focus on the rhyme scheme of the cheers. Perhaps grouping them with students who are enthusiastic will help. Also, when working in a group, these students may prefer to record the group's ideas.

Direct attention to the *Think about it!* section and have students discuss the questions.

Answers will vary.

Additional Resources

- Heritage Learner Workbook: 2A-7

La cultura en vivo

Aficionados al fútbol

El fútbol (soccer) is the favorite sport in most Spanish-speaking countries. In fact, it is the most popular sport in the entire world. It has grown in popularity in the United States over the past years. As with other sports you are familiar with, *fútbol* has loyal fans, cheers, team songs, and sometimes cheerleaders. If you attended a game in Venezuela at the Escuela Secundaria Bolívar you might hear the following chant:

Jugando al fútbol en la Ciudad Universitaria, Madrid, España

Chiquitibúm a la bim bom bam
A la bío
A la bao
A la bim bom bam
¡Bolívar! ¡Bolívar!
¡Ra, ra, ra!

Except for the school name, the words of this chant do not have any meaning.

Here's another cheer:

¡Se ve! ¡Se siente!	**You see it, you feel it!**
¡Bolívar está presente!	**Bolívar is here!**
¡Que sí, que no!	**Oh, yes, oh, no!**
¡Bolívar ya ganó!	**Bolívar has already won!**
¡A la bío, a la bao!	**¡A la bío! ¡A la bao!**
¡El otro está cansao!	**The other team is tired!**

Try it out! In groups of five, select one of the chants and use it for a model to create a chant for one of your school teams. Present it to the class.

Think about it! How are these cheers and fan enthusiasm similar to or different from the cheers at your school?

Aficionados al fútbol

Universal Access

Multiple Intelligences

Bodily / Kinesthetic: Encourage students to make up moves to accompany their cheers. Allow them to present their cheers to the class.

Heritage Language Learners

Some students may be familiar with cheers from their heritage country. Allow them time to ask family and friends about them and then to bring the information to share with the class.

Presentación oral

Mis clases

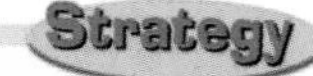

Task
Imagine that a student from Costa Rica has just arrived at your school. Tell the student about some of your classes.

1. **Prepare** Make a chart similar to the one below and fill in information for three of your classes. You will use this chart to think through what you may want to say about these classes.

Strategy

Using graphic organizers
Simple charts can help you organize your thoughts for a presentation.

Hora	Clase	Comentarios	Profesor(a)
primera	la clase de español	me gusta hablar español	la Sra. Salinas
cuarta	la clase de arte	difícil	el Sr. Highsmith
octava	la clase de ciencias naturales	divertida	la Srta. Huerta

2. **Practice** Go through your presentation several times. You can use your notes in practice, but your teacher may not want you to use them when you present. Try to:
   - mention the information on your classes and your teachers
   - use complete sentences
   - speak clearly

Modelo

En la primera hora tengo la clase de español. Me gusta hablar español. La Sra. Salinas es la profesora.

3. **Present** Describe the three classes you selected.

4. **Evaluation** Your teacher may give you a rubric for how the presentation will be graded. You probably will be graded on:
   - how complete your preparation is
   - how much information you communicate
   - how easy it is to understand you

Presentación oral

Presentation

Standards: 1.3

Resources: Voc. & Gram. Transparencies: 56

Focus: Speaking about classes

Suggestions: Review the task and the four steps with the students. You might want to model a top-scoring presentation. Then, to get students started, have them brainstorm vocabulary they can use to describe classes. Have students practice their presentation with a partner, focusing on fluency and pronunciation.

Portfolio

Record students' oral presentations on cassette or videotape for inclusion in their portfolios.

Additional Resources

- Heritage Learner Workbook: 2A-8

Assessment

- Cap. 2A, Rubrics

Give students copies of the rubric before they begin the activity. Go over the descriptions of the different levels of performance. After assessing students, help individuals understand how their performance could be improved.

Enriching Your Teaching

RUBRIC	Score 1	Score 3	Score 5
How complete your preparation is	Your information is written down but without use of chart.	Your chart is used but only partially completed.	Your chart is used and all information provided.
Amount of information you give	You describe three classes but only provide one piece of information about each class.	You describe three classes but only provide two pieces of information about each class.	You describe five classes and include all requested information.
How easily you are understood	You are very difficult to understand, using only isolated words and phrases.	You are understandable but have frequent errors in vocabulary and / or grammar.	You are easily understood. Your teacher does not have to "decode" what you are trying to say.

2A Culture

El mundo hispano

Presentation

Standards: 2.1, 2.2, 3.2, 4.2
Resources: Voc. & Gram. Transparencies: 12 (map)

Focus: Reading about Mexico's heritage

Presentation: After students read the text, show a map of Mexico. Have them note that Mexico borders the Gulf of Mexico on the east and the Pacific Ocean on the west. Locate Mexico City and the Yucatan peninsula. Have students identify Mexico's three neighbors. Point out that Belize—once known as British Honduras—is an English-speaking country.

Focus on the first paragraph. Have students hypothesize about the ways in which the United States and Mexico have influenced each other.

Direct attention to the large background photo. Have students identify it. Point out its approximate location on the map. Ask students what advantage there would be in having a port built on a cliff. When discussing the Mayan civilization, highlight its years of existence and its achievements. Have students do the math to get a clearer understanding of how long the civilization flourished. Imagine the conditions and lifestyle during those years. On a map, indicate the expanse of the Mayan civilization. Remind students that the present borders between countries did not exist at that time. Point out that there are approximately thirty languages that evolved from ancient Mayan.

Direct attention to the photo of Mexico City and to its location on a map. Have students discuss the advantages and disadvantages of its location. Point out that, like the port in the background photo, it was built by indigenous people (the Aztecs) before the arrival of the Spaniards. When the Spaniards arrived in 1519, the city was already larger than most European cities. Today it is the largest city in the world.

Focus on the picture of the Ballet Folklórico. Ask students to compare this troupe to what they know about ballet companies in the United States. If necessary, point out the traditional clothing, emphasizing the wide, colorful skirts and the white embroidered blouses.

El mundo hispano

México

With a population of more than 100 million people, Mexico is the most populous Spanish-speaking country. It has been shaped by ancient indigenous civilizations, European colonialism, and immigration, as well as by its proximity to the United States.

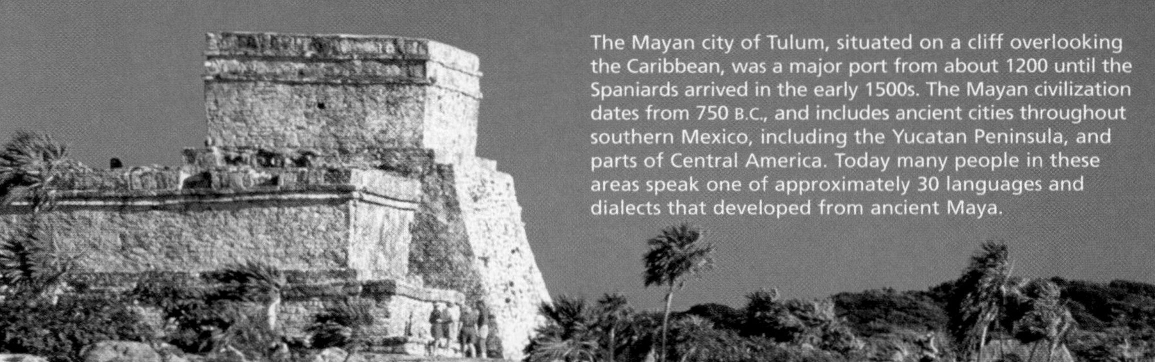

The Mayan city of Tulum, situated on a cliff overlooking the Caribbean, was a major port from about 1200 until the Spaniards arrived in the early 1500s. The Mayan civilization dates from 750 B.C., and includes ancient cities throughout southern Mexico, including the Yucatan Peninsula, and parts of Central America. Today many people in these areas speak one of approximately 30 languages and dialects that developed from ancient Maya.

¿Sabes que . . . ?

The butterfly reserve at El Rosario, Michoacán, lies in the mountains not far from Mexico City. From November through February every year, millions of monarch butterflies migrate to this area from the north, covering the branches of the area's tall pine trees.

Para pensar

These two pages show a brief overview of Mexico. If you were asked to create a similar overview of the United States, what would you highlight? Select five photographs and write a brief caption for each one. Share your results with a small group or the whole class.

Go Online PHSchool.com
For: Online Atlas
Visit: www.phschool.com
Web Code: jae-0002

Universal Access

Advanced Learners

Have students research and compare the Mayan and Aztec civilizations. Help them focus on when they existed, what they were like at their heights, and some achievements and accomplishments of each.

Heritage Language Learners

Students whose heritage country is Mexico may enjoy researching the hometown of their ancestors. Perhaps they can find answers to such questions as: Who were the indigenous peoples of the area? What, if any, traces of those peoples still exist today?

Mexico's most famous dance company, el Ballet Folklórico de México, is a world-class troupe of more than 75 dancers and musicians. For more than five decades, this company has been touring the globe and performing traditional Mexican dances, such as the *jarabe tapatío*, (better known in the United States as the Mexican hat dance), *la culebra*, and the *chilingo lingo*.

Mexico's capital is one of the largest cities in the world. It is also one of the oldest, dating back to 1500 B.C. It was here that the Aztecs built their capital, Tenochtitlán, in the 1300s. When the Spaniards arrived in 1519, Tenochtitlán had a population of more than 100,000—making it larger than most European cities of that time.

Many families in Mexico spend Sundays together. A popular spot for families in Mexico City is Xochimilco, where they can relax on colorful boats while enjoying a meal and music. The canals of Xochimilco are remnants of *chinampas*, the "floating gardens" that helped feed Tenochtitlán and other ancient cities in the valley of Mexico.

Focus on the boat in the middle picture. Note that many families spend Sundays relaxing together, a time that is very important to them. The photo reflects a modern-day use of a canal system built centuries ago.

Direct students to the *¿Sabes qué ...?* section. Ask who has seen a monarch butterfly. Elicit from students the importance of protecting the butterflies' habitat.

Suggestions: Some students may have difficulty computing the duration of the Mayan civilization. You may want to have a volunteer do the math on the board.

When discussing the time period, help students realize that there were no modern tools or machines. All work was done by manual labor and with beasts of burden, and many people were needed to build the great cities.

Have students make a timeline showing when each civilization was prominent in Mexico.

Direct attention to the *Para pensar* section and have students work in groups to discuss the question. Allow each group to present their ideas to the class.

Answers will vary.

Go Online

The Online Atlas will provide a more detailed map of Mexico and the neighboring areas.

Theme Project

Students can perform step 3 at this point. (For more information, see p. 84-a.)

Enriching Your Teaching

Culture Note

In the summer, the monarch butterfly lives in Canada and the United States. In fall, however, all the monarchs fly to their winter home; a mountain in Angangueo, Mexico. Here so many butterflies gather that they weigh down the tree branches. When the sun hits them and they take flight, you can hear their wings flap. What is perhaps most amazing is the fact that the monarchs who migrate have never made the journey before. Each trip is made by a new generation that somehow knows how to find the way.

2A Review

Review Activities

To talk about your school day: Have students bring in books from other classes. Randomly select a few and call on volunteers to tell what class each is from. For example, using the Spanish book, ask *¿Es para la clase de ciencias naturales? (No. Es para la clase de español.)*

To talk about the order of things and things you need for school: Have students make a list of their classes for that day, numbering them in order. Have Student A point to a specific class in Student B's list, and have Student B say what time the class is and then to describe it. For example, *En la tercera hora tengo la clase de matemáticas. Es divertida.* Be sure to have students include items they need from the list in *To talk about things you need for school.*

To describe your classes and Other useful words: Using the list created above, have students work in pairs to compare classes. For example, *La clase de tecnología es más difícil que la clase de inglés.* Be sure they use a variety of descriptions and comparisons.

Portfolio

Invite students to review the activities they completed in this chapter, including written reports, posters or other visuals, tapes of oral presentations, or other projects. Have them select one or two items that they feel best demonstrate their achievements in Spanish. Include these products in students' portfolios. Have them include this with the Chapter Checklist and Self-Assessment Worksheet.

Additional Resources

- Audio Program: CD Cap. 2A, Track 14
- Resource Book: Cap. 2A, Clip Art
- Resource Book: Cap. 2A, Situation Cards
- Assessment Program: Cap. 5A, Chapter Checklist and Self-Assessment Worksheet

Chapter Review

Repaso del capítulo

Vocabulario y gramática

To prepare for the test, check to see if you...

- know the new vocabulary and grammar
- can perform the tasks on p. 115

to talk about your school day

el almuerzo	lunch
la clase	class
la clase de...	...class
arte	art
español	Spanish
ciencias naturales	science
ciencias sociales	social studies
educación física	physical education
inglés	English
matemáticas	mathematics
tecnología	technology / computers
el horario	schedule
en la...hora	in the...hour (class period)
la tarea	homework

to describe school activities

enseñar	to teach
estudiar	to study
hablar	to talk

to talk about the order of things

***primero, -a**	first
segundo, -a	second
***tercero, -a**	third
cuarto, -a	fourth
quinto, -a	fifth
sexto, -a	sixth
séptimo, -a	seventh
octavo, -a	eighth
noveno, -a	ninth
décimo, -a	tenth

*Changes to *primer, tercer* before a masculine singular noun.

to talk about things you need for school

la calculadora	calculator
la carpeta de argollas	three-ring binder
el diccionario	dictionary
necesitas	you need
necesito	I need

For *Vocabulario adicional,* see pp. 268–269.

to describe your classes

aburrido, -a	boring
difícil	difficult
divertido, -a	amusing, fun
fácil	easy
favorito, -a	favorite
interesante	interesting
más... que	more...than
práctico, -a	practical

other useful words

a ver...	let's see...
mucho	a lot
para	for
¿Quién?	Who?
(yo) tengo	I have
(tu) tienes	you have

subject pronouns

yo	I	**nosotros** **nosotras**	we we
tú	you *(fam.)*	**vosotros** **vosotras**	you you
usted (Ud.)	you *(form.)*	**ustedes (Uds.)**	you *(form.)*
él **ella**	he she	**ellos** **ellas**	they they

hablar *to talk*

hablo	**hablamos**
hablas	**habláis**
habla	**hablan**

Más práctica

Practice Workbook Puzzle 2A-8
Practice Workbook Organizer 2A-9

Universal Access

Heritage Language Learners

Since much of the vocabulary and grammar will already be familiar to students, you may want to encourage them to focus on spelling and accuracy.

Multiple Intelligences

Interpersonal / Social: If students have mastered most of the vocabulary and grammar points in this chapter, suggest that they act as "leader" in study groups, assisting other students and reinforcing their own knowledge.

For: Test preparation
Visit: www.phschool.com
Web Code: jad-0206

Preparación para el examen

On the exam you will be asked to . . .	Here are practice tasks similar to those you will find on the exam . . .	If you need review . . .
1 Escuchar Listen and understand as people talk about their new schedules and what they think of their classes	Listen to two students who have just attended some of the classes on their new schedules. a) Which class does each one like? Why? b) Which class does each one dislike? Why?	**pp. 86–91** *A primera vista* **p. 87** Actividades 1–2 **p. 93** Actividad 7 **p. 96** Actividades 10–11
 **2 Hablar** Talk about activities you and your friends have in common	To get to know you, your homeroom advisor asks you to talk or write about what you and your friends have in common, such as school subjects that you all study, and music or activities that you all like. For example, *cantamos.* You might also tell how you and your friends are different. For example, *Yo toco la guitarra y ellos practican deportes.*	**p. 96** Actividad 11 **p. 103** Actividad 21 **pp. 104–105** Actividad 23 **p. 111** *Presentación oral*
 **3 Leer** Read and understand someone's e-mail description of his classes	Read this e-mail that your friend received from his e-pal. What does the e-pal study in school? What does he think of his classes? Do you agree or disagree? Why? ¿Cómo son mis clases? A ver . . . Yo tengo ocho clases. Estudio ciencias naturales, inglés, español, educación física, geografía, matemáticas, tecnología y ciencias sociales. ¡Me gusta más la clase de inglés! Necesito hablar inglés aquí en Ecuador, pero es MUY difícil. Mi clase de geografía es muy aburrida y mi clase de educación física es muy divertida. Y, ¿cómo son tus clases? 	**pp. 86–91** *A primera vista* **p. 92** Actividad 5 **p. 108–109** *Lectura*
 **4 Escribir** Write your schedule including hour, class, and teacher's name, and give opinions about the classes	Write a note to a counselor listing reasons why you want to drop two of the classes on your schedule. What might be some reasons for wanting to change classes? You might say that your first hour class is boring and that your second hour class is difficult for you.	**p. 94** Actividad 8 **p. 95** Actividad 9 **p. 96** Actividad 10 **p. 111** *Presentación oral*
 **5 Pensar** Demonstrate an understanding of cultural practices concerning sports	Think about the sports at your school that attract the most fans. Are these the same sports that are most popular in Spanish-speaking countries? How do spectators show their enthusiasm?	**p. 110** *La cultura en vivo*

Enriching Your Teaching

Teacher-to-Teacher

Assign another students' name to each person. then have students generate humorous schedules for one another. They might have the same class multiple times, or several lunch periods, or the wrong teachers, or bizarre starting and ending times. Hand the schedules to the individuals for whicih they were written, and then have students describe to the class what their new schedules are like. Encourage exaggerated responses and use of descriptive adjectives to show their reactions.

 *Standards:* 1.2, 1.3, 2.1, 4.2

Performance Tasks

Resources: Audio Program: CD Cap. 2A, Track 15; Resource Book: Cap. 2A, Audio Script; Practice Answers on Transparencies

1. Escuchar

Suggestions: Use the *Audio CD* or read the script.

Script:

Boy: Me gusta mucho la clase de arte. Me gusta dibujar. Es una clase fantástica. Pero la clase de matemáticas ... ¡Uf! Es mucho más difícil que mi clase de arte. A veces hay mucha tarea.

Girl: ¡La clase de matemáticas no es difícil! La tarea es muy fácil. Me gusta mucho el profesor. Él es muy divertido. Pero no me gusta la clase de educación física. No soy atlética.

Answers:

Boy: a) Art class, because he likes to draw. b) Math, because it's difficult and has lots of homework.

Girl: a) Math, because the homework is easy and she likes the teacher. b) Physical education, because she's not athletic.

2. Hablar

Suggestions: Brainstorm vocabulary needed to describe and compare classes with students. Write the list on the board.

Answers will vary.

3. Leer

Suggestions: Remind students that almost all the vocabulary can be found on p. 114.

Answers:

He studies science, English, Spanish, physical education, geography, math, technology, and social studies. He likes English and thinks that geography is boring. Answers will vary.

4. Escribir

Suggestions: Brainstorm with students about words to use for this activity.

Answers will vary.

5. Pensar

Suggestions: Remind students that they may use a Venn diagram to organize their information before writing.

Answers will vary.

Assessment

- Examen del capítulo: 2A
- Audio Program: CD 20, Track 5

Alternative Assessment

- ExamView Test bank CD-ROM
- Resource Book: Cap. 5A, Situation Cards
- Resource Book: Cap. 5A, Communicative Activities

Capítulo 2B

Overview

Chapter Overview

A primera vista INPUT	Manos a la obra PRACTICE	¡Adelante! APPLICATION	Repaso del capítulo REVIEW
Objectives Read, listen to, and explain information about: • the classroom • where objects are located	**Objectives** • Communicate about a classroom • Ask and tell how someone feels • Talk about where someone or something is located • Use the verb ***estar,*** the plurals of nouns, and the plurals of articles	**Objectives** • Read about an important program of the United Nations • Talk about cultural differences in schools • Write a note describing your classroom • Discuss facts about Central America	**Objectives** • Prepare for the chapter test
Vocabulary • Classroom items, furniture, and parts • Prepositions of location	**Vocabulary** • Practice and learn new vocabulary	**Vocabulary** • Application	**Vocabulary** • Review
Grammar Lexical use of: • the verb ***estar*** • plural nouns and articles	**Grammar** • The verb ***estar*** • The plurals of nouns and articles	**Grammar** • Application	**Grammar** • Review
Culture • Sor Juana Inés de la Cruz	**Culture** • School uniforms • Currency exchange rates • P.E. class in Spanish-speaking countries	**Culture** • Cultural perspectives on school • Facts about Central America	**Culture** • Demonstrate an understanding of cultural perspectives on school

Learner Support

Strategies

- Predicting the outcome
- Predicting outcomes
- Creating visuals

Recycling

- Using the verb ***estar*** to ask how someone is
- Singular definite and indefinite articles

Pronunciación

- The letter ***g***

Exploración del lenguaje

- Language through gestures

Conexiones

- Math: Currencies of the Spanish-speaking world

Beyond the Classroom

Countries

- Spain
- Mexico
- Guatemala
- Nicaragua
- Costa Rica
- Panama
- Puerto Rico
- Belize
- Peru
- Chile

El español en el mundo del trabajo

- School district employees that speak Spanish

Internet

- Vocabulary activities
- Grammar activities
- Internet links
- Self-tests

Print Components

TEACHER

Teacher's Resource Book
- Chapter Resource Checklist
- Input Script
- Video Script
- Audio Script
- Answer Keys
- *GramActiva* Blackline Master
- Communicative Activities Blackline Masters
- Situation Cards Blackline Masters
- School-to-Home Connection Letter
- Vocabulary Clip Art

TPR Storytelling Book
- Cap. 2B

STUDENT

Practice Workbook
- Vocabulary: 2B-1 – 2B-4
- Grammar: 2B-5 – 2B-7
- Puzzle: 2B-8
- Organizer: 2B-9

Writing, Audio & Video Workbook
- Writing: 2B-1 – 2B-4
- Audio: 2B-5 – 2B-10
- Video: 2B-11

Realidades para hispanohablantes
- Cap. 2B

Transparencies

Vocabulary & Grammar Transparencies
- Chapter Opener: 12–20 (maps)
- *A primera vista:* 57–58
- *Videohistoria:* 12 (map), 59–60
- Grammar: 61–63
- Presentation: 64
- *Cultura:* 13 (map)

Practice Answers on Transparencies
- Cap. 2B

Fine Art Transparencies
- Transparencies
- Teacher's Guide

Assessment

Assessment Program
- *Pruebas:*
  - Vocabulary recognition: 2B-1
  - Vocabulary production: 2B-2
  - The verb ***estar:*** 2B-3
  - The plurals of nouns and articles: 2B-4
- *Examen del capítulo:* 2B

ExamView Test Bank CD-ROM

Test Preparation Workbook
- Cap. 2B Reading #1
- Cap. 2B Reading #2

Alternative Assessment
- Performance-Based Speaking
- Assessment Program: Rubrics
- Internet Self-Test
- Situation Cards Blackline Masters
- TPR Storytelling Book: Speaking Task

Technology

iText

Mind Point Quiz Show CD-ROM

Resource Pro CD-ROM
- Lesson Planner
- Teacher Resources
- Clip Art

Video Program VHS and DVD
- *A primera vista* video: *Un ratón en la clase*
- *GramActiva* Videos:
  - the verb ***estar***
  - the plurals of nouns and articles

Audio Program CDs
- *A primera vista*
- *Escucha y escribe* activities
- Audio Activities
- *Pronunciación*
- *Repaso*
- Chapter Listening Test
- Songs

Capítulo 2B

Lesson Plans

Regular Schedule (50 minutes)

For electronic lesson plans: Resource Pro CD-ROM

	Warm-up / Assess	Preview / Present / Practice / Communicate	Wrap-up / Homework Options
DAY 1	**Return Examen del capítulo (10 min.)**	**A primera vista (35 min.)** • Objectives • Presentation: *Vocabulario y gramática en contexto* • *Actividades* 1, 2 • *Fondo cultural*	**Wrap-up and Homework Options (5 min.)** • Practice Workbook 2B-1, 2B-2 • Go Online • Heritage Language Learner Workbook • Vocabulary Clip Art
DAY 2	**Warm-up (5 min.)** • Homework check	**A primera vista (40 min.)** • Review: *Vocabulario y gramática en contexto* • Presentation: *Videohistoria Un ratón en la clase* • View: Video *Un ratón en la clase* • Video Activities • *Actividades* 3, 4	**Wrap-up and Homework Options (5 min.)** • *Prueba* 2B-1: Vocabulary recognition • Practice Workbook 2B-3, 2B-4 • Go Online
DAY 3	**Warm-up (5 min.)** • Homework check **✔Assessment (10 min.)** • *Prueba* 2B-1: Voc. recognition	**Manos a la obra (30 min.)** • Objectives • *Actividades* 5, 6	**Wrap-up and Homework Options (5 min.)** • *Actividad* 7
DAY 4	**Warm-up (5 min.)** • Homework check • Return *Prueba* 2B-1: Voc. recognition	**Manos a la obra (40 min.)** • *Exploración del lenguaje* • *Actividad* 8 • *Fondo cultural* • *Juego: Actividad* 9	**Wrap-up and Homework Options (5 min.)** • *Actividad* 10
DAY 5	**Warm-up (5 min.)** • Homework check	**Manos a la obra (40 min.)** • Presentation: The verb ***estar*** • *GramActiva* Video • *Actividades* 11, 13	**Wrap-up and Homework Options (5 min.)** • *Actividad* 12 • Practice Workbook 2B-5
DAY 6	**Warm-up (5 min.)** • Homework check	**Manos a la obra (40 min.)** • Review: The verb ***estar*** • *Actividades* 14, 15, 16	**Wrap-up and Homework Options (5 min.)** • *Actividad* 20
DAY 7	**Warm-up (5 min.)** • Homework check	**Manos a la obra (40 min.)** • Review: The verb ***estar*** • *Actividad* 17 • *Juego: Actividad* 18 • *Conexiones: Actividad* 19	**Wrap-up and Homework Options (5 min.)** • *Prueba* 2B-3: The verb ***estar*** • Go Online
DAY 8	**Warm-up (5 min.)** • Homework check **✔Assessment (10 min.)** • *Prueba* 2B-3: The verb ***estar***	**Manos a la obra (30 min.)** • Presentation: The plurals of nouns and articles • *GramActiva* Video • *Actividades* 21, 22, 24	**Wrap-up and Homework Options (5 min.)** • Practice Workbook 2B-6, 2B-7 • *Actividad* 23 • *Prueba* 2B-2: Vocabulary production

Day	Warm-up / Assess	Preview / Present / Practice / Communicate	Wrap-up / Homework Options
DAY 9	**Warm-up** (5 min.) • Homework check • Return *Prueba* 2B-3: The verb ***estar*** ✔**Assessment** (10 min.) • *Prueba* 2B-2: Voc. production	**Manos a la obra** (30 min.) • Review: The plurals of nouns and articles • *Actividades* 25, 26, 27, 29	**Wrap-up and Homework Options** (5 min.) • *Actividad* 28 • *Prueba* 2B-4: The plurals of nouns and articles
DAY 10	**Warm-up** (5 min.) • Homework check • Return *Prueba* 2B-2: Voc. production ✔**Assessment** (10 min.) • *Prueba* 2B-4: The plurals of nouns and articles	**Manos a la obra** (30 min.) • *Actividad* 30 • *El español en el mundo del trabajo* • *Pronunciación*	**Wrap-up and Homework Options** (5 min.) • Go Online • Practice Workbook
DAY 11	**Warm-up** (5 min.) • Homework check • Return *Prueba* 2B-4: The plurals of nouns and articles	**¡Adelante!** (40 min.) • *Presentación escrita:* Prewrite • *Lectura* • *Fondo cultural*	**Wrap-up and Homework Options** (5 min.) • *¿Comprendes?* • Go Online
DAY 12	**Warm-up** (5 min.) • Homework check	**¡Adelante!** (40 min.) • *Presentación escrita:* Draft, revise • *Perspectivas del mundo hispano*	**Wrap-up and Homework Options** (5 min.) • Go Online • *Presentación escrita:* Publish
DAY 13	**Warm-up** (5 min.) • Homework check	**¡Adelante!** (40 min.) • *Presentación escrita:* Present	**Wrap-up and Homework Options** (5 min.) • Writing Activities • Practice Workbook 2B-8, 2B-9
DAY 14	**Warm-up** (5 min.) • Homework check	**¡Adelante!** (20 min.) • *El mundo hispano* **Repaso** (20 min.) • *Vocabulario y gramática* • *Preparación para el examen*	**Wrap-up and Homework Options** (5 min.) • Go Online: Self-test • *Examen del capítulo*
DAY 15	**Warm-up** (5 min.) • Answer questions ✔**Assessment** (45 min.) • *Examen del capítulo*		

2B Preview

Standards for *Capítulo* 2B

- To achieve the goals of the Standards, students will:

Communication

1.1 Interpersonal
- Talk about personal and classroom items and furniture
- Talk about offices and classrooms
- Talk about the the locations and spatial relationships of people and objects

1.2 Interpretive
- Read and listen to information about classroom items and furniture
- Listen to information about the use of location words
- Read a picture-based story
- Listen to and watch a video about a classroom prank
- Compare a photo to oral descriptions of a Spanish club
- Read a journalistic article about UNICEF
- Read a note about a students request for information

1.3 Presentational
- Present information about classroom items and furniture; retell portions of a story they have heard
- Present a dialogue requiring understanding of articles
- Write a paragraph about their classroom; write a letter to a pen pal; write an e-mail-style note to a friend about classes

Culture

2.1 Practices and Perspectives
- Learn about women's access to education in seventeenth century Mexico
- Learn about the widespread use of school uniforms
- Learn that school lockers are rare in Latin America
- Learn how phys-ed and team sports are conducted
- Learn that most students spend more time in school
- Understand Costa Rican efforts to protect endangered species
- Understand the communicative functions of the ***huipil***

2.2 Products and Perspectives
- Understand the structure educational systems
- Learn about the ***huipil***

Connections

3.1 Cross-curricular
- Learn about the seventeenth century Mexican intellectual, Sor Juana Inés de la Cruz
- Learn about currency of Spanish-speaking countries
- Read a journalistic article about UNICEF

Comparisons

4.1 Language
- Learn vocabulary through the recognition of cognates
- Learn the verbal and nonverbal expression, ***¡Ojo!***
- Learn about the irregular verb ***estar***
- Understand number agreement with nouns and articles
- Learn the pronunciation of the letter ***g***

4.2 Culture
- Compare the use of school uniforms and school lockers
- Compare influence of women writers on perspectives
- Compare the design of physical education class
- Compare commitments to and behavior in school
- Consider the hypothetical result of United States expansion south to Panama in the nineteenth century

Communities

5.1 Beyond the School
- Consider the need for Spanish-speakers in different types of jobs in the educational field

Fondo cultural

Sor Juana Inés de la Cruz (1648–1695), born near Mexico City, was one of the greatest intellectuals of her time. She wrote poetry, essays, music, and plays. Sor Juana also defended a woman's right to an education at a time when few women had access to it. She entered a convent at the age of 19 and over the years built a library of several thousand books. Sor Juana's living quarters in the convent became a meeting place for other writers and intellectuals, who were drawn to her because of her intelligence and knowledge.

- How are various aspects of Sor Juana's life represented in this painting? If you were to pose for a portrait, what objects would represent you and your interests?

Sor Juana Inés de la Cruz, arte mexicano del siglo XVII
Institut Amatller d'Art Hispanic-Arxiu Mas

Universal Access

Personalizing the Theme

Have students write three sentences in English to describe the location of objects or people in the classroom. Point out that we often need to tell where things are so that people can locate them or so that they know what we are referring to. Have volunteers read their sentences. Write a few of them on the board and identify the prepositional phrases.

Tu sala de clases

Chapter Objectives

- Describe a classroom
- Indicate where things are located
- Talk about more than one object or person
- Understand cultural perspectives on school

Video Highlights

A primera vista: ***Un ratón en la clase***
GramActiva Videos: **the verb *estar;* the plurals of nouns and articles**

Country Connection

As you learn how to describe your classroom, you will make connections to these countries and places:

For: Online Atlas
Visit: www.phschool.com
Web Code: jae-0002

Estudiantes en una sala de clases en Cuzco, Perú

Preview 2B

Chapter Opener

Presentation

Resources: Voc. & Gram. Transparencies: 12–18, 20 (maps)

Suggestions: Review the objectives. Explain to students that they will be learning to talk about classroom objects and locations. The video story is about what happens when a hamster escapes in a classroom. The *GramActiva* Video will help students learn the present tense of ***estar*** and the plurals of nouns and articles. Show the transparencies to help students locate the places featured in the chapter.

 *Standards:* 2.1, 2.2, 4.2

Resources: Fine Art Transparencies; Fine Art Transparencies Teacher's Guide

Suggestions: Point out the dates of Sor Juana's birth and death and ask students what they know about the culture of that era (science, arts, and historical events). What opportunities did women have in the seventeenth century to be independent professionals, artists, and scientists?

Answers will vary.

Enriching Your Teaching

Planning for Instruction

Resources:

- Teacher Express CD-ROM or Resource Book
  - Teaching resources
  - Lesson Planner
  - Chapter Resource Checklist
  - School-to-Home Connection Letter

Culture Note

Direct attention to the photo and point to the insignia that the students have on their sweaters and vests. In addition to uniforms, some schools require their students to wear the official school seal. Others may require school-specific uniform colors as well.

Vocabulario y gramática

Presentation

 *Standards:* 1.2

Resources: Voc. & Gram. Transparencies: 57–58; Resource Book: 2B, Input Script; Resource Book: Cap. 2B, Clip Art; TPR Storytelling Book: Cap. 2B; Audio Program: CD Cap. 2B, Tracks 1–2

Focus: Presenting vocabulary for classroom items, furniture, and location; introducing use of ***estar,*** gender and number of nouns, plural articles

Suggestions: Use the Input Script from the *Teacher's Resource Book* or use the *TPR Storytelling Book* to introduce the new vocabulary. Show the transparencies. Have students look at the picture of the classroom in their books and touch the pictures as you describe the scene. Use the new vocabulary to name items in your classroom and have volunteers touch the objects you name.

If possible, use your classroom computer to identify the computer parts. Have students move around the room to touch objects or move objects in response to your directions.

Additional Resources

- Audio Program: Song CD

A primera vista

Vocabulario y gramática en contexto

Objectives

Read, listen to, and understand information about
- the classroom
- where objects are located

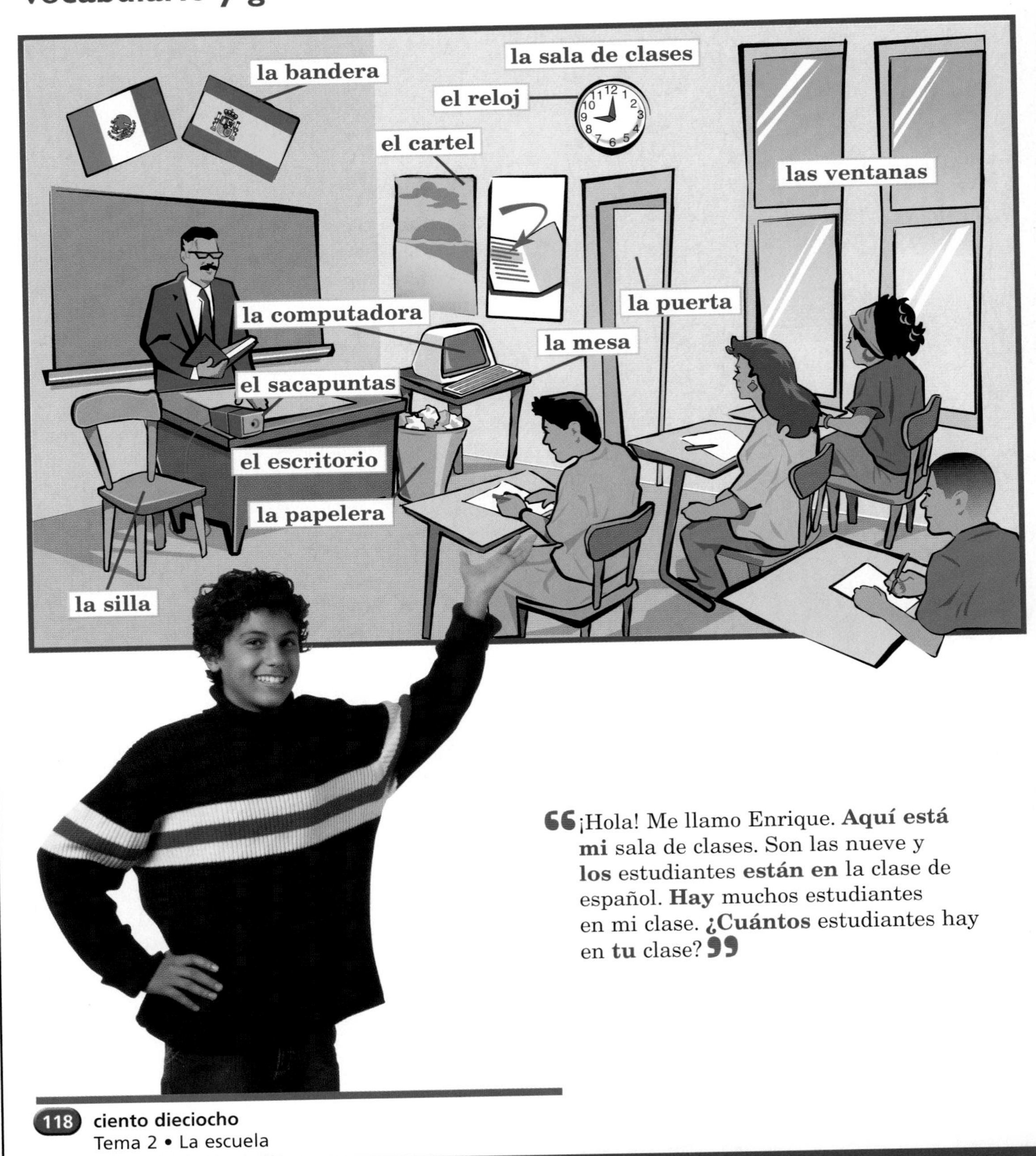

“¡Hola! Me llamo Enrique. **Aquí está mi** sala de clases. Son las nueve y **los** estudiantes **están en** la clase de español. **Hay** muchos estudiantes en mi clase. **¿Cuántos** estudiantes hay en **tu** clase?”

Universal Access

Heritage Language Learners

Have students make their own vocabulary lists of classroom objects, adding other words they know. If necessary, help them with spelling.

Multiple Intelligences

Logical / Mathematical: Have students count objects in their classroom for which they've learned the vocabulary. Have them write sentences: *Hay tres computadoras en la sala de clases. Hay treinta pupitres,* etc. The class can listen to the sentences and tell whether they are accurate.

El cuaderno está **debajo de** la calculadora.
La calculadora está **encima del** cuaderno.
Los bolígrafos están **al lado del** diccionario.
La bandera está **detrás de** la computadora.
La silla está **delante de** la mesa.

—Elena, ¿es tu disquete?
—No, es el disquete **de** David.

Escuchar

¿Qué hay en la sala de clases?

Look at Enrique's classroom. You will be asked if certain things are there. If you see the item mentioned, raise your hand and give a "thumbs-up" sign. If you don't see it, give a "thumbs-down" sign.

Escuchar

En la sala de clases

Look at the picture of Enrique's classroom again. Listen to a description of various items in the room. As soon as you recognize an item, touch it.

Más práctica

Practice Workbook 2B-1, 2B-2

For: Vocabulary practice
Visit: www.phschool.com
Web Code: jad-0211

Enriching Your Teaching

Teacher-to-Teacher

Have students make decorative labels for objects in the classroom. Call on a volunteer to place the label on an object as another student describes where it is located: *El sacapuntas está al lado del diccionario.* When all labels are placed on the objects, have students close their eyes while you switch the labels. Ask students to tell you what is wrong and how to correct it: *El sacapuntas está debajo la silla. Está al lado del diccionario.*

Standards: 1.2 (Actividad 1)

Resources: Audio Program: CD Cap. 2B, Track 3; Resource Book: Cap. 2B, Audio Script; Practice Answers on Transparencies

Focus: Listening to and recognizing vocabulary for classroom objects and locations

Suggestions: Explain to students that they will be listening for the name of the object, and that it might appear in either of the large pictures. Allow students to listen more than once.

Script and Answers:

1. **¿Hay una computadora en la sala de clases? *(up)***
2. **¿Hay un teclado? *(up)***
3. **¿Hay una tele? *(down)***
4. **¿Hay un sacapuntas? *(up)***
5. **¿Hay una mochila? *(down)***
6. **¿Hay una ventana? *(up)***
7. **¿Hay un cartel? *(up)***
8. **¿Hay una puerta? *(up)***
9. **¿Hay una guitarra? *(down)***
10. **¿Hay un reloj? *(up)***

Standards: 1.2 (Actividad 2)

Resources: Audio Program: CD Cap. 2B, Track 4; Resource Book: Cap. 2B, Audio Script; Practice Answers on Transparencies

Focus: Listening to and recognizing vocabulary for classroom objects and locations

Suggestions: Tell students that most of the objects referred to in this exercise are pictured on p. 119.

Script and Answers:

1. **La computadora está debajo del profesor.**
2. **La silla está al lado del escritorio del profesor.**
3. **La bandera está detrás de la computadora.**
4. **La papelera está al lado del escritorio del profesor.**
5. **El cartel está en la pared.**
6. **El reloj está al lado del sacapuntas.**

Videohistoria

Presentation

 *Standards:* 1.2, 4.1

Resources: Voc. & Gram. Transparencies: 59–60; Audio Program: CD Cap. 2B, Track 5

Focus: Presenting additional vocabulary about classroom objects and location.

Suggestions:

Pre-reading: Direct students' attention to the *Strategy.* Remind them that pictures can often help in predicting what will happen in a story. Have students close their books. Using the transparencies with the dialogues covered up, go panel by panel and ask students to predict the outcome of the story. Why did Manolo pull a prank? *(Manolo no tiene la tarea.)*

Answers:

Strategy: **A hamster is loose in the classroom.**

1. **Answers will vary but may include:** ***hámster, idea, impaciente, disquetes, silencio, oficina.***
2. **Answers will vary.**

Videohistoria

Un ratón en la clase

¿Qué pasa en la clase de ciencias sociales? Lee la historia.

Antes de leer

 **Predicting outcomes** Look at the pictures before you read to help you predict what will happen.

- What is causing the disturbance in Teresa's class?

1. Find at least five cognates in the *Videohistoria*. How do these cognates help you understand the story?
2. Look at the photos in the *Videohistoria* and try to predict if Manolo will get away with his prank.

Universal Access

Students with Learning Difficulties

To help students with vocabulary for location, bring in a toy mouse and place it in the classroom according to where the hamster is in the *Videohistoria*. Have a student read the appropriate panels aloud as you place the toy, or ask a volunteer to place it as you give the locations. You may want to use the toy mouse throughout the chapter to review prepositions of location.

1 **Claudia:** **¿Qué es esto?**
Teresa: Es mi hámster. Es para la clase de ciencias naturales.
Claudia: ¿Cómo se llama?
Teresa: Paquito.

2 **Manolo:** ¡Carlos! No tengo mi tarea.
Carlos: ¿Qué?
Manolo: Tengo una idea . . .

3 **Carlos:** ¡Un ratón! Profesora, ¡hay un ratón debajo del escritorio!
Profesora: ¿Un ratón en la clase de ciencias sociales? **¿Dónde** está? ¿Dónde?

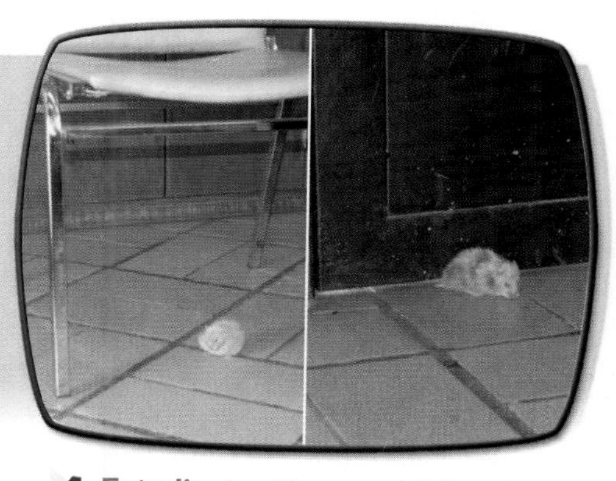

4 **Estudiante:** Ahora está debajo de la silla.
Manolo: Y ahora está al lado de la puerta. **Es un** ratón muy impaciente.
Teresa: ¡No es un ratón! Es mi hámster, y se llama Paquito.

Suggestions:

Reading: Using the transparencies and pantomime, help students understand the new words in blue type. Discuss how the word ***ratón*** has multiple meanings, both in English and Spanish. Be sure students understand that the animal in the story is actually a hamster, and that Manolo is exaggerating by calling it ***un ratón.***

Post-reading: Complete the activities on p. 123 to check comprehension.

Additional Resources

- Writing, Audio & Video Workbook: Cap. 2B, Video Activity 1

Enriching Your Teaching

Teacher-to-Teacher

Have students put their heads down on their desks while one student moves an object in the classroom. When the object is placed, everyone raises their heads, and the student who moved the object asks: *¿Dónde está (la papelera)?* The first student to spot it must accurately describe its location and then becomes "It."

Video

Presentation

Standards: 1.2, 4.1, 4.2

Resources: Video Program: Cap. 2B; Resource Book: Cap. 2B, Video Script

Focus: Listening to contextualized vocabulary

Suggestions:

Pre-viewing: Review prepositions of location with students. Ask them if they have ever been in a class that was disrupted by a spider, bee, or other insect. If so, what happened?

Viewing: Show the video without pausing. Then go back and show it again, stopping along the way to check comprehension. Ask students which parts of the video were easier to understand than others. Why? Which words did they recognize as being similar to English words?

Post-viewing: Complete the Video Activities in the *Writing, Audio & Video Workbook.*

Additional Resources

- Writing, Audio & Video Workbook: Cap. 2B, Video Activities 2–4
- Heritage Learner Workbook: 2B-1, 2B-2

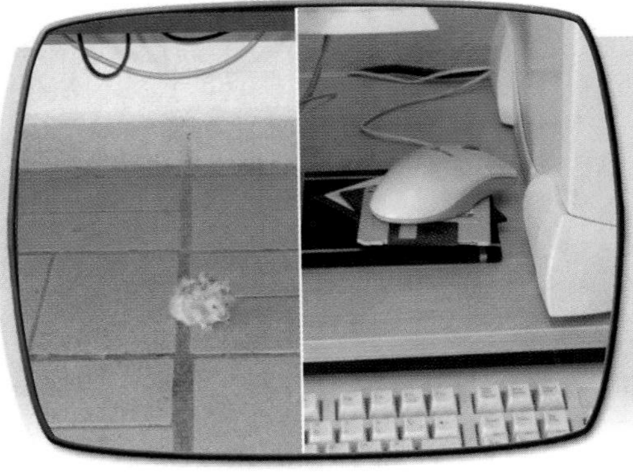

5 **Claudia:** ¡Está **allí**, delante de la mesa!

Teresa: ¡Ay, mi Paquito!

Manolo: Pues, ahora está detrás de la computadora, encima de los disquetes.

Teresa: ¡Manolo! Es el ratón de la computadora. No es mi Paquito.

6 *El director de la escuela, el Sr. Treviño, entra en la clase.*

Carlos: ¡Ay! ¡Aquí está! Está en mi **mochila.**

Sr. Treviño: ¡Silencio, por favor!

7 **Sr. Treviño:** Teresa, hablamos en mi oficina.

Teresa: Sí, señor.

8 **Profesora:** Y ahora, Manolo, ¿tu tarea?

Manolo: Pues, profesora . . .

Universal Access

Heritage Language Learners

Have students extend the story by writing Manolo's excuse to the *Profesora*. Check students' work and provide feedback as necessary.

Multiple Intelligences

Visual / Spatial: Have students draw classroom objects on note cards. On the back of each card, students should write the Spanish word. Have students work in pairs to arrange the note cards next to, underneath, in front of, or behind another card on their desktops. Students then take turns asking the locations of the objects.

Actividad 3 **Leer**

¿Comprendes?

Match each of the sentences with the *Videohistoria* character whom it describes.

el Sr. Treviño

Paquito

Claudia

Teresa

Manolo

1. No tiene la tarea.
2. Está debajo de la silla.
3. Tiene un hámster.
4. Es amiga de Teresa.
5. Es muy serio.

Actividad 4 **Leer/Escribir**

Un hámster en la escuela

It's not a typical day at Claudia's school. Find out what is going on by putting the sentences below in the correct order. Rewrite the story on a separate sheet of paper.

a. El Sr. Treviño entra en la clase.

b. El hámster está debajo de la silla.

c. El Sr. Treviño y Teresa hablan en la oficina.

d. La profesora quiere *(wants)* la tarea de Manolo.

e. Teresa habla con *(with)* Claudia del ratón para la clase de ciencias naturales.

f. El hámster está en la mochila de Carlos.

Más práctica

Practice Workbook 2B-3, 2B-4

For: Vocabulary practice
Visit: www.phschool.com
Web Code: jad-0212

Actividad 3 *Standards:* 1.2

Resources: Practice Answers on Transparencies

Focus: Reading to check comprehension of the *Videohistoria*

Suggestions: Have students read the five sentences that describe the characters and make a list of keywords that they will need to look for in the *Videohistoria.* Tell them to scan the reading to find the information.

Answers:
1. Manolo
2. Paquito
3. Teresa
4. Claudia
5. el Sr. Treviño

Actividad 4 *Standards:* 1.2, 1.3

Resources: Practice Answers on Transparencies

Focus: Reading and writing to check comprehension

Suggestions: Have students read all of the sentences before skimming the *Videohistoria.* On a sheet of paper have them list the corresponding letters in the correct order to use when rewriting the paragraph.

Answers:
1. e
2. b
3. a
4. f
5. c
6. d

Assessment
- Prueba 2B-1: Vocabulary recognition

Enriching Your Teaching

Culture Note

Although many schools in Central and South America use modern technology, there are schools that do not have access to computers or other forms of audiovisual technology. Discuss the advantages and disadvantages of using technology in the classroom.

Standards: 1.2

Resources: Practice Answers on Transparencies

Focus: Comprehending vocabulary words

Suggestions: Remind students that they need to decide if the sentence is logical or not. They should not base their responses on the photo.

Answers:

1. no
2. sí
3. no
4. sí
5. sí
6. no

Extension: Have students tell what items they have in their backpacks.

Standards: 1.3

Resources: Practice Answers on Transparencies

Focus: Writing to identify classroom objects

Suggestions: Remind students that ***hay*** means "there is" or "there are," and that no other verb is required.

Answers:

1. Hay un sacapuntas.
2. ... un reloj.
3. ... una silla.
4. ... una mochila.
5. ... un cartel.
6. ... una papelera.
7. ... ventanas.
8. ... una mesa.

Manos a la obra

Vocabulario y gramática en uso

Objectives

- Communicate about a classroom
- Ask and tell how someone feels
- Talk about where someone or something is located
- Learn to use the verb *estar* and the plurals of nouns and articles

Leer

¿Es lógico o no?

Juan Carlos is telling you about what he has in his backpack. Decide if what he is saying is logical or not. Number your paper from 1–6 and write *sí* if it is logical or *no* if it is not.

1. Un teclado está en mi mochila.
2. Hay un disquete en mi mochila.
3. Hay una mesa en mi mochila.
4. Un bolígrafo está en mi mochila.
5. Mi tarea está en mi mochila.
6. Hay una papelera en mi mochila.

Escribir

¿Qué hay?

Write the names of the things you see.

Modelo

Hay una bandera.

1. 

2.  

3. 

4. 

5. 

6. 

7. 

8. 

Universal Access

Students with Learning Difficulties
Make a list of the items mentioned in *Actividad* 5. Point to each item and ask students ***cierto / falso*** questions to help them with the vocabulary. For example, point to a table and say: *Es un teclado, ¿cierto o falso?*

Advanced Learners
Have students write a brief description of where things in their room are located. Encourage them to supplement their description with vocabulary from prior chapters.

Actividad 7 Leer/Escribir

¿Dónde está?

Write the numbers from 1–9 on a sheet of paper. Complete the sentences to tell where the following items are located in Beto's bedroom. Choose from the words below and add the correct definite article.

al lado de
debajo de
delante de
detrás de
encima de

Modelo

El escritorio está debajo de la ventana.
La computadora está encima del escritorio.

1. El reloj está ___ mesa.
2. La papelera está ___ escritorio.
3. La silla está ___ escritorio.
4. El teclado está ___ disquete.
5. La computadora está ___ mesa.
6. El ratón está ___ teclado.
7. El cartel está ___ ventana.
8. La mochila está ___ silla.

Nota

When the preposition *de* is followed by the masculine definite article *el*, the contraction *del* must be used.

- La papelera está al lado **del** escritorio.

Actividad 7  *Standards:* 1.2, 1.3

Resources: Practice Answers on Transparencies

Focus: Writing about locations of items in a bedroom

Suggestions: Direct students' attention to the *Nota* and provide additional examples. Allow students time to study the picture before beginning.

Answers:

1. encima de la
2. al lado del
3. delante del
4. debajo del
5. al lado de la
6. al lado del
7. al lado de la
8. detrás de la

Enriching Your Teaching

Culture Note

Since many Spanish-speaking countries have an evening class schedule (in addition to a day schedule), most evening school students will do their homework in the morning. Ask students to imagine doing their homework at 8:00 A.M., instead of later in the day. What advantages and disadvantages are there?

Teacher-to-Teacher

Have students work in pairs. Provide them with two very similar pictures of a classroom but with five or six differences. Without looking at each other's pictures, have students ask one another questions about the objects and their locations until they have identified all the differences.

Rapid Review

Point to items in your classroom that are listed in *Actividad* 8 and have students name them.

Standards: 1.3

Actividad 8

Focus: Practicing vocabulary for classroom items in a personalized context

Suggestions: Encourage students to add items to personalize their lists. Remind them to use the contraction ***del*** when necessary.

Answers will vary.

Standards: 1.1, 1.2

Resources: Resource Book: Cap. 2B, GramActiva BLM

Focus: Describing and listening for locations of objects

Recycle: Classroom items

Suggestions: Remind students that the vocabulary provided in the *Para decir más...* will be helpful to them in completing an activity, but that it is not tested. Demonstrate how to play the game. Walk around the room, prompting students if necessary and monitoring their accuracy.

Answers will vary.

Escribir

¿Estás preparado(a) para la clase?

You want to make sure that you are prepared for class. Copy the checklist below onto your own paper. Place a check mark next to the items that you have and tell where they are.

el libro	✔	encima del escritorio
un cuaderno		
un disquete		
la tarea		
un lápiz		
un bolígrafo		
un sacapuntas		
una mochila		
un diccionario		

Hablar/Escribir

Juego

1. Work with a partner. Your partner will face away from you and have a blank piece of paper and a pen or a pencil.
2. Choose four classroom items and arrange them on your desk, putting objects on top of others, next to each other, and so forth.
3. Your partner will ask you questions about what is on your desk and how the items are positioned. Based on your answers, he or she will try to draw the arrangement on your desk.
4. When your teacher calls time, see how closely the picture matches the actual arrangement. Then switch roles.

Modelo

A —*¿Tienes un disquete?*
B —*No, no tengo un disquete.*
A —*¿Tienes una calculadora?*
B —*Sí, tengo una calculadora.*
A —*¿Dónde está?*
B —*Está encima de la carpeta.*

Para decir más . . .

a la izquierda de to the left of
a la derecha de to the right of

Universal Access

Heritage Language Learners

Have students make a list of appropriate gestures used in Spanish-speaking communities. Then have them compare these with body language expressed by people in the United States.

Multiple Intelligences

Visual / Spatial: If possible, have students watch Spanish-language TV shows and identify gestures. As they watch, tell them to take notes describing each gesture. Ask them to interview a Spanish speaker to clarify the meaning of the gestures.

Exploración del lenguaje

Language through gestures

In Spanish, just as in English, nonverbal body language in the form of gestures, or *gestos,* is very important to communication.

You saw the expression *¡Ojo!* in the video *Un ratón en la clase*. The word literally means "eye," but it is used to mean "be careful" or "pay attention." It is usually accompanied by a gesture, and often people use the *¡Ojo!* gesture without saying the word.

¡Ojo!

Unas estudiantes en uniforme

Fondo cultural

School uniforms Many schools in Spanish-speaking countries require their students to wear uniforms. Often students wear a full uniform, like the ones you see in the photo. Sometimes the uniform consists of something more like a smock that is worn over a student's regular clothes and helps protect them from becoming dirty or torn during the school day.

- How are these uniforms similar to or different from those worn by high school students in the United States?

Actividad 10 **Escribir/Hablar**

Y tú, ¿qué dices?

Describe your classroom.

1. ¿Dónde está la puerta?
2. ¿Hay un reloj en tu clase? ¿Dónde está?
3. ¿Cuántos escritorios y sillas hay?
4. ¿Hay una bandera en tu clase? ¿Dónde está?
5. ¿Qué más *(What else)* hay en tu clase?

Enriching Your Teaching

Teacher-to-Teacher

Demonstrate how important body language can be by telling students a story using only Spanish. Even though students don't have the vocabulary or grammar to understand the entire story, use gestures to help them. For example: *¡Vamos! Ya es tarde* (point to your watch impatiently) *y tengo hambre* (rub your stomach). *Tengo ganas de comer* (place your fingertips together and bring your hand up close to your mouth. Repeat the motion several times). See Level B, p. 302 for more gestures.

Practice and Communicate

Exploración del lenguaje

Presentation

 *Standards:* 4.1

Suggestions: Demonstrate the ***¡Ojo!*** gesture. Have students discuss what kinds of gestures they use to communicate with or are familiar with. Do different age groups have different types of body language? Are there different types of body language to indicate different relationships between people?

 *Standards:* 2.1, 4.2

Suggestions: Have students look at the picture. Ask them to discuss the advantages and disadvantages of uniforms. Remind them about the insignias on the Chapter Opener photo.

Answers will vary.

 *Standards:* 1.2

Focus: Writing and talking about the classroom

Suggestions: Have students write their answers at the beginning of the class period while you take attendance.

Answers will vary.

Additional Resources

- Writing, Audio & Video Workbook: Cap. 2B, Audio Activities 5–6, Tracks 7–8
- Writing, Audio & Video Workbook: Cap. 2B, Writing Activity 10
- Resource Book: Cap. 2B, Communicative Activity BLM

Assessment

- Prueba 2B-2: Vocabulary production

Practice and Communicate

Gramática

Presentation

Standards: 4.1

Resources: Voc. & Gram. Transparencies: 61; Video Program: Cap. 2B; Resource Book: Cap. 2B, Video Script

Suggestions: Direct attention to the *¿Recuerdas?* Point out additional examples of ***estar*** that students have encountered. Show the *GramActiva* Video to reinforce the presentation. Ask questions for each verb form: *¿Cómo estás? Yo estoy muy bien. ¿Cómo está(n) usted(es)?* Be sure students notice the accents, and that they understand the importance of including them when writing.

Standards: 1.2

Actividad 11

Resources: Practice Answers on Transparencies

Focus: Reading sentences to find out who is in class

Suggestions: Remind students to use the ***nosotros*** form of the verb for ***Carmen y yo.***

Answers:

1. **Tú no estás en clase hoy.**
2. **Martina y Clarisa no están...**
3. **Carmen y yo estamos...**
4. **Guillermo está...**
5. **Yo estoy...**

Extension: Choose a volunteer to tell who is and isn't in class.

Standards: 1.2, 1.3

Actividad 12

Resources: Practice Answers on Transparencies

Focus: Completing a dialogue using forms of ***estar***

Suggestions: Have students read the exercise through before giving the answers. Have them identify the subject of each statement. Have volunteers perform the dialogue.

Answers:

1. **están**
2. **estamos**
3. **Estoy**
4. **están**
5. **está**
6. **está**

Gramática

The verb *estar*

The *-ar* verbs you have used until now are called **regular verbs** because they follow a regular pattern. Verbs that do not follow a regular pattern are called **irregular verbs.**

Estar is irregular because the *yo* form doesn't follow a regular pattern and because the forms *estás, está,* and *están* require accent marks.

Use *estar* to tell how someone feels or where someone or something is located.

(yo)	estoy	(nosotros) (nosotras)	estamos
(tú)	estás	(vosotros) (vosotras)	estáis
Ud. (él) (ella)	está	Uds. (ellos) (ellas)	están

¿Recuerdas?

You have used the verb *estar* to ask how someone is.

- ¿Cómo **estás?**
- ¿Cómo **está** Ud.?

GramActiva VIDEO

Want more practice with the verb *estar?* Watch the **GramActiva** video.

Actividad 11 Gramática **Leer**

¿Están en clase hoy?

Your teacher asks you to take attendance. Find out who is present and who isn't by matching the people in the first column with the completion of the sentence in the second column.

1. Tú
2. Martina y Clarisa
3. Carmen y yo
4. Guillermo
5. Yo

a. está en clase hoy.
b. estoy en clase hoy.
c. no estás en clase hoy.
d. estamos en clase hoy.
e. no están en clase hoy.

Actividad 12 Gramática **Escribir**

¡Hola! ¿Cómo estás?

Write the correct forms of *estar* on a separate sheet of paper.

Marcos: ¡Buenos días! ¿Cómo __1.__ Uds.?

Paula y Roberta: ¡Hola, Marcos! Nosotras __2.__ bien, gracias. ¿Y tú?

Marcos: __3.__ muy bien. ¿Dónde __4.__ Pedro y Juana?

Roberta: Pedro __5.__ en la sala de clases. Juana __6.__ en la oficina.

Universal Access

Students with Learning Difficulties

From time to time, allow students to refer to the vocabulary section of their notebooks when doing activities that require memorization. For *Gramática,* have them write all forms of ***estar*** into their grammar notebook section. Understanding and mastering verb forms can prove difficult and may require numerous reinforcement exercises.

Actividad 13 Gramática Hablar

¿En qué clase están?

Following the model, take turns with a partner to give the correct forms of *estar*.

ella

Modelo

Ella está en la clase de tecnología.

1. 

yo

2. 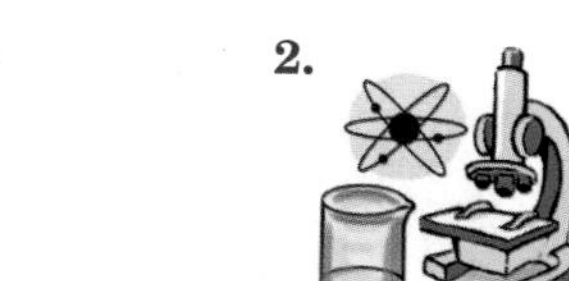

los profesores

3. 

la profesora

4. 

nosotros

5. 
ella

6. 
tú

Actividad 14 Gramática Hablar

¿Están los amigos allí?

The following people are supposed to study together in the library, but nobody is there. Explain that they are not there and tell where they are by using the correct form of *estar* and any of the places listed below.

Modelo

Paco no está allí. Está en la clase de educación física.

1. Yo
2. María
3. Tú
4. Natalia y Roberto
5. Uds.
6. Timoteo

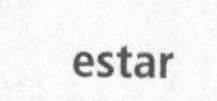

en la clase de inglés
en la oficina del director
en la clase de matemáticas
en la sala de clases
en la clase de español
en la clase de arte

Actividad 15 Hablar/Escribir

En mi clase

Look around your classroom. Tell where the following people and things are located in relationship to the word in parentheses. Use the verb *estar*, and follow the model.

Modelo

yo (mi silla)
Yo estoy en mi silla.

1. la papelera (el escritorio)
2. el teclado (la computadora)
3. los estudiantes (la sala de clases)
4. yo (mi escritorio)
5. mi mochila (la silla)
6. los estudiantes (el/la profesor(a))

Enriching Your Teaching

Teacher-to-Teacher

Have students write a sentence describing their location in relation to another student or a classroom object. Example: *Yo estoy al lado de la ventana.* Tell them to write their name on top of the paper, fold it in half, and put it in a box or hat. Have students randomly choose a description and read it aloud without giving the name of the student who wrote it. The student who guesses the name of the person being described gets a point.

Actividad 13 *Standards:* 1.1

Resources: Practice Answers on Transparencies

Focus: Using correct forms of ***estar*** in a school context

Recycle: Names of classes

Suggestions: Review the school subjects before students begin the activity.

Answers:

1. (Yo) estoy en la clase de español.
2. Los profesores están en la clase de ciencias naturales.
3. La profesora está en la clase de matemáticas.
4. Nosotros estamos en la clase de inglés.
5. Ella está en la clase de arte.
6. Tú estás en la clase de educación física.

Actividad 14 *Standards:* 1.1

Resources: Practice Answers on Transparencies

Focus: Talking about where people are

Suggestions: Remind students that they don't need to repeat the subject or subject pronoun in the second sentence.

Answers will vary but will include:

1. Yo no estoy allí. Estoy...
2. María no está allí. Está...
3. Tú no estás allí. Estás...
4. Natalía y Roberto no están allí. Están...
5. Uds. no están allí. Están...
6. Timoteo no está allí. Está...

Actividad 15 *Standards:* 1.1, 1.3

Focus: Talking and writing about where people and things are in the classroom

Suggestions: Review the prepositions of location with students before they begin.

Answers will vary.

2B Practice and Communicate

Rapid Review
Use Transparency 63 to quickly review location of classroom objects.

Standards: 1.2

Actividad 16

Resources: Audio Program: CD Cap. 2B, Track 6; Resource Book: Cap. 2B, Audio Script; Practice Answers on Transparencies

Focus: Listening to information about a photo and responding based on comprehension

Suggestions: Allow students time to study the photo before beginning.

Script and Answers:

1. Yo estoy detrás de Sara. *(cierto)*
2. El señor Salas está debajo del escritorio. *(falso)*
3. Julián y Mateo están delante de Rosa. *(falso)*
4. Sara y yo estamos al lado del escritorio. *(cierto)*
5. José y Lucita están encima del escritorio. *(cierto)*
6. Benito está delante del señor Salas. *(cierto)*

Standards: 1.1

Resources: Practice Answers on Transparencies

Focus: Speaking about the locations of people in a photo

Suggestions: Be sure students understand that they are describing locations from Javier's perspective.

Answers will vary but may include:

1. Están detrás de Rosa.
2. Rosa está al lado del escritorio.
3. Sara está delante de Javier.
4. Yo estoy detrás de Sara.
5. Está al lado del escritorio.
6. Están encima del escritorio.
7. Benito está delante del escritorio.
8. Estamos a la izquierda del escritorio.

Standards: 1.1

Focus: Asking questions to determine the identity of a classmate

Suggestions: Point out the *Para decir más...* and demonstrate the words. Model the questions before students begin.

Answers will vary.

Actividad 16 Gramática Escuchar

¿Cierto o falso?

Write the numbers 1–6 on a sheet of paper. Listen to the statements about Javier's Spanish club photo and write *cierto* or *falso* based on the information provided as you view the photograph from *your* perspective.

Actividad 17 Gramática Hablar

¿Y dónde están todos?

Work with a partner. Using the club picture above, find out where the various students are located from *Javier's* perspective.

Modelo
A —*¿Y dónde está Lucita?*
B —*Lucita está encima de la mesa.*

1. Julián y Mateo
2. Rosa
3. Sara
4. yo
5. el Sr. Salas
6. Lucita y José
7. Benito
8. Sara y yo

Actividad 18 Escribir/Hablar

Juego

Work with a partner. Write down the name of someone in the classroom. Your partner can only ask *sí* or *no* questions to find out the name. When your partner has guessed the mystery student's identity, switch roles.

Modelo
A —*¿Está al lado de Tomás?*
B —*No.*
A —*¿Está detrás de mí?*
B —*Sí.*
A —*¿Es Patricia?*
B —*Sí.*

Para decir más . . .

a la izquierda to the left
a la derecha to the right
detrás de mí behind me
detrás de ti behind you

Universal Access

Heritage Language Learners
Have students bring in photographs and describe where they are with small groups. Encourage students to use the verb ***estar*** and vocabulary to indicate location.

Students with Special Needs
Some students may have difficulty visualizing spatial relationships from a photo. Bring in small dolls, name them, and place them in order in front of the student. This will make the relationships more concrete.

Leer/Pensar

Los precios de las mochilas en el mundo hispano

Conexiones **Las matemáticas**

Most countries have their own currencies. In Mexico, people pay in *pesos,* in Peru they use *nuevos soles,* and so on. The value of each currency can go up or down daily in relation to other countries' currencies. For example, a dollar might be worth 10 Mexican *pesos* one day and 9.5 *pesos* the following day. Read the prices for *una mochila* in six different countries.

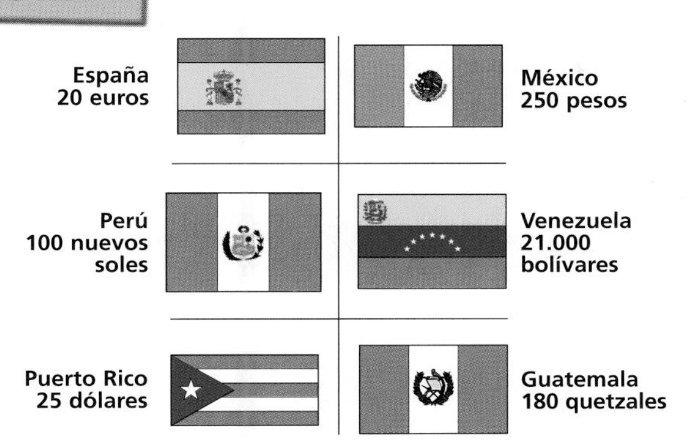

1. How much does a typical *mochila* cost in your community?
2. Convert the prices for *una mochila* into dollars. You can find a currency converter on the Internet.
3. How do these prices compare to those in your community? Why might the same item have different values in different countries?

Pensar/Escribir

De vacaciones

The following people are spending their vacations in various Spanish-speaking countries. Based on the currency they are using, say where they are. Use the information in Actividad 19 to help you.

Modelo

Clara usa quetzales.
Clara está en Guatemala.

1. Yo uso euros.
2. Ellos usan pesos.
3. Tú usas nuevos soles.
4. Ustedes usan quetzales.
5. Federico usa bolívares.

Más práctica
Practice Workbook 2B-5

For: Practice with *estar*
Visit: www.phschool.com
Web Code: jad-0214

Enriching Your Teaching

Culture Note

The official currency of Venezuela, the ***bolívar,*** is named after Simón Bolívar, the Great Liberator. The ***quetzal,*** the official unit of money in Guatemala, is named after a rare, exotic bird found only in Central American rain forests. Have students research these and other currencies to see what they look like.

Internet Search

Keywords:

currency converter; exchange rates

Actividad 19 *Standards:* 3.1

Focus: Reading and calculating international currencies; making a cross-curricular connection

Suggestions: Bring in prices of other school supplies that you've found on the Internet (or have students do a search themselves) to reinforce the concept that items not only have different prices but also different values in various countries.

Answers will vary.

Actividad 20 *Standards:* 3.1

Resources: Practice Answers on Transparencies

Focus: Thinking and writing about where people are based on the currency they are using

Suggestions: Before beginning, review the names of the countries and currencies in *Actividad* 19.

Answers:

1. Estoy en España.
2. Están en México.
3. Estás en Perú.
4. Están en Guatemala.
5. Está en Venezuela.

Theme Project

Students can perform step 4 at this point. Be sure they understand your corrections and suggestions. (For more information, see p. 84-a.)

Additional Resources

- Writing, Audio & Video Workbook: Cap. 2B, Audio Activity 7, Track 11
- Writing, Audio & Video Workbook: Cap. 2B, Writing Activity 11
- Resource Book: Cap. 2B, Communicative Activity BLM

Assessment

- Prueba 2B-3: The verb *estar*

Practice and Communicate

Gramática

Presentation

Standards: 4.1

Resources: Voc. & Gram. Transparencies: 62; Video Program: Cap. 2B; Resource Book: Cap. 2B, Video Script

Suggestions: Direct attention to the *¿Recuerdas?* Show the *GramActiva* Video to reinforce the presentation. ***Unos / unas*** is difficult for many English speakers to grasp, so you will want to give additional examples. Use the transparency for additional practice.

Standards: 1.2, 1.3

Actividad 21

Resources: Practice Answers on Transparencies

Focus: Practicing definite article agreement

Suggestions: Encourage students to work together to select the appropriate articles before they carry on the conversation. Be sure they use the definite article in all cases.

Answers:

1. los
2. la
3. los
4. los
5. la
6. las
7. los
8. las
9. la
10. las

Standards: 1.2

Actividad 22

Resources: Audio Program: CD Cap. 2B, Track 9; Resource Book: Cap. 2B, Audio Script; Practice Answers on Transparencies

Focus: Listening and speaking using plural nouns and articles

Suggestions: Play the *Audio CD* or read the script and have the class respond with the appropriate plural.

Script and Answers:

1. la mesa *(las mesas)*
2. la ventana *(las ventanas)*
3. el escritorio *(los escritorios)*
4. la mochila *(las mochilas)*
5. el teclado *(los teclados)*
6. el reloj *(los relojes)*
7. la bandera *(las banderas)*
8. el disquete *(los disquetes)*

Gramática

The plurals of nouns and articles

In Spanish, to make nouns plural you usually add *-s* to words ending in a vowel and *-es* to words ending in a consonant.

silla → sillas   teclado → teclados   cartel → carteles

Singular nouns that end in *z* change the *z* to *c* in the plural.

el lápiz → los lápices

The plural definite articles are *los* and *las*. Like *el* and *la*, they both mean "the."

las sillas   *the chairs*

The plural indefinite articles are *unos* and *unas*. They both mean "some" or "a few."

unos carteles   *some posters*

Singular	Plural
el reloj la ventana	los relojes las ventanas
un disquete una mesa	unos disquetes unas mesas

¿Recuerdas?

You have used the definite and indefinite articles in the singular form.

el, la *the*

un, una *a (an)*

GramActiva VIDEO

Want more help with the plurals of nouns and articles? Watch the **GramActiva** video.

Actividad 21 Gramática **Leer/Hablar**

¡A estudiar!

Marta and Berta are getting ready for school. Read the dialogue with a partner, completing the sentences with the correct definite articles.

Marta: ¿Dónde están __1.__ lápices?

Berta: Aquí están, en __2.__ mochila.

Marta: ¿Y tienes __3.__ bolígrafos y __4.__ libros?

Berta: No. Están allí, encima de __5.__ mesa, y debajo de __6.__ ventanas.

Marta: Ah, sí. ¿Y __7.__ cuadernos y __8.__ carpetas? ¿Dónde están?

Berta: Están encima de __9.__ mesa, y detrás de __10.__ computadoras.

Actividad 22 Gramática **Escuchar/Hablar**

Las palabras plurales

You will hear eight words. Say the plural form of the words as you hear them.

Modelo

You will hear: *el libro*
You will say: *los libros*

Universal Access

Students with Learning Difficulties

Provide students with a two-column graphic organizer. Have them write examples of singular nouns in one column and the corresponding plural forms in the next. Have them record this information in their grammar notebook section. Provide numerous examples of situations when ***el, la, los,*** and ***las*** are used.

Multiple Intelligences

Interpersonal / Social: Have students work in groups to write a short dialogue in which they ask a parent to help them find their things before they leave for school. They can videotape their dialogues for their portfolios.

Escribir

Más plurales

On a sheet of paper, write the plural forms of the articles and nouns below.

1. el cuaderno
2. una clase
3. la bandera
4. una mochila
5. la papelera
6. un escritorio
7. el profesor
8. un pupitre

Hablar

Una mesa desordenada

Sometimes your classmates are disorganized and they leave their things all over the table. With a partner, look at the drawing and take turns asking and telling where different things are located.

Modelo

A —*¿Dónde están las carpetas?*
B —*Las carpetas están debajo de los disquetes.*

Enriching Your Teaching

Teacher-to-Teacher

Use the Clip Art from the *Teacher's Resource Book* or the *Teacher Express CD-ROM* to create flashcards to practice articles and plurals. Some cards should show single objects. Others should show multiple copies of one object.

Practice and Communicate

2B

Resources: Practice Answers on Transparencies

Focus: Writing plural forms of nouns and articles

Recycle: School vocabulary

Suggestions: Encourage students to try chanting the singular and then the plural with a rap-like cadence to make the pattern second-nature: ***el cuaderno, los cuadernos, la bandera, las banderas,*** etc. Then have them go back and forth between definite and indefinite articles.

Answers:

1. los cuadernos
2. unas clases
3. las banderas
4. unas mochilas
5. las papeleras
6. unos escritorios
7. los profesores
8. unos pupitres

Focus: Asking and answering questions about the location of classroom objects

Suggestions: Remind students to use the third-person plural of ***estar*** if they are asking or telling about the location of something plural.

Answers will vary.

Standards: 2.1, 4.2

Suggestions: Have students describe the photo before they begin reading. Ask them to predict what the reading will be about. Point out that since schools differ from place to place, it is possible to find a school with lockers in other countries, but it is not as common as in the United States.

Answers will vary.

Standards: 1.2

Actividad 25

Resources: Practice Answers on Transparencies

Focus: Writing about objects found in a locker

Recycle: School vocabulary

Suggestions: Ask students to guess the meaning of ***armario*** by looking at the picture and reading the direction line. Point out that the word for a real mouse and a computer mouse is the same.

Answers will vary but may include:

Hay unos disquetes. Hay unos bolígrafos. Hay unos libros. Hay una calculadora. Hay unos lápices. Hay unas carpetas de argollas. Hay unos ratones. Hay unos papeles. Hay unas banderas. Hay unos carteles.

Estudiantes mexicanas

Fondo cultural

In some countries such as Mexico, Colombia, Costa Rica, and Chile, students attending public schools generally do not have lockers in which to store their things before each class. Most students carry the books and school supplies they need for the day in book bags. In some countries, such as Mexico, students will wear their gym clothes instead of their required school uniforms on the days they have physical education.

- If you didn't have a locker at school, what books and schools supplies would you bring every day and which ones would you leave at home?

Actividad 25 Gramática

Escribir

El armario de Ramón

You are looking at Ramón's messy locker. Write five sentences about what you see. Be sure to use the indefinite articles.

Modelo

Hay unos disquetes.

Universal Access

Heritage Language Learners

If you have students who attended school in a Spanish-speaking country, have them write a short paragraph describing their school and what a typical classroom was like.

Multiple Intelligences

Interpersonal / Introspective: Have students write a description of their own lockers. Remind them to use ***armario*** for "locker."

  Escribir

Necesito mucho

You need some of the things that the following people have. Look at the photos and write eight sentences following the model.

Flor

Modelo

Necesito los cuadernos de Flor.

> **Nota**
>
> In Spanish, you can express possession by using *de* and the name of the owner of the item.
>
> - el escritorio **de** la profesora *the teacher's desk*

1.   Ricardo
2.   el profesor
3. 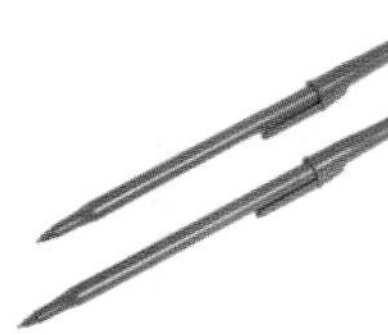 Carmen
4. 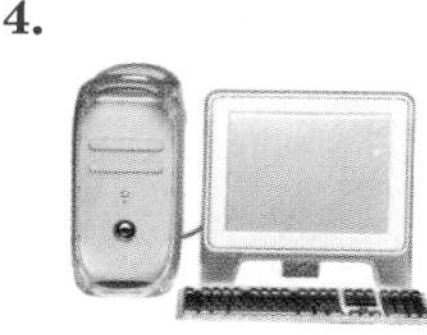 el director
5.  Milagros
6.  Rosa
7.  Enrique
8.  Juan

  Hablar

Es el cuaderno de . . .

Work in a group of four. Each of you should choose a classroom object you have brought to class. Show your group what you have chosen. Your teacher will collect all the items, then place them in view in different parts of the classroom. Ask your group where your object is.

Modelo

A —*¿Dónde está mi calculadora?*
B —*Tu calculadora está debajo de la silla de Margarita.*

Enriching Your Teaching

Teacher-to-Teacher

Have students use a shoebox and art supplies to create a diorama of a messy locker. Have them work in groups to describe the lockers they made, using *Actividad* 25 as a model. Keep the dioramas to use as a rapid review of vocabulary throughout the chapter.

Actividad 26  *Standards:* 1.3

Resources: Practice Answers on Transparencies

Focus: Writing about classroom items that people need

Recycle: ***necesito***

Suggestions: Direct students' attention to the *Nota* and practice possessive phrases by talking about objects that belong to students in the class. Emphasize that in Spanish, *'s* is never used to indicate possession.

Answers:

1. Necesito la calculadora de Ricardo.
2. ...la papelera del profesor.
3. ...los bolígrafos de Carmen.
4. ...la computadora del director.
5. ...la silla de Milagros.
6. ...la mochila de Rosa.
7. ...las carpetas de Enrique.
8. ...el sacapuntas de Juan.

Actividad 27  *Standards:* 1.1, 1.2

Focus: Speaking about the locations of classroom objects; ***mi, tu,*** and possessive with ***de***

Suggestions: Be sure students don't volunteer anything of any value. Return all items to students before the end of the class period.

Answers will vary.

Standards: 1.3

Focus: Writing sentences to describe a classroom

Suggestions: Before students identify locations of the classroom objects, have them make a list of all of the objects they see in the picture. Remind students of the *Nota* on p. 135.

Answers will vary.

Standards: 1.1, 1.3

Focus: Asking and answering questions in authentic context

Suggestions: Be sure students understand that they can choose among the options to create their questions.

Answers will vary.

Extension: Have students compare their classroom to the one in the picture. Or, bring in other photos of classrooms to have students describe.

Theme Project

Students can perform step 5 at this point. (For more information, see p. 84-a.)

Escribir

Una clase de inglés

Look at this picture of an English class in Chile and write five sentences about what you see.

Modelo

Los disquetes de Claudia están encima del escritorio.

Escribir/Hablar

En el dibujo hay . . .

Write at least three questions about the picture in Actividad 28, and then ask your partner those questions. Use some of the phrases in the box below.

¿Qué es esto?	¿Quién está . . . ?
¿Cuántos(as) . . . hay?	¿Hay . . . ?
¿Dónde está(n) . . . ?	¿Qué hay . . . ?

Modelo

A —*¿Cuántos estudiantes hay en la clase?*
B —*Hay cuatro estudiantes.*
A —*¿Dónde está la profesora?*
B —*Está al lado de la bandera.*

Universal Access

Advanced Learners

Have students choose a Latin American country and research the educational system. They should include information about requirements for attendance, if schools are primarily private or public, how schools are divided based on ages, and the country's literacy rate. Encourage them to try to find school Web sites on the Internet and photos of different schools. Ask them to bring in photos of students from the country they choose and to describe them.

El español en el mundo del trabajo

School districts in the United States have many positions in which employees need to speak Spanish. For example, school counselors work with new students and parents from Spanish-speaking countries. Counselors help them set up schedules, talk about school policies, and answer questions. Both the parents and the new students feel much more comfortable when the counselor can communicate with them in Spanish.

- Does your district need employees who speak Spanish? In what other jobs within a school system would speaking Spanish be helpful?

Actividad 30 Escribir

Y tú, ¿qué dices?

Look around your classroom and write at least five sentences describing objects and people that you see. Be sure to tell where they are located.

Más práctica
Practice Workbook 2B-6, 2B-7

For: Practice with plurals
Visit: www.phschool.com
Web Code: jad-0213

Pronunciación

The letter *g*

In Spanish, the letter *g* sounds like *g* in *go* when it is followed by *a*, *o*, or *u*, although it often has a slightly softer sound than in English. Listen to and say the following words:

Gustavo	domin**go**	ten**go**
a**go**sto	pre**gu**nta	lue**go**
ami**go**	ar**go**llas	**ga**to

In Spanish, the letter *g* sounds like the letter *h* in *hot* when it is followed by *e* or *i*. Listen to and say the following words. Some of these words you have not yet heard or seen. Can you guess the meanings of these cognates?

inteli**ge**nte	**ge**neroso	**ge**neral
gimnasio	tecnolo**gí**a	biolo**gí**a

Try it out! See if you can guess how to pronounce the following Spanish first names. Say each name in Spanish, keeping in mind the pronunciation rules for the *g* sound.

Gabriela	Ángela	Gerardo
Gilberto	Gustavo	Rodrigo
Olga	Rogelio	Gregorio

Enriching Your Teaching

Teacher-to-Teacher

Have students interview school employees who speak Spanish. Have them find out how each person learned Spanish, why it is necessary for his or her job, and how knowing Spanish has helped him or her in general. Have students present the information to the class.

Teacher-to-Teacher

Have students work in pairs or groups to create tongue twisters using words with both hard and soft ***g*** and present them the to class.

El español en el mundo del trabajo

Presentation

Standards: 5.1

Suggestions: Have students brainstorm a list of jobs in education that they think would require knowing Spanish. Have them come up with a list of people who work for your school who speak Spanish.

Answers will vary.

Actividad 30 *Standards:* 1.1, 1.3

Focus: Writing a paragraph about the classroom

Suggestions: Assign this as homework. Students should list or outline what they want to talk about and some of the words they want to use.

Answers will vary.

Pronunciación

Presentation

Standards: 4.1

Resources: Audio Program: CD Cap. 2B, Track 10

Suggestions: Have students practice the syllables ***ga-***, ***go-***, and ***gu-***, perhaps singing them on a tone. Then have students practice ***gi-*** and ***ge-***, alternating between them with each breath, emphasizing the exhaling.

Additional Resources

- Writing, Audio & Video Workbook: Audio Activities 8–9, Tracks 12–13
- Writing, Audio & Video Workbook: Writing Activities 12–13
- Heritage Learner Workbook: 2B-3, 2B-4, 2B-5

Assessment

- Prueba 2B-4: The plurals of nouns and articles

2B Communicate: Reading

Lectura

Presentation

Standards: 1.2, 3.1

Focus: Reading a narrative about UNICEF

Suggestions:

Pre-reading: Direct students' attention to the *Strategy*. Have students scan the reading for cognates and to tell what the main ideas are in this text. Ask students to take a good look at the illustration and predict how they might relate to the reading.

Reading: Have students read the article, stopping to make note of the important information in each paragraph. Tell students to refer to their list of predictions as they read and make a checkmark next to each one that is mentioned in the article.

Post-reading: Invite students to share which of their predictions were mentioned in the article. Then have them complete the *¿Comprendes?* questions in class or as homework.

Additional Resources

- Heritage Learner Workbook: 2B-6

¡Adelante!

Lectura

Lee este artículo sobre el UNICEF.

Objectives

- Read about an important program of the United Nations
- Learn about cultural differences in schools
- Write a note describing your classroom
- Learn facts about Central America

Strategy

Predicting outcomes
Think about what you would consider to be basic rights for children around the world. Jot down four of them on a piece of paper. As you read the article, see if your ideas are included.

El UNICEF y una convención para los niños[1]

¿Sabes que es un privilegio estar en una escuela, tener una mochila con libros, unos lápices, una calculadora, unas hojas de papel y un profesor bueno? En ciertas[2] naciones, ir a la escuela es difícil o no es posible.

El UNICEF es la organización internacional de las Naciones Unidas que trabaja para los niños. UNICEF es una sigla[3] inglesa que significa "Fondo Internacional de Emergencia de las Naciones Unidas para los Niños." Tiene siete oficinas regionales en diversas naciones y un Centro de Investigaciones en Italia.

El 20 de noviembre de 1989, la Organización de las Naciones Unidas escribió[4] "una convención para los niños" en inglés, árabe, chino, ruso y francés.

[1]children [2]certain [3]acronym [4]wrote

Esta convención dice que[5] los niños de todas[6] las naciones necesitan:

- dignidad
- una casa
- protección
- una buena dieta
- la práctica de deportes
- atención especial para los niños con problemas físicos
- amor y la comprensión de la familia
- expresar sus opiniones
- una comunidad sin[7] violencia
- ir a la escuela para ser inteligentes y sociables

[5]says that [6]all [7]without

Universal Access

Students with Learning Difficulties

Point out the *Strategy* and provide examples of the concept of "basic rights." Before reading, go through the *¿Comprendes?*, highlighting key words and phrases. Students might need to read through the passage a number of times to comprehend information. Doing guided reading with students may be useful.

Advanced Learners

Have students research other organizations that provide aid to children. Can they find Spanish-language information about the organizations? Have them bring in examples to share with the class.

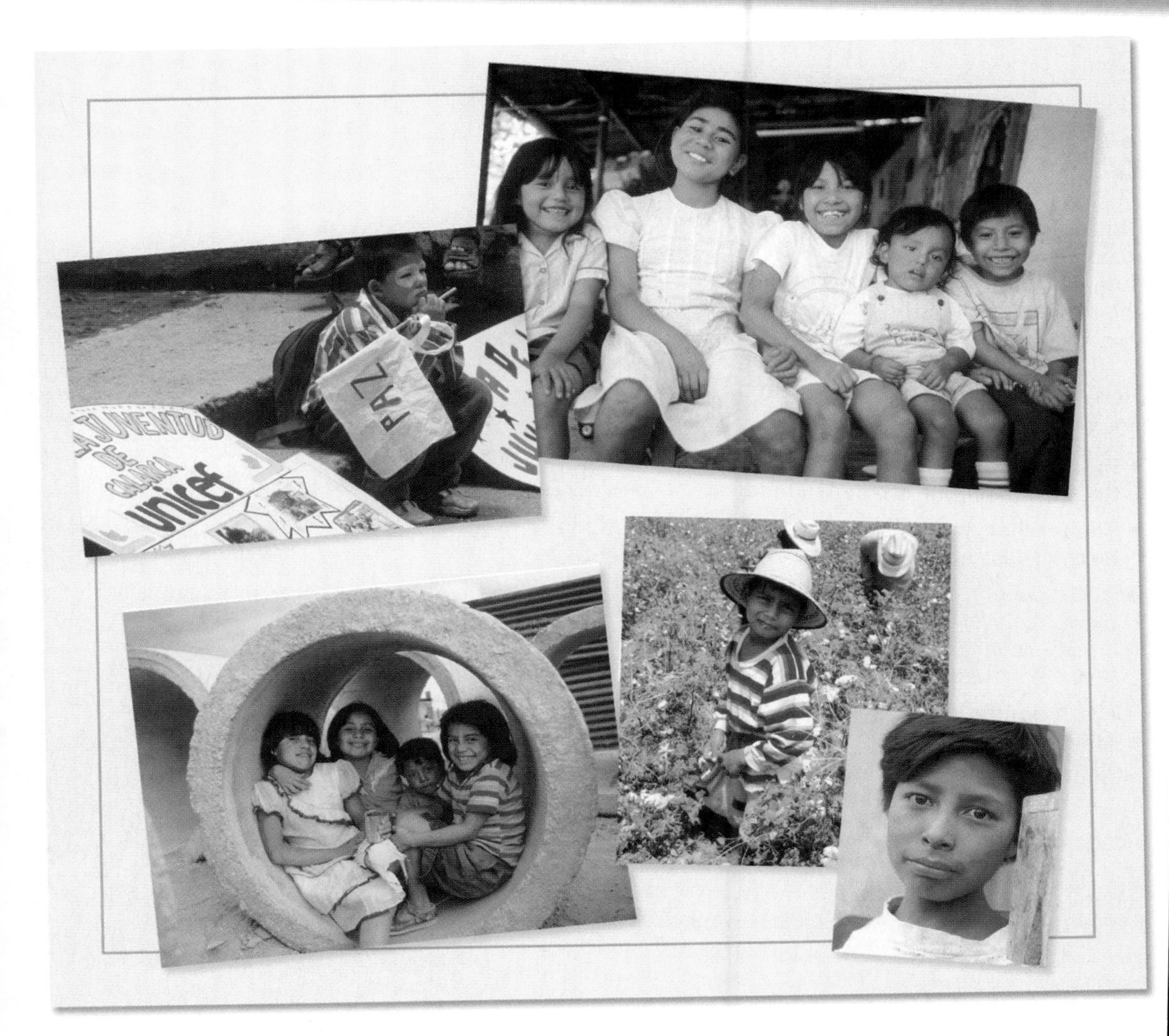

¿Comprendes?

1. It is easy for students of every nation to attend school and own a backpack. True or false?
2. How many offices in different nations does UNICEF have?
3. What do the letters UNICEF stand for?
4. Where is the *Centro de Investigaciones?*
5. The convention is for children of all nations. True or false?
6. According to the convention, what are four things that children need?

For: Internet link activity
Visit: www.phschool.com
Web Code: jad-0215

Enriching Your Teaching

Culture Note

UNICEF is a private, nonprofit organization supported by volunteers who help raise funds selling the well-known UNICEF greeting cards and conducting the "Trick or Treat for UNICEF" program. The agency seeks to generate understanding of the rights and needs of children everywhere. UNICEF helps children get the care they need as infants and encourages families to educate girls as well as boys. Funds are used to reduce infant deaths and illnesses and to protect children from war or natural disasters.

 *Standards:* 1.1, 1.3

¿Comprendes?

Resources: Practice Answers on Transparencies

Focus: Demonsstrating reading comprehension

Suggestions: Help students understand the questions that contain cognates and decodable words. Have students discuss the questions and answers in small groups.

Answers:

1. false
2. seven
3. United Nations International Children's Emergency Fund
4. The *Centro de Investigaciones* is in Italy.
5. true
6. Answers will vary but will include any of the items in the list on p. 138.

2B Culture

Perspectivas del mundo hispano

Presentation

Standards: 2.1, 2.2, 4.2

Focus: Reading about school in Spanish-speaking countries

Presentation: Have students vote about whether they spend too much time, too little time, or just the right amount of time in school. Tally the results on the board. Tell them that the school year in Spanish-speaking countries is usually longer than in the United States. Call attention to the graph. Point out the variations. Tell students that the way classes are run is different, too. Have volunteers read the bulleted items. Are there any that students find preferable to what they experience? Have students complete the *Check it out!* section.

Suggestions: Many students will not like the idea of spending more time in school, but have them enumerate possible benefits to a longer school year. How would they like the added time spent? Ask how the rules might affect students and classes. Find out if students like the idea of wearing a uniform or having class lectures instead of class discussion, and why.
Direct attention to the *Think about it!* section and have students discuss the questions.

Answers will vary.

Additional Resources

- Heritage Learner Workbook: 2B-7

Perspectivas del mundo hispano

¿Cómo es la escuela?

Did you know that students in many Spanish-speaking countries spend more time in school than you do? The graph to the right shows the length of the school year in various countries.

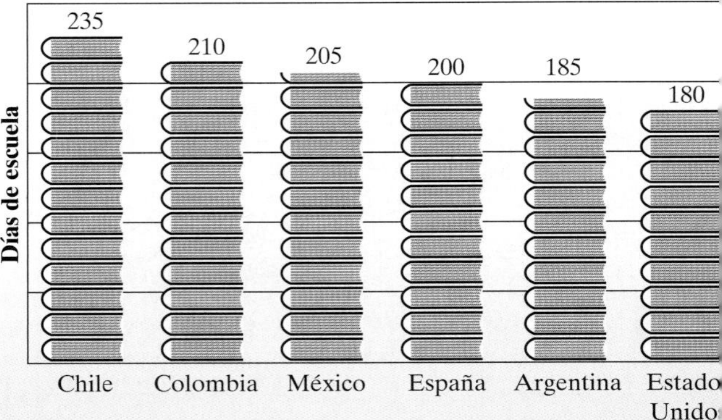

Here are some other facts you may not know:

- In many schools, when a teacher enters the classroom, the students stand.
- The teacher may call the students by their last name.
- The students, on the other hand, are more likely to address their teacher simply as *maestro(a), profesor(a),* or just *profe,* without a last name.
- Class time is generally spent with the teacher lecturing rather than with class discussion.
- Many public and private schools require uniforms.

Check it out! How are other schools in your area similar to or different from yours? How are they similar to or different from those in Spanish-speaking countries? Make a list of schools in your area and describe these similarities and differences. Are some schools more formal? Do students take classes that are different from the ones you take?

Think about it! Based on the information above, what might you assume are the attitudes toward school in Spanish-speaking cultures? How are these the same or different from attitudes in your community? List five suggestions that might help an exchange student from Mexico City adjust to your school's system.

Universal Access

Multiple Intelligences

Logical / Mathematical: Have students find out about the length of the school day and year in a Spanish-speaking country not included in the graph. Ask them to compare their own curriculum with that of students of the same age in the country of their choice. Have them present this information to the class in the form of a graph.

Heritage Language Learners

Some students may have gone to school in their heritage country. If so, ask them to tell what adjustments they found difficult when they came to school in the United States. Ask them to share what they prefer about each system.

Presentación escrita

Tu sala de clases

Task
Your pen pal from Mexico is coming to visit your school next semester and would like to know what to expect. Write her a note describing your Spanish classroom.

1. **Prewrite** Draw a simple sketch of your classroom, showing the classroom items you intend to describe in your note. Label the items.

2. **Draft** Write the first draft of your note. Your sketch will help you remember which items you want to describe and where they are located. Use the model to help you organize your writing.

Creating visuals
Creating a sketch or a drawing can help you remember the things you want to write about in a description.

Modelo

En mi sala de clases hay cuatro ventanas. Mi pupitre está delante del escritorio de la profesora. La bandera está al lado de la puerta. Las computadoras están encima de la mesa.

3. **Revise** Read through your paragraph and check for correct spelling as well as for the criteria under Evaluation.

   Share your work with a partner. Your partner should check the following:
   - Is your paragraph easy to understand?
   - Is there other information you could add?
   - Are there are any errors?

   Rewrite your paragraph making any necessary changes.

4. **Publish** Make a final copy of your note. You may exhibit it in the classroom or add it to your portfolio.

5. **Evaluation** Your teacher may give you a rubric for how the paragraph will be graded. You probably will be graded on:
   - use of vocabulary
   - correct use of the verb *estar*
   - amount of information provided

Communicate: Writing

Presentación escrita

Presentation

Standards: 1.3

Focus: Writing to a Mexican pen pal about an American classroom

Suggestions: Introduce the task to the class and then have them work through each step of the process. You may want to provide a model of a top-scoring note.

Portfolio

Have students include their notes in their portfolios.

Additional Resources

- Heritage Learner Workbook: 2B-8

Assessment

- Asssessment Program: Cap. 2B, Rubrics

Give students copies of the rubric before they begin the activity. Review the different levels of performance. After assessing students, help individuals understand how their performance could be improved.

Teacher-to-Teacher

Several pen pal Web sites serve to connect pen pals from different countries. Some of these Web sites are geared for classrooms and students. Find out about setting students up with pen pals through school or home computers. You might prefer to contact a school in a Spanish-speaking city and set up a "sister" class for exchanging letters through regular mail service.

Enriching Your Teaching

RUBRIC	Score 1	Score 3	Score 5
Use of newly acquired vocabulary	You use very little variation of vocabulary with frequent usage errors.	You use limited vocabulary, but with some usage errors.	You use an extended variety of vocabulary with very few usage errors.
Correct use of the verb *estar*	You use many repetitions of incorrect verb forms.	You use frequent repetitions of incorrect verb forms.	You use very few incorrect verb forms.
Amount of information provided	You provide information about two or fewer items in the classroom.	You provide information about three or fewer items in the classroom.	You provide information about four or more items in the classroom.

El mundo hispano

Presentation

Standards: 2.1, 2.2, 4.2

Resources: Voc. & Gram. Transparencies: 13 (map)

Focus: Reading about the countries of Central America

Suggestions: After students have read the text, show a map of Central America and identify the seven countries. Have students locate Belize and explain why Spanish is not the language of that country. Point out the narrowness of this stretch of land and the Caribbean Sea and the Pacific Ocean on either side. Only Belize and El Salvador do not have access to both bodies of water. How might this affect trade and other aspects of life in those countries?

Direct attention to the photo in the middle of p. 142. Discuss sea turtles and the efforts of Costa Rica to protect the environment. Since there are rainforests in this part of the world, ask what we can tell about the climate.

Note the photo of the women and discuss the indigenous Mayan population of Guatemala. This picture shows how certain traditions have survived the centuries. Discuss the messages in the clothing these women are wearing. How might this have been useful?

The top photo focuses on the modern city of Granada, Nicaragua; an important trading center. What may have helped this city become so important? Discuss whether Nicaragua would have been a good alternative site for the canal. Which do students think would have been the better choice? Why?

Direct attention to the bottom picture. Have students explain why forts to protect the ships and their cargo were built along this coast. Ask why they think the silver and gold from Peru was carried overland to the coast. Was this really the best route?

Direct students to the *¿Sabes que...?* section. Discuss possible reasons for Spain to have had an interest in a canal. How many years passed before it was built?

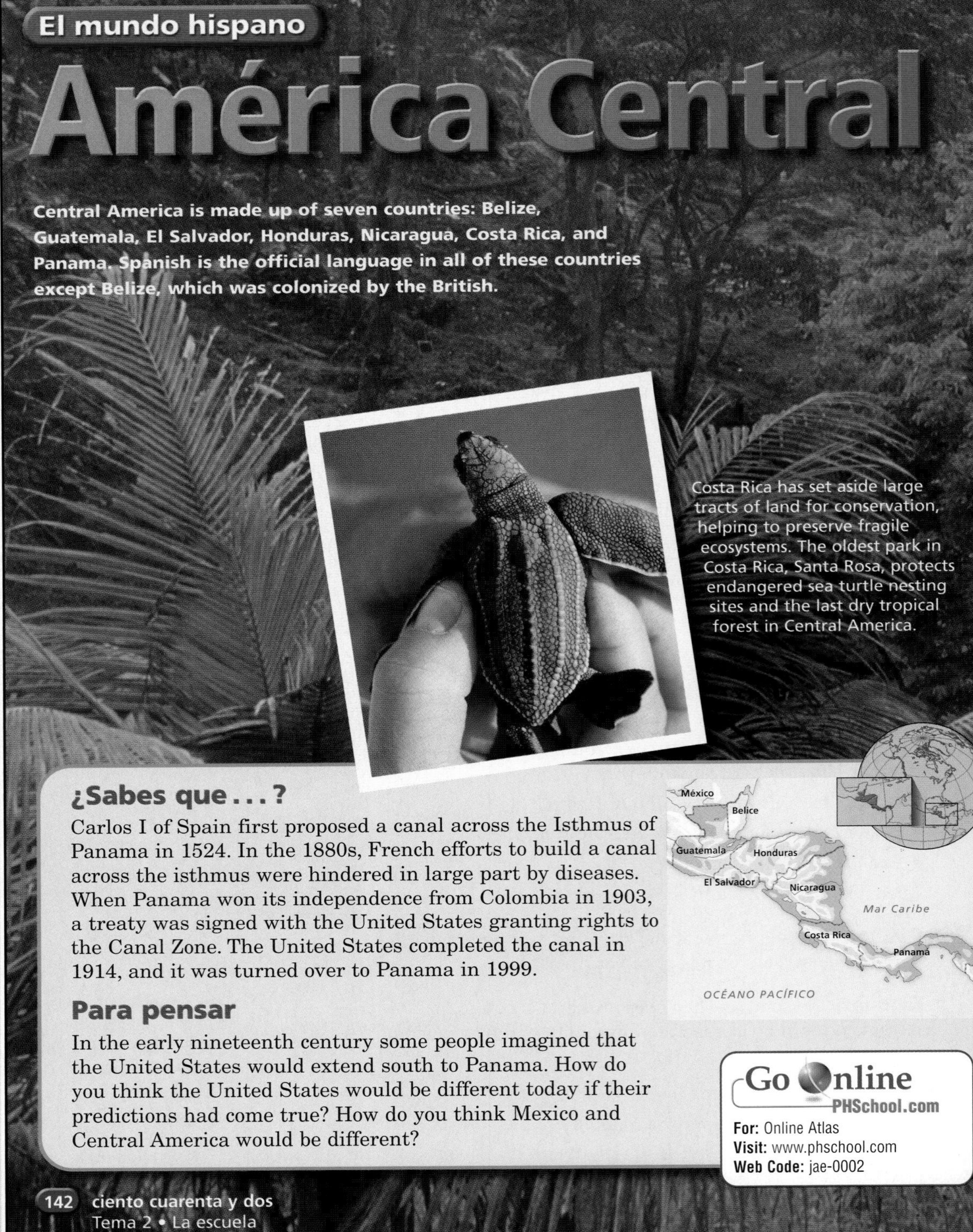

El mundo hispano

América Central

Central America is made up of seven countries: Belize, Guatemala, El Salvador, Honduras, Nicaragua, Costa Rica, and Panama. Spanish is the official language in all of these countries except Belize, which was colonized by the British.

Costa Rica has set aside large tracts of land for conservation, helping to preserve fragile ecosystems. The oldest park in Costa Rica, Santa Rosa, protects endangered sea turtle nesting sites and the last dry tropical forest in Central America.

¿Sabes que . . . ?

Carlos I of Spain first proposed a canal across the Isthmus of Panama in 1524. In the 1880s, French efforts to build a canal across the isthmus were hindered in large part by diseases. When Panama won its independence from Colombia in 1903, a treaty was signed with the United States granting rights to the Canal Zone. The United States completed the canal in 1914, and it was turned over to Panama in 1999.

Para pensar

In the early nineteenth century some people imagined that the United States would extend south to Panama. How do you think the United States would be different today if their predictions had come true? How do you think Mexico and Central America would be different?

Go Online
PHSchool.com
For: Online Atlas
Visit: www.phschool.com
Web Code: jae-0002

Universal Access

Multiple Intelligences

Visual / Spatial: Have students create a map of Central America, including major cities, rainforests, indigenous wildlife, and other facts or phenomena they find interesting or important.

Heritage Language Learners

Have students find out about the indigenous people of their heritage country or of another Spanish-speaking country of their choice. Does the Spanish spoken there today have words that came from the indigenous language(s)?

Culture

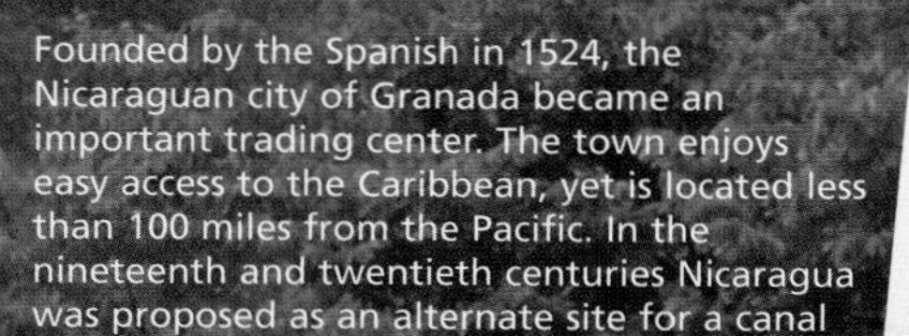

Founded by the Spanish in 1524, the Nicaraguan city of Granada became an important trading center. The town enjoys easy access to the Caribbean, yet is located less than 100 miles from the Pacific. In the nineteenth and twentieth centuries Nicaragua was proposed as an alternate site for a canal linking the Atlantic and Pacific oceans.

Much of Guatemala's large indigenous population is of Mayan descent. These women are wearing the traditional hand-woven *huipil*, which is a very "communicative" part of their clothing. The *huipil* identifies the wearer's village, her marital status, her religious beliefs, wealth, and personality. A well-woven *huipil* may last between 20 to 30 years.

From the 1500s to the end of the 1700s, the coasts of Spanish America were plagued by pirates. Panamanian ports were perfect targets, since the silver and gold mined in Peru were loaded on Panama's Pacific coast and carried overland to the Atlantic, where they were put on ships bound for Spain. Fuerte San Lorenzo, on Panama's Atlantic coast, was part of a network of forts that were meant to protect ships and their precious cargo.

Suggestions: Help students see the value of a canal connecting the Caribbean and the Pacific Ocean—and of canals in general.

Some students may not understand how it is possible that Belize was colonized by the British, yet is surrounded by countries colonized by the Spanish. Discuss how the English, the Spanish, and the French colonized most of the Americas.

Direct attention to the *Para pensar* section and have students discuss the questions.

Answers will vary.

Go Online

The Online Atlas will provide more detailed maps of Central America.

Enriching Your Teaching

Teacher-to-Teacher

Have students research the Panama Canal. They should find out when it was finally built, who built it and under what circumstances, and the status of the Canal today.

2B Review

Review Activities

Resources: Audio Program: CD Cap. 2B, Track 14

Suggestions:

To talk about classroom items: Point to classroom items and have students tell you what they are. Call on volunteers to tell what vocabulary items aren't found in their classroom. For example: *En la sala de clase hay una mesa pero no hay un sacapuntas.*

To talk about classroom furniture: Have students make a list of the furniture that should be in a classroom. Have Student A point to a specific piece of furniture and have Student B say what it is. For example: *¿Es una mesa? No. Es una silla.*

To talk about parts of a classroom and ***To indicate location:*** Using the list created above, have students work in pairs, asking and telling where different items are located relative to the parts of the classroom. For example: *¿Dónde está el escritorio? Está al lado de la ventana.*

To indicate possession, to identify (description, quantity) and ***To identify gender and quantity of nouns:*** Have students work in groups. Tell them to put several classroom objects in front of them. Have Student A point to an item and ask what it is and Student B will name the item and say whose it is. For example: *¿Qué es esto? Es una calculadora. Es tu calculadora.*

Portfolio

Invite students to review the activities they completed in this chapter, including written reports, posters or other visuals, and tapes of oral presentations, or other projects. Have them select one or two items that they feel best demonstrate their achievements in Spanish to include in their portfolios. Have them include this with the Chapter Checklist and Self-Assessment Worksheet.

Additional Resources

- Resource Book: Cap. 2B, Clip Art
- Resource Book: Cap. 2B, Situation Cards
- Audio Program: CD Cap. 2B, Track 14
- Assessment Program: Chapter Checklist and Self-Assessment Worksheet

Repaso del capítulo

Chapter Review

To prepare for the test, check to see if you . . .

- know the new vocabulary and grammar
- can perform the tasks on p. 145

Vocabulario y gramática

to talk about classroom items

la bandera	flag
el cartel	poster
la computadora	computer
el disquete	diskette
la mochila	bookbag, backpack
la pantalla	(computer) screen
la papelera	wastepaper basket
el ratón	(computer) mouse
el reloj	clock
el sacapuntas	pencil sharpener
el teclado	(computer) keyboard

to talk about classroom furniture

el escritorio	desk
la mesa	table
la silla	chair

to talk about parts of a classroom

la puerta	door
la sala de clases	classroom
la ventana	window

to indicate location

al lado de la / del	next to, beside
allí	there
aquí	here
debajo de la/del	underneath
delante de la/del	in front of
detrás de la/del	behind
¿Dónde?	Where?
en	in, on
encima de la/del	on top of

to indicate possession

de	of
mi	my
tu	your

For *Vocabulario adicional,* see pp. 268–269.

to identify (description, quantity)

¿Cuántos, -as?	How many?
Es un(a) . . .	It's a (an) . . .
Hay	There is, There are
¿Qué es esto?	What is this?

to identify gender and quantity of nouns

los, las	the
unos, unas	some

estar *to be*

estoy	**estamos**
estás	**estáis**
está	**están**

Más práctica

Practice Workbook Puzzle 2B-8
Practice Workbook Organizer 2B-9

Universal Access

Students with Learning Difficulties

To help kinesthetic learners review vocabulary, have them place labels on items. Before students arrive in the classroom on the day of the review, place labels for classroom objects on your desk. Call on volunteers to come up and choose a label and place it on the appropriate item.

Multiple Intelligences

Kinesthetic: If students have mastered most of the vocabulary and grammar oints in this chapter, suggest that they put it all together to act out a brief conversation using all the elements in the chapter.

For: Test preparation
Visit: www.phschool.com
Web Code: jad-0216

Preparación para el examen

On the exam you will be asked to . . .	Here are practice tasks similar to those you will find on the exam . . .	If you need review . . .
1 Escuchar Listen to and identify classrooms and locations	Listen as a student frantically asks some of his friends where he left his homework. Can you identify all the classrooms and places they suggest that he look?	**pp. 118–123** *A primera vista* **p. 124** Actividades 5–6 **p. 135** Actividad 27
2 Hablar Talk about where someone is located by describing where that person is in relation to objects in the classroom	You are trying to find out the name of someone in your class. You ask the person next to you, but he doesn't understand whom you are talking about. Give at least three statements that would help him identify the person. You might include where he or she is in relation to the teacher's desk, the window, someone else's desk, and so on.	**pp. 118–123** *A primera vista* **p. 125** Actividad 7 **p. 126** Actividad 9 **p. 130** Actividades 16–17 **p. 133** Actividad 24 **p. 135** Actividad 27 **p. 136** Actividad 29
3 Leer Read and understand a letter that contains questions and concerns about school issues	The school counselor has asked you to help out read a note written by a new Spanish-speaking student at school. After reading it, tell the counselor what questions the student has about her classes? *Necesito una clase para la primera hora. ¿Cómo es la clase de tecnología, fácil o difícil? ¿Qué necesito para la clase? ¿Cuántos alumnos hay en las clases? ¿Hay mucha tarea?*	**pp. 118–122** *A primera vista* **p. 128** Actividad 11 **pp. 138–139** *Lectura*
 **4 Escribir** Write an e-mail to a friend about one of her classes	You have just moved to a new town and are sending an e-mail to a friend from your old school. You have lots of questions for your friend about her classes. Write at least three questions about one of her classes: whether she likes it, how many students are in it, where her desk is in the room, what else is in the room, etc.	**pp. 118–123** *A primera vista* **p. 124** Actividad 6 **p. 125** Actividad 7 **p. 136** Actividad 28 **p. 137** Actividad 30
 **5 Pensar** Demonstrate an understanding of cultural differences in schools	Think about how students and teachers interact within a typical classroom in a Spanish-speaking country. What are at least four things that you might find different from most schools in the United States?	**p. 127** *Fondo cultural* **p. 134** *Fondo cultural* **p. 140** *Perspectivas del mundo hispano*

Performance Tasks

Standards: 1.1, 1.2, 1.3, 4.2

Resources: Audio Program: CD Cap. 2B, Track 15; Resource Book: Cap. 2B, Audio Script; Practice Answers on Transparencies

1. Escuchar

Suggestions: Play the *Audio CD* or read the script.

Script:

Juan: ¡Ay! Mi tarea ... ¿Dónde está? Necesito mi tarea para la clase de matemáticas. Ana, ¿dónde está mi tarea?
Ana: ¿Tu tarea? Está en la clase de ciencias sociales, en el escritorio del profesor.
Juan: Gracias, Ana. ¡Ay! No está aquí. Daniel, ¿dónde está mi tarea de matemáticas?
Daniel: Está en la clase de tecnología ... al lado de la computadora.
Juan: Gracias.

Answer:

En la clase de ciencias sociales, en el escritorio del profesor. En la clase de tecnología . . . al lado de la computadora.

2. Hablar

Suggestions: Pair students for this activity. Give them time to prepare before they speak.

Answers will vary.

3. Leer

Suggestions: If students have difficulty reading and understanding this note, refer them to the vocabulary list to study words they do not recognize.

4. Escribir

Suggestions: Have students try this activity without consulting the vocabulary list, notes, or completed activities.

5. Pensar

Suggestions: Encourage students to read the *Perspectivas del mundo hispano* and *Fondos culturales* to prepare for this task.

Assessment

- Examen del capítulo: 2B
- Audio Program: CD 20, Track 6

Alternative Assessment

- ExamView Test Bank CD-ROM
- Resource Book: Cap. 2B, Situation Cards
- Resource Book: Cap. 2B, Communicative Activities

Enriching Your Teaching

Teacher-to-Teacher

Have students work in groups to create a board game. Have them draw eight adjoining squares on a sheet of paper and label each square with a classroom item. Then have students create 20 cards with different locations in the classroom. For example: ***encima del escritorio.*** Have students take turns choosing cards. If the location on the card describes the location of the object written on their space, they move ahead. If not, it's the next student's turn. The first student to get through all eight squares wins.

Tema 3

La comida

THEME OVERVIEW

3A ¿Desayuno o almuerzo?

- Foods and beverages for breakfast and lunch

Vocabulary: foods; beverages; adverbs of frequency; expressions to show surprise

Grammar: present tense of ***-er*** and ***-ir*** verbs; ***me gusta(n), me encanta(n)***

Cultural Perspectives: meals in the Spanish-speaking world

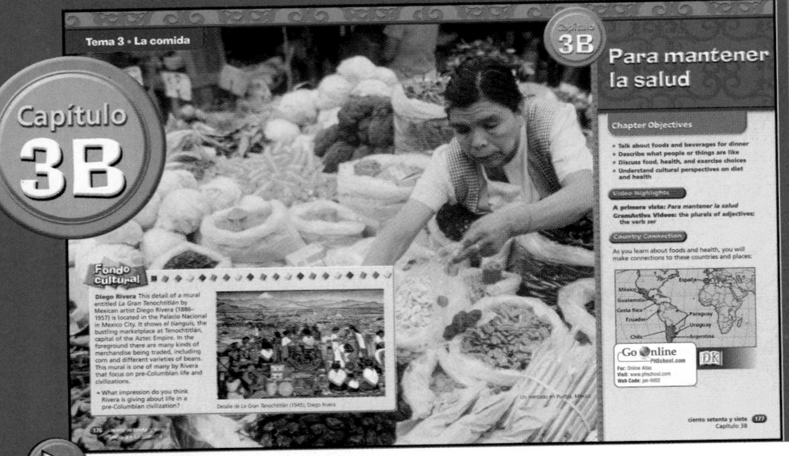

3B Para mantener la salud

- Foods and beverages for dinner and food, health, and exercise choices

Vocabulary: food; beverages; expressions to discuss health and indicate preference, agreement, disagreement, and quantity; adjectives to describe food

Grammar: the plural of adjectives; the verb ***ser***

Cultural Perspectives: opinions regarding diet and health

Theme Project

Vacaciones para la salud

Overview: Students create a brochure describing a typical day at a health resort. The brochure includes a schedule of the day's activities and descriptions of breakfast, lunch, and dinner. Photos or drawings accompany each meal and one of the activities listed. Students then present the brochures to the class as if they were sales representatives from the resort.

Materials: construction paper, magazines, scissors, glue, colored pencils ,markers

Sequence: (suggestions for when to do each step are found throughout the chapters)

3A ▶ STEP **1.** Review instructions so students know what is expected of them. Hand out the "Theme 3 Project Instructions and Rubric" from the *Teacher's Resource Book.*

STEP **2.** Students submit a rough sketch of their brochure. Return the sketches with your suggestions. For vocabulary and grammar practice, ask students to partner and present their sketches to each other.

STEP **3.** Students do layouts on construction paper. Encourage students to work in pencil first and to try different arrangements before drawing pictures or gluing magazine clippings and writing the content of the brochure.

3B ▶ STEP **4.** Students submit a draft of their meal descriptions and schedule. Note your corrections and suggestions, then return the drafts to students.

STEP **5.** Students complete and present their brochure to the class, trying to "sell" their health resort to classmates.

Options:

1. Students design a one-week lunch plan for the school cafeteria using the Food Guide Pyramid.
2. Students create a diet and exercise guide for someone who wants to get in shape.

Assessment:

Here is a detailed rubric for assessing this project:

Theme 3 Project: *Vacaciones para la salud*

RUBRIC	Score 1	Score 3	Score 5
Evidence of planning	You provided no written draft or page layout.	Your draft was written and your layout created, but not corrected.	You corrected your draft and layout.
Your use of illustrations	You included no photos / visuals.	You included photos / visuals, but your layout was unorganized.	Your brochure was easy to read, complete, and accurate.
Your presentation	You included little of the required information for the brochure and made no attempt to "sell" the product.	You included most of the required information for the brochure and made some attempt to "sell" the product.	You included all of the required information for the brochure and tried to "sell" the product.

Bulletin Boards

Theme: ***La comida***

Ask students to cut out, copy, or download photos of foods and beverages from around the world, people engaged in various forms of exercise, and recipes in Spanish. Cluster photos according to the following themes: healthy foods and beverages, unhealthy foods and beverages, exercise, and recipes.

Bibliography

Goldstein, Ernest, and Diego Rivera. *The Journey of Diego Rivera.* Minneapolis: Lerner Publications, 1996. A look at Rivera's art, with color prints.

DK Hornby, Hugh. *Soccer.* DK Eyewitness Books. New York: Dorling Kindersley, 2000. The inside story of soccer, from its origins to the latest World Cup finals.

DK Kindersley, Anabel, and Barnabas Kindersley. *Children Just Like Me: Celebrations.* New York: Dorling Kindersley, 1997. Cultural traditions of children around the world, including Spain.

McKay, Susan. *Spain.* Milwaukee: Gareth Stevens, 1999. Festivals of the world.

Parnell, Helga. *Cooking the South American Way: Revised and Expanded to Include New Low-fat and Vegetarian Recipes.* Minneapolis: Lerner Publications, 2002. Recipes and descriptions of the land, people, and food of South America.

Step-By-Step Cooking Series. *Spanish Cooking.* Murdoch Books, 1993. Step-by-step recipes for the traditional dishes of Spain.

Hands-on Culture

Recipe: ***Tortilla española***

This popular dish from Spain can be eaten at breakfast, as an appetizer, or as a light supper.

Ingredients:

4 eggs
3 potatoes
1 small onion
$\frac{1}{2}$ c. olive oil
$\frac{3}{8}$ T. salt

1. Scrub the potatoes and peel the onion. Slice the potatoes and onion.
2. In a frying pan, sauté the potatoes and onion in the olive oil until they are lightly browned. Add the salt.
3. Beat the eggs thoroughly. Pour them over the potatoes and onion.
4. Cook the mixture over low heat for three to four minutes, until the eggs set.
5. Place a plate over the frying pan, and flip the tortilla onto the plate. Slide the tortilla back into the pan, the uncooked side down. Continue cooking over low heat for three to four minutes.
6. Place the tortilla on a serving plate and allow it to come to room temperature before serving.

Internet Search

Use the keywords to find more information.

3A **Keywords:**

Bartolomé Murillo, recetas, frutas y verduras de las Américas

3B **Keywords:**

Diego Rivera, pirámide alimenticia, tomatina, World Cup soccer, alternative medicine

Game

Categorías

This game is a timed relay race. Play it to review vocabulary before the Vocabulary production quiz.

Players: the entire class

Materials: paper, pens

Rules:

1. Arrange students' desks in five rows. Ask students to clear their desks. Give the first student in each row a sheet of paper and a pen.
2. Call out one of the following categories: ***desayuno, almuerzo, cena, bebidas,*** or ***salud.*** Tell students they have one minute to write as many words from the category as they can on their row's sheet of paper.
3. After you say ***"empiecen,"*** the first student in each row writes a word, then passes the paper and pen to the next student. That student writes another word, then passes it to the third student, and so on until the paper reaches the end of the row. The last student brings the paper to the first student, and the relay begins again until you call time.
4. Rows exchange papers for correction. The team with the most words spelled correctly wins a point.
5. Continue play until all the categories have been completed. If there is a tie at the end of play, have students define each word on their row's list. The winner is the row that defines all words correctly first.

Variation: Have a relay spelling bee. Call out a vocabulary word or expression, and have each student in a row write one letter of the word.

Overview

Chapter Overview

A primera vista — INPUT	Manos a la obra — PRACTICE	¡Adelante! — APPLICATION	Repaso del capítulo — REVIEW
Objectives Read, listen to, and explain information about: • foods and beverages for breakfast and lunch	**Objectives** • Talk about foods and beverages for breakfast and lunch • Ask and tell what people eat and drink for breakfast and lunch • Express likes and dislikes • Use the present tense of *-er* and *-ir* verbs and ***me gustan, me encantan***	**Objectives** • Read about fruits that are native to the Americas • Talk about a snack in Spanish-speaking countries, ***churros y chocolate*** • Maintain a conversation about what you like, including your food preferences • Discuss facts about the northern part of South America	**Objectives** • Prepare for the chapter test
Vocabulary • Foods and beverages for breakfast and lunch • Verbs to talk about eating and drinking • Adverbs	**Vocabulary** • Practice and learn new vocabulary	**Vocabulary** • Application	**Vocabulary** • Review
Grammar Lexical use of: • present tense of *-er* and *-ir* verbs • ***me gusta(n), me encanta(n)***	**Grammar** • Present tense of *-er* and *-ir* verbs • ***me gusta(n), me encanta(n)***	**Grammar** • Application	**Grammar** • Review
Culture • Bartolomé Murillo	**Culture** • ***El desayuno*** in the Spanish-speaking world • Recipes for common dishes in the Spanish-speaking world	**Culture** • Fruits and vegetables that the United States imports from Chile • ***Churros y chocolate***	**Culture** • Demonstrate an understanding of cultural perspectives on popular snacks

Learner Support

Strategies

- Using prior experience
- Skimming
- Making guesses
- Making lists

Recycling

- Present tense of *-ar* verbs
- ***gustar***
- Expressions of agreement and disagreement

Pronunciación

- The letters ***h*** and ***j***

Exploración del lenguaje

- Using a noun to modify another noun

Conexiones

- History: food exchange between Europe and the Americas

Beyond the Classroom

Countries

- Chile
- Bolivia
- Peru
- Ecuador
- Colombia
- Costa Rica
- Venezuela
- Spain

El español en la comunidad

- Foods from Spanish-speaking countries in the grocery store

Internet

- Vocabulary activities
- Grammar activities
- Internet links
- Self-tests

Print Components

TEACHER

Teacher's Resource Book
- Chapter Resource Checklist
- Input Script
- Video Script
- Audio Script
- Answer Keys
- *GramActiva* Blackline Master
- Communicative Activity Blackline Masters
- Situation Cards Blackline Masters
- School-to-Home Connection Letter
- Vocabulary Clip Art

TPR Storytelling Book
- Cap. 3A

STUDENT

Practice Workbook
- Vocabulary: 3A-1 – 3A-4
- Grammar: 3A-5 – 3A-7
- Puzzle: 3A-8
- Organizer: 3A-9

Writing, Audio & Video Workbook
- Writing: 3A-1 – 3A-4
- Audio: 3A-5 – 3A-10
- Video: 3A-11

Realidades para hispanohablantes
- Cap. 3A

Transparencies

Vocabulary & Grammar Transparencies
- Chapter Opener: 13, 15–18 (maps)
- *A primera vista:* 65–66
- *Videohistoria:* 9 (graphic organizer), 13 (map), 67–68
- Grammar: 69–72
- *Lectura:* 16 (map)
- *Culture:* 17 (map)

Practice Answers on Transparencies
- Cap. 3A

Fine Art Transparencies
- Transparencies
- Teacher's Guide

Assessment

Assessment Program
- *Pruebas:*
  – Vocabulary recognition: 3A-1
  – Vocabulary production: 3A-2
  – Present tense of ***-er*** and ***-ir*** verbs: 3A-3
  – ***me gustan, me encantan:*** 3A-4
- *Examen del capítulo*: 3A

ExamView Test Bank CD-ROM

Test Preparation Workbook
- Cap. 3A Reading #1
- Cap. 3A Reading #2

Alternative Assessment
- Performance-Based Speaking
- Assessment Program: Rubrics
- Internet Self-Test
- Situation Cards Blackline Masters
- TPR Storytelling Book: Speaking Task

Technology

iText

Mind Point Quiz Show CD-ROM

Resource Pro CD-ROM
- Lesson Planner
- Teacher Resources
- Clip Art

Video Program VHS and DVD
- *A primera vista* video: *El desayuno*
- *GramActiva* Videos:
  – present tense of ***-er*** and ***-ir*** verbs
  – ***me gusta(n), me encanta(n)***

Audio Program CDs
- *A primera vista*
- *Escucha y escribe*
- Audio Activities
- *Pronunciación*
- *Repaso*
- Chapter Listening Test
- Songs

Capítulo 3A

Lesson Plans

Regular Schedule (50 minutes)

For electronic lesson plans: Resource Pro CD-ROM

	Warm-up / Assess	Preview / Present / Practice / Communicate	Wrap-up / Homework Options
DAY 1	**Return Examen del capítulo (10 min.)**	**A primera vista (35 min.)** • Objectives • Presentation: *Vocabulario y gramática en contexto* • *Actividades* 1, 2	**Wrap-up and Homework Options (5 min.)** • Practice Workbook 3A-1, 3A-2 • Go Online • Heritage Language Learner Workbook • Vocabulary Clip Art
DAY 2	**Warm-up (5 min.)** • Homework check	**A primera vista (40 min.)** • Review: *Vocabulario y gramática en contexto* • Presentation: *Videohistoria El desayuno* • View: Video *El desayuno* • Video Activities • *Actividades* 3, 4	**Wrap-up and Homework Options (5 min.)** • *Prueba* 3A-1: Vocabulary recognition • *Actividad* 5 • Practice Workbook 3A-3, 3A-4 • Go Online
DAY 3	**Warm-up (5 min.)** • Homework check ✔**Assessment (10 min.)** • *Prueba* 3A-1: Voc. recognition	**Manos a la obra (30 min.)** • Objectives • *Actividades* 6, 7, 8	**Wrap-up and Homework Options (5 min.)** • *Actividad* 9
DAY 4	**Warm-up (10 min.)** • Homework check • Return *Prueba* 3A-1: Voc. recognition	**Manos a la obra (35 min.)** • *Actividades* 10, 11, 12 • *Exploración del lenguaje*	**Wrap-up and Homework Options (5 min.)** • *Exploración del lenguaje:* Try it out!
DAY 5	**Warm-up (10 min.)** • Homework check	**Manos a la obra (35 min.)** • *Juego: Actividad* 13 • *Conexiones: Actividad* 14 • *Actividad* 15	**Wrap-up and Homework Options (5 min.)** • *Conexiones:* Questions
DAY 6	**Warm-up (5 min.)** • Homework check	**Manos a la obra (40 min.)** • Presentation: Present tense of ***-er*** and ***-ir*** verbs • *GramActiva* Video • *Actividades* 16, 17	**Wrap-up and Homework Options (5 min.)** • *Actividad* 18 • Practice Workbook 3A-5
DAY 7	**Warm-up (5 min.)** • Homework check	**Manos a la obra (40 min.)** • *Actividades* 19, 20, 21, 22 • *Fondo cultural*	**Wrap-up and Homework Options (5 min.)** • *Prueba* 3A-3: Present tense of ***-er*** and ***-ir*** verbs • Go Online
DAY 8	**Warm-up (5 min.)** • Homework check ✔**Assessment (10 min.)** • *Prueba* 3A-3: Present tense of ***-er*** and ***-ir*** verbs	**Manos a la obra (30 min.)** • Presentation: ***Me gusta(n), me encanta(n)*** • *GramActiva* Video • *Actividades* 23, 24	**Wrap-up and Homework Options (5 min.)** • *Actividad* 25 • *Prueba* 3A-2: Vocabulary production • Go Online • Practice Workbook 3A-6, 3A-7

	Warm-up / Assess	Preview / Present / Practice / Communicate	Wrap-up / Homework Options
DAY 9	**Warm-up (5 min.)** • Homework check • Return *Prueba* 3A-3: Present tense of ***-er*** and ***-ir*** verbs ✔**Assessment (10 min.)** • *Prueba* 3A-3: Voc. production	**Manos a la obra (30 min.)** • *Actividades* 26, 27, 28 • *El español en la comunidad* • *Pronunciación*	**Wrap-up and Homework Options (5 min.)** • Go Online • *Prueba* 3A-4: ***Me gusta(n), me encanta(n)***
DAY 10	**Warm-up (5 min.)** • Homework check ✔**Assessment (10 min.)** • *Prueba* 3A-4: ***Me gusta(n), me encanta(n)***	**¡Adelante! (30 min.)** • *Lectura* • *Fondo cultural*	**Wrap-up and Homework Options (5 min.)** • Go Online • *¿Comprendes?*
DAY 11	**Warm-up (5 min.)** • Homework check • Return *Prueba* 3A-4: ***Me gusta(n), me encanta(n)***	**¡Adelante! (40 min.)** • *Presentación oral:* Prepare • *La cultura en vivo*	**Wrap-up and Homework Options (5 min.)** • Go Online
DAY 12	**Warm-up (5 min.)** • Homework check	**¡Adelante! (40 min.)** • *Presentación oral:* Practice	**Wrap-up and Homework Options (5 min.)** • Go Online
DAY 13	**Warm-up (5 min.)** • Homework check	**¡Adelante! (40 min.)** • *Presentación oral:* Present	**Wrap-up and Homework Options (5 min.)** • Writing Activities • Practice Workbook 3A-8, 3A-9
DAY 14	**Warm-up (5 min.)** • Homework check	**¡Adelante! (20 min.)** • *El mundo hispano* **Repaso (20 min.)** • *Vocabulario y gramática* • *Preparación para el examen*	**Wrap-up and Homework Options (5 min.)** • Go Online: Self-test • *Examen del capítulo*
DAY 15	**Warm-up (5 min.)** • Answer questions ✔**Assessment (45 min.)** • *Examen del capítulo*		

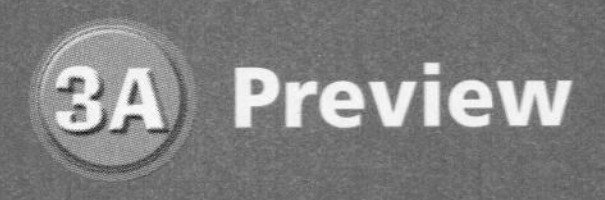

3A Preview

Standards for *Capítulo* 3A

- To achieve the goals of the Standards, students will:

Communication

1.1 Interpersonal

- Talk about: preferences concerning foods and beverages; eating habits during different meals; favorite activities; ***churros y chocolate***

1.2 Interpretive

- Listen to and understand information about food items
- Listen to information about breakfast and lunch
- Read a picture-based story
- Listen to and watch a video about breakfast foods
- Read recipes for meals and beverages in Spanish
- Read information about eating habits during different meals; Read and respond to a magazine food quiz
- Read a restaurant menu; Read about fruits and vegetables of Spanish-speaking countries

1.3 Presentational

- Present information about: foods and beverages; eating habits during meals; the origins of food items; a restaurant menu; food and drink preferences

Culture

2.1 Practices and Perspectives

- Understand: value of fresh fruit from a historical, socioeconomic perspective; breakfast habits; Learn about the ingredients of ***enchiladas***

2.2 Products and Perspectives

- Learn about Bartolomé Murillo and his painting
- Understand many Latin American meals result from the Colombian Exchange of produce items
- Understand the connection between produce exports and economics in Latin American countries
- Learn about ***churros y chocolate***

Connections

3.1 Cross-curricular

- Learn about important artists and their work: Murillo
- Learn about the ingredients of ***enchiladas***
- Learn about the nutritional values of tropical fruits
- Learn how to make ***churros y chocolate***; Learn about geological features of South America
- Learn about Machu Picchu; Learn about the Galápagos Islands and tortoise

Comparisons

4.1 Language

- Learn: new vocabulary through the recognition of cognates; the usage of ***me gusta(n)*** and ***me encanta(n)***
- Understand: the present tense of ***-er*** and ***-ir*** verbs; that nouns can modify other nouns; the pronunciation of the letters ***h*** and ***j***

4.2 Culture

- Compare typical breakfast habits; ***churros y chocolate*** to popular food and drink combinations in the United States
- Understand the Colombian Exchange of produce items
- Compare creation of environmentally protected areas

Communities

5.1 Beyond the School

- Discover the local availability of foods from Spanish-speaking countries

5.2 Life Long Learner

- Realize the value of being able to read a restaurant menu

Tema 3 • La comida

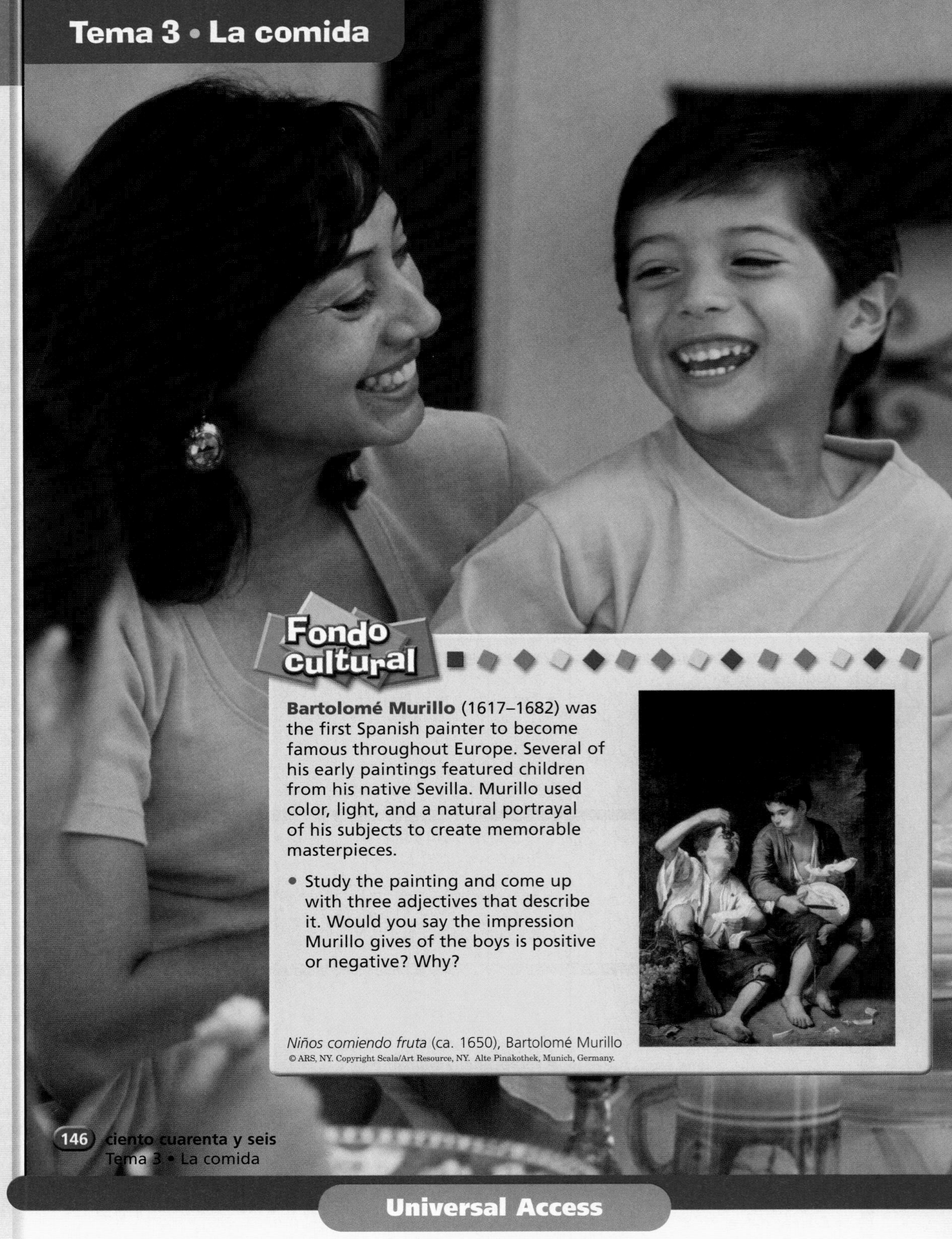

Fondo cultural

Bartolomé Murillo (1617–1682) was the first Spanish painter to become famous throughout Europe. Several of his early paintings featured children from his native Sevilla. Murillo used color, light, and a natural portrayal of his subjects to create memorable masterpieces.

- Study the painting and come up with three adjectives that describe it. Would you say the impression Murillo gives of the boys is positive or negative? Why?

Niños comiendo fruta (ca. 1650), Bartolomé Murillo

Universal Access

Personalizing the Theme

Ask students to describe what they usually eat and drink for breakfast and lunch. What do they eat for breakfast if they are in a hurry? What do they eat for lunch on the weekends?

Heritage Language Learners

Ask students to name fruits, vegetables, and meats that are popular in their heritage countries. Are they available in the United States? If so, have them give an example of where these products are available in your community.

Capítulo 3A

¿Desayuno o almuerzo?

joven familia desayunando en la Ciudad de México, México

Chapter Objectives

- Talk about foods and beverages for breakfast and lunch
- Talk about likes and dislikes
- Express how often something is done
- Understand cultural perspectives on meals

Video Highlights

A primera vista: ***El desayuno***
GramActiva Videos: **present tense of *-er* and *-ir* verbs; *me gustan, me encantan***

Country Connection

As you learn about foods and meals, you will make connections to these countries and places:

For: Online Atlas
Visit: www.phschool.com
Web Code: jae-0002

Enriching Your Teaching

Planning for Instruction

Resources:

- Teacher Express CD-ROM or Resource Book
  - Teaching resources
  - Lesson Planner
  - Chapter Resource Checklist
  - School-to-Home Connection Letter

Culture Note

In Spain, families generally have meals together. Often, lunch is the primary meal. Even in Madrid, offices and stores usually close at 2 P.M. so that workers may go home to have lunch. Work generally resumes around 4 P.M. As a result, people tend to get home around 8 P.M. and eat dinner later. In many families, dinner tends to be more informal than lunch.

Chapter Opener

Presentation

Resources: Voc. & Gram. Transparencies: 13, 15–18 (maps)

Suggestions: Point out the chapter title. Students already know the word ***almuerzo.*** Can they guess the meaning of ***desayuno****?* As students read through the objectives, tell them that they will be learning vocabulary for different foods and beverages and how to say what they like and don't like for breakfast and lunch. In the *Videohistoria*, students will see a comical episode about cultural misunderstandings about what people eat. Explain that different cultures have different practices associated with meals, and that students will explore some of these in this chapter.

The *GramActiva* Videos will reinforce key grammar points taught in the chapter, such as formation of ***-er*** and ***-ir*** verbs. Use the transparencies or refer to the maps at the beginning of the book to locate countries in this chapter.

Standards: 2.1, 2.2, 3.1

Fondo cultural

Resources: Fine Art Transparencies; Fine Art Transparencies Teacher's Guide

Suggestions: To help students answer the question, remind them of the techniques and themes mentioned in the reading. As they choose adjectives, have them keep in mind both content and style.

Answers will vary but may include adjectives such as *touching, simple,* or *realistic*. Students may suggest that Murillo is portraying the boys in a positive sense, as they appear content, despite their possible hardships.

Teaching with Art

Resources: Fine Art Transparencies; Fine Art Transparencies Teacher's Guide

To guide discussion of the painting, ask: How old do you think the boys are? What do you think their relationship is to one another? What is the general feeling that they give off in the painting—distress or contentment? How is that feeling portrayed?

Vocabulario y gramática

Presentation

Standards: 1.2

Resources: Voc. & Gram. Transparencies: 65–66; Resource Book: 3A, Input Script; Resource Book: Cap. 3A, Clip Art; TPR Storytelling Book: Cap. 3A; Audio Program: CD Cap. 3A, Tracks 1–2

Focus: Presenting new vocabulary for foods and beverages eaten for breakfast and lunch

Suggestions: Use the Input Script for *Capítulo* 3A. Tell students what you like and don't like to eat for breakfast, using the short narrative at the bottom of the page as a framework. Have students point to the items in their books as they hear them. You can use transparency 65, pointing to the pictures to confirm students' understanding. Then ask a volunteer to read the narrative. Make a list on the board or overhead of words that cannot be identified through visuals. Have the class work together to understand their meanings. Point out the footnote about the word ***agua.***

Bring in food items and containers or magazine pictures of these foods and ask volunteers to identify each item.

Tell students that they have $8.00 to buy lunch with at *El Restaurante de la Plaza.* Ask them to say what they would like to order.

Additional Resources

- Audio Program: Song CD

A primera vista

Vocabulario y gramática en contexto

Objectives

Read, listen to, and understand information about

- foods and beverages for breakfast and lunch

*Note that *agua* is a feminine noun. However, you use the masculine article *el* to make it easier to say.

"**El desayuno** es mi **comida** favorita. **En el desayuno,** yo **como** cereal **con** leche, tocino y **pan tostado. Todos los días bebo** jugo de naranja. **Nunca** bebo té **sin** leche. Y tú, ¿qué **comes** en el desayuno?"

Universal Access

Students with Learning Difficulties

You may wish to provide students with a two-column chart to help them organize vocabulary. Charts can be found in the *Voc. & Gram. Transparencies* or on the *Teacher Express CD-ROM*. Have students label the columns ***Para beber*** and ***Para comer*** and the rows ***El desayuno*** and ***El almuerzo.***

Multiple Intelligences

Interpersonal / Social: Have students write grocery lists with four or five items that they see in the advertisement. Then, have students work in pairs. Tell students to take turns reading prices from the advertisement while their partner checks items off of the list. This activity will recycle numbers and reinforce vocabulary.

"**Me encanta** el Restaurante de la Plaza. La comida es muy buena. **En el almuerzo,** como una ensalada de frutas o un sándwich de jamón y queso. **Siempre** bebo agua. Es importante **beber** mucha agua, ¿verdad?"

Escuchar

¿Beber o comer?

Listen to the names of ten foods or beverages. If an item is a food, pantomime eating. If it's a beverage, pantomime drinking.

Escuchar

¿El desayuno o el almuerzo?

Listen as different people tell what they are eating. Hold up one hand if the meal is *el desayuno* and hold up both hands if it is *el almuerzo.*

Más práctica

Practice Workbook 3A-1, 3A-2

For: Vocabulary practice
Visit: www.phschool.com
Web Code: jad-0301

Standards: 1.2

Resources: Audio Program: CD Cap. 3A, Track 3; Resource Book: Cap. 3A, Audio Script; Practice Answers on Transparencies

Focus: Listening to food and beverage vocabulary

Suggestions: Use the *Audio CD* or read the script. You may want to decide on standard gestures for eating and drinking, then model them for the class.

Script and Answers:

1. la pizza *(eating)*
2. el perrito caliente *(eating)*
3. el agua *(drinking)*
4. el jamón *(eating)*
5. el té *(drinking)*
6. el pan *(eating)*
7. el queso *(eating)*
8. la limonada *(drinking)*
9. la leche *(drinking)*
10. el cereal *(eating)*

Standards: 1.2

Resources: Audio Program: CD Cap. 3A, Track 4; Resource Book: Cap. 3A, Audio Script; Practice Answers on Transparencies

Focus: Listening to food vocabulary and distinguishing between breakfast and lunch

Suggestions: Use the *Audio CD* or read the script aloud. Pause to check students' progress after each item. Remind students that they should focus on the vocabulary for food and beverages, and that they should not worry about understanding every word.

Script and Answers:

1. Como un sándwich de jamón y queso. *(both hands)*
2. Yo como el pan tostado y jugo de naranja. *(one hand)*
3. Y yo como los huevos con tocino. ¡Mmmm! *(one hand)*
4. Me gusta comer las hamburguesas. *(both hands)*
5. Yo como la ensalada de frutas y pan. *(both hands)*
6. Y yo siempre como el cereal con leche y salchichas. *(one hand)*

Enriching Your Teaching

Culture Note

Often, soft drinks from Spanish-speaking cultures tend to be fruitier and sweeter than drinks consumed in the United States Drinks with natural ingredients are very popular. For example, ***horchata*** is a well known drink in Spain and Mexico. Although the name is the same, the ingredients differ in each location.

Throughout Mexico, it is possible to find ***horchata*** made with water or milk, rice, almonds, cinnamon, and sugar; while in Valencia, Spain, ***horchata*** is made with ***chufa*** (also known as *tiger nut*), water, a touch of cinnamon, and sugar.

Teacher-to-Teacher

Have students write the new food and beverage vocabulary on individual index cards. Collect the cards, fold them two times, and put them into a box. Then assign each student either breakfast or lunch. Tell them to choose three cards out of the box, and tell you if their choices are logical or not, based on the meal that you assigned them.

Presentation

Standards: 1.2

Resources: Voc. & Gram. Transparencies: 67–68; Audio Program: CD Cap. 3A, Track 5

Focus: Presenting additional contextualized vocabulary and grammar; recognizing similarities and differences between breakfast and lunch in Costa Rica and the United States; previewing the video

Suggestions:

Pre-reading: Discuss the questions in the *Strategy.* Making sure that students' books are closed, use the transparencies to ask them to determine what attitudes Tomás and the others have about breakfast. Also, ask them to make predictions about what is going to happen following the end of the story.

Answers will vary but may include:

fruta, pan tostado, huevos, salchicas, tocino, jugo, leche, cereal

1. **How awful!**
2. **He doesn't want to eat a big breakfast, but he doesn't want to insult anyone either.**

Videohistoria

El desayuno

Tomás es de los Estados Unidos. Está en Costa Rica para estudiar. ¿Qué come el primer día? Lee la historia.

Antes de leer

Using prior experience You can use experiences that you have already had to help you understand what you read. Think about eating breakfast. Do you like a big breakfast? A small one? No breakfast at all?

- What do you think Tomás and Raúl have for breakfast?

1. Look at photo 2. Can you figure out from the picture what *¡Qué asco!* means?
2. Look at the photos and describe the problem Tomás is having at breakfast.

Universal Access

Students with Special Needs

You may wish to provide hearing-impaired students with a copy of the video script so that they may follow along and engage in post-viewing activities.

Multiple Intelligences

Verbal / Linguistic: Have students prepare a short dialogue based on the *Videohistoria*, in which they change the foods that are discussed. Encourage them to be comical in their selections. Then have students present their dialogues to the class.

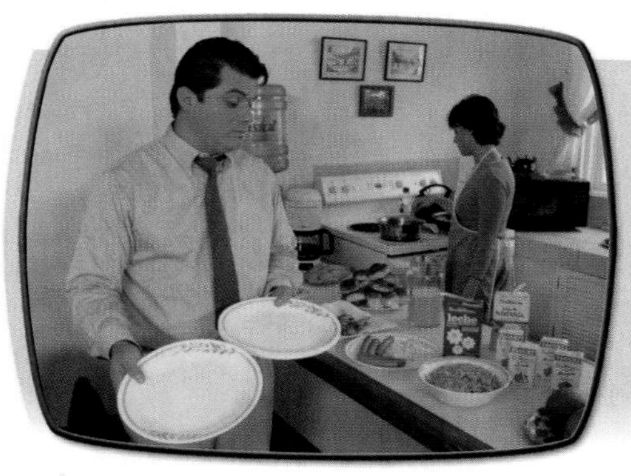

1 **Mamá:** A ver . . . tocino, salchichas, huevos . . .

Papá: ¡Uy! Es mucha comida. No **comprendo.** Tú nunca comes el desayuno.

Mamá: No es mi desayuno. Es para Tomás, **por supuesto.** Los americanos comen mucho en el desayuno.

2 **Raúl:** No comes mucho en el desayuno, ¿verdad?

Tomás: ¡No! **¡Qué asco!**

3 **Tomás:** No me gusta nada el desayuno. A veces bebo jugo de naranja y como pan tostado.

Raúl: Yo tampoco como mucho.

4 **Mamá:** Buenos días, Tomás. Aquí tienes tu desayuno. Huevos, tocino, salchichas, pan tostado, cereal con leche . . .

Tomás: Gracias. Es un desayuno muy bueno. **Me encantan** los huevos y el tocino.

Suggestions:

Reading: Model the dialogue for the first panel with a volunteer. Begin the reading again with volunteers playing the roles of the characters. Using the transparencies, help students understand the new words in blue type.

Post-reading: Complete the activities on p. 153 to check comprehension.

Additional Resources

- Writing, Audio & Video Workbook: Cap. 3A, Video Activity 1

Enriching Your Teaching

Culture Note

Meals in Spanish-speaking countries vary by country and region. In some cities, it is common to have a light breakfast and to have lunch as the main meal. In rural areas, however, families tend to eat what they produce for themselves. Breakfast might include steak, corn, milk, eggs, or beans.

In Costa Rica, breakfast usually includes ***gallo pinto*** (a mix of rice and black beans), eggs, toast, and tropical fruit juice. Have students compare their breakfast with a Costa Rican breakfast, and talk about why such differences might exist.

Video

Presentation

Standards: 1.2

Resources: Video Program: Cap. 3A; Resource Book: Cap. 3A, Video Script

Focus: Listening to new vocabulary presented in story form; using visuals to understand new vocabulary

Suggestions:

Pre-viewing: Tell students that this video is called *El desayuno*. Ask them to list words that they think they will hear in the video.

Viewing: Show the video once without pausing. Show it again, stopping to ask questions and check comprehension. Remind students that they may not understand every word in the video, but that they should listen and watch for overall understanding. Show the segment a final time without pausing. See the *Teacher's Resource Book* for more ways to teach with video.

Post-viewing: Complete Video Activities in the *Writing, Audio & Video Workbook*.

Additional Resources

- Writing, Audio & Video Workbook: Cap. 3A, Video Activities 2–4
- Heritage Learner Workbook: 3A-1, 3A-2

5 **Tomás: Comparto** los huevos, el tocino y las salchichas.

Raúl: ¿Compartes tu desayuno? Muchas gracias, Tomás.

6 **Raúl:** ¿Y qué **bebes?**

Tomás: Jugo de naranja, por favor.

Mamá: Te gusta la leche, ¿no?

Tomás: Más o menos.

7 **Raúl:** Papá, ¿unos huevos?

Papá: No, gracias. ¡La comida es para Uds.!

8 **Mamá: ¿Cuál** es tu almuerzo favorito, Tomás?

Tomás: Me gustan las hamburguesas, la pizza, **la ensalada . . .**

Mamá: Bueno . . . ¡pizza, hamburguesas y ensalada en el almuerzo!

Universal Access

Multiple Intelligences

Visual / Spatial: Have students use the clip art from the *Teacher's Resource Book* or *Teacher Express CD-ROM* to create their own supermarket advertisement based on the example on p. 148. Suggest that they give their supermarket a name, and have them provide a price for each item. As an extension to *Actividad* 3, have students use their advertisements to tell which items Raúl's mother could find at their supermarket and how much she would spend on each item.

Actividad 3 Escribir

La lista

Copy Raúl's mother's shopping list on a separate sheet of paper. Then scan the *Videohistoria* and place a check mark next to the items that she uses to make breakfast for Raúl and Tomás.

Lista para el supermercado

yogur	tocino
queso	jugo de naranja
salchichas	huevos
jamón	pan
galletas	cereal
plátanos	leche

Actividad 4 Leer/Hablar

Los gustos de Tomás

Read the following sentences and tell how Tomás would react, according to the *Videohistoria*. If he would like what is mentioned, say "*¡Me encanta!*" If he wouldn't like it, say "*¡Qué asco!*"

1. En el desayuno hay pan tostado.
2. En el desayuno hay jugo de naranja.
3. En el almuerzo hay pizza.
4. Hoy hay un desayuno muy grande.
5. Hoy hay ensalada en el almuerzo.

Actividad 5 Leer

¿Comprendes?

Read the following sentences. Write the numbers 1–6 on your paper and write *C (cierto)* if a sentence is true, or *F (falso)* if it is false.

1. Tomás está en Costa Rica.
2. La mamá de Raúl siempre come mucho en el desayuno.
3. A Tomás le gusta comer mucho en el desayuno.
4. Hoy Tomás no come mucho en el desayuno.
5. Tomás comparte el desayuno con Raúl.
6. A Tomás le gustan las hamburguesas y la pizza.

Más práctica
Practice Workbook 3A-3, 3A-4

For: Vocabulary practice
Visit: www.phschool.com
Web Code: jad-0302

Enriching Your Teaching

Teacher-to-Teacher

Have students search the Internet for supermarkets in Spanish-speaking countries. Tell them to provide specific brand names and prices for as many of the items on the shopping list in *Actividad* 3 as they can find. Assign students a specific food item and ask them to make a replica using the brand name they found in their search. For example, using art supplies and cardboard, students could make a milk carton with the appropriate Spanish label. Use the products students make as props for later activities.

Actividad 3

Standards: 1.2

Resources: Practice Answers on Transparencies

Focus: Recognizing new vocabulary; reading for comprehension

Suggestions: To be sure students understand the vocabulary, have volunteers come to the board and draw and label each item on the grocery list.

Answers:
salchichas, tocino, jugo de naranja, huevos, pan, cereal, leche

Actividad 4

Standards: 1.1, 1.2

Resources: Practice Answers on Transparencies

Focus: Reading for understanding

Suggestions: Have students skim the *Videohistoria* and make a list of the type of breakfast and lunch foods Tomás likes and another list of those he dislikes. Have students use their lists for this activity.

Answers:
1. ¡Me encanta!
2. ¡Me encanta!
3. ¡Me encanta!
4. ¡Qué asco!
5. ¡Me encanta!

Actividad 5

Standards: 1.2

Resources: Practice Answers on Transparencies

Focus: Reading for comprehension

Suggestions: You may want to do this as a listening activity. Read the sentences aloud and have students write ***cierto*** or ***falso.***

Answers:
1. C
2. F
3. F
4. F
5. C
6. C

Extension: When students answer ***falso,*** have them supply the correct information and identify the panel number in which it is found.

Assessment

- Prueba 3A-1: Vocabulary recognition

Standards: 1.3

Resources: Practice Answers on Transparencies

Focus: Identifying food and beverage-related items

Suggestions: Have students make a list of all of the items in *la cocina de Ana* and use it when they compare the two pictures. Tell students to use ***en vez de*** to say "instead of."

Answers may vary but should include:

en la cocina de Lola:

1. **No hay jamón.**
2. **Hay leche en vez de queso.**
3. **No hay tocino.**
4. **Hay ensalada de frutas en vez de ensalada.**
5. **Hay galletas en vez de cereal.**
6. **Hay sopa en vez de manzanas.**
7. **Hay pizza en vez de un perrito caliente.**

Standards: 1.3

Resources: Voc. & Gram. Transparencies: 2; Practice Answers on Transparencies

Focus: Writing names of breakfast and lunch foods; using a Venn diagram to organize ideas

Suggestions: Ask questions such as: *¿Comes una hamburguesa en el desayuno? ¿Comes yogur en el almuerzo?* By answering these questions, students will begin to classify the foods. Once they have two or three examples, they can fill in the rest of the vocabulary.

Answers may vary but should include:

el desayuno: **los huevos, el tocino, el cereal, el pan tostado, las salchichas**

el almuerzo: **la hamburguesa, las papas fritas, el perrito caliente, la sopa de verduras, los refrescos, el té helado, la limonada, las galletas**

los dos: **el yogur de fresa, el jamón, los plátanos, el café, los jugos, el té, el agua, la leche, el queso, el pan**

Manos a la obra

Vocabulario y gramática en uso

Objectives

- Talk about foods and beverages for breakfast and lunch
- Ask and tell what people eat and drink for breakfast and lunch
- Express likes and dislikes
- Learn to use the present tense of *-er* and *-ir* verbs and *me gustan* / *me encantan*

Pensar/Escribir

Las diferencias

The two kitchens below look identical, but there are several differences. Make a list of as many differences between *la cocina de Ana* and *la cocina de Lola* as you can find.

Modelo

No hay papas fritas en la cocina de Lola.

la cocina de Ana

la cocina de Lola

Universal Access

Advanced Learners

Ask students to think of three brand names of food or drink items. Have them say only the brand name, and call on a volunteer to explain what it is. The student who responds should continue the game by saying another brand name and calling on another volunteer to describe it.

Students with Special Needs

For *Actividad* 7, pair visually impaired students with other students who will say the name of the items pictured in Spanish. Then have the visually impaired students say whether or not the item is appropriate for ***desayuno, almuerzo,*** or ***los dos.***

Actividad 7 **Pensar/Escribir**

El desayuno y el almuerzo

Think about what people usually eat for breakfast and lunch. Copy the Venn diagram on a sheet of paper. Which foods pictured in Actividad 6 would usually be eaten for breakfast or lunch? Write the Spanish words in the appropriate oval for *el desayuno* or *el almuerzo*. Which items could be eaten for either breakfast or lunch? Write them in the overlapping area.

Modelo

el desayuno los dos el almuerzo

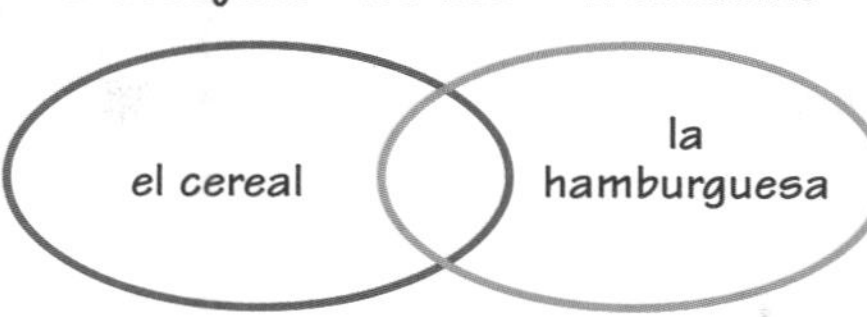

Actividad 8  **Escuchar/Escribir**

¿Dónde están?

You will hear eight descriptions of the drawing of *la cocina de Ana* in Actividad 6. Write the numbers 1–8 on your paper and write the correct food or beverage.

 **Escribir**

¿Qué bebes?

1. On a sheet of paper, make three columns with these headings: *Todos los días, A veces, Nunca.* Under each heading, write the names of the beverages pictured below based on how often you drink them.

1. 
2. 
3. 
4. 
5. 
6. 
7. 

2. Write complete sentences telling how often you drink these beverages.

Modelo

Bebo limonada todos los días.

Practice and Communicate

Rapid Review

To review prepositions, provide a word bank of prepositions on the board. Placing a food prop on, in front of, or behind a desk and ask: *¿Dónde está...?*

 Standards: 1.2

Resources: Audio Program: CD Cap. 3A, Track 6; Resource Book: Cap. 3A, Audio Script; Practice Answers on Transparencies

Focus: Listening to descriptions of foods

Recycle: Location prepositions

Suggestions: Use the *Audio CD* or read the script aloud. Explain that the items near the bottom of the page are in the front, and those near the top are in the back.

Script and Answers:

1. Los huevos están al lado de la ensalada. *(F)*
2. El queso está al lado del jamón. *(F)*
3. La hamburguesa está al lado de las papas fritas. *(C)*
4. Las manzanas están detrás de los plátanos. *(F)*
5. El sándwich está detrás del perrito caliente. *(F)*
6. Las salchichas y el tocino están debajo de los huevos y la ensalada. *(C)*
7. El pan tostado está delante del cereal. *(F)*
8. El yogur está al lado del jamón. *(C)*

 Standards: 1.3

Focus: Writing about food in a personalized context

Suggestions: Draw a sample chart on the board to show students how to set up their papers for this activity. Review the meanings of ***todos los días, a veces,*** and ***nunca.***

Answers will vary.

Enriching Your Teaching

Culture Note

In Mexico, ***limonada*** isn't the only kind of refreshing drink made with fresh fruit juice, water, and sweetener. ***Aguas frescas*** or ***aguas de frutas*** are found throughout Mexico and include three main ingredients: fruit (sometimes seeds or flowers), water, and sugar. They are easy to make and there is no need for a blender.

Follow this easy recipe to make ***agua de melón:***
- 1/2 cantaloupe melon, diced
- 1 quart water
- 1/4 cup sugar to taste

Mash the melon to a coarse pulp and transfer it to a pitcher. Add the water and sugar, stir, and enjoy.

Standards: 1.1

Actividad 10

Focus: Asking and answering questions about eating habits

Suggestions: Have volunteers read the model on the page. Then have them use a vocabulary word not given in the activity to personalize the roles of Student A and Student B. They can also add ***en el desayuno*** or ***en el almuerzo*** to their questions and answers: *¿Comes cereal en el desayuno? Sí, a veces como cereal en el desayuno.*

Answers will vary.

Exploración del lenguaje

Presentation

Standards: 4.1

Resources: Voc. & Gram. Transparencies: 70

Suggestions: Provide an example of a noun modifying another noun in English, such as "peanut butter sandwich." Have students come up with additional examples in English in order to internalize the concept. Refer students to the vocabulary presented on pp.148–149 to complete the *Try it out!* Ask volunteers to share their answers.

You may want to point out that ***la ensalada de frutas*** and ***la sopa de verduras*** have plural modifiers because they are made from a combination of ingredients, while ***la sopa de tomate*** uses the singular because there is only one main ingredient.

Answers will vary but should include:
el yogur de fresa; el jugo de naranja; el jugo de manzana; la ensalada de frutas; el sándwich de jamón y queso; la sopa de verduras
la sopa de tomate **la ensalada de lechuga**
el jugo de piña **el sándwich de pollo**

Extension: Have students create other examples, such as *un sándwich de tocino, lechuga y tomate; un sándwich de huevos y tocino; el jugo de tomate; el yogur de plátano.*

Actividad 10 **Hablar**

¿Qué comes?

Working with a partner, discuss the things that you eat and don't eat.

Modelo

A —*¿Comes cereal?*
B —*Sí, como cereal todos los días.*
o: *No, nunca como cereal.*

Estudiante A

Estudiante B

Sí, todos los días . . .
Sí, a veces . . .
Sí, siempre . . .
No, nunca . . .
No, ¡qué asco!

Exploración del lenguaje

Using a noun to modify another noun

In English, we often use one noun to describe another noun: *vegetable soup, strawberry yogurt.* Notice that the noun that is being described comes second.

In Spanish, however, the noun that is being described comes first and is followed by *de* + the describing noun: *sopa **de** verduras, yogur **de** fresa.* Notice that you don't use a definite article in front of the second noun.

The form of the noun following *de* does not change even when the first noun becomes plural.

el sándwich de **jamón**
los sándwiches de **jamón**

Try it out! Name five or more examples of foods or beverages from this chapter that follow this pattern.

- Now that you know the pattern, say what the food or beverage would be in Spanish using the words paired with the pictures below.

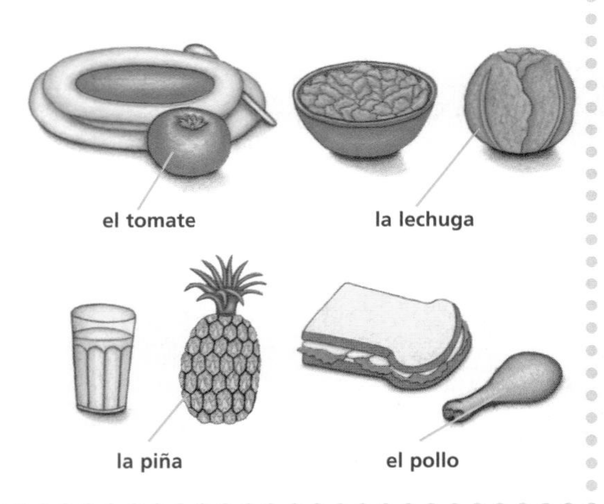

Universal Access

Multiple Intelligences

Visual / Spatial: A fun way to illustrate some of the word combinations in the *Exploración del lenguaje* is to have students cut images from a magazine and paste them on a poster board. For example, students could illustrate ***un sándwich de queso*** by using a photo of a sandwich, the word ***de,*** and a photo of cheese. Have students illustrate the food combinations they create in *Actividad* 11, and post them in the classroom.

Hablar

¿Qué preparas?

You are preparing a meal for your friend. Use *de* and any of the words in the box below to come up with something special. (Some of your combinations may be a bit strange!) Tell your partner what you are making and he or she will respond with *¡Qué asco!* or *¡Me encanta(n)!*

Modelo

un sándwich
A —*Preparo un sándwich de manzanas y huevos.*
B —*¡Qué asco!*
o: *¡Me encanta!*

1. un sándwich
2. una sopa
3. un jugo
4. una ensalada
5. un yogur

verduras	salchichas	plátanos	frutas
fresas	jamón	tocino	perritos calientes
manzanas	queso	huevos	

También se dice . . .

la naranja = la china *(el Caribe)*
el sándwich = el bocadillo *(España)*; la torta *(México)*
el plátano = la banana, el guineo *(el Caribe)*
las papas = las patatas *(España)*
el jugo = el zumo *(España)*
beber = tomar *(México)*

Hablar

Mis comidas favoritas

With a partner, talk about the foods you like and don't like.

Modelo

A —*Te gustan los plátanos, ¿verdad?*
B —*Sí, ¡por supuesto! Me encantan.*

Estudiante A

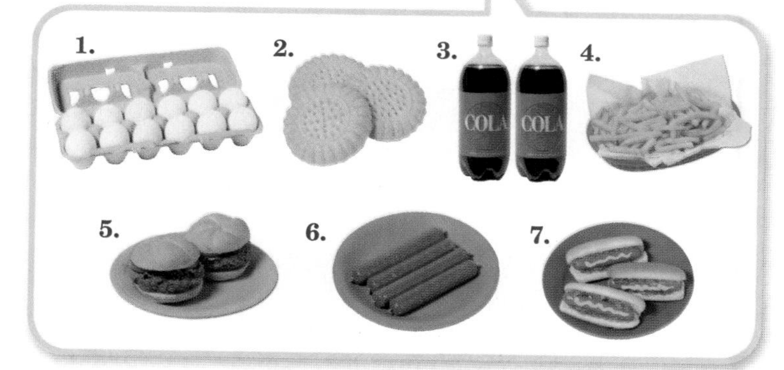

Estudiante B

Sí, ¡por supuesto! Me encantan.
Sí, más o menos.
No, no me gustan.
No, ¡qué asco!
¡Respuesta personal!

Practice and Communicate

3A

Standards: 1.1

Focus: Talking about food in a personalized context

Suggestions: Tell students to use their imagination when creating food combinations. Explain to them that not all of their creations will be appetizing.

Answers will vary.

Extension: Have students report their partner's most creative food combination and have the class vote on the most outrageous creation.

Standards: 1.1

Resources: Practice Answers on Transparencies

Focus: Talking about food

Suggestions: Encourage Student B to respond using *¡Respuesta personal!* along with the words from the Student B list. Have students switch roles.

Answers for Student B will vary. Student A asks:

1. **Te gustan los huevos, ¿verdad?**
2. **Te gustan las galletas, ¿verdad?**
3. **Te gustan los refrescos, ¿verdad?**
4. **Te gustan las papas fritas, ¿verdad?**
5. **Te gustan las hamburguesas, ¿verdad?**
6. **Te gustan las salchichas, ¿verdad?**
7. **Te gustan los perritos calientes, ¿verdad?**

Extension: Have students repeat the activity using drinks, which are sometimes singular. They should say ***me gusta*** and ***me encanta,*** when appropriate. You may want to provide the vocabulary transparency to remind students of vocabulary options.

Enriching Your Teaching

Culture Note

Sandwiches in Spain and Mexico differ in more than just name. In Spain, ***un bocadillo*** may be composed of a hard roll with a piece of cheese, cured beef, or a ***tortilla española***—a Spanish omelette. In Mexico, ***una torta*** almost always contains refried beans, chile, lettuce, tomato, and ham, chicken, or cheese.

Internet Search

Keywords:

Spanish restaurants; Mexican restaurants; bocadillo; tortilla española; torta

Rapid Review

Review the vocabulary for foods and beverages by holding up pictures or homemade flashcards of the items and asking students to respond with the correct word.

Standards: 1.1, 1.3

Focus: Asking and answering questions about food and drink preferences

Suggestions: Be sure that students have made their bingo cards correctly before they begin the game.

Give students a time limit and tell them that they can only speak Spanish. Explain to students that anyone who speaks English will be disqualified. Announce how much time remains in thirty-second to one-minute intervals.

Have the winner read his or her sentences aloud and ask students who responded to verify that the information is correct.

Answers will vary.

Extension: Have students continue the game or start a new game and play "Blackout." Tell students to continue to interview their classmates until all of the squares are filled. Depending on the size of the class, you may want to allow students to enter the name of the same students on more than one square.

Escribir/Hablar

Juego

1. Copy this blank Bingo card on a separate piece of paper. You will need to make it big enough to write a vocabulary word and a person's name in each square.

2. After you have made your Bingo card, write the name of a food or drink from the *Repaso del capítulo* on p. 174 in any order that you want. Be sure to leave enough space at the bottom of each square to write a person's name.

3. Now that you have made your game card, you are ready to interview your classmates. Ask a classmate if he or she drinks a beverage or eats a food item that you have on your card. If the answer is *no,* you will need to ask someone else the same question. If the answer is *sí,* write the classmate's name at the bottom of that square. You can only have a classmate's name on your card once, so after you have found a classmate who says *"sí,"* look for a different person for each of the remaining items on your card. The first person to say *"¡Bingo!"* after completing a horizontal or vertical row wins.

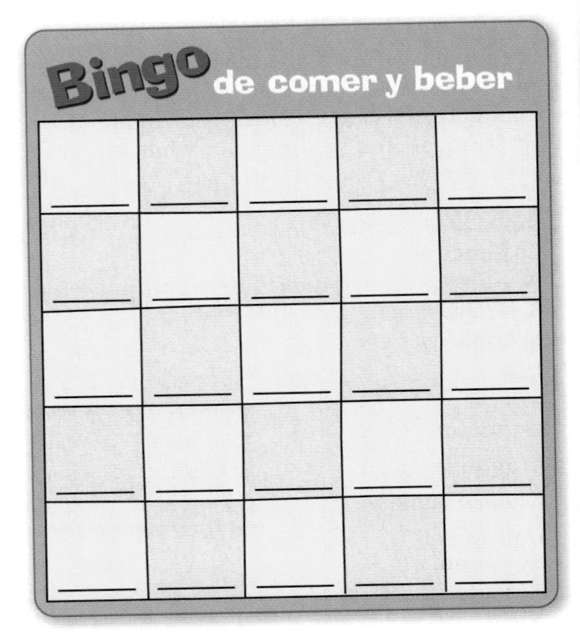

Modelo

A —*Marco, ¿bebes limonada?*
B —*No, ¡qué asco!*
A —*Sarita, ¿bebes limonada?*
C —*Sí. Me encanta.*

You write: *Sarita*

Universal Access

Students with Learning Difficulties

Throughout the book, there are activities that build upon each other, such as *Actividad* 14 and *Actividad* 15. Make sure students are aware of this feature. Reinforce the information learned in the previous activity as students continue with the next one, especially when the activities are completed on different days.

Advanced Learners

Have students use the *Conexiones* reading in *Actividad* 14 to start a research project about the development of the Spanish colonies in Central and South America after the arrival of Columbus. Have students focus on the trade that occurred between Spain and the New World.

Practice and Communicate

Standards: 2.2, 4.2

Actividad 14

Focus: Making a cross-curricular connection to Social Studies / History, focusing on the Columbian Exchange

Suggestions: Before you begin, you may wish to make a list of some of the foods mentioned, and ask students if they have any insights into their origins. After the activity, check to see if students were correct in their predictions. Ask students to tell who they think benefited more from the exchange—the Europeans or the Americans.

Standards: 1.2, 1.3, 2.2, 3.1

Actividad 15

Resources: Practice Answers on Transparencies

Focus: Reading a Mexican recipe and writing about intercultural ingredients.

Suggestions: Have students make a two-column chart labeled "Americas" in the first column, and "Europe" in the second. Have students fill in the chart with the correct foods. Tell students you're going to be making ***enchiladas de pollo*** for dinner and need to make a shopping list. Have volunteers tell you what to put on your list as you write it on the board. Guide students through pronunciation and meaning.

Answers:

Americas:	*Europe:*
tortillas de maíz	pollo
tomates	queso
aceite de maíz	crema

Actividad 14 Leer/Pensar

El intercambio entre dos mundos

Conexiones La historia

Think about how your meals would be different without chicken, pork, beef, milk, cheese, sugar, grapes, and food made from the grains wheat and barley. Europeans brought all these foods to the Americas.

Both sides of the Atlantic Ocean benefited from a product exchange. Starting in the fifteenth century, Columbus took back to Europe a wide range of foods from the Americas that Europeans had never seen before. These foods included corn, beans, squash, tomatoes, limes, avocados, chiles, peanuts, cashews, turkey, pineapples, yams, potatoes, vanilla, and chocolate. Today these foods are found in dishes in many countries.

- What is your favorite meal? Do the ingredients originally come from the Americas, Europe, or elsewhere?

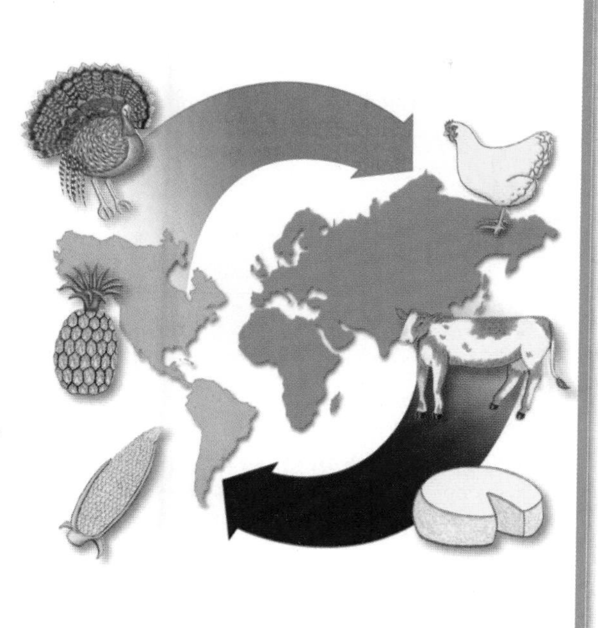

Actividad 15 Leer/Escribir

Enchiladas de pollo

Read the list of ingredients for a traditional Mexican dish of *enchiladas.* Based upon the information you just read and saw in the map, write which ingredients had their origins in the Americas and which came from Europe.

Enchiladas de pollo[1] con salsa de tomate

Ingredientes

12 tortillas de maíz[2]
1 taza[3] de pollo
1 taza de queso fresco[4]
6 tomates grandes[5]
2 cebollas[6] no muy grandes
crema
aceite[7] de maíz

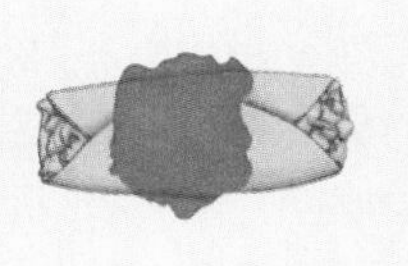

[1]chicken [2]corn [3]cup [4]fresh [5]large [6]onions [7]oil

Enriching Your Teaching

Culture Note

Corn, tomatoes, and chiles are staples of the Mexican kitchen. Tortillas are present at every meal and are even used to make delicious soups. Chiles, tomatoes, and onions are used in many different ways, both raw and cooked, to make a variety of ***salsas*** that may be included in any meal—even breakfast.

Additional Resources

- Writing, Audio & Video Workbook: Cap. 3A, Audio Activities 5–6
- Writing, Audio & Video Workbook: Cap. 3A, Writing Activity 10
- Heritage Language Learner Workbook: 3A-1, 3A-2
- Resource Book: Cap. 3A, Communicative Activity BLM

Assessment

- Prueba 3A-2: Vocabulary production

Practice and Communicate

Rapid Review

Write an ***-ar*** verb on an overhead transparency or on the board, and ask a volunteer to review the conjugation process.

Gramática

Presentation

Standards: 4.1

Resources: Voc. & Gram. Transparencies: 69; Video Program: Cap. 3A; Resource Book: Cap. 3a, Video Script

Suggestions: Direct students' attention to the *¿Recuerdas?* Use the transparency to reinforce the verb forms. Use the lists of familiar infinitives to give students practice with creating the forms of the verbs. Use the *GramActiva* Video to introduce the grammar or to reinforce your own grammar explanation.

Actividad 16

Standards: 1.2, 1.3

Resources: Practice Answers on Transparencies

Focus: Writing complete sentences with forms of an ***-ir*** verb

Suggestions: Point out that each sentence will use a form of the verb ***compartir.*** Remind students that ***tú + yo*** requires the ***nosotros(as)*** form of the verb.

Answers:

1. **Tomás comparte una pizza con María.**
2. **Tú compartes unos sándwiches con Ramón.**
3. **Nosotros compartimos unas papas fritas con los estudiantes.**
4. **Uds. comparten unas galletas con el profesor.**
5. **Ellas comparten unos perritos calientes con nosotros.**
6. **Tú y yo compartimos unos plátanos con Luis y Roberta.**
7. **Yo comparto *(student's choice)* con mi amigo.**

Gramática

Present tense of *-er* and *-ir* verbs

To create the present-tense forms of *-er* and *-ir* verbs, drop the endings from the infinitives, then add the verb endings *-o, -es, -e, -emos / -imos, -éis / -ís,* or *-en* to the stem.

Here are the present-tense forms of *-er* and *-ir* verbs using *comer* and *compartir:*

(yo)	**como**	(nosotros) (nosotras)	**comemos**
(tú)	**comes**	(vosotros) (vosotras)	**coméis**
Ud. (él) (ella)	**come**	Uds. (ellos) (ellas)	**comen**

(yo)	**comparto**	(nosotros) (nosotras)	**compartimos**
(tú)	**compartes**	(vosotros) (vosotras)	**compartís**
Ud. (él) (ella)	**comparte**	Uds. (ellos) (ellas)	**comparten**

¿Recuerdas?

The pattern of present-tense *-ar* verbs is:

toco	tocamos
tocas	tocáis
toca	tocan

- Regular *-er* verbs that you know are *beber, comer, comprender, correr,* and *leer.*
- Regular *-ir* verbs that you know are *compartir* and *escribir.*
- You also know the verb *ver*. It is regular except in the *yo* form, which is *veo.*

GramActiva VIDEO

Want more practice with *-er* and *-ir* verbs? Watch the **GramActiva** video.

Actividad 16 Gramática **Escribir**

¿Quiénes comparten el almuerzo?

On a separate sheet of paper, write complete sentences saying what each person is sharing and with whom.

Modelo

Elena / una manzana / Raúl
Elena comparte una manzana con Raúl.

1. Tomás / una pizza / María
2. tú / unos sándwiches / Ramón
3. nosotros / unas papas fritas / los estudiantes
4. Uds. / unas galletas / el profesor
5. ellas / unos perritos calientes / nosotros
6. tú y yo / unos plátanos / Luis y Roberta
7. yo / ¿–? / mi amigo

Una familia almorzando

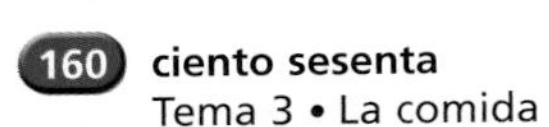

Universal Access

Students with Learning Difficulties

When presenting the *Gramática*, point out the infinitives and demonstrate how the ***-er*** and ***-ir*** are removed and new endings added. Ask students to recall the process of changing verb forms with ***-ar*** verbs. Some students may benefit from repeating the conjugations with new endings until they have internalized the process.

Multiple Intelligences

Visual / Spatial: Have students draw pictures to illustrate the ***-er*** and ***-ir*** verbs they know. Ask them to write a subject pronoun for each illustration. Have pairs exchange papers and say what the people are doing in the drawings.

Actividad 17 Gramática **Leer/Escribir**

Una tarjeta postal

Read the following postcard from your friend Carolina in Venezuela. Number your paper from 1–8 and write the correct form of the appropriate verb in parentheses.

¡Hola!

Elena y yo estamos en Caracas. Nosotras __1.__ (*comprender / correr*) todos los días y __2.__ (*comer / ver*) muy bien.

Los estudiantes aquí __3.__ (*comer / leer*) mucha pizza y __4.__ (*ver / beber*) mucho café. Ellos __5.__ (*leer / beber*) muchos libros y __6.__ (*escribir / ver*) mucho también para las clases. Las clases son difíciles pero me encantan.

En la clase de español nosotros __7.__ (*correr / leer*) revistas y cuentos en español. Elena __8.__ (*comprender / beber*) muy bien pero para mí es un poco difícil.

Tengo que estudiar. Hasta luego.

Tu amiga,
Carolina

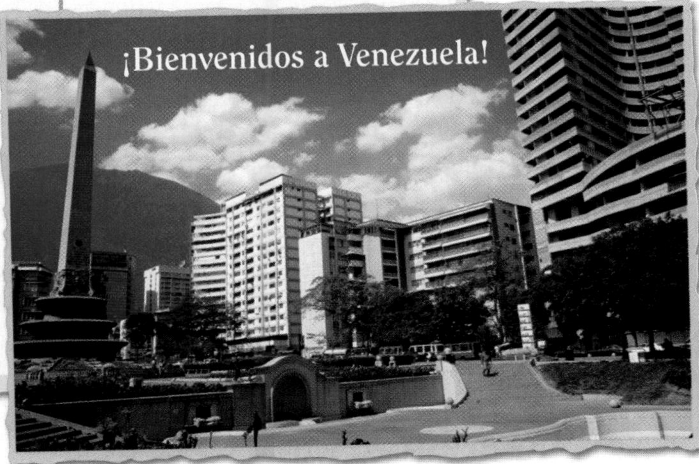

Actividad 18 Gramática **Escribir**

El desayuno con la familia Acevedo

You have been invited to Sunday breakfast at the Acevedo house. Write five sentences to describe what everyone is doing. Be sure to use a different subject and a different verb for each sentence.

Modelo
Nosotros vemos la tele.

- el Sr. Acevedo
- yo
- Francisco y Marta
- la Sra. Acevedo
- nosotros

- ver la tele
- leer una revista
- correr a la puerta
- compartir un desayuno muy bueno
- beber jugo de manzana
- comer yogur de fresas
- **¡Respuesta personal!**

Standards: 1.2, 1.3

Actividad 17

Resources: Practice Answers on Transparencies

Focus: Reading a letter and writing correct verb forms

Suggestions: Encourage students to scan the paragraph before writing the verb forms. Remind students to use context and prior knowledge for comprehension when reading. This can be assigned as homework.

Answers:

1. **corremos**
2. **comemos**
3. **comen**
4. **beben**
5. **leen**
6. **escriben**
7. **leemos**
8. **comprende**

Common Errors: Students may conjugate a verb incorrectly when given a proper name instead of a subject pronoun. Help these students see the connection by writing the appropriate pronoun for each subject.

Extension: Ask students to write three statements about Elena's postcard, which can be true or false. Have them read the sentences aloud, and ask the other students to determine if they're true.

Standards: 1.3

Actividad 18

Resources: Practice Answers on Transparencies

Focus: Describing a family breakfast

Suggestions: Be sure students understand that this activity is not based on a specific scenario and that there could be several sentence combinations for the same subject. Encourage students to use the *¡Respuesta personal!*

Answers will vary but may include:
El Sr. Acevedo lee la revista.
Yo veo la tele.
Francisco y Marta corren a la puerta.
La Sra. Acevedo come yogur de fresas.
Nosotros bebemos jugo de manzana.

Enriching Your Teaching

Culture Note

In Latin America, to say what they eat for breakfast, people often use the verb ***desayunar:*** *Desayunamos huevos con tocino.* ***Comer*** can be used for any meal, but it's generally used when referring to lunch, and ***cenar*** is used to refer to the evening meal. ***Almuerzo*** is another word used throughout Latin America to describe lunch.

Rapid Review

Use transparency 70 to quickly review food vocabulary.

Standards: 1.1, 1.2

Resources: Practice Answers on Transparencies

Focus: Asking questions using ***comer*** and ***beber***

Suggestions: Ask volunteers to demonstrate the models. Point out that no article is necessary in front of the names of the foods and drinks. Remind students that in item 6, Student B's answers will vary.

Answers:

1. **¿Qué comen Raúl y Gloria en el desayuno? Raúl y Gloria comen huevos.**
2. **¿Qué comes tú en el almuerzo? Yo como hamburguesas.**
3. **¿Qué comen Graciela y Carlos en el desayuno? Graciela y Carlos comen cereal.**
4. **¿Qué come Carolina en el almuerzo? Carolina come yogur con fresas.**
5. **¿Qué beben tu familia y tú en el desayuno? Nosotros bebemos jugo de naranja.**
6. **¿Qué comes tú en el almuerzo? Yo como *(answers will vary).***

Extension: When students complete the dialogues, have volunteers repeat them for the class. Ask whether they themselves eat or drink the items mentioned.

Standards: 1.1, 1.3

Resources: Resource Book: Cap. 3A, GramActiva BLM

Focus: Writing and talking about foods in a personalized context

Suggestions: Give students a copy of the chart or have them create their own. You might also provide a list of other words that students want to use. Have students complete the activity and keep the chart for *Actividad* 21.

Answers will vary.

Theme Project

Give students copies of the Theme Project outline and rubric from the *Teacher's Resource Book.* Explain the task to them, and have them perform step 1. (For more information, see p. 146-a.)

Actividad 19 Gramática — Hablar

¿Qué beben y qué comen?

Work with a partner. Use the verbs *comer* and *beber* to ask questions. Then answer them, following the models.

Juan / desayuno

Modelo

A —*¿Qué come Juan en el desayuno?*
B —*Juan come pan tostado.*

Miguel y Carlos / almuerzo

Modelo

A —*¿Qué beben Miguel y Carlos en el almuerzo?*
B —*Miguel y Carlos beben limonada.*

Para decir más . . .

la crema de cacahuates peanut butter
el pan dulce breakfast pastry
el panqueque pancake
el pollo chicken

1. Raúl y Gloria / desayuno

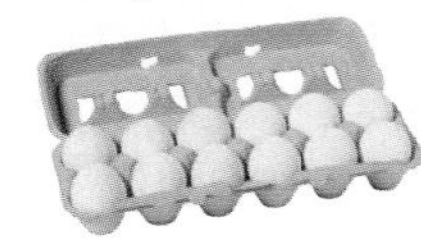

2. tú / almuerzo

3. Graciela y Carlos / desayuno

4. Carolina / almuerzo
5. tu familia y tú / desayuno
6. tú / almuerzo

¡Respuesta personal!

Actividad 20 — Hablar/Escribir

Los sábados y la comida

Talk about what you and your classmates eat and drink for breakfast and lunch on Saturdays. Make a chart like the one below on a sheet of paper and complete each box with information about yourself. Then survey two classmates to find out what their habits are. Record the information in the chart.

Modelo

Los sábados, ¿qué comes en el desayuno? ¿Qué bebes?
¿Qué comes en el almuerzo? ¿Qué bebes?

	¿Qué comes?	¿Qué bebes?
el desayuno	yo: huevos, pan tostado, tocino Sandra: cereal, plátanos	
el almuerzo		

Universal Access

Students with Learning Difficulties

To help students organize the information in *Actividad* 20, provide them with colored pencils. Have them use a different colored pencil for each classmate they include in their survey. This will make it easier for students to find information on their charts.

Advanced Learners

Tell students to keep a one-week record of what they have for breakfast and lunch. Each day they should list all of the items they eat and drink. At the end of the week ask them to share their journals with the class. Discuss what the most popular foods and drinks are among students.

Actividad 21 Escribir/Hablar

Los hábitos de la clase

Use your completed chart from Actividad 20 to write summary statements based on your survey. Be prepared to read your sentences to the class.

Modelo

Sandra y yo comemos huevos y cereal en el desayuno.
Gregorio no bebe jugo de naranja en el desayuno y le gusta mucho la leche.
Sofía come cereal y bebe leche en el desayuno.

Actividad 22 Escribir/Hablar

Y tú, ¿qué dices?

1. ¿Qué comen tú y tus amigos en el almuerzo?
2. ¿Compartes la comida con tus amigos? ¿Qué compartes?
3. ¿Qué bebes en el desayuno?
4. ¿Qué libros lees en tu clase de inglés?
5. ¿Quién corre rápido *(fast)* en tu clase de educación física?
6. ¿Ves la tele en tu clase de ciencias sociales? ¿Qué ves?

¿Recuerdas?

Since the verb endings indicate who is doing the action, you can often use the verb without the subject pronoun.

- **escribo** *I write*
- **escribimos** *we write*

Fondo cultural

¿Qué comen en el desayuno?

El desayuno From the popular *churros* (fried dough rolled in sugar) and hot chocolate in Spain to the *pan dulce* served in many countries, a wide variety of foods can be found on the breakfast table in the Spanish-speaking world. Most often, people prefer a light breakfast of bread or a roll, coffee or tea, and possibly juice. Items such as cereal, milk, eggs, ham, or sausage are less common.

- In Spain you can ask for a *desayuno americano*. What do you think you would be served?

Más práctica
Practice Workbook 3A-5

Go Online PHSchool.com
For: Practice with *-er* and *-ir* verbs
Visit: www.phschool.com
Web Code: jad-0303

Enriching Your Teaching

Culture Note

Pan dulce is a dome-shaped pastry traditionally topped with sweet vanilla or chocolate crumbles. As the name implies, it is sweet bread, but not as sweet as American pastries. It is often eaten with ***chocolate,*** a thick, frothy hot chocolate lightly flavored with cinnamon and ground almonds.

Internet Search

Keywords:

pan dulce + history + Mexico

Actividad 21 *Standards:* 1.3

Focus: Writing and reading sentences based on chart information

Suggestions: Remind students to use the chart from *Actividad* 20 to complete this activity. Be sure that sentences include correct verb forms. Write a sample sentence on the board to get students started. Ask volunteers to say their completed sentences for the class.

Answers will vary.

Actividad 22 *Standards:* 1.1, 1.3

Focus: Writing and speaking about meals, activities, and classes

Recycle: Classroom vocabulary

Suggestions: When students complete the activity, have volunteers ask the questions and call on classmates to respond.

Answers will vary.

Standards: 1.2, 2.1, 4.2

Fondo cultural

Suggestions: Have students discuss what they typically eat for breakfast, and tell what their idea of an American breakfast is.

Answers: will vary but may include cereal, bacon, eggs, sausages, waffles, and pancakes.

Additional Resources

- Writing, Audio & Video Workbook: Cap. 3A, Audio Activity 7, Track 11
- Writing, Audio & Video Workbook: Cap. 3A, Writing Activity 11
- Resource Book: Cap. 3A, Communicative Activity BLM

Assessment

- Prueba 3A-3: Present tense of ***-er*** and ***-ir*** verbs

3A Practice and Communicate

Gramática

Presentation

Standards: 4.1

Resources: Video Program: 3A; Resource Book: Cap. 3A, Video Script

Suggestions: Use the *GramActiva* Video either as an initial introduction or as a follow-up to your explanation. Have students brainstorm foods and drinks and write them in the plural on the board. Ask volunteers to tell their likes and dislikes using ***me gustan, no me gustan,*** or ***me encantan*** and the words listed on the board. Then provide some singular nouns to show the contrast.

Standards: 1.2

Resources: Audio Program: CD Cap. 3A, Track 9; Resource Book: Cap. 3A, Audio Script; Practice Answers on Transparencies

Focus: Listening to food vocabulary and indicating likes and dislikes using manipulatives

Suggestions: Use the *Audio CD* or read the script aloud. Pause after each item to check the responses.

Script:

1. la sopa
2. las hamburguesas
3. el tocino
4. las fresas
5. el pan
6. el yogur
7. las galletas
8. los huevos

Answers will vary but should include:

1. gusta
2. gustan
3. gusta
4. gustan
5. gusta
6. gusta
7. gustan
8. gustan

Standards: 1.3

Focus: Writing personalized sentences about food preferences

Suggestions: Assign this activity for homework. When students have finished the sentences, ask volunteers to express their opinions to the class. For each statement, ask a follow-up question to another student, such as: *¿Y a ti? ¿Te gustan también...?*

Answers will vary but should include: ***me gusta(n), no me gusta(n) nada,*** or ***me encantan.***

Gramática

Me gustan, me encantan

Use *me gusta* and *me encanta* to talk about a singular noun.

Me gusta **el té** pero me encanta **el té helado.**

Use *me gustan* and *me encantan* to talk about plural nouns.

Me encantan **las fresas** pero no me gustan mucho **los plátanos.**

When you use *me gusta(n)* and *me encanta(n)* to talk about a noun, include *el, la, los,* or *las.*

Me encanta **el** jugo de naranja pero no me gusta **la** leche.

¿Qué te gustan más, **las** hamburguesas o **los** perritos calientes?

GramActiva VIDEO

Want more help with *me gusta(n)/ me encanta(n)?* Watch the **GramActiva** video.

Actividad 23 Gramática Escuchar/GramActiva

¿Gusta o gustan?

1. Tear a sheet of paper in thirds. On the first piece, write *No.* On the second piece write *me gusta.* On the third piece, write *n.*
2. You will hear eight food items. Indicate when you like or don't like the items by holding up one, two, or all three pieces of paper. Remember to use *me gustan* when the item you hear is plural.

Actividad 24 Gramática Escribir

¿Qué te gusta?

Indicate how much you do or do not like the following foods.

Modelo

Me gustan las manzanas.
o: *No me gustan nada las manzanas.*
o: *Me encantan las manzanas.*

1. 
2. 
3. 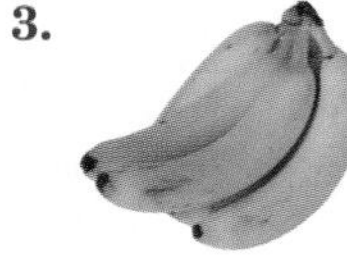
4.
5. 
6. 

Universal Access

Students with Special Needs

For *Actividad* 23, some students may have difficulty manipulating three pieces of paper. It may be better for you to provide students with four different index cards, saying ***me gusta, me gustan, no me gusta,*** and ***no me gustan.***

Advanced Learners

Have students save the manipulatives from *Actividad* 23 to use in other activities in this chapter. Ask students to use them when you are reviewing activities such as *Actividad* 24. You can also have students make cards with ***te gusta*** and ***le gusta*** as well as others using ***encantar.***

  Leer/Escribir

Un *quiz* personal

A popular magazine has provided this survey to see how much you and a friend have in common. Read the survey. Then, for each item on the quiz, write a sentence describing which choice you like the most. Write your sentences on a sheet of paper.

Modelo

Me gusta más la comida italiana.

¿Qué te gusta más?

¿Tu amigo(a) y tú son muy similares o muy diferentes?

Completa este quiz y compara tus respuestas con las de un(a) amigo(a).

1. la comida mexicana o la comida italiana
2. el desayuno o el almuerzo
3. el cereal con fruta o el cereal sin fruta
4. las revistas o los libros
5. la música rock o la música rap
6. los amigos graciosos o los amigos serios
7. las hamburguesas con queso o las hamburguesas sin queso

Respuestas similares:

7–6	¡Uds. son gemelos![1]
5–4	Tienen mucho en común, ¿verdad?
3–2	¡Un poco similar y un poco diferente!
1–0	¿Los opuestos[2] se atraen?[3] ¡Por supuesto!

[1]twins [2]opposites [3]attract

  Hablar

¿Amigos similares o diferentes?

Working in pairs, take turns asking your partner about the survey items in Actividad 25. Keep track of your similarities and differences. See how the magazine rates you.

Modelo

A —*¿Qué te gusta más, la comida mexicana o la comida italiana?*
B —*Me gusta más la comida italiana.*
o: *No me gusta ni la comida mexicana ni la comida italiana.*
A —*A mí me gusta la comida mexicana.*
o: *A mí también.*
o: *A mí tampoco.*

Practice and Communicate

 *Standards:* 1.1, 1.3

Resources: Voc. & Gram. Transparencies: 71

Focus: Answering survey questions about likes and dislikes

Recycle: Definite articles

Suggestions: Have students read the entire survey for comprehension before writing their answers. You may wish to provide your own preferences as a model for the students.

Answers will vary.

Extension: Using the survey as a model, have students create their own survey, consisting of five to seven questions. They should include items that have to do with food, school, and leisure time activities.

 *Standards:* 1.1

Focus: Comparing preferences

Recycle: ***ni...ni; a mí también; a mí tampoco;*** vocabulary from previous chapters

Suggestions: Before beginning the activity, choose one of the items on the quiz and call on a volunteer. Follow the model to compare your preference with that of the volunteer.

Answers will vary.

Enriching Your Teaching

Teacher-to-Teacher

For more practice with the concept of ***me gustan*** and ***me encantan,*** write a list of specific people, places, and things that students can identify. You can use sports teams, individual athletes, individual singers, musical groups, or other celebrities. Have students work in pairs to ask and say whether or not they like the items on the list. Have students make their own survey like the one in *Actividad* 25. Encourage them to be creative with their questions.

Standards: 1.1, 1.2, 1.3

Focus: Talking about what you need at the supermarket

Suggestions: Review the numbers from 1–100 with students. Point out that the ad is from the United States, so they will be using ***dólares*** and ***centavos*** to talk about prices.

Answers: will vary.

El español en la comunidad

Presentation

Standards: 5.1

Focus: Enhancing Spanish language and cultural knowledge through community experiences

Suggestion: Have students talk about items they have eaten that are typical of Spanish-speaking cultures. Can they identify what specific culture each food comes from? Ask them to brainstorm a list of items that might not be well-known in the United States. Compile students' findings into one list, type it, and distribute copies to each student as a shopping list of new items to try.

Leer/Hablar/Escribir

Necesito mucho del supermercado

You and your friend are going food shopping in San Antonio, Texas. Look at the following advertisement and decide with your partner what items you should put on your shopping list. When you decide that you need an item, write it on your list.

Modelo

A —*¿Necesitamos huevos?*
B —*Sí, me encantan los huevos.*
o: *No, ¡qué asco! No me gustan los huevos.*

El español en la comunidad

Foods from different Spanish-speaking countries have become very popular in the United States. Visit a local grocery store and make a list of different foods that come from Spanish-speaking countries.

- Which of these foods have you tried? How do they compare to foods that you normally eat?

Universal Access

Students with Learning Difficulties

For *Actividad* 28, have students read the *¿Comprendes?* questions first, then refer them to the visuals before asking them to read the menu.

Heritage Language Learners

Be sure to emphasize the distinction between ***h*** and ***j*** with students. It is not uncommon to see the silent ***h*** left out in writing, so monitor this carefully when checking student work.

Pronunciación

The letters *h* and *j*

In Spanish, the letter *h* is never pronounced. Listen to and say these words:

hora	hablar	hasta	hola
hoy	hace	hacer	hotel

The letter *j* is pronounced like the letter *h* in *hat* but with more of a breathy sound. It is made far back in the mouth—almost in the throat. Listen to and say these words:

trabajar	dibujar	jugar	videojuegos
hoja	jueves	junio	julio

Try it out! Find and say five or more examples of foods or beverages from this chapter that have *h* or *j* in their spelling.

Try it out! Say this *trabalenguas* (tongue twister) three times, as fast as you can:

Debajo del puente de Guadalajara había un conejo debajo del agua.

Actividad 28 **Leer/Escribir**

¿Qué comida hay en el Ciberc@fé @rrob@?

Menú del Ciberc@fé @rrob@

Desayunos

No. 1 Huevos: *(jamón, tocino, chorizo[1])* $18.00
Con cóctel de fruta $20.00

No. 2 Sincronizadas: *(tortilla de harina,[2] queso amarillo, jamón)* $22.00
Con cóctel de fruta $24.00

No. 3 Cuernitos: *(jamón, queso, tomate y lechuga)* $20.00
Con cóctel de fruta $22.00

No. 4 Chilaquiles: *verdes o rojos (con pollo o huevos)* $14.00
Con cóctel de fruta $16.00

No. 5 Omelet: *(con pollo, jamón, tomate, cebolla, champiñones[3] o queso)* $18.00

No. 6 Crepas *(champiñones, jamón, pollo)* $12.50

Refrescos $5.00 Café $4.00 Jugos $7.50 Té o té helado $4.00

Tel: 212 03 95 **16 de septiembre #65, Col. Centro**

[1]spicy sausage [2]flour [3]mushrooms

Strategy

Skimming
Look quickly through the menu. What meal is featured? Find three dishes you recognize and two that are new to you.

1 Read the menu and answer the questions on a separate sheet of paper.

1. Comes el desayuno No. 1 con té. ¿Cuál es el precio *(price)* del desayuno?
2. No te gustan nada los huevos. ¿Qué comes del menú?
3. Te encanta la fruta. ¿Qué bebes?

2 Use the cyber café menu as a model menu to create a lunch menu using the vocabulary in this chapter.

Más práctica
Practice Workbook 3A-6, 3A-7

Go Online PHSchool.com
For: Practice with *me gusta(n)/me encanta(n)*
Visit: www.phschool.com
Web Code: jad-0304

Practice and Communicate

Pronunciación

Presentation

Standards: 4.1

Resources: Audio Program: CD Cap. 3A, Track 10; Resource book: Cap. 3A, Audio Script

Suggestions: Use an exaggerated tone to emphasize the pronunciation distinctions as you read through the list. If you choose to use the *Audio CD,* pause it after each word and repeat the word. Have students say it with you a third time.

Try it out! Have the class refer to pp. 148–149 for food vocabulary. Ask them to say examples of ***h*** and ***j*** words.

Try it out! Read through the ***trabalenguas*** slowly with class. Use the picture to help students grasp the meaning. You may want to explain that ***había*** means "there was." Then have them read it together a few times. Finally, ask volunteers to say the ***trabalenguas*** for the class.

Actividad 28 *Standards:* 1.2, 1.3, 4.1, 5.2

Resources: Voc. & Gram. Transparencies: 72; Practice Answers on Transparencies

Focus: Reading a menu

Suggestions: Direct students' attention to the *Strategy*. Have the class list familiar foods and identify new ones using the footnotes at the bottom of the menu. After students have written the answers to the questions, ask volunteers to read and answer the questions for the class.

Answers:

1. **$22.00 *(veintidós dólares)***
2. **Como sincronizadas, chilaquiles con pollo, cuernitos o crepas.**
3. **Bebo jugos.**

Enriching Your Teaching

Culture Note

There are several Mexican dishes made from leftover tortillas, including one called ***chilaquiles.*** The tortillas are cut into strips, dried, fried, and then cooked in a sauce made from tomato, onion and lots of chile. They are then covered with cheese and heavy cream. This is a breakfast favorite.

Cuernitos are croissants and are often served as a sandwich with ham, cheese, and tomato. ***Sincronizadas*** are two flour tortillas with ham and cheese in the middle. They are first grilled on both sides, then cut into four even pieces.

Theme Project

Students can perform step 2 at this point. Be sure they understand your corrections. (For more information, see p. 146-a.)

Additional Resources

- Writing, Audio & Video Workbook: Audio Activity 8–9, Tracks 12–13
- Writing, Audio & Video Workbook: Writing Activity 12–2
- Heritage Learner Workbook: 3A-3, 3A-4, 3A-5

Assessment

- Prueba 3A-4: ***Me gustan, me encantan***

Lectura

Presentation

Standards: 1.2, 1.3, 3.1, 4.1

Focus: Reading about fruits and vegetables native to the Americas; reading a recipe for a ***licuado***

Suggestions:

Pre-reading: Direct students' attention to the *Strategy*. Have students look at the photos and ask if they recognize the fruits and vegetables. Have them look at the recipe on p. 169 and identify which part lists ingredients and which part is the instructions.

Reading: Remind students that it is not important to understand every word, but rather the passage as a whole. Have students discuss the question about which of these fruits they enjoy eating, or if they have not tried them, which look interesting. Have students predict what the recipe makes. As they read, ask them to write down unknown words on a separate sheet of paper. Then have them go back and attempt to find the meanings of these words based on their background knowledge and visual cues.

Post-reading: Have students write their answers to the *¿Comprendes?* questions as homework and then share them in class the next day.

Additional Resources

- Heritage Learner Workbook: 3A-6

¡Adelante!

Objectives

- Read about fruits that are native to the Americas
- Learn about a snack in Spanish-speaking countries, *churros y chocolate*
- Maintain a conversation about what you like, including your food preferences
- Learn facts about the northern part of South America

Lectura

Frutas y verduras de las Américas

Hay muchas frutas y verduras que son originalmente de las Américas que hoy se comen en todos los países. Las verduras más populares son la papa, el maíz, los frijoles y muchas variedades de chiles. También hay una gran variedad de frutas como la papaya, la piña y el aguacate. Estas frutas y verduras son muy nutritivas, se pueden preparar fácilmente y son muy sabrosas. La papaya y la piña son frutas que se comen en el desayuno o de postre. ¿Cuáles de estas frutas comes?

Strategy

Making guesses
When you find an unknown word, try to guess the meaning. Is it a cognate? What might it mean within the context of the reading and other words around it? Keep reading and the meaning may become clear.

la papaya
Es una fruta con mucha agua. Es perfecta para el verano. Tiene más vitamina C que la naranja.

el aguacate
La pulpa del aguacate es una fuente de energía, proteínas, vitaminas y minerales. Tiene vitaminas A y B.

el mango
Aunque[1] el mango es originalmente de Asia, se cultiva en las regiones tropicales de muchos países de las Américas. Tiene calcio y vitaminas A y C como la naranja.

[1]Although

Universal Access

Students with Learning Difficulties

When students are given longer reading passages, it may be beneficial to pair students with learning difficulties with a more skillful reader who can help them to apply the reading strategies that they have learned. These strategies might include sing their prior knowledge, visual cues, or cognates to deduce meaning.

Multiple Intelligences

Visual / Spatial: Have students research fruits from Latin America and prepare a poster showing pictures and informative captions in Spanish.

Licuado de plátano

El licuado es una bebida muy popular en los países tropicales. ¡Es delicioso y muy nutritivo!

Ingredientes:
1 plátano
2 vasos de leche
1 cucharadita de azúcar
hielo

Preparación:
1. Cortar el plátano.
2. Colocar los ingredientes en la licuadora.
3. Licuar por unos 5 ó 10 segundos.

¿Comprendes?

1. ¿Qué vitaminas tienen las frutas en la página anterior?
2. De las frutas y verduras en el artículo, ¿cuáles *(which ones)* te gustan? ¿Cuáles no te gustan?
3. ¿Qué otras frutas te gustan? ¿Comes estas frutas en el desayuno o en el almuerzo?
4. ¿Qué fruta no es originalmente de las Américas?

Frutas y verduras During winter, the United States imports a wide range of fruits from Chile such as cherries, peaches, and grapes. When you purchase grapes from a supermarket in January, look to see if they have a label that says *Producto de Chile* or *Importado de Chile.*

- What are some other fruits and vegetables in your local market that are products of other countries?

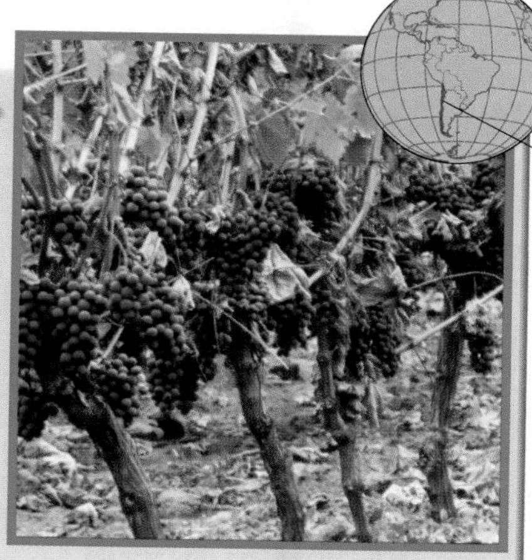

Go Online PHSchool.com
For: Internet link activity
Visit: www.phschool.com
Web Code: jad-0305

Enriching Your Teaching

Culture Note

In Latin America there are many little shops that sell ***licuados*** made from different fruits. A ***licuado*** can serve as a quick meal any time during the day.

Teacher-to-Teacher

If you plan to prepare a variety of foods and beverages for your students, you may want to submit your class lists to the school nurse first. Ask him or her to check for any allergies that are on record for your students. That way, you'll know who needs to avoid anything you are preparing.

Licuado de plátano

Suggestions: If possible, have volunteers bring in the ingredients and supplies to make the recipe in class. Be absolutely certain that students do not have food allergies before doing this. Have students read the ingredients and point to each item. Ask the class to read the recipe and tell you what to do. Provide them with the phrase ***Ud. necesita...*** so that they are able to give you instructions.

Standards: 1.2, 1.3

¿Comprendes?

Resources: Practice Answers on Transparencies

Focus: Writing and talking about the information in the reading

Suggestions: Have students read each question and then re-read the text, looking for key words to answer the questions. When students complete the activity, have one student ask the questions and volunteers give their answers.

Answers:
1. **Las frutas tienen vitaminas A, B y C.**
2. **Answers will vary.**
3. **Answers will vary.**
4. **el mango**

Standards: 2.2, 5.1

Suggestions: After reading the passage, you may wish to ask students to begin a sticker collection. Reward them with a point or other compensation for every sticker that they bring in from fruits imported from a Spanish-speaking country. Title a blank piece of poster board *Las frutas importadas*, have students add the stickers, and display it in class.

Answers will vary but may include citrus fruits, pears, avocados, papayas, and guava fruit.

3A Culture

La cultura en vivo

Presentation

 *Standards:* 2.2, 3.1, 4.2

Focus: Reading about making ***churros*** and ***chocolate***

Presentation: Begin a class discussion about snack foods. Talk about foods sold by sidewalk vendors in the United States. Encourage students to talk about what snacks they like, where and when they tend to eat them, and whether they eat them alone or in a group. Introduce the idea of ***churros*** and ***chocolate.*** Have students read the first paragraph. If any students have tried ***churros,*** let them share their experience with the class.

Continue the discussion and remind students that people in Spanish-speaking countries often sit and socialize with friends and enjoy a snack. ***Churros*** are not as sweet as doughnuts and are often dipped in hot chocolate. The chocolate mentioned here is thicker and richer than that usually served in the United States. Point out the recipe. Tell students they might like to try making this at home with an adult.

Direct attention to the *Think about it!* section and have students discuss the questions.

Answers will vary.

Suggestions: Preparing hot foods in the classroom may not be an option. However, you may be able to get some ***churros*** for the students to taste. Another option is to prepare ***churros*** and ***chocolate*** for a food festival. Some parents may be willing to participate and help prepare the food. Be sure that students are not allergic to any foods brought into the classroom.

Point out that ***churros*** are bought in a ***churrería,*** not a grocery store. Compare ***churrerías*** to doughnut shops. Ask why people might prefer to get doughnuts from a doughnut shop rather than an all-purpose grocery store. (Answers will vary but might include: more variety, it's their specialty so is apt to be better, freshness, a place to sit and chat.)

Additional Resources

- Heritage Learner Workbook: 3A-7

La cultura en vivo

Churros y chocolate

Chocolate y churros

In many Spanish-speaking countries, a popular snack is the combination of *churros y chocolate. Churros* are long, slender doughnut-like pastries fried in hot oil. Small restaurants called *churrerías* specialize in *churros* and cups of delicious hot chocolate. You can also find *churros* being sold in stands on the street.

Try it out! Here's the recipe to try. *Churros* are high in fat and calories, so you won't want to sample too many of them!

Churros

1 cup water	$\frac{1}{2}$ cup unsalted butter *(= 1 stick)*
$\frac{1}{4}$ teaspoon salt	1 cup all-purpose flour
4 large eggs	oil for deep-frying
1 cup sugar	

Un molinillo

In a heavy saucepan, bring water, butter, and salt to a full boil. Remove from heat. Add the flour all at once, stirring briskly. Stir until the mixture pulls away from the side of the pan and forms a ball. Put the mixture in a bowl. With an electric mixer on medium speed, add one egg at a time. After adding the last egg, beat the mixture for one more minute.

With adult supervision, heat 2–3 inches of oil to 375° F in a deep, heavy pan. Fit a pastry bag or cookie press with a $\frac{1}{2}$-inch star tip. Pipe out 6 inch-long tubes of dough into the oil. ***Be extremely cautious adding dough to the oil, because the oil may spatter and burn you!*** Fry, turning a few times, for 3–5 minutes or until golden brown. Place the sugar on a plate. Drain the *churros* well on paper towels and then roll them in the sugar.

Chocolate caliente

To make hot chocolate in Mexico, cacao beans are ground to a powder. Cinnamon, powdered almonds, and sugar are then added, and hot milk is poured in. The mixture is whipped with a wooden whisk called *un molinillo* or *un batidor.* You can find Mexican-style chocolate for making *chocolate caliente* in many supermarkets.

Think about it! What kinds of food and drink do you and your friends like? Is chocolate among the popular choices? Can you think of combinations of food and drink that are popular with many people in the United States? Are these combinations popular elsewhere?

Universal Access

Heritage Language Learners

Students may be familiar with other snacks from Spanish-speaking countries. If so, allow them to describe the snack and tell whether there is a special way to eat it. If not, they might enjoy researching snacks from their heritage country.

Presentación oral

¿Y qué te gusta comer?

Task
An exchange student from the United States is going to Uruguay. You and a partner will role-play a telephone conversation in which you each take one of the roles and gather information about the other person.

1 Prepare You will role-play this conversation with a partner. Be sure to prepare for both roles. Here's how to prepare:

Host Student: Make a list of at least four questions that you might ask the exchange student. Find out what he or she likes to study, his or her favorite activities, and what he or she likes to eat and drink for breakfast and lunch.

> **Strategy**
> **Making lists**
> Making lists of questions can help you in conversations where you need to find out specific information.

Exchange Student: Jot down some possible answers to questions that the host student might ask and be prepared to provide information about yourself.

2 Practice Work in groups of four in which there are two exchange students and two host students. Work together to practice different questions and different responses. Here's how you might start your phone conversation:

Host Student:	¡Hola, Pablo! Soy Rosa.
Exchange Student:	Hola, Rosa. ¿Cómo estás?
Host Student:	Bien, gracias. Pues Pablo, ¿te gusta . . . ?

Continue the conversation using your notes. You can use your notes in practice, but not during the role-playing.

3 Present You will be paired with another student, and your teacher will tell you which role to play. The host student begins the conversation. Listen to your partner's questions and responses and keep the conversation going.

4 Evaluation Your teacher may give you a rubric for how the presentation will be graded. You probably will be graded on:

- completion of task
- how well you were understood
- your ability to keep the conversation going

Presentación oral

Presentation

Standards: 1.1, 1.3

Focus: Role-playing a telephone conversation between an American exchange student and a host student in Uruguay

Suggestions: Point out the *Strategy*. Tell Students that the *Strategy* will be helpful to them as they prepare their presentation. Read through the assignment and the four-step approach with students.

1. Prepare Provide time for students to complete this step individually. Students may need to refer to *Capítulos* 1A and 1B to guide them while writing their questions and answers. Students may want to keep their written questions and answers to add to their portfolio.

2. Practice Pair up students and then tell them to work with another pair of students. Allow adequate time for students to practice both roles.

3. Present Students should not use their notes for this part of the presentation. Remind them to listen carefully to the questions and answers so they can answer accurately.

4. Evaluation Your students may want to place a copy of the rubric in their portfolios, along with their grade, your comments, and the questions they prepared in advance.

Portfolio

Record students' oral presentations on cassette or videotape for inclusion in their portfolios.

Additional Resources

- Heritage Learner Workbook: 3A-8

Assessment

- Assessment Program: Cap. 3A, Rubrics

Give students copies of the rubric before they begin the activity. Review the different levels of performance. After assessing students, help individuals understand how their performance could be improved.

Enriching Your Teaching

RUBRIC	Score 1	Score 3	Score 5
Completion of task	You ask or answer two questions during the conversation.	You ask or answer three questions during the conversation.	You ask or answer four or more questions during the conversation.
How easily you are understood	You are extremely difficult to understand. Your teacher could only recognize isolated words and phrases.	You are understandable, but have frequent errors in vocabulary and/or grammar that hinder your comprehensibility.	You are easily understood. Your teacher does not have to "decode" what you are trying to say.
Your ability to keep the conversation going	You provide no conversational response or follow-up to what your partner says.	You provide frequent response or follow-up to what your partner says.	You always respond to your partner, listen and ask follow-up questions or volunteer additional information.

El mundo hispano

Presentation

Standards: 2.2, 3.1, 4.2

Resources: Voc. & Gram. Transparencies: 15 (map)

Focus: Reading about the countries in northern South America

Suggestions: After students read the text, display a map of South America. Focus on the northern part of the continent, and draw attention to the five countries featured here. Point out that this is a region of contrasts. Focus on the topography. Draw attention to the mountains and valleys, the rainforests and deserts. Note that the steep, rugged mountains make farming difficult. Point out the background photo of the terraced fields. Help students understand that terracing, an ancient system of agriculture, was necessary for successful farming. Terracing created shelves that slowed the course of the water, allowing it to soak into the ground, and thus making it possible to cultivate crops. Scientists have discovered that these ancient systems work better than some modern techniques.

Point out that these mountains are at a very high altitude, and that South America has the highest navigable body of water in the world. (Show Lake Titicaca on the map.) Guide students to understand that, in comparison, very little takes place in the United States at 12,500 ft. Note that Bolivia is one of two landlocked countries in South America.

Theme Project

Students can perform step 3 at this point. (For more information, see p. 146-a.)

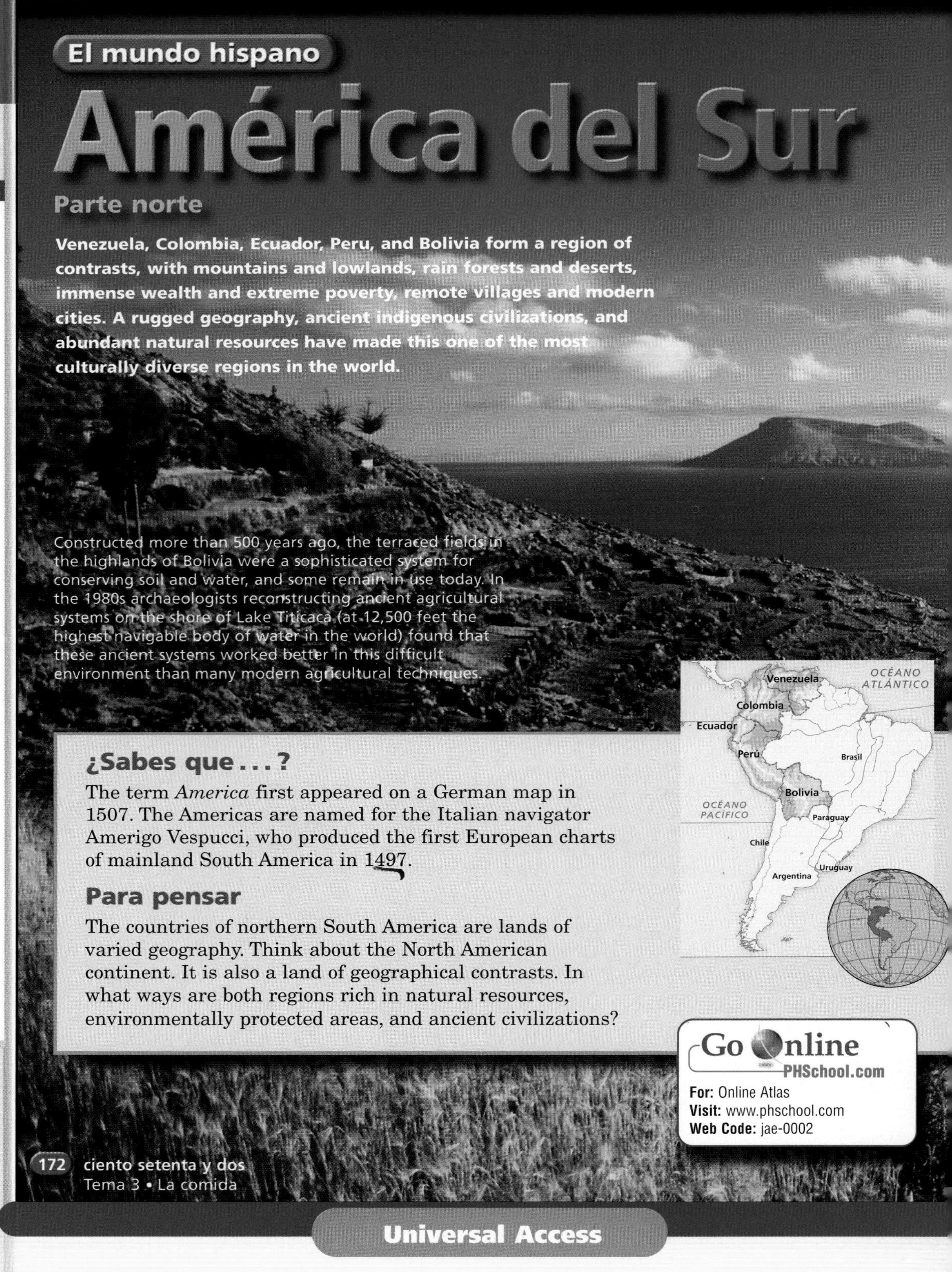

El mundo hispano

América del Sur

Parte norte

Venezuela, Colombia, Ecuador, Peru, and Bolivia form a region of contrasts, with mountains and lowlands, rain forests and deserts, immense wealth and extreme poverty, remote villages and modern cities. A rugged geography, ancient indigenous civilizations, and abundant natural resources have made this one of the most culturally diverse regions in the world.

Constructed more than 500 years ago, the terraced fields in the highlands of Bolivia were a sophisticated system for conserving soil and water, and some remain in use today. In the 1980s archaeologists reconstructing ancient agricultural systems on the shore of Lake Titicaca (at 12,500 feet the highest navigable body of water in the world) found that these ancient systems worked better in this difficult environment than many modern agricultural techniques.

¿Sabes que . . . ?

The term *America* first appeared on a German map in 1507. The Americas are named for the Italian navigator Amerigo Vespucci, who produced the first European charts of mainland South America in 1497.

Para pensar

The countries of northern South America are lands of varied geography. Think about the North American continent. It is also a land of geographical contrasts. In what ways are both regions rich in natural resources, environmentally protected areas, and ancient civilizations?

Go Online PHSchool.com
For: Online Atlas
Visit: www.phschool.com
Web Code: jae-0002

Universal Access

Advanced Learners

Have students research the Inca empire. Allow them to focus on a specific topic of their choice, such as the rediscovered city of Machu Picchu. Encourage them to present their findings to the class, or to create a display.

Heritage Language Learners

The heritage country of some students may have been presented here. If so, have them research the natural resources of that country, and make a brief presentation of their findings.

"Rediscovered" in 1911, the mountaintop city of Machu Picchu in Peru was part of the Incan empire, which in the sixteenth century extended from present-day Ecuador to Chile. Machu Picchu's buildings were made of huge, precisely carved stone blocks that were hauled into place without wheels or heavy draft animals.

Venezuela is one of the most important sources of oil consumed in the United States. Other important Latin American oil producers include Mexico, Colombia, Ecuador, and Peru, with new deposits being found every year. Latin America and Canada account for approximately 48 percent of oil imports to the United States. In contrast, the Middle East accounts for approximately 30 percent.

The Galapagos Islands, also called *las islas encantadas* (the enchanted islands), lie 600 miles off the coast of Ecuador. It is believed that the Incas may have traveled to the islands in large ocean-going rafts. In 1835, the naturalist Charles Darwin spent weeks here studying the islands' unique animal life. *Galápagos* are giant tortoises that are native to these islands, which are now a national park and wildlife sanctuary.

Culture 3A

Direct attention to the top photo on p. 173. Have students hypothesize about how the Inca managed to precisely carve huge stone blocks and move them into place. Help them understand what an achievement this was. Use the map to show the extent of the Inca civilization.

Direct attention to the middle photo on p. 173. Venezuela is rich in oil. It contributes 13% to 18% of the oil used in the United States. Have students discuss how the discovery of oil in Venezuela has affected its economy.

Point out the bottom photo on p. 173. Have students locate the Galápagos Islands on a map. Explain that these islands have animals that are not known to exist anywhere else in the world. As a result, the islands are now a wildlife sanctuary and national park.

Direct attention to the *¿Sabes que ...?* section. Discuss Vespucci with students. Have them compare the dates of his travels and those of Columbus. Let them give an opinion about the naming of the continents.

Point out that this section only talks about the northern part of the continent. The southern part will be discussed later. Make sure students understand that much of South America is rural and that many descendants of the original indigenous people still live there and speak their own language rather than Spanish. The big cities, however, are very much like cities elsewhere.

Direct attention to the *Para pensar* section and have students discuss the question.

Answers will vary.

Go Online

The Online Atlas will provide more detailed maps of the locations.

Enriching Your Teaching

Teacher-to-Teacher

As an ongoing project, have students create a bulletin board on South America. They may wish to begin by making a large map of the continent. As they learn about a country, they can label it and research principal products, major cities, and historical information.

Internet Search

Keywords:

Venezuela, Colombia, Ecuador, Peru, Bolivia, Lake Titicaca, Galapagos, Inca

Review Activities

To talk about breakfast and lunch, to talk about beverages: Have students work in pairs to quiz each other on the vocabulary. They may find it useful to create flashcards with pictures on them.

To talk about eating and drinking: Have students ask others what they like to eat and drink.

To indicate how often: Have students make a list of their favorite foods and beverages and talk about how often they eat them.

To show surprise, to say that you like/love something: Have students brainstorm a list of foods and beverages that they like and dislike. Ask them to read their lists to a partner and react using one of these phrases.

Portfolio

Invite students to review the activities they completed in this chapter, including written reports, posters or other visuals, and tapes of oral presentations, or other projects. Have them select one or two items that they feel best demonstrate their achievements in Spanish to include in their portfolios. Have them include this with the Chapter Checklist and Self-Assessment Worksheet.

Additional Resources

- Audio Program: CD Cap. 3A, Track 14
- Resource Book: Cap. 3A, Clip Art
- Resource Book: Cap. 3A, Situation Cards
- Assessment Program: Chapter Checklist and Self-Assessment Worksheet

Assessment

- Examen del capítulo: 3A
- Audio Program: CD 20, Track 7

Alternative Assessment

- ExamView Test Bank CD-ROM
- Resource Book: Cap. 5A, Situation Cards
- Resource Book: Cap. 5A, Communicative Activities

Chapter Review

Repaso del capítulo

To prepare for the test, check to see if you . . .
- know the new vocabulary and grammar
- can perform the tasks on p. 175

Vocabulario y gramática

to talk about breakfast

en el desayuno	for breakfast
el cereal	cereal
el desayuno	breakfast
los huevos	eggs
el pan	bread
el pan tostado	toast
el plátano	banana
la salchicha	sausage
el tocino	bacon
el yogur	yogurt

to talk about lunch

en el almuerzo	for lunch
la ensalada	salad
la ensalada de frutas	fruit salad
las fresas	strawberries
la galleta	cookie
la hamburguesa	hamburger
el jamón	ham
la manzana	apple
las papas fritas	French fries
el perrito caliente	hot dog
la pizza	pizza
el queso	cheese
el sándwich de jamón y queso	ham and cheese sandwich
la sopa de verduras	vegetable soup

to talk about beverages

el agua *f.*	water
el café	coffee
el jugo de manzana	apple juice
el jugo de naranja	orange juice
la leche	milk
la limonada	lemonade
el refresco	soft drink
el té	tea
el té helado	iced tea

Más práctica

Practice Workbook Puzzle 3A-8
Practice Workbook Organizer 3A-9

For *Vocabulario adicional,* see pp. 268–269.

to talk about eating and drinking

beber	to drink
comer	to eat
la comida	food, meal
compartir	to share

to indicate how often

nunca	never
siempre	always
todos los días	every day

to say that you like / love something

Me / te encanta(n) ____.	I / you love ____.
Me / te gusta(n) ____.	I / you like ____.

other useful words

comprender	to understand
con	with
¿Cuál?	Which? What?
más o menos	more or less
por supuesto	of course
¡Qué asco!	How awful!
sin	without
¿Verdad?	Really?, Right?

present tense of *-er* verbs

como	comemos
comes	coméis
come	comen

present tense of *-ir* verbs

comparto	compartimos
compartes	compartís
comparte	comparten

Universal Access

Students with Learning Difficulties

When reviewing for the test, be sure to discuss not only the test content, but also the format. Look at the test for *Capítulo* 3A, and provide sample questions to help students with individual assessment needs.

Advanced Learners

Have students write a paragraph or create a graph they can use to compare their typical diet and favorite foods to those of someone they know (a relative or a friend). Students can present the information to the class orally or turn in a report.

Go Online PHSchool.com
For: Test preparation
Visit: www.phschool.com
Web Code: jad-0306

Preparación para el examen

On the exam you will be asked to . . .	Here are practice tasks similar to those you will find on the exam . . .	If you need review . . .
1 Escuchar Listen and understand as people describe what they eat and drink for lunch	Listen as three students describe what they typically eat and drink for lunch. Which is most like the kind of lunch you eat? Did they mention anything you could not buy in your school cafeteria?	**pp. 148–153** *A primera vista* **p. 149** Actividades 1–2 **p. 155** Actividad 8
2 Hablar Tell someone what you typically eat for breakfast and ask the same of others	Your Spanish club is meeting for breakfast before school next week. Find out what other people in your class typically eat for breakfast. After you tell at least two people what you eat for breakfast, ask what they like to eat. Does everyone eat the same kind of breakfast or do you all like to eat different things?	**p. 156** Actividad 10 **p. 157** Actividad 12 **p. 162** Actividades 19–20 **p. 163** Actividad 21 **p. 171** *Presentación oral*
 **3 Leer** Read and understand words that are typically found on menus	You are trying to help a child order from the lunch menu below, but he is very difficult to please. He doesn't like any white food. And he refuses to eat anything that grows on trees. Which items from the menu do you think he would refuse to eat or drink? ALMUERZO hamburguesa, pizza, ensalada, plátanos, manzana, leche	**pp. 148–153** *A primera vista* **p. 159** Actividad 15 **p. 167** Actividad 28 **pp. 168–169** *Lectura*
4 Escribir Write a list of foods that you like and others that you dislike	Your Spanish club is sponsoring a "Super Spanish Saturday." Your teacher wants to know what foods the class likes and dislikes so that the club can buy what most people like. Write the headings *Me gusta(n)* and *No me gusta(n)* in two columns. List at least four items that you like to eat and drink for breakfast and four items for lunch. Then list what you don't like to eat and drink for these same meals.	**p. 155** Actividades 7, 9 **p. 160** Actividad 16 **p. 163** Actividad 21 **p. 164** Actividad 24
 **5 Pensar** Demonstrate an understanding of cultural differences regarding snacks	Think about food combinations in the United States. What combination in Spanish-speaking countries is similar to coffee and doughnuts? Where are you able to buy it?	**p. 170** *La cultura en vivo*

Enriching Your Teaching

Teacher-to-Teacher

Have students create a memory game to review vocabulary and expressions from this chapter. Ask students to write the Spanish word on one square of paper, and its English equivalent on the other. They should choose between 10 and 15 words from the list. Once the cards are made, they can mix them up and place them face down in rows face down on the desk. Working with a partner, students must take turns looking for pairs. In order to keep their pair, they must use the word in a sentence. The person with the most pairs wins.

Performance Tasks

Standards: 1.1, 1.2, 1.3, 4.2

Resources: Audio Program: CD Cap. 3A, Track 15; Resource Book: Cap. 3A, Audio Script; Practice Answers on Transparencies

1. Escuchar

Suggestions: Play the *Audio CD* or use the script. Ask students to answer the questions.

Script:

Marco: Siempre como una hamburguesa y papas fritas en el almuerzo. Por supuesto, necesito comer frutas y verduras, pero no me gustan.

Elena: ¡Qué asco! ¡Una hamburguesa y papas fritas! Nunca como papas fritas. Todos los días como una ensalada de frutas o sopas de verduras, ¡con una galleta, claro!

Tomás: ¿Cuál es mi comida favorita? Pues, no como mucho en el almuerzo. Como pizza o un perrito caliente y bebo un refresco.

Answers will vary.

2. Hablar

Suggestions: Allow time for students to work on this task in class. If students have difficulty with spontaneous conversation, have them write their messages and practice speaking them until they can say them without consulting their notes.

Answers will vary.

3. Leer

Suggestions: Have students read their answers to the class. Ask which items the boy would eat or drink.

Answers:

Eat: ensalada, hamburguesa y pizza
Not eat: plátanos, manzana y leche

Extension: Have students list food or drink items from the list on p. 174 that the boy would eat or drink.

4. Escribir

Suggestions: Have students try this activity without consulting the vocabulary list, notes, or completed activities.

5. Pensar

Suggestions: Remind students that in the United States we often snack on brand-name packaged foods. How does this differ from what they have learned about students in Spanish-speaking cultures?

Answers: ***Churros*** and ***chocolate*** can be purchased in ***churrerías*** or at street stands.

Capítulo 3B

Overview

Chapter Overview

A primera vista — INPUT	Manos a la obra — PRACTICE	¡Adelante! — APPLICATION	Repaso del capítulo — REVIEW
Objectives Read, listen to, and explain information about: • food groups and foods on the Food Guide Pyramid • activities to maintain good health • ways to describe food	**Objectives** • Talk about dinner foods • Express food preferences • Describe people and foods • Talk about healthy and unhealthy lifestyles • Use the plurals of adjectives and the verb ***ser***	**Objectives** • Read about a specialized sports diet and learn some facts about an athlete • Explain cultural perspectives on healthcare • Make a poster about good health habits • Discuss facts about the southern part of South America	**Objectives** • Prepare for the chapter test
Vocabulary • Foods and beverages • Health and exercise vocabulary • Expressions to indicate hunger, thirst, a preference, agreement and disagreement • Quantities	**Vocabulary** • Practice and learn new vocabulary	**Vocabulary** • Application	**Vocabulary** • Review
Grammar Lexical use of: • plural adjectives • the verb ***ser***	**Grammar** • The plurals of adjectives • The verb ***ser***	**Grammar** • Application	**Grammar** • Review
Culture • Diego Rivera's mural of *el tianguis*	**Culture** • ***el mate*** • ***la Tomatina*** • ***los mercados***	**Culture** • Soccer and the World Cup • Facts about alternative, natural medicine	**Culture** • Demonstrate an understanding of cultural perspectives on alternative medicine and herbal remedies

Learner Support

Strategies
- Using visuals to make predictions
- Using cognates
- Skimming
- Gathering information

Recycling
- Gender agreement of adjectives and nouns
- Using ***ser*** to talk about what a person is like
- Present tense of ***-ar*** verbs
- ***me gusta(n)***

Pronunciación
- The letters ***l*** and ***ll***

Exploración del lenguaje
- Word origins

Conexiones
- Math: creating a bar graph

Beyond the Classroom

Countries
- Mexico
- Guatemala
- Costa Rica
- Ecuador
- Chile
- Spain
- Paraguay
- Uruguay
- Argentina

El español en el mundo del trabajo
- Profile of a Mexican chef

Internet
- Vocabulary activities
- Grammar activities
- Internet links
- Self-tests

Print Components

TEACHER

Teacher's Resource Book
- Chapter Resource Checklist
- Input Script
- Video Script
- Audio Script
- Answer Keys
- *GramActiva* Blackline Master
- Situation Cards Blackline Masters
- School-to-Home Connection Letter
- Communicative Activity Blackline Masters
- Vocabulary Clip Art

TPR Storytelling Book
- Cap. 3B

STUDENT

Practice Workbook
- Vocabulary: 3B-1 – 3B-4
- Grammar: 3B-5 – 3B-7
- Puzzle: 3B-8
- Organizer: 3B-9

Writing, Audio & Video Workbook
- Writing: 3B-1 – 3B-4
- Audio: 3B-5 – 3B-10
- Video: 3B – 11

Realidades para hispanohablantes
- Cap. 3B

Transparencies

Vocabulary & Grammar Transparencies
- Chapter Opener: 12–20 (maps)
- *A primera vista:* 73–74
- *Videohistoria:* 13 (map), 75–76
- Grammar: 11 (graphic organizer), 77–79
- *Lectura:* 15 (map), 80
- *Cultura:* 16 (map)

Practice Answers on Transparencies
- Cap. 3B

Fine Art Transparencies
- Transparencies
- Teacher's Guide

Assessment

Assessment Program
- *Pruebas:*
  - Vocabulary recognition: 3B-1
  - Vocabulary production: 3B-2
  - Plurals of adjectives: 3B-3
  - The verb ***ser:*** 3B-4
- *Examen del capítulo:* 3B

ExamView Test Bank CD-ROM

Test Preparation Workbook
- Cap. 3B Reading #1
- Cap. 3B Reading #2

Alternative Assessment
- Performance-Based Speaking
- Assessment Program: Rubrics
- Internet Self-Test
- Situation Cards Blackline Masters
- TPR Storytelling Book: Speaking Task

Technology

iText

Mind Point Quiz Show CD-ROM

Resource Pro CD-ROM
- Lesson Planner
- Teacher Resources
- Clip Art

Video Program VHS and DVD
- *A primera vista* video: *Para mantener la salud*
- *GramActiva* Videos:
  - plurals of adjectives
  - the verb ***ser***

Audio Program CDs
- *A primera vista*
- *Escucha y escribe*
- Audio Activities
- *Pronunciación*
- *Repaso*
- Chapter Listening Test
- Songs

Capítulo 3B

Lesson Plans

Regular Schedule (50 minutes)

For electronic lesson plans: Resource Pro CD-ROM

	Warm-up / Assess	Preview / Present / Practice / Communicate	Wrap-up / Homework Options
DAY 1	**Return Examen del capítulo (10 min.)**	**A primera vista (35 min.)** • Objectives • Presentation: *Vocabulario y gramática en contexto* • *Actividades* 1, 2 • *Fondo cultural*	**Wrap-up and Homework Options (5 min.)** • Practice Workbook 3B-1, 3B-2 • Go Online • Heritage Language Learner Workbook • Vocabulary Clip Art
DAY 2	**Warm-up (5 min.)** • Homework check	**A primera vista (40 min.)** • Review: *Vocabulario y gramática en contexto* • Presentation: *Videohistoria Para mantener la salud* • View: Video *Para mantener la salud* • Video Activities • *Actividades* 3, 4	**Wrap-up and Homework Options (5 min.)** • *Prueba* 3B-1: Vocabulary recognition • Practice Workbook 3B-3, 3B-4 • Go Online
DAY 3	**Warm-up (5 min.)** • Homework check ✔**Assessment (10 min.)** • *Prueba* 3B-1: Voc. recognition	**Manos a la obra (30 min.)** • Objectives • *Actividad* 5 • *Juego: Actividad* 6 • *Fondo cultural*	**Wrap-up and Homework Options (5 min.)** • *Actividad* 7
DAY 4	**Warm-up (5 min.)** • Homework check • Return *Prueba* 3B-1: Voc. recognition	**Manos a la obra (40 min.)** • *Actividades* 8, 10, 11	**Wrap-up and Homework Options (5 min.)** • *Actividad* 13
DAY 5	**Warm-up (5 min.)** • Homework check	**Manos a la obra (40 min.)** • *Actividades* 12, 14, 15	**Wrap-up and Homework Options (5 min.)** • *Actividad* 9
DAY 6	**Warm-up (5 min.)** • Homework check	**Manos a la obra (40 min.)** • Presentation: The plurals of adjectives • *GramActiva* Video • *Actividades* 16, 17, 18 • *Pronunciación*	**Wrap-up and Homework Options (5 min.)** • Practice Workbook 3B-5 • Go Online • *Prueba* 3B-3: The plurals of adjectives
DAY 7	**Warm-up (5 min.)** • Homework check ✔**Assessment (10 min.)** • *Prueba* 3B-3: The plurals of adjectives	**Manos a la obra (30 min.)** • Presentation: The verb *ser* • *GramActiva* Video • *Actividades* 19, 20	**Wrap-up and Homework Options (5 min.)** • Go Online • Practice Workbook 3B-6, 3B-7
DAY 8	**Warm-up (5 min.)** • Homework check • Return *Prueba* 3B-3: The plurals of adjectives	**Manos a la obra (40 min.)** • *Actividades* 21, 22 • *Fondo cultural*	**Wrap-up and Homework Options (5 min.)** • *Prueba* 3B-2: Vocabulary production

Day	Warm-up / Assess	Preview / Present / Practice / Communicate	Wrap-up / Homework Options
DAY 9	**Warm-up** (5 min.) • Homework check ✔**Assessment** (10 min.) • *Prueba* 3B-2: Voc. production	**Manos a la obra** (30 min.) • *Actividades* 23, 24 • *Fondo cultural* • *Exploración del lenguaje*	**Wrap-up and Homework Options** (5 min.) • Go Online • *Prueba* 3B-4: The verb ***ser***
DAY 10	**Warm-up** (5 min.) • Homework check • Return *Prueba* 3B-2: Voc. production ✔**Assessment** (10 min.) • *Prueba* 3B-4: The verb ***ser***	**Manos a la obra** (30 min.) • *Actividades* 25, 26 • *El español en el mundo del trabajo* • *Conexiones: Actividad* 27	**Wrap-up and Homework Options** (5 min.) • Go Online
DAY 11	**Warm-up** (5 min.) • Homework check • Return *Prueba* 3B-4: The verb ***ser***	**¡Adelante!** (40 min.) • *Presentación escrita:* Prewrite • *Lectura* • *Fondo cultural*	**Wrap-up and Homework Options** (5 min.) • *¿Comprendes?* • Go Online
DAY 12	**Warm-up** (5 min.) • Homework check	**¡Adelante!** (40 min.) • *Presentación escrita:* Draft, revise • *Perspectivas del mundo hispano*	**Wrap-up and Homework Options** (5 min.) • Go Online • *Presentación escrita:* Publish
DAY 13	**Warm-up** (5 min.) • Homework check	**¡Adelante!** (40 min.) • *Presentación escrita:* Present	**Wrap-up and Homework Options** (5 min.) • Writing Activities • Practice Workbook 3B-8, 3B-9
DAY 14	**Warm-up** (5 min.) • Homework check	**¡Adelante!** (20 min.) • *El mundo hispano* **Repaso** (20 min.) • *Vocabulario y gramática* • *Preparación para el examen*	**Wrap-up and Homework Options** (5 min.) • Go Online: Self-test • *Examen del capítulo*
DAY 15	**Warm-up** (5 min.) • Answer questions ✔**Assessment** (45 min.) • *Examen del capítulo*		

3B Preview

Standards for *Capítulo* 3B

- To achieve the goals of the Standards, students will:

Communication

1.1 Interpersonal

- Talk about food groups and healthy diet
- Talk about food preferences and meals
- Talk about healthy lifestyle choices
- Talk about the personality traits of various people

1.2 Interpretive

- Read and listen to information about food groups
- Read and listen to information about health habits
- Listen to ways to describe food
- Read a picture-based story
- Listen to and watch a video about healthy diet
- Read an advertisement for a pizza parlor
- Read about ***fútbol*** star Edwin Tenorio

1.3 Presentational

- Present information about foods and beverages
- Present information about healthy lifestyle choices
- Present information about personality traits of people
- Present information ***fútbol*** star Edwin Tenorio

Culture

2.1 Practices and Perspectives

- Understand past and present open-air markets
- Learn about the communal nature of mate
- Learn about ***La Tomatina*** festival
- Understand the popularity of ***fútbol***
- Learn that alternative and herbal medicine is common
- Understand how Spanish imports of livestock created a cowboy culture in parts of South America

2.2 Products and Perspectives

- Learn about Diego Rivera and his painting
- Learn about ***mate***
- Learn about writers and dances of Argentina

Connections

3.1 Cross-curricular

- Learn about important artists and their work: Rivera
- Learn about nutrition and good health habits
- Reinforce math and graphing abilities skills
- Learn about the history and geography of South America

3.2 Target Culture

- Watch and listen to a video

Comparisons

4.1 Language

- Learn new vocabulary through the recognition of cognates
- Understand gender agreement in use of Adjectives
- Understand the pronunciation of the letters ***l*** and ***ll***
- Understand number agreement in use of adjectives
- Learn the present tense of the irregular verb ***ser***

4.2 Culture

- Compare mate to its counterpart in the United States
- Compare ***La Tomatina*** to festivals in the United States
- Compare places people shop for produce
- Compare ***fútbol*** to baseball
- Compare attitudes and access to alternative therapies

Communities

5.1 Beyond the School

- Understand the value of Spanish-speaking ability in a ...er such as culinary arts

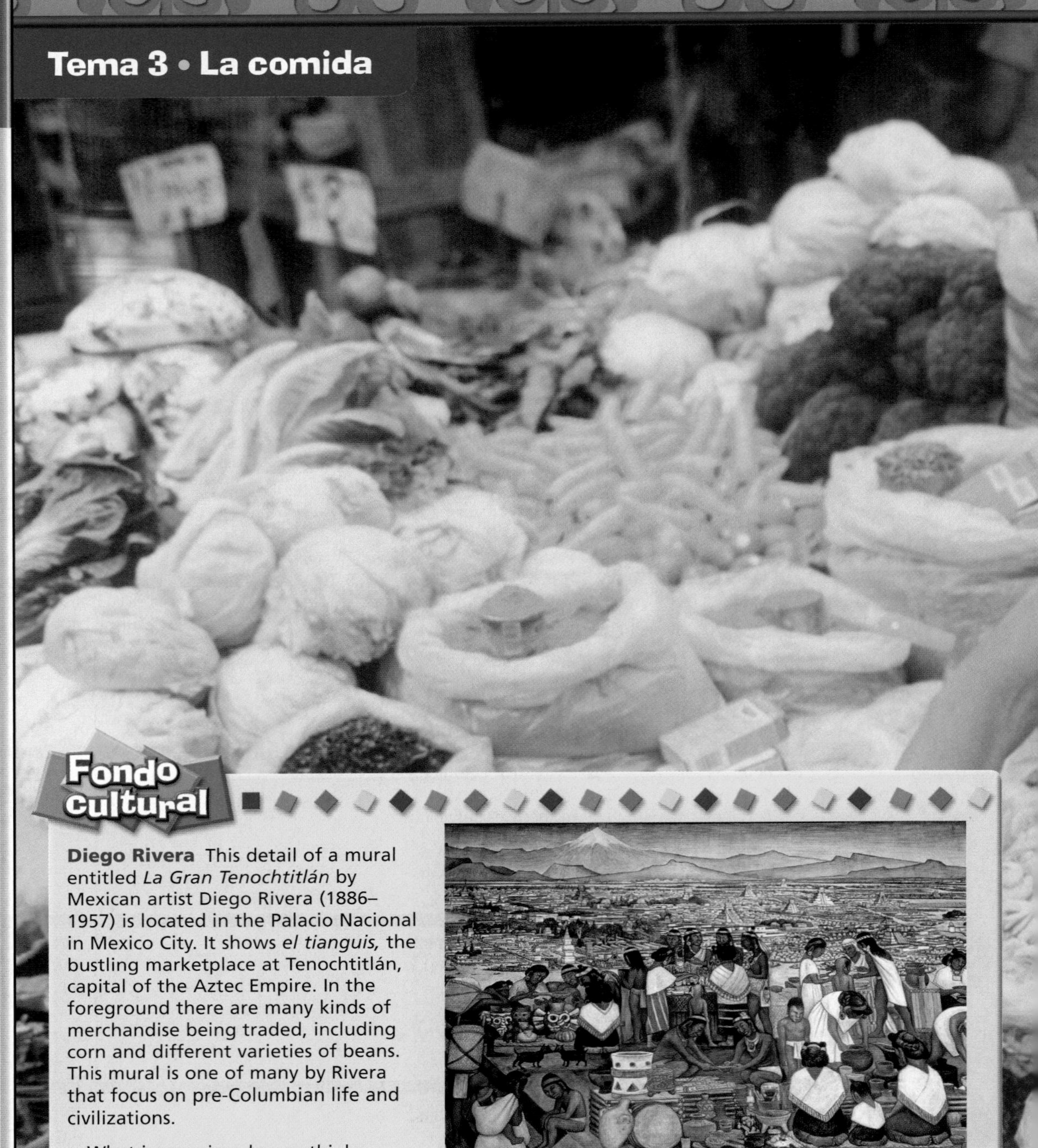

Fondo cultural

Diego Rivera This detail of a mural entitled *La Gran Tenochtitlán* by Mexican artist Diego Rivera (1886–1957) is located in the Palacio Nacional in Mexico City. It shows *el tianguis,* the bustling marketplace at Tenochtitlán, capital of the Aztec Empire. In the foreground there are many kinds of merchandise being traded, including corn and different varieties of beans. This mural is one of many by Rivera that focus on pre-Columbian life and civilizations.

- What impression do you think Rivera is giving about life in a pre-Columbian civilization?

Detalle de *La Gran Tenochtitlán* (1945), Diego Rivera

Universal Access

Personalizing the Theme

Ask students to talk about their eating habits and the way diet can affect personal health. What kinds of foods do they eat? Where is the food purchased? Is the food they eat at home or at school different from the food they eat in other places? What foods are important for good health?

Heritage Language Learners

Ask students if they have ever been to a market that sold products typically found in their heritage countries. Have they noticed the same products in local supermarkets? How are traditional markets different from and similar to supermarkets?

Capítulo 3B

Para mantener la salud

Chapter Objectives

- Talk about foods and beverages for dinner
- Describe what people or things are like
- Discuss food, health, and exercise choices
- Understand cultural perspectives on diet and health

Video Highlights

A primera vista: ***Para mantener la salud***

GramActiva Videos: the plurals of adjectives; the verb *ser*

Country Connection

As you learn about foods and health, you will make connections to these countries and places:

Go Online
PHSchool.com
For: Online Atlas
Visit: www.phschool.com
Web Code: jae-0002

Un mercado en Puebla, México

Chapter Opener

Presentation

Resources: Voc. & Gram. Transparencies: 12–18, 20 (maps)

Suggestions: Introduce the chapter theme and review the objectives. Tell students they will be learning to talk about healthy habits. Brainstorm a list of healthy foods and "junk" foods that students eat, and discuss eating habits. The *A Primera vista* video is about a similar topic.

Standards: 2.1, 2.2, 3.1

Resources: Fine Art Transparencies; Fine Art Transparencies Teacher's Guide

Suggestions: Explain that ***el tianguis*** was a central marketplace for the Aztecs. In modern Mexico these markets have the same name, and many of the same goods. Have students discuss markets in the United States, including any local markets.

Answers will vary.

Teaching with Art

Resources: Fine Art Transparencies; Fine Art Transparencies Teacher's Guide

Suggestions: Share with students that Tenochtitlán was located in what is now Mexico City. It was the capital of the Aztec civilization until 1521, when the Spanish defeated the Aztecs. Mexico City went through tremendous turmoil again during the Mexican Revolution (1910–1940). Diego Rivera and other artists were asked to paint large murals in Mexico City to convey a sense of pride in Mexico's past and hope for her future.

Teacher-to-Teacher

Tell students that many countries have open-air markets, where food, fabrics, clothing, tools, kitchen utensils, furniture, and many other items are sold. In some countries these markets offer fresher foods and homemade items and more profit for the producer of the goods.

Enriching Your Teaching

Planning for Instruction

Resources:

- Teacher Express CD-ROM or Resource Book
  - Teaching resources
  - Lesson Planner
  - Chapter Resource Checklist
  - School-to-Home Connection Letter

Culture Note

The word "mural" comes from the Latin word *murus,* which means "wall". A mural is painted directly on a wall, not hung like a framed painting. Murals often depict the concerns, hopes, and values of the community where the murals are painted. Mural art is particularly important in Mexican culture.

Vocabulario y gramática

Presentation

Standards: 1.2, 3.1

Resources: Voc. & Gram. Transparencies: 73–74; Resource Book: Cap. 3B, Input Script; Resource Book: Cap. 3B, Clip Art; TPR Storytelling Book: Cap. 3B; Audio Program: CD Cap. 3B, Tracks 1–2

Focus: Presenting vocabulary and information about food groups

Suggestions: Use the story in the *TPR Storytelling Book* to present the new vocabulary and grammar, or use the Input Script from the *Teacher's Resource Book.* Bring plastic foods to class like those you would find in a child's toy kitchen. Present the vocabulary in three sets: fruits and vegetables, meats and starches, and words to discuss health. Have students look at the pictures and guess what the words mean. Ask questions that require a limited verbal response: *¿Te gustan las verduras? ¿Comes muchas uvas? ¿Los pasteles son buenas para la salud?* Have students "shop" for the plastic food items. Be sure they take foods from each of the food groups. Have them organize the items as you call out food groups.

Hand out copies of the Vocabulary Clip Art. Have students tear the images into individual food items. Describe different meals to students and have them group the foods as they would on a cafeteria tray. (If your class is small, you might be able to borrow real trays from the cafeteria.) Then ask if the meal you described is good or bad for one's health.

Additional Resources

- Audio Program: Song CD

Teacher-to-Teacher

Have students create posters illustrating the Food Guide Pyramid. They can cut out pictures from magazines or grocery store ads. Encourage them to find additional foods and place them in the appropriate categories. They should label their posters and explain them to the class.

A primera vista

Vocabulario y gramática en contexto

Objectives

Read, listen to, and understand information about
- food groups and foods on the Food Guide Pyramid
- activities to maintain good health
- ways to describe food

La pirámide nutritiva es la forma más práctica de indicar la comida que **debes** comer **cada día. Para mantener la salud,** es importante comer de **todos** los grupos.

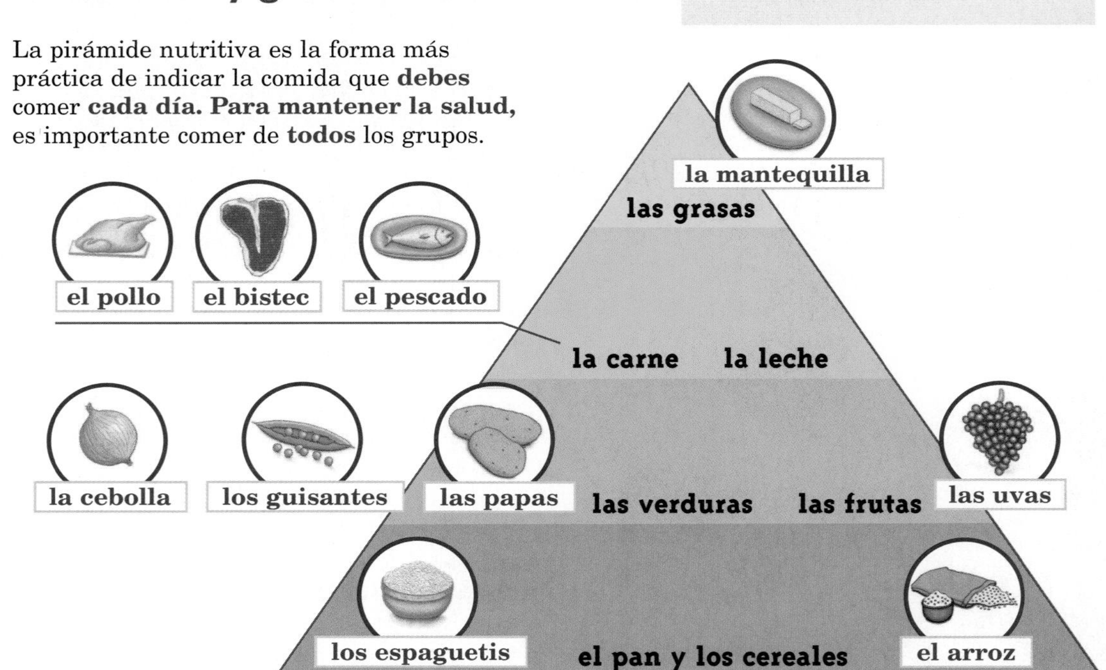

"¡Mi amiga Claudia no come comida buena **para la salud!** Come muchos pasteles y helado. **Son horribles.**"

el helado

los pastel

Universal Access

Students with Learning Difficulties

Have students write the new vocabulary in the vocabulary section of their notebooks, accompanied by pictures and English translations, if needed. For *Actividad* 1, you might prepare students by naming individual items and having the students touch them before they hear them in context.

Heritage Language Learners

Have students make two lists: one of their favorite foods and the other of foods they think they should be eating. Using their lists, have students discuss what they know about diet and activities to maintain good health. Check the lists for spelling.

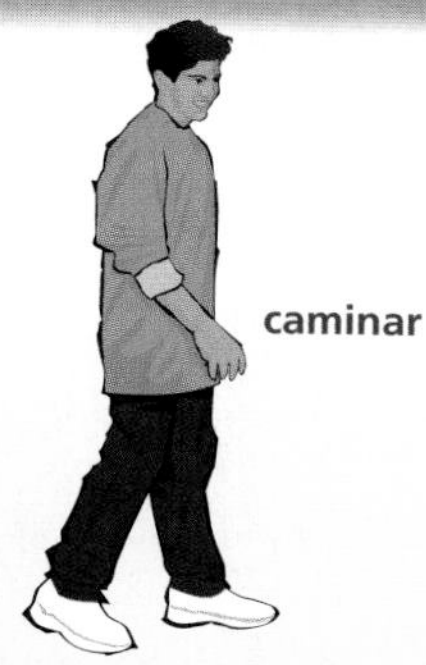

—¿Qué **haces** para mantener la salud?

—Pues, cada día **hago ejercicio.** Camino, monto en bicicleta y practico deportes.

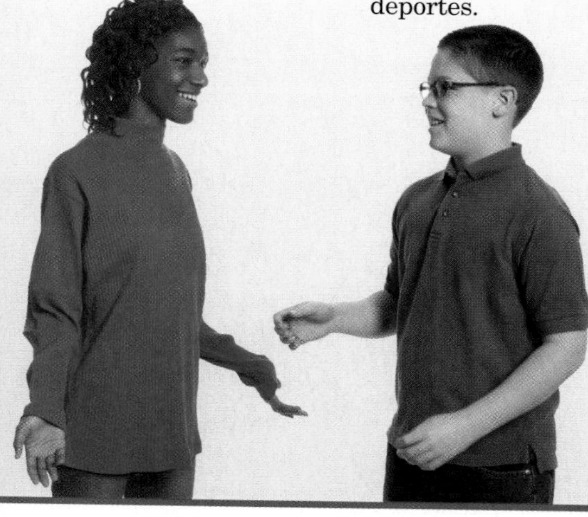

—¡Uf! **Tengo hambre. ¿Por qué** no comemos **algo** en el restaurante "A tu salud"? Los sándwiches son muy **sabrosos.**

—¡Por supuesto!

Actividad 1 **Escuchar**

Debes comer . . .

Your teacher is giving a lecture on foods that you should eat from the Food Guide Pyramid. Touch each item as it is mentioned. You won't understand everything in the sentences, so listen carefully for the names of the foods.

Más práctica
Practice Workbook 3B-1, 3B-2

Actividad 2 **Escuchar**

Para mantener la salud

Listen to students talk about things they do. Give a "thumbs-up" sign if they are describing things that are healthy and a "thumbs-down" sign if the things are unhealthy.

Go Online PHSchool.com
For: Vocabulary practice
Visit: www.phschool.com
Web Code: jad-0311

Actividad 1 *Standards:* 1.2, 3.1

Resources: Audio Program: CD Cap. 3B, Track 3; Resource Book: Cap. 3B, Audio Script; Practice Answers on Transparencies

Focus: Listening comprehension about the Food Guide Pyramid

Suggestions: Play the *Audio CD* or use the script to read the activity aloud. Tell students that some of the sentences contain more than one food item.

Script and Answers:
1. Necesitas beber leche o comer queso. *(milk)*
2. El pescado y el pollo son buenos para la salud. *(fish, chicken)*
3. Las judías verdes y las zanahorias son verduras importantes. *(green beans, carrots)*
4. No debes comer mucho helado. *(ice cream)*
5. Las papas son buenas para la salud. *(potatoes)*
6. El arroz es bueno para la salud. *(rice)*
7. No es bueno comer muchos pasteles. *(pastries)*
8. Debes comer uvas u otra fruta cada día. *(grapes)*

Actividad 2 *Standards:* 1.2, 3.1

Resources: Audio Program: CD Cap. 3B, Track 4; Resource Book: Cap. 3B, Audio Script; Practice Answers on Transparencies

Focus: Listening comprehension about food and health

Suggestions: Play the *Audio CD* or read the script. Repeat the activity until students indicate understanding.

Script and Answers:
1. Me gusta mucho correr. *(up)*
2. Nunca hago ejercicio. *(down)*
3. Practico deportes. *(up)*
4. Como pasteles cada día. *(down)*
5. Mis amigos y yo levantamos pesas. *(up)*
6. Bebo agua cada día. *(up)*
7. Nunca como verduras. ¡Son horribles! *(down)*
8. Me gustan los espaguetis con tomate. *(up)*

Enriching Your Teaching

Culture Note

Food items may have many different names across cultures. Green beans, for example, may be called ***judías verdes, ejotes, habas, alubias,*** and ***habichuelas.*** Some may assume the term ***judías verdes*** is a reference to Jewish people. It is in fact from the Arabic *yudiyaa,* the word for "bean."

Internet Search

Keywords:

La Guía Pirámide de Alimentos

Teacher-to-Teacher

Make a Food Guide Pyramid chart and display it in the classroom. Have students add labels of foods they eat to the different parts of the pyramid.

Videohistoria

Presentation

Standards: 1.2

Resources: Voc. & Gram. Transparencies: 75–76; Audio Program: CD Cap. 3B, Track 5; Practice Answers on Transparencies

Focus: Presenting additional contextualized vocabulary and grammar; previewing the video

Suggestions:

Pre-reading: Direct attention to the *Strategy.* Have students look at the pictures, panel by panel, and write their predictions. Do students notice what Mamá is serving in panel 8? Do they remember that Mamá was planning this meal in the last chapter?

Answers:

1. **No, Tomás does not.**
2. **Tomás lifts weights and walks.**
3. **Tomás is feeling hungry.**

Videohistoria

Para mantener la salud

¿Qué hacen Raúl, Tomás y Gloria para mantener la salud? Lee la historia.

Antes de leer

Strategy **Using visuals to make predictions** Use the pictures to try to predict what will happen before you read the story. As you read, predicting what will happen next will help you understand the story better.

- How did your predictions compare with what you read?

1. Look at photo 1. Does Tomás think that coffee is good for your health?
2. Look at photo 5. What does Tomás do for exercise?
3. Look at photo 6. How is Tomás feeling?

Universal Access

Students with Special Needs

Some students may have difficulty matching the characters' speech in the *Videohistoria* dialogues with the people in the photos. As students read, use the transparencies and point to the characters. Have students do the same in their books.

Multiple Intelligence

Visual / Spatial: Ask students to create a poster with foods they eat and exercises they do to stay healthy. Have them include activities from *Cap.* 1A. The poster should include information about why the foods and exercises are healthy. Display the posters in class.

1 **Tomás: Tengo sed . . .**
Raúl: ¿Qué **prefieres?** ¿Te gusta el café? El café de Costa Rica es muy bueno.
Tomás: ¡Pero el café es **malo** para la salud! **Prefiero** una **bebida** como . . . un jugo de fruta.

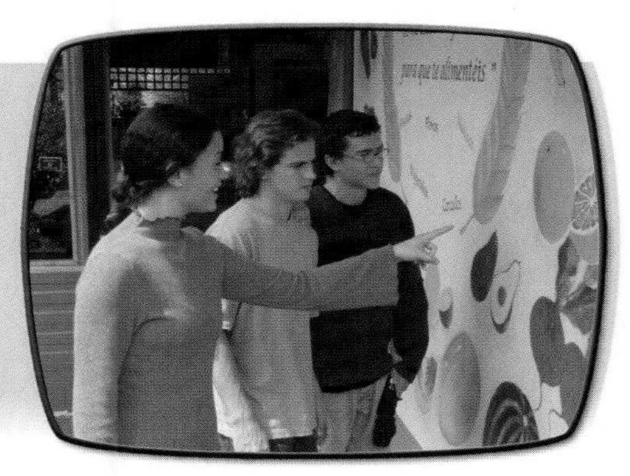

2 **Raúl:** ¡Ah! **Estoy de acuerdo,** un refresco.
Tomás: Raúl, ¿por qué hablas de *refrescos?* A mí me gustan los jugos de fruta.
Gloria: Porque, Tomás, ¡un *refresco* en Costa Rica *es* un jugo de fruta!

3 **Raúl:** Dos refrescos de mango con leche.
Gloria: Y un refresco de mango con agua, por favor.

4 **Tomás:** ¡Es *muuuy* sabroso!
Gloria y Raúl: Sí, sí . . . ¡y todos los refrescos aquí son buenos para la salud!
Gloria: Tomás, ¿qué haces para mantener la salud?

Reading: Read the captions or play the *Audio CD.* Using the transparencies and non-verbal clues, help students understand the new words in blue type.

Post-reading: Complete the activities on p.183 to check comprehension.

Additional Resources

- Writing, Audio & Video Workbook: Cap. 3B, Video Activity 1

Enriching Your Teaching

Culture Note

In Costa Rica, ***gallo pinto,*** the national dish of fried rice and black beans, is served as a breakfast food. Many meals are derivatives of *gallo pinto,* including ***arroz con pollo*** or ***arroz con atún***. At lunch, ***gallo pinto*** becomes ***casado:*** rice and beans accompanied by cabbage and tomato salad, fried plantains, and meat.

Teacher-to-Teacher

Make cloze activities out of the *Videohistoria* panels by copying them onto index cards and deleting some of the words. Write the missing words on the board. Divide students into eight groups (one for each panel) and have them complete the dialogues using the words on the board, rather than referring to their books.

Video

Presentation

 *Standards:* 1.2

Resources: Video Program: Cap. 3B; Resource Book: Cap. 3B, Video Script

Focus: Comprehending contextualized language about healthy eating habits

Suggestions:

Pre-viewing: Review the *Videohistoria* reading, and have students list the key ideas. Play a video excerpt with the sound muted, and ask students which panel of the *Videohistoria* it corresponds to.

Divide the class into eight groups and assign each group one of the panels from the reading. During the video, when they see the action or hear the dialogue from their assigned panel, they will "do the wave" in their group. (One student waves both arms in front of himself or herself, setting off a chain reaction of the rest of the students who do the same, one at a time.) Practice before showing the video by calling out the first lines of the panels.

Viewing: Show the video without pausing, then show it again, stopping along the way to check new vocabulary. Ask students to identify unfamiliar words or behavior. Were any parts of the video easier to understand? Why? Which words were similar to English words?

Post-viewing: Complete the Video Activities in the *Writing, Audio & Video Workbook*.

Additional Resources

- Writing, Audio & Video Workbook: Cap. 3B, Video Activities 2–4
- Heritage Learner Workbook: 3B-1, 3B-2

5 **Tomás:** ¡Me gusta hacer algo cada día! Hago ejercicio, levanto pesas o camino todos los días.

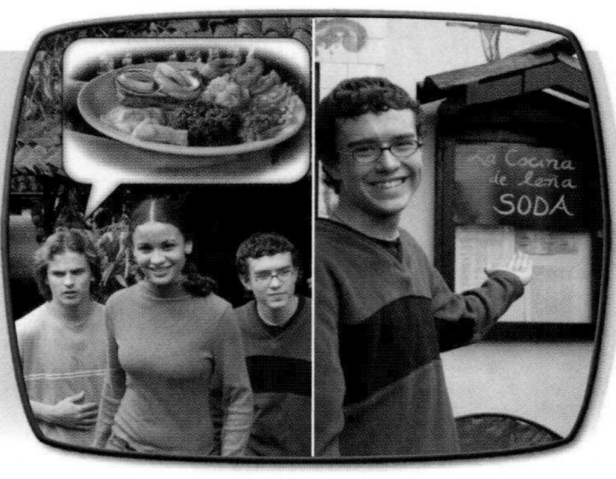

6 **Tomás:** Tengo hambre.
Raúl: ¿Por qué no comemos en la soda?*

**La soda* is the word for a casual restaurant in Costa Rica.

7 **Tomás:** La comida aquí es muy buena. Ahora no tengo hambre. ¿Y tú?
Raúl: **¡Creo que no!**
Gloria: Pues, **creo que** debemos ir a casa.

8 **Mamá:** ¡A comer **la cena!**
Los jóvenes: *¡Uf!*

Universal Access

Multiple Intelligence

Interpersonal / Social: Have students write other statements the characters might make. Students will exchange their statements with a classmate and guess who would make each statement.

Heritage Language Learners

Have students describe a dish they eat at home that other students may not have tried. If possible, have them give a cooking demonstration in your home economics department kitchen or the cafeteria. Be cautious about sampling, however, due to the risk of food allergies.

Leer/Escribir

¿Quién dice . . . ?

Number your paper 1–6. Based on what you read in the *Videohistoria,* write the name(s) of the character(s) who would make each of these statements.

1. Prefiero el café de Costa Rica.
2. Creo que es bueno hacer ejercicio.
3. Prefiero jugo de fruta.
4. Creo que los refrescos en Costa Rica son sabrosos.
5. Creo que el café es malo para la salud.
6. No debemos comer la cena.

Raúl

Gloria

Tomás

Leer/Escribir

¿Estás de acuerdo?

Read each statement, and write *Cierto* if the statement is true, or *Falso* if it is not. Base your answers on what you read in the *Videohistoria.*

1. Raúl tiene sed.
2. Según Tomás, el café es bueno para la salud.
3. Un refresco en Costa Rica es un jugo de fruta.
4. Gloria bebe un refresco de mango con leche.
5. Tomás nada todos los días.
6. A Tomás no le gusta nada la comida de la soda.
7. Según Gloria, los jóvenes deben ir a casa.
8. La mamá de Raúl y Gloria no prepara *(doesn't prepare)* la cena.

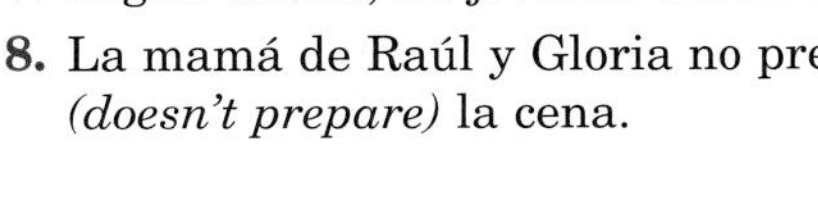

Más práctica

Practice Workbook 3B-3, 3B-4

For: Vocabulary practice
Visit: www.phschool.com
Web Code: jad-0312

Enriching Your Teaching

Culture Note

Point out to students that ***un refresco*** in Costa Rica is made with tropical fruit juices, water or milk, and sugar. Water is recommended with tamarind, passion fruit, and star fruit juices, while milk is preferred with papaya and blackberry juices.

Teacher-to-Teacher

If you have a specialty foods market in your area, bring some mangoes, papayas, and other tropical fruits to class for your students to see. Be cautious about sampling, however, because of the risk of food allergies.

Standards: 1.2

Resources: Practice Answers on Transparencies

Focus: Reading comprehension

Suggestions: Tell students that they will not find the exact sentences in *Actividad* 3 in the *Videohistoria*. Read through the sentences and have students look for the keywords that will help them do the activity.

Answers:

1. Raúl
2. Tomás
3. Tomás y Raúl
4. Tomás
5. Tomás
6. los jóvenes

Extension: Write the sentences on flashcards, with one word written on each flashcard. Shuffle the flashcards for one sentence and give them to a student to arrange correctly on the chalktray.

Standards: 1.2, 1.3

Resources: Practice Answers on Transparencies

Focus: Reading comprehension

Suggestions: Point out to students the two meanings of the word ***nada*** in items 5 and 6.

Answers:

1. falso
2. falso
3. cierto
4. falso
5. falso
6. falso
7. cierto
8. falso

Extension: Have students rewrite the false statements to make them true.

Teacher-to-Teacher

Review foods introduced in *Capítulo* 3A. Have students work in small groups to create menus for three meals in a health food restaurant. Have students think of a creative name for their restaurant, write their menus, and decorate them with drawings or pictures. Display the menus.

Assessment

- Prueba 3B-1: Vocabulary recognition

Rapid Review
Review the use of ***el, los, la, las.***

Standards: 1.3

Resources: Practice Answers on Transparencies

Focus: Reading and writing food vocabulary

Suggestions: To help students organize their answers, have them make a two-column chart labeled ***No*** and ***Sí.*** Have volunteers give answers for each item. Accept any logical answer for the replacement items.

Answers: The second item in each set may vary.

1. el arroz...el bistec
2. los pasteles...la lechuga
3. ver la televisión...levantar pesas
4. comer mucho...mantener la salud
5. los tomates...el arroz
6. las papas...el pescado
7. el pescado...el pastel

Standards: 1.2, 1.3

Focus: Demonstrating comprehension of food vocabulary

Suggestions: If classroom management is a concern, do *Actividad* 6 as an individual, rather than a group, activity.

Answers will vary but should reflect vocabulary from p. 178.

Extension: Write the food items on index cards. Take students outside and use chalk to draw a large food pyramid on a sidewalk. Play hopscotch by having a student toss a pebble onto the food pyramid. He or she will choose a food card for that food group, hop out to the food group on the pyramid say the word, deposit the card, pick up the pebble, and hop back.

Manos a la obra

Vocabulario y gramática en uso

Objectives

- Talk about dinner foods
- Express food preferences
- Describe people and foods
- Talk about healthy and unhealthy lifestyles
- Learn to use the plurals of adjectives and the verb *ser*

Leer/Escribir

¡Claro que no!

For each group of words, choose the word or expression that doesn't belong and write it on your paper. Then write one more word or expression that would fit with the group.

Modelo

la cebolla   la lechuga   las uvas
las uvas . . . las zanahorias

1.	el pollo	el pescado	el arroz
2.	las zanahorias	los pasteles	las judías verdes
3.	caminar	correr	ver la televisión
4.	comer mucho	levantar pesas	hacer ejercicio
5.	los tomates	el pan	los espaguetis
6.	el bistec	las papas	el pollo
7.	la mantequilla	el helado	el pescado

Escribir/Leer

Juego

1. Working in a group, make one large food pyramid identical to the one you see on the right.
2. Cut or tear a sheet of paper into ten small pieces, and write the word for one food or drink item on each piece of paper. Exchange the pieces of paper with another group.
3. When your teacher tells you to start, correctly place each of the vocabulary words in the appropriate spot on the food pyramid you have created. The first group to fill in a correct pyramid wins!

las grasas
la carne   la leche
las verduras   las frutas
el pan y los cereales

Universal Access

Heritage Language Learners
Have students talk about the ethnic foods they are familiar with. What are some of the ingredients? At what special occasions are these dishes served?

Multiple Intelligence
Logical / Mathematical: Have students research the fat grams and calories of the foods they have learned about in this chapter. Have them prepare a food pyramid that includes this information.

Fondo cultural

El mate is the national beverage of Argentina, Paraguay, and Uruguay. This herbal tea is shared among family and friends. It is served hot in a hollow gourd, also called *un mate,* with a straw called *una bombilla.*

- What national beverage does the United States have that compares to *mate?*

Escribir

La fiesta

You and a friend are preparing a surprise meal for your parent's birthday, using what's already in your kitchen. Look in the refrigerator at right, and make a list of eight items that you would use to prepare the meal. Be creative!

Hablar

¿Qué comemos en la fiesta?

Compare your list from Actividad 7 with your partner's list. Tell your partner what you think you need for the party. Your partner will agree or disagree.

Modelo

A —*Creo que necesitamos queso.*
B —*Estoy de acuerdo. ¡Me encanta!*
o: *No estoy de acuerdo. ¡Qué asco!*

Standards: 2.1, 2.2, 4.2

Suggestions: Explain that leaves from the ***yerba mate*** tree are used to make the herbal tea. The ***bombilla*** is a filtered metal straw to strain leaf fragments. The gourd is passed from person to person. Ask: What qualifies a beverage or food as "national"? What are some "national" beverages?

Answers will vary, but the second question may include coffee, iced tea, or soft drinks.

Standards: 1.3

Focus: Writing a list of food items

Suggestions: Call on individual students to identify the items in the refrigerator before they do the activity.

Answers will vary.

Common Errors: Students may confuse gender and say: ***las tomates, los papas.*** Remind them that gender must be learned for these words.

Extension: Tell students that they will prepare a surprise breakfast for their parent. Call out items in the refrigerator and have students give you a "thumbs-up" sign for items they would use to prepare breakfast and "thumbs-down" sign for items they would not use.

Standards: 1.1

Focus: Expressing need; agreeing and disagreeing

Suggestions: Tell students that when they compare lists, they should draw a circle around items on their own list that do not appear on their partner's list. These are the items they will use in their conversation.

Answers will vary.

Extension: Have pairs ask and tell the locations of the food items in the refrigerator. *(¿Dónde está el queso? Está al lado de la leche.)*

Enriching Your Teaching

Culture Note

The names of many foods in Mexico come from ***náhuatl,*** the language spoken by the Aztecs and still spoken today. Words from ***náhuatl*** often end in ***-te*** (from ***-tl***). Some examples include: ***chocolate, cacahuate, ejote*** (string bean), ***elote*** (corn), and ***tomate.***

Teacher-to-Teacher

Create a "refrigerator" out of a cardboard box with a flap for the door. Bring real food items, or empty packaging that suggests these items, to class. Place several of the items in the refrigerator, then open the door for students to see for three seconds. Close the door and have them list as many items as they can remember.

Standards: 1.3

Focus: Using food vocabulary to create meal menus

Recycle: Breakfast, lunch, and dinner food items

Suggestions: Tell students that they should use the food items from *Capítulo.* 3A for this activity, also.

Answers will vary but may include:

el desayuno: **el pan, el café, la mantequilla, la leche, la papaya, las frutas;** ***el almuerzo:*** **el pescado, el arroz, las zanahorias, el jamón, el pollo;** ***la cena:*** **los espaguetis, las papas, los guisantes, las tortillas, el bistec**

Extension: Have students copy the food items they listed for one meal onto a piece of paper. Tell them to scramble the letters. Students will exchange lists and unscramble each other's food items.

Standards: 1.1, 1.3

Resources: Practice Answers on Transparencies

Focus: Talking about maintaining good health

Recycle: Vocabulary from prior chapters

Suggestions: Discuss what kinds of foods should be eaten daily and which should not be eaten in excess. Ask volunteers to perform their conversations.

Answers:

1. **—¿Debo comer papas fritas cada día para mantener la salud?**
   —Creo que no.
2. **¿...verduras...? Creo que sí.**
3. **¿...pan y mantequilla...? Creo que no.**
4. **¿...frutas...? Creo que sí.**
5. **¿...helado...? Creo que no.**
6. **¿...yogur...? Creo que sí.**
7. **¿...beber agua...? Creo que sí.**

Extension: Have students reverse roles and use ***necesito*** instead of ***debo.***

  **Escribir**

Menú del día

You're in charge of the menu! Decide what you would serve your family for each meal. Copy the chart below on a sheet of paper, and fill in items that you would serve. Be sure to include at least five logical items for each one.

el desayuno	el almuerzo	la cena

Una cena grande con toda la familia

  **Pensar/Hablar**

¿Sí o no?

With a partner, talk about the things that you should eat and drink in order to be healthy.

Modelo

A —*¿Debo beber leche cada día para mantener la salud?*
B —*Creo que sí.*
o: *Creo que no.*

Estudiante A

Estudiante B

Creo que . . .

Universal Access

Advanced Learners

Have Student B extend the *Creo que sí* responses in *Actividad* 10 by saying *Y también, debemos beber / comer. . . .*

Heritage Language Learners

Have students write a nursery rhyme, a poem, a song, or a rap that would help young children learn which foods are good for one's health and which ones are not.

  Hablar

¿Qué prefieres?

Ask your partner which of two foods he or she prefers. Your partner will answer and ask you which one you prefer.

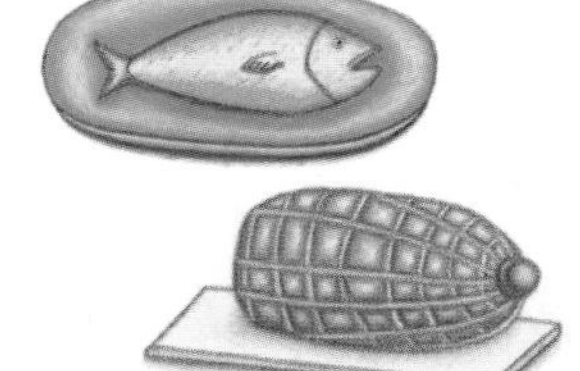

Modelo

A —*¿Qué prefieres, carne o pescado?*
B —*Prefiero carne. Y tú, ¿qué prefieres?*
o: *No como ni carne ni pescado. Y tú, ¿qué prefieres?*
A —*Prefiero pescado.*

Estudiante B

¡Respuesta personal!

En los supermercados de Texas hay muchas frutas y verduras de México.

Practice and Communicate

Standards: 1.1

Resources: Practice Answers on Transparencies

Focus: Talking about food preferences

Suggestions: Discuss the options in the *Modelo* with students. Be sure they understand that they are to answer truthfully.

Answers will vary, but will include:

1. **¿Qué prefieres, pescado o pollo?**
2. **¿...pizza o espaguetis?**
3. **¿...papas o arroz?**
4. **¿...zanahorias o tomates?**
5. **¿...guisantes o judías verdes?**
6. **¿...cebollas o lechuga?**
7. **¿...helado o uvas?**

Extension: Have students figure out their partner's favorite food among those listed by asking about the foods their partner said he or she preferred. For example, if Student B says he or she prefers the chicken in item 1 and the pizza in item 2, Student A will ask if Student B prefers the chicken or the pizza, and so forth.

Teaching with Photos

Suggestions: Have students identify as many of the fruits and vegetables in the photo as they can.

Enriching Your Teaching

Culture Note

Texas was once a part of Mexico, and many people living in Texas are of Mexican heritage. One result of the blending of European-American and Mexican-American cultures is Tex-Mex cuisine. Some examples of Tex-Mex cuisine include tacos, nachos, burritos, fajitas, and chili.

Internet Search

Keyword: Tex-Mex cuisine 

Standards: 1.1

Resources: Practice Answers on Transparencies

Focus: Talking about foods and beverages appropriate for certain times of day

Recycle: Telling time

Suggestions: Point out the *Para decir más...* Students are not held responsible for these words but should use them in their answers. Show the transparencies with food vocabulary while students practice the conversation. Point out that Student B should give a personal response.

Answers will vary but will include:

1. Son las doce (es mediodía)...
2. Son las diez de la noche...
3. Son las nueve de la mañana...
4. Son las siete de la mañana...
5. Son las seis de la tarde...
6. Son las tres de la tarde...

Standards: 1.2, 1.3

Focus: Reading comprehension and writing new vocabulary

Suggestion: While students are working, walk around the room to support students who need assistance. Tell students to keep their work for *Actividad* 14.

Answers will vary.

Standards: 1.1

Focus: Talking about maintaining good health

Suggestion: When students have discussed all seven items, have them reverse roles and practice again.

Answers will vary.

Extension: Have students write four more sentences telling two things one should do for good health and two things one should not do.

   **Hablar**

¿Hay algo para comer?

Working with a partner, talk about what you should eat and drink at the following times.

Para decir más...

de la mañana	in the morning
de la tarde	in the afternoon
de la noche	in the evening

Modelo

A —*Son las ocho de la mañana y tengo hambre y sed. ¿Qué debo comer y beber?*
B —*Debes comer cereal y debes beber té.*

Estudiante A

Estudiante B

¡Respuesta personal!

 **Leer/Escribir**

Los buenos consejos

Give advice about what's good or bad for your health. Copy and complete each sentence.

1. Para mantener la salud, debes ___ todos los días.
2. Necesitas beber ___ cada día.
3. Debes comer ___ en la cena.
4. ___ es malo para la salud.
5. El jugo de zanahoria es ___.
6. Debes comer ___ todos los días.
7. Nunca debes comer ___.

  **Hablar**

Compartir consejos

Compare the advice you gave in Actividad 13 with the advice your partner gave. If you disagree with your partner's advice, suggest something else.

Modelo

A —*Para mantener la salud, debes practicar deportes todos los días.*
B —*Estoy de acuerdo.*
o: *No estoy de acuerdo. Debes correr todos los días.*

También se dice...

los guisantes = los chícharos *(México)*; las arvejas *(Argentina)*
las papas = las patatas *(España)*
el tomate = el jitomate *(México)*

Universal Access

Students with Special Needs

Some students may be unable to read clock faces as in *Actividad* 12, so you may want to give them pictures of digital clocks instead. Others may need help filling in the blanks in *Actividad* 13. Offer a list of three choices for each blank and allow students to choose the one they prefer.

Advanced Learners

Have students write a letter giving nutrition advice either to a friend who wants to gain weight before football season or to a friend who wants to lose weight before wrestling season.

Leer/Escribir/Hablar

Un "quiz" para la salud

1. Take the following quiz on healthy activities. Write your answers in complete sentences on a sheet of paper.

¿Qué haces para mantener la salud?

Contesta las preguntas según las actividades que haces cada día. Cada "sí" = 1 punto.

- ❑ **1.** ¿Haces ejercicio?
- ❑ **2.** ¿Practicas deportes?
- ❑ **3.** ¿Comes verduras?
- ❑ **4.** ¿Comes frutas?
- ❑ **5.** ¿Caminas o corres?
- ❑ **6.** ¿Comes un buen desayuno?
- ❑ **7.** ¿Comes comida que es buena para la salud?
- ❑ **8.** ¿Bebes cinco vasos* de agua?
- ❑ **9.** ¿Pasas tiempo con amigos?
- ❑ **10.** ¿No ves más de tres horas de televisión?

9–10 puntos *¡Felicidades! ¡Haces mucho para mantener la salud!*

6–8 puntos *Bueno, pero debes hacer más para mantener la salud.*

0–5 puntos *¡Ay, ay, ay! Necesitas hacer algo para mantener la salud.*

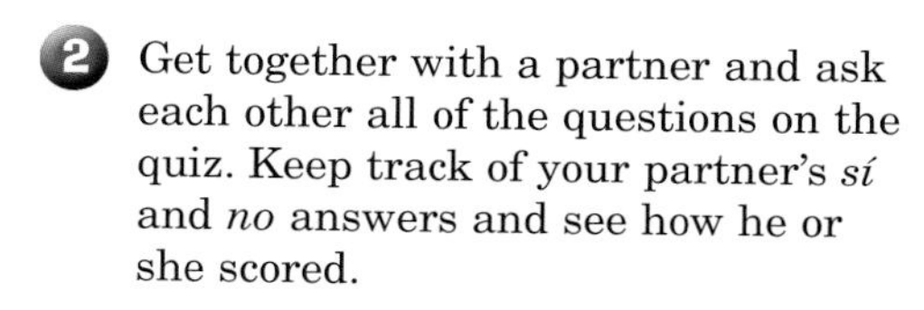

*glasses

2. Get together with a partner and ask each other all of the questions on the quiz. Keep track of your partner's *sí* and *no* answers and see how he or she scored.

3. Write five recommendations suggesting what your partner should do every day to have a healthier lifestyle.

Modelo

Debes hacer ejercicio todos los días.

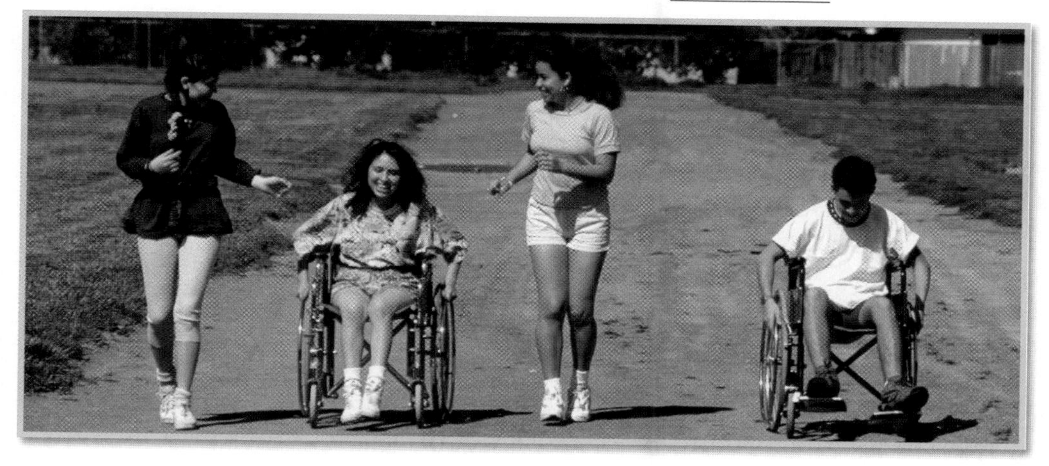

Actividad 15 *Standards:* 1.1, 1.2, 1.3

Resources: Voc. & Gram, Transparencies: 78

Focus: Reading comprehension; giving written recommendations about health

Recycle: Present-tense ***yo*** form of verbs ***hacer, practicar, comer, caminar, beber, pasar,*** and ***ver***

Suggestions: Have students skim the questionnaire and clarify any difficulties with the vocabulary. Use Transparency 78 to do the reading as a class.

Answers will vary.

Common Errors: Remind students to answer in complete sentences.

Extension: Have students interview family members and report to the class.

Additional Resources

- Writing, Audio & Video Workbook: Cap. 3B, Audio Activities 5–6, Tracks 6–7
- Writing, Audio & Video Workbook: Cap. 3B, Writing Activity 10
- Resource Book: Cap. 3B, Communicative Activity BLM

Assessment

- Prueba 3B-2: Vocabulary production

Theme Project

Students can perform step 4 at this point. Be sure they understand your corrections and suggestions. (For more information, see p. 146-a.)

Enriching Your Teaching

Culture Note

Spain is an active member of the International Paralympic Committee. This committee sponsors Olympic-style competitions for athletes around the world who face physical challenges. Athletes with the following disabilities can compete in various sports: severe back problems, blindness, motor impairment, amputated limbs, and cerebral palsy.

Teacher-to-Teacher

Bring a lunchbox and food props of healthy and unhealthy foods to class. Have students act out a skit between a parent who insists on packing his or her child's lunchbox with healthy food and a child who says he or she dislikes every item the parent puts in the lunchbox. The child will use the unhealthy food props to tell what he or she prefers.

3B Practice and Communicate

Presentation

 *Standards:* 4.1

Resources: Video Program: Cap. 3B; Resource Book: Cap. 3B, Video Script

Suggestions: Remind students that adjectives agree in gender with nouns and point out the *¿Recuerdas?*. Explain that adjectives also agree in number with the noun they modify. Remind students that a mixed-gender group of people also takes the masculine form. Reinforce the use of the plurals of adjectives by showing the *GramActiva* Video.

 *Standards:* 4.1

Resources: Resource Book: Cap. 3B, GramActiva BLM

Focus: Reading adjectives and adding the correct gender and plural ending

Recycle: Adjectives

Suggestions: Give students copies of the *GramActiva* BLM to use for their cards. Use the transparencies or the Clip Art to provide the cues. Allow adequate time for them to select the correct cards.

Answers will vary.

 *Standards:* 1.3

Resources: Practice Answers on Transparencies

Focus: Applying knowledge of gender and plural endings

Suggestions: Make sure that students know that they will need to change the verb ***es*** to ***son*** in each sentence.

Answers:

1. **Todas las estudiantes son deportistas.**
2. **Todos los helados son muy populares.**
3. **Todas las bebidas son horribles.**
4. **Todos los pasteles son malos para la salud.**
5. **Todas las frutas son buenas para la salud.**
6. **Todos los refrescos son sabrosos.**

Gramática

The plurals of adjectives

Just as adjectives agree with a noun depending on whether it's masculine or feminine, they also agree according to whether the noun is singular or plural. To make adjectives plural, just add an *-s* after the vowel at the end of the adjective. If the adjective ends in a consonant, add *-es*.

La hamburguesa es sabros**a**. Las hamburguesas son sabros**as**.

El pastel es muy popular. Los pasteles son muy popular**es**.

When an adjective describes a group including both masculine and feminine nouns, use the masculine plural form.

La lechuga, **las** zanahorias y **los** tomates son buen**os** para la salud.

Don't forget that in the singular form, *mucho(a)* means "much," but in the plural form, *muchos(as)* means "many."

No como mucha carne, pero como much**as** verduras.

¿Recuerdas?

Adjectives agree in gender with the masculine or feminine nouns they modify:

- **El** bistec es sabros**o**.
- **La** ensalada es sabros**a**.

GramActiva VIDEO

Want more help with the the plurals of adjectives? Watch the **GramActiva** video.

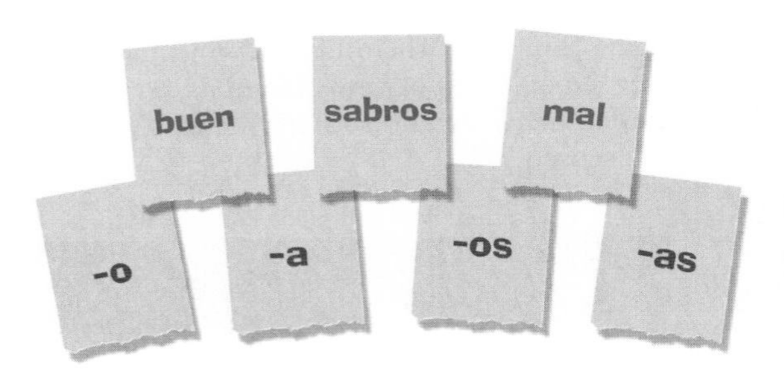

  **Pensar/Leer/GramActiva**

¿Sabroso o sabrosa?

Your teacher will give you a GramActiva worksheet. Tear or cut apart the different adjective stems and endings that are printed on the sheet. Then your teacher will show you pictures of several foods. Show how you feel about each food item by holding up the appropriate adjective stem and the appropriate ending.

buen | sabros | mal

-o | -a | -os | -as

 **Escribir**

Exageramos un poco

Exaggerate a little by rewriting the following sentences in plural form.

Modelo

La hamburguesa es sabrosa.
Todas las hamburguesas son sabrosas.

1. La estudiante es deportista.
2. El helado es muy popular.
3. La bebida es horrible.
4. El pastel es malo para la salud.
5. La fruta es buena para la salud.
6. El refresco es sabroso.

Universal Access

Heritage Language Learners
Have students write ten adjectives used to describe foods. They should think of taste, color, and texture. Have them write sentences using the adjectives and hand them in for correction.

Students with Learning Difficulties
Have students refer to pp. 82 and 114 for a list of adjectives to add to the following nouns. Students should select adjectives appropriate for the noun and make sure that the endings are correct in number and gender. Nouns: *las señoritas; los profesores; las calculadoras; las clases.*

Actividad 18 Gramática · Hablar

En el club deportivo

In many parts of Latin America, young people exercise, practice sports, and get together for after-school activities at sports clubs. Work with a partner to describe the following kids who go to the Club Deportivo Águila.

Luis y Ricardo

Modelo

A —*¿Cómo son Luis y Ricardo?*
B —*Ellos son atrevidos.*

Estudiante A

Flor y Carlos

Lisa y Pilar

Andrés y Carmen

Marco y Tomás

Paqui y Ramón

Micaela y Luisa

Estudiante B

perezoso	serio
artístico	atrevido
gracioso	talentoso
deportista	

Más práctica
Practice Workbook 3B-5

For: Practice with plural of adjectives
Visit: www.phschool.com
Web Code: jad-0313

Pronunciación

The letters *l* and *ll*

In Spanish, the letter *l* is pronounced much like the letter *l* in the English word *leaf*. Listen to and say these words:

lechuga	lunes	pasteles	helado
almuerzo	sol	abril	difícil

For most Spanish speakers, the letter combination *ll* is similar to the sound of the letter *y* in *yes*. Listen to and say these words:

llamo	silla	allí	llueve
cebolla	pollo	ella	mantequilla

Try it out! Listen to this song and then sing it.

Canta el gallo, canta el gallo
con el kiri, kiri, kiri, kiri, kiri;
La gallina, la gallina
con el cara, cara, cara, cara, cara;
Los polluelos, los polluelos
con el pío, pío, pío, pío, pío, pío, pí.

Practice and Communicate 3B

Rapid Review

Call out the personality traits from *Actividad* 18 and have students tell you the name of a character from a book, TV show, or movie who has that personality trait.

Actividad 18 — *Standards:* 1.1

Resources: Practice Answers on Transparencies

Focus: Using plural adjectives to describe people

Suggestions: Have students switch roles after each description.

Answers:
Student A:
All answers will begin with ¿Cómo son...?
Student B:
Ellos son deportistas.
Ellas son serias.
Ellos son talentosos *(artísticos).*
Ellos son perezosos.
Ellos son graciosos.
Ellas son artísticas *(talentosas).*

Pronunciación

Presentation

Standards: 4.1

Resources: Audio Program: CD Cap. 3B, Tracks 8–9

Focus: Pronouncing the letters ***l*** and ***ll***

Suggestions: Demonstrate the difference between pronunciation of ***l*** and ***ll.*** Have students repeat the words. Play the song from the *Audio CD.*

Try it out! Before listening to the song, have students look at the picture and match **gallo, gallina,** and **polluelos** with the correct images.

Enriching Your Teaching

Teacher-to-Teacher

Tell students that the song uses onomatopoeia ***(onomatopeya),*** words formed by imitating sounds. Students may enjoy learning how Spanish represents the sounds made by other animals. These provide very good pronunciation practice.

Internet Search

Keyword: onomatopoeia

Additional Resources

- Writing, Audio & Video Workbook: Cap. 3B, Audio Activity 7, Track 10
- Writing, Audio & Video Workbook: Cap. 3B, Writing Activity 11
- Resource Book: Cap. 3b, Communicate Activity BLM

Assessment

- Prueba 3B-3: The plurals of adjectives

Presentation

Standards: 4.1

Resources: Voc. & Gram. Transparencies: 77; Video Program: Cap. 3B; Resource Book: Cap. 3B, Video Script

Suggestions: Direct attention to the *¿Recuerdas?* Have students practice ***ser*** by first saying their own names *(**Soy...**)*. Then point to or group other students to demonstrate the other forms.

Standards: 1.3

Resources: Practice Answers on Transparencies

Focus: Writing sentences using the correct forms of ***ser***

Suggestions: Look at the first item together and ask students which two clues will help them choose the ending (the verb form ***es,*** and ***deportista,*** which is singular).

Answers:

1. c
2. e
3. a
4. b
5. d

Common Errors: Students might look for a feminine plural subject when they see the ending to item 3 *(Son muy deportistas...)*. Remind them that ***deportista*** ends with ***-a*** regardless of the gender of the noun it modifies.

Standards: 1.2, 1.3

Resources: Practice Answers on Transparencies

Focus: Using the correct forms of ***ser***

Suggestions: Before students do the activity, show how to find the correct verb on the chart when the subject of the sentence is a common noun **(*la fruta*)** or a proper noun **(*El Sr. y la Sra. Zarzalejos*)**.

Answers:

1. soy
2. es
3. son
4. son
5. somos
6. es
7. son
8. eres

Gramática

The verb *ser*

Ser, which means "to be," is an irregular verb. Use *ser* to describe what a person or thing is like. Here are the present-tense forms:

(yo)	soy	(nosotros) (nosotras)	somos
(tú)	eres	(vosotros) (vosotras)	sois
Ud. (él) (ella)	es	Uds. (ellos) (ellas)	son

¿Recuerdas?

In previous chapters, you learned how to talk about what a person is like.

—Tú **eres** muy deportista, ¿no?

—Sí, **soy** deportista.

—Mi amigo Pablo **es** deportista también.

GramActiva VIDEO

Want more help with the verb *ser?* Watch the **GramActiva** video.

Actividad 19 Gramática Escribir

Amigos deportistas

Juan Pablo thinks that he and his friends are very athletic. Find out why by combining the appropriate phrases. Write the completed sentences on a sheet of paper.

1. Es muy deportista . . .
2. Somos muy deportistas . . .
3. Son muy deportistas . . .
4. Soy muy deportista . . .
5. Eres muy deportista . . .

a. porque ellos caminan todos los días.
b. porque yo corro cada tarde.
c. porque ella hace mucho ejercicio.
d. porque tú levantas pesas.
e. porque nosotros nadamos todas las noches.

Actividad 20 Gramática Leer/Escribir

En el mercado de fruta

Rafe's mother is explaining to him how she likes to buy fruit at the local market. Complete her explanation by using the correct form of the verb *ser.* Write your answers on a separate sheet of paper.

Yo __1.__ muy práctica. Me gusta mucho comprar la fruta en el mercado Zarzalejos. La fruta nunca __2.__ mala. Los plátanos __3.__ sabrosos y las fresas __4.__ muy buenas también. La Sra. Zarzalejos y yo __5.__ buenas amigas. Ella trabaja en el mercado y __6.__ muy trabajadora. El Sr. y la Sra. Zarzalejos __7.__ muy simpáticos. Rafe, tú __8.__ muy trabajador, ¿por qué no trabajas en el mercado con ellos en el verano?

Universal Access

Advanced Learners

Some students may notice that *¿Cómo estás?* and *¿Cómo está Ud.?* use a different verb for "to be" from the one shown above. If so, it is appropriate to go ahead and give them a limited explanation of the difference between ***ser*** and ***estar.*** The formal explanation is in *Realidades B, Capítulo* 5B.

Un mercado guatemalteco

Fondo cultural

Los mercados, or open-air markets, are common throughout Latin America. Many towns have a central market, held on a given day of the week, where people come from all around to buy and sell food, as well as flowers, crafts, and clothing.

- How does this market compare with the ways in which fruits and vegetables are bought in your community?

21 Escuchar/Escribir

Escucha y escribe

You will hear comments from five customers about the food being sold in a market. On a sheet of paper, write the numbers 1–5. As you listen, write the comments next to the numbers.

Un mercado de fruta

22 Gramática Escribir

En la cafetería

Write eight original sentences to describe the following people and things that you see while eating lunch in the cafeteria. Your sentences all need to make sense!

yo el almuerzo las verduras mis amigos y yo la leche los profesores tú el helado	ser	inteligente deportista talentoso simpático popular	sabroso malo para la salud horrible perezoso bueno para la salud

¡Respuesta personal!

Enriching Your Teaching

Culture Note

The variety of fresh fruits and vegetables sold in open-air and interior markets in Spanish-speaking countries is amazingly assorted. A number of markets also serve hot meals at reasonable prices. Many people like to visit the markets during lunchtime.

Teacher-to-Teacher

Bring in the weekly menu from your school cafeteria. Have students give their opinions of the foods that are served. Which ones do they eat? Which ones do they not eat? Students are likely to have strong opinions. Have a volunteer keep track of the reactions and give a rating for each item.

Standards: 2.1, 4.2

Fondo cultural

Suggestions: Ask students what they find interesting about the picture. Discuss the differences between open-air markets and supermarkets. Ask if there are open-air markets in your community.

Answers will vary.

Standards: 1.2

Actividad 21

Resources: Audio Program: CD Cap. 3B, Track 11; Resource Book: Cap. 3B, Audio Script; Practice Answers on Transparencies

Focus: Listening comprehension about food sold in a market

Suggestions: Play the *Audio CD* or read the script two or three times to allow students to focus on the comments before they write.

Script and Answers:

1. **Las zanahorias son muy buenas.**
2. **La papa es sabrosa.**
3. **Las cebollas son malas.**
4. **Señor, los guisantes son horribles.**
5. **El pescado no es bueno.**

Standards: 1.3

Actividad 22

Resources: Practice Answers on Transparencies

Focus: Writing personalized sentences to practice ***ser*** and adjective agreement

Suggestion: Review the adjectives, asking students if an adjective could apply to a person, to a food item, or to both before having students do the activity.

Answers will vary but will include:

yo soy...	**la leche es...**
el almuerzo es...	**los profesores son...**
las verduras son...	**tú eres...**
mis amigos y yo somos...	**el helado es...**

Teaching with Photos

Suggestions: Ask students to compare and contrast the markets shown here with the photograph of the market and the painting of a market on pp. 176–177.

3B Practice and Communicate

Exploración del lenguaje

 *Standards:* 4.1

Resources: Practice Answers on Transparencies

Suggestions: You may want to discuss word origins in English with the class before reading the *Exploración del lenguaje*. Have students match the obvious words first, and discuss the similarities between the words.

Answers:

1. agua...*aqua*
2. arroz...*óryza*
3. pan...*panis*
4. bistec...*beefsteak*
5. salchichas...*salciccia*
6. pescado...*piscatu*
7. café...*kahvé*
8. pollo...*pullu*

Rapid Review

Have students call out the names of the foods in *Actividad* 23 as you call out the numbers in random order.

Resources: Practice Answers on Transparencies

Focus: Giving opinions about foods

Recycle: Foods and beverages

Suggestions: Model the options in the answers. Brainstorm possible *¡Respuesta personal!* answers.

Answers will include:

1. ¿Comes pescado en la cena?
2. ¿...uvas...?
3. ¿...guisantes...?
4. ¿Bebes leche...?
5. ¿Comes mantequilla...?
6. ¿...judías verdes...?
7. ¿...yogur...?
8. ¿...pasteles...?
9. ¿...papas...?
10. ¿...tocino...?
11. ¿...fresas...?

Exploración del lenguaje

Where did it come from?

The names of many foods in Spanish come from Latin as well as from other languages as diverse as Arabic, Italian, Greek, Turkish, and English. While it's clear that the word *espaguetis* comes from the Italian word *spaghetti,* it's not obvious that the word *zanahoria* comes from the Arabic word *safunariya*.

Try it out! Read the Spanish words on the left and match them up to their counterparts in their language of origin on the right.

agua	*piscatu* (Latin)
arroz	*aqua* (Latin)
pan	*beefsteak* (English)
bistec	*pane* (Latin)
salchichas	*pullu* (Latin)
pescado	*kahvé* (Turkish)
café	*salciccia* (Italian)
pollo	*óryza* (Greek)

Hablar

¿Sabroso u horrible?

Work with a partner and express your opinions on various foods and beverages.

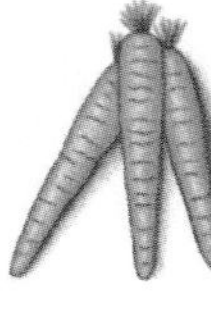

Modelo

A —*¿Comes zanahorias en la cena?*
B —*No, no como zanahorias en la cena porque son horribles.*
o: *Sí, como zanahorias en la cena porque son buenas para la salud.*

Estudiante A

Estudiante B

(muy) sabroso
bueno para la salud
malo para la salud
horrible

¡Respuesta personal!

Universal Access

Multiple Intelligences

Verbal / Linguistic: Have students conjecture as to why food items often have names borrowed from other cultures. Have them research the origins of some of their favorite food items and the etymology of the names.

Heritage Language Learners

Have students choose four food items and explore the different names they have in different Spanish-speaking countries. How did these differences arise? Where did the names come from? If the name is borrowed from another language, what is the historical connection?

Fondo cultural

La Tomatina How would you like to attend a festival where a gigantic food fight with tomatoes is the highlight of the day? That's what happens at the annual *Fiesta de la Tomatina* in Buñol, Spain. After the town council distributes more than 130 tons of ripe tomatoes to participants, the two-hour-long tomato-throwing festival begins.

- Describe any festivals unique to your community or your state. How do they compare to *La Tomatina?*

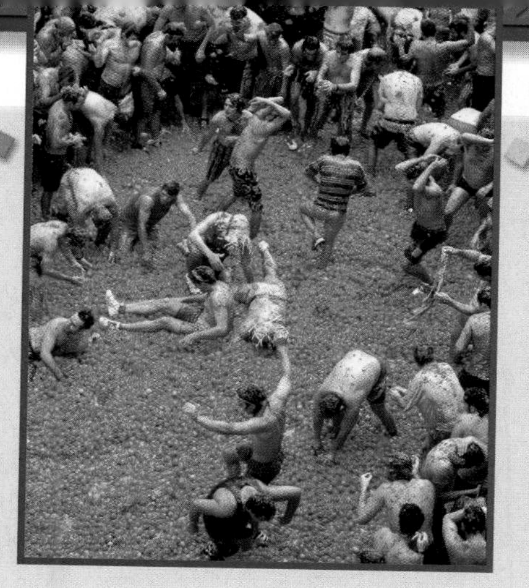

La Tomatina en Buñol, España

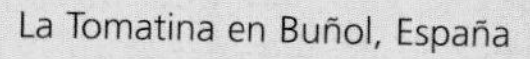

Leer/Escribir

En el festival

Your friend Juanito has just attended the *Tomatina* festival and has written a postcard to tell you all about it. However, there were so many tomatoes flying around that some got on the postcard, and now you have to figure out what it says.

1. Number your paper 1–5 and write the forms of the verb *ser* that best complete the postcard.

2. Write your own postcard to a friend and describe people you know and things you are familiar with. Use Juanito's postcard as a model.

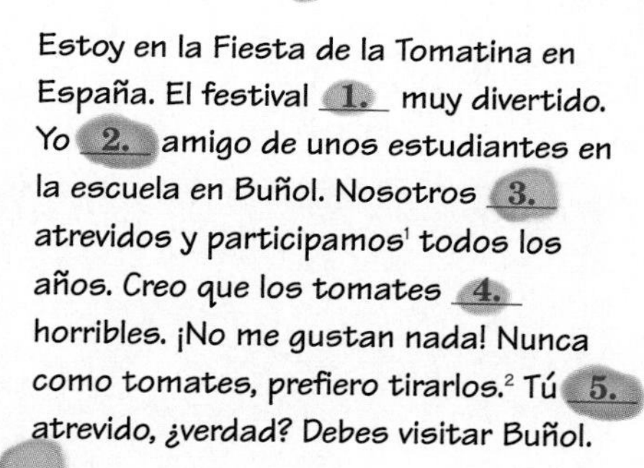

¡Hola!

Estoy en la Fiesta de la Tomatina en España. El festival __1.__ muy divertido. Yo __2.__ amigo de unos estudiantes en la escuela en Buñol. Nosotros __3.__ atrevidos y participamos[1] todos los años. Creo que los tomates __4.__ horribles. ¡No me gustan nada! Nunca como tomates, prefiero tirarlos.[2] Tú __5.__ atrevido, ¿verdad? Debes visitar Buñol.

Hasta pronto,

Juanito

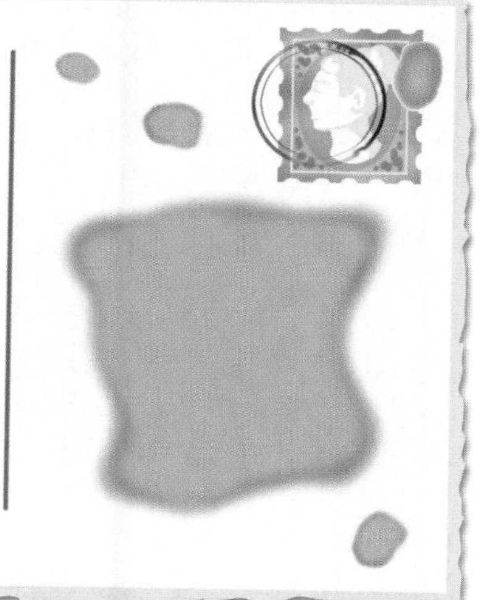

[1]we participate [2]to throw them

Enriching Your Teaching

Culture Note

The tomato has been cultivated in the Andes since prehistoric times. Tomato growing spread from South America to Mexico more than 3,000 years ago. Tomatoes were then brought to Europe. By 1550, tomatoes were being grown in Italy.

Teacher-to-Teacher

Have students think about milk or orange juice ads they have seen. Have them create an ad that endorses a vegetable or fruit from this chapter. Display their posters in the room.

Standards: 2.1, 4.2

Fondo cultural

Suggestions: Ask: Would you participate in a festival like this? Why or why not? How might a celebration like *La Tomatina* be good or bad for a community?

Answers will vary.

Standards: 1.2, 1.3

Actividad 24

Resources: Practice Answers on Transparencies

Focus: Reading and writing contextualized vocabulary

Suggestions: Encourage students to write a humorous letter for step 2. Have volunteers read their letters to the class.

Answers:

Step 1
1. es
2. soy
3. somos
4. son
5. eres

Step 2
Answers will vary.

Standards: 1.2, 4.1

Resources: Voc. & Gram. Transparencies: 79

Focus: Reading and writing with contextualized vocabulary

Recycle: Food vocabulary from *Cap.* 3A.

Suggestions: Point out the *Strategy* and have students scan the text for cognates. Have students read the ad and list the health benefits of each ingredient. Can students guess the meaning of ***saludable?***

Answers will vary, but may include:

1. **pizza, ingredientes, calorías, variedad, usamos, nutritivos, combinación, sodio**
2. **It should have less cheese. It should have lots of vegetables. It should have chicken.**

Extension: Have students write their own ads for a vegetarian restaurant, a juice bar, or a gourmet sandwich shop. Have them list words related to health and food, then work in pairs to draft the ad. Ads should include an original name for the business and an address and telephone number.

Standards: 1.1, 1.3

Focus: Reading and speaking about food, likes and dislikes

Recycle: Leisure activities

Suggestions: Students may like ingredients not listed in the vocabulary from *Capítulos* 3A or 3B. Encourage them to use a dictionary to find words such as ***jalapeño, pimiento, piña, aceituna, oliva,*** and ***hongo.***

Answers will vary.

Theme Project

Students can perform step 5 at this point. (For more information, see p.146-a.)

Leer/Escribir

Una pizza para la buena salud

Read this ad for pizza and answer the questions that follow.

Using cognates
Be sure to look for cognates to help you read this ad.

Pizzería Lilia
¡Pizzas saludables!

A veces la pizza tiene muchas calorías y grasas que no son buenas para la salud.

La Pizzería Lilia tiene una variedad de pizzas con ingredientes que son buenos y saludables.

- Menos queso
- Usamos ingredientes nutritivos
  - Más verduras (tienen pocas calorías y son muy nutritivas)
- Evita[1] la combinación de carnes
  - Las carnes tienen mucho sodio y grasas
  - El pollo o el jamón es mejor[2] que las salchichas

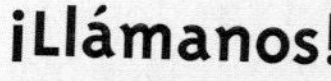

¡Llámanos!
¡Estamos aquí para servirte!
372 42 89
Calle Independencia 28

[1]Avoid [2]better

1. Find and list three cognates in this ad.
2. Write three recommendations for a healthier pizza.

Escribir/Hablar

Y tú, ¿qué dices?

1. ¿Qué prefieres en tu pizza, cebolla o pollo?
2. Describe tu pizza favorita.
3. ¿Crees que la pizza es buena o mala para la salud? ¿Por qué?
4. ¿Qué verduras prefieres? ¿Qué verduras no te gustan?
5. ¿Qué comes cuando tienes hambre?

Universal Access

Heritage Language Learners

Have students research fast-food restaurants in Spanish-speaking countries. How many are there? Are they popular? Where do most people prefer to eat? What are some of the slogans used to sell the food? Students can present their findings in the form of a poster, a report, or an oral presentation.

El español en el mundo del trabajo

Rick Bayless's career as a world-class Mexican chef began at the age of 14, when he visited Mexico and decided to study Spanish. Since 1978, Rick has opened gourmet Mexican restaurants, created and starred in cooking shows, written cookbooks, and won many awards.

- How would Rick's Spanish skills be helpful in his career?

  Leer/Escribir

Las calorías y la salud

Para decir más . . .

doscientos	two hundred	**seiscientos**	six hundred
trescientos	three hundred	**setecientos**	seven hundred
cuatrocientos	four hundred	**ochocientos**	eight hundred
quinientos	five hundred	**novecientos**	nine hundred

Conexiones — **La salud**

You've probably noticed that the nutritional labels on the bottle of juice that you drink, the energy bar that you eat, or even the gum that you chew all have a listing for calories. Our bodies burn calories even when we are sleeping. We can burn more or fewer calories depending on how much we weigh and what kind of activities we do. Look at the chart at right and answer the questions that follow.

Promedio[1] de calorías quemadas[2] en una hora de ejercicio

Actividad	Peso[3] 55–59 kg	Peso 77–82 kg
Básquetbol	170–515	400–800
Bailar	115–400	160–560
Correr 10 km/h	575	800
Fútbol	290–690	400–960
Nadar	230–690	320–900
Tenis	230–515	320–720
Caminar 6 km/h	250	340

[1]Average [2]burned (*quemar* = to burn) [3]weight

1. ¿En qué actividad quemas más calorías si pesas *(you weigh)* 78 kilogramos?
2. Pablo nada por una hora y Paco corre por una hora. Ellos queman el máximo *(maximum)* número de calorías. ¿Quién quema más calorías?
3. Tú pesas 55 kg. Bailas por dos horas y quemas el máximo número de calorías. ¿Cuántas quemas?
4. Una barra de chocolate *(chocolate bar)* tiene 320 calorías. Pesas 59 kg. ¿Por cuántos minutos tienes que caminar para quemar las calorías? ¿Es mucho?

Más práctica
Practice Workbook 3B-6, 3B-7

For: Practice with *ser*
Visit: www.phschool.com
Web Code: jad-0314

El español en el mundo del trabajo

 *Standards:* 5.1

Suggestions: Have students research the names of restaurants in your area that serve food from Spanish-speaking cultures.

Answers will vary.

Rapid Review
Call out three-digit page numbers in Spanish and have students turn to those pages in their books.

Actividad 27 *Standards:* 1.2, 1.3

Resources: Practice Answers on Transparencies

Focus: Understanding information presented in a chart

Recycle: Physical activities

Suggestions: Direct students' attention to the *Para decir más*.... Then call out numbers from the chart and have students point in their books to the numbers you say. Finally, ask students to identify the three kinds of information given on the chart: the activities, a person's weight in kilograms, and the range of calories a person would burn doing the activities.

Answers will vary but may include:
1. **fútbol**
2. **Pablo**
3. **400 calorías**
4. **77 minutos (Second answer will vary.)**

Extension: Call out simple math questions involving numbers by the hundreds and have students tell you the answers in Spanish.

Enriching Your Teaching

Culture Note
Although they share a language, the cuisine in Spanish-speaking countries is far from identical. For example, Mexican cuisine can be very spicy, relying heavily on hot chili peppers such as jalapeños and habaneros and spices like cumin, whereas Costa Rican cuisine is much milder and uses fewer spices.

Teacher-to-Teacher
Have students look at a newspaper's food section to get ideas for their own food article or advertisement. They can write a recipe, draw a food comic strip, or create supermarket ads. If they create an ad, be sure that it endorses a vegetable or fruit in this chapter. Display their posters.

Additional Resources
- Writing, Audio & Video Workbook: Audio Activities 8–9, Tracks 12–13
- Writing, Audio & Video Workbook: Writing Activities 12–13
- Heritage Learner Workbook: 3B-3, 3B-4, 3B-5

Assessment
- Prueba 3B-4: The verb *ser*

3B Communicate: Reading

Lectura

Presentation

 *Standards:* 1.2, 1.3, 3.1

Resources: Voc. & Gram. Transparencies: 80

Focus: Reading an article about athletes' diets

Suggestions:

Pre-reading: Point out the *Strategy* and be sure students understand skimming. Remind them that using prior knowledge and prediction will help them understand new texts. Use the transparency to make this a whole-class activity. Have students also find cognates.

Reading: Have students read the pie chart. As they read, have them tell you in which segment the various food items fall.

Post-reading: Have students review their skimming predictions and see how accurate they were. Have them identify cognates they noticed in the reading.

Teacher-to-Teacher

Have students keep a weekly list of what they eat to track carbohydrate, protein, and fat intake. At the end of the week, ask them to draw a pie chart to display the information.

Additional Resources

- Heritage Learner Workbook: 3B-6

¡Adelante!

Lectura

La comida de los atletas

Lee este artículo *(article)* de una revista deportiva. ¿Qué comen y qué beben los atletas profesionales para mantener la salud y estar en buena forma?

Objectives

- Read about a sports diet and learn some facts about an athlete
- Understand about cultural perspectives on healthcare
- Make a poster about good health habits
- Learn facts about the southern part of South America

Strategy

Skimming
List three things that you would expect to find in an article about athletes' eating habits. Skim the article to find the information.

¿Qué come un jugador de fútbol?

Los jugadores[1] de fútbol comen comidas equilibradas con muchos carbohidratos, minerales y vitaminas. Ellos consumen cerca de 5.000 calorías en total todos los días.

17% Proteínas
13% Grasas
70% Carbohidratos

Para el desayuno el día de un partido,[2] un jugador típico come mucho pan con mantequilla y jalea,[3] yogur y té.

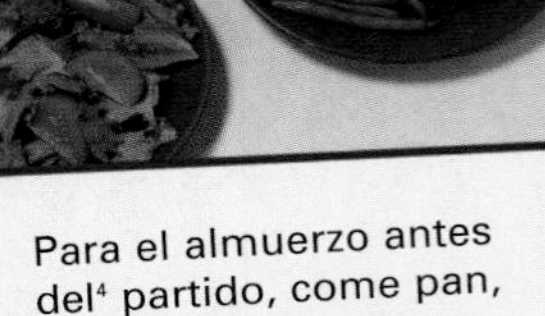

Para el almuerzo antes del[4] partido, come pan, pasta, pollo sin grasa, verduras, frutas y una ensalada.

Para la cena después del[5] partido, el atleta come papas, carne sin grasa y más verduras y frutas.

También es muy importante beber muchos líquidos. La noche antes del partido, el jugador bebe un litro de jugo de naranja y durante el partido bebe hasta[6] dos litros de agua y bebidas deportivas.

[1]players [2]game [3]jam [4]before the [5]after the [6]up to

Universal Access

Heritage Language Learners
Remind students to pay close attention to the correct spelling of words that are frequently spelled incorrectly: ***mantequilla*** (not *mantequiya*), ***pollo*** (not *poyo*), ***jalea*** (not *jallea*), and ***atleta*** (not *athleta*). Keep track of words that give them spelling difficulties and do a dictation periodically to check them.

Students with Learning Difficulties
Many students have problems skimming. Suggest that they move their fingers along the lines to find any information they understand. The strategy of using expectations to aid in reading can be very helpful. Stress that they will not understand every word, nor will they need to.

¿Comprendes?

1. ¿Qué debe comer Edwin Tenorio antes de un partido de fútbol?
2. ¿Qué debe beber?
3. ¿Qué comida no debe comer Edwin?
4. ¿Es tu dieta diferente de la dieta de un jugador de fútbol profesional? ¿Cómo?
5. ¿Cuál es la fecha de nacimiento *(birth date)* de Edwin? Escribe tu fecha de nacimiento como lo hacen en los países hispanohablantes.

For: Internet link activity
Visit: www.phschool.com
Web Code: jad-0315

Fondo cultural

¡Goooooooooooool! Scoring the winning *gol* is the most exciting moment of the game. *El fútbol* is the most popular sport in the world, and it has many *fanáticos* (fans) in every Spanish-speaking country. Every four years, teams throughout the world compete regionally in order to become one of the 32 teams to advance to the World Cup *(la Copa Mundial)* competition. Many Spanish-speaking countries compete in what has become the most widely watched sporting event in the world. Since the competition began in 1930, two Spanish-speaking countries have won the World Cup competition: Uruguay in 1930 and 1950 and Argentina in 1978 and 1986.

- How does the enthusiasm for soccer in the United States compare with the rest of the world's view of this sport? Why do you think this is so?

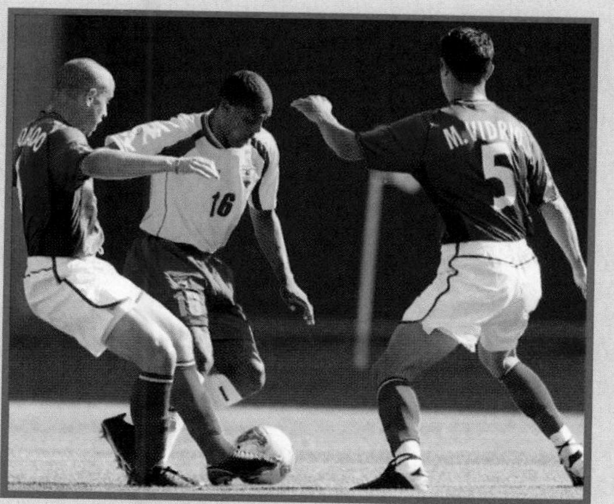

Jugadores de fútbol

Standards: 1.1, 1.2, 1.3

¿Comprendes?

Resources: Practice Answers on Transparencies

Focus: Demonstrating reading comprehension; learning to write dates using Spanish language conventions

Suggestions: Review the verb ***deber*** with students. Have students refer back to the reading as they write their answers.

Answers:

1. **pan y mantequilla y jalea, yogur, pasta, pollo, verduras, frutas, y una ensalada**
2. **Debe beber un litro de jugo de naranja y hasta dos litros de agua y bebidas deportivas.**
3. **Answers will vary.**
4. **Answers will vary.**
5. **El 16 de junio. Answers will vary.**

Standards: 2.1, 4.1, 4.2

Suggestions: Ask if students have seen a World Cup soccer match. Discuss how soccer has become popular in the United States. Find out who plays soccer in your class and invite them to talk about the sport.

Answers will vary.

Enriching Your Teaching

Culture Note

Soccer is quickly gaining a strong following in the United States, and many youth soccer clubs have developed across the country. Soccer historians give the credit to Pelé, the star soccer player from Brazil who, in the 1970s, fascinated sports fans in the United States with his finesse and agility.

Teacher-to-Teacher

It might be fun to have students make a poster showing a soccer field with the players' positions labeled. Have students search the internet for the Spanish names of the positions, such as: ***delantero*** ("forward"), ***centrocampista*** ("center"), and ***portero*** or ***arquero*** ("goalie" or "goalkeeper"). This may be a project for soccer enthusiasts in the class.

Perspectivas del mundo hispano

Presentation

*Standards:* 2.1, 4.2

Focus: Reading about traditional remedies as medical treatments

Suggestions: Point out that finding ways to stay healthy is a perennially popular topic. Natural remedies and herbs are among those often mentioned. Neither of them is really new, and many, such as eating chicken soup for a cold, have been passed down from generation to generation. Have students read the text. Discuss what they may know about the remedies mentioned. Also discuss researching herbal remedies as modern-day solutions. Assign the *Check it out!* section for homework. Discuss their responses at a later time.

Locate the Amazon rainforest on a map. Point out that a great deal of research into the benefits of herbal remedies takes place there. Discuss how scientists feel the rainforest has so much to offer because of its abundance of plants and animals, many of which are still not generally known elsewhere.

Direct attention to the *Think about it!* section and have students discuss the questions.

Answers will vary.

Additional Resources

- Heritage Learner Workbook: 3B-7

Perspectivas del mundo hispano

¿Qué haces para mantener la salud?

Have you ever eaten chicken soup when you have a cold? How about putting aloe on a sunburn? In many countries, including those in the Spanish-speaking world, traditional remedies consisting of medicinal herbs have been used for centuries to treat common medical problems. In Mexico, a mint known as *yerbabuena* may be made into tea and given to someone with a stomachache. Remedies such as these may not be prescribed by licensed physicians, but people have confidence in them because they have been passed down through the generations. Many of those herbs are very safe, though some may have harmful side effects.

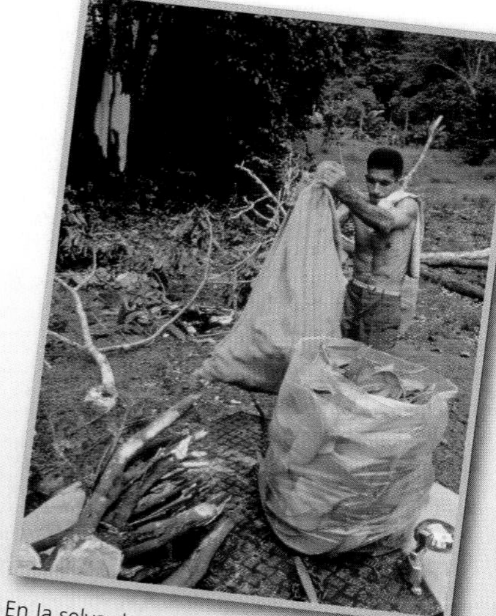

En la selva de Amazonas, Perú

Researchers are studying traditional herbal remedies to find modern-day medical solutions. In the Amazon rainforest in South America, an amazing abundance of plant life may hold the key to treating a wide variety of common ailments and diseases. Drug companies are looking for cures found in these plants and herbs that could be reproduced in today's modern drugs.

Increasingly, medicinal herbs are accepted not only as the basis for pharmaceutical drugs, but also for their own inherent healing qualities. In many countries, including the United States, herbal remedies are sometimes used in combination with conventional healthcare.

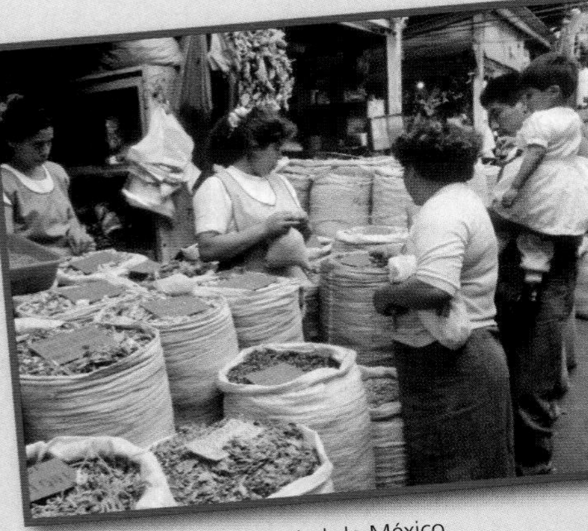

En un mercado en la Ciudad de México

Check it out! What alternatives to conventional medical care are available in your community? Make a list of all the healthcare services you can think of that are not traditional physicians. Are there health stores that sell herbal medicines? What types of herbal medicines are being sold and what remedies are attributed to these medicines?

Think about it! In many Spanish-speaking cultures, herbal remedies have been accepted for centuries. Do you think that medicinal herbs can provide relief and cures? Why or why not?

Universal Access

Advanced Learners

Have students learn about the Amazon rainforest, where it is located, and why scientists are interested in the plants and animals that live there. Ask students to give a short explanation about possible medicines and cures that might come from the region.

Students with Special Needs

If students are not able to make a poster for the *Presentación escrita* because of physical impairments, pair students and have them work collaboratively to create the product for the presentation.

Presentación escrita

Para mantener la salud

Task
You are doing some research for your health class on good eating and exercise habits. Make a poster in Spanish with five suggestions for better health.

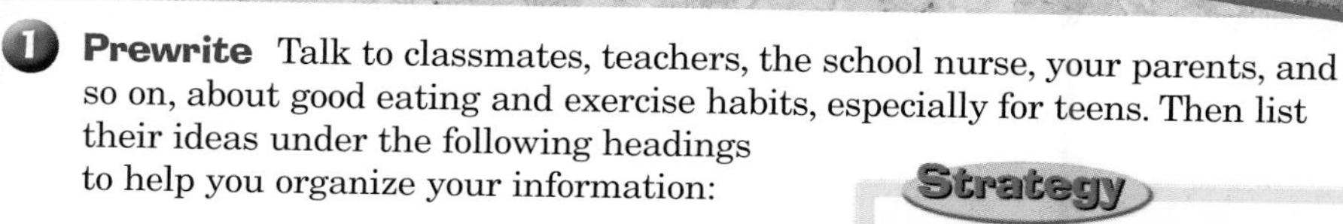

1 Prewrite Talk to classmates, teachers, the school nurse, your parents, and so on, about good eating and exercise habits, especially for teens. Then list their ideas under the following headings to help you organize your information:

- Debes comer . . .
- Debes beber . . .
- No debes comer mucho(a) . . .
- No debes beber mucho(a) . . .
- Debes ____ para mantener la salud.

Strategy

Gathering information
Gathering information from a variety of sources helps you create a more complete presentation on a topic.

2 Draft Write the first draft. Decide how to present the information in a logical manner. Think about using visuals for clarity. Sketch them on your draft. Give the poster a title.

3 Revise Share your draft with a partner. Your partner should check the following:

- Have you communicated the five suggestions well?
- Do the visuals help convey meaning and make the poster attractive?
- Are the vocabulary and grammar correct?

Decide whether to use your partner's suggestions, and then rewrite your poster.

4 Publish Make a final copy, adding attractive illustrations or designs and making necessary changes. You might want to:

- post it in the nurse's office, at a local community center, or in your classroom
- include it in your portfolio

5 Evaluation Your teacher may give you a rubric for how the poster will be graded. You probably will be graded on:

- completion of task
- accuracy of vocabulary and grammar
- effective use of visuals

Presentación escrita

Presentation

Standards: 1.3

Focus: Writing about good eating habits and exercise; adding illustrations or designs to enhance a presentation

Suggestions: Review the task and steps with students. Point out that students should use reliable sources that know about health. Encourage students to make their posters eye-appealing as well as persuasive. Review the rubric with the class to explain how you will grade the posters. Make and display a poster of your own as a model. Use a sample poster and show how it would be graded.

Have students present their posters to the class. Ask them how they might change their habits after completing this project.

Additional Resources

- Heritage Learner Workbook: 3B-8

Assessment

- Assessment Program: Cap. 3B, Rubrics

Give students copies of the rubric before they begin the activity. Review the different levels of performance. After assessing students, help individuals understand how their performance could be improved.

Portfolio

Have students include their posters in their portfolios.

Enriching Your Teaching

RUBRIC	Score 1	Score 3	Score 5
Completion of task	You included at least three suggestions for a healthy lifestyle.	You included at least four suggestions for a healthy lifestyle.	You included five or more suggestions for a healthy lifestyle.
Accurate use of vocabulary and grammar	You had very little variation of vocabulary use with many grammar errors.	You had limited usage of vocabulary, and some grammar errors.	You had extended use of a variety of vocabulary with very few grammar errors.
Effective use of visuals	You included only three visuals that clearly connect to information.	You included only four visuals that clearly connect to information.	You included five visuals that clearly connect to the information.

3B Culture

El mundo hispano

Presentation

 *Standards:* 2.1, 3.1, 2.2

Resources: Voc. & Gram. Transparencies: 16 (map); Heritage Language Learner Workbook: 3B-7

Focus: Reading about the countries in southern South America

Suggestions: After students read the selection, display a map of South America. Point out the four countries highlighted in this section. Note characteristics such as coastal access or mountainous areas. Point out that, unlike the South American countries discussed earlier, the populations of these countries with the exception of Paraguay live mainly in large cities. Note that these cities, like those of the United States, were shaped largely by mass immigration from southern and eastern Europe. Ask if students would expect to see a large indigenous population.

Direct attention to the photo at the top of p. 203. Ask students to hypothesize where in Chile they imagine these people might live.

Point out that when the Spanish arrived, they brought with them not only their language and culture, but their animals as well. Ask students to describe how these animals may have affected the land and the environment, as well as the present-day culture. Entertain the idea that perhaps some indigenous animals of the time when the Spanish arrived no longer exist because of the animals brought from Europe.

Focus on the photo at the bottom of p. 203. Point out that Buenos Aires is one of the most cosmopolitan cities in the world. Locate it on a map. Guide students to understand that prior to mass transportation and air travel, coastal cities had more immigrants than interior cities. People arrived by boat at a port city and many of them stayed. Have students think about why the citizens of Buenos Aires are known as ***porteños.***

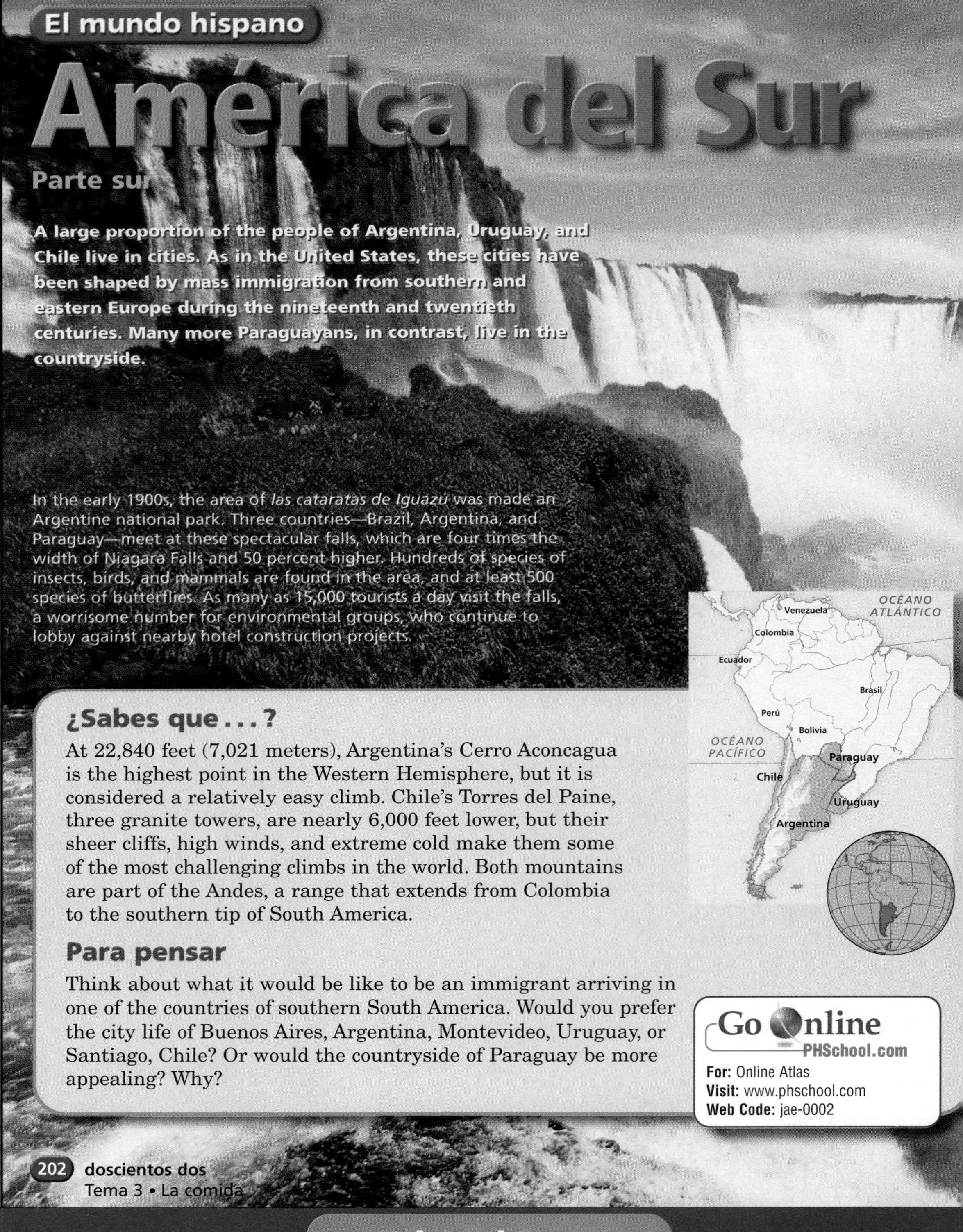

El mundo hispano

América del Sur

Parte sur

A large proportion of the people of Argentina, Uruguay, and Chile live in cities. As in the United States, these cities have been shaped by mass immigration from southern and eastern Europe during the nineteenth and twentieth centuries. Many more Paraguayans, in contrast, live in the countryside.

In the early 1900s, the area of *las cataratas de Iguazú* was made an Argentine national park. Three countries—Brazil, Argentina, and Paraguay—meet at these spectacular falls, which are four times the width of Niagara Falls and 50 percent higher. Hundreds of species of insects, birds, and mammals are found in the area, and at least 500 species of butterflies. As many as 15,000 tourists a day visit the falls, a worrisome number for environmental groups, who continue to lobby against nearby hotel construction projects.

¿Sabes que . . . ?

At 22,840 feet (7,021 meters), Argentina's Cerro Aconcagua is the highest point in the Western Hemisphere, but it is considered a relatively easy climb. Chile's Torres del Paine, three granite towers, are nearly 6,000 feet lower, but their sheer cliffs, high winds, and extreme cold make them some of the most challenging climbs in the world. Both mountains are part of the Andes, a range that extends from Colombia to the southern tip of South America.

Para pensar

Think about what it would be like to be an immigrant arriving in one of the countries of southern South America. Would you prefer the city life of Buenos Aires, Argentina, Montevideo, Uruguay, or Santiago, Chile? Or would the countryside of Paraguay be more appealing? Why?

Go Online PHSchool.com
For: Online Atlas
Visit: www.phschool.com
Web Code: jae-0002

202 doscientos dos
Tema 3 • La comida

Universal Access

Heritage Language Learners

Have students choose a South American country and research foods and regional dishes. If possible, students should relate them to the geography of the region.

The Spanish were able to topple large, centralized empires such as those of the Aztecs and Incas quickly, but they were never able to conquer the smaller indigenous groups in the more remote regions. Chile's Pehuenche suffered defeats in the nineteenth century, but they still struggle to maintain their lands and culture.

Spain introduced horses, cows, sheep, and pigs to the Americas in the sixteenth century, transforming the ecology, culture, and economy of the region. In the nineteenth century, the growth of cities, the expansion of railways, and improvements in shipping created a worldwide market for South American meat and hides—and helped spur the development of the cowboy culture throughout the Americas. As on ranches in the western United States and northern Mexico, the main house of an Argentine or Uruguayan *estancia* served as a residence, office, and military stronghold.

With its wide boulevards, parks, museums, and diverse cultural life, Buenos Aires is considered one of the most cosmopolitan cities in the world. Argentina has produced world-class writers such as Jorge Luis Borges, Julio Cortázar, and José Hernández, who wrote a classic about the life of the *gauchos*. The tango, the first dance from Latin America to gain international popularity, is a favorite of the *porteños*—the residents of Buenos Aires.

Culture

Locate Paraguay on the map. Unlike the other countries in southern South America, it is mostly rural. Most people do not live in large cities. Have students hypothesize as to why this might be. If necessary, point to the fact that it is landlocked. Can students recall the other landlocked South American country? (Bolivia)

Direct attention to the background photo. Based on their reading, have students identify it. Emphasize that South America has a great deal of natural beauty and an abundance of remarkable wildlife.

Have students focus on the *¿Sabes que...?* section. Use the map to show the path of the Andes. Point out the extreme differences in the two points mentioned in the text. Have students calculate the height of Chile's Torre del Paine. Note that this is still at a very high altitude.

Discuss the concerns of the environmentalist groups at Iguazú Falls. The number of tourists who visit is large, and the balance of nature is delicate. Sometimes just the presence of people is enough to destroy some aspect of a natural site. Once gone, it is often gone for good. Discuss how construction and population growth cause changes in nature. Can students relate this to any environmental issues in their community, state, or region?

Direct attention to the *Para pensar* section and have students discuss the questions.

Answers will vary.

Go Online

The Online Atlas will provide more detailed maps of the locations mentioned here.

Enriching Your Teaching

Teacher-to-Teacher

Have students add to the bulletin board display on South America. (See notes for p. 173.) They can fill in facts about ***gauchos*** and the Iguazú Falls. Encourage them to include information on artistic contributions of all the countries.

Internet Search

Keywords:

Argentina; Uruguay; Paraguay; Chile; gaucho; Iguazú Falls; waterfall

Review Activities

To talk about food and beverages: Have students work in pairs to quiz each other on the vocabulary. They may use flashcards or use the Food Guide Pyramid. Use classroom posters, plastic foods, or magazines to help students review the vocabulary. Have them include *Tengo hambre* and *Tengo sed* in practicing the foods and beverages.

To discuss health: Have students work in pairs and give each other recommendations using *Para mantener la salud* ____. Have them agree or disagree, saying what is good or bad.

To indicate preference or agreement / disagreement: Give students choices of two items and ask their preference. Then have them agree or disagree with statements you make about whether something is good or bad for health.

To describe something: Give names of activities or foods and have students describe them.

Portfolio

Invite students to review the activities completed in this chapter, including written reports, posters, or other visuals, and tapes of oral presentations or other projects. Have them select a few items that they feel best demonstrate their achievements in Spanish to include in their portfolios. Have them include this with the Chapter Checklist and Self Assessment Worksheet.

Additional Resources

- Audio Program: CD Cap. 3B, Track 14
- Resource Book: Cap. 3B, Clip Art
- Resource Book: Cap. 3B, Situation Cards
- Assessment Program: Cap. 3B, Chapter Checklist and Self-Assessment Worksheet

Chapter Review

Repaso del capítulo

Vocabulario y gramática

To prepare for the test, check to see if you . . .

- know the new vocabulary and grammar
- can perform the tasks on p. 205

to talk about food and beverages

la cena	dinner
el bistec	beefsteak
la carne	meat
el pescado	fish
el pollo	chicken
la cebolla	onion
los guisantes	peas
las judías verdes	green beans
la lechuga	lettuce
las papas	potatoes
los tomates	tomatoes
las uvas	grapes
las zanahorias	carrots
el arroz	rice
los cereales	grains
los espaguetis	spaghetti
las grasas	fats
la mantequilla	butter
el helado	ice cream
los pasteles	pastries
las bebidas	beverages

to talk about being hungry and thirsty

Tengo hambre.	I'm hungry.
Tengo sed.	I'm thirsty.

to discuss health

caminar	to walk
hacer ejercicio	to exercise
(yo) hago	I do
(tú) haces	you do
levantar pesas	to lift weights
para la salud	for one's health
para mantener la salud	to maintain one's health

For *Vocabulario adicional*, see pp. 268–269.

to indicate a preference

(yo) prefiero	I prefer
(tú) prefieres	you prefer
deber	should, must

to indicate agreement or disagreement

Creo que . . .	I think (that) . . .
Creo que sí / no.	I (don't) think so.
(No) estoy de acuerdo.	I (don't) agree.

to express a question or an answer

¿Por qué?	Why?
porque	because

to express quantity

algo	something
muchos, -as	many
todos, -as	all

to describe something

horrible	horrible
malo, -a	bad
sabroso, -a	tasty, flavorful

other useful words

cada día	every day

plurals of adjectives

Masculine	Feminine
Singular/Plural	**Singular/Plural**
sabroso/sabrosos	sabrosa/sabrosas
popular/populares	popular/populares

ser *to be*

soy	**somos**
eres	**sois**
es	**son**

Más práctica

Practice Workbook Puzzle 3B-8
Practice Workbook Organizer 3B-9

Universal Access

Students with Learning Difficulties

Give students the format of the actual test and the point values of different parts. This will help take much of the stress out of the testing situation. Help them decide which parts they need to study most. Consider study sessions in class or at a special time.

Multiple Intelligences

Visual / Spatial: Encourage students to prepare a picture dictionary of the food items from this chapter and from *Capítulo* 3A. Students will number the words to show their alphabetical order, then draw and label the items in that order, with 5–10 entries on each page of their dictionary.

Go Online
PHSchool.com
For: Test preparation
Visit: www.phschool.com
Web Code: jad-0316

Preparación para el examen

On the exam you will be asked to . . .	Here are practice tasks similar to those you will find on the exam . . .	If you need review . . .
1 Escuchar Listen and understand as people describe a healthy or unhealthy lifestyle	Listen as two people are interviewed about their habits. See if you can tell which one is an Olympic skier and which one is a drummer. Be prepared to explain your "educated guesses."	**pp. 178–183** *A primera vista* **p. 179** Actividad 2
2 Hablar Express your opinion about food preferences	During a telephone survey, you are asked some questions in Spanish about your food preferences. Say whether you think each food choice is good or bad for your health.	**p. 187** Actividad 11 **p. 188** Actividades 12, 14 **p. 194** Actividad 23 **p. 197** Actividad 27
3 Leer Read and compare what people do and eat in order to determine whether they lead a healthy or unhealthy lifestyle	Read the online conversation that you have just joined in a chat room. Decide whether each person has a healthy or unhealthy lifestyle, based on what they tell each other. Chato: ¿Qué hago yo? Cuando hace buen tiempo, corro por treinta minutos. Cuando llueve, levanto pesas. Chispa: No me gusta hacer ejercicio. Prefiero comer papas fritas. Son muy sabrosas. Andrés: ¿Papas fritas? Son horribles para la salud. Para mantener la salud, nunca debes comer papas fritas.	**pp. 178–183** *A primera vista* **p. 188** Actividad 13 **p. 189** Actividad 15 **p. 196** Actividad 25 **pp. 198–199** *Lectura*
4 Escribir Write a list of things a person should do to maintain a healthy lifestyle	Many people think that teens don't know anything about a healthy lifestyle. You and your friends are compiling a top-ten list of ways to improve teens' health. Write at least three suggestions for the list.	**p. 188** Actividad 13 **p. 189** Actividad 15 **p. 196** Actividad 25 **p. 201** *Presentación escrita*
 **5 Pensar** Demonstrate an understanding of cultural perspectives regarding healthcare	Give an example of an herbal remedy that is accepted in a Spanish-speaking country as a remedy for a common ailment. Compare this with a similar herbal/natural remedy believed by many in the United States to be a cure for a common ailment.	**p. 200** *Perspectivas del mundo hispano*

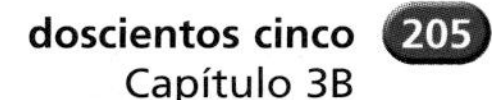

Enriching Your Teaching

Culture Note

While Spanish explorers took many products from the Americas back to Europe, they also introduced some products from Europe into the Americas. One of these was aloe vera, a plant originally from Africa whose healing properties had been appreciated by many early civilizations, including ancient Greece.

Teacher-to-Teacher

Place real or plastic food in a grocery bag. Have students reach in and select an item. Ask students questions, such as *¿Qué vas a comer? ¿Qué comes en la cena?* or *¿Como son los tomates?* Students should respond based upon the food item they select.

Performance Tasks

Standards: 1.1, 1.2, 1.3, 3.1, 4.2

Resources: Audio Program: CD Cap. 3B, Track 15; Resource Book: Cap. 3B, Audio Script; Practice Answers on Transparencies

1. Escuchar

Suggestions: Play the *Audio CD* or read the script.

Script and Answers:

1. **—Cada día, a las cinco y media de la mañana, levanto pesas por treinta minutos y camino por una hora. Nunca como los pasteles ni las papas fritas porque son malos para la salud. *(Olympic skier)***
2. **—Nunca como el desayuno porque no tengo tiempo para comer. Para el almuerzo prefiero la comida rápida: una hamburguesa con un refresco. *(drummer)***

2. Hablar

Suggestions: Remind students that adjectives must agree with nouns in gender and number.

Answers will vary.

3. Leer

Suggestions: Have students list the clues to the answers as they read.

Answers:

Chato and Andrés lead healthy lifestyles. Chispa leads an unhealthy lifestyle.

4. Escribir

Suggestions: Have students write their suggestions, then exhange their answers with a partner and correct any mistakes.

Answers will vary.

5. Pensar

Suggestions: Have students reread the del mundo hispano information as homework.

Assessment

- Examen del capítulo: 3B
- Audio Program: CD 20, Track 8
- Alternative Assessment head

Alternative Assessment

- ExamView Test Bank CD-ROM
- Resource Book: Cap. 3B, Situation Cards
- Resource Book: Cap. 3B, Communicative Activities

Tema 4

Los pasatiempos

THEME OVERVIEW

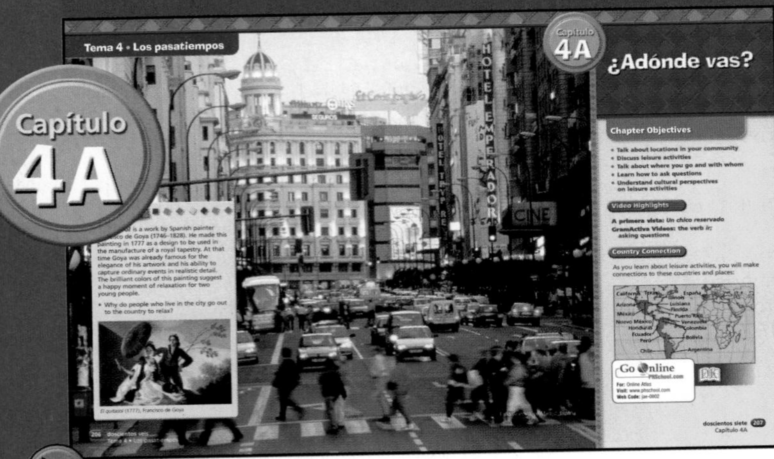

4A ¿Adónde vas?
- Leisure activities and locations in your community

Vocabulary: leisure activities; places; expressions to tell where and with whom you go; expressions to talk about when things are done

Grammar: the verb *ir;* interrogative words

Cultural Perspectives: leisure activities in the Spanish-speaking world

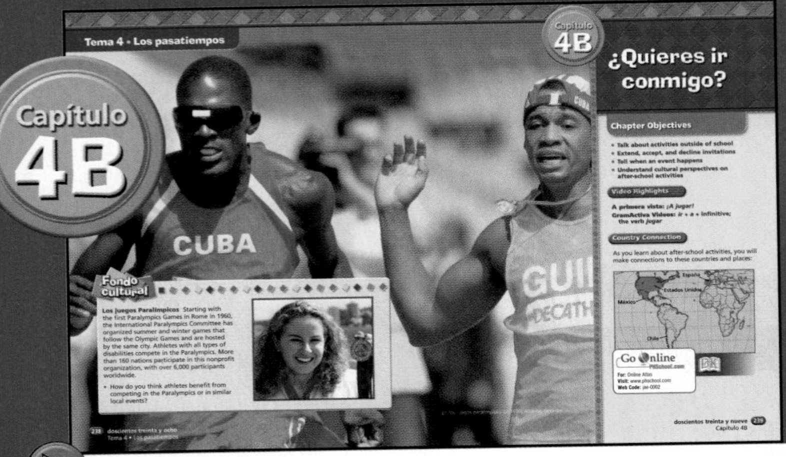

4B ¿Quieres ir conmigo?
- Activities outside of school and invitations

Vocabulary: leisure activities; feelings; expressions for extending, accepting, and declining invitations; expressions to tell when something happens

Grammar: *ir* + *a* + infinitive; the verb *jugar*

Cultural Perspectives: opinions on after-school activities

Theme Project

Guía del ocio

Overview: Students create a weekend entertainment guide, featuring the times and locations of six different events and an illustration of each event. They then present their guide to the class.

Materials: construction paper, magazines, scissors, glue, colored markers

Sequence: (suggestions for when to do each step appear throughout the chapters)

4A **STEP 1.** Review instructions so students know what is expected of them. Hand out the "Theme 4 Project Instructions and Rubric" from the *Teacher's Resource Book*.

STEP 2. Students look at examples of entertainment guides on the Internet or in their local newspaper. They then brainstorm what to include in their guide.

STEP 3. Students submit a rough sketch of their guide. Return the sketches with your suggestions.

4B **STEP 4.** Students create layouts on construction paper. Encourage students to work in pencil first, before gluing magazine clippings or drawing illustrations and writing the content of the guide.

STEP 5. Students submit a draft of the information in their guide. Note your corrections and suggestions, then return the drafts to students. For additional oral practice, students use their guides to invite a partner to one of the events.

STEP 6. Students complete and present their guide to the class, describing each of the events featured.

Options:
1. Students write and act out a script for a television entertainment show describing upcoming events.
2. Students make a collage of their favorite leisure activities and write a paragraph about when and where they do them.

Assessment:
Here is a detailed rubric for assessing this project:
Theme 4 Project: *Guía del ocio*

RUBRIC	Score 1	Score 3	Score 5
Evidence of planning	You provided no written draft or page layout.	Your draft was written and your layout created, but not corrected.	You corrected your draft and layout.
Your use of illustrations	You included no photos or illustrations.	You included photos or illustrations, but your layout was disorganized.	Your guide was easy to read, complete, and accurate.
Your poster presentation	Your guide and presentation included little of the required information.	Your guide and presentation included most of the required information.	Your guide and presentation included all of the required information.

Bulletin Boards

Theme: *Tiempo libre*

Ask students to cut out, copy, or download photos of buildings and outdoor locations in Spanish-speaking countries and people engaged in leisure activities. Cluster photos of activities around photos of places where the activities might take place.

Bibliography

Bolton, Leslie. *The Everything Classical Mythology Book: Greek and Roman Gods, Goddesses, Heroes, and Villains from Ares to Zeus.* Avon, Mass.: Adams Media Corporation, 2002.

DK Campbell, Malcolm. *The New Encyclopedia of Golf.* New York: Dorling Kindersley, 2001. Everything about golf: history, courses, tournaments, and stars.

McHugh, A. Rose. *Rebecca Lobo.* Basketball Stars Series. Chanhassen, Minn.: Child's World, 2001. Biography of Rebecca Lobo.

Stone, Rob. *Spanish Cinema: Inside Film.* New York: Longman, 2001. Broad introduction to Spanish cinema, tracing themes and film movements.

Wilson, Patricia L., Rick Graetz, and Susie Graetz. *Old San Juan, El Morro, San Cristobal.* Helena, Mont.: Farcountry Press, 1995. Photo essay on the old city of San Juan, Puerto Rico.

Hands-on Culture

Craft: *Migajón*

Migajón is the soft part of bread. It is used throughout Latin America as the base for a modeling material to create decorations and miniature toys.

Materials:

2 slices of white bread per student
2 tablespoons of white glue per student
acrylic paints
paint brushes

Steps:

1. Trim the crust from the bread and tear it into pieces.
2. Knead the glue into the bread. Continue to work the bread until the stickiness disappears and it becomes clay-like.
3. Shape the ***migajón*** into a small figure, such as an animal, car, or flower.
4. Set the figure aside for two to three days to let it air dry and become hard.
5. Decorate the figure with paint.

Internet Search

Use the keywords to find more information.

***4A* Keywords:**

Old San Juan; Pilsen, Chicago; Morazán; Andean music

***4B* Keywords:**

Paralympics, Sergio García, Lorena Ochoa Reyes, Rebecca Lobo

Game

Pregúntame

Play this game after you present *Gramática: Asking questions* in *Capítulo* 4A.

Players: the entire class

Materials: paper, pens, 2 paper bags

Steps:

1. Write all the question words and phrases from the *Gramática* on the chalkboard.
2. Divide the class into two teams. Teams write 11 sentences that would answer questions using the words and phrases from the board. Teams write one sentence for each question word or phrase.
   Question word: ¿Adónde?
   Team writes: Voy a la biblioteca.
   Question phrase: ¿Con quién?
   Team writes: Ella va con Roberto.
3. Collect the strips of paper and place them in two paper bags, one for each team.
4. Toss a coin to determine which team begins the game.
5. Draw a sentence from the Team 1 bag and read it aloud. Students from Team 2 have ten seconds to confer, then ask a question the sentence would answer. If the question is correct, Team 2 earns a point. If more than one question is possible, Team 2 may ask a second question to earn another point.
   Sentence: Él va a la playa a las diez.
   First question: ¿Adónde va?
   Second question: ¿Cuándo va a la playa?
6. Repeat step 5 for the other team.
7. The winner is the team with the most points after both bags have been emptied.

Variation: You write the sentences, making some of them simple and others more complex. Begin play with the simple sentences and progress to the more complex ones.

Chapter Overview

A primera vista INPUT	Manos a la obra PRACTICE	¡Adelante! APPLICATION	Repaso del capítulo REVIEW
Objectives Read, listen to, and explain information about: • places to go when you're not in school	**Objectives** • Communicate about leisure activities • Tell where you go and with whom • Use the verb *ir* and ask questions	**Objectives** • Read about after-school and weekend activities offered at a mall • Talk about some nursery rhymes • Role-play a new student's first day at school • Discuss facts about the history of the United States	**Objectives** • Prepare for the chapter test
Vocabulary • Leisure activities • Places • Expressions for where you go and with whom • Expressions for when things are done and where someone is from	**Vocabulary** • Practice and learn new vocabulary	**Vocabulary** • Application	**Vocabulary** • Review
Grammar Lexical use of: • the verb *ir* • interrogative words	**Grammar** • The verb *ir* • Asking questions	**Grammar** • Application	**Grammar** • Review
Culture • Francisco de Goya	**Culture** • *la plaza* • Popularity of sports clubs and gyms • Tradition of going to the movies • Old San Juan	**Culture** • Andean music • Chants and songs	**Culture** • Demonstrate an understanding of rhymes, songs, and games from Spanish-speaking cultures

Learner Support

Strategies
- Scanning
- Using prior knowledge
- Using models

Recycling
- The verb *ir*
- The present tense of *-ar* verbs
- The present tense of *-er* and *-ir* verbs
- Infinitives

Pronunciación
- Stress and accents

Exploración del lenguaje
- Origins of the Spanish days of the week

Conexiones
- Math: creating a bar graph to show how often students participate in various activities
- History: Old San Juan

Beyond the Classroom

Countries
- Honduras
- Puerto Rico
- Peru
- Mexico
- Chile
- Colombia
- Argentina
- Spain
- Venezuela
- United States

El español en la comunidad
- Spanish-speaking neighborhoods' expressions of community

Internet
- Vocabulary activities
- Grammar activities
- Internet links
- Self-tests

Print Components

TEACHER

Teacher's Resource Book
- Chapter Resource Checklist
- Input Script
- Video Script
- Audio Script
- Answer Keys
- *GramActiva* Blackline Masters
- Communicative Activity Blackline Masters
- Situation Cards Blackline Masters
- School-to-Home Connection Letter
- Vocabulary Clip Art

TPR Storytelling Book
- Cap. 4A

STUDENT

Practice Workbook
- Vocabulary: 4A-1 – 4A-4
- Grammar: 4A-5 – 4A-7
- Puzzle: 4A-8
- Organizer: 4A-9

Writing, Audio & Video Workbook
- Writing: 4A-1 – 4A-4
- Audio: 4A-5 – 4A-10
- Video: 4A-11

Realidades para hispanohablantes
- Cap. 4A

Transparencies

Vocabulary & Grammar Transparencies
- Chapter Opener: 12–18, 20 (maps)
- *A primera vista:* 81–82
- *Videohistoria:* 83–84
- Grammar: 11 (graphic organizer), 14–15 (maps), 85–87
- *Lectura:* 17 (map)
- *Cultura:* 20 (map)

Practice Answers on Transparencies
- Cap. 4A

Fine Art Transparencies
- Transparencies
- Teacher's Guide

Assessment

Assessment Program
- *Pruebas:*
  - Vocabulary recognition: 4A-1
  - Vocabulary production: 4A-2
  - The verb ***ir:*** 4A-3
  - Asking questions: 4A-4
- *Examen del capítulo:* 4A

ExamView Test Bank CD-ROM

Test Preparation Workbook
- Cap. 4A Reading #1
- Cap. 4A Reading #2

Alternative Assessment
- Performance-Based Speaking
- Assessment Program: Rubrics
- Internet Self-Test
- Situation Cards Blackline Masters
- TPR Storytelling Book: Speaking Task

Technology

iText

Mind Point Quiz Show CD-ROM

Resource Pro CD-ROM
- Lesson Planner
- Teacher Resources
- Clip Art

Video Program VHS and DVD
- *A primera vista* video: *Un chico reservado*
- *GramActiva* Videos:
  - the verb ***ir***
  - asking questions

Audio Program CDs
- *A primera vista*
- *Escucha y escribe* activities
- Audio Activities
- *Pronunciación*
- *Repaso*
- Chapter Listening Test
- Songs

Regular Schedule (50 minutes)

For electronic lesson plans:
Resource Pro CD-ROM

	Warm-up / Assess	Preview / Present / Practice / Communicate	Wrap-up / Homework Options
DAY 1	**Return Examen del capítulo (10 min.)**	**A primera vista (35 min.)** • Objectives • Presentation: *Vocabulario y gramática en contexto* • *Actividades* 1, 2 • *Fondo cultural*	**Wrap-up and Homework Options (5 min.)** • Practice Workbook 4A-1, 4A-2 • Go Online • Heritage Language Learner Workbook • Vocabulary Clip Art
DAY 2	**Warm-up (5 min.)** • Homework check	**A primera vista (40 min.)** • Review: *Vocabulario y gramática en contexto* • Presentation: *Videohistoria Un chico reservado* • View: Video *Un chico reservado* • Video Activities • *Actividades* 3, 4	**Wrap-up and Homework Options (5 min.)** • *Prueba* 4A-1: Vocabulary recognition • Practice Workbook 4A-3, 4A-4 • Go Online
DAY 3	**Warm-up (5 min.)** • Homework check **✓Assessment (10 min.)** • *Prueba* 4A-1: Voc. recognition	**Manos a la obra (30 min.)** • Objectives • *Actividades* 5, 7, 8	**Wrap-up and Homework Options (5 min.)** • *Actividad* 6
DAY 4	**Warm-up (10 min.)** • Homework check • Return *Prueba* 4A-1: Voc. recognition	**Manos a la obra (35 min.)** • *Actividades* 9, 10 • *Exploración del lenguaje*	**Wrap-up and Homework Options (5 min.)** • *Exploración del lenguaje:* Try it out! • *Actividad* 11
DAY 5	**Warm-up (10 min.)** • Homework check	**Manos a la obra (35 min.)** • Presentation: The verb ***ir*** • *GramActiva* Video • *Actividades* 12, 13	**Wrap-up and Homework Options (5 min.)** • *Actividad* 14 • Practice Workbook 4A-5
DAY 6	**Warm-up (5 min.)** • Homework check	**Manos a la obra (40 min.)** • Review: The verb ***ir*** • *Fondo cultural* • *Actividades* 16, 17	**Wrap-up and Homework Options (5 min.)** • *Actividad* 15
DAY 7	**Warm-up (5 min.)** • Homework check	**Manos a la obra (40 min.)** • *Juego: Actividad* 18 • *El español en la comunidad* • *Pronunciación*	**Wrap-up and Homework Options (5 min.)** • *Prueba* 4A-3: The verb ***ir*** • Go Online
DAY 8	**Warm-up (5 min.)** • Homework check **✓Assessment (10 min.)** • *Prueba* 4A-3: The verb ***ir***	**Manos a la obra (30 min.)** • Presentation: Asking questions • *GramActiva* Video • *Actividades* 19, 20	**Wrap-up and Homework Options (5 min.)** • *Actividad* 21 • *Prueba* 4A-3: Vocabulary production • Go Online • Practice Workbook 4A-6, 4A-7

	Warm-up / Assess	Preview / Present / Practice / Communicate	Wrap-up / Homework Options
DAY 9	**Warm-up** (5 min.) • Homework check • Return *Prueba* 4A-3: The verb ***ir*** ✔**Assessment** (10 min.) • *Prueba* 4A-2: Voc. production	**Manos a la obra** (30 min.) • *Actividades* 22, 24, 25, 27 • *Juego: Actividad* 26 • *Fondo cultural*	**Wrap-up and Homework Options** (5 min.) • *Actividad* 23 • *Prueba* 4A-4: Asking questions
DAY 10	**Warm-up** (5 min.) • Homework check • Return Prueba 4A-2: Voc. production ✔**Assessment** (10 min.) • Prueba 4A-4: Asking questions	**Manos a la obra** (10 min.) • *Conexiones: Actividad* 28 • *Juego: Actividad* 26 **¡Adelante!** (20 min.) • *Lectura* • *Fondo cultural*	**Wrap-up and Homework Options** (5 min.) • Go Online • *¿Comprendes?*
DAY 11	**Warm-up** (5 min.) • Homework check • Return Prueba 4A-4: Asking questions	**¡Adelante!** (40 min.) • *Presentación oral:* Prepare • *La cultura en vivo*	**Wrap-up and Homework Options** (5 min.) • Go Online
DAY 12	**Warm-up** (5 min.) • Homework check	**¡Adelante!** (40 min.) • *Presentación oral:* Practice	**Wrap-up and Homework Options** (5 min.) • Go Online
DAY 13	**Warm-up** (5 min.) • Homework check	**¡Adelante!** (40 min.) • *Presentación oral:* Present	**Wrap-up and Homework Options** (5 min.) • Writing Activities • Practice Workbook 4A-8, 4A-9
DAY 14	**Warm-up** (5 min.) • Homework check	**¡Adelante!** (20 min.) • *El mundo hispano* **Repaso** (20 min.) • *Vocabulario y gramática* • *Preparación para el examen*	**Wrap-up and Homework Options** (5 min.) • Go Online: Self-test • *Examen del capítulo*
DAY 15	**Warm-up** (5 min.) • Answer questions ✔**Assessment** (45 min.) • *Examen del capítulo*		

Standards for *Capítulo 4A*

- To achieve the goals of the Standards, students will:

Communication

1.1 Interpersonal

- Talk about leisure activities and locations
- Talk about where they go on different days of the week
- Talk about people and their destinations

1.2 Interpretive

- Read and listen to information about leisure activities and locations
- Read: a picture-based story; a magazine-style interview; a letter telling how an exchange student spends her time; an advertisement for a cinema; about Old San Juan, Puerto Rico
- Listen to and watch a video about leisure activities
- Listen to information about Plaza Morazán
- Read a mall advertisement about scheduled activities

1.3 Presentational

- Present information about: leisure activities and locations; Tegucigalpa; cinema; the history of Puerto Rico
- Reply to an email message
- Perform a short skit about a student's first day of school

Culture

2.1 Practices and Perspectives

- Understand leisure enjoyment in the eighteenth-century Spanish aristocracy
- Learn about: the social aspect of the town square in Tegucigalpa; school-based exercise; movie-going habits; restoration of historic districts in Puerto Rico

2.2 Products and Perspectives

- Learn about: Francisco de Goya and his painting; José Antonio Velásquez and his painting; the muscial styles ***bomba*** and ***plena;*** Andean music and instruments; Spanish architecture in the United States

Connections

3.1 Cross-curricular

- Learn about: important artists and their work: Goya, Velásquez; the history of Puerto Rico; Spain's colonial influence on the United States
- Read a street map of Madrid
- Reinforce math and graphing abilities skills

3.2 Target Culture

- Recite the Mexican folk song, "La Bamba"
- Practice children songs

Comparisons

4.1 Language

- Learn new vocabulary through cognates
- Origins of the Spanish days of the week
- Understand the verb ***ir***
- Learn the correct placement of stress and accents
- Understand the use of interrogatives

4.2 Culture

- Compare: social gathering places to Plaza Morazán; school-based sports and exercise activities; movie-going habits of teens; restoration of historic districts; the influence of musical intruments; children's songs; ***bomba*** and ***plena*** to local music styles

Communities

5.1 Beyond the School

- Identify opportunities to explore local Spanish-speaking communities

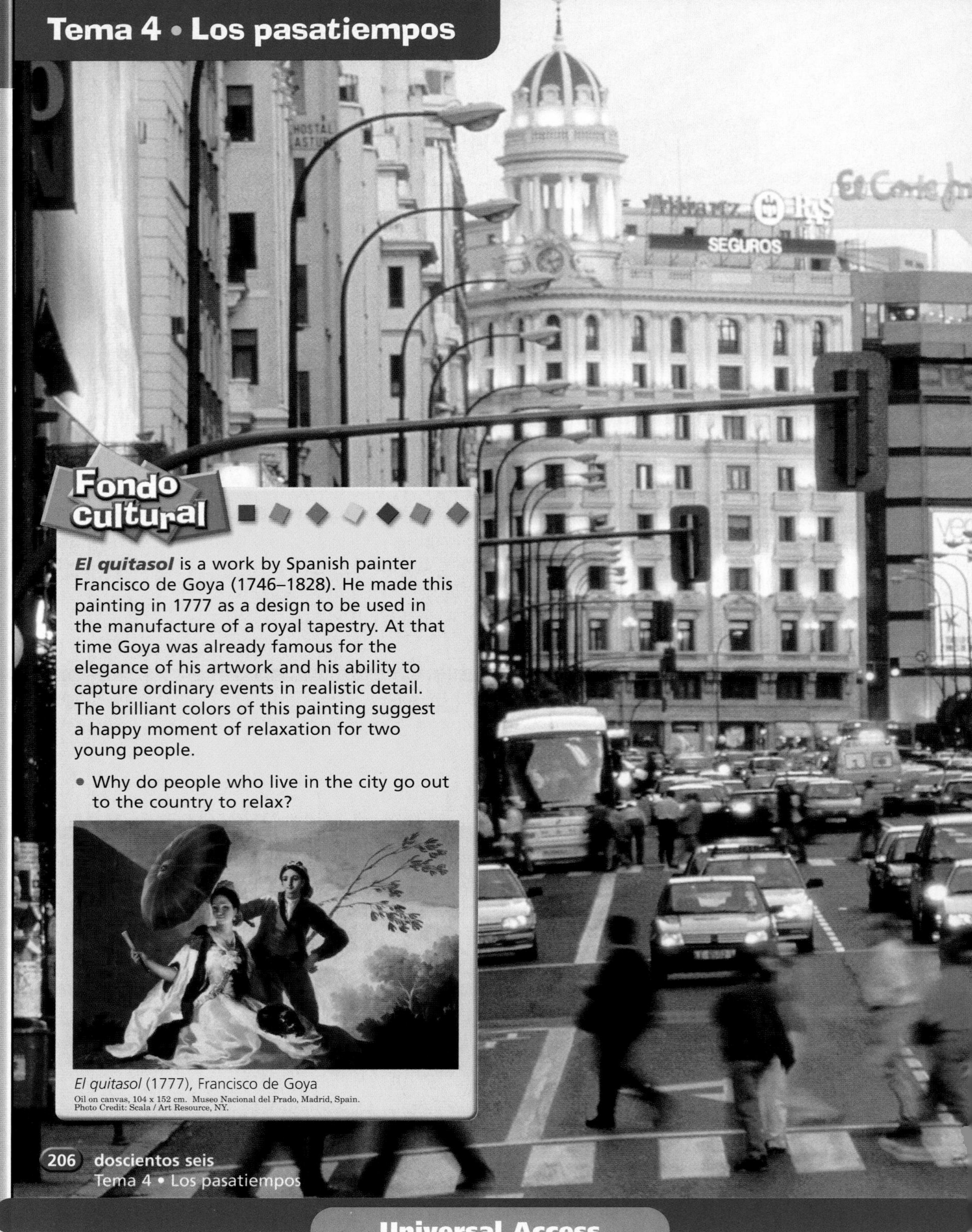

Fondo cultural

El quitasol is a work by Spanish painter Francisco de Goya (1746–1828). He made this painting in 1777 as a design to be used in the manufacture of a royal tapestry. At that time Goya was already famous for the elegance of his artwork and his ability to capture ordinary events in realistic detail. The brilliant colors of this painting suggest a happy moment of relaxation for two young people.

- Why do people who live in the city go out to the country to relax?

El quitasol (1777), Francisco de Goya
Oil on canvas, 104 x 152 cm. Museo Nacional del Prado, Madrid, Spain.
Photo Credit: Scala / Art Resource, NY.

Universal Access

Personalizing the Theme

Ask students to name places that they go in the evening or on weekends. With whom do they go? At what times? What questions do their parents or guardians ask when students tell them they're going somewhere? Explain that this chapter will focus on leisure activities and places to go.

Advanced Learners

Have students use maps, guidebooks, and the Internet to research the major streets and monuments of Madrid. Have them use presentation software to create a slideshow introduction to the city. They could also do this by making posters.

Capítulo 4A

¿Adónde vas?

En la Gran Vía de Madrid, España

Chapter Objectives

- Talk about locations in your community
- Discuss leisure activities
- Talk about where you go and with whom
- Learn how to ask questions
- Understand cultural perspectives on leisure activities

Video Highlights

A primera vista: *Un chico reservado*

GramActiva Videos: the verb *ir;* asking questions

Country Connection

As you learn about leisure activities, you will make connections to these countries and places:

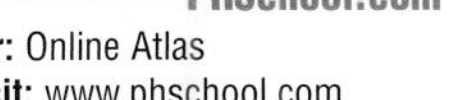

For: Online Atlas
Visit: www.phschool.com
Web Code: jae-0002

Preview 4A

Chapter Opener

Presentation

Resources: Voc. & Gram. Transparencies: 12–18, 20 (maps)

Suggestions: Have students list the places in your community where they go for leisure activities. Explain that in this chapter, they will be learning to talk about the places they go for fun. They will also learn to ask questions of others. The *A primera vista* video focuses on a group of Spanish teens introducing themselves to a new student and talking about their preferred activities.

Standards: 2.1, 2.2, 3.1

Resources: Fine Art Transparencies; Fine Art Transparencies Teacher's Guide

Suggestions: Explain that Goya is one of the greatest Spanish painters. Bring in additional examples of his work to share with students. Individuals can choose their favorites to explain to the class.

Answers will vary, but may include that people enjoy being in a quieter, less polluted environment, surrounded by nature.

Enriching Your Teaching

Planning for Instruction

Resources:

- Teacher Express CD-ROM or Resource Book
  - Teaching resources
  - Lesson Planner
  - Chapter Resource Checklist
  - School-to-Home Connection Letter

Culture Note

Madrid is a bustling city full of monuments, parks, museums, and fountains. One of the main thoroughfares is the Gran Vía, pictured above. Ask students how this looks different from American cities they know. Point out the Corte Inglés sign and explain that this is an elegant department store.

4A Language Input

Vocabulario y gramática

Presentation

Standards: 1.2, 4.1

Resources: Resource Book: 4A, Input Script; Voc. & Gram. Transparencies: 81–82; Resource Book: Cap. 4A, Clip Art; TPR Storytelling Book: Cap. 4A; Audio Program: CD Cap. 4A, Tracks 1–2

Focus: Presenting new vocabulary about places to go

Suggestions: Use the story in the *TPR Storytelling Book* to present the new vocabulary and grammar, or use the Input Script from the *Teacher's Resource Book.* Present the vocabulary in two sets: places to go during the week and places to go on weekends. Use the transparencies to reinforce meaning as you describe places to go. Draw a map of your town on the board or overhead and locate the various locales as you describe them. Have students raise their hands if you mention a place that they go. Remind students that they will be held responsible for the words in the *Más vocabulario.*

Teacher-to-Teacher

Divide students into groups of five or six. Allow each group to have one open book. Students take turns secretly writing down one of the places shown. The others ask, *¿Vas a(l)...?* until they guess the destination. When it is guessed, the first student confirms the answer: *Sí, voy a(l)....* Continue until all have had a turn.

Additional Resources

- Audio Program: Song CD

A primera vista

Objectives

Read, listen to, and understand information about

- places to go to when you're not in school

Vocabulario y gramática en contexto

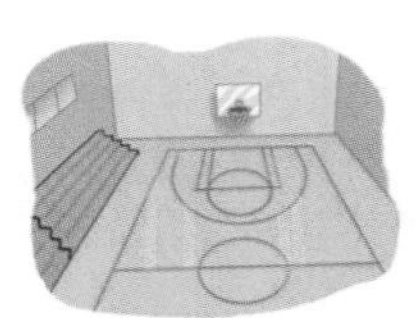
el gimnasio

el parque

el centro comercial

ir de compras

el trabajo

la lección de piano

el cine

ver una película

la biblioteca

la piscina

—En tu **tiempo libre después de** las clases, ¿qué haces?

—**Voy al** gimnasio **para** levantar pesas y al parque para correr. ¿Y tú?

—Hoy voy **a** mi trabajo. No voy a mi lección de piano.

—**¿Con quién** vas al centro comercial?

—Voy con Guillermo, y **después vamos** al cine. ¿Y tú?

—Voy a la biblioteca para estudiar. Después voy al **Café** del Mundo con Lucila.

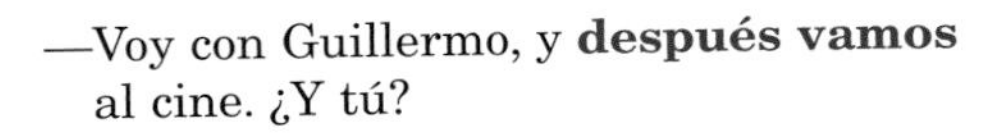

Universal Access

Students with Learning Difficulties

To help students acquire the structure ***a* + *el* = *al*,** use the Clip Art from the *Teacher Express CD-ROM* or the *Teacher's Resource Book* and provide each student with copies of the various pictures. Help them label the pictures with the appropriate prepositions: ***al, a la,*** and ***a las.*** They can use these as flashcards for drill. Be sure to point out the *Nota* on p. 215.

Advanced Learners

Have students create a calendar for the coming month on which they label where they are going and at what times. They can quiz one another: *¿Qué haces los (domingos)? ¿Qué haces el (18)?*

la playa

el restaurante

el campo

las montañas

—¿Qué haces **los** domingos?

—Voy **con mis amigos** a la playa. Allí comemos el almuerzo. Hay un restaurante muy bueno. ¿Y tú?

—**Generalmente** voy al campo o a las montañas.

Más vocabulario

la iglesia	church
la mezquita	mosque
la sinagoga	synagogue
el templo	temple; Protestant church

Actividad 1 **Escuchar**

¿Estás de acuerdo?

You will hear Elena describe where she does seven activities. If a statement is logical, give a "thumbs-up" sign. If it is not logical, give a "thumbs-down" sign.

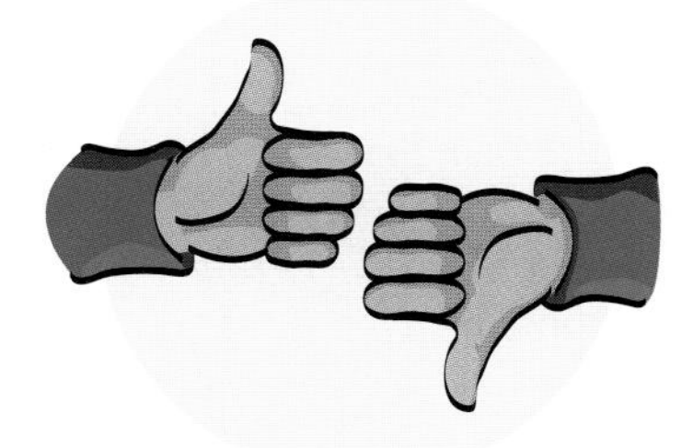

Actividad 2 **Escuchar**

¡Muchas actividades!

Listen to Antonio describe his weekly list of after-school activities. As he names his activities, touch the corresponding picture(s).

Más práctica

Practice Workbook 4A-1, 4A-2

For: Vocabulary practice
Visit: www.phschool.com
Web Code: jad-0401

Enriching Your Teaching

Culture Note

On Sundays in many Spanish-speaking countries, it is common for entire families to go out together. Often, they will attend a religious service, then have something to eat at a restaurant, and then spend time in a park or at the movies. They may also gather at the home of a family member or friend.

Teacher-to-Teacher

Prepare a map handout with various places in your community pictured on it. Include places where your students work. As you describe an imaginary itinerary for one of your students, have students trace the route on the map. Put up a transparency with a completed map so that they can check their work.

Actividad 1 *Standards:* 1.2

Resources: Audio Program: CD Cap. 4A, Track 3; Resource Book: Cap. 4A, Audio Script; Practice Answers on Transparencies

Focus: Listening comprehension about locations for activities

Suggestions: Play the *Audio CD* or read the script. Repeat the activity. Then ask the class to name the seven activities that Elena describes.

Script and Answers:

1. **Me gusta esquiar en la piscina. *(down)***
2. **Voy a la biblioteca para leer. *(up)***
3. **Bailamos en casa. *(up)***
4. **Practico deportes en el gimnasio. *(up)***
5. **Veo una película en el parque. *(down)***
6. **Nado en el cine. *(down)***
7. **Bebo café en el restaurante. *(up)***

Actividad 2 *Standards:* 1.2

Resources: Audio Program: CD Cap. 4A, Track 4; Resource Book: Cap. 4A, Audio Script; Practice Answers on Transparencies

Focus: Listening comprehension and identification of place

Suggestions: Play the *Audio CD* or read the script. As students listen and point, walk around the classroom and note whether or not they point to the correct picture. Explain that some sentences contain two activities or places. Confirm answers using the transparencies.

Script and Answers:

1. **Voy a la biblioteca para estudiar. *(library)***
2. **Me gusta correr en el parque. *(park)***
3. **Voy de compras al centro comercial. *(shopping / mall)***
4. **El viernes voy al cine con Paco. *(movie theater)***
5. **El sábado voy a mi trabajo en el restaurante. *(work / restaurant)***
6. **El domingo voy a la playa. *(beach)***

Videohistoria

Presentation

Standards: 1.2

Resources: Voc. & Gram. Transparencies: 83–84; Audio Program: CD Cap. 4A, Track 5

Focus: Presenting additional contextualized vocabulary and grammar; previewing the video

Suggestions:

Pre-reading: Direct attention to the *Strategy.* Point out that scanning the text before reading in a detailed way can help in understanding the whole story. Use the transparencies to go panel by panel. Cover the dialogue and ask students to predict what activities are being talked about. Uncover the dialogue and have students scan to find the phrases that support their predictions. Show students where Madrid and Salamanca are located, using the map on Transparency 18.

Answers:

1. Answers will vary. Javier.
2. Answers will vary.

Videohistoria

Un chico reservado

¿Qué pasa cuando Ignacio, Elena y Ana hablan con el estudiante nuevo *(new)*? Lee la historia.

Antes de leer

Using visuals You can use visuals to predict what might happen in a story.

- Use the photos in the *Videohistoria* to predict what different activities Ana, Elena, Ignacio, and Javier are talking about. Then, look in the dialogues and find the corresponding word or phrase that describes each activity.

1. Does your school get many new students each year? If so, do you make a point to get to know them? Can you tell from the photos which person is the new student at this school?
2. What do you usually do after school? Do you have the same routine, or do your activities vary? Use the photos to compare the activities that these students participate in with your own pastimes.

Universal Access

Advanced Learners

Ask students to come to the front of the class and read the parts of the four students in the *Videohistoria.* Give them a few minutes to practice before they come up.

Students with Learning Difficulties

Students with visual field difficulties may need extra help in focusing on details in the photos. To eliminate distraction, use the transparencies and cover all the pictures except the one you want students to focus on. Point to or otherwise highlight the people or objects that convey the information.

1 **Ignacio:** Mira, el estudiante nuevo es un poco reservado, ¿verdad?

Elena: Ah sí. . . Está allí **solo.** ¿Por qué no hablamos con él?

Ignacio: Sí, ¡vamos!

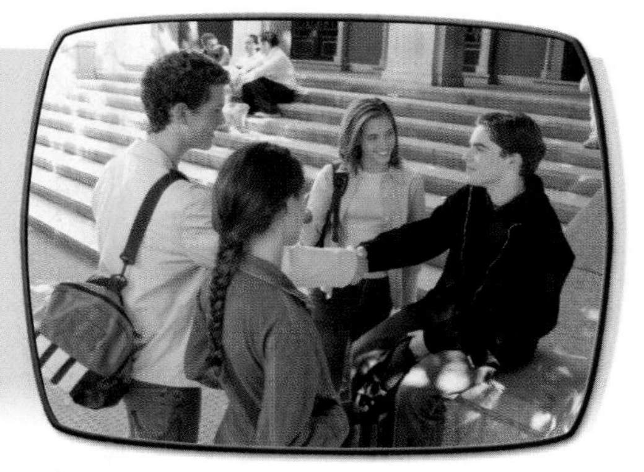

2 **Elena:** Hola. Me llamo Elena. Él es Ignacio, y ella es Ana.

Javier: Mucho gusto. Me llamo Javier.

Elena: Encantada . . . **¿De dónde eres?**

Javier: Soy **de** Salamanca.

3 **Ana:** Pues, Javier, ¿vas después de las clases **con tus amigos?**

Javier: No, voy **a casa.**

4 **Javier:** **¿Adónde** vais* vosotros después de las clases?

Elena: Los lunes, miércoles y viernes voy a mi trabajo en el centro comercial.

Ignacio: Generalmente voy al gimnasio. Me gusta levantar pesas.

*Remember that in Spain, the *vosotros(as)* form of the verb is used when speaking to a group of people you would address individually with *tú*.

Suggestions:

Reading: Use the *Audio CD* or have volunteers read the parts aloud. Stop periodically to check comprehension. Give students verbal and nonverbal clues to help them understand the new words in blue.

Post-reading: Complete *Actividades* 3 and 4 on p. 213 to check comprehension.

Additional Resources

- Writing, Audio & Video Workbook: Cap. 4A, Video Activity 1

Enriching Your Teaching

Culture Note

Salamanca, located northwest of Madrid, is one of the oldest university cities in Europe. The university was founded in 1218. Salamanca was originally a Roman military camp called Salmantica. It is located on the Tormes River and is the setting for one of the classics of Spanish literature, *Lazarillo de Tormes.*

Internet Search

Keywords:

fútbol in Salamanca; Salmantica; Lazarillo de Tormes

Video

Presentation

Standards: 1.2

Resources: Video Program: Cap. 4A; Resource Book: Cap. 4A, Video Script

Focus: Comprehending a story about a new student meeting classmates and talking about leisure activities

Suggestions:

Pre-viewing: Ask students if they've experienced being in a new location, or if they've befriended new students. Explain that the video deals with this situation. Remind them that they will not understand every word, and that they will be hearing the ***vosotros*** form of certain verbs.

Viewing: Show the video once without pausing. Then go back and show it again, using the graphics-supported version. Stop along the way to check comprehension. Show the segment a final time without pausing.

Post-viewing: Complete the video activities in the *Writing, Audio & Video Workbook.*

Additional Resources

- Writing, Audio & Video Workbook: Cap. 4A, Video Activities 2–4
- Heritage Learner Workbook: 4A-1, 4A-2

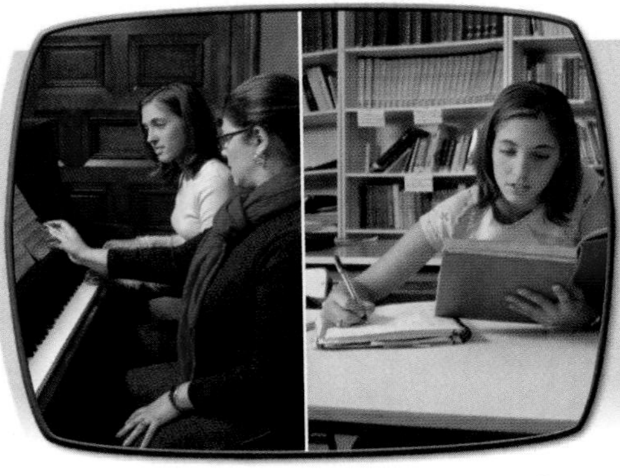

5 **Ana:** Los lunes voy a mi lección de piano y los martes, miércoles y jueves voy a la biblioteca para estudiar. Y Javier, ¿qué haces **los fines de semana?**

6 **Javier:** ¿Los fines de semana? **Me quedo en casa.** No tengo muchos amigos aquí.

Ignacio: ¿Qué te gusta hacer?

Javier: ¡Me gusta el fútbol!

7 **Ana:** **¡No me digas!** Pues, nosotros vamos al parque para practicar fútbol.

Javier: **¿Cuándo?**

Ana: El sábado.

Javier: Está bien.

8 **Elena:** Pero Ana, ¿fútbol?

Ana: ¿Por qué no? ¡No tiene muchos amigos y le gusta el fútbol!

Universal Access

Advanced Learners

Have students rewrite the dialogue for the various characters, substituting other activities or places that they've learned. They could also personalize it using names of classmates. Have them perform their dialogues for the class. Encourage creativity.

Heritage Language Learners

Have students write a short paragraph telling what they usually do each day of the week. Allow them to use vocabulary that has not yet been taught, if they desire. Verify their spelling and have them make necessary corrections before placing the paragraphs in their portfolios.

 Actividad 3 Leer/Escribir

¿Comprendes?

Number your paper 1–6. Based on the *Videohistoria,* choose the response that best completes each statement below. Write the completed sentences on your paper.

1. Javier es de . . .
   - **a.** Madrid.
   - **b.** Barcelona.
   - **c.** Salamanca.
2. Después de las clases Javier va . . .
   - **a.** a la biblioteca para estudiar.
   - **b.** a casa.
   - **c.** al cine.
3. Después de las clases Ignacio va . . .
   - **a.** al gimnasio.
   - **b.** al centro comercial.
   - **c.** al restaurante.
4. El jueves Ana va . . .
   - **a.** a la lección de piano.
   - **b.** a la biblioteca.
   - **c.** a la iglesia.
5. A Javier le gusta practicar . . .
   - **a.** el fútbol.
   - **b.** el golf.
   - **c.** el español.
6. Todos van al parque el . . .
   - **a.** martes.
   - **b.** jueves.
   - **c.** sábado.

Actividad 4 Leer/Escribir

La rutina de los estudiantes

You are trying to organize everybody's schedule. Copy the chart below onto a sheet of paper. Based on information in the *Videohistoria,* write what each person does on the various days of the week. Not all of the spaces on the chart will be filled.

	Ignacio	Elena	Ana	Javier
lunes				
martes				
miércoles				
jueves				
viernes				
sábado				
domingo				

Más práctica
Practice Workbook 4A-3, 4A-4

Go Online PHSchool.com
For: Vocabulary practice
Visit: www.phschool.com
Web Code: jad-0402

Enriching Your Teaching

Culture Note

Schools in the United States often offer a variety of after-school extracurricular activities such as language clubs, chess clubs, quiz bowl teams, and sports teams. Most schools in Spanish-speaking countries don't offer extracurricular activities. Students participate in these kinds of activities at private and city clubs.

Teacher-to-Teacher

Create a chart like the one in *Actividad* 4 on the computer and photocopy it for students. That way they don't have to use class time creating the chart and can simply fill in the targeted vocabulary.

 Actividad 3 — *Standards:* 1.2, 1.3

Resources: Practice Answers on Transparencies

Focus: Demonstrating comprehension of the *Videohistoria*

Suggestions: Tell students that they can refer to the *Videohistoria* captions when they answer the questions. Have them tell in what panel they found the information to complete the sentences.

Answers:
1. c. Salamanca. *(panel 2)*
2. b. a casa. *(panel 3)*
3. a. al gimnasio. *(panel 4)*
4. b. a la biblioteca. *(panel 5)*
5. a. el fútbol. *(panel 6)*
6. c. sábado. *(panel 7)*

 Actividad 4 — *Standards:* 1.2, 1.3

Resources: Practice Answers on Transparencies

Focus: Reading and organizing information about the *Videohistoria*

Suggestions: Ask students to first complete the chart at their seats. Then have them pair up to compare and correct answers.

Answers:
Ignacio:
Most days: va al gimnasio
sábado: jugar al fútbol
Elena:
lunes, miércoles, viernes: ir al trabajo
sábado: jugar al fútbol
Ana:
lunes: ir a la lección de piano
martes, miércoles, jueves: estudiar en la biblioteca
sábado: jugar al fútbol
Javier:
Every day: ir a casa

Extension: Have students create a chart similar to the one in *Actividad* 4, using their own names and the names of two classmates. Have them interview those classmates to find out where they go after school on different days.

Assessment

- Prueba 4A-1: Vocabulary recognition

Standards: 1.2, 1.3

Resources: Practice Answers on Transparencies

Focus: Reading and completing sentences about where certain activities take place

Suggestions: Review the places pictured before students begin. Brainstorm logical responses for the *¡Respuesta personal!*

Answers:

1. ...el gimnasio.
2. ...la piscina.
3. ...el cine.
4. ...la biblioteca.
5. ...las montañas.
6. ...casa.

Extension: Have students create illogical sentences, e.g., *Nado en la biblioteca.* Ask volunteers to write theirs on the board and have the class correct them.

Standards: 1.3

Resources: Resource Book: Cap. 4A, GramActiva BLM

Focus: Writing about frequency of going certain places

Recycle: Expressions of frequency

Suggestions: Have students identify each picture before they begin. As students work, walk around the room, checking that they understand what to do.

Answers will vary.

Extension: Draw the line diagram on the board and have volunteers write places they go under the correct time expression.

Manos a la obra

Vocabulario y gramática en uso

Objectives

- Communicate about leisure activities
- Tell where you go and with whom
- Learn to use the verb *ir* and how to ask questions

Escribir

¿Qué haces en . . . ?

Using the pictures at right, complete the following sentences logically. Write the completed sentences on your paper.

1. Hago ejercicio en . . .
2. Nado en . . .
3. Veo películas en . . .
4. Leo libros y revistas en . . .
5. Esquío en . . .
6. Como el desayuno en . . .

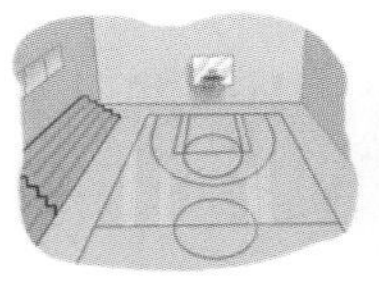

¡Respuesta personal!

Escribir

¿Vas mucho a . . . ?

On a sheet of paper, copy the diagram below and write the names of the places you go under the appropriate time expressions.

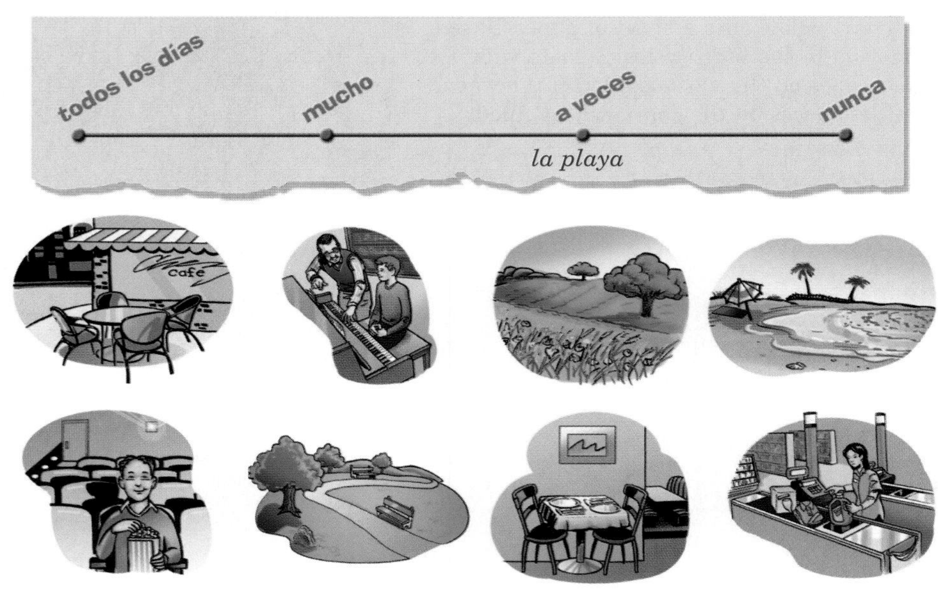

Universal Access

Advanced Learners

Have students write an original sentence using each of the places mentioned in *Actividad* 5. Ask students to read their sentences to the class.

Students with Special Needs

Students who have difficulty writing can be given copies of the pictures from the Clip Art on the *Resource Pro CD-ROM* or the *Teacher's Resource Book.* Prepare a large version of the diagram. Have students place the pictures under the appropriate expressions and name them as they place them.

  Hablar

¡No me digas!

Work with a partner. Using what you wrote for Actividad 6, take turns saying where you go and how often. React to your partner's statements. Follow the model.

Modelo

A —*Voy a la playa a veces.*
B —*¡No me digas! Yo voy a la playa a veces también.*
o: *¡No me digas! Yo nunca voy a la playa.*
o: *Pues, yo voy a la playa todos los días.*

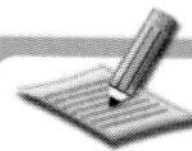

Nota

When *a* is used before *el,* the two words form the contraction *al (to the):*

a + el = al

- Voy **al** centro comercial a veces pero voy **a la** piscina mucho.

También se dice . . .

la piscina = la alberca *(México);* la pileta *(América del Sur)*

el restaurante = el restaurán *(América del Sur)*

  Escuchar/Escribir

Escucha y escribe

Look at this painting of Plaza Morazán in Tegucigalpa. You will hear six statements about the painting. Number your paper from 1–6 and write what you hear.

Fondo cultural

La Plaza Strolling through the main square, *la plaza,* of most towns and cities in Spanish-speaking countries is a popular activity for young and old alike. Plaza Morazán is the main square in Tegucigalpa, the capital city of Honduras. The square is named after Francisco Morazán (1792–1842), a Honduran general and head of state.

- What social gathering place in your community is similar to *la plaza?*

Plaza Morazán en Tegucigalpa (1969), José Antonio Velásquez

Enriching Your Teaching

Culture Note

General Francisco Morazán (1792–1842) was key in forming the *Unión de las Provincias de Centroamérica* (later to become *la República Federal de Centroamérica)* after Honduras, Nicaragua, Guatemala, El Salvador, and Costa Rica gained independence from Spain in 1821. For ten years Morazán served as president of the *Unión,* which collapsed in 1839. He was forced into exile within a year. He then became president of Costa Rica, but was betrayed by his troops and killed. His birthday is celebrated each October 3rd as a national holiday in Honduras.

 *Standards:* 1.1

Actividad 7

Focus: Talking about places people go and how often in a personalized context

Recycle: Expressions of frequency

Suggestions: Point out the *Nota* if you have not already explained this concept. Remind students of the examples they saw earlier. Show the transparencies and have students tell you the preposition for each place or activity. Be sure Student B understands the options in the *Modelo.*

Answers will vary.

 *Standards:* 1.2, 1.3

Actividad 8

Resources: Audio Program: CD Cap. 4A, Track 6; Resource Book: Cap. 4A, Audio Script; Practice Answers on Transparencies

Focus: Listening to and writing information about a painting

Suggestions: Play the *Audio CD* or read the script. Allow students to listen several times. Use the *Fine Art Transparencies* to guide students' attention as they listen.

Script and Answers:

1. **Hay muchas personas en la plaza.**
2. **Hace buen tiempo hoy.**
3. **¿Ves la bandera de Honduras?**
4. **Muchas personas hablan en el parque.**
5. **Voy a la plaza con mis amigos.**
6. **Me encanta la iglesia.**

 *Standards:* 2.1, 4.2

Suggestions: Point out that the main ***plaza*** is the hub of most towns or cities, and that people often arrange to meet at the plaza, both for business and pleasure.

Answers will vary, but may include such things as malls, post offices, downtown shopping areas, etc.

Practice and Communicate

Exploración del lenguaje

Presentation

Standards: 4.1

Resources: Practice Answers on Transparencies

Suggestions: Remind students that what is now Spain was a Roman province for centuries. Have students research the origins of the English days of the week and make comparisons with the Latin / Spanish versions.

Answers:

1. c
2. e
3. a
4. g
5. b
6. f
7. d

The Latin word for day is *dies.*

Standards: 1.1

Focus: Asking and telling about where you go on specific days

Recycle: Vocabulary for leisure activities

Suggestions: Direct attention to the *Nota.* Point out that the article is required, unlike in English. Go through possible answers that Student B might give.

Answers will vary.

Common errors: Students often try to use ***en*** before days of the week. To reinforce the correct structure, have Student B include the article and day of the week in the answers.

Extension: Have the classroom brainstorm places and activites they have learned and write them on the board. Then write, ***¿Cuándo vas...?*** and give a possible answer (***los jueves, los sábados,*** etc.). Then have volunteers ask and answer the question.

Exploración del lenguaje

Origins of the Spanish days of the week

The word *sábado,* like many Spanish words, is based on Latin. The Spanish days of the week come from the Latin names for the gods, planets, sun, and moon, all of which were important in Roman daily life.

Try it out! Match the Spanish days of the week with their Latin origins.

1. lunes	**a.** *dies Mercurii:* named after Mercury, the god of commerce and travelers
2. martes	**b.** *dies Veneris:* named after Venus, the goddess of beauty and love
3. miércoles	**c.** *dies lunae:* the day dedicated to the moon *(luna)*
4. jueves	**d.** *dies solis:* named after the sun *(sol),* but later changed to *dies Dominicus,* which means "the Lord's day"
5. viernes	**e.** *dies Martis:* dedicated to Mars, the god of war
6. sábado	**f.** *dies Saturni:* named after Saturn; also called *dies Sabbati,* based on the Hebrew word *shabbath,* or "day of rest"
7. domingo	**g.** *dies Jovis:* named after Jove, or Jupiter, the ruler of the gods

- Since you know *día* means "day" in Spanish, what is the word for "day" in Latin?

Hablar

¿Adónde vas?

With a partner, talk about the places you go at different times during the week.

Modelo

los lunes

A —*¿Adónde vas los lunes?*

B —*Generalmente voy a la lección de piano.*

o: *Generalmente me quedo en casa.*

Nota

To say that something usually happens on a certain day every week, use ***los*** with the plural of the day of the week:

- Generalmente ellos van al campo **los viernes** o **los sábados.**

Estudiante A

1. los miércoles
2. los viernes
3. los sábados
4. los domingos
5. los fines de semana
6. después de las clases

Estudiante B

¡Respuesta personal!

Universal Access

Students with Learning Difficulties

For *Actividad* 10 some students may need help understanding how a grid works. Show them how to trace down with their fingers to the letter, and then across to the number.

Advanced Learners

Have students research the origins of the Spanish names of the months. Have them prepare a poster or handout with a two-column chart like the one in the *Exploración del lenguaje.* They could also create a matching exercise like the one there.

  Pensar/Hablar

Leer un mapa no es difícil

When you visit a new city or town in a Spanish-speaking country, you will often use a map to help you get to where you want to go. Although maps may vary from place to place, you will usually find some standard features that will help you find your way around. You should always look for the key *(la clave)*. This will give you the symbols and other information that you need to read the map. Some maps are set up as a grid so that you can use an index to help you find streets or places of interest.

Conexiones — La geografía

You are visiting Madrid. With a partner, take turns asking and answering where you are going, based on the grid locations and the map.

1. F4 **2.** B7 **3.** E1 **4.** B8 **5.** E9 **6.** C10

Modelo

D9
A —*Estoy en D9. ¿Adónde voy?*
B —*Vas al restaurante.*

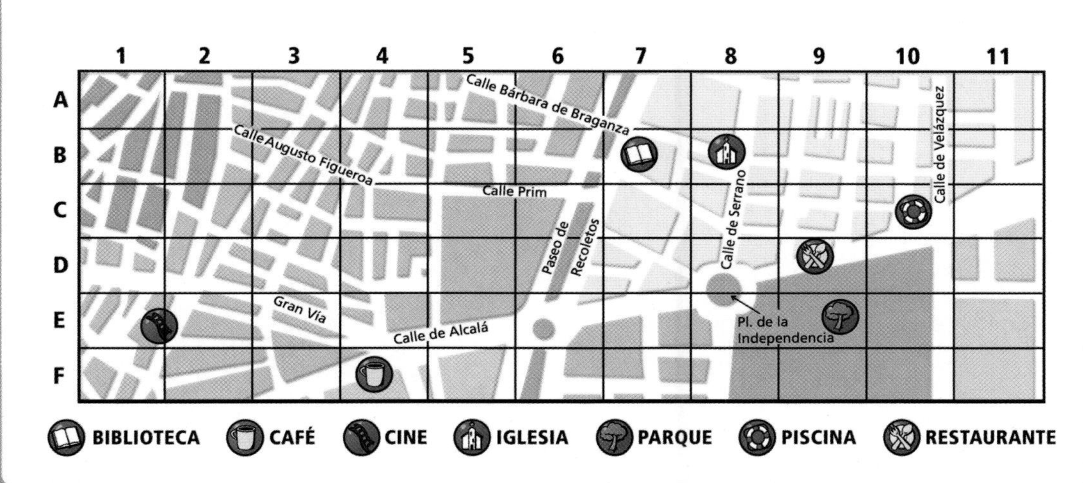

 Escribir/Hablar

Y tú, ¿qué dices?

1. ¿Dónde ves más películas, en casa o en el cine?
2. Cuando vas de compras, ¿adónde vas?
3. ¿Adónde vas los fines de semana? ¿Vas solo(a) o con tus amigos?

Enriching Your Teaching

Culture Note

Although many cities in the United States were carefully planned and developed around a grid, many cities in Spain, like Sevilla, were built around historic city centers that date back to the Roman era. These areas have winding, narrow streets that cars can barely drive through. Some streets are so narrow that a person can touch the buildings on each side with outstretched arms.

Internet Search

Keywords:

Sevilla + centro histórico + Calle Sierpes

 *Standards:* 1.1, 3.1 (Actividad 10)

Resources: Practice Answers on Transparencies

Focus: Reading a map and talking about going places; making a cross-curricular connection with geography

Recycle: ***estoy***

Suggestions: Model how to locate items on a map. Have Student A ask the questions for a–c, and Student B give the answers. Have Student B ask the questions for d–f and Student A will give the answers.

Answers:

1. **—Estoy en F4. ¿Adónde voy? —Vas al café.**
2. **...a la biblioteca.**
3. **...al cine.**
4. **...a la iglesia.**
5. **...al parque.**
6. **...a la piscina.**

  *Standards:* 1.1, 1.2 (Actividad 11)

Focus: Writing and speaking in a personalized context

Suggestions: Have students deduce the meaning of ***solo(a)*** in item 3 using context (it's the opposite of ***con tus amigos***) or cognate recognition.

Answers will vary but will include: **ves, veo, corres, corro, usas, uso, vas, voy.**

Additional Resources

- Writing, Audio & Video Workbook: Cap. 4A, Audio Activities 5–6, Tracks 7–8
- Writing, Audio & Video Workbook: Cap. 4A, Writing Activity 10
- Resource Book: Cap. 4A, Communicative Activity BLM

Assessment

- Prueba 4A-2: Vocabulary production

Presentation

 *Standards:* 4.1

Resources: Voc. & Gram. Transparencies: 85; Video Program: Cap. 4A; Resource Book: Cap. 4A, Video Script

Suggestions: Direct attention to the *¿Recuerdas?* Use the transparency to reinforce the verb forms or write them on the board. Ask the question *¿Adónde vas?* of several students. Then point to another student and ask, *¿Adónde va?* Continue through the verb forms. For additional reinforcement, play the *GramActiva* Video.

Standards: 1.3

Resources: Practice Answers on Transparencies

Focus: Matching the forms of the verb ***ir*** with the appropriate subject

Suggestions: Point out the note that says *Mario* and ask the students to look at the chart for the verb ***ir.*** Ask students which subject pronoun would best represent *Mario,* and therefore, which form of the verb ***ir*** would go with *Mario.* If necessary, repeat this process with the other notes on the left side of the refrigerator. Then have students write the sentences.

Answers:

1. **Mario va a la lección de piano.**
2. **Luisa y Carlos van a la biblioteca.**
3. **Papá y yo vamos al templo.**
4. **Yo voy a casa después del templo.**
5. **Tú vas al café.**

Teacher-to-Teacher

Have students write a list of five places they go. Divide the class into groups of five. Name a leader in each group. The leader asks the person to the right, *¿Vas a (la biblioteca)?* The person responds with *Sí, voy...* or *No, no voy...* according to his or her list. The leader continues asking questions twice around the circle, and then must try to restate where everyone is going without making any errors. Play continues around the circle.

Gramática

The verb *ir*

To say where someone is going, use the verb *ir.* Here are its present-tense forms:

(yo)	voy	(nosotros) (nosotras)	vamos
(tú)	vas	(vosotros) (vosotras)	vais
Ud. (él) (ella)	va	Uds. (ellos) (ellas)	van

The verb *ir* is almost always followed by *a.* To ask where someone is going, use *¿Adónde?*

¿Adónde vas? ***Where** are you going?*

- You will often hear people say *¡Vamos!* This means, "Let's go!"

¿Recuerdas?

You have used the infinitive *ir* to talk about going to school.

- Me gusta **ir** a la escuela.

GramActiva VIDEO

Want more help with the verb *ir?* Watch the **GramActiva** video.

Actividad 12 Gramática **Escribir**

¿Adónde va la familia?

The members of the Li family are always busy. They have to leave messages on the refrigerator to let the others know where they are going. Find out where everyone is going by putting the messages together. Write the complete sentences on a separate sheet of paper.

Universal Access

Multiple Intelligences

Visual / Spatial: Have students research places to go in Chile and present their information as a postcard telling where they are going with their Chilean friends. Students can use pictures from magazines or the Internet to make the postcard look authentic.

Heritage Language Learners

Students may frequently confuse the letters ***b*** and ***v*** when they write, because of the similarity in pronunciation. Give them a short dictation that includes several of the present-tense forms of ***ir*** as well as words containing the letter ***b.***

Actividad 13 Gramática **Leer/Escribir**

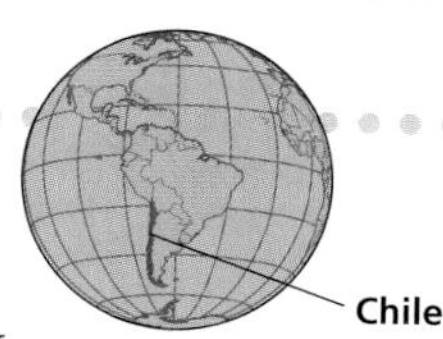

Un año en Chile

María, a student from Corpus Christi, Texas, is spending a year with a family in Santiago, Chile. Read the letter that she wrote to her friends back home and write the correct forms of the verb *ir* on a separate sheet of paper.

17 de julio

Querida Sonia,

¿Cómo estás? Yo, bien. Generalmente, paso tiempo en casa los fines de semana, pero a veces yo __1.__ a Portillo con mi familia para esquiar. Hace mucho frío allí y por eso la mamá no __2.__ siempre con nosotros. En Portillo hay una escuela para los esquiadores y muchos chicos simpáticos __3.__ a las lecciones. También hay un cibercafé con computadoras. Muchas personas __4.__ allí para pasar tiempo con los amigos. Nosotros __5.__ el domingo. Y tú, ¿ __6.__ a la playa todos los días con tus amigos?

Hasta luego,

María

Actividad 14 Gramática **Leer/Hablar**

La carta

Read the letter in Actividad 13 again and answer the following questions about María's experience in Chile.

1. ¿Quién no va siempre con la familia a Portillo?
2. ¿Por qué a María le gusta ir a las lecciones de esquí?
3. ¿Adónde van para usar las computadoras?
4. ¿Cuándo van al cibercafé?
5. ¿Adónde van muchas personas para pasar tiempo con los amigos?

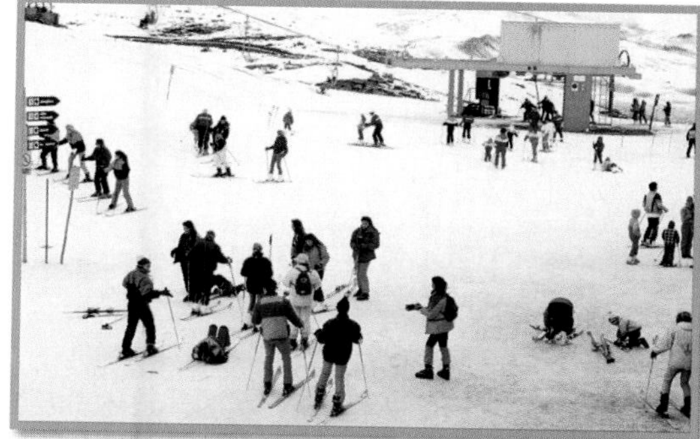

Esquiadores en Portillo, Chile

Practice and Communicate

Actividad 13

Standards: 1.2, 3.1

Resources: Practice Answers on Transparencies

Focus: Reading and writing forms of the verb ***ir*** in context

Suggestions: Have students number their papers 1–6 and complete the assignment. Walk around the room as they work, assisting with comprehension. When students have finished, ask volunteers to read a sentence using the correct form of the verb.

Answers:

1. voy	3. van	5. vamos
2. va	4. van	6. vas

Actividad 14

Standards: 1.2, 1.3

Resources: Practice Answers on Transparencies

Focus: Reading a letter and orally answering questions about it

Suggestions: Have students take turns reading the letter in *Actividad* 13 aloud. Then ask the class the questions.

Answers:

1. La mamá chilena no va a veces con la familia.
2. Porque muchos chicos simpáticos van a las lecciones.
3. Van a un cibercafé.
4. Van el domingo.
5. Van a la playa.

Enriching Your Teaching

Culture Note

Portillo is recognized as one of the finest resorts in South America but it offers much more than just skiing and snowboarding. You can relax in one of two lodges, take a yoga class, go to the movie theater, visit the game room, or use the gym. Portillo provides a relaxing vacation atmosphere for skiers and non-skiers alike.

Internet Search

Keywords:

Portillo + Chile; Gran + Catedral; Cerro + Catedral; Bariloche + Argentina

Standards: 1.3

Resources: Practice Answers on Transparencies

Focus: Writing about where people go

Suggestions: Suggest that students write the word bank on their paper so that they can check off the words as they use them. Tell students to keep their work to use for *Actividad* 16.

Answers:

1. Luis va al gimnasio.
2. Yo voy al parque.
3. Carlitos y Sandrina van al cine.
4. Nosotros vamos al restaurante.
5. Tú vas a la piscina.
6. Uds. van al centro comercial.

Common Errors: Students may not properly match the verb conjugation with the subject. Refer them to the ***ir*** chart on p. 218 to refresh their memory.

Rapid Review

Have students look at the places listed in the word bank for *Actividad* 15. Then act out the activity that you would do at one of the places. For example, pretend to be swimming. The student who guesses ***piscina*** comes to the front of the room and acts out another activity from one of the places until all the places have been reviewed.

Standards: 1.3

Resources: Practice Answers on Transparencies

Focus: Writing about why people go places

Recycle: Leisure activities

Suggestions: Ask volunteers to read the sentences they wrote for *Actividad* 15. After a student reads a sentence, ask why someone would go to that place. Tell students that there are various answers for each item.

Answers:

1. Luis va al gimnasio para levantar pesas.
2. Yo voy al parque para correr.
3. Carlitos y Sandrina van al cine para ver películas.
4. Nosotros vamos al restaurante para comer.
5. Tú vas a la piscina para nadar.
6. Uds. van al centro comercial para ir de compras.

Actividad 15 Gramática **Escribir**

¿Adónde van todos?

Look at the pictures below. Number your paper 1–6 and, using the places in the word bank, write complete sentences telling where the following people are going.

Elena

Modelo

Elena va a la biblioteca.

la piscina	el cine	la biblioteca
el restaurante	el centro comercial	el parque
el gimnasio		

1.

Luis

2.

yo

3.

Carlitos y Sandrina

4.

nosotros

5.

tú

6.

Uds.

Actividad 16 Gramática **Escribir**

¿Por qué van allí?

Where you go often depends on what you like to do. Using the sentences you wrote in Actividad 15, explain why the people go to those places.

Modelo

Elena va a la biblioteca porque lee muchos libros.

Universal Access

Heritage Language Learners

Have students name additional places and activities that they enjoy. Have them write five sentences describing these. Check spelling and verb agreement carefully.

Advanced Learners

Have students write five personalized sentences telling where they like to go and why, following the format of the sentences in *Actividad* 16.

  Hablar

Voy allí porque me gusta . . .

Choose five of the following places. Working in pairs, ask your partner if he or she goes there and why.

Modelo

A —*¿Vas al café?*
B —*Sí, por supuesto.*
o: *Claro que no.*
A —*¿Por qué (no) vas al café?*
B —*Voy porque me gusta pasar tiempo con mis amigos.*
o: *No voy porque no me gusta beber café.*

Estudiante A

el café
la playa
la biblioteca
las montañas
el parque
la casa
el cine
la escuela
el centro comercial
el restaurante

Estudiante B

comer
beber
pasar tiempo con mis amigos
estudiar
leer
ver
hablar
comprar
nadar
esquiar

¡Respuesta personal!

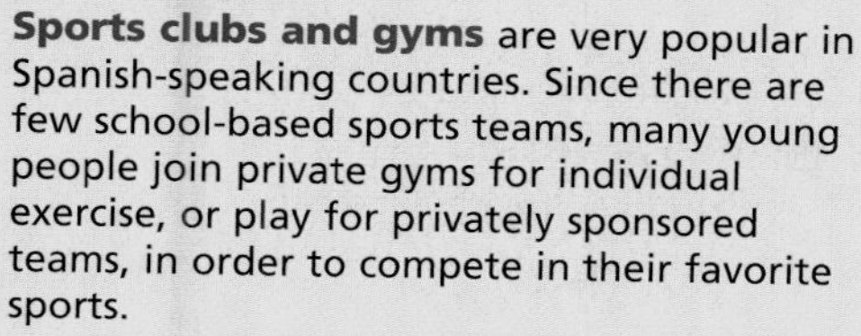

Estudiantes en el gimnasio

Sports clubs and gyms are very popular in Spanish-speaking countries. Since there are few school-based sports teams, many young people join private gyms for individual exercise, or play for privately sponsored teams, in order to compete in their favorite sports.

- What do you think students would do if your school did not offer opportunities for playing and competing in sports?

Enriching Your Teaching

Culture Note

While baseball and basketball are popular in Spanish-speaking countries, soccer is by far the favorite sport. Other favorite sports are walking, jogging, and swimming. In the countryside, horseback riding is popular.

Rapid Review

To prepare the students for *Actividad* 17, review ***me gusta*** with them. Then quickly ask various students if they like to do the activities in the Student B bubble in *Actividad* 17. For example: *¿Te gusta comer? ¿Te gusta beber café?*

  *Standards:* 1.1

Focus: Talking about where you like or don't like to go and why

Suggestions: Read the affirmative *Modelo* with a volunteer reading the part of Student B. Repeat with the negative *Modelo*. Have students write down the five places that they have chosen to discuss. Circulate through the room during practice to help students who appear stuck or are having problems.

Answers will vary.

 *tandards:* 2.1, 4.2

Suggestions: Students may have difficulty imagining the situation posed in the question. Point out that students in other countries find outlets for exercise and sports despite the lack of school-sponsered competitions.

Answers will vary.

Standards: 1.1, 1.2, 1.3

Focus: Writing and talking about what people like to do and where they do it

Suggestions: Point out to students that they need to write ten sentences, five stating what they like to do and five telling where they do each activity. Stress that they should not let other teams see their sentences. As students work in their groups of four, walk around the room to monitor understanding and correct sentence formation, speaking and pronunciation.

Answers will vary.

El español en la comunidad

Standards: 5.1

Suggestions: Ask a student to read *El español en la comunidad.* When students discuss the question, ask: If you have not visited a neighborhood with a Spanish-speaking community, what would you expect to find in one? Correct any misconceptions.

Answers will vary.

Additional Resources

- Writing, Audio & Video Workbook: Cap. 4A, Audio Activity 7, Track 11
- Writing, Audio & Video Workbook: Cap. 4A, Writing Activity 11
- Resource Book: Cap. 4A, Communicative Activity BLM

Assessment

- Prueba 4A-3: The verb *ir*

Actividad 18 Gramática — Escribir/Hablar

Juego

1. With a partner, write five sentences telling what the two of you do in your free time and when. On a separate sheet of paper, write sentences telling where you go to do these activities.

Modelo

Nosotros corremos después de las clases. Vamos al gimnasio.

2. Get together with another pair of students and tell them what you and your partner do in your free time. Be sure not to tell them where you go! It's their job to guess where you go. If they guess correctly, their team gets a point. The team that earns the most points wins.

Modelo

A —*Nosotros corremos después de las clases.*
B —*Uds. van al gimnasio, ¿verdad?*
A —*Sí, vamos al gimnasio para correr.*
o: *No, no vamos al gimnasio para correr. Vamos al parque.*

Más práctica

Practice Workbook 4A-5

For: Practice with *ir*
Visit: www.phschool.com
Web Code: jad-0403

El español en la comunidad

In many businesses and neighborhoods in the United States, you can hear Spanish being spoken. For example, the Pilsen neighborhood in Chicago, Illinois, is home to one of the nation's largest Mexican communities. Colorful murals, thriving businesses, and popular restaurants give Pilsen its character.

- Are there areas near you where you can see expressions of community for Spanish speakers like those in Pilsen? What are they?

Un mural en la comunidad de Pilsen en Chicago

Universal Access

Students with Special Needs

Students with hearing impairments may benefit from seeing hand signals to indicate where syllabic stress falls. You might use an open hand to indicate a stressed syllable and a closed one to indicate an unstressed one.

Heritage Language Learners

Students may have trouble remembering to use written accents on words. Dictate a mixture of words that require accent marks and those that do not. Ask students to write the words, inserting necessary accent marks based on the rules they've learned.

Pronunciación

Stress and accents

How can you tell which syllable to stress, or emphasize, when you see words written in Spanish? Here are some general rules.

1. **When words end in a vowel, *n*, or *s*** place the stress on the **next-to-last syllable.** Copy each of these words and draw a line under the next-to-last syllable. Then listen to and say these words, making sure you stress the underlined syllable:

centro	pasteles	piscina
computadora	trabajo	parque
mantequilla	escriben	generalmente

2. **When words end in a consonant (except *n* or *s*)** place the stress on the **last syllable.** Listen to and say these words, making sure you stress the last syllable:

señor	nariz	escribir
profesor	reloj	arroz
español	trabajador	comer

3. **When a word has a written accent** place the stress on the **accented syllable.** One reason for written accents is to indicate exceptions to the first two rules. Listen to and say these words. Be sure to emphasize the accented syllable:

café	número	teléfono
difícil	película	lápiz
fácil	plátano	artístico

Try it out! Listen to the first verse of the song "La Bamba" and say each word with the stress on the correct syllable. Then listen to the recording again and see if you can sing along with the first verse.

Para bailar la bamba, para bailar la bamba
se necesita una poca de gracia,
una poca de gracia y otra cosita
y arriba y arriba,
y arriba y arriba y arriba iré,
yo no soy marinero, yo no soy marinero,
por ti seré, por ti seré, por ti seré.

Enriching Your Teaching

Culture Note

"La Bamba" is a folk song that was popularized by Ritchie Valens (1941–1959), a young singer from a Mexican American family in California. His last name was Valenzuela, but he changed it when he became a performer. He had a million-seller hit single, "Donna." *"La Bamba"* was on the other side of the record and became an unexpected hit as well. Valens died in a small-plane crash with Buddy Holly, shortly before his eighteenth birthday.

Rapid Review

Review the five basic vowel sounds in Spanish with this quick rhyme: *A, E, I, O, U, ¿Adónde vas tú?* Ask one student. After he or she answers, have that student ask another student, until several students have correctly pronounced the vowels.

Pronunciación

Presentation

Standards: 4.1

Resources: Audio Program: CD Cap. 4A, Tracks 9–10

Suggestions: Take each of the rules separately. Spend time drilling each stress pattern and its rules before moving on to the next step. Play the *Audio CD* as many times as necessary.

Try it out! After students have completed the activity, ask two students to read one line at a time together. Correct pronunciation errors. Play the song (Track 11) and encourage students to sing.

Have students write the words to the song *"La Bamba"* and highlight accent and stress points mentioned in steps 1, 2, and 3.

Teaching with Music

Songs are an excellent means of teaching rhythm and stress as students acquire a second language. Use the Song CD from the *Audio Program* or bring in other music with easy, singable lyrics from your collection or from libraries.

Theme Project

Give students copies of the Theme Project outline and rubric from the *Teacher's Resource Book*. Explain the task to them, and have them perform step 1. (For more information, see p. 206-2.)

4A Practice and Communicate

Presentation

 *Standards:* 4.1

Resources: Voc. & Gram. Transparencies: 86; Video Program: Cap. 4A; Resource Book: Cap. 4A, Video Script

Suggestions: Be sure that students understand how questions are formed in English, and the relationship between the kind of information you are seeking and the way a question is asked. Go through the list of questions. Point out the use of the double question marks. Then point out the written accent marks on question words and explain that they are extra clues to the fact that a question is being asked. Use the transparency and cover the English to check comprehension. When students seem to be grasping the concept, give them a statement and see if they can tell you what question they would ask to get that answer. Show the *GramActiva* Video to reinforce the concept.

 *Standards:* 1.2, 1.3

Resources: Practice Answers on Transparencies

Focus: Matching questions and answers

Suggestion: Tell students to read all the questions and answers before they make their selections. Point out that subject and verb agreement can help them choose some of the answers. Tell them to eliminate the easy or most obvious matches first.

Answers:

1. d	3. b	5. a
2. c	4. f	6. e

Gramática

Asking questions

You use interrogative words *(who, what, where,* and so on) to ask questions.

¿Qué?	*What?*	¿Adónde?	*(To) Where?*
¿Cómo?	*How?, What?*	¿De dónde?	*From where?*
¿Quién?	*Who?*	¿Cuál?	*Which?, What?*
¿Con quién?	*With whom?*	¿Por qué?	*Why?*
¿Dónde?	*Where?*	¿Cuándo?	*When?*
¿Cuántos, -as?	*How many?*		

In Spanish, when you ask a question with an interrogative word, you put the verb before the subject.

¿Qué **come Elena** en el restaurante? — *What* ***does Elena eat*** *at the restaurant?*

¿Adónde **van Uds.** después de las clases? — *Where* ***do you go*** *after classes?*

¿Por qué **va Ignacio** a la playa todos los días? — *Why* ***does Ignacio go*** *to the beach every day?*

You have already used several interrogative words. Notice that all these words have a written accent mark.

For simple questions that can be answered by *sí* or *no,* you can indicate with your voice that you're asking a question:

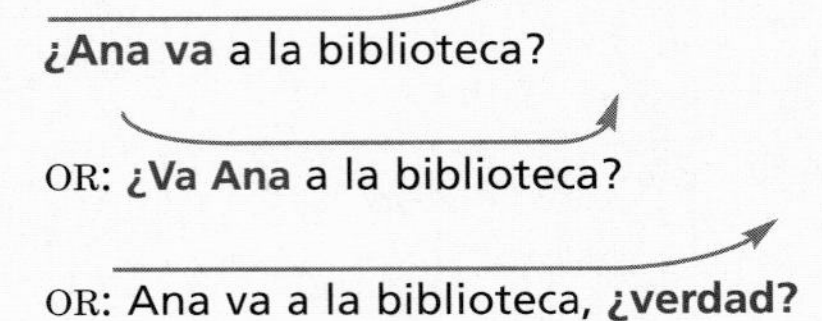

¿Ana va a la biblioteca?

OR: ¿**Va Ana** a la biblioteca?

OR: Ana va a la biblioteca, **¿verdad?**

GramActiva VIDEO

Use the **GramActiva** video to help you learn more about asking questions.

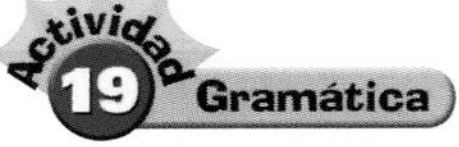

Actividad 19 Gramática **Leer/Escribir**

Un chico curioso

Joaquín is always asking you questions. Read his questions. Then, number your paper from 1–6 and write the appropriate responses.

1. ¿Qué haces tú después de las clases?
2. ¿Adónde van tú y tus amigos los fines de semana?
3. ¿Con quién comes tú en la cafetería?
4. ¿Por qué vas tú al gimnasio todos los días?
5. ¿Cuándo estudias tú?
6. ¿Quién es tu profesor favorito?

a. Yo estudio después de la cena.
b. Como el almuerzo con mis amigos.
c. Los sábados nosotros vamos a la biblioteca y los domingos estamos en casa.
d. Generalmente yo voy al centro comercial o al gimnasio.
e. Mi profesor favorito es el señor Rodríguez.
f. Voy porque me gusta mantener la salud.

Universal Access

Heritage Language Learners

Using the interrogative words taught on this page, have students prepare a list of questions they would like to ask their favorite singer, actor, athlete, or another person. Have students exchange lists and answer the questions as if they were the well-known individuals.

Students with Special Needs

Write the words in *Actividad* 20 on individual cards and help students sort them into proper order. Use a different color card for the interrogative words so that they stand out. Emphasize the accent marks so students notice them.

Actividad 20 Gramática Pensar/Escribir

Preguntas revueltas

Your new pen pal from Bolivia has sent you an e-mail, but all of his questions are scrambled. Unscramble the words and write the questions in a logical order on a separate sheet of paper. Then answer your pen pal's questions.

1. ¿/ eres / de dónde / tú /?
2. ¿/ clases / tienes / cuántas /?
3. ¿/ Uds. / adónde / van / los fines de semana /?
4. ¿/ tú / qué / después de las clases / haces /?
5. ¿/ al centro comercial / cuándo / van / Uds. /?
6. ¿/ vas / tú / con quién / al centro comercial /?

Actividad 21 Gramática Leer/Pensar/Escribir

¿Cómo es el cine?

Read the advertisement for the *Cine Parque Arauco*. Then read the questions and answers below the advertisement. Number your paper from 1–5 and write the appropriate question words, based on what you read.

1. ¿___ es la calidad de la proyección en el cine? *Es excelente.*
2. ¿___ comen muchas personas allí? *Comen palomitas.*
3. ¿___ es el nombre del cine? *Es el Cine Parque Arauco.*
4. ¿___ van las personas a ver películas muy tarde *(late)* en la noche? *Van los miércoles, viernes y sábados.*
5. ¿___ está el cine? *Está delante del Centro Comercial Gigante.*

Cuándo	Cuál
Por qué	Dónde
Cómo	Qué

Enriching Your Teaching

Teacher-to-Teacher

Tell students that they are going to match up the perfect friends in the class. To do so, they must create a survey questionnaire with questions that reveal people's personalities and interests, where they like to go, etc. Have them work in small groups to come up with six questions in each group. When they're done, have the groups report their questions as you write them on the board or overhead. Have the class vote on the ten best questions. Create a survey form that students can answer for homework. Have volunteers tally the results and match up the people who have the most similar answers.

Actividad 20 *Standards:* 1.2, 1.3

Resources: Voc. & Gram. Transparencies: 87; Practice Answers on Transparencies

Focus: Identifying interrogatives and word order

Suggestions: Write the words on strips of paper and show students how to resequence them. Tell them to be sure to capitalize appropriate words. Be sure they understand that they are to answer the questions truthfully.

Answers:

1. ¿De dónde eres tú?
2. ¿Cuántas clases tienes?
3. ¿Adónde van Uds. los fines de semana?
4. ¿Qué haces tú después de las clases?
5. ¿Cuándo van Uds. al centro comercial?
6. ¿Con quién vas tú al centro comercial?

Answers to the questions will vary.

Actividad 21 *Standards:* 1.2, 1.3

Resources: Practice Answers on Transparencies

Focus: Reading a theater ad and completing questions about it using appropriate interrogatives

Suggestions: Read through the ad with the class, activating prior knowledge, using cognates, and using context to help with meaning. Remind students that they do not have to know the meaning of every word to understand the general message. Point out the interrogatives in the word bank. Help students see how the words in italics are key to knowing which interrogative to choose.

Answers:

1. Cómo
2. Qué
3. Cuál
4. Cuándo
5. Dónde

Common Errors: Students often forget to write accent marks on question words. Demonstrate that omitting them can change meaning.

Standards: 1.1, 1.3

Focus: Writing and speaking about weekend activities; reviewing forms of ***ir***

Suggestions: Give students copies of the chart to fill out to save time. If they are drawing their own charts, be sure that they understand to omit the information shown in the example.

Answers will vary.

Extension: Have students do the activity a second time, using places they go after school. Ask students to work with different classmates for step 2 of the activity.

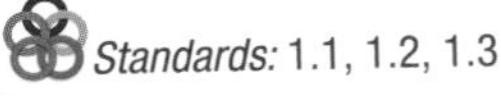
Standards: 1.1, 1.2, 1.3

Resources: Practice Answers on Transparencies

Focus: Reading for comprehension; practicing interviewing skills

Suggestions: Students can read this interview on their own. Review the interrogatives that they will need to form questions for step 2. Change the names in step 3 to match gender. Ask volunteers to act out their interview.

Steps 1 and 2 are good homework assignments. At the beginning of the next class go over the answers and pair students to complete step 3.

Answers:

1. He's from San Juan, Puerto Rico.
2. His new movie comes out on Sept. 15.
3. His co-stars.
4. He goes to the gym or to restaurants. He stays home when he's not working.
5. He's an actor because he loves movies and thinks he's talented.

Escribir/Hablar

Los fines de semana

1. Copy a chart like this one on a separate sheet of paper. Write *yo* in the first column, and the name of a place that you go on the weekends in the second column. If there are people who go with you, write their names in the third column.

Nombre	¿Adónde vas?	¿Con quién?
yo	a la lección de guitarra	solo(a)
Laura	al centro comercial	con Selena

2. Follow the model to find out the same information about three of your classmates. Write the information on your chart.

Modelo

A —*¿Adónde vas los fines de semana?*
B —*Voy al centro comercial.*
A —*¿Con quién vas?*
B —*Voy con Selena.*
o: *Voy solo(a).*

3. Report the information you find to the class.

Modelo

Yo voy a mi lección de guitarra solo(a).
Laura va al centro comercial con Selena.

Leer/Escribir/Hablar

Una estrella de cine

1. *Estrella* magazine interviewed Luis Ramos, a famous movie star. Read the interview, then answer the questions below.

¿Comprendes?

1. What city is Luis Ramos from?
2. What is happening on September 15?
3. Who are María Rúa and Lorena Herrera?
4. What does Luis Ramos like to do in his free time?
5. Why is he an actor?

2. Write two additional questions that you might add to the interview with Luis Ramos.

3. Work with a partner to take turns playing the role of Luis or his co-star María. Ask him or her the additional questions that you wrote.

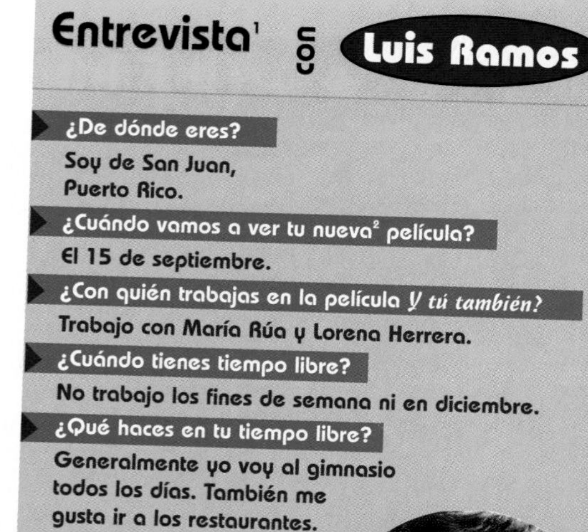

Entrevista[1] con Luis Ramos

¿De dónde eres?
Soy de San Juan, Puerto Rico.

¿Cuándo vamos a ver tu nueva[2] película?
El 15 de septiembre.

¿Con quién trabajas en la película *Y tú también*?
Trabajo con María Rúa y Lorena Herrera.

¿Cuándo tienes tiempo libre?
No trabajo los fines de semana ni en diciembre.

¿Qué haces en tu tiempo libre?
Generalmente yo voy al gimnasio todos los días. También me gusta ir a los restaurantes. Me quedo en casa cuando no trabajo en una nueva película.

¿Por qué eres actor?
Soy actor porque me encantan las películas, y creo que soy talentoso.

¡Gracias!
¡Gracias a usted! ¡Nos vemos!

[1]Interview [2]new

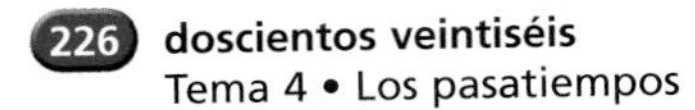

Universal Access

Heritage Language Learners

Following the model of *Actividad* 23, have students write a six-question interview for one of their favorite Spanish-speaking celebrities. Then have them research the celebrity and fill in the answers to their questions.

Students with Learning Difficulties

In *Actividad* 22, some students may have trouble switching from the ***tú / yo*** forms of the questions and answers in part 2 to the third-person answers in part 3. Provide additional models for them to follow.

Actividad 24 **Leer/Escribir**

Estudiantes desordenados

At the Colegio de Ponce, a public school in Puerto Rico, the school newspaper staff is extremely disorganized today. They have the answers to the questions that they asked in an interview with a new student, but they lost the questions. Help them complete the article by reading the answers at right and then writing a logical question for each one.

Modelo

Me llamo Juliana Ramírez.
¿Cómo te llamas?

Me llamo Juliana Ramírez.
Yo soy de San Juan.
Yo estudio con mis amigos.
Mi clase favorita es matemáticas.
Después de las clases, voy al centro comercial.
Porque soy deportista y me gusta mucho practicar deportes.
Los sábados, voy a la playa o voy al cine para ver una película.

Hablar/Escribir

Una entrevista con un amigo

Use the questions that you wrote for Actividad 24 to interview a partner. Present the information you find out to the class.

Modelo

Jaime es de Houston. Él va a la lección de piano después de las clases . . .

Escribir/Hablar/GramActiva

Juego

1. With a partner, cut a sheet of blank paper into twelve squares, making sure that each square is the same size.
2. Write six questions, each on a different square. Use a different question word for each one. On the remaining six squares of paper, write a logical answer for each question.
3. Mix up the questions and answers, and spread them out facedown on the desk. Take turns turning two cards faceup, and read what they say aloud. If the cards are a logical question and answer match, pick them up and take another turn. If not, turn them facedown again and let your partner take a turn. The person with the most pairs wins. When you finish your game, switch cards with another pair of students.

Modelo

¿Cómo es Ana?

Ella es inteligente.

Enriching Your Teaching

Teacher-to-Teacher

Some students might enjoy doing a more extensive survey of their classmates' leisure preferences. Help them create lists of activities or places that are popular in your community. They can include some humorous choices. Ask them to use their lists to create a written survey with questions for everyone to answer. Have them compile the information and give a presentation of their findings to the class complete with bar charts produced using presentation software.

Standards: 1.2, 1.3

Resources: Practice Answers on Transparencies

Focus: Reading for comprehension; forming written questions

Suggestions: Have students number their papers from 1–7. They should write the *Modelo* answer as number 1.

Answers will vary but may include:

1. **¿Cómo te llamas?**
2. **¿De dónde eres?**
3. **¿Con quién estudias?**
4. **¿Cuál es tu clase favorita?**
5. **¿Adónde vas después de las clases?**
6. **¿Por qué vas al gimnasio?**
7. **¿Qué haces los sabados?**

Standards: 1.1, 1.3

Focus: Interviewing a partner and reporting the results

Suggestions: Circulate through the room to help with pronunciation. Ask a few volunteers to present their partners to the class.

Answers will vary.

Standards: 1.1

Focus: Playing a game to match interrogatives and appropriate responses

Suggestions: Tell students to place the pieces of paper in two separate grid patterns (one for the questions and one for the answers) so that they can more easily remember the location of the cards they have turned and read. Tell students that the answers cannot "sort of" make sense, but must be the correct answer for the question. If not, there will likely be cards at the end that won't match.

Answers will vary.

4A Practice and Communicate

Rapid Review

To quickly review question words, make statements, mumbling over part of the sentence. Students should ask the correct question to get the rest of the information. For example: *(Mumble, mumble) va a la escuela.* The students ask: *¿Quién?*

Standards: 1.1

Actividad 27

Focus: Writing and talking about a photo

Recycle: Vocabulary for leisure activities

Suggestions: Have the class study the picture and discuss its important features. Then have students work individually on step 1. While students are conversing in pairs for step 2, walk around the room to monitor correct word usage, syntax, and pronunciation. Then have volunteers ask their questions in front of the class while others answer.

Answers will vary.

Standards: 2.2, 4.2

Fondo cultural

Suggestions: Students may not immediately recognize that the music they listen to may have roots in other cultures. Have them list their favorite songs or types of music and point out any connections to other cultures' music.

Answers will vary.

Actividad 27 — **Escribir/Hablar**

Y tú, ¿qué preguntas?

1. Look at the photo and write four questions about the beach, the people, and the activities.
2. Ask your partner your questions and he or she will respond. Then switch roles.

Para decir más . . .

el hombre man
la mujer woman
la persona person
tomar el sol to sunbathe

Mucho jóvenes pasan el día en la playa en Perú.

Fondo cultural

La música puertorriqueña In Puerto Rico, as in much of the Caribbean, music is an extremely important part of the identity of the people. Two of the musical styles that are often associated with Puerto Rico are *bomba* and *plena*. *Bomba* is a style of music with African roots where various people tend to call out and respond to the accompaniment of drums. *Plena* is a style of music where a singer tells a story or recounts an event to a musical accompaniment.

- What style of music do you listen to that is similar to *bomba* or *plena?*

Universal Access

Students with Learning Difficulties

If students have trouble deciding what to ask about the photo in *Actividad* 27, you might give them a list of statements from which they can derive questions. If this is still difficult, help them identify the appropriate interrogative words and have them create the questions from those.

Multiple Intelligences

Intrapersonal / Introspective: Some students might enjoy a personalized version of *Actividad* 27. Invite students to bring in a few vacation photos to share. Pair students and have them ask and answer questions about their photos.

Actividad 28 **Leer/Escribir**

¡Vamos al Viejo San Juan!

Puerto Rico has been a commonwealth of the United States since 1952. It is an island with a fascinating past. Look at the pictures and read about a historic section of Puerto Rico's capital. Then answer the questions below.

El Viejo[1] San Juan es una zona histórica, pintoresca,[2] colonial y muy popular en la capital de Puerto Rico. Los jóvenes[3] pasan el tiempo con sus amigos en los parques, cafés y plazas. Allí cantan, bailan y comen en los restaurantes típicos.

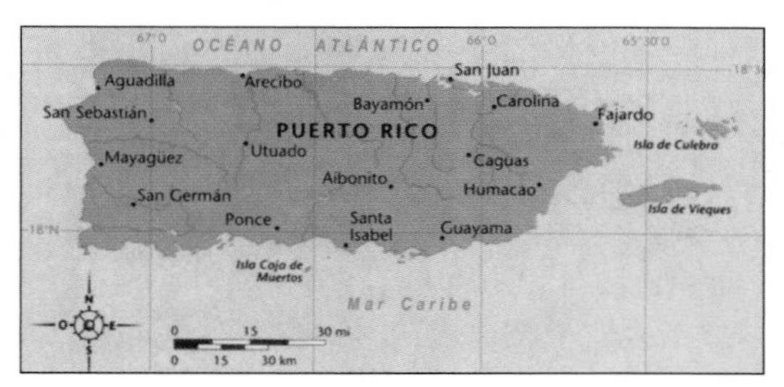

Datos importantes:

- Cristóbal Colón llega[4] aquí durante su segunda visita a las Américas en 1493.
- El Viejo San Juan llega a ser[5] la capital de Puerto Rico en 1521.

El Morro fue construido[6] en el siglo[7] XVI para combatir los ataques de los piratas ingleses y franceses.[8]

La Catedral de San Juan tiene muchas obras de arte.[9] Allí descansan[10] los restos[11] de Juan Ponce de León, famoso explorador de la Florida.

[1]Old [2]picturesque [3]young people [4]arrives [5]becomes [6]was constructed [7]century [8]French [9]works of art [10]lie [11]remains

¿Comprendes?

1. For how many years has San Juan been the capital of Puerto Rico?
2. On which of his voyages did Christopher Columbus land on Puerto Rico?
3. Why did the Spaniards build *El Morro?*
4. What are two things you'll see when you visit the cathedral?

Más práctica

Practice Workbook 4A-6, 4A-7

For: Practice with questions
Visit: www.phschool.com
Web Code: jad-0404

Standards: 1.2, 1.3, 3.1

Resources: Practice Answers on Transparencies; Voc. & Gram Transparencies: 14 (map)

Focus: Reading about Old San Juan, making a cross-curricular connection

Suggestions: Show Transparency 14 for another view of Puerto Rico. Have students read the English questions before they begin to read. Be sure they know that they are to answer in English.

Answers:

1. **San Juan has been the capital of Puerto Rico since 1521.**
2. **Christopher Columbus landed on Puerto Rico during his second voyage to the Americas.**
3. **The Spaniards built El Morro to combat the attack of English and French pirates.**
4. **Two things that one can see in the cathedral are the remains of Juan Ponce de León and many works of art.**

Theme Project

Students can perform step 2 at this point. Be sure students understand the task. (For more information, see p. 206-2.)

Additional Resources

- Writing, Audio & Video Workbook: Audio Activities 8–9
- Writing, Audio & Video Workbook: Writing Activities 12–13
- Heritage Language Learner Workbook: 4A-4, 4A-5

Assessment

- Prueba 4A-4: Asking questions

Enriching Your Teaching

Culture Note

Puerto Ricans are American citizens. However, they do not have the right to vote for president or for full representation in Congress. Puerto Rico does send an observer to the U.S. House of Representatives. This individual votes in Congressional committees. The question of Puerto Rico becoming the 51st state has long been debated, and Puerto Ricans remain divided on the issue.

Teacher-to-Teacher

Have students plan a trip to Puerto Rico using guidebooks, encyclopedias, and the Internet. They can work in small groups to write sentences saying where they plan to go while they are there. They can use a digital camera to take pictures of themselves "visiting" various spots.

Lectura

Presentation

Standards: 1.2, 1.3, 4.1

Resources: Voc. & Gram. Transparencies: 88

Focus: Reading a mall advertisement about available activities

Suggestions:

Pre-reading: Direct students to the *Strategy.* Point out the words in the glosses. To activate students' prior knowledge, bring in brochures from a local mall with similar information and have students identify the events. Have them scan the *Lectura* to see if any of the events are similar. Have them identify the calendar organization of the brochure.

Reading: Have students take turns reading sections of the brochure. Remind them that context and cognates can help them understand what they read. Help them decode unfamiliar words.

Post-reading: Have students answer the *¿Comprendes?* questions to check comprehension. When they have finished, discuss the questions and answers in class.

Additional Resources

- Heritage Learner Workbook: 4A-6

¡Adelante!

Lectura

Al centro comercial

Lee las actividades diferentes que puedes hacer en la semana del 11 al 17 de enero durante tu tiempo libre.

Objectives

- Read about after-school and weekend activities offered at a mall
- Learn some nursery rhymes
- Role-play a new student's first day at school
- Learn facts about the history of the United States

Strategy

Using prior knowledge
Think about what you know about special-event weeks at shopping centers. List events from this calendar that you think might be offered at a mall.

¡Vamos a la Plaza del Sol!

Aquí en la Plaza del Sol, ¡siempre hay algo que hacer!

Actividades para el 11 al 17 de enero

Fecha	Día	Hora	Actividad
11	lunes	8.00 P.M.	Música andina
12	martes	7.00 P.M.	Clase de yoga
13	miércoles	8.00 P.M.	Noche de jazz
14	jueves	7.00 P.M.	Clase de repostería[1]
15	viernes	8.00 P.M.	Música andina
16	sábado	1.30 P.M.	Exposición de fotografía
		2.00 P.M.	Show infantil
		4.00 P.M.	Exhibición de yoga
		8.00 P.M.	Sábado flamenco
17	domingo	1.30 P.M.	Exposición de fotografía
		2.00 P.M.	Show infantil
		4.00 P.M.	Exhibición de yoga
		8.00 P.M.	Noche de tango

Música andina
El grupo Sol Andino toca música andina fusionada con bossa nova y jazz los lunes y los viernes a las 8.00 P.M. Abierto[2] al público.

Clase de yoga
La práctica de yoga es todos los martes desde las 7.00 hasta las 9.00 P.M. La instructora Lucía Gómez Paloma enseña los secretos de esta disciplina. Inscríbase[3] al teléfono 224-24-16. Vacantes limitadas.

[1] pastry making [2] Open [3] Register

Universal Access

Students with Learning Difficulties
Some students may have difficulty sorting out information when it is presented in an advertisement like this. Help them identify that it's a calendar by pointing out the days and dates. Help them see that the four featured events are among those mentioned in the calendar portion.

Advanced Learners
Have students go on the Internet to find shopping malls or cultural centers in Spanish-speaking countries that feature activities similar to those in the reading. Have them print out the schedules and identify in English the basic information.

Sábado flamenco

El Sábado flamenco es el programa más popular de la semana. María del Carmen Ramachi baila acompañada por el guitarrista Ernesto Hermoza el sábado a las 8.00 P.M. Es una noche emocionante y sensacional de música y danza. Abierto al público.

Clase de repostería

Inscríbase gratis[4] en la clase de repostería programada para el jueves a las 7.00 P.M. Preparamos unos pasteles deliciosos gracias a la Repostería Ideal y al maestro Rudolfo Torres. Inscríbase al teléfono 224-24-16. Vacantes limitadas.

[4] free

¿Comprendes?

1. You will be in town from January 9 through February 2. Will you be able to take part in these activities?
2. Which events require you to sign up in advance? Which don't?
3. You have to baby-sit your six-year-old sister. Which day(s) would be best to go?
4. According to the interests of these people, to what events mentioned in the *Lectura* are they going?

Raquel:	Me gusta mucho hacer ejercicio.
Roberto:	Me encantan los pasteles.
Teresa:	Estudio baile. Tomo lecciones todos los jueves.
Alejandro:	Me gusta escuchar música . . . toda clase de música.

5. What activities mentioned interest you the most?

For: Internet link activity
Visit: www.phschool.com
Web Code: jad-0405

Fondo cultural

Andean music Andean music has become popular worldwide. This style originated in the Andes mountains of Peru, Ecuador, Bolivia, and Chile. The music has a slightly haunting sound. Performers often wear typical Andean attire. Instruments commonly used in Andean music include the *quena* flute, *siku* panpipes, and a small guitar called a *charango.*

- The Andean sound is created using a particular set of instruments. What instruments define the music you enjoy?

 *Standards:* 1.3

¿Comprendes?

Resources: Practice Answers on Transparencies

Answers:

1. Yes, in all of them.
2. Yoga and the pastry class have limited spaces available; the Andean music and flamenco are open to the public.
3. Saturday the 16th and Sunday the 17th, because there's a children's show.
4. Raquel: yoga; Roberto: pastry-making class; Teresa: flamenco and tango; Alejandro: the Andean music and the jazz
5. Answers will vary.

 *Standards:* 2.2, 4.2

Resources: Voc. & Gram. Transparencies: 15–17 (map)

Suggestions: Use the transparencies to point out the Andean region. Bring in examples of Andean music for students to enjoy. Explain that flutes like the ***quena*** and ***siku*** are very ancient, and that similar instruments developed in many parts of the world.

Answers will vary.

Teaching with Music

Play some Andean music for the class and point out the instruments mentioned in the *Fondo cultural.*

Theme Project

Students can perform step 3 at this point. Be sure that students understand your suggestions. (For more information, see p. 206-2.)

Enriching Your Teaching

Culture Note

Shopping malls are common in many parts of the Spanish-speaking world. You will find very elegant ones, for example, in cities like Mexico City. Many of the stores would be familiar to students, either because they are American chain stores or because they are similar in style.

Internet Search

Keywords:

Andean music, Alturas, Titicaca, Poco a poco

Culture

La cultura en vivo

Presentation

Standards: 3.2, 4.2

Resources: Audio Program: CD Cap. 4A, Track 14; Resource Book: Cap. 4A, Audio Script

Focus: Reading about and learning children's rhymes

Suggestions: Begin class by reciting a few words from an English nursery rhyme that students would likely know. Ask them to identify it. Ask if they remember any jump-rope rhymes. If students are unfamiliar with these, elicit something they do know and use it. Direct attention to the top photo of children jumping rope. Point out that it is easier to jump rope to a chant, as it helps you keep the beat and jump at the right time. Have students read the first two paragraphs. Practice the rhyme and the chant with the class.

If you can, go outdoors for this activity. A real jump rope works best. In the classroom, use a short piece of rope or string with a paper clip in the middle and a volunteer to demonstrate how a song helps to keep the beat while jumping rope. Students will hear the rope or paper clip hit the desk or floor.

Have students work in three groups. For the first chant, one student can say it, indicating another group member with each word, and the last person is "it." That person takes the role of saying the rhyme and the first one moves on to group 2. Students in group 2 jump rope to the chant, moving on to group 3 when their turn is over. Students in group 3 play the game described while singing the song. Each moves on to group 1 when the turn is over. Students continue until all have had a chance.

Direct attention to the *Think about it!* section and have students discuss the questions.

Answers will vary.

Additional Resources

- Heritage Learner Workbook: 4A-7

La cultura en vivo

Rimas infantiles

Niños saltando a la cuerda

Can you remember the chants and songs you learned as a child? Or do you remember the rhymes you or your friends recited while jumping rope?

Here are some chants and songs that children in the Spanish-speaking world use when they play. The first one is a Spanish-language equivalent to "Eenie, meenie, minie, moe . . ." It is a nonsense rhyme used to select the person who will be "It" in various games.

Tin Marín de dopingüé
cucaramanga titirifuera.
Yo no fui,
fue Teté.
Pégale, pégale,
que ella fue.

Niños jugando en San Sebastián, España

Here's a chant for jumping rope:

Salta, salta la perdiz	**The partridge jumps and jumps**
por los campos de maíz.	**Through the cornfields.**
Ten cuidado, por favor,	**Be careful, please!**
¡porque viene el cazador!	**Here comes the hunter!**
	(The jump rope then turns faster.)

Try it out! Here's a traditional game that combines Spanish, math, and hopping over a board. Place a long, narrow board on the floor. Take turns hopping with both feet from one side of the board to the other. Go forward as you hop. When you get to the end of the board, jump and turn in the air, facing the direction you came from. Continue hopping from side to side back to the other end. Be very careful! Try this in an area where you won't hurt yourself. As you are hopping, sing this song:

Brinca la tablita	**Jump over the board**
que yo la brinqué.	**That I already jumped.**
Bríncala tú ahora	**Now you jump**
que yo me cansé.	**Since I'm tired.**
Dos y dos son cuatro,	**Two and two are four,**
cuatro y dos son seis.	**Four and two are six.**
Seis y dos son ocho,	**Six and two are eight,**
y ocho dieciséis,	**And eight are sixteen,**
y ocho veinticuatro,	**And eight are twenty-four,**
y ocho treinta y dos.	**And eight are thirty-two.**
Y diez que le sumo	**And ten that I add**
son cuarenta y dos.	**Equals forty-two.**

Think about it! What rhymes and songs do you know? What purpose do they serve in play?

Universal Access

Multiple Intelligences

Musical / Rhythmic: Have students learn other songs or rhymes from a Spanish-speaking country. Have them research this topic, learn one rhyme or song, and present it to the class, telling where it came from and when children use it.

Heritage Language Learners

Students may be familiar with these or other children's songs and rhymes. If so, allow them to present them to the class with an explanation of when and how the song or rhyme is used.

Presentación oral

Un estudiante nuevo

Task

This is a new student's first day at school. You and a partner will play the roles of a new student and a student who has been at the school for awhile. Find out information about the new student.

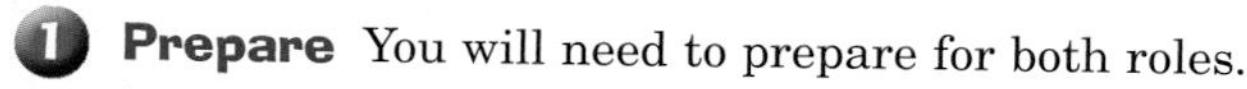

1 Prepare You will need to prepare for both roles.

Experienced student: Make a list of at least four questions. Find out where the new student is from, activities he or she likes to do and on what days of the week, and where he or she goes and with whom. Plan to greet the new student and introduce yourself.

New student: Look at the questions the experienced student will ask you and jot down answers.

Using models

It helps to go back and review models that prepare you for a task like this role-play. Reread *A primera vista* (pp. 208–213). Pay attention to the different questions and answers that will help you with this task.

2 Practice Work in groups of four, with two experienced students and two new students. Practice different questions and responses. Be sure you are comfortable in both roles. Go through your presentation several times. You can use your notes in practice, but not during the role-play. Try to:

- obtain or provide information
- keep the conversation going
- speak clearly

3 Present Your teacher will tell you which role to play. The experienced student begins the conversation by greeting the new student. Listen to your partner's questions or responses and keep the conversation going.

4 Evaluation Your teacher may give you a rubric for how the presentation will be graded. You probably will be graded on:

- completion of task
- ability to keep the conversation going
- how well you were understood

Enriching Your Teaching

RUBRIC	Score 1	Score 3	Score 5
Completion of Task	You ask or answer two questions.	You ask or answer three questions.	You ask or answer four or more questions.
Your ability to keep the conversation going	You have no conversational response or follow-up to what partner says.	You have frequent response or follow-up to what partner says.	You always respond to partner, listen and ask follow-up questions.
How easily you are understood	You are very difficult to understand. Your teacher could only recognize isolated words and phrases.	You are understandable, but have frequent errors in vocabulary and/or grammar that hinder understanding.	You are easily understood. Your teacher does not have to "decode" what you are trying to say.

Presentación oral

Presentation

Standards: 1.1, 1.3

Focus: Talking about a new student's first day of class

Suggestions: Go over the task and the 4-step approach with students. Point out the *Strategy.* Give students time to do the review suggested. Help them identify the questions that will be most important for them. Review the rubric with the class (see *Assessment* below) to explain how you will grade the performance task. Do a presentation of your own to model a top-scoring presentation.

Step 1: Pair the students. The experienced student may need to review *A primera vista,* pp. 208–209 and *Videohistoria,* pp. 210–212 to complete his or her role.

Step 2: Allow students adequate time to practice both roles. Monitor their progress.

Step 3: Students should not use their notes for this part of the presentation. Remind the new student to listen carefully to the questions so that he or she can answer accurately.

Step 4: Students may want to keep their written questions and answers to add to their portfolio.

Portfolio

Record students' oral presentations on cassette or videotape for inclusion in their portfolios.

Additional Resources

- Heritage Learner Workbook: 4A-8

Assessment

- Assessment Program: Cap. 4A, Rubrics

Give students copies of the rubric before they begin the activity. Review the different levels of performance. After assessing students, help individuals understand how their performance could be improved.

El mundo hispano
Presentation

 *Standards:* 2.2, 3.1

Resources: Voc. & Gram. Transparencies: 20 (map)

Focus: Reading about historical Spanish influences in the United States

Suggestions: Display a map of the United States. Locate St. Augustine, Florida, and Plymouth, Massachusetts, as you discuss the first colonists. Using a world map, point out the origins of the colonists in Spain and England. As you discuss the lands held by Spain, locate them on a world map so that students can see the vastness of the Spanish holdings.

Direct attention to the top left photo on p. 235. Tell students that the English and Spanish were joined by the French in colonizing North America. Can students name a French-speaking region in North America? (Quebec) Discuss the French Quarter in New Orleans. Even today the French influence can be seen in the city and in the names of other places in Louisiana. Point out that although the French left their mark, the Spanish rebuilt the city and their influence is found in the architecture. For example, many homes there are built around courtyards and feature wrought-iron grilles and balconies, both very indicative of Spanish influence.

Focus attention on the picture of the Castillo, a national monument since 1924. Discuss its original purpose, and have students give their ideas as to why ships returning to Spain needed protection. Help them understand that the ships were carrying riches from America to Spain.

Point out the picture of the Alamo on p. 234. Most students will have heard of it, but many may not know that it was built as a mission. Then note the photo of the mission on p. 235, and have students reread the paragraph. At one time a network of missions extended throughout the Americas. Cities often grew up around the missions (San Diego, Los Angeles, San Francisco). Some missions still exist and are open to visitors.

El mundo hispano
Estados Unidos
Histórico

The oldest permanent European settlement in the United States, St. Augustine, Florida, was established by Spain in 1565—55 years before the Pilgrims landed at Plymouth Rock. For more than two centuries after that, the Spanish controlled a large territory in North America that included what is now Mexico, parts of the southern United States, the states of Texas, New Mexico, Arizona, California, and Nevada, and parts of Colorado and Utah.

Constructed as a mission in 1718, the Alamo (in San Antonio, Texas) today is best known as a key battleground in the secession of Texas from Mexico in 1836. The defeat of the Texans at the Alamo became a rallying cry for Texas independence, and Texas gained its freedom from Mexico two months later. ▶

¿Sabes que . . . ?

The language of the Nahua peoples of central Mexico, which included the Aztecs, is related to the languages of the Shoshone, Comanche, and Hopi tribes in the United States. When Spaniards pushed north from the newly conquered central Mexico, they often followed ancient Native American trade routes and used Nahua people as guides.

Para pensar

You can find many Spanish names of cities, counties, and states in the United States. Work with a partner and write a list of at least ten places with Spanish names and then try to guess what they mean in English.

Go Online PHSchool.com
For: Online Atlas
Visit: www.phschool.com
Web Code: jae-0002

Universal Access

Advanced Learners
Have students research Fray Junípero Serra on the Internet and report back to the class. Who was he? When did he live? What is his importance in the history of California?

Heritage Language Learners
Have students research the architecture in one of the following states: Texas, New Mexico, Arizona, or California. Have them look for architecture that shows a Spanish influence and write a report about their findings.

The French Quarter in New Orleans was named after the French who first settled here. In spite of its name, most of the buildings date to when Spain ruled Louisiana (1763–1803). Fires ravaged the area in 1788 and 1794, so when the rebuilding was done, the architectural style was Spanish. This can be seen in the landscaped patios and iron grillwork on balconies.

A network of Spanish Catholic missions once extended throughout the Americas. Many cities in the southwestern United States, including San Francisco, San Diego, and Santa Fe, were originally built around Catholic missions, which in turn were often located at Native American villages or religious sites. The Mission San Xavier del Bac, in Arizona, combines the name of a Catholic saint (San Xavier) with the name of the Papago village where it was built (Bac, which means "where the water emerges"). Constructed in the early 1700s, the mission is still used by the Papago people and is considered one of the world's architectural treasures.

Spain built the Castillo de San Marcos to protect both St. Augustine (Florida) and the sea routes for ships returning to Spain from enemy attacks. This fort was started in 1672 and took 23 years to build. When Spain sold Florida to the United States in 1821, the fort was renamed Fort Marion. The Castillo has been a National Monument since 1924.

Have students read the *¿Sabes que…?* section. Discuss possible explanations about how these languages could be related.

Discuss the battle of the Alamo, in San Antonio. Point out its location on the map. Point out its proximity to Mexico and remind students that Texas was at that time part of Mexico. Mexico won the battle for the Alamo, but Texas won its independence soon thereafter.

Discuss the missions that extended throughout the Americas. Point out that the missionaries' goal was to convert the indigenous people to Christianity.

Direct attention to the *Para pensar* section and have students discuss the questions.

Answers will vary.

Go Online
The Online Atlas will provide detailed maps of the locations mentioned here.

Enriching Your Teaching

Teacher-to-Teacher
Have students work in groups to find the locations of the missions in California. Have them note the locations on a map and estimate the number of miles from one to the next. This mileage is the distance a rider could cover on horseback in a day.

Teacher-to-Teacher
Have groups of students choose one of the cities or buildings featured here to research. Have them prepare posters and reports complete with photographs and drawings. When students have finished, make these available in a resource center in your classroom so that others can learn from and enjoy them.

Review Activities

To talk about leisure activities and places: Have students work in pairs to quiz each other on the vocabulary. They can create flashcards, writing the Spanish word on one side of an index card and the English meaning on the other. Provide copies of the Clip Art for this purpose.

To ask and tell where, with whom, and when you go: Have students work in pairs to practice asking and answering questions about their leisure activities.

Portfolio

Invite students to review the activities they completed in this chapter, including written reports, posters or other visuals, and tapes of oral presentations, or other projects. Have them select one or two items that they feel best demonstrate their achievements in Spanish to include in their portfoliios. Have them include this with the Chapter Checklist and Self-Assessment Worksheet.

Additional Resources

- Audio Program: CD Cap. 4A, Track 15
- Resource Book: Cap. 4A, Clip Art
- Resource Book: Cap. 4A, Situation Cards
- Assessment Program: Cap. 4A, Chapter Checklist and Self-Assessment Worksheet

Repaso del capítulo

Vocabulario y gramática

To prepare for the test, check to see if you . . .

- know the new vocabulary and grammar
- can perform the tasks on p. 237

to talk about leisure activities

ir de compras	to go shopping
ver una película	to see a movie
la lección de piano	piano lesson (class)
Me quedo en casa.	I stay at home.

to talk about places

la biblioteca	library
el café	café
el campo	countryside
la casa	home, house
en casa	at home
el centro comercial	mall
el cine	movie theater
el gimnasio	gym
la iglesia	church
la mezquita	mosque
las montañas	mountains
el parque	park
la piscina	swimming pool
la playa	beach
el restaurante	restaurant
la sinagoga	synagogue
el templo	temple, Protestant church
el trabajo	work, job

For *Vocabulario adicional,* see pp. 268–269.

to ask and tell where you go

a	to *(prep.)*
a la, al *(a + el)*	to the
¿Adónde?	(To) Where?
a casa	(to) home

to ask and tell with whom you go

con mis/tus amigos	with my/your friends
¿Con quién?	With whom?
solo, -a	alone

to talk about when things are done

¿Cuándo?	When?
después	afterwards
después (de)	after
los fines de semana	on weekends
los lunes, los martes . . .	on Mondays, on Tuesdays . . .
tiempo libre	free time

to talk about where someone is from

¿De dónde eres?	Where are you from?
de	from, of

to indicate how often

generalmente	generally

other useful words and expressions

¡No me digas!	You don't say!
para + *infinitive*	in order to + *infinitive*

ir *to go*

voy	vamos
vas	vais
va	van

Más práctica

Practice Workbook Puzzle 4A-8
Practice Workbook Organizer 4A-9

Universal Access

Students with Learning Difficulties

Have students use the Organizer in the *Practice Workbook* as a basis for review. Have them fill it in carefully, and then check their work for accuracy.

Heritage Language Learners

Have students create a list of all the interrogatives that were explained in the *Gramática*. They can add these to their ongoing list of accented words.

Preparación para el examen

For: Test preparation
Visit: www.phschool.com
Web Code: jad-0406

On the exam you will be asked to . . .	Here are practice tasks similar to those you will find on the exam . . .	If you need review . . .
1 Escuchar Listen and understand as people ask questions about weekend events	Two friends are trying to make plans for the weekend. Based on their dialogue, what do they finally agree on? a) who is going b) where they are going c) when they are going	**pp. 208–213** *A primera vista* **p. 226** Actividad 22
2 Hablar Talk about places to go and things to do on the weekend	Your parents want to know what you're doing this weekend. Mention at least three places you plan to go or things you plan to do. For example, you might say *Voy de compras con mis amigos.*	**pp. 208–213** *A primera vista* **p. 215** Actividad 7 **p. 216** Actividad 9 **p. 221** Actividad 17 **p. 222** Actividad 18 **p. 226** Actividad 22
3 Leer Read about what a person does on particular days of the week	Someone has left his or her planner at your house. Read the schedule for two days to try to figure out what type of person owns it. Indicate whether you agree or disagree with the statements about the person. MARTES: 6:00 Desayuno 4:00 Lección de piano 5:00 Trabajo 8:30 Clase aeróbica JUEVES: 3:30 Gimnasio 4:30 Piscina 6:00 Trabajo 8:00 Biblioteca *¿Estás de acuerdo o no?* *a) Es muy perezoso(a).* *b) Es atlético(a).* *c) Le gusta ir de compras.*	**pp. 208–213** *A primera vista* **p. 214** Actividad 5 **p. 219** Actividad 13 **pp. 230–231** *Lectura*
4 Escribir Write a short note to a friend to let him or her know where you are going after school	Your friend is taking a make-up test after school, so you need to write her a short note to tell her what you are doing after school today. In the note, tell her where you are going and then at what time you are going home.	**p. 214** Actividad 5 **p. 217** Actividad 11 **p. 220** Actividad 15 **p. 222** Actividad 18 **p. 228** Actividad 27
 **5 Pensar** Demonstrate an understanding of rhymes, songs, and games from Spanish-speaking cultures	Think about your favorite childhood game. How does it compare to the children's games you learned about in this chapter? Describe a traditional game from a Spanish-speaking country.	**p. 232** *La cultura en vivo*

Enriching Your Teaching

Teacher-to-Teacher

You might enjoy playing the role of a concerned parent who is asking many, many questions of a teenager. Keep asking questions and demanding answers about what your "child" is going to do, with whom, when, etc.

Teacher-to-Teacher

Organize a "vocabulary bee." Have students stand around the room. One by one, ask them to identify the correct word when you prompt them. Give a student an English word and ask its Spanish equivalent, or give a Spanish word and ask for its English meaning. When a student does not know a word, ask him or her to sit down. The last student standing is the "winner."

Performance Tasks

Standards: 1.1, 1.2, 1.3, 4.2

Resources: Audio Program: CD Cap. 4A, Track 16; Resource Book: Cap. 4A, Audio Script; Practice Answers on Transparencies

1. Escuchar

Suggestions: Play the *CD* or read from the script until all students know the answers. Ask students to suggest answers to the questions.

Script:

—¿Adónde vas el fin de semana?
—El sábado me quedo en casa, pero el domingo voy al cine.
—¿A qué hora vas?
—A las nueve y media. Y tú, ¿qué haces el fin de semana?
—Yo también voy al cine el domingo.
—¿Por qué no vamos a las nueve y media?
—Yo prefiero ir a las siete.

Answers:

a) Two boys. b) To the movies. c) Sunday at 7:00.

2. Hablar

Suggestions: Allow individual study time in class. If students have difficulty with spontaneous conversation, have them write what they're going to say and practice until they can say it without consulting their notes.

Answers will vary.

3. Leer

Suggestions: Some students will understand this better if they transcribe it in planner form.

Answers:

a) no b) yes c) no

4. Escribir

Suggestions: Have students try this activity without consulting the vocabulary list, notes, or completed activities.

5. Pensar

Suggestions: Have students reread the *La cultura en vivo* if they need to.

Answers will vary.

Assessment

- Examen del capítulo: 4A
- Audio Program: CD 20, Track 9

Alternative Assessment

- ExamView Test Bank CD-ROM
- Resource Book: Cap. 4A, Situation Cards
- Resource Book: Cap. 4A, Communicative Activities

Capítulo 4B Overview

Chapter Overview

	A primera vista INPUT	Manos a la obra PRACTICE	¡Adelante! APPLICATION	Repaso del capítulo REVIEW
Objectives	Read, listen to, and explain information about: • activities outside of school	• Talk about activities outside of school • Extend, accept, and decline invitations • Tell when an event happens • Say what you are going to do • Use ***ir*** + ***a*** + infinitive and the verb ***jugar***	• Read about and compare the lives of two famous golfers • Recognize specialized sports vocabulary • Explain cultural perspectives regarding extracurricular activities • Write an invitation to an event • Discuss facts about the contemporary United States	• Prepare for the chapter test
Vocabulary	• Leisure activities • Adjectives for how someone feels • Expressions to extend, accept, or decline invitations • Expressions for what time something happens	• Practice and learn new vocabulary	• Application	• Review
Grammar	Lexical use of: • ***ir*** + ***a*** + infinitive • the verb ***jugar***	• ***ir*** + ***a*** + infinitive • The verb ***jugar***	• Application	• Review
Culture	• The Paralympics	• ***fiestas***	• Rebecca Lobo • Leisure activities	• Demonstrate an understanding of cultural differences regarding extracurricular activities

Learner Support

Strategies
- Looking to find key questions
- Cognates
- Organizing information

Recycling
- Telling time
- The verb ***estar***
- The verb ***ir***
- Infinitives

Pronunciación
- The letter ***d***

Exploración del lenguaje
- Spanish words borrowed from English

Conexiones
- Math: converting kilometers to miles

Beyond the Classroom

Countries
- Mexico
- Spain
- United States
- Chile

El español en el mundo del trabajo
- Volunteer work for which speaking Spanish is helpful

Internet
- Vocabulary activities
- Grammar activities
- Internet links
- Self-tests

Print Components

TEACHER

Teacher's Resource Book
- Chapter Resource Checklist
- Input Script
- Video Script
- Audio Script
- Answer Keys
- *GramActiva* Blackline Masters
- Communicative Activity Blackline Masters
- Situation Cards Blackline Masters
- School-to-Home Connection Letter
- Vocabulary Clip Art

TPR Storytelling Book
- Cap. 4B

STUDENT

Practice Workbook
- Vocabulary: 4B-1 – 4B-4
- Grammar: 4B-5 – 4B-7
- Puzzle: 4B-8
- Organizer: 4B-9

Writing, Audio & Video Workbook
- Writing: 4B-1 – 4B-4
- Audio: 4B-5 – 4B-10
- Video: 4B-11

Realidades para hispanohablantes
- Cap. 4B

Transparencies

Vocabulary & Grammar Transparencies
- Chapter Opener: 12, 16–18, 20 (maps)
- *A primera vista:* 89–90
- *Videohistoria:* 91–92
- Grammar: 18 (map), 93–95
- *Lectura:* 2 (graphic organizer)
- *Cultura:* 12,14, 20 (maps)

Practice Answers on Transparencies
- Cap. 4B

Fine Art Transparencies
- Transparencies
- Teacher's Guide

Assessment

Assessment Program
- *Pruebas:*
  - Vocabulary recognition: 4B-1
  - Vocabulary production: 4B-2
  - ***ir*** + ***a*** + infinitive: 4B-3
  - The verb ***jugar:*** 4B-4
- *Examen del capítulo:* 4B

ExamView Test Bank CD-ROM

Test Preparation Workbook
- Cap. 4B Reading #1
- Cap. 4B Reading #2

Alternative Assessment
- Performance-Based Speaking
- Assessment Program: Rubrics
- Internet Self-Test
- Situation Cards Blackline Masters
- TPR Storytelling Book: Speaking Task

Technology

iText

Mind Point Quiz Show CD-ROM

Resource Pro CD-ROM
- Lesson Planner
- Teacher Resources
- Clip Art

Video Program VHS and DVD
- *A primera vista* video: *¡A jugar!*
- *GramActiva* Videos:
  - ***ir*** + ***a*** + infinitive
  - the verb ***jugar***

Audio Program CDs
- *A primera vista*
- *Escucha y escribe* activities
- Audio Activities
- *Pronunciación*
- *Repaso*
- Chapter Listening Test
- Songs

Regular Schedule (50 minutes)

For electronic lesson plans:
Resource Pro CD-ROM

	Warm-up / Assess	Preview / Present / Practice / Communicate	Wrap-up / Homework Options
DAY 1	**Return Examen del capítulo (10 min.)**	**A primera vista (35 min.)** • Objectives • Presentation: *Vocabulario y gramática en contexto* • *Actividades* 1, 2 • *Fondo cultural*	**Wrap-up and Homework Options (5 min.)** • Practice Workbook 4B-1, 4B-2 • Go Online • Heritage Language Learner Workbook • Vocabulary Clip Art
DAY 2	**Warm-up (5 min.)** • Homework check	**A primera vista (40 min.)** • Review: *Vocabulario y gramática en contexto* • Presentation: *Videohistoria ¡A jugar!* • View: Video *¡A jugar!* • Video Activities • *Actividades* 3, 4	**Wrap-up and Homework Options (5 min.)** • *Prueba* 4B-1: Vocabulary recognition • Practice Workbook 4B-3, 4B-4 • Go Online
DAY 3	**Warm-up (5 min.)** • Homework check **✔Assessment (10 min.)** • *Prueba* 4B-1: Voc. recognition	**Manos a la obra (30 min.)** • Objectives • *Actividades* 5, 6, 7 • *Fondo cultural*	**Wrap-up and Homework Options (5 min.)** • *Actividad* 8
DAY 4	**Warm-up (5 min.)** • Homework check • Return *Prueba* 4B-1: Voc. recognition	**Manos a la obra (40 min.)** • *Actividades* 9, 10, 12 • *Exploración del lenguaje*	**Wrap-up and Homework Options (5 min.)** • *Exploración del lenguaje:* Try it out!
DAY 5	**Warm-up (5 min.)** • Homework check	**Manos a la obra (40 min.)** • *Actividades* 13, 14, 15	**Wrap-up and Homework Options (5 min.)** • *Actividad* 11
DAY 6	**Warm-up (5 min.)** • Homework check	**Manos a la obra (40 min.)** • Presentation: ***Ir*** + ***a*** + infinitive • *GramActiva* Video • *Actividades* 17, 18, 19	**Wrap-up and Homework Options (5 min.)** • *Actividad* 16 • Practice Workbook 4B-5
DAY 7	**Warm-up (5 min.)** • Homework check	**Manos a la obra (40 min.)** • Review: ***Ir*** + ***a*** + infinitive • *Actividades* 20, 21, 22, 23 • *Pronunciación*	**Wrap-up and Homework Options (5 min.)** • Go Online • *Prueba* 4B-3: ***Ir*** + ***a*** + infinitive
DAY 8	**Warm-up (5 min.)** • Homework check **✔Assessment (10 min.)** • *Prueba* 4B-3: ***Ir*** + ***a*** + infinitive	**Manos a la obra (30 min.)** • Presentation: The verb ***jugar*** • *GramActiva* Video • *Actividad* 24 • *Juego: Actividad* 25	**Wrap-up and Homework Options (5 min.)** • *Prueba* 4B-2: Vocabulary production • Practice Workbook 4B-6, 4B-7

	Warm-up / Assess	Preview / Present / Practice / Communicate	Wrap-up / Homework Options
DAY 9	**Warm-up** (5 min.) • Homework check • Return Prueba 4B-3: ***Ir*** + ***a*** + infinitive ✔**Assessment** (10 min.) • Prueba 4B-2: Voc. production	**Manos a la obra** (30 min.) • *Actividades* 26, 28	**Wrap-up and Homework Options** (5 min.) • Go Online • *Prueba* 4B-4: The verb ***jugar***
DAY 10	**Warm-up** (5 min.) • Homework check • Return Prueba 4B-2: Voc. production ✔**Assessment** (10 min.) • *Prueba* 4B-4: The verb ***jugar***	**Manos a la obra** (30 min.) • *Conexiones: Actividad* 27 • *El español en el mundo del trabajo*	**Wrap-up and Homework Options** (5 min.) • Go Online
DAY 11	**Warm-up** (5 min.) • Homework check • Return Prueba 4B-4: The verb ***jugar***	**¡Adelante!** (40 min.) • *Presentación escrita:* Prewrite • *Lectura* • *Fondo cultural*	**Wrap-up and Homework Options** (5 min.) • Go Online
DAY 12	**Warm-up** (5 min.) • Homework check	**¡Adelante!** (40 min.) • *Presentación escrita:* Draft, revise • *Perspectivas del mundo hispano*	**Wrap-up and Homework Options** (5 min.) • Go Online • *Presentación escrita:* Publish
DAY 13	**Warm-up** (5 min.) • Homework check	**¡Adelante!** (40 min.) • *Presentación escrita:* Present	**Wrap-up and Homework Options** (5 min.) • Writing Activities • Practice Workbook 4B-8, 4B-9
DAY 14	**Warm-up** (5 min.) • Homework check	**¡Adelante!** (20 min.) • *El mundo hispano* **Repaso** (20 min.) • *Vocabulario y gramática* • *Preparación para el examen*	**Wrap-up and Homework Options** (5 min.) • Go Online: Self-test • *Examen del capítulo*
DAY 15	**Warm-up** (5 min.) • Answer questions ✔**Assessment** (45 min.) • *Examen del capítulo*		

4B Preview

Standards for *Capítulo* 4B

• To achieve the goals of the Standards, students will:

Communication

1.1 Interpersonal
- Talk about: sports and pastimes; emotions and states of being; when certain events and activities occur; cellular phone usage; experiences of family immigration
- Extend, accept, or decline invitations

1.2 Interpretive
- Read and listen to information about sports and pastimes
- Listen to information about how people are feeling
- Read a picture-based story
- Listen to and watch a video about sports and pastimes
- Read: about emotions and states of being; an advertisement for a sports training school; an advertisement for a campground; about golfers Sergio García and Lorena Ochoa Reyes

1.3 Presentational
- Present information about: sports and pastimes; emotions and states of being; when certain activities occur; a sports training school; Sergio García and Lorena Ochoa Reyes
- Write about cellular phone usage
- Present an account of an interview about immigration

Culture

2.1 Practices and Perspectives
- Talk about: the festival, ***La Noche de los rábanos;*** how students traditionally engage in activities outside of school

2.2 Products and Perspectives
- Talk about the elaborate radish-sculpting of ***La Noche de los rábanos***

Connections

3.1 Cross-curricular
- Talk about: international sports; writer and basketball star Rebecca Lobo
- Reinforce math and metric conversion skills
- Apply knowledge of geography and current events

3.2 Target Culture
- Read an advertisement for a sports training school

Comparisons

4.1 Language
- Learn: new vocabulary through the recognition of cognates; the use of ***ir*** + ***a*** and infinitive; the pronunciation of the letter ***d***
- Explain that words are borrowed across languages
- Compare the use of ***jugar*** idioms with English

4.2 Culture
- Compare: international and local athletic events; specialized, regional crafts and products; how students engage in activities outside of school

Communities

5.1 Beyond the School
- Consider local opportunities for Spanish-speakers in the health care professions
- Interview a Spanish-speaker about the immigrant experience

5.2 Lifelong Learner
- Read about golfers Sergio García and Lorena Ochoa Reyes
- Explain the current influence of Spanish-speakers in areas like politics, music, poetry, and science

Tema 4 • Los pasatiempos

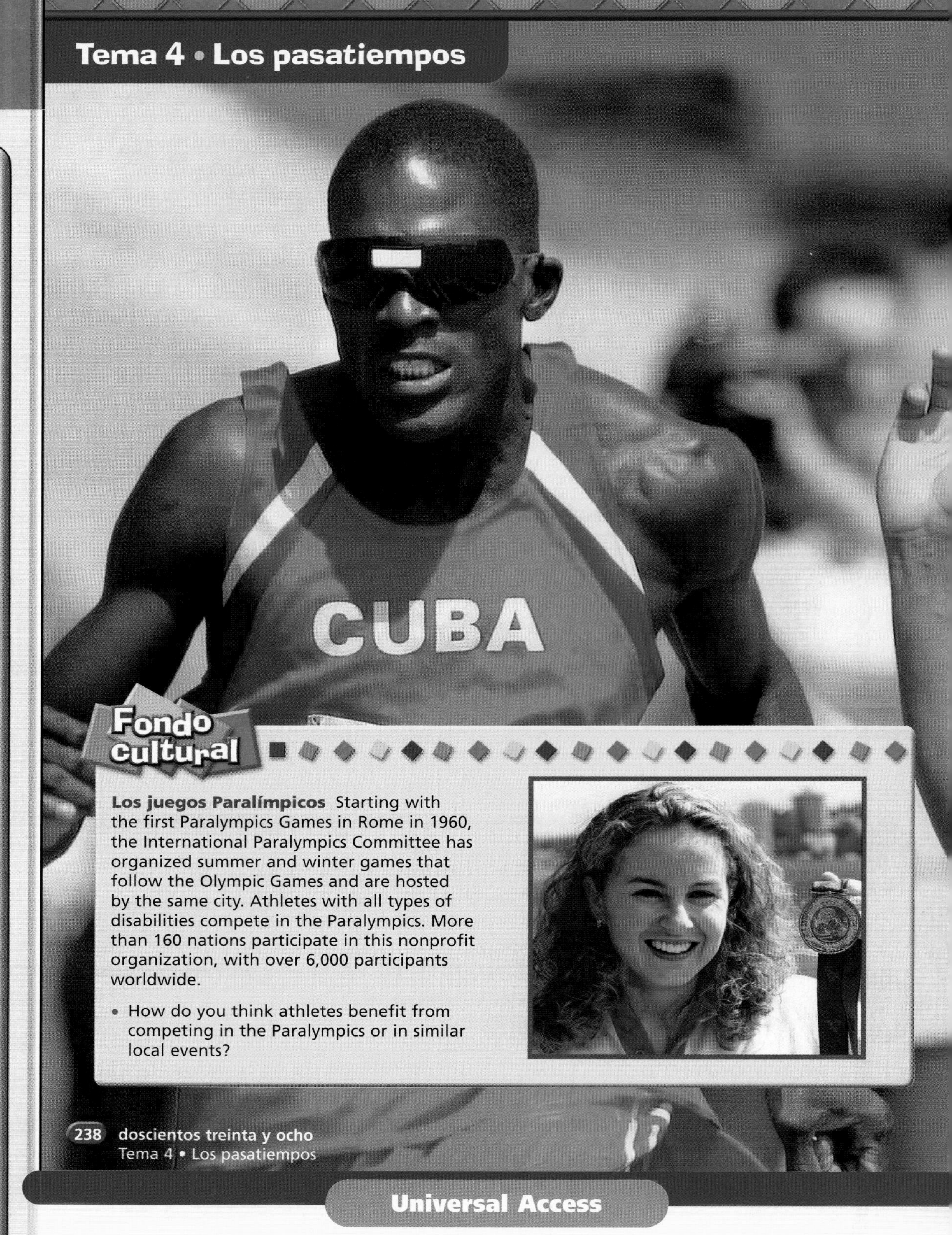

Fondo cultural

Los juegos Paralímpicos Starting with the first Paralympics Games in Rome in 1960, the International Paralympics Committee has organized summer and winter games that follow the Olympic Games and are hosted by the same city. Athletes with all types of disabilities compete in the Paralympics. More than 160 nations participate in this nonprofit organization, with over 6,000 participants worldwide.

- How do you think athletes benefit from competing in the Paralympics or in similar local events?

Universal Access

Personalizing the Theme

More and more disabled athletes are now competing against the able-bodied (in marathons, tennis, golf, etc.). Some disabled runners, for example, are as fast as their non-disabled colleagues. Discuss with students the impact that such a breaking down of barriers has on a society.

Heritage Language Learners

Ask students to describe sports events they may have attended in their countries of origin. Have them compare leisure-time activities in the two countries.

¿Quieres ir conmigo?

Chapter Objectives

- Talk about activities outside of school
- Extend, accept, and decline invitations
- Tell when an event happens
- Understand cultural perspectives on after-school activities

Video Highlights

A primera vista: ***¡A jugar!***
GramActiva Videos: ***ir + a +*** **infinitive; the verb *jugar***

Country Connection

As you learn about after-school activities, you will make connections to these countries and places:

For: Online Atlas
Visit: www.phschool.com
Web Code: jae-0002

los juegos paralímpicos de 1996, Atlanta, Georgia

Preview

Chapter Opener

Presentation

Resources: Voc. & Gram. Transparencies: 12, 16–18, 20 (maps)

Suggestions: As you go over the objectives of the chapter, point out that the video segments will introduce more leisure-time vocabulary. Introduce the theme of the chapter by asking students what they like to do in their free time. How many enjoy concerts? How many participate in sports or other outdoor activities? Brainstorm a list of activities.

Help students locate the cities, states, land countries featured in the chapter by using the map transparencies.

Standards: 3.1, 4.2

Suggestions: Emphasize that the Paralympic Games promote international competition and friendship among athletes with disabilities. Ask students to name similar local competitions and the events in which those athletes compete.

Answers will vary.

Enriching Your Teaching

Planning for Instruction

Resources:
- Teacher Express CD-ROM or Resource Book
  - Teaching resources
  - Lesson Planner
  - Chapter Resource Checklist
  - School-to-Home Connection Letter

Teacher-to-Teacher

Bring Spanish-language sports or leisure magazines to class. Share photos of the activities with your students, encouraging a discussion about how these activities compare with those that they enjoy. Ask students to identify cognates in the headlines, captions, and articles.

Vocabulario y gramática

Presentation

 *Standards:* 1.2, 4.1

Resources: Voc. & Gram. Transparencies: 89–90; Resource Book: Cap. 4B, Input Script; Resource Book: Cap. 4B, Clip Art; TPR Storytelling Book: Cap. 4B; Audio Program: CD Cap. 4B, Tracks 1-2

Focus: Presenting vocabulary about non-school activities

Suggestions: Use the Input Script from the *Teacher's Resource Book* or the story in the *TRP Storytelling Book* to help present the new vocabulary and grammar. Or you can use the transparencies to present the new vocabulary and to talk about what activities you like to do. Ask such questions as: *¿Qué te gusta practicar más—el béisbol o el fútbol americano?* Continue the questions until students seem comfortable with the vocabulary. Have students look at the schedule, and point out that it uses the 24-hour clock, which is common in Spanish-speaking cultures. Ask students to recall this concept, and have them tell you what time 13:00 and 16:00 are.

Have students predict what is happening in the pictures on p. 241. Ask volunteers to read the parts of Rosa and her friends. Then have students list words they recognize in the conversation.

Variation: *Cámping* may be written with or without an accent mark. We have chosen to use *cámping* with an accent mark, following the regular rules of accentuation in Spanish.

Additional Resources

- Audio Program: Song CD

A primera vista

Vocabulario y gramática en contexto

Objectives

Read, listen to, and understand information about
- activities outside of school

—¿Qué **quieres** hacer **a las ocho de la mañana, jugar al** fútbol o al vóleibol?

—A ver . . . No **quiero** jugar al fútbol. **Juego muy mal.** Prefiero jugar al vóleibol. Necesito practicar más. ¿Y qué **te gustaría** hacer a las cuatro **esta tarde?**

—**Me gustaría** jugar al fútbol americano.

Universal Access

Students with Special Needs

If students are unable to act out the vocabulary for *Actividad* 2 on p. 241, ask them to write each adjective on a sheet of paper or say it aloud.

Students with Learning Difficulties

Have students add new words to their vocabulary notebook and accompany these words with pictures and English translations if needed. For *Actividad* 2, provide students with examples of what is expected of them.

el concierto

la fiesta

el baile

el partido

—¡Hola! Soy Rosa. ¿Quieres hacer algo **conmigo este fin de semana?** Hay un concierto en el parque.

—**Lo siento,** pero no **puedo.** Estoy **demasiado ocupado** y tengo mucha tarea.

—No puedo porque **tengo que** trabajar. Trabajo **esta noche** a las siete y mañana trabajo **a la una de la tarde. Voy a estar** un poco **cansada. ¡Ay! ¡Qué pena!**

—¡Qué **triste!** No, no puedo ir **contigo.** Estoy **un poco enferma.**

ir de cámping

ir de pesca

—**¡Qué buena idea!** Pero no me gustan los conciertos. Prefiero ir de cámping. Siempre estoy muy **contenta** cuando voy de cámping. **¿A qué hora?** ¿Mañana a las cinco de la tarde? **Entonces,** nos vemos.

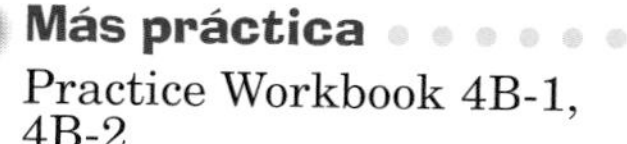

Actividad 1 **Escuchar**

¡Deportemanía!

Marcela is a sports fanatic! As she lists the days on which she will play the various sports, touch the picture of each sport.

Actividad 2 **Escuchar**

¿Cómo estás?

You will hear how five people are feeling. Act out the adjectives that you hear.

Más práctica

Practice Workbook 4B-1, 4B-2

Go Online PHSchool.com

For: Vocabulary practice
Visit: www.phschool.com
Web Code: jad-0411

Actividad 1 *Standards:* 1.2

Resources: Audio Program: CD Cap. 4B, Track 3; Resource Book: Cap. 4B, Audio Script; Practice Answers on Transparencies

Focus: Listening comprehension

Suggestions: Play the *Audio CD* or read the script. Monitor to verify that students are correctly identifying the sports.

Script and Answers:

1. El lunes tengo que practicar el golf. *(golf)*
2. El martes hay un partido de básquetbol. *(basketball)*
3. El miércoles juego al tenis con Lorenzo. *(tennis)*
4. El jueves tengo que jugar al béisbol. *(baseball)*
5. El viernes hay un partido de vóleibol. *(volleyball)*
6. El sábado tengo que jugar al fútbol. *(soccer)*

Actividad 2 *Standards:* 1.2

Resources: Audio Program: CD Cap. 4B, Track 4; Resource Book: Cap. 4B, Audio Script; Practice Answers on Transparencies

Focus: Listening comprehension

Suggestions: First agree on the body language to represent the different feelings. In a large class, you may wish to have volunteers act out the words, and ask the rest of the class whether or not they agree with what they see.

Script and Answers:

1. ¡Uf! Estoy muy cansada. *(tired)*
2. Lo siento pero estoy muy mal, muy enfermo. *(sick)*
3. No tengo tarea esta noche. Estoy muy contenta. *(happy)*
4. ¿La señora Sánchez no enseña la clase de español? Estoy triste. *(sad)*
5. Tengo mucho que hacer. Estoy ocupado. *(busy)*

Extension: Give students three situations using known vocabulary, such as *Tengo que estudiar* or *No hay clases*. Ask them to give you at least one adjective to describe how they might feel in each situation.

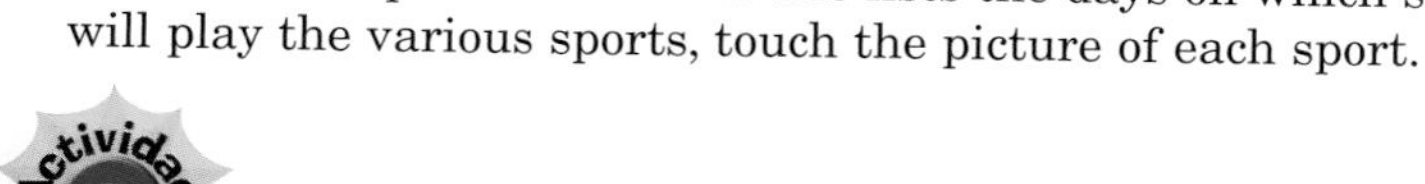

Enriching Your Teaching

Culture Note

The musical sounds of Latin America have a variety of origins, most linked to regional history. Instruments include panpipes, steel drums, ***marimba, maracas,*** and ***guitarrón***. Ask students to list some singers who have a distinct Latin American sound.

Internet Search

Keywords:

Latin American music, Carlos Santana, Gloria Estefan, Tito Puentes

Videohistoria

Presentation

Standards: 1.2

Resources: Voc. & Gram. Transparencies: 91–92; Audio Program: CD Cap. 4B, Track 5

Focus: Extending the presentation of contextualized vocabulary and grammar; previewing the language video

Suggestions:

Pre-reading: Direct students' attention to the instructions in the *Strategy*. Have students identify the questions they think are invitations. Then have students close their books. Using the transparencies, go panel by panel and ask students who seems to be doing the inviting, who is accepting, and what they think will happen next.

Videohistoria

¡A jugar!

Ignacio, Javier, Ana y Elena están en el Parque del Retiro en Madrid. ¿Qué van a jugar y hacer? ¿De qué hablan? Lee la historia.

Antes de leer

Look to find key questions Before you read the story, skim to find where the characters are asking questions. The answers may point to important information in the story.

- Look at the questions. Which characters are offering invitations? What do you think they will do?

1. Look through the text for words that you already know. What clues do they give you about how the students are spending their weekend?
2. Think about how you spend your weekends. How does your weekend compare with what you see the students doing in the pictures?
3. Using the pictures, try to determine what each person is like. What can you tell about each student's interests based on what you see?

Universal Access

Heritage Language Learners

Have students write three sentences about their favorite sport, including teams and athletes that they follow. Collect the first draft of their sentences, and correct any spelling and grammar mistakes.

Multiple Intelligences

Verbal / Linguistic: Ask students to write a few short lines of dialogue to change the ending of the *Videohistoria*. In the new ending, Javier should not accept the invitation to the party, and he should give at least one reason why he will not go.

1 *Hoy es sábado y hace buen tiempo. Ignacio, Javier, Ana y Elena están en el parque para jugar al fútbol.*

2 **Ignacio:** **¡Oye,** Javier! **¡Sabes** jugar muy bien al fútbol!

Javier: Y tú también . . . pero necesito practicar más. Ana, ¿quieres jugar?

Ana: ¡Por supuesto! Vamos a jugar.

3 **Elena:** Estoy demasiado cansada y tengo sed. ¿Por qué no tomamos un refresco?

Ignacio: **¡Genial!** Yo también estoy un poco cansado.

4 **Ana:** ¿Juegas al vóleibol esta tarde?

Elena: Sí, a las seis.

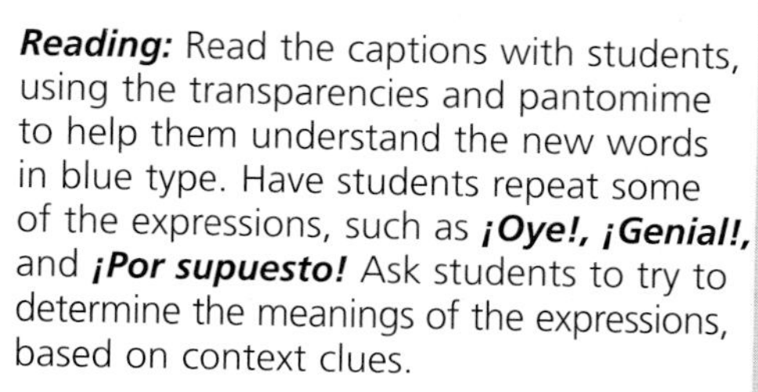

Reading: Read the captions with students, using the transparencies and pantomime to help them understand the new words in blue type. Have students repeat some of the expressions, such as ***¡Oye!, ¡Genial!,*** and ***¡Por supuesto!*** Ask students to try to determine the meanings of the expressions, based on context clues.

Post-reading: Complete *Actividades* 3 and 4 to check comprehension.

Additional Resources

- Writing, Audio & Video Workbook: Cap. 4B, Video Activity 1

Enriching Your Teaching

Culture Note

Call attention to the word ***vais*** on panel 5 of the video. Remind students that ***vais*** is the informal way to say "you go" or "you are going" when referring to more than one person. This plural informal verb form is used much more often in Spain than in other Spanish-speaking countries, where ***ustedes van*** would most likely be used instead. Since the video story takes place in Madrid, it is natural for the characters to use ***vais.***

Video

Presentation

Standards: 1.2

Resources: Video Program: Cap. 4B; Resource Book: Cap. 4B, Video Script

Focus: Viewing and understanding the classroom language input video

Suggestions:

Pre-viewing: Remind students that they do not need to get every word in order to understand what is happening. Remind them that body language and gestures can aid in comprehension. Show them a short clip of the video with the volume muted. Discuss how the characters' body language helps express their feelings.

Viewing: Show the video without pausing. Show it again, stopping along the way to verify new vocabulary and to check general understanding.

Post-viewing: Complete video activities in the *Writing, Audio & Video Workbook.*

Additional Resources

- Writing, Audio & Video Workbook: Cap. 4B, Video Activities 2–4
- Heritage Learner Workbook: 4B-1, 4B-2

5 **Ignacio:** Oye, hay una fiesta esta noche. Ana, tú y Elena vais, ¿verdad?

Ana: ¡Claro!

Elena: Javier, ¿quieres ir con nosotros a la fiesta?

Ana: ¡Qué buena idea!

6 **Javier:** ¿A qué hora es la fiesta?

Ana: A las nueve **de la noche,** en la escuela.

7 **Javier:** ¿Tengo que bailar?

Ana: Pues, sí. Puedes bailar conmigo y con Elena.

Javier: No **sé** bailar muy bien.

Ana: ¡Vamos, Javier!

Javier: Bien, voy.

8 **Javier:** Hasta las nueve entonces.

Ignacio: ¡Genial! Hasta más tarde.

Universal Access

Advanced Learners

For *Actividad* 3, on p. 245, have students cover the word bank with a sheet of paper and complete the activity unassisted.

Heritage Language Learners

Have students write a short story in which they describe what happens at the party. They must use the characters from the *Videohistoria,* but can create any scenario. Post students' final copies in the classroom.

Actividad 3 Leer/Escribir

Una postal de Javier

Before going to the party, Javier decides to write a postcard to his friend in Salamanca, telling him about his new friends in Madrid. Number your paper from 1–6. Use the words in the box to complete his postcard. Base your answers on the *Videohistoria*.

fiesta	bailar
Elena	fútbol
sábado	nueve

Querido José,

¿Cómo estás? Estoy bien en mi nueva[1] escuela. Tengo tres amigos: Ignacio, Ana y __1.__. Ellos son muy divertidos. Hoy es __2.__, y fuimos[2] al parque para jugar al __3.__. Esta noche, vamos a una __4.__. Vamos a las __5.__ de la noche. Según mi amiga, yo tengo que __6.__. ¡Pero no sé bailar muy bien! Bueno, son las ocho y media y debo ir.

¡Hasta pronto!
Javier

José Romero-Manterola
15-D, c/Luchana
37008 Salamanca

[1] new [2] we went

Actividad 4 Escribir/Hablar

¿Quién habla?

Who is speaking: Ana, Ignacio, Elena, or Javier?

Ana

Ignacio

Elena

Javier

1. No sé bailar bien.
2. Juego al vóleibol a las seis.
3. Necesito beber algo después de jugar al fútbol.
4. Necesito practicar más el fútbol.
5. Voy a la fiesta a las nueve.
6. Sé jugar al fútbol muy bien.

Más práctica
Practice Workbook 4B-3, 4B-4

For: Vocabulary practice
Visit: www.phschool.com
Web Code: jad-0412

Actividad 3 *Standards:* 1.2, 1.3

Resources: Practice Answers on Transparencies

Focus: Reading for comprehension; verifying understanding of the *Videohistoria*

Suggestions: Tell students to read the entire postcard once before filling in their answers. Remind them that they can find answers in the postcard in the same order that they appear in the *Videohistoria.*

Answers:
1. **Elena**
2. **sábado**
3. **fútbol**
4. **fiesta**
5. **nueve**
6. **bailar**

Actividad 4 *Standards:* 1.2, 1.3

Resources: Practice Answers on Transparencies

Focus: Reading for comprehension

Suggestions: When reviewing the answers, have students give the number of the panel and read the sentence that supports each one. Have students read answers as if they were the person. For example: *No sé bailar bien. Soy Javier.*

Answers:
1. **Javier**
2. **Elena**
3. **Elena**
4. **Javier**
5. **Ana**
6. **Ignacio**

Assessment
- Prueba 4B-1: Vocabulary recognition

Enriching Your Teaching

Teacher-to-Teacher

Have students create advertisements for a sports club or outdoor recreation facility. They should include a variety of activities, hours of operation, and contact information. Suggest that they illustrate the advertisements, and post them in the room to be used to guide further conversations about sports and leisure-time activities.

Internet Search

Keywords:

recreación, ocio, parques, atracciones

Actividad 5 — *Standards:* 1.1

Resources: Practice Answers on Transparencies

Focus: Expressing what you would and wouldn't like to do

Suggestions: Emphasize that students will be using ***Me gustaría*** ("I would like") as opposed to ***Me gusta.***

Answers will vary but should include:

(No) me gustaría...
1. ir al concierto.
2. ir al baile.
3. ir al partido.
4. ir de cámping.
5. ir de pesca.

Actividad 6 — *Standards:* 1.1, 1.2

Resources: Practice Answers on Transparencies

Focus: Communicating about sports

Suggestions: Tell students that they will need this information for *Actividad* 7.

Answers will vary but should include:

Sé / No sé jugar al ...
1. básquetbol
2. fútbol americano
3. vóleibol
4. tenis
5. golf
6. fútbol

Actividad 7 — *Standards:* 1.1

Focus: Using new vocabulary in personal contexts and conversations

Suggestions: Have students move around the room and interact with several different classmates during the activity.

Answers will vary.

Manos a la obra

Vocabulario y gramática en uso

Objectives

- Talk about activities outside of school
- Extend, accept, and decline invitations
- Tell when an event happens
- Say what you are going to do
- Learn to use *ir* + *a* + infinitive and the verb *jugar*

Actividad 5 — **Hablar**

Me gustaría ir . . .

Say whether or not you would like to do these things this weekend.

Modelo

Me gustaría ir a una fiesta este fin de semana.
o: *No me gustaría ir a una fiesta este fin de semana.*

1. 
2. 
3. 
4. 
5. 

Actividad 6 — **Escribir/Hablar**

No sé jugar . . .

Number your paper from 1–6. Indicate whether or not you know how to play the sports pictured below.

Modelo

Sé jugar al béisbol muy bien.
o: *No sé jugar al béisbol.*

1. 
2. 

3. 
4. 
5. 
6. 

Actividad 7 — **Hablar**

¿Qué deportes practicas?

Using the information from Actividad 6, ask and tell about which sports you know, or don't know, how to play.

Modelo

A —*¿Sabes jugar al béisbol?*
B —*¡Por supuesto! Sé jugar al béisbol muy bien.*
o: *No, no sé jugar al béisbol.*

Universal Access

Advanced Learners
Ask students to use the Internet to research a well-known athlete of Spanish-speaking origin. Have them write a short profile of the athlete, including which sports he or she plays, his or her statistics, and what team he or she plays for, if appropriate.

Heritage Language Learners
Have students prepare a profile as suggested in the *Advanced Learners* section. If appropriate, suggest that they write the information about a well-known athlete from their heritage country.

Actividad 8 Escribir

La fiesta de Marta

Marta is having a party, and many of her classmates in her class are there. While some people are having a great time, others are not. Number your paper from 1–6. Use the adjectives in the word box to write six sentences describing the people in the picture below.

triste ocupado, -a cansado, -a contento, -a enfermo, -a mal

Modelo

Felipe y María están contentos.

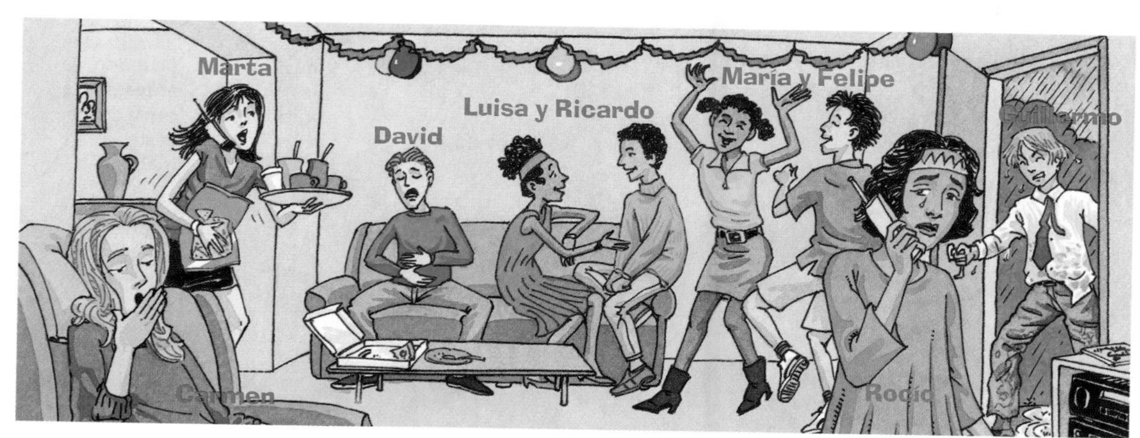

Fondo cultural

La noche de los rábanos is just one of the many kinds of *fiestas* in the Spanish-speaking world. On the evening of December 23, people set up booths around the *zócalo* (town square) of Oaxaca, Mexico, to display and sell radishes *(los rábanos)* sculpted into a fantastic array of shapes. *Oaxaqueños* and visitors alike crowd the square to view the amazing creations.

- Do you know communities or regions in the United States that are known for particular crafts or products?

Rábanos esculpidos *(sculpted)*, Oaxaca, México

Enriching Your Teaching

Culture Note

A wide range of handicrafts is produced in Oaxaca, including black pottery, blown glass, weavings, and brightly colored woodcarvings of animals *(**alebrijes**)*. Artisans bring their wares to the ***zócalos*** to sell. Artisans pass their skill from one generation to another.

Internet Search

Keywords:

La noche de los rábanos; Oaxaca, Mexico

Rapid Review

Ask students to use the words in the box to describe how they are feeling today.

Standards: 1.3

Actividad 8

Resources: Practice Answers on Transparencies

Focus: Writing sentences using contextualized vocabulary

Suggestions: Before beginning, ask students to name a situation in which they might feel each of the adjectives in the box. Remind students that they need to make sure that the adjectives agree with the subjects in their sentences.

Answers:

1. **Marta está ocupada.**
2. **Guillermo está mal.**
3. **Ricardo y Luisa están contentos.**
4. **David está enfermo.**
5. **Rocío está triste.**
6. **Carmen está cansada.**

Standards: 2.1, 2.2, 4.2

Fondo cultural

Resources: Voc. & Gram. Transparencies: 12 (map)

Suggestions: Locate Oaxaca on the map transparency. Ask students if they have seen foods carved into shapes. When is this done, and why? How does this practice in the United States differ from what is done with the ***rábanos*** in Oaxaca?

Answers will vary.

4B Practice and Communicate

Standards: 1.1

Resources: Practice Answers on Transparencies

Focus: Extending and declining invitations

Recycle: Activities vocabulary

Suggestions: Before beginning, talk about excuses students use to avoid doing things.

Answers:

Student A:
1. —¡Oye! ¿Quieres ir de pesca conmigo...?
2. —¡Oye! ¿Quieres jugar al básquetbol conmigo...?
3. —¡Oye! ¿Quieres ir de compras conmigo...?
4. —¡Oye! ¿Quieres montar en bicicleta conmigo...?
5. —¡Oye! ¿Quieres jugar al fútbol conmigo...?

Student B:
—Lo siento. Hoy no puedo. Estoy *(answers will vary.)*

Standards: 1.2

Resources: Audio Program: CD Cap. 4B, Track 6; Resource Book: Cap. 4B, Audio Script; Practice Answers on Transparencies

Focus: Listening comprehension

Suggestions: Before the activity, remind students to listen for intonations that indicate a positive or negative reaction.

Script and Answers:
1. A —¿Puedes ir conmigo al baile esta noche? *(going to a dance)*; B —¡Qué pena! Tengo que trabajar. *(no)* 2. A—¿Te gustaría ir conmigo al partido esta tarde? *(going to a game)*; B —¡Qué buena idea! Me gustaría mucho. *(sí)* 3. A —Voy a jugar al golf el domingo. ¿Quieres jugar? *(playing golf)*; B —¿Contigo? ¡Genial! *(sí)*

Standards: 1.1

Resources: Practice Answers on Transparencies

Focus: Accepting and declining invitations

Recycle: Activities vocabulary.

Suggestions: Remind students that they need to look at the time mentioned before deciding upon their excuse.

Answers:
1. No puedo. Tengo que ir a la lección de piano. 2. . . . que jugar al básquetbol con Silvia y Jaime. 3. . . . que ir al baile. 4. . . . que ir a la biblioteca con Ramón. 5. . . . que ir a la fiesta de Julia. 6. . . . que jugar al fútbol americano con mis amigos.

   Hablar

Lo siento

Ask your partner if he or she wants to do these activities with you. Your partner can't go and will offer excuses to explain why.

Modelo

A —*¡Oye! ¿Quieres patinar conmigo esta tarde?*
B —*Lo siento. Hoy no puedo. Estoy demasiado enfermo(a).*

Estudiante B

muy	ocupado, -a
demasiado	enfermo, -a
un poco	cansado, -a
	triste
	mal

¡Respuesta personal!

 Escuchar/Escribir

Escucha y escribe

You will hear three invitations to events and the responses given. On a sheet of paper, write the numbers 1–3. As you listen, write what each invitation is for and whether the person accepted it (write *sí)* or turned it down (write *no*).

  Escribir

Un estudiante muy popular

You have a busy Saturday and your friends are asking you to do things. Respond by telling them why you cannot accept.

Modelo

¿Quieres ir al cine a la una y media de la tarde?
No puedo. Tengo que ir a la biblioteca con Ramón.

1. ¿Te gustaría ir al café a las diez de la mañana?
2. ¿Puedes jugar al vóleibol a las tres de la tarde?
3. ¿Quieres ir al concierto esta noche a las siete?
4. ¿Puedes ir al restaurante con la clase esta tarde?
5. ¿Quieres ir a la fiesta de Beto esta noche?
6. ¿Te gustaría ir de pesca a las doce del mediodía?

sábado: el 26 de abril

10:00	ir a la lección de piano
12:00	jugar al fútbol americano con mis amigos
1:30	ir a la biblioteca con Ramón
3:00	jugar al básquetbol con Silvia y Jaime
5:30	comer en casa
7:00	ir al baile
9:30	ir a la fiesta de Julia

Universal Access

Students with Learning Difficulties

Actividad 10 requires students to listen, process, and write at the same time, which can be challenging. You may want to divide this into two separate tasks: first listening for the event, and then listening for the response.

Heritage Language Learners

Refer students to the *Exploración del lenguaje* at the bottom of p. 249. Ask students to identify additional Spanish words and expressions borrowed from English.

  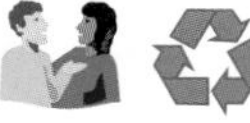 Hablar

¿A qué hora?

Take turns asking and telling what time the following activities take place.

 8:00 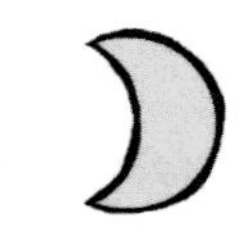

Modelo

A —*¿A qué hora es la película?*
B —*A las ocho de la noche.*

1.  9:00 
2.  2:30 
3.  1:30 
4.  8:30 
5.  7:30 
6.  7:00 

Nota

To ask and tell what time something happens, you say:

- **¿A qué hora** vas?
- Voy **a la** una.
- Voy **a las** tres y media.

To specify what part of the day, add:

de la mañana* in the morning (A.M.)
de la tarde in the afternoon (P.M.)
de la noche in the evening, at night (P.M.)

**Mañana* means "tomorrow"; *la mañana* means "morning."

Exploración del lenguaje

Spanish words borrowed from English

Languages often borrow words from one another. For example, *rodeo* and *patio* are Spanish words that have found their way into English. There are also many examples of English words that have entered Spanish. By recognizing these familiar words, you can increase your vocabulary in Spanish.

Try it out! Read the sentences and identify the "borrowed words." Don't forget to pronounce the words correctly in Spanish.

Quiero hacer videos.
¿Quieres jugar al básquetbol conmigo?
Practico el rugby y el ráquetbol.
Juego al fútbol cuando voy de cámping.
¡Me encantan los sándwiches!

Enriching Your Teaching

Culture Note

If you are invited to a party, a dinner, or other event in a Spanish-speaking country and you cannot accept the invitation, it is usually best to offer an explanation. Just saying *Lo siento. Ya tengo planes* ("I'm sorry. I already have plans") may be seen as rude. It is also traditional to bring the host or hostess a gift.

Teacher-to-Teacher

Using visuals of activities, have students write three sentences saying why they cannot do them. Tell them that their excuses do not always have to be logical. For example: *No puedo montar en monopatín. Estoy demasiado contenta.* Have the class decide whether or not the excuse makes sense.

 *Standards:* 1.1

Resources: Practice Answers on Transparencies

Focus: Using visualized vocabulary; expressing what time an event occurs

Recycle: Telling time

Suggestions: Have students look at the *Nota* on p. 249, and remind them to use it as a reference while doing the activity.

Answers:

1. —¿A qué hora es el concierto?
 —A las nueve de la noche.
2. —¿A qué hora es la fiesta?
 —A las dos y media de la tarde.
3. —¿A qué hora es el partido?
 —A la una y media de la tarde.
4. —¿A qué hora es el baile?
 —A las ocho y media de la noche.
5. —¿A qué hora es la cena?
 —A las siete y media de la noche.
6. —¿A qué hora es el desayuno?
 —A las siete de la mañana.

Exploración del lenguaje

Presentation

 *Standards:* 4.1

Suggestions: Review the *Try it out!* with students. For further practice, have them work with a partner to the glossary for additional borrowed words.

Standards: 1.1

Resources: Practice Answers on Transparencies

Focus: Using contextualized vocabulary in conversation

Recycle: ***ir;*** place names

Suggestions: Ask volunteers to read the model as it is written. Then, ask them to read it again, this time having Student B decline the invitation.

Answers will vary but should include the following:

1. —¿Te gustaría ir al baile?
   —¿A qué hora?
   —A las siete y media de la noche.
   —Answers will vary.
2. —¿Te gustaría ir a la piscina?
   —¿A qué hora?
   —A la una de la tarde.
   —Answers will vary.
3. —¿Te gustaría ir a la fiesta?
   —¿A qué hora?
   —A las ocho y media de la noche.
   —Answers will vary.
4. —¿Te gustaría ir al partido de fútbol?
   —¿A qué hora?
   —A las cuatro y cuarto de la tarde.
   —Answers will vary.
5. —¿Te gustaría ir al cine?
   —¿A qué hora?
   —A las cinco y media de la tarde.
   —Answers will vary.
6. —¿Te gustaría ir al centro comercial?
   —¿A qué hora?
   —A las once de la mañana.
   —Answers will vary.

Hablar

Una invitación para el sábado

Invite your partner to these places, and tell at what time you will go. Your partner will accept or decline. Follow the model.

1:30

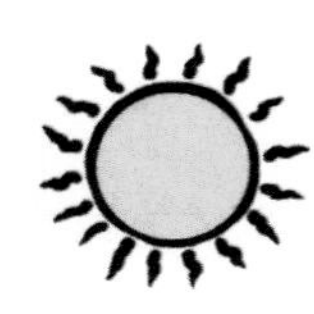

Modelo

A —*¿Te gustaría ir al concierto el sábado?*
B —*¿A qué hora?*
A —*A la una y media de la tarde.*
B —*¡Genial! Nos vemos el sábado.*

Estudiante A

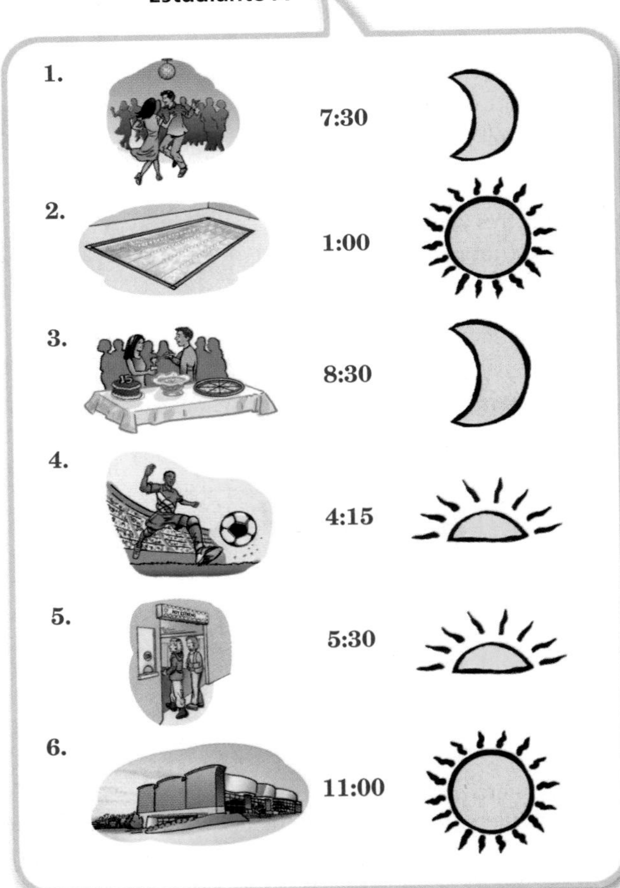

Estudiante B

¡Por supuesto! Me gustaría mucho.
Lo siento, pero no puedo.
¡Ay! ¡Qué pena! Tengo que trabajar.
¡Genial! Nos vemos el sábado.
¡Qué buena idea! ¡Gracias!

¡Respuesta personal!

Universal Access

Multiple Intelligences

Visual / Spatial: Have students draw a three-paneled cartoon. In their cartoon, they should write a dialogue in which one character invites the other(s) to do something. There should be a response, and then a comment or a conclusion. Ask students to post their cartoons or to present them to the class.

Heritage Language Learners

Have students keep an interactive journal of their activities for a week. Encourage them to include details about each activity, such as where they will go, who will be with them, and what they need. Maintain a dialogue with students by writing responses that provide feedback and ask for additional output.

  **Escribir/Hablar**

Una invitación para mi amigo

viernes, el ________ de ________

la mañana ________

la tarde ________

la noche ________

sábado, el ________ de ________

la mañana ________

la tarde ________

la noche ________

domingo, el ________ de ________

la mañana ________

la tarde ________

la noche ________

1. Copy this page of an agenda book onto a sheet of paper. Then, fill in each space with what you will be doing this weekend. Try to include specific times whenever possible.
2. After you have completed your schedule, work with a partner to invite him or her to various activities. Your partner will accept or decline, based on the information in his or her agenda book.

Actividad 15 **Escribir/Hablar**

Y tú, ¿qué dices?

1. ¿Qué haces los fines de semana?
2. ¿Qué prefieres, practicar un deporte o ver la televisión? ¿Por qué?
3. ¿Cómo estás después de practicar tu deporte favorito? ¿Cómo estás cuando pasas tiempo con tus amigos?
4. ¿Qué te gustaría hacer esta noche? ¿Y mañana?
5. ¿Qué tienes que hacer este fin de semana?

Enriching Your Teaching

Teacher-to-Teacher

Provide authentic texts as a supplement to activities. For example, in *Actividad* 14, provide students with a movie listing from a Spanish-language newspaper. Have students invite their classmate to see a movie of their choice, and then have the partner accept or decline based on what is written in their agenda book. Authentic texts make language meaningful to students, as they are able to see how what they are learning is applied to sources outside of the textbook.

Standards: 1.1, 1.3

Focus: Writing an agenda based on recently learned vocabulary, including times of events

Suggestions: To save time, you may wish to supply students with copies of the agenda page. For step 2, encourage students to use a variety of expressions for accepting and declining invitations.

Answers will vary.

Rapid Review

Write the expression ***tengo que*** on the board, and have students share things that they have to do after school.

Standards: 1.1, 1.3

Focus: Using vocabulary in a personalized context

Suggestions: Encourage students to be as detailed as possible in their answers.

Answers will vary.

Extension: Have students create one additional question to ask their classmates. This could be done as a homework assignment. As a class, have volunteers read their questions and select students to answer them.

Theme Project

Students can perform step 4 at this point. (For more information, see p. 206-a.)

Additional Resources

- Writing, Audio & Video Workbook: Cap. 4B, Audio Activities 5–6, Tracks 7–8
- Writing, Audio & Video Workbook: Cap. 4B, Writing Activity 10
- Resource Book: Cap. 4B, Communicative Activity BLM

Assessment

- Prueba 4B-2: Vocabulary production

Practice and Communicate

Gramática

Presentation

 *Standards:* 4.1

Resources: Video Program: Cap. 4B; Resource Book: Cap. 4B, Video Script

Suggestions: Emphasize that the second verb is always in the infinitive and that only the forms of ***ir*** change. Use the *GramActiva* Video either as an initial introduction or as a follow-up to your own presentation of the grammar.

 *Standards:* 1.3

Focus: Combining phrases to express what is going to happen

Suggestions: Encourage students to answer with *¡Respuesta personal!*

Answers will vary.

Standards: 1.3

Resources: Audio Program: CD Cap. 4B, Track 9; Resource Book: Cap. 4B, Audio Script; Practice Answers on Transparencies

Focus: Listening for comprehension

Suggestions: Use the *Audio CD* or read the script aloud. Have students listen to the messages without taking notes the first time.

Script and Answers:

Rosario:

1. ¡Hola! Soy Rosario. ¿Qué pasa? Tomás y yo vamos a patinar esta tarde. ¿Te gustaría ir con nosotros? Vamos a estar en el parque a las cuatro. Hasta luego.
1. al parque 2. patinar 3. a las cuatro

Pablo:

2. ¡Oye! ¿Cómo estás? Soy Pablo. ¿Puedes ir al gimnasio conmigo? No tengo que trabajar hoy. Muchos estudiantes van a jugar al vóleibol a las siete. Háblame por teléfono si puedes ir.
1. al gimnasio 2. jugar vóleibol 3. a las siete

Gramática

Ir + *a* + infinitive

Just as you use "going" + infinitive in English to say what you are going to do, in Spanish you use a form of the verb ***ir* + *a* +** an infinitive to express the same thing:

Voy a jugar al tenis hoy.
I'm going to play *tennis today.*

¿Tú **vas a jugar** al golf esta tarde?
Are you going to play *golf this afternoon?*

Mis amigas **van a ir de cámping** mañana.
My friends ***are going camping*** *tomorrow.*

Javier: **¿Van a jugar** conmigo, o no?
Ana: Sí, **vamos a jugar** contigo.

GramActiva VIDEO

Want more help with *ir* + *a* + infinitive? Watch the **GramActiva** video.

Actividad 16 Gramática **Escribir**

¿Qué van a hacer todos?

You and the people you know have a lot to do this weekend. Tell what everyone is going to do by matching the people in the first column with any of the activities in the third column. Use the appropriate form of the verb *ir*. Write the sentences you create on a sheet of paper.

1. yo	ir a	ver una película
2. mis amigos		ir de pesca
3. mi mamá		jugar al golf
4. mi papá y yo		estudiar
5. mi profesor(a) y director(a)		trabajar
6. tú		pasar tiempo con amigos
		¡Respuesta personal!

Actividad 17 Gramática **Escuchar/Escribir**

Escucha y escribe

Rosario and Pablo have left messages on your answering machine telling you what they are going to do and inviting you to join them. Copy this chart on your paper. As you listen to each message, complete the chart with information given in the message.

	Rosario	Pablo
1. ¿Adónde quiere ir?		
2. ¿Qué va a hacer?		
3. ¿A qué hora va a ir?		

Universal Access

Advanced Learners

Have students create a mini-journal in which they tell what they are going to do each day of the week after school. Have them include the phrases ***de la mañana, de la tarde,*** and ***de la noche.*** Suggest that they include details such as with whom they will do the activities, where they will go, and why they are going to do them. Encourage journal-writing as a warm-up activity to help get students focused and on task before beginning the lesson.

  Escribir

Este fin de semana vamos a . . .

On your paper, write sentences telling what the Ríos family is going to do this weekend.

Esteban /  / 8:00 

Modelo
Esteban va a estudiar a las ocho de la noche.

1. Angélica /  / 3:30 
2. Angélica y el Sr. Ríos /  / 7:00 
3. yo /  / 4:00 
4. Los señores Ríos /  / 7:30 
5. Esteban y un amigo /  / 10:00 
6. Angélica, Esteban y yo /  / 8:00 

   Hablar

En mi tiempo libre voy a . . .

Work with a partner and talk about what you are going to do in your free time and when.

Modelo
A —*¿Cuándo vas a correr?*
B —*Voy a correr esta tarde.*
o: *Nunca voy a correr.*

Estudiante A

correr en el parque
estudiar español
hacer ejercicio
trabajar
comer en un restaurante
ver una película

¡Respuesta personal!

Estudiante B

a la(s) . . .
esta tarde
esta noche
este fin de semana
nunca

¡Respuesta personal!

Enriching Your Teaching

Practice and Communicate 4B

 *Standards:* 1.3

Resources: Practice Answers on Transparencies

Focus: Using context to write what people are going to do

Recycle: Telling time and activities vocabulary

Suggestions: If you have a large clock manipulative that you use to teach telling time, use it to review these answers. Put the clock hands at any of the times given in the activity, and have students say what the people will do.

Answers:

1. **Angélica va a trabajar a las tres y media de la tarde.**
2. **Angélica y el Sr. Ríos van a ir de pesca a las siete de la mañana.**
3. **Yo voy a jugar al vóleibol a las cuatro de la tarde.**
4. **Los señores Ríos van a ir de compras a las siete y media de la noche.**
5. **Esteban y un amigo van a jugar al fútbol a las diez de la mañana.**
6. **Angélica, Esteban y yo vamos a ir al cine a las ocho de la noche.**

Common Errors: In expressions using ***ir*** + ***a*** + infinitive, when ***ir*** is the infinitive, students frequently omit the second ***ir,*** changing the sentence to the present tense. Give students several examples to help them internalize the correct structure.

 *Standards:* 1.1

Focus: Talking about what people are going to do in their free time

Recycle: Activities vocabulary

Suggestions: Encourage students to create original answers for both parts of the dialogue.

Answers will vary.

Pronunciación

Presentation

Standards: 4.1

Resources: Audio Program: CD Cap. 4B, Track 13

Suggestions: Read the *Pronunciación* with students or use the *Audio CD.* Model the two sounds of the letter *d,* exaggerating the *d* sound in ***doce*** and the *th* sound in ***cansado.*** Then have the class repeat.

Actividad 20

Standards: 1.1, 1.3

Resources: Resource Book: Cap. 4B, GramActiva BLM

Focus: Saying when and with whom something will be done

Recycle: Activities vocabulary

Suggestions: Brainstorm a few activities to help students recall a variety of actions. Give students copies of the chart. Point out that they should not include the example on the page unless it is true for them.

Answers will vary.

Extension: Encourage students to continue their conversations by asking for more details, such as where their partner is going and how he or she is getting there.

Theme Project

Students can perform step 5 at this point. Be sure they understand your corrections and suggestions. (For more information, see p. 206-a.)

Pronunciación

The letter *d*

In Spanish, the pronunciation of the letter *d* is determined by its location in a word. When *d* is at the beginning of a word, or when it comes after *l* or *n,* it sounds similar to the *d* in "dog." Listen to and say these words:

diccionario	doce	donde
domingo	desayuno	día
deportes	calendario	bandera

When *d* comes between vowels and after any consonant except *l* or *n,* it sounds similar to the *th* of "the." Listen to and say these words:

cansado	ocupado	puedes
idea	sábado	partido
tarde	ensalada	atrevido

Try it out! Here is a tongue twister to give you practice in pronouncing the letter *d,* and also to give you something to think about!

Porque puedo, puedes,
porque puedes, puedo;
Pero si no puedes,
yo tampoco puedo.

Actividad 20

 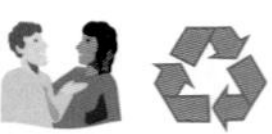
Escribir/Hablar

¿Qué vas a hacer?

1. Make a chart like this one to describe five things you're going to do, when you're going to do them, and with whom. Use the following words to say when you're going to do these things: *esta tarde, esta noche, mañana, el (jueves), este fin de semana.*

¿Qué?	¿Cuándo?	¿Con quién?
tocar la guitarra	esta tarde	mis amigos

2. Ask your partner what his or her plans are.

Modelo

A —*¿Qué vas a hacer esta tarde?*
B —*Esta tarde mis amigos y yo vamos a tocar la guitarra.*

Universal Access

Students with Learning Difficulties

Some students may have difficulty hearing the difference between the two *d* sounds when they are looking at the words. Have them close their eyes as they listen to you read the words.

In addition, some students may have difficulty reproducing the *th* sound for *d*. Have them say English words such as *rather* and *bother*, then substitute the Spanish words.

Leer/Escribir

El teléfono celular

Answer the following questions about this ad for a cellular phone. Then create your own ad by writing at least five things that you want to do.

1. ¿Por qué es bueno tener un teléfono celular?
2. ¿Te gusta hablar por teléfono celular? ¿Con quién?
3. ¿Crees que es bueno o malo usar un teléfono celular en un restaurante? ¿Por qué?

Hablar

Una conversación por teléfono celular

You're calling a friend to invite him or her to do something. Your friend turns down the invitation and explains why. Make at least three invitations each.

Modelo

A —*Hola, Sara. Soy Rosa. ¿Puedes jugar al tenis conmigo esta tarde?*
B —*Lo siento, hoy no puedo. Voy a estudiar para mi clase de inglés.*
A —*¡Ay! ¡Qué pena!*

Escribir/Hablar

Y tú, ¿qué dices?

1. ¿Con quién te gustaría ir a una fiesta? ¿Por qué?
2. ¿Qué prefieres: ir de pesca o ir a un baile?
3. ¿Qué vas a hacer mañana a las ocho de la noche?
4. ¿Qué vas a hacer este fin de semana?
5. ¿Te gustaría ver un partido de fútbol o ir a un concierto?

Más práctica
Practice Workbook 4B-5, 4B-6

Go Online PHSchool.com
For: Practice with *ir* + *a* + infinitive
Visit: www.phschool.com
Web Code: jad-0413

Enriching Your Teaching

Teacher-to-Teacher

Have students write out a conversation beween two people on the phone. After corrections have been made, have the students record the conversation. Copy the best dialogues, omitting various words and expressions from this lesson. Distribute them to the class. As you play the recordings, have the students fill in the blanks on their papers based on what they hear.

Actividad 21 *Standards:* 1.1, 1.2, 1.3

Resources: Voc. & Gram. Transparencies: 95; Practice Answers on Transparencies

Focus: Reading for comprehension and writing with accuracy

Suggestions: Form groups of students with varying abilities to interpret the ad. Discuss the questions as a class.

Answers:
1. **¡Con un teléfono celular puedes hacer planes para hacerlo todo!**
2. **Answers will vary.**
3. **Answers will vary.**

Actividad 22 *Standards:* 1.1

Focus: Having a telephone conversation

Recycle: Activities vocabulary

Suggestions: Encourage students to present their lines without a script, pretending to be on an actual phone. You may want to bring in toy phones for students to use as props.

Answers will vary.

Actividad 23 *Standards:* 1.1, 1.3

Focus: Using vocabulary to express opinions in a personalized context

Suggestions: If students are only given the option to choose between two items, ask follow-up questions, such as why they feel that way about the activity.

Answers will vary.

Additional Resources

- Writing, Audio & Video Workbook: Cap. 4B, Audio Activity 7, Track 11
- Writing, Audio & Video Workbook: Cap. 4B, Writing Activity 11
- Resource Book: Cap. 4B, Communicative Activity BLM

Assessment

- Prueba 4B-3: ***Ir*** + ***a*** + infinitive

4B Practice and Communicate

Gramática

Presentation

Standards: 4.1

Resources: Voc. & Gram. Transparency: 93; Video Program: Cap. 4B; Resource Book: Cap. 4B, Video Script

Suggestions: Highlight the difference between a stem-changing verb, such as ***jugar,*** and a regular ***-ar*** verb, such as ***hablar,*** by using a different color chalk or pen for the stem changes. Play the *GramActiva* Video as an introduction or to review your own presentation of the verb ***jugar.***

Standards: 1.3

Resources: Practice Answers on Transparencies

Focus: Using the verb ***jugar*** to say what sports people play

Suggestions: Have students identify all of the sports before they begin.

Answers:

1. Natalia juega al golf.
2. Los estudiantes en mi clase juegan al fútbol americano.
3. Nosotros jugamos al fútbol.
4. Sara juega al vóleibol.
5. Ustedes juegan al básquetbol.
6. Tú juegas al tenis.

Common Errors: With stem-changing verbs, students may overgeneralize and change all of the forms.

Extension: For homework, have students choose two sports and write a sentence about one or more famous athletes who play each one.

Gramática

The verb *jugar*

Use the verb *jugar* to talk about playing a sport or a game. Even though *jugar* uses the same endings as the other *-ar* verbs, it has a different stem in some forms. For those forms, the *u* becomes *ue.* This kind of verb is called a "stem-changing verb." Here are the present-tense forms:

(yo)	juego	(nosotros) (nosotras)	jugamos
(tú)	juegas	(vosotros) (vosotras)	jugáis
Ud. (él) (ella)	juega	Ud. (ellos) (ellas)	juegan

Nota

Many Spanish speakers always use *jugar a* and the name of the sport or game:

- ¿Juegas **al** vóleibol?

Others do not use the ***a:***

- ¿Juegas vóleibol?

GramActiva VIDEO

Use the **GramActiva** video to help you learn more about the verb *jugar.*

Actividad 24 Gramática Escribir

¿A qué juegan?

Write sentences telling what sports the following people play.

Alejandro

Modelo

Alejandro juega al béisbol.

También se dice . . .

el básquetbol = el baloncesto *(muchos países)*
el fútbol = el balompié *(muchos países)*
el vóleibol = el balonvolea *(España)*

1. 
Natalia

2. 
los estudiantes en mi clase

3. 
nosotros

4. 
Sara

5. 
Uds.

6. 
tú

Universal Access

Heritage Language Learners

Have students prepare an oral presentation on their favorite sport or athlete. Students should use the verb ***jugar.*** If students present a new sport not covered in this chapter, have them provide a poster to support their oral presentation.

Advanced Learners

Have students collaborate to make a sports magazine, including photos and illustrations, statistics, and a short article featuring a well-known athlete. Make the magazines available for all students to see.

  **Dibujar/Escribir/Hablar/GramActiva**

Juego

1. On each of two index cards, draw a picture that represents a sport or game and write *muy bien, bien,* or *mal* to show how well you play that sport or game. Don't let your classmates see your cards.
2. Get together with five other students. Put all the cards face down in the center of your group. Choose a card and try to identify who drew it by asking the others how well they play what is pictured. Keep track of what you learn about your classmates.

Modelo

A —*Enrique, ¿juegas bien al tenis?*
B —*No, juego muy mal al tenis.*

3. Write six sentences describing the sports and games the students in your group play.

Modelo

Óscar y Nacho juegan muy bien al fútbol.
Teresa y yo jugamos bien al béisbol.

Estos jugadores de Managua, Nicaragua juegan muy bien al béisbol.

Practice and Communicate

Rapid Review

Use transparency 94 to quickly review sports activities. You may want to have students say the answers aloud, instead of having to write sentences.

 *Standards:* 1.1, 1.3

Focus: Writing and speaking in personalized contexts; using the verb ***jugar***

Suggestions: You may want to bring in old sports magazines for students to cut up as an alternative to illustrations. Point out the placement of ***muy mal*** and remind students to place the adverb between the verb and the direct object. Encourage students to create a chart in their notebooks to organize the information about their classmates for their paragraph.

Answers will vary.

Teacher-to-Teacher

Have your class create a bulletin board honoring well-known baseball players from Spanish-speaking countries. Have students find pictures of their favorite players and then write two sentences about the person and for whom they play.

Enriching Your Teaching

Culture Note

Baseball was first introduced to Cuba well over 100 years ago. From there its popularity spread to other Spanish-speaking countries of the Caribbean, in particular, the Dominican Republic. The Dominican Republic has produced many baseball superstars, including the great Sammy Sosa, named Most Valuable Player of the National League in 1998. The Dominican government finances the building and maintenance of stadiums and local fields and pays the coaches' salaries. Baseball is more than just a sport in the Dominican Republic; it is a way of life.

Actividad 26

Standards: 1.2, 1.3, 3.2

Resources: Practice Answers on Transparencies

Focus: Reading comprehension

Suggestions: Have students scan the text for cognates to help them prepare for the reading. Read the passage to the students, and then ask a volunteer to reread it. Have students work with a partner to answer the questions.

Answers:

1. **Quiere una ciudad dedicada al deporte, a la familia y a los niños. Quiere servicios de calidad internacional, con profesores de excelencia.**
2. **fútbol, tenis y hockey**
3. **el 23 de marzo, a las ocho**
4. **a las dos de la tarde**
5. **Answers will vary.**

El español en el mundo del trabajo

Presentation

Standards: 5.1

Suggestion: Have students determine the meaning of the quotation in the reading and use it as a model to say how they feel about volunteer work. To help students answer the questions, brainstorm different volunteer opportunities on the board.

Answers will vary.

Extension: If possible, invite a health care worker to your class to talk about ways in which knowledge of Spanish is helpful in his or her job.

Leer/Escribir/Hablar

La ciudad deportiva

Read about Iván Zamorano's dream and answer the questions.

1. ¿Qué es el sueño de Iván Zamorano?
2. ¿Qué deportes juegan en la Ciudad Deportiva de Iván?
3. ¿Qué día empieza *(begins)* la inscripción para las escuelas? ¿A qué hora?
4. ¿A qué hora empiezan las actividades?
5. ¿Te gustaría ir a la Ciudad Deportiva de Iván Zamorano? ¿Por qué?

Mi sueño[1]

Quiero una ciudad[2] dedicada al deporte, a la familia y a los niños.[3] Quiero servicios de calidad internacional, con profesores de excelencia. En mi sueño, los niños y jóvenes juegan y practican deportes para ser mejores.[4] Este sueño ya es realidad y quiero compartirlo contigo.

El lugar[5] para hacer deporte en familia.

Escuelas de Fútbol, Tenis, Hockey

Inicio de Inscripción[6]: 23 de marzo, a las 8
Inicio de Actividades: 1 de abril, a las 14 horas

Avenida Pedro Hurtado 2650, Las Condes, Santiago, Chile
Teléfono: 212 2711

[1]dream [2]city [3]children [4]better [5]place [6]Registration

El español en el mundo del trabajo

There are many opportunities to use Spanish in the health care field—in hospitals, emergency rooms, and neighborhood clinics. This young woman volunteers in a California hospital. Since many of the patients come from Spanish-speaking homes, she is able to speak with them and their families in Spanish. *"Para mí, trabajar como voluntaria es una de mis actividades favoritas. Creo que mi trabajo es importante."*

- What opportunities are there in your community to do volunteer work where speaking Spanish is helpful?

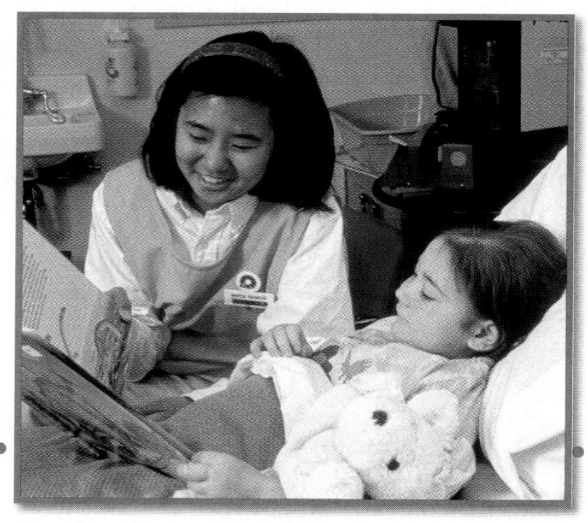

Una voluntaria en un hospital

Universal Access

Heritage Language Learners

Have students create a poster for a community organization that is looking for volunteers who know how to speak Spanish.

Students with Learning Difficulties

The readings in *Actividad*es 26 and 27 might intimidate students because of the unknown vocabulary. Help them review the ad for vocabulary they already know. Then read through the ad with students, and emphasize words and phrases that will help them understand the meaning.

Leer/Pensar/Escribir

¡Vamos de cámping!

Tourism is an important industry in Spain. Many tourists prefer to go camping rather than stay in hotels. Read the following brochure about a campground and then answer the questions.

Conexiones
Las matemáticas

Cámping Playa Tropicana

Alcossebre (Castellón)
Teléfono: 462 41 42 73   Fax: 964 01 55 05

240 kilómetros al sur de Barcelona
52 kilómetros al norte de Castellón

- Un cámping verdaderamente recomendable
- Siempre algo nuevo
- La mejor opción para su dinero

Con abundante vegetación y mucha sombra,[1] directamente sobre una fabulosa playa. Ideal para niños. La mejor zona de pesca de la Costa de Azahar.

[1]shade

1. ¿Qué distancia en millas[2] hay entre[3] Barcelona y el Cámping Playa Tropicana?
2. ¿Qué distancia hay entre Castellón y el Cámping Playa Tropicana?

(Para convertir kilómetros en millas, es necesario dividir el número de kilómetros por 1.6.)

[2]miles [3]between

Para decir más . . .
200 doscientos

Escribir/Hablar

Y tú, ¿qué dices?

1. ¿Qué deporte juegas bien? ¿Qué deporte juegas mal?
2. ¿Quién juega al básquetbol muy bien? ¿Al golf?
3. ¿Dónde juegan tú y tus amigos al vóleibol?
4. ¿Qué deportes juegan tú y tus amigos para la escuela?
5. ¿Qué deportes juegan tú y tus amigos en invierno?

Más práctica
Practice Workbook 4B-7

For: Practice with *jugar*
Visit: www.phschool.com
Web Code: jad-0414

Enriching Your Teaching

Culture Note

Because Spain has a variety of landscapes, there are many different kinds of sporting activities for tourists—fishing, swimming, parasailing, hiking, cave exploring, and canoeing. In addition to all the activities, tourists enjoy the wonderful food, museums, architecture, and climate.

Teacher-to-Teacher

Before beginning a lesson, choose a question from *Y tú, ¿qué dices?*, or create a similar one, to ask students as they prepare to start class. If you present them with a question upon entering, communication starts immediately.

Standards: 1.2, 3.1

Resources: Voc. & Gram. Transparency: 18 (map); Practice Answers on Transparencies

Focus: Reading comprehension

Suggestions: Before beginning, have students talk about the title and the photograph. Ask them to compare what they see to vacations and camping trips they have been on. Remind students that they will not know every word. Have them identify cognates such as ***fabulosa*** and ***ideal.***

Answers:
Entre Barcelona y el Cámping Playa Tropicana hay 150 millas. Entre Castellón y Playa Tropicana hay 32.5 millas.

Standards: 1.1, 1.3

Focus: Answering questions about sports

Suggestions: After students have written their answers, have them work with a partner to ask and answer the questions.

Answers will vary.

Theme Project

Students can perform step 6 at this point. Record their presentations on cassette or videotape for inclusion in their portfolios. (For more information, see p. 206-a.)

Additional Resources

- Writing, Audio & Video Workbook: Audio Activities 8–9, Tracks 12–13
- Writing, Audio & Video Workbook: Writing Activities 12–13
- Heritage Language Learner Workbook: 4B-3, 4B-4, 4B-5

Assessment

- Prueba 4B-4: The verb *jugar*

4B Communicate: Reading

Lectura

Presentation

Standards: 1.2, 1.3, 5.2, 4.1

Focus: Developing reading strategies and interpretive skills; comparing the lives of two people

Suggestions:

Pre-reading: Direct attention to the *Strategy.* Have students skim the two articles and write a list of cognates. Have them share their lists with the class and write them on the board. Encourage students to use other context clues that can help them, such as dates and numbers.

Reading: Ask students to read the article about Sergio García first. Have them make a list of words they do not understand. Then have students read the article about Lorena Ochoa Reyes. Did they find similar words they did not understand, or were there new unfamiliar words?

Post-reading: Ask students what they learned about Sergio García. What did they learn about Lorena Ochoa Reyes? Discuss how these two athletes are alike. Then have students think about what makes each one unique.

Additional Resources

- Heritage Learner Workbook: 4B-6

¡Adelante!

Lectura

Sergio y Lorena: El futuro del golf

Lee este artículo de una revista deportiva. Vas a conocer a[1] Sergio García y a Lorena Ochoa Reyes, dos atletas famosos.

Objectives

- Read about and compare the lives of two famous golfers
- Recognize specialized sports vocabulary
- Understand cultural perspectives regarding extracurricular activities
- Write an invitation to an event
- Learn facts about the contemporary United States

Strategy

Cognates
Use the cognates in the following articles to help you understand what is being said about the golfers.

Sergio García

Nombre: Sergio García
Fecha de nacimiento: 9/1/80
Lugar de nacimiento: Borriol, Castellón (España)
Club: Club de Campo del Mediterráneo
Su objetivo: Ser el mejor del mundo
Profesional: Desde abril del 99
Aficiones[2]: Real Madrid, tenis, fútbol, videojuegos

Sergio García es uno de los golfistas más populares en el mundo del golf profesional.

Sergio juega para el Club de Campo del Mediterráneo en Borriol, Castellón, donde su padre Víctor es golfista profesional. Juega al golf desde la edad[3] de tres años y a los 12 años es campeón[4] del Club de Campo. Es el golfista más joven en competir en el campeonato PGA desde Gene Sarazen en 1921 y gana[5] segundo lugar.[6] Tiene el nombre "El niño". A los 15 años, juega en un torneo del circuito europeo de profesionales. Y a la edad de 17 años gana su primer torneo de profesionales.

Es evidente que este español tiene el talento para realizar su objetivo.

[1]You will meet [2]Interests [3]age [4]champion [5]he wins [6]second place

Universal Access

Advanced Learners
Have students choose an athlete in the school to interview. Suggest that they find out information similar to what they have read about Sergio and Lorena. Tell them that they can conduct the interview in English if the athlete is not a Spanish student, but that they should write a summary in Spanish to share with the class.

Heritage Language Learners
Ask students to discuss athletes they are familiar with from a variety of sports. As they are talking, guide their discussion by asking: How old is this person? Where was he or she born? What are some of his or her biggest accomplishments? Do you think he or she is a good role model? Why or why not?

Nombre: Lorena Ochoa Reyes

Fecha de nacimiento: 15/11/81

Lugar de nacimiento: Guadalajara, México

Su objetivo: Ser la golfista número uno del mundo

Universidad: Universidad de Arizona

Aficiones: básquetbol, tenis, bicicleta de montaña, correr, nadar, comida italiana

Lorena es la mejor golfista de México. Juega al golf desde los seis años de edad. A los 21 años, gana su primer torneo de profesionales. Es la única[7] mexicana en calificar al torneo U.S. Women's Open. Ella dice que está muy emocionada porque quiere jugar mejor[8] y competir en los Estados Unidos. Ella dice que es importante practicar y entrenar[9] todos los días. Un día ella quiere ser la golfista número uno del mundo.

[7]only [8]better [9]to train

¿Comprendes?

Copy this Venn diagram on a sheet of paper. Make a list in English of at least eight facts that you learned about Sergio and Lorena. Write the facts on your Venn diagram. Include information about Sergio in the left oval, information about Lorena in the right oval, and any fact that applies to both of them in the overlapping oval.

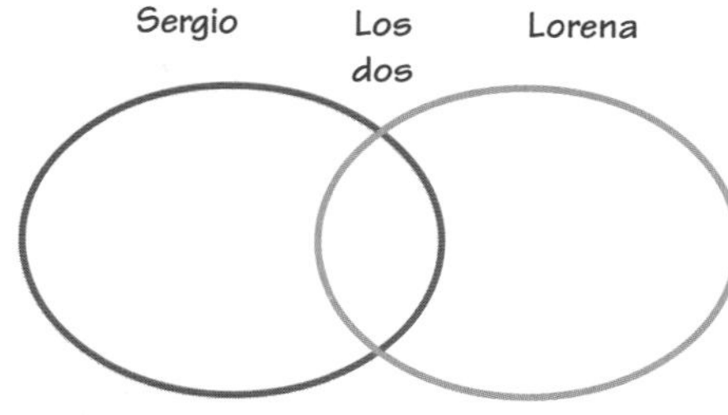

Go Online PHSchool.com
For: Internet link activity
Visit: www.phschool.com
Web Code: jad-0415

Fondo cultural

Una jugadora profesional Rebecca Lobo is a professional basketball player. After winning a gold medal in the 1996 Olympics, she became one of the WNBA's original players. Rebecca wrote a book called The Home Team, which tells about her life and her mother's struggle against breast cancer. In 2001, she established a college scholarship fund to assist minority students who plan to pursue careers in the healthcare field.

- Rebecca Lobo is a popular motivational speaker. What message do you think she gives to her audiences?

Enriching Your Teaching

Culture Note

In the 1950s, the "*Ticas*" of Costa Rica formed the first women's soccer team in Latin America. However, it wasn't until 1982 that the Federation of International Football Associates decided to make women's soccer official. By 1985, only one South American country had a team—Brazil. Today almost all South American countries have women's soccer teams. Despite a long struggle for acceptance, women's professional sports teams are gaining popularity.

Standards: 1.3

¿Comprendes?

Resources: Voc. & Gram. Transparency; Practice Answers on Transparencies

Focus: Comparing Sergio García and Lorena Ochoa Reyes

Suggestions: Use the transparency for a blank venn diagram. Remind students to look at both the profiles and the paragraphs to find facts about the two athletes. When reviewing answers, ask students questions such as *¿Quién juega en el Club de Campo del Mediterráneo?*

Answers will vary but may include:

Sergio García:
from Spain
professional golfer
his father is a golfer

Los dos:
they both want to be the best
they both like tennis

Lorena Ochoa Reyes:
from Mexico
younger
plays golf for her university

Extension: Have students write a short autobiographical "snapshot" of themselves. They can follow the format used in the boxes in the article. Encourage students to use vocabulary from this chapter.

Standards: 3.1

Suggestions: After reading the text, discuss the question with students. Encourage them to think about how Rebecca Lobo's struggles and accomplishments may affect her message. Ask students to name other celebrities or athletes who have overcome struggles. How do they compare with Rebecca Lobo?
Answers will vary.

Teacher-to-Teacher

Have students write a short autobiographical "snapshot." They can follow the format used in the boxes to the right of the photos. Encourage them to use vocabulay from this chapter.

Perspectivas del mundo hispano

Presentation

 *Standards:* 2.1, 4.2

Focus: Reading about leisure activities of students in Spanish-speaking countries

Suggestions: Ask students what they do in their spare time. Tell them that in many Spanish-speaking countries, spare time is not necessarily free time. Many students use it to learn a foreign language or practice a sport in an athletic club. Have students read the text and point out similarities and differences between their experience and that of the students described. Direct attention to the photos. Of course many students in the United States also participate in these and similar activities. Mention that in general, high-school students in Spanish-speaking countries do not have jobs.

Have students think about how a schedule like the one described would affect their lives. What would change? Would they have to stop doing something? Ask if this schedule sounds enjoyable. Remember that many students today hold jobs out of necessity, and that many have very full schedules, much like the one described here.

Direct attention to the *Think about it!* section and have students discuss the question.

Answers will vary.

Additional Resources

- Heritage Learner Workbook: 4B-7

Perspectivas del mundo hispano

¿Qué haces en tu tiempo libre?

Jugando al hockey en Buenos Aires, Argentina

In many Spanish-speaking countries, extracurricular activities traditionally play a much smaller role in school life than in the United States. Students usually participate in activities such as music and athletics at clubs and institutions outside of school.

Although some schools have teams, many students who are interested in sports attend clubs such as el Club Deportivo General San Martín. At these clubs teens practice and compete on teams. They also participate in individual sports such as tennis. The competition between clubs is sometimes more intense than the competition between schools.

¿Te gusta jugar al ajedrez?

Students with artistic talents often go to a private institute to take music, dance, or art lessons. They might attend el Instituto de Música Clásica or el Instituto de Danza Julio Bocca.

Many students spend their time outside of classes studying a foreign language. They might learn English at la Cultura Inglesa or French at la Alianza Francesa.

In general, students do not hold jobs. They spend their time studying, being with family and friends, and participating in different activities.

Check it out! Take a survey of your friends to find out what they do after school. Do they work a part-time job? Do they participate in a sport with a school team or in extracurricular activities at school? Do they belong to a club or organization outside of school?

Think about it! How do the practices in your community compare with what you have learned about young people's after-school activities in Spanish-speaking countries?

Trabajando después de las clases

Universal Access

Advanced Learners

Have students research schools in the United States where students can go if they have artistic talents; for example, the Juilliard School, music conservatories, etc. Have them find out more about the schools listed in the text. Ask them to compare the schools and make a short presentation to the class.

Students with Special Needs

Students may participate in special activities or groups. If they wish, invite them to share their experiences with the class.

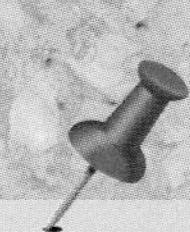

Presentación escrita

Una invitación

Task
A special event is coming up on the calendar and you want to invite a friend to go with you.

1 Prewrite Think about an event that you would invite a friend to attend, such as a concert, sporting event, or party. Write an invitation that includes:

- the name of the event
- when, where, and at what time the event is taking place
- who is going

Strategy

Organizing information
Thinking about the correct format and necessary information beforehand will help you create a better invitation.

2 Draft Use the information from Step 1 to write a first draft of your invitation. Begin your invitation with *¡Hola . . . !* and close with *Tu amigo(a)* and your name.

3 Revise Read your note and check for correct spelling and verb forms. Share your invitation with a partner. Your partner should check the following:

- Did you give all the necessary information?
- Is there anything you should add or change?
- Are there any errors?

4 Publish Write a final copy of your invitation, making any necessary changes. You may want to give it to your friend or include it in your portfolio.

5 Evaluation Your teacher may give you a rubric for how the invitation will be graded. You probably will be graded on:

- how complete the information is
- use of vocabulary expressions
- accuracy of sentence structures

Communicate: Writing 4B

Presentación escrita

Presentation

Standards: 1.3

Focus: Writing an invitation

Suggestions: Review the assignment, the 5-step approach, and the rubric with the class. Make an invitation of your own as a model for students to use. Refer students to the *Strategy*, and have them write the information to be included in their invitations before beginning. You may wish to have them give you rough drafts.

In Spanish, review the *5-Ws—Who, What, Where, When, Why*—with students, and have volunteers suggest how these could be included in an invitation.

Encourage students to make their invitations appealing with artwork or calligraphy.

Teacher-to-Teacher

Have students work in groups to create a singing telegram inviting a special friend to an event. The class can evaluate the telegrams based on a variety of categories, such as most original, best singing, and most humorous. The class can vote on the top telegram.

Portfolio

Attach a copy of the grading rubric to the final copy of the invitation, and include within the students' portfolios.

Additional Resources

- Heritage Learner Workbook: 4B-8

Assessment

- Assessment Program: Cap. 4B, Rubrics

Give students copies of the rubric before they begin the activity and examples that demonstrate the different levels of performance. After assessing students, help individuals understand how they could improve their performance.

Enriching Your Teaching

RUBRIC	Score 1	Score 3	Score 5
Amount of information	You give very few or no details or examples about locations and activities.	You give only a few details or examples about locations and activities.	You give many details and examples about locations, times and activities.
Use of vocabulary expressions	You have very little variation of vocabulary use with frequent incorrect usage.	You have limited usage of vocabulary, but with some usage errors.	You have extended use of a variety of vocabulary with very few usage errors.
Accuracy of sentence structures	You have at least three sentences with many grammar errors.	You have at least three sentences but with some grammar errors.	You have at least three sentences with very few grammar errors.

El mundo hispano

Presentation

Standards: 1.1, 1.3, 2.1, 5.1, 5.2

Resources: Voc. & Gram. Transparency: 20 (map)

Focus: Reading about the current influence of Spanish speakers in the United States

Suggestions: Have students read the selection. Locate Mexico, Cuba, and Puerto Rico on the maps. Discuss the latest census results in the United States and how most Spanish speakers in this country say they are from one of these locations. Have students think about the reasons people from Spanish-speaking countries now immigrate to the United States.

Have students read about the astronauts featured and discuss their achievements. Direct attention to the photo at the top of p. 265. Discuss the contribution of Spanish speakers to the arts. New York City has a large concentration of Puerto Ricans. Locate Puerto Rico and New York City on the maps. Ask students to hypothesize as to why so many Puerto Ricans went to New York City when other parts of the country are so much closer. Have students consider the idea that people go where they have family. Moving to a new country is difficult; being with family greatly eases the transition. Remind students that Puerto Rico is a territory of the United States, which means that Puerto Ricans have an automatic right to immigrate.

El mundo hispano

Estados Unidos

Contemporáneo

According to the 2000 census, 32,800,000 people (about 12 percent of the total population of the United States) classified themselves as being of Spanish or Hispanic descent. Out of that number, 30,700,800 indicated that they were of either Mexican, Puerto Rican, or Cuban descent. The remaining 2,099,200 people checked "Other Spanish/Hispanic" on their census questionnaires. This broad category included people who came from or who had ancestral ties to other Spanish-speaking countries in the Caribbean, Central and South America, or Spain.

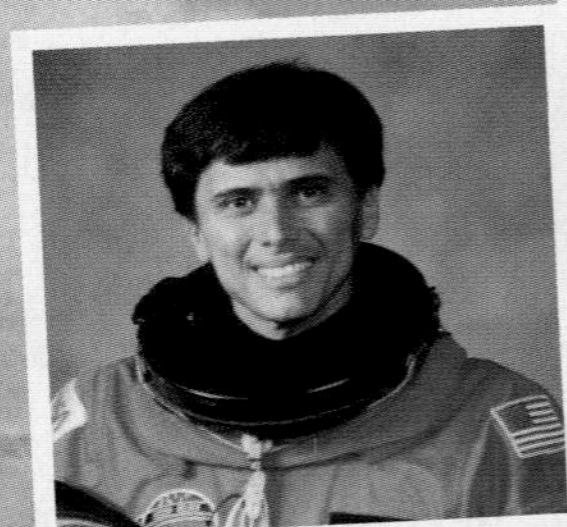

Born in Costa Rica, Dr. Franklin Chang-Díaz (left) was the first Hispanic astronaut to fly in space. He was selected by NASA in 1980 and is a veteran of seven space flights. In 1990, Californian Dr. Ellen Ochoa (right) became the first Hispanic female astronaut. Since then she has logged more than 480 hours in space. Her dream is to help build a space station, which she considers "critical . . . to human exploration in space." Both Dr. Ochoa and Dr. Chang-Díaz are the recipients of many honors for their technical contributions and their scholarship.

¿Sabes que . . . ?

The influence of Spanish-speaking cultures is evident throughout the United States. Musical artists such as Enrique Iglesias, Shakira, and Marc Anthony sell millions of CDs. Actors such as Salma Hayek, Jennifer Lopez, Benjamin Bratt, and Edward James Olmos earn great acclaim for their work. And in politics, Spanish-speaking Americans serve in Congress and top-level Cabinet posts.

Para pensar

Work with a partner and interview a classmate, friend, or acquaintance who is Spanish-speaking or who has ties to a Spanish-speaking country. What is the person's name? Where did the family come from, and when? Why did the family move to your community? If this person had one thing to say to you and your classmates about the immigrant experience and cultural differences, what might that be? Write a short account of the interview and present it to your class or to a small group.

For: Online Atlas
Visit: www.phschool.com
Web Code: jae-0002

Universal Access

Advanced Learners

Have students choose a major city or region in the United States with a large Spanish-speaking population, research celebrations and businesses that reflect the Spanish-speaking culture, and prepare a short report indicating their findings.

Heritage Language Learners

Have students find out if there is a city or region in the United States that has a large concentration of people from their heritage country. Have them identify the place and find out why people from their heritage country concentrated there.

The music and poetry of New York City's Puerto Rican community are a creative blend of English and Spanish. *Nuyoricans* of the *Loisaida* (Lower East Side) rub shoulders with people of diverse ethnic backgrounds creating sounds and rhythms unlike any other in the world. The Nuyorican Poets Café has become an institution on the *Loisaida,* where poets, writers, performance artists, musicians, and visual artists of all nationalities can find an outlet for their work.

More than half of Miami's population is of Spanish-speaking descent. Calle Ocho is the heart of Little Havana, the largest Cuban American community in the United States. The Calle Ocho Festival, which takes place at the end of Carnaval Miami, is a great time to sample Cuban food and dance to some of the world's greatest salsa artists.

More Mexicans visit the border town of Laredo, Texas, than any other city in the United States; and more United States citizens visit the Mexican border town of Tijuana than any other foreign city. Most of the visitors come from nearby areas and stay for only a few hours to visit or shop.

Culture 4B

Have students read the middle paragraph on p. 265. Discuss Miami and Calle Ocho. This street has become famous for its Cuban flavor and festivals. Help students see the proximity of Cuba and Miami on the map. Mention that because of the political situation in Cuba, many Cubans left their country and arrived on the shores of Florida. The Cuban influence is evident throughout Miami.

Have students focus on the information under the photo of the road signs. Discuss how people who live near the Mexico–United States border often go to the other country for brief visits.

Direct students to the *¿Sabes que...?* section. Discuss the people mentioned and highlight their achievements.

Emphasize that people emigrate for a variety of reasons. Some students may not understand that many people emigrate for political reasons. Explain, if necessary, that not all countries offer the same opportunities and freedoms.

Direct attention to the *Para pensar* section. Have students complete it and present it to the class another day.

Answers will vary.

Go Online

The Online Atlas will provide more detailed maps of the locations mentioned here.

Enriching Your Teaching

Teacher-to-Teacher

Latin American foods are very popular in the United States. Have students research one or two major cities across the nation for restaurants that offer cuisine from Spanish-speaking countries. Have them sort the restaurants according to the country of origin and make a bar graph indicating the countries represented. Which country has the most widespread representation?

Review Activities

Talking about leisure activities and describing how someone feels: Have students work in pairs to quiz each other. They should take turns being Student A and Student B. Student A can pantomime an activity, and Student B will say the word in Spanish.

Extending, accepting and declining invitations; telling what time something happens: Student A will invite Student B to an activity and state what time it will take place. Student B will make up an excuse for why he or she cannot go based on how he or she feels.

Jugar: Have students write the six pronouns on separate note cards, shuffle the cards and hold them up one at a time. Student pairs will take turns saying the appropriate form of ***jugar.*** To reinforce vocabulary, ask them to add a sport to their sentences, for example: *Ellos juegan al tenis.*

Portfolio

Invite students to review the activities they completed in this chapter, including written reports, posters or other visuals, and tapes of oral presentations or other projects. Have them select one or two items that they feel best demonstrate their achievements in Spanish to include in their portfolios. Have them include this with the Chapter Checklist and Self-Assessment Worksheet.

Additional Resources

- Audio Program: CD Cap. 4B, Track 14
- Resource Book: Cap. 4B, Clip Art
- Resource Book: Cap. 4B, Situation Cards
- Assessment Program: Cap. 4B, Chapter Checklist and Self-Assessment Worksheet

Chapter Review

Repaso del capítulo

Vocabulario y gramática

To prepare for the test, check to see if you . . .
- **know the new vocabulary and grammar**
- **can perform the tasks on p. 267**

to talk about leisure activities

el baile	dance
el concierto	concert
la fiesta	party
ir + a + *infinitive*	to be going + infinitive
ir de cámping	to go camping
ir de pesca	to go fishing
jugar al básquetbol	to play basketball
jugar al béisbol	to play baseball
jugar al fútbol	to play soccer
jugar al fútbol americano	to play football
jugar al golf	to play golf
jugar al tenis	to play tennis
jugar al vóleibol	to play volleyball
el partido	game, match
(yo) sé	I know (how)
(tú) sabes	you know (how)

to describe how someone feels

cansado, -a	tired
contento, -a	happy
enfermo, -a	sick
mal	bad, badly
ocupado, -a	busy
triste	sad

For *Vocabulario adicional,* see pp. 268–269.

to extend, accept, or decline invitations

conmigo	with me
contigo	with you
(yo) puedo	I can
(tú) puedes	you can
¡Ay! ¡Qué pena!	Oh! What a shame!
¡Genial!	Great!
lo siento	I'm sorry
¡Oye!	Hey!
¡Qué buena idea!	What a good/nice idea!
(yo) quiero	I want
(tú) quieres	you want
¿Te gustaría?	Would you like?
Me gustaría	I would like
Tengo que ___.	I have to ___.

to tell what time something happens

¿A qué hora?	(At) what time?
a la una	at one (o'clock)
a las ocho	at eight (o'clock)
de la mañana	in the morning
de la noche	in the evening, at night
de la tarde	in the afternoon
esta noche	this evening
esta tarde	this afternoon
este fin de semana	this weekend

other useful words and expressions

demasiado	too
entonces	then
un poco (de)	a little

jugar (a) *to play (games, sports)*

juego	**jugamos**
juegas	**jugáis**
juega	**juegan**

Más práctica
Practice Workbook Puzzle 4B-8
Practice Workbook Organizer 4B-9

Universal Access

Multiple Intelligences

Bodily / Kinesthetic: Have students elaborate on their responses to invitations by creating a skit on the topic. Ask them to exaggerate expressions of enthusiasm or disappointment.

Students with Learning Difficulties

As for other *Repaso* sections, break this information down into more manageable segments. You might need to modify the test or create alternative tests that meet the individual needs of different students.

For: Test preparation
Visit: www.phschool.com
Web Code: jad-0416

Preparación para el examen

On the exam you will be asked to . . .	Here are practice tasks similar to those you will find on the exam . . .	If you need review . . .
1 Escuchar Listen to and understand messages that give information about when and where to meet someone	On your answering machine, you hear your friend asking if you can go somewhere with her this weekend. Based on her message, try to tell: a) where she is going; b) what she is going to do; and c) what time she wants to go.	**pp. 240–245** *A primera vista* **p. 248** Actividad 10 **p. 252** Actividad 17
 **2 Hablar** Make excuses for not accepting an invitation	You and a friend have planned a camping trip this weekend, but another friend now wants you to do something with him. With a partner, take turns rehearsing excuses for declining his invitation.	**p. 246** Actividad 5 **p. 248** Actividad 9 **p. 250** Actividad 13 **p. 255** Actividad 22
 **3 Leer** Read and understand short messages about accepting or declining invitations	You find notes under your desk that were written to the person who was sitting there before you. Read them to see why people declined an invitation to a party: (a) Me gustaría, pero no puedo. Tengo que estudiar para un examen. (b) ¡Genial! ¡Una fiesta! Ay, pero no puedo— voy de cámping. (c) ¿A las siete? No puedo. Juego un partido de vóleibol a las siete y media. Lo siento.	**pp. 240–245** *A primera vista* **pp. 260–261** *Lectura*
 **4 Escribir** Write a short note telling what you are going to do during the week	As a counselor for an after-school program for children, you must write a note to the parents telling them at least three things their children are going to do during the week. (Hint: Start your note with *¡Hola! Esta semana . . .*)	**pp. 240–245** *A primera vista* **p. 253** Actividad 18 **p. 254** Actividad 20 **p. 263** *Presentación escrita*
 **5 Pensar** Demonstrate an understanding of cultural differences regarding extracurricular activities	Think about what you and your friends typically do after school. Are your activities usually school-related? How would you compare what you do to what some Spanish-speaking teens do in their after-school time?	**p. 262** *Perspectivas del mundo hispano*

Enriching Your Teaching

Teacher-to-Teacher

Have students create a picture book in which the characters discuss what their plans are, invite others to join them, and accept or decline offers. Students may illustrate their books with their own drawings or find pictures from magazines to include.

Performance Tasks

 *Standards:* 1.1, 1.2, 1.3, 4.2

Resources: Audio Program: CD Cap. 4B, Track 15; Resource Book: Cap. 4B, Audio Script; Practice Answers on Transparencies

1. Escuchar

Suggestions: You may wish to use the *Audio CD* or read the script yourself.

Script:

Hola, Toni, soy Susi. Oye. Yo voy al centro comercial después de las clases a las cuatro de la tarde. ¿Te gustaría ir conmigo? Voy a comprar algo para un amigo.

Answers:

a. Susi is going to the mall.
b. Susi is going to buy something for her friend.
c. Susi is wants to go at 4:00 in the afternoon.

2. Hablar

Suggestions: Remind students that their excuses should sound legitimate. Ask them to tell how they feel and to tell about another activity that is preventing them from attending.

Answers will vary.

3. Leer

Suggestions: Tell students to scan the readings for the key word that says why the person cannot go, and then have them read the entire passage.

Answers:

a. The person has to study for a test.
b. The person is going camping.
c. The person is going to a volleyball game.

4. Escribir

Suggestions: Remind students that the verbs will be in the third person since they are describing what students will do.

Answers will vary.

3. Pensar

Suggestions: Remind students to refer to *Perspectivas del mundo hispano* on p. 262.

Answers will vary.

Assessment

- Examen del capítulo: 4B
- Audio Program: CD 20, Track 10

Alternative Assessment

- ExamView Test Bank CD-ROM
- Resource Book: Cap 4B, Situation Cards
- Resource Book: Cap 4B, Communicative Activities

Vocabulario adicional

Las actividades

coleccionar sellos / monedas to collect stamps / coins

jugar al ajedrez to play chess

patinar sobre hielo to ice-skate

practicar artes marciales *(f.)* to practice martial arts

tocar to play *(an instrument)*

- **el bajo** bass
- **la batería** drums
- **el clarinete** clarinet
- **el oboe** oboe
- **el saxofón,** *pl.* **los saxofones** saxophone
- **el sintetizador** synthesizer
- **el trombón,** *pl.* **los trombones** trombone
- **la trompeta** trumpet
- **la tuba** tuba
- **el violín,** *pl.* **los violines** violin

Las clases

el alemán German

el álgebra *(f.)* algebra

el anuario yearbook

la banda band

la biología biology

el cálculo calculus

el drama drama

la fotografía photography

el francés French

la geografía geography

la geometría geometry

el latín Latin

la química chemistry

la trigonometría trigonometry

Las cosas para la clase

la grapadora stapler

las grapas staples

el sujetapapeles, *pl.* **los sujetapapeles** paper clip

las tijeras scissors

Las comidas

Las frutas

el aguacate avocado
la cereza cherry
la ciruela plum
el coco coconut
el durazno peach
la frambuesa raspberry
el limón, *pl.* **los limones** lemon
el melón, *pl.* **los melones** melon
la pera pear
la sandía watermelon
la toronja grapefruit

Las verduras

el apio celery
el brócoli broccoli
la calabaza pumpkin
el champiñón, *pl.* **los champiñones** mushroom
la col cabbage
la coliflor cauliflower
los espárragos asparagus
las espinacas spinach
el pepino cucumber

La carne

la chuleta de cerdo pork chop
el cordero lamb
la ternera veal

Los condimentos

la mayonesa mayonnaise
la mostaza mustard
la salsa de tomate ketchup

Otro tipo de comidas

los fideos noodles

Los lugares y actividades

el banco bank
el club club
el equipo de . . . ___ team
la farmacia pharmacy
la oficina office
la práctica de . . . ___ practice
la reunión, *pl.* **las reuniones de . . .** ___ meeting
el supermercado supermarket

Resumen de gramática

Grammar Terms

Adjectives describe nouns: *a **red** car.*

Adverbs usually describe verbs; they tell when, where, or how an action happens: *He read it **quickly.*** Adverbs can also describe adjectives or other adverbs: ***very** tall, **quite well.***

Articles are words in Spanish that can tell you whether a noun is masculine, feminine, singular, or plural. In English, the articles are *the, a,* and *an.*

Commands are verb forms that tell people to do something: ***Study!, Work!***

Comparatives compare people or things.

Conjugations are verb forms that add endings to the stem in order to tell who the subject is and what tense is being used: *escrib**o**, escrib**iste.***

Conjunctions join words or groups of words. The most common ones are ***and, but,*** and ***or.***

Direct objects are nouns or pronouns that receive the action of a verb: *I read the **book.** I read **it.***

Gender in Spanish tells you whether a noun, pronoun, or article is masculine or feminine.

Indirect objects are nouns or pronouns that tell you to whom / what or for whom / what something is done: *I gave **him** the book.*

Infinitives are the basic forms of verbs. In English, infinitives have the word "to" in front of them: ***to walk.***

Interrogatives are words that ask questions: ***What** is that? **Who** are you?*

Nouns name people, places, or things: ***students, Mexico City, books.***

Number tells you if a noun, pronoun, article, or verb is singular or plural.

Prepositions show relationship between their objects and another word in the sentence: *He is **in** the classroom.*

Present tense is used to talk about actions that always take place, or that are happening now: *I always **take** the bus; I **study** Spanish.*

Present progressive tense is used to emphasize that an action is happening *right now: I **am doing** my homework; he **is finishing** dinner.*

Preterite tense is used to talk about actions that were completed in the past: *I **took** the train yesterday; I **studied** for the test.*

Pronouns are words that take the place of nouns: ***She** is my friend.*

Subjects are the nouns or pronouns that perform the action in a sentence: ***John** sings.*

Superlatives describe which things have the most or least of a given quality: *She is the **best** student.*

Verbs show action or link the subject with a word or words in the predicate (what the subject does or is): *Ana **writes;** Ana **is** my sister.*

Nouns, Number, and Gender

Nouns refer to people, animals, places, things, and ideas. Nouns are singular or plural. In Spanish, nouns have gender, which means that they are either masculine or feminine.

Singular Nouns	
Masculine	**Feminine**
libro	carpeta
pupitre	casa
profesor	noche
lápiz	ciudad

Plural Nouns	
Masculine	**Feminine**
libros	carpetas
pupitres	casas
profesores	noches
lápices	ciudades

Definite Articles

El, la, los, and *las* are definite articles and are the equivalent of "the" in English. *El* is used with masculine singular nouns; *los* with masculine plural nouns. *La* is used with feminine singular nouns; *las* with feminine plural nouns. When you use the words *a* or *de* before *el,* you form the contractions *al* and *del: Voy* ***al*** *centro; Es el libro* ***del*** *profesor.*

Masculine	
Singular	Plural
el libro	los libros
el pupitre	los pupitres
el profesor	los profesores
el lápiz	los lápices

Feminine	
Singular	Plural
la carpeta	las carpetas
la casa	las casas
la noche	las noches
la ciudad	las ciudades

Indefinite Articles

Un and *una* are indefinite articles and are the equivalent of "a" and "an" in English. *Un* is used with singular masculine nouns; *una* is used with singular feminine nouns. The plural indefinite articles are *unos* and *unas*.

Masculine	
Singular	Plural
un libro	unos libros
un escritorio	unos escritorios
un baile	unos bailes

Feminine	
Singular	Plural
una revista	unas revistas
una mochila	unas mochilas
una bandera	unas banderas

Pronouns

Subject pronouns tell who is doing the action. They replace nouns or names in a sentence. Subject pronouns are often used for emphasis or clarification: *Gregorio escucha música.*
Él *escucha música.*

After most prepositions, you use *mí* and *ti* for "me" and "you." The forms change with the preposition *con: conmigo, contigo.* For all other persons, you use subject pronouns after prepositions.

Subject Pronouns		Objects of Prepositions	
Singular	Plural	Singular	Plural
yo	nosotros, nosotras	(para) mí, conmigo	nosotros, nosotras
tú	vosotros, vosotras	(para) ti, contigo	vosotros, vosotras
usted (Ud.)	ustedes (Uds.)	Ud.	Uds.
él, ella	ellos, ellas	él, ella	ellos, ellas

Interrogative Words

You use interrogative words to ask questions. When you ask a question with an interrogative word, you put the verb before the subject. All interrogative words have a written accent mark.

¿Adónde?	¿Cuándo?	¿Dónde?
¿Cómo?	¿Cuánto, -a?	¿Por qué?
¿Con quién?	¿Cuántos, -as?	¿Qué?
¿Cuál?	¿De dónde?	¿Quién?

Adjectives

Words that describe people and things are called adjectives. In Spanish, most adjectives have both masculine and feminine forms, as well as singular and plural forms. Adjectives must agree with the noun they describe in both gender and number. When an adjective describes a group including both masculine and feminine nouns, use the masculine plural form.

Masculine	
Singular	**Plural**
alto	altos
inteligente	inteligentes
trabajador	trabajadores
fácil	fáciles

Feminine	
Singular	**Plural**
alta	altas
inteligente	inteligentes
trabajadora	trabajadoras
fácil	fáciles

Shortened Forms of Adjectives

When placed before masculine singular nouns, some adjectives change into a shortened form.

bueno	buen chico
malo	mal día
primero	primer trabajo
tercero	tercer plato
grande	gran señor

One adjective, ***grande,*** changes to a shortened form before any singular noun: *una gran señora, un gran libro.*

Possessive Adjectives

Possessive adjectives are used to tell what belongs to someone or to show relationships. Like other adjectives, possessive adjectives agree in number with the nouns that follow them.

Only *nuestro* and *vuestro* have different masculine and feminine endings. *Su* and *sus* can have many different meanings: *his, her, its, your,* or *their.*

Singular	Plural
mi	mis
tu	tus
su	sus
nuestro, -a	nuestros, -as
vuestro, -a	vuestros, -as
su	sus

Demonstrative Adjectives

Like other adjectives, demonstrative adjectives agree in gender and number with the nouns that follow them. Use *este, esta, estos, estas* ("this" / "these") before nouns that name people or things that are close to you. Use *ese, esa, esos, esas* ("that" / "those") before nouns that name people or things that are at some distance from you.

Singular	Plural
este libro	estos libros
esta casa	estas casas

Singular	Plural
ese niño	esos niños
esa manzana	esas manzanas

Verbos

Regular Present Tense

Here are the conjugations for regular *-ar, -er,* and *-ir* verbs in the present tense.

Infinitive	Present	
estudiar	estudio estudias estudia	estudiamos estudiáis estudian
correr	corro corres corre	corremos corréis corren
escribir	escribo escribes escribe	escribimos escribís escriben

Stem-changing Verbs

Here is an alphabetical list of the stem-changing verbs.

Infinitive	Present	
doler (o → ue)	duele	duelen
dormir (o → ue)	duermo duermes duerme	dormimos dormís duermen
empezar (e → ie)	empiezo empiezas empieza	empezamos empezáis empiezan
jugar (u → ue)	juego juegas juega	jugamos jugáis juegan
llover (o → ue)	llueve	
nevar (e → ie)	nieva	
pensar (e → ie)	pienso piensas piensa	pensamos pensáis piensan
preferir (e → ie)	prefiero prefieres prefiere	preferimos preferís prefieren

Irregular Verbs

These verbs have irregular patterns.

Infinitive	Present	
estar	estoy estás está	estamos estáis están
hacer	hago haces hace	hacemos hacéis hacen
ir	voy vas va	vamos vais van
poder	puedo puedes puede	podemos podéis pueden
querer	quiero quieres quiere	queremos queréis quieren
saber	sé sabes sabe	sabemos sabéis saben
ser	soy eres es	somos sois son
tener	tengo tienes tiene	tenemos tenéis tienen
ver	veo ves ve	vemos veis ven

Expresiones útiles para conversar

The following are expressions that you can use when you find yourself in a specific situation and need help to begin, continue, or end a conversation.

Greeting someone

Buenos días. Good morning.

Buenas tardes. Good afternoon.

Buenas noches. Good evening. Good night.

Making introductions

Me llamo . . . My name is . . .

Soy . . . I'm . . .

¿Cómo te llamas? What's your name?

Éste es mi amigo *m.* **. . .** This is my friend . . .

Ésta es mi amiga *f.* **. . .** This is my friend . . .

Se llama . . . His / Her name is . . .

¡Mucho gusto! It's a pleasure!

Encantado, -a. Delighted.

Igualmente. Likewise.

Asking how someone is

¿Cómo estás? How are you?

¿Cómo andas? How's it going?

¿Cómo te sientes? How do you feel?

¿Qué tal? How's it going?

Estoy bien, gracias. I'm fine, thank you.

Muy bien. ¿Y tú? Very well. And you?

Regular. Okay. Alright.

Más o menos. More or less.

(Muy) mal. (Very) bad.

¡Horrible! Awful!

¡Excelente! Great!

Talking on the phone

Aló. Hello.

Diga. Hello.

Bueno. Hello.

¿Quién habla? Who's calling?

Habla . . . It's [name of person calling].

¿Está . . . , por favor? Is . . . there, please?

¿De parte de quién? Who is calling?

¿Puedo dejar un recado? May I leave a message?

Un momento. Just a moment.

Llamo más tarde. I'll call later.

¿Cómo? No le oigo. What? I can't hear you.

Making plans

¿Adónde vas? Where are you going?

Voy a . . . I'm going to . . .

¿Estás listo, -a? Are you ready?

Tengo prisa. I'm in a hurry.

¡Date prisa! Hurry up!

Sí, ahora voy. OK, I'm coming.

Todavía necesito . . . I still need . . .

¿Te gustaría . . . ? Would you like to . . . ?

Sí, me gustaría . . . Yes, I'd like to . . .

¡Claro que sí (no)! Of course (not)!

¿Quieres . . . ? Do you want to . . . ?

Quiero . . . I want to . . .

¿Qué quieres hacer hoy? What do you want to do today?

¿Qué haces después de las clases? What do you do after school (class)?

¿Qué estás haciendo? What are you doing?

Te invito. It's my treat.

¿Qué tal si . . . ? What about . . . ?

Primero . . . First . . .

Después . . . Later . . .

Luego . . . Then . . .

Making an excuse

Estoy ocupado, -a. I'm busy.

Lo siento, pero no puedo. I'm sorry, but I can't.

¡Qué lástima! What a shame!

Ya tengo planes. I already have plans.

Tal vez otro día. Maybe another day.

Being polite

Con mucho gusto. With great pleasure.

De nada. You're welcome.

Disculpe. Excuse me.

Lo siento. I'm sorry.

Muchísimas gracias. Thank you very much.

Te (Se) lo agradezco mucho. I appreciate it a lot.

Muy amable. That's very kind of you.

Perdón. Pardon me.

¿Puede Ud. repetirlo? Can you repeat that?

¿Puede Ud. hablar más despacio? Can you speak more slowly?

Keeping a conversation going

¿De veras? Really?

¿Verdad? Isn't that so? Right?

¿En serio? Seriously?

¡No lo puedo creer! I don't believe it!

¡No me digas! You don't say!

Y entonces, ¿qué? And then what?

¿Qué hiciste? What did you do?

¿Qué dijiste? What did you say?

¿Crees que . . . ? Do you think that . . . ?

Me parece bien. It seems alright.

Perfecto. Perfect.

¡Qué buena idea! What a good idea!

¡Cómo no! Of course!

De acuerdo. Agreed.

Está bien. It's all right.

Giving a description when you don't know the name of someone or something

Se usa para . . . It's used to / for . . .

Es la palabra que significa . . . It's the word that means . . .

Es la persona que . . . It's the person who . . .

Ending a conversation

Bueno, tengo que irme. Well, I have to go.

Chao. (Chau.) Bye.

Hasta pronto. See you soon.

Hasta mañana. See you tomorrow.

Vocabulario español-inglés

The *Vocabulario español-inglés* contains all active vocabulary from the text, including vocabulary presented in the grammar sections.

A dash (—) represents the main entry word. For example, **pasar la —** after **la aspiradora** means **pasar la aspiradora.**

The number following each entry indicates the chapter in which the word or expression is presented. The letter *P* following an entry refers to the *Para empezar* section.

The following abbreviations are used in this list: *adj.* (adjective), *dir. obj.* (direct object), *f.* (feminine), *fam.* (familiar), *ind. obj.* (indirect object), *inf.* (infinitive), *m.* (masculine), *pl.* (plural), *prep.* (preposition), *pron.* (pronoun), *sing.* (singular).

A

a to *(prep.)* (4A)
- **— casa** (to) home (4A)
- **— la una de la tarde** at one (o'clock) in the afternoon (4B)
- **— las ocho de la mañana** at eight (o'clock) in the morning (4B)
- **— las ocho de la noche** at eight (o'clock) in the evening / at night (4B)
- **— mí también** I do (like to) too (1A)
- **— mí tampoco** I don't (like to) either (1A)
- **¿— qué hora?** (At) what time? (4B)
- **— veces** sometimes (1B)
- **— ver** Let's see (2A)
- **al** *(a + el),* **a la,** to the (4A)
- **al lado de** next to (2B)

abril April (P)
aburrido, -a boring (2A)
acuerdo:
- **Estoy de —.** I agree. (3B)
- **No estoy de —.** I don't agree. (3B)

¡Adiós! Good-bye! (P)
¿Adónde? (To) where? (4A)
agosto August (P)
el **agua** *f.* water (3A)
al *(a + el),* **a la,** to the (4A)
- **— lado de** next to (2B)

algo something (3B)
allí there (2B)
el **almuerzo** lunch (2A)
- **en el —** for lunch (3A)

el **año** year (P)
aquí here (2B)
el **arroz** rice (3B)
el **arte:**
la clase de — art class (2A)
artístico, -a artistic (1B)
asco:
¡Qué —! How awful! (3A)
atrevido, -a daring (1B)
¡Ay! ¡Qué pena! Oh! What a shame / pity! (4B)

B

bailar to dance (1A)
el **baile** dance (4B)
la **bandera** flag (2B)
el **básquetbol: jugar al —** to play basketball (4B)
beber to drink (3A)
las **bebidas** beverages (3B)
béisbol: jugar al — to play baseball (4B)
la **biblioteca** library (4A)
bien well (P)
el **bistec** beefsteak (3B)
la **boca** mouth (P)
el **bolígrafo** pen (P)
el **brazo** arm (P)
bueno (buen), -a good (1B)
- **Buenas noches.** Good evening. (P)
- **Buenas tardes.** Good afternoon. (P)
- **Buenos días.** Good morning. (P)

C

la **cabeza** head (P)
cada día every day (3B)
el **café** coffee (3A); café (4A)
la **calculadora** calculator (2A)
calor: Hace —. It's hot. (P)
caminar to walk (3B)
el **campo** countryside (4A)
cansado, -a tired (4B)
cantar to sing (1A)
la **carne** meat (3B)
la **carpeta** folder (P)
- **la — de argollas** three-ring binder (2A)

el **cartel** poster (2B)
la **casa** home, house (4A)
- **a —** (to) home (4A)
- **en —** at home (4A)

catorce fourteen (P)
la **cebolla** onion (3B)
la **cena** dinner (3B)
el **centro: el — comercial** mall (4A)
el **cereal** cereal (3A)
cero zero (P)
la **chica** girl (1B)
el **chico** boy (1B)
cien one hundred (P)
las **ciencias:**
- **la clase de — naturales** science class (2A)
- **la clase de — sociales** social studies class (2A)

cinco five (P)
cincuenta fifty (P)
el **cine** movie theater (4A)
la **clase** class (2A)
- **la sala de clases** classroom (P)

comer to eat (3A)
la **comida** food, meal (3A)

¿Cómo?:

¿— eres? What are you like? (1B)

¿— es? What is he / she like? (1B)

¿— está Ud.? How are you? *formal* (P)

¿— estás? How are you? *fam.* (P)

¿— se dice . . . ? How do you say . . . ? (P)

¿— se escribe . . . ? How is . . . spelled? (P)

¿— se llama? What's his / her name? (1B)

¿— te llamas? What is your name? (P)

compartir to share (3A)

comprender to understand (3A)

la **computadora** computer (2B)

usar la — to use the computer (1A)

con with (3A)

— mis / tus amigos with my / your friends (4A)

¿— quién? With whom? (4A)

el **concierto** concert (4B)

conmigo with me (4B)

contento, -a happy (4B)

contigo with you (4B)

correr to run (1A)

creer:

Creo que . . . I think . . . (3B)

Creo que no. I don't think so. (3B)

Creo que sí. I think so. (3B)

el **cuaderno** notebook (P)

¿Cuál? Which?, What? (3A)

¿— es la fecha? What is the date? (P)

¿Cuándo? When? (4A)

¿Cuántos, -as? How many? (P)

cuarenta forty (P)

cuarto, -a fourth (2A)

y — quarter past *(in telling time)* (P)

menos — *(time)* quarter to (P)

cuatro four (P)

D

de of (2B); from (4A)

¿— dónde eres? Where are you from? (4A)

— la mañana / la tarde / la noche in the morning / afternoon / evening (4B)

debajo de underneath (2B)

deber should, must (3B)

décimo, -a tenth (2A)

decir to say, to tell

¿Cómo se dice . . . ? How do you say . . . ? (P)

¡No me digas! You don't say! (4A)

¿Qué quiere — . . . ? What does . . . mean? (P)

Quiere — . . . It means . . . (P)

Se dice . . . You say . . . (P)

el **dedo** finger (P)

delante de in front of (2B)

demasiado too (4B)

deportista athletic, sports-minded (1B)

el **desayuno** breakfast (3A)

en el — for breakfast (3A)

desordenado, -a messy (1B)

después (de) after, afterwards (4A)

detrás de behind (2B)

el **día** day (P)

Buenos —s. Good morning. (P)

cada — every day (3B)

¿Qué — es hoy? What day is today? (P)

todos los —s every day (3A)

dibujar to draw (1A)

el **diccionario** dictionary (2A)

diciembre December (P)

diecinueve nineteen (P)

dieciocho eighteen (P)

dieciséis sixteen (P)

diecisiete seventeen (P)

diez ten (P)

difícil difficult (2A)

el **disquete** diskette (2B)

divertido, -a amusing, fun (2A)

doce twelve (P)

domingo Sunday (P)

dónde:

¿—? Where? (2B)

¿De — eres? Where are you from? (4A)

dos two (P)

E

educación física: la clase de — physical education class (2A)

el **ejercicio: hacer —** to exercise (3B)

el the *m. sing.* (1B)

él he (1B)

ella she (1B)

ellas they *f. pl.* (2A)

ellos they *m. pl.* (2A)

en in, on (2B)

— casa at home (4A)

— la . . . hora in the . . . hour (class period) (2A)

encantado, -a delighted (P)

encantar to please very much, to love

me / te encanta(n) . . . I / you love . . . (3A)

encima de on top of (2B)

enero January (P)

enfermo, -a sick (4B)

la **ensalada** salad (3A)

la — de frutas fruit salad (3A)

enseñar to teach (2A)

entonces then (4B)

¿Eres . . . ? Are you . . . ? (1B)

es is (P); (he / she / it) is (1B)

— el *(number)* **de** *(month)* it is the . . . of . . . *(in telling the date)* (P)

— el primero de *(month)*. It is the first of . . . (P)

— la una. It is one o'clock. (P)

— un(a) . . . it's a . . . (2B)

escribir:

- **¿Cómo se escribe . . . ?** How is . . . spelled? (P)
- **— cuentos** to write stories (1A)
- **Se escribe . . .** It's spelled . . . (P)

el escritorio desk (2B)

escuchar música to listen to music (1A)

los espaguetis spaghetti (3B)

el español: la clase de — Spanish class (2A)

esquiar (i → í) to ski (1A)

la estación, *pl.* **las estaciones** season (P)

estar to be (2B)

- **¿Cómo está Ud.?** How are you? *formal* (P)
- **¿Cómo estás?** How are you? *fam.* (P)
- **Estoy de acuerdo.** I agree. (3B)
- **No estoy de acuerdo.** I don't agree. (3B)

este, esta this

- **esta noche** this evening (4B)
- **esta tarde** this afternoon (4B)
- **este fin de semana** this weekend (4B)

el estómago stomach (P)

estos, estas these

- **¿Qué es esto?** What is this? (2B)

Estoy de acuerdo. I agree. (3B)

el/la estudiante student (P)

estudiar to study (2A)

estudioso, -a studious (1B)

F

fácil easy (2A)

favorito, -a favorite (2A)

febrero February (P)

la fecha: ¿Cuál es la —? What is the date? (P)

la fiesta party (4B)

el fin de semana:

- **este —** this weekend (4B)
- **los fines de semana** on weekends (4A)

las fresas strawberries (3A)

frío: Hace —. It's cold. (P)

el fútbol: jugar al — to play soccer (4B)

el fútbol americano: jugar al — to play football (4B)

G

la galleta cookie (3A)

generalmente generally (4A)

¡Genial! Great! (4B)

el gimnasio gym (4A)

el golf: jugar al — to play golf (4B)

gracias thank you (P)

gracioso, -a funny (1B)

los guisantes peas (3B)

gustar:

- **(A mí) me gusta . . .** I like to . . . (1A)
- **(A mí) me gusta más . . .** I like to . . . better (I prefer to . . .) (1A)
- **(A mí) me gusta mucho . . .** I like to . . . a lot (1A)
- **(A mí) no me gusta . . .** I don't like to . . . (1A)
- **(A mí) no me gusta nada . . .** I don't like to . . . at all. (1A)
- **Le gusta . . .** He / She likes . . . (1B)
- **Me gusta . . .** I like . . . (3A)
- **Me gustaría . . .** I would like . . . (4B)
- **No le gusta . . .** He / She doesn't like . . . (1B)
- **¿Qué te gusta hacer?** What do you like to do? (1A)
- **¿Qué te gusta hacer más?** What do you like better (prefer) to do? (1A)
- **Te gusta . . .** You like . . . (3A)
- **¿Te gusta . . . ?** Do you like to . . . ? (1A)
- **¿Te gustaría . . . ?** Would yo like . . . ? (4B)

H

hablar to talk (2A)

- **— por teléfono** to talk on th phone (1A)

hacer to do (3B)

- **Hace calor.** It's hot. (P)
- **Hace frío.** It's cold. (P)
- **Hace sol.** It's sunny. (P)
- **— ejercicio** to exercise (3B)
- **¿Qué tiempo hace?** What's the weather like? (P)
- **(yo) hago** I do (3B)
- **(tú) haces** you do (3B)

hambre: Tengo —. I'm hungry. (3B)

la hamburguesa hamburger (3A)

hasta:

- **— luego.** See you later. (P)
- **— mañana.** See you tomorrow. (P)

Hay There is, There are (2B)

el helado ice cream (3B)

la hoja de papel sheet of paper (P

¡Hola! Hello! (P)

la hora:

- **en la . . . —** in the . . . hour (class period) (2A)
- **¿A qué hora?** (At) what time? (4B)

el horario schedule (2A)

horrible horrible (3B)

hoy today (P)

los huevos eggs (3A)

I

la iglesia church (4A)

igualmente likewise (P)

impaciente impatient (1B)

el inglés: la clase de — English class (2A)

inteligente intelligent (1B)
interesante interesting (2A)
el **invierno** winter (P)
ir to go (4A)
— **a** + *inf.* to be going to + *verb* (4B)
— **a la escuela** to go to school (1A)
— **de cámping** to go camping (4B)
— **de compras** to go shopping (4A)
— **de pesca** to go fishing (4B)

J

las **judías verdes** green beans (3B)
jueves Thursday (P)
jugar (a) (u → ue) to play *(games, sports)* (4B)
— **al básquetbol** to play basketball (4B)
— **al béisbol** to play baseball (4B)
— **al fútbol** to play soccer (4B)
— **al fútbol americano** to play football (4B)
— **al golf** to play golf (4B)
— **al tenis** to play tennis (4B)
— **al vóleibol** to play volleyball (4B)
— **videojuegos** to play video games (1A)
el **jugo:**
— **de manzana** apple juice (3A)
— **de naranja** orange juice (3A)
julio July (P)
junio June (P)

L

la the *f. sing.* (1B)
lado: al — de next to, beside (2B)
el **lápiz,** *pl.* **los lápices** pencil (P)
las the *f. pl.* (2B)
le (to / for) him, her
— **gusta . . .** He / She likes . . . (1B)
No — gusta . . . He / She doesn't like . . . (1B)
la **lección,** *pl.* **las lecciones de piano** piano lesson (class) (4A)
la **leche** milk (3A)
la **lechuga** lettuce (3B)
leer revistas to read magazines (1A)
levantar pesas to lift weights (3B)
el **libro** book (P)
la **limonada** lemonade (3A)
llamar:
¿Cómo se llama? What's his / her name? (1B)
¿Cómo te llamas? What is your name? (P)
Me llamo . . . My name is . . . (P)
llover (o → ue): Llueve. It's raining. (P)
lo it, him
— **siento.** I'm sorry. (4B)
los the *m. pl.* (2B)
— **fines de semana** on weekends (4A)
— **lunes, los martes . . .** on Mondays, on Tuesdays . . . (4A)
lunes Monday (P)
los lunes on Mondays (4A)

M

mal bad, badly (4B)
malo, -a bad (3B)
la **mano** hand (P)
mantener: para — la salud to maintain one's health (3B)
la **mantequilla** butter (3B)
la **manzana** apple (3A)
el jugo de — apple juice (3A)
mañana tomorrow (P)
la **mañana:**
a las ocho de la — at eight (o'clock) in the morning (4B)
de la — in the morning (4B)
martes Tuesday (P)
los martes on Tuesdays (4A)
marzo March (P)
más:
— **. . . que** more . . . than (2A)
— **o menos** more or less (3A)
las **matemáticas: la clase de —** mathematics class (2A)
mayo May (P)
me (to / for) me
— **gustaría** I would like (4B)
— **llamo . . .** My name is . . . (P)
— **quedo en casa.** I stay at home. (4A)
media, -o half (P)
y — thirty, half past *(in telling time)* (P)
menos: más o — more or less (3A)
el **mes** month (P)
la **mesa** table (2B)
la **mezquita** mosque (4A)
mi my (2B)
mí:
a — también I do (like to) too (1A)
a — tampoco I don't (like to) either (1A)
miércoles Wednesday (P)
la **mochila** bookbag, backpack (2B)
las **montañas** mountains (4A)
montar:
— **en bicicleta** to ride a bicycle (1A)
— **en monopatín** to skateboard (1A)
mucho, -a a lot (2A)
— **gusto** pleased to meet you (P)
muchos, -as many (3B)
muy very (1B)
— **bien** very well (P)

N

nada nothing (P)

(A mí) no me gusta — . . . I don't like to . . . at all. (1A)

nadar to swim (1A)

la **naranja: el jugo de —** orange juice (3A)

la **nariz,** *pl.* **las narices** nose (P)

necesitar:

(yo) necesito I need (2A)

(tú) necesitas you need (2A)

nevar (e → ie) Nieva. It's snowing. (P)

ni . . . ni neither . . . nor, not . . . or (1A)

No estoy de acuerdo. I don't agree. (3B)

¡No me digas! You don't say! (4A)

noche:

a las ocho de la — at eight (o'clock) in the evening, at night (4B)

Buenas —s. Good evening. (P)

de la — in the evening, at night (4B)

esta — this evening (4B)

nos (to / for) us

¡— vemos! See you later! (P)

nosotros, -as we (2A)

noveno, -a ninth (2A)

noventa ninety (P)

noviembre November (P)

nueve nine (P)

nunca never (3A)

O

o or (1A)

ochenta eighty (P)

ocho eight (P)

octavo, -a eighth (2A)

octubre October (P)

ocupado, -a busy (4B)

el **ojo** eye (P)

once eleven (P)

ordenado, -a neat (1B)

el **otoño** fall, autumn (P)

¡Oye! Hey! (4B)

P

paciente patient (1B)

el **pan** bread (3A)

el — tostado toast (3A)

la **pantalla** (computer) screen (2B)

las **papas** potatoes (3B)

las — fritas French fries (3A)

la **papelera** wastepaper basket (2B)

para for (2A)

— + *inf.* in order to (4A)

— la salud for one's health (3B)

— mantener la salud to maintain one's health (3B)

el **parque** park (4A)

el **partido** game, match (4B)

pasar:

— tiempo con amigos to spend time with friends (1A)

¿Qué pasa? What's happening? (P)

los **pasteles** pastries (3B)

patinar to skate (1A)

la **película:** film, movie

ver una — to see a movie (4A)

perezoso, -a lazy (1B)

pero but (1B)

el **perrito caliente** hot dog (3A)

pesas: levantar — to lift weights (3B)

el **pescado** fish (3B)

el **pie** foot (P)

la **pierna** leg (P)

la **piscina** pool (4A)

la **pizza** pizza (3A)

el **plátano** banana (3A)

la **playa** beach (4A)

poco: un — (de) a little (4B)

poder (o → ue) to be able

(yo) puedo I can (4B)

(tú) puedes you can (4B)

el **pollo** chicken (3B)

por:

¿— qué? Why? (3B)

— supuesto of course (3A)

porque because (3B)

practicar deportes to play sports (1A)

práctico, -a practical (2A)

preferir (e → ie) to prefer

(yo) prefiero I prefer (3B)

(tú) prefieres you prefer (3B

la **primavera** spring (P)

primer (primero), -a first (2A)

el **profesor, la profesora** teacher (P)

puedes: (tú) — you can (4B)

puedo: (yo) — I can (4B)

la **puerta** door (2B)

pues well *(to indicate pause)* (1A)

el **pupitre** student desk (P)

Q

Qué:

¡— asco! How awful! (3A)

¡— buena idea! What a good / nice idea! (4B)

¿— día es hoy? What day is today? (P)

¿— es esto? What is this? (2B)

¿— hora es? What time is it? (P)

¿— pasa? What's happening? (P)

¡— pena! What a shame / pity! (4B)

¿— quiere decir . . . ? What does . . . mean? (P)

¿— tal? How are you? (P)

¿— te gusta hacer? What do you like to do? (1A)

¿— te gusta hacer más? What do you like better (prefer) to do? (1A)

¿— tiempo hace? What's the weather like? (P)

querer (e → ie) to want

¿Qué quiere decir . . . ? What does . . . mean? (P)

Quiere decir . . . It means . . . (P)

(yo) quiero I want (4B)

(tú) quieres you want (4B)

¿Quién? Who? (2A)

quince fifteen (P)

quinto, -a fifth (2A)

R

el ratón, *pl.* **los ratones** (computer) mouse (2B)

el refresco soft drink (3A)

regular okay, so-so (P)

el reloj clock (2B)

reservado, -a reserved, shy (1B)

el restaurante restaurant (4A)

S

sábado Saturday (P)

saber to know (how)

(yo) sé I know (how to) (4B)

(tú) sabes you know (how to) (4B)

sabroso, -a tasty, flavorful (3B)

el sacapuntas, *pl.* **los sacapuntas** pencil sharpener (2B)

la sala de clases classroom (P)

la salchicha sausage (3A)

la salud:

para la — for one's health (3B)

para mantener la — to maintain one's health (3B)

el sándwich de jamón y queso ham and cheese sandwich (3A)

sé: (yo) — I know (how to) (1B)

sed: Tengo —. I'm thirsty. (3B)

según according to (1B)

— mi familia according to my family (1B)

segundo, -a second (2A)

seis six (P)

la semana week (P)

este fin de — this weekend (4B)

los fines de — on weekends (4A)

señor (Sr.) sir, Mr. (P)

señora (Sra.) madam, Mrs. (P)

señorita (Srta.) miss, Miss (P)

septiembre September (P)

séptimo, -a seventh (2A)

ser to be (3B)

¿Eres . . . ? Are you . . . ? (1B)

es he / she is (1B)

no soy I am not (1B)

soy I am (1B)

serio, -a serious (1B)

sesenta sixty (P)

setenta seventy (P)

sexto, -a sixth (2A)

sí yes (1A)

siempre always (3A)

siento: lo — I'm sorry (4B)

siete seven (P)

la silla chair (2B)

simpático, -a nice, friendly (1B)

sin without (3A)

la sinagoga synagogue (4A)

sociable sociable (1B)

el sol: Hace —. It's sunny. (P)

solo, -a alone (4A)

Son las . . . It is . . . *(in telling time)* (P)

la sopa de verduras vegetable soup (3A)

soy I am (1B)

supuesto: por — of course (3A)

T

tal: ¿Qué —? How are you? (P)

talentoso, -a talented (1B)

también also, too (1A)

a mí — I do (like to) too (1A)

tampoco: a mí — I don't (like to) either (1A)

tarde afternoon (4B)

a la una de la — at one (o'clock) in the afternoon (4B)

Buenas —s. Good afternoon. (P)

de la tarde in the afternoon (4B)

esta — this afternoon (4B)

la tarea homework (2A)

te (to / for) you

¿— gusta . . . ? Do you like to . . . ? (1A)

¿— gustaría . . . ? Would you like . . . ? (4B)

el té tea (3A)

el — helado iced tea (3A)

el teclado (computer) keyboard (2B)

la tecnología technology / computers (2A)

la clase de — technology / computer class (2A)

el templo temple; Protestant church (4A)

tener to have

(yo) tengo I have (2A)

(tú) tienes you have (2A)

Tengo hambre. I'm hungry. (3B)

Tengo que . . . I have to . . . (4B)

Tengo sed. I'm thirsty. (3B)

el tenis: jugar al — to play tennis (4B)

tercer (tercero), -a third (2A)

ti you *fam. after prep.*

¿Y a —? And you? (1A)

el tiempo:

el — **libre** free time (4A)

pasar — con amigos to spend time with friends (1A)

¿Qué — hace? What's the weather like? (P)

tocar la guitarra to play the guitar (1A)

el **tocino** bacon (3A)

todos, -as all (3B)

— los días every day (3A)

los **tomates** tomatoes (3B)

trabajador, -ora hardworking (1B)

trabajar to work (1A)

el **trabajo** work, job (4A)

trece thirteen (P)

treinta thirty (P)

treinta y uno thirty-one (P)

tres three (P)

triste sad (4B)

tu your (2B)

tú you *fam.* (2A)

U

Ud. (usted) you *formal sing.* (2A)

Uds. (ustedes) you *formal pl.* (2A)

un, una a, an (1B)

un poco (de) a little (4B)

la **una: a la —** at one o'clock (4B)

uno one (P)

unos, -as some (2B)

usar la computadora to use the computer (1A)

usted (Ud.) you *formal sing.* (2A)

ustedes (Uds.) you *formal pl.* (2A)

las **uvas** grapes (3B)

V

veinte twenty (P)

veintiuno (veintiún) twenty-one (P)

la **ventana** window (2B)

ver:

a — Let's see (2A)

¡Nos vemos! See you later! (P)

— la tele to watch television (1A)

— una película to see a movie (4A)

el **verano** summer (P)

¿Verdad? Really?, Right? (3A)

la **vez,** *pl.* **las veces:**

a veces sometimes (1B)

los **videojuegos: jugar —** to play video games (1A)

viernes Friday (P)

el **vóleibol: jugar al —** to play volleyball (4B)

vosotros, -as you *pl.* (2A)

Y

y and (1A)

¿— a ti? And you? (1A)

— cuarto quarter past *(in telling time)* (P)

— media thirty, half past *(in telling time)* (P)

¿— tú? And you? *fam.* (P)

¿— usted (Ud.)? And you? *formal* (P)

yo I (1B)

el **yogur** yogurt (3A)

Z

las **zanahorias** carrots (3B)

English-Spanish Vocabulary

The *English-Spanish Vocabulary* contains all active vocabulary from the text, including vocabulary presented in the grammar sections.

A dash (—) represents the main entry word. For example, **to play —** after **baseball** means **to play baseball.**

The number following each entry indicates the chapter in which the word or expression is presented. The letter *P* following an entry refers to the *Para empezar* section.

The following abbreviations are used in this list: *adj.* (adjective), *dir. obj.* (direct object), *f.* (feminine), *fam.* (familiar), *ind. obj.* (indirect object), *inf.* (infinitive), *m.* (masculine), *pl.* (plural), *prep.* (preposition), *pron.* (pronoun), *sing.* (singular).

A

a, an un, una (1B)
- **a little** un poco (de) (4B)
- **a lot** mucho, -a (2A)

according to según (1B)
- **— my family** según mi familia (1B)

after después (de) (4A)

afternoon:
- **at one (o'clock) in the afternoon** a la una de la tarde (4B)
- **Good —.** Buenas tardes. (P)
- **in the —** de la tarde (4B)
- **this —** esta tarde (4B)

afterwards después (4A)

agree:
- **I —.** Estoy de acuerdo. (3B)
- **I don't —.** No estoy de acuerdo. (3B)

all todos, -as (3B)

alone solo, -a (4A)

also también (1A)

always siempre (3A)

am:
- **I —** (yo) soy (1B)
- **I — not** (yo) no soy (1B)

amusing divertido, -a (2A)

and y (1A)
- **¿— you?** ¿Y a ti? *fam.* (1A); ¿Y tú? *fam.* (P); ¿Y usted (Ud.)? *formal* (P)

apple la manzana (3A)
- **— juice** el jugo de manzana (3A)

April abril (P)

Are you . . . ? ¿Eres . . . ? (1B)

arm el brazo (P)

art class la clase de arte (2A)

artistic artístico, -a (1B)

at:
- **— eight (o'clock)** a las ocho (4B)
- **— eight (o'clock) at night** a las ocho de la noche (4B)
- **— eight (o'clock) in the evening** a las ocho de la noche (4B)
- **— eight (o'clock) in the morning** a las ocho de la mañana (4B)
- **— home** en casa (4A)
- **— one (o'clock)** a la una (4B)
- **— one (o'clock) in the afternoon** a la una de la tarde (4B)
- **— what time?** ¿A qué hora? (4B)

athletic deportista (1B)

August agosto (P)

autumn el otoño (P)

B

backpack la mochila (2B)

bacon el tocino (3A)

bad malo, -a (3B); mal (4B)

badly mal (4B)

banana el plátano (3A)

baseball: to play — jugar al béisbol (4B)

basketball: to play — jugar al básquetbol (4B)

to **be** ser (3B); estar (2B)
- **to — going to** + *verb* ir a + *inf.* (4B)

beach la playa (4A)

because porque (3B)

beefsteak el bistec (3B)

behind detrás de (2B)

beverages las bebidas (3B)

bicycle: to ride a — montar en bicicleta (1A)

binder: three-ring — la carpeta de argollas (2A)

book el libro (P)

bookbag la mochila (2B)

boring aburrido, -a (2A)

boy el chico (1B)

bread el pan (3A)

breakfast el desayuno (3A)
- **for —** en el desayuno (3A)

busy ocupado, -a (4B)

but pero (1B)

butter la mantequilla (3B)

C

café el café (4A)

calculator la calculadora (2A)

can:
- **I —** (yo) puedo (4B)
- **you —** (tú) puedes (4B)

carrots las zanahorias (3B)

cereal el cereal (3A)

chair la silla (2B)

chicken el pollo (3B)

church la iglesia (4A)
- **Protestant —** el templo (4A)

class la clase (2A)

classroom la sala de clases (P)

clock el reloj (2B)

coffee el café (3A)

cold: It's —. Hace frío. (P)

computer la computadora (2B)
- **— keyboard** el teclado (2B)
- **— mouse** el ratón (2B)
- **— screen** la pantalla (2B)
- **—s / technology** la tecnología (2B)
- **to use the —** usar la computadora (1A)

concert el concierto (4B)
cookie la galleta (3A)
countryside el campo (4A)

D

dance el baile (4B)
to **dance** bailar (1A)
daring atrevido, -a (1B)
date: What is the —? ¿Cuál es la fecha? (P)
day el día (P)
every — todos los días (3A); cada día (3B)
What — is today? ¿Qué día es hoy? (P)
December diciembre (P)
delighted encantado, -a (P)
desk el pupitre (P); el escritorio (2B)
dictionary el diccionario (2A)
difficult difícil (2A)
dinner la cena (3B)
diskette el disquete (2B)
to **do** hacer (3B)
— you like to . . . ? ¿Te gusta . . . ? (1A)
I — (yo) hago (3B)
you — (tú) haces (3B)
door la puerta (2B)
to **draw** dibujar (1A)
to **drink** beber (3A)

E

easy fácil (2A)
to **eat** comer (3A)
eggs los huevos (3A)
eight ocho (P)
eighteen dieciocho (P)
eighth octavo, -a (2A)
eighty ochenta (P)
either tampoco (1A)
I don't (like to) — a mí tampoco (1A)
eleven once (P)
English class la clase de inglés (2A)
evening:
Good —. Buenas noches. (P)
in the — de la noche (4B)
this — esta noche (4B)
every day cada día (3B); todos los días (3A)
to **exercise** hacer ejercicio (3B)
eye el ojo (P)

F

fall el otoño (P)
favorite favorito, -a (2A)
February febrero (P)
fifteen quince (P)
fifth quinto, -a (2A)
fifty cincuenta (P)
finger el dedo (P)
first primer (primero), -a (2A)
fish el pescado (3B)
to go —ing ir de pesca (4B)
five cinco (P)
flag la bandera (2B)
flavorful sabroso, -a (3B)
folder la carpeta (P)
food la comida (3A)
foot el pie (P)
football: to play — jugar al fútbol americano (4B)
for para (2A)
— breakfast en el desayuno (3A)
— lunch en el almuerzo (3A)
forty cuarenta (P)
four cuatro (P)
fourteen catorce (P)
fourth cuarto, -a (2A)
free time el tiempo libre (4A)
French fries las papas fritas (3A)
Friday viernes (P)
friendly simpático, -a (1B)
from de (4A)
Where are you —? ¿De dónde eres? (4A)
fruit salad la ensalada de frutas (3A)
fun divertido, -a (2A)
funny gracioso, -a (1B)

G

game el partido (4B)
generally generalmente (4A)
girl la chica (1B)
to **go** ir (4A)
to be —ing to + *verb* ir a + *inf.* (4B)
to — camping ir de cámping (4B)
to — fishing ir de pesca (4B)
to — shopping ir de compras (4A)
to — to school ir a la escuela (1A)
golf: to play — jugar al golf (4B)
good bueno (buen), -a (1B)
— afternoon. Buenas tardes. (P)
— evening. Buenas noches. (P)
— morning. Buenos días. (P)
Good-bye! ¡Adiós! (P)
grapes las uvas (3B)
Great! ¡Genial! (4B)
green verde
— beans las judías verdes (3B)
guitar: to play the — tocar la guitarra (1A)
gym el gimnasio (4A)

H

half media, -o (P)
— past y media *(in telling time)* (P)
ham and cheese sandwich el sándwich de jamón y queso (3A)
hamburger la hamburguesa (3A)
hand la mano (P)
happy contento, -a (4B)
hardworking trabajador, -ora (1B)

to have: I — to . . . tengo que + *inf.* (4B)
he él (1B)
he / she is es (1B)
head la cabeza (P)
health:
for one's — para la salud (3B)
to maintain one's — para mantener la salud (3B)
Hello! ¡Hola! (P)
here aquí (2B)
Hey! ¡Oye! (4B)
home la casa (4A)
at — en casa (4A)
(to) — a casa (4A)
homework la tarea (2A)
horrible horrible (3B)
hot:
— dog el perrito caliente (3A)
It's —. Hace calor. (P)
hour: in the . . . — en la . . . hora (class period) (2A)
house la casa (4A)
how: — awful! ¡Qué asco! (3A)
How? ¿Cómo? (P)
— are you? ¿Cómo está Ud.? *formal* (P); ¿Cómo estás? *fam.* (P); ¿Qué tal? *fam.* (P)
— do you say . . . ? ¿Cómo se dice . . . ? (P)
— is . . . spelled? ¿Cómo se escribe . . . ? (P)
— many? ¿Cuántos, -as? (P)
hundred: one — cien (P)
hungry: I'm —. Tengo hambre. (3B)

I

I yo (1B)
— am soy (1B)
— am not no soy (1B)
— do too a mí también (1A)
— don't either a mí tampoco (1A)
— don't think so. Creo que no. (3B)
— stay at home. Me quedo en casa. (4A)
— think . . . Creo que . . . (3B)
— think so. Creo que sí. (3B)
— would like Me gustaría (4B)
—'m hungry. Tengo hambre. (3B)
—'m sorry. Lo siento. (4B)
—'m thirsty. Tengo sed. (3B)
ice cream el helado (3B)
iced tea el té helado (3A)
impatient impaciente (1B)
in en (P, 2B)
— front of delante de (2B)
— order to para + *inf.* (4A)
— the . . . hour en la . . . hora (class period) (2A)
intelligent inteligente (1B)
interesting interesante (2A)
is es (P)
he / she — es (1B)
it la, lo
— is . . . Son las *(in telling time)* (P)
— is one o'clock. Es la una. (P)
— is the . . . of . . . Es el *(number)* de *(month) (in telling the date)* (P)
— is the first of . . . Es el primero de *(month).* (P)
—'s a . . . es un / una . . . (2B)
—'s cold. Hace frío. (P)
—'s hot. Hace calor. (P)
—'s raining. Llueve. (P)
—'s snowing. Nieva. (P)
—'s sunny. Hace sol. (P)

J

January enero (P)
job el trabajo (4A)
juice:
apple — el jugo de manzana (3A)
orange — el jugo de naranja (3A)
July julio (P)
June junio (P)

K

keyboard (computer) el teclado (2B)
to know saber (4B)
I — (how to) (yo) sé (4B)
you — (how to) (tú) sabes (4B)

L

later: See you — ¡Hasta luego!, ¡Nos vemos! (P)
lazy perezoso, -a (1B)
leg la pierna (P)
lemonade la limonada (3A)
Let's see A ver . . . (2A)
lettuce la lechuga (3B)
library la biblioteca (4A)
to lift weights levantar pesas (3B)
to like:
Do you — to . . . ? ¿Te gusta . . . ? (1A)
He / She doesn't — . . . No le gusta . . . (1B)
He / She —s . . . Le gusta . . . (1B)
I don't — to . . . (A mí) no me gusta . . . (1A)
I don't — to . . . at all. (A mí) no me gusta nada . . . (1A)
I — . . . Me gusta . . . (3A)
I — to . . . (A mí) me gusta . . . (1A)
I — to . . . a lot (A mí) me gusta mucho . . . (1A)
I — to . . . better (A mí) me gusta más . . . (1A)
I would — Me gustaría (4B)
What do you — better (prefer) to do? ¿Qué te gusta hacer más? (1A)
What do you — to do? ¿Qué te gusta hacer? (1A)

Would you —? ¿Te gustaría? (4B)
You — . . . Te gusta . . . (3A)
likewise igualmente (P)
to **listen to music** escuchar música (1A)
little: a — un poco (de) (4B)
lot: a — mucho, -a (2A)
to **love** encantar
I / You — . . . Me / Te encanta(n) . . . (3A)
lunch el almuerzo (2A)
for — en el almuerzo (3A)

M

madam (la) señora (Sra.) (P)
to **maintain one's health** para mantener la salud (3B)
mall el centro comercial (4A)
many muchos, -as (3B)
How —? ¿Cuántos, -as? (P)
March marzo (P)
match el partido (4B)
mathematics class la clase de matemáticas (2A)
May mayo (P)
me me
— too a mí también (1A)
with — conmigo (4B)
meal la comida (3A)
to **mean:**
It —s . . . Quiere decir . . . (P)
What does . . . —? ¿Qué quiere decir . . . ? (P)
meat la carne (3B)
messy desordenado, -a (1B)
milk la leche (3A)
miss, Miss (la) señorita (Srta.) (P)
Monday lunes (P)
on Mondays los lunes (4A)
month el mes (P)
more:
— . . . than más . . . que (2A)
— or less más o menos (3A)
morning:
Good —. Buenos días. (P)
in the — de la mañana (4B)
mosque la mezquita (4A)
mountains las montañas (4A)
mouse (computer) el ratón (2B)
mouth la boca (P)
movie la película
to see a — ver una película (4A)
— theater el cine (4A)
Mr. (el) señor (Sr.) (P)
Mrs. (la) señora (Sra.) (P)
music: to listen to — escuchar música (1A)
must deber (3B)
my mi (2B)
— name is . . . Me llamo . . . (P)

N

name:
My — is . . . Me llamo . . . (P)
What is your —? ¿Cómo te llamas? (P)
What's his / her —? ¿Cómo se llama? (1B)
neat ordenado, -a (1B)
to **need**
I — necesito (2A)
you — necesitas (2A)
neither . . . nor ni . . . ni (1A)
never nunca (3A)
next to al lado de (2B)
nice simpático, -a (1B)
night: at — de la noche (4B)
nine nueve (P)
nineteen diecinueve (P)
ninety noventa (P)
ninth noveno, -a (2A)
nose la nariz, *pl.* las narices (P)
not . . . or ni . . . ni (1A)
notebook el cuaderno (P)
nothing nada (P)
November noviembre (P)

O

o'clock:
at eight — a las ocho (4B)
at one — a la una (4B)
October octubre (P)
of de (2B)
— course por supuesto (3A)
Oh! What a shame / pity! ¡Ay! ¡Qué pena! (4B)
okay regular (P)
on en (2B)
— Mondays, on Tuesdays . . los lunes, los martes . . . (4A)
— top of encima de (2B)
— weekends los fines de semana (4A)
one uno (un), -a (P)
at — (o'clock) a la una (4B)
one hundred cien (P)
onion la cebolla (3B)
or o (1A)
orange: — juice el jugo de naranja (3A)

P

paper: sheet of — la hoja de papel (P)
park el parque (4A)
party la fiesta (4B)
pastries los pasteles (3B)
patient paciente (1B)
peas los guisantes (3B)
pen el bolígrafo (P)
pencil el lápiz, *pl.* los lápices (P)
— sharpener el sacapuntas, *pl.* los sacapuntas (2B)
phone: to talk on the — hablar por teléfono (1A)
physical education class la clase de educación física (2A)
piano lesson (class) la lección, *pl.* las lecciones de piano (4A)
pizza la pizza (3A)
to **play** jugar (a) (u → ue) *(games, sports)* (4B); tocar *(an instrument)* (1A)

to — baseball jugar al béisbol (4B)
to — basketball jugar al básquetbol (4B)
to — football jugar al fútbol americano (4B)
to — golf jugar al golf (4B)
to — soccer jugar al fútbol (4B)
to — sports practicar deportes (1A)
to — tennis jugar al tenis (4B)
to — the guitar tocar la guitarra (1A)
to — video games jugar videojuegos (1A)
to — volleyball jugar al vóleibol (4B)
pleased to meet you mucho gusto (P)
pool la piscina (4A)
poster el cartel (2B)
potatoes las papas (3B)
practical práctico, -a (2A)
to prefer preferir (e → ie)
I — (yo) prefiero (3B)
I — to . . . (a mí) me gusta más . . . (1A)
you — (tú) prefieres (3B)

Q

quarter past y cuarto *(in telling time)* (P)

R

rain: It's —ing. Llueve. (P)
to read magazines leer revistas (1A)
Really? ¿Verdad? (3A)
reserved reservado, -a (1B)
restaurant el restaurante (4A)
rice el arroz (3B)
to ride: to — a bicycle montar en bicicleta (1A)
Right? ¿Verdad? (3A)
to run correr (1A)

S

sad triste (4B)
salad la ensalada (3A)
fruit — la ensalada de frutas (3A)
sandwich: ham and cheese — el sándwich de jamón y queso (3A)
Saturday sábado (P)
sausage la salchicha (3A)
to say decir
How do you —? ¿Cómo se dice? (P)
You — . . . Se dice . . . (P)
You don't —! ¡No me digas! (4A)
schedule el horario (2A)
science: — class la clase de ciencias naturales (2A)
screen: computer — la pantalla (2B)
season la estación, *pl.* las estaciones (P)
second segundo, -a (2A)
to see ver
Let's — A ver . . . (2A)
— you later! ¡Nos vemos!, Hasta luego. (P)
— you tomorrow. Hasta mañana. (P)
to — a movie ver una película (4A)
September septiembre (P)
serious serio, -a (1B)
seven siete (P)
seventeen diecisiete (P)
seventh séptimo, -a (2A)
seventy setenta (P)
to share compartir (3A)
she ella (1B)
sheet of paper la hoja de papel (P)
should deber (3B)
shy reservado, -a (1B)
sick enfermo, -a (4B)
to sing cantar (1A)
sir (el) señor (Sr.) (P)
six seis (P)
sixteen dieciséis (P)
sixth sexto, -a (2A)
sixty sesenta (P)
to skate patinar (1A)
to skateboard montar en monopatín (1A)
to ski esquiar (i → í) (1A)
snow: It's —ing. Nieva. (P)
so-so regular (P)
soccer: to play — jugar al fútbol (4B)
sociable sociable (1B)
social studies class la clase de ciencias sociales (2A)
soft drink el refresco (3A)
some unos, -as (2B)
something algo (3B)
sometimes a veces (1B)
sorry: I'm —. Lo siento. (4B)
soup: vegetable — la sopa de verduras (3A)
spaghetti los espaguetis (3B)
Spanish class la clase de español (2A)
to spell:
How is . . . spelled? ¿Cómo se escribe . . . ? (P)
It's spelled . . . Se escribe . . . (P)
to spend time with friends pasar tiempo con amigos (1A)
sports:
to play — practicar deportes (1A)
— -minded deportista (1B)
spring la primavera (P)
to stay: I — at home. Me quedo en casa. (4A)
stomach el estómago (P)
stories: to write — escribir cuentos (1A)

strawberries las fresas (3A)

student el / la estudiante (P)

studious estudioso, -a (1B)

to **study** estudiar (2A)

summer el verano (P)

Sunday domingo (P)

sunny: It's —. Hace sol. (P)

to **swim** nadar (1A)

synagogue la sinagoga (4A)

T

table la mesa (2B)

talented talentoso, -a (1B)

to **talk** hablar (2A)

  to — on the phone hablar por teléfono (1A)

tasty sabroso, -a (3B)

tea el té (3A)

  iced — el té helado (3A)

to **teach** enseñar (2A)

teacher el profesor, la profesora (P)

technology / computers la tecnología (2A)

technology / computer class la clase de tecnología (2A)

television: to watch — ver la tele (1A)

temple el templo (4A)

ten diez (P)

tennis: to play — jugar al tenis (4B)

tenth décimo, -a (2A)

thank you gracias (P)

the el, la (1B); los, las (2B)

theater: movie — el cine (4A)

then entonces (4B)

there allí (2B)

  — is / are hay (2B)

they ellos, ellas (2A)

to **think** pensar (e → ie)

  I don't — so. Creo que no. (3B)

  I — . . . Creo que . . . (3B)

  I — so. Creo que sí. (3B)

third tercer (tercero), -a (2A)

thirsty: I'm —. Tengo sed. (3B)

thirteen trece (P)

thirty treinta (P); y media *(in telling time)* (P)

thirty-one treinta y uno (P)

this este, esta

  — afternoon esta tarde (4B)

  — evening esta noche (4B)

  — weekend este fin de semana (4B)

  What is —? ¿Qué es esto? (2B)

three tres (P)

three-ring binder la carpeta de argollas (2A)

Thursday jueves (P)

time:

  At what —? ¿A qué hora? (4B)

  free — el tiempo libre (4A)

  to spend — with friends pasar tiempo con amigos (1A)

  What — is it? ¿Qué hora es? (P)

tired cansado, -a (4B)

to a *(prep.)* (4A)

  in order — para + *inf.* (4A)

  — the a la, al (4A)

toast el pan tostado (3A)

today hoy (P)

tomatoes los tomates (3B)

tomorrow mañana (P)

  See you —. Hasta mañana. (P)

too también (1A); demasiado (4B)

  I do (like to) — a mí también (1A)

  me — a mí también (1A)

top: on — of encima de (2B)

Tuesday martes (P)

  on —s los martes (4A)

twelve doce (P)

twenty veinte (P)

twenty-one veintiuno (veintiún) (P)

two dos (P)

U

underneath debajo de (2B)

to **understand** comprender (3A)

to **use: to — the computer** usar la computadora (1A)

V

vegetable soup la sopa de verduras (3A)

very muy (1B)

  — well muy bien (P)

video games: to play — jugar videojuegos (1A)

volleyball: to play — jugar al vóleibol (4B)

W

to **walk** caminar (3B)

to **want** querer (e → ie)

  I — (yo) quiero (4B)

  you — (tú) quieres (4B)

wastepaper basket la papelera (2B)

to **watch television** ver la tele (1A)

water el agua *f.* (3A)

we nosotros, -as (2A)

weather: What's the — like? ¿Qué tiempo hace? (P)

Wednesday miércoles (P)

week la semana (P)

weekend:

  on —s los fines de semana (4A)

  this — este fin de semana (4B)

well bien (P); pues *(to indicate pause)* (1A)

  very — muy bien (P)

What? ¿Cuál? ¿Qué? (3A)

  — are you like? ¿Cómo eres? (1B)

  (At) — time? ¿A qué hora? (4B

  — day is today? ¿Qué día es hoy? (P)

  — do you like better (prefer) to do? ¿Qué te gusta hacer más? (1A)

— **do you like to do?** ¿Qué te gusta hacer? (1A)

— **does . . . mean?** ¿Qué quiere decir . . . ? (P)

— **is she / he like?** ¿Cómo es? (1B)

— **is the date?** ¿Cuál es la fecha? (P)

— **is this?** ¿Qué es esto? (2B)

— **is your name?** ¿Cómo te llamas? (P)

— **time is it?** ¿Qué hora es? (P)

—**'s happening?** ¿Qué pasa? (P)

—**'s his / her name?** ¿Cómo se llama? (1B)

—**'s the weather like?** ¿Qué tiempo hace? (P)

What!:

— **a good / nice idea!** ¡Qué buena idea! (4B)

— **a shame / pity!** ¡Qué pena! (4B)

When? ¿Cuándo? (4A)

Where? ¿Dónde? (2B)

— **are you from?** ¿De dónde eres? (4A)

(To) —? ¿Adónde? (4A)

Which? ¿Cuál? (3A)

Who? ¿Quién? (2A)

Why? ¿Por qué? (3B)

window la ventana (2B)

winter el invierno (P)

with con (3A)

— **me** conmigo (4B)

— **my / your friends** con mis / tus amigos (4A)

— **whom?** ¿Con quién? (4A)

— **you** contigo (4B)

without sin (3A)

work el trabajo (4A)

to **work** trabajar (1A)

Would you like . . . ? ¿Te gustaría . . . ? (4B)

to **write: to — stories** escribir cuentos (1A)

Y

year el año (P)

yes sí (1A)

yogurt el yogur (3A)

you *fam. sing.* tú (2A); *formal sing.* usted (Ud.) (2A); *fam. pl.* vosotros, -as (2A); *formal pl.* ustedes (Uds.) (2A); *fam. after prep.* ti (1A)

And —? ¿Y a ti? (1A)

with — contigo (4B)

— **don't say!** ¡No me digas! (4A)

— **say . . .** Se dice . . . (P)

your *fam.* tu (2B)

Z

zero cero (P)

Grammar Index

Structures are most often presented first in *A primera vista*, where they are practiced lexically. They are then explained later in a *Gramática* section or a *Nota*. Light face numbers refer to the pages where structures are initially presented or, after explanation where student reminders occur. **Bold face numbers** refer to pages where structures are explained or are otherwise highlighted.

a 26–30, 218
- + definite article 208–209, **215**
- after **jugar** 240, **256**
- in time telling 240–241, **250**
- with **ir** + infinitive 241, **252**

accent marks **13,** 38, **223**
- in interrogative words **224**

adjectives:
- agreement and formation 56–57, **64,** 82, **190,** 204
- comparative 87
- demonstrative 240–241
- plural. *See* adjectives: agreement and formation
- position of **72**
- possessive 29, 118, 144

alphabet 12

-ar verbs 36
- present 87, 89–90, **100,** 114, 160

articles:
- definite **11, 70,** 82, **132,** 144
- definite, with **a** 208–209, **215**
- definite, with days of the week 216
- definite, with **de 125**
- definite, with titles of respect 94
- indefinite **70,** 82, **132,** 144

cognates 40, 68

comparison 87

compound subject **98**

dates 14–15

de:
- + definite article 125
- in compound nouns **156**
- in prepositional phrases 119, 125
- possessive 119, **135**

derivation of words 94, 194, 216, 249

encantar 149, **164**

-er verbs 36
- present 148–149, **160,** 174

estar 118–119, **128,** 144

Exploración del lenguaje:
- Cognates **40**
- Cognates that begin with **es** + consonant **68**
- Connections between Latin, English, and Spanish **94**
- Language through gestures **127**
- Origins of the Spanish days of the week **216**
- Punctuation and accent marks **13**
- Señor, señora, señorita **2**
- Spanish words borrowed from English **249**
- **Tú** vs. **usted 5**
- Using a noun to modify another noun **156**
- Where did it come from? **194**

gender **11**
- of adjectives agreeing with nouns **64,** 82, **190,** 204
- of articles **70,** 82
- of pronouns **98**

gustar 26, 52, **164**

hacer 26, 179
- use of in weather expressions 18

hay 14

infinitive **36**
- after **ir a** 241, **252**
- after **para** 208
- after **tener que** 241

interrogative words **224**

ir 30, 208, **218,** 236
- + **a** + infinitive 241, **252**
- with future meaning 241, **252**

-ir verbs 36
- present 152, **160,** 174

jugar 27, 240, **256,** 266

negative 27, **42, 44,** 72, 105
- **nada** used for emphasis 27, **42**
- **ni . . . ni** 27, **42**
- **tampoco** 27, **44**

nouns **11,** 64
- compound **156**
- plural **132,** 190
- used with **gustar / encantar 164**

numbers 7
- in dates 15
- in telling time **8**
- ordinal 86

plurals:
- of adjectives **190,** 204
- of nouns **132,** 190

poder 241

possession:
- adjectives 29, 118
- with **de** 119, 135

preferir 181

prepositions 119

present. *See individual verb listings*

pronouns:
- **conmigo / contigo** 241
- prepositional, used for agreement, clarity, or emphasis 26–27, **44**

subject 56, 60, **98,** 114
subject, omission of **100,** 163
subject, use of for clarification or emphasis 100
Pronunciation:
a, e, i 35
accent marks 223
c 107
d 254
g 137
h/j 167
l/ll 191
o/u 71
stress 223
punctuation marks **13**
querer 240

question formation **224**
accent marks 224
with **¿no?** 90
with **¿verdad?** 149

saber 243–244
ser 28, 57, **192,** 204
in telling time 8
stem-changing verbs. *See* verbs, stem-changing
subject, of a sentence **98.** *See also* pronouns, subject

tener 86, 89
expressions with 179, 181
with **que** + infinitive 241

time telling **8,** 240–241, **250**
tú vs. **usted** 4, **5, 98**

ver 27, **160**
verbs 36
-ar 87, **100,** 114, 160
-er 148, **160,** 174
-ir 152, **160,** 174
irregular. *See individual listings*
stem-changing **u → ue** 240, **256,** 266

weather expressions 18
word order with adjectives **72,** 82

Acknowledgments

Cover Design Tamada Brown & Associates

Program Graphic Development Herman Adler Design

Maps Mapping Specialists
Technical Illustration/Additional Graphics Herman Adler Design; New England Typographic Services; Publicom; John Reece; Joseph Taylor

Ilustrations Wilkinson Studios Artists; Bob Brugger: **pp. 167, 254**; Dennis Dzielak: **pp. 8, 79, 94, 118, 119**; Seitu Hayden: **pp. 6, 12, 16, 27, 32, 34, 36, 208, 209, 214, 246, 248, 249**; Reggie Holladay: **pp. 43, 67, 103, 230, 231**; Tim Jones: **pp. 16, 26, 62, 65, 74, 86, 91, 95, 134, 136, 191, 220, 241, 247, 253,** Victor Kennedy: **p. 35**; Gary Krejca: **pp. 32, 36**; Miguel Luna: **pp. 7, 191**; Jonathan Massie: **p. 179**; Tom Mc Kee: **pp. 2, 15, 188, 232, 257**; Donna Perrone: **pp.103, 154, 156, 159, 178, 185, 186, 187, 194**; Judy Stead: **pp. 3, 18, 70, 125, 240, 250**; Nicole Wong: **pp. 8, 209, 214**

Photography Front and back covers: Parque del Buen Retiro, Madrid, Spain, Lonely Planet Images; (front cover inset) Café on the waterfront, Barcelona, Spain, Robert Frerck/Odyssey/Chicago;
Photographers who contributed to the studio/location photography: Bill Burlingham, Burlingham Photography and John Morrison, Morrison Photography.

x–xi, José Fuste Raga/CORBIS; **x inset,** Danny Lehman/CORBIS; **xi inset,** www.corbis.com/Phil Schermeister; **xiii–xiii,** Danny Lehman/CORBIS; **xiv–xv,** David Zimmerman/CORBIS; **xiv inset,** Stuart Westmorland/CORBIS; **xvi–xvii,** Jim Erickson/CORBIS; **xviii-xix,** ©Galen Rowell/CORBIS; **xx–xxi,** Paul Hardy/CORBIS; **xx inset,** Mark L. Stephenson; **xxi inset,** José Fuste Raga/CORBIS; **xxii-xxiii,** ©Craig Turtle/CORBIS; **xxii inset,** Strauss/Curtis/CORBIS; **xxiii br inset,** Ron Watts/CORBIS; **xxiii bl inset,** Corbis Royalty Free; **xxiv tl,** Pablo Picasso (1881-1973) ©ARS, NY ©Erich Lessing/Art Resource, NY; **xxiv tr,** Paul Barton/CORBIS; **xxiv bm,** ©S. P. Gillette/CORBIS; **xxvi,** LatinFocus.com; **1 t,** Robert Frerck/Odyssey Productions, Inc.; **1 br,** Bill Bachmann/PhotoEdit; **3 (1),** Bob Daemmrich/Stock Boston; **3 (2),** Spencer Grant/Stock Boston; **3 (3),** David Young-Wolff/PhotoEdit; **3 (4),** M. Ferguson/PhotoEdit; **3 (5),** Bachmann/Stock Boston; **3 (6),** Mary Kate Denny/PhotoEdit; **5,** Spencer Grant/Stock Boston; Mary Kate Denny/PhotoEdit; **8,** A.K.G., Berlin/SuperStock; **13,** Museo Nacional de Antropología, Mexico City, Mexico/Bridgeman Art Library International, Ltd.; **15,** David Young-Wolff/PhotoEdit; **16,** A. Ramey/PhotoEdit; **17,** Peter Wilson/Dorling Kindersley Media Library © CONACULTA-INAH-MEX. Authorized reproduction by the *Instituto Nacional de Antropología e Historia*; **18 all,** George Gold/SuperStock, Inc.; **19 (1),** © Gordon R. Gainer/CORBIS; **19 (2),** Rocio Escobar; **19 (3),** Joseph Nettis/Photo Researchers, Inc.; **19 (4),** *Causes and Effects*, Philip Steele; **20 tl,** Spencer Swanger/Tom Stack & Associates, Inc.; **20 tr,** Ann Duncan/Tom Stack & Associates, Inc.; **20 bl,** J. Schulte/D. Donne Bryant Stock Photography; **20 br,** Ricardo Carrasco/D. Donne Bryant Stock Photography; **20 m,** © ESA/ELI/CORBIS; **24–25,** David Young-Wolff/Photo Edit ; **24 inset,** Picasso, Pablo (1881-1973). (c) ARS, NY. *Three Musicians*. 1921. Oil on canvas, 6' 7" x 7' 3 3/4". Mrs. Simon Guggenheim Fund. (55.1949). Museum of Modern Art, New York, N.Y., U.S.A./The Bridgeman Art Library International, Ltd.; **28 m,** Roberto M. Arakaki/ImageState/International Stock Photography Ltd.; **29 tm,** Spencer Grant/PhotoEdit; **29 bm,** SuperStock, Inc.; **30 r,** Buddy Mays/ImageState/International Stock Photography, Ltd.; **33,** Peter Menzel/Stock Boston; **35 tl,** Ernest Manewal/SuperStock, Inc.; **35 tr,** M. Paganelli/Woodfin Camp & Associates; **38,** David Simson/Stock Boston; **40 m,** Museo Bellapart; **41 ml,** Bonnie Kamin/PhotoEdit; **41 bl,** PictureQuest; **41 t,** Blaine Harrington; **41 mr,** David Young-Wolff/PhotoEdit; **41 br,** HIRB/Index Stock Imagery; **45,** Getty Images, Inc.; **45 b,** Wolfgang Kaehler/CORBIS; **45 tl,** Larry Prosor/SuperStock, Inc.; **46 t,** David Young-Wolff/PhotoEdit; **46 b,** Marisol Diaz/Latin Focus Photo Agency; **47 t,** © Robert Frerck/Odyssey/Chicago; **47 ml,** Myrleen Ferguson Cate/PhotoEdit Inc. **48,** Danilo Boschung/eStock Photography LLC; **49 t,** Bob Daemmrich Photography, Inc.; **49 b,** Kathy Ferguson-Johnson/PhotoEdit; **50–51, background image** Reinhard Eisele/CORBIS, **inset tr,** Richard Bickel, **inset mr,** Roger Resmeyer/CORBIS, **inset br,** Jan Burchofsky-Houser/CORBIS; **51 t,** Robert Frerck/Woodfin Camp & Associates; **51,** Dave Bartruff/Stock Boston; **51 m,** Patrick Ward/CORBIS; **51 b,** Robert Frerck/Odyssey Productions, Inc.; **52,** Robert Frerck/Odyssey Productions, Inc.; **54–55,** David Simson/Stock Boston; **54 inset,** Albright-Knox Art Gallery; **57 b,** Paul Mark Smith/Panos Pictures; **63 (1, 2, 3, 7, 8)** Ulrike Welsch Photography; **63 (4),** Robert Frerck/Odyssey Productions, Inc.; **63 (5),** PhotoDisc/GettyImages; **63 (6),** Robert Frerck/Odyssey Productions, Inc.; **66,** Copyright © Mary Kate Denny/PhotoEdit All rights reserved; **68 t,** The Bridgeman Art Library International, Ltd.; **68 b,** David Simson/Stock Boston; **69 b,** David Sanger Photography; **73 t,** Robert Fried Photography/Stock Boston; **73 b,** H. Huntly Hersch/D. Donne Bryant Stock Photography; **75,** Robert Fried Photography; **77,** Robert Frerck/Odyssey/Chicago; **78 tr,** Rhoda Sidney/Stock Boston; **78 br,** David Simson/Stock Boston; **78 tl,** Tony Arruza/CORBIS; **78 bl,** Robert Fried Photography; **78,** H. Huntly Hersch/D.Donne Bryant Stock Photography; **79 t,** David Young-Wolff/PhotoEdit; **79 b,** David Young-Wolff/PhotoEdit; **80–81,** Reinhard Eisele/CORBIS; **81 t inset,** Richard Bickel/COR-

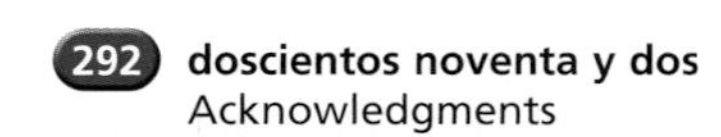

BIS; **81 m inset,** Roger Resmeyer/CORBIS; **81 b inset,** Jan Burchofsky-Houser/CORBIS; **84–85,** Owen Franken/Stock Boston; **84 inset,** Marlborough Gallery, Inc.; **95,** Dave Bartruff/Stock Boston; **97 t,** Jeff Greenberg/PhotoEdit; **97 b,** H. Huntly Hersch/D.Donne Bryant Stock Photography; **99 (1, 8),** ©Robert Frerck/Odyssey Productions, Inc.; **99 (2, 6),** ©Robert Fried Photography; **99 (3),** Charlie Marsden/Panos Pictures; **99 (4),** Jeff Greenberg/PhotoEdit; **99 (5),** Owen Franken/Stock Boston; **99 (7),** Richard Pasley/Stock Boston; **102 b,** Carlos S. Pereyra/D. Donne Bryant Stock Photography; **103 t,** Ulrike Welsch/PhotoEdit; **103 b,** Paul Conklin/PhotoEdit; **104–105,** John Post/Panoramic Images; **107,** Charlie Marsden/Panos Pictures; **108 m,** ©José Fuste Raga/CORBIS; **108 inset,** Bob Deammrich/Stock Boston; **109 t,** Ulrike Welsch/Stock Boston; **109 b,** Robert Fried Photography; **110 t,** Robert Fried Photography; **110 b,** Joe Viesti/The Viesti Collection, Inc.; **111 t,** Ulrike Welsch/Stock Boston; **111 b,** Jeff Greenberg/PhotoEdit; **112–113,** José Fuste Raga/CORBIS; **113 tr inset,** Lindsay Hebberd/CORBIS; **113 mr inset,** Danny Lehman/CORBIS, **br inset,** ©Randy Faris/CORBIS; **113,** Spencer Grant/PhotoEdit; **116–117,** Robert Fried/Stock Boston; **116 inset,** Institut Amatller de Arte Hispanico; **114,** Ulrike Welsch Photography; **127 m,** Jeff Greenberg/PhotoEdit; **128 b,** Ulrike Welsch Photography; **128,** Carlos S. Pereyra/D.Donne Bryant Photography; **131 m,** PhotoDisc/GettyImages; **134,** Robert Fried Photography; **134,** June Concord/D.donne Bryant Stock Photgraphy; **137 t,** Jeff Greenberg/PhotoEdit; **137 b,** © 2004 Ulrike Welsch; **138 t,** Wolfgang Kaehler Photography; **138 b,** Sean Sprague/Panos Pictures; **139 tl, tr,** Jeremy Horner/Panos Pictures; **139 bl,** Jon Spaul/Panos Pictures; **139 bm,** Jean-Leo Dugast/Panos Pictures; **139 br,** Sean Sprague/Panos Pictures; **140 t,** Jeff Greenberg/PhotoEdit; **140 b,** Carlos S. Pereyra/D. Donne Bryant Stock; **141,** Panos Pictures;**142-143,** Gail Shumway/Getty Images, **142 inset,** Kennan Ward/CORBIS; **143 tr inset,** Shepard Sherbell/CORBIS; **143 m inset,** Bill Gentile/CORBIS, **143 br inset,** José Angel Murillo; **146–147,** Ronnie Kaufman/CORBIS; **146 inset,** Murillo, Bartolomeo Esteban. (1618-1682) (c) ARS, NY. *Children Eating Sweets*. Copyright Scala/Art Resource, NY. Alte Pinakothek, Munich, Germany; **160,** Ivonne Barreto/Latin Focus Photo Agency; **161,** Robert Fried Photography; **165 b,** PhotoDisc/GettyImages; **169,** M. Barlow/Trip/ The Viesti Collection; **170 t,** Richard Hutchings/PhotoEdit; **170,** David-Young Wolff/PhotEdit; **171 t,** PatrickRamsey/ImageState/International Stock Photography Ltd.; **171 b,** David Shopper/Stock Boston; **172-173,** ©James Spartshatt/CORBIS, **173 tr inset,** Jim Zuckerman/CORBIS; **173 mr inset,** Caroline Penn/CORBIS; **176–177,** Latin Focus.com; **176 inset,** Robert Frerck/Odyssey Productions, Inc.; **185 t,** Carlos Goldwin/Focus/D. Donne Bryant Stock Photography; **186,** Jose Carillo/PhotoEdit; **187,** Robert Frerck/Odyssey Productions, Inc.; **187,** Owen Franken/Stock Boston; **189,** Robert Fried/D. Donne Bryant Stock Photography; **193 t,** James Nelson/Tony Image Studio; **193 b,** Look GMBH/eStock Photography, LLC; **195,** Roberto Arakaki/ImageState/International Stock Photography Ltd.; **196 b,** Ulrike Welsch/PhotoEdit; **197 t,** AP/Wide World Photos; **199 tl,** AP/Wide World Photos; **199 b,** David Cannon/Hulton Archive/GettyImages; **200 t,** Martin Rogers/Stock Boston; **200 b,** ©Robert Frerck/Odyssey/Chicago; **201 t,** Jimmy Dorantes/Latin Focus Photo Agency; **201 b,** The Stock Market; **202–203,** Larry Lee/CORBIS; **203 tr inset,** Hubert Stadler/CORBIS; **203 mr inset,** Yann Arthus-Bertrand/CORBIS; **203 br inset,** Pablo Corral/CORBIS; **206–207,** Spencer Grant/PhotoEdit; **206 inset,** Paul Conklin/PhotoEdit; **215 inset,** Art Museum of The Americas/Audio Visual Program; **219,** Fernando Pastene; **219,** Latin Focus.com; **221,** Bob Daemmrich Photography, Inc.; **222,** Vic Bider/PhotoEdit; **226,** Robert Frerck/Odyssey Productions, Inc.; **228 t,** Robert Fried Photography; **228 b,** David Young-Wolff/PhotoEdit; **229 both,** ©Robert Frerck/OdysseyChicago; **231,** Malcolm Fife/eStock Photography, LLC; **232 all,** Robert Fried Photography; **233 both,** Latin Focus.com; **234–235,** Wolfgang Kaehler/CORBIS; **234–235 tm inset,** Alan Schein/CORBIS; **234 ml inset,** D. Boone/CORBIS, **234 bm inset,**Richard Cummins/CORBIS; **234,** Super Stock, Inc.; **236,** ©Robert Frerck/Odyssey/Chicago; **238 inset,** ©AFP/Greg Wood/CORBIS; **238–239,** REUTERS/Will Burgess/CORBIS; **247,** ©Robert Frerck/Odyssey/Chicago; **254 b,** PhotoDisc/GettyImages; **255,** ©Robert Frerck/Odyssey/Chicago; **255 b,** David Young-Wolff/PhotoEdit; **257,** Peter Chartran/D. Donne Bryant Stock Photography; **257,** Peter Chart; pal; **258 t,** ©Reuters NewMedia Inc./CORBIS; **258 b,** Myrleen Ferguson Cate/PhotoEdit; **259,** Robert Frerck/Woodfin Camp & Associates; **260,** Chris Trotman/Duomo Photography Incorporated; **261 t,** AP/Wide World Photos; **261 b,** Chris Trotman/Duomo Photography Incorporated; **262 t,** Robert Frerck/Odyssey/Latin Focus, **262 b,** Jimmy Dorantes/Latin Focus **263 t,** Bob Daemmrich/Stock Boston; **263 m,** David Young-Wolff/PhotoEdit; **263 b,** Richard V. Procopio/Stock Boston; **264–265,** Nik Wheeler/CORBIS; **264 tl inset,** Tiziou Jacques/CORBIS/Sygma; **264 tr inset,** ©CORBIS; **265 tr inset** ©Kevin Fleming/CORBIS **265 mr inset,** Randy Faris/CORBIS

Text Chapter 4B, p. 259: Playa Tropicana.

Note: Every effort has been made to locate the copyright owner of material used in this textbook. Omissions brought to our attention will be corrected in subsequent editions.